A FIRE BELL IN THE PAST

A FIRE BELL IN THE PAST

The Missouri Crisis at 200

Volume I
Western Slavery, National Impasse

Edited By

Jeffrey L. Pasley and John Craig Hammond

UNIVERSITY OF MISSOURI PRESS

COLUMBIA

Publication of this volume made possible with the generous support of the Kinder Institute on Constitutional Democracy

Library of Congress Cataloging-in-Publication Data
Names: Pasley, Jeffrey L., 1964- editor. | Hammond, John Craig, 1974-
    editor.
Title: A fire bell in the past : the Missouri Crisis at 200 / edited by
    Jeffrey L. Pasley, and John Craig Hammond.
Description: Columbia : University of Missouri Press, [2021-] | Series:
    Studies in constitutional democracy; 1 | Includes bibliographical
    references and index. | Contents: v. 1. Western slavery, national
    impasse --
Identifiers: LCCN 2021003501 (print) | LCCN 2021003502 (ebook) | ISBN
    9780826222312 (v. 1 ; hardcover) | ISBN 9780826274588 (v. 1 ; ebook)
Subjects: LCSH: Missouri compromise. | Missouri
    compromise.--Historiography. | Slavery--Political aspects--United
    States--History--19th century. | Slavery--United States--Extension to
    the territories. | United States--Politics and government--1817-1825. |
    United States--Territorial expansion--History--19th century. |
    Sectionalism (United States)--History--19th century. |
    Missouri--Politics and government--To 1865.
Classification: LCC E373 .F74 2021 (print) | LCC E373 (ebook) | DDC
    973.5/4--dc23
LC record available at https://lccn.loc.gov/2021003501
LC ebook record available at https://lccn.loc.gov/2021003502

Typeface: Minion

STUDIES IN CONSTITUTIONAL DEMOCRACY

Justin B. Dyer and Jeffrey L. Pasley, Series Editors

The Studies in Constitutional Democracy Series explores the origins and development of American constitutional and democratic traditions, as well as their applications and interpretations throughout the world. The often subtle interaction between constitutionalism's commitment to the rule of law and democracy's emphasis on the rule of the many lies at the heart of this enterprise. Bringing together insights from history and political theory, the series showcases interdisciplinary scholarship that traces constitutional and democratic themes in American politics, law, society, and culture, with an eye to both the practical and theoretical implications.

Previous Titles in Studies in Constitutional Democracy

To John L. Pasley (1936–2020)—engineer, public servant, sometimes star-crossed businessman, and beloved father. His Missouri crises have ended. Hope the better place he's gone to has an ocean.

For Pep Hammond—father, grandfather, union steamfitter.

CONTENTS

CONTRIBUTORS

Christa Dierksheide is an associate professor and Brockman Foundation Jefferson Scholars Foundation Professor of History at the University of Virginia. She is the author of *Amelioration and Empire: Progress and Slavery in the Plantation Americas, 1770–1840* (2014) as well as numerous essays and articles on Jefferson, slavery, and race.

David N. Gellman is a professor of history at DePauw University. Among his books are *American Odysseys: A History of Colonial North America* (2014, coauthored with Timothy J. Shannon) and a forthcoming multigenerational study of slavery and abolitionism in the Jay family.

Sarah L. H. Gronningsater is an assistant professor of history at the University of Pennsylvania. She is the author of several publications, including "'On Behalf of His Race and the Lemmon Slaves': Louis Napoleon, Northern Black Legal Culture, and the Politics of Sectional Crisis," *Journal of the Civil War Era* (June 2017) and "'Expressly Recognized by Our Election Laws': Certificates of Freedom and the Multiple Fates of Black Citizenship in the Early Republic," *William and Mary Quarterly* (July 2018). She is working on a book that traces the long history of emancipation in the United States, with a focus on New York State and the generation of black children born during gradual abolition.

John Craig Hammond is an associate professor of history and assistant director of academic affairs at Penn State University–New Kensington. He is author and editor of numerous books and articles about slavery and politics in the early American republic and the middle Mississippi Valley. He lives in suburban Pittsburgh but daydreams about the Mississippi River and its tributaries.

Robert Lee is a lecturer in American history and a fellow of Selwyn College at the University of Cambridge. His research on the interconnected histories of Indigenous dispossession and U.S. states has appeared in the *Journal of American History*, *High Country News*, and the *New York Times*. After earning a PhD in history from the University of California, Berkeley, and an MA in American studies from the Universität Heidelberg, he was a junior fellow at the Harvard Society of Fellows.

Jeffrey L. Pasley is a professor of history, and associate director of the Kinder Institute on Constitutional Democracy, at the University of Missouri. He previously taught at Florida State University. He is the author of *"The Tyranny of Printers": Newspaper Politics in the Early American Republic* (2001) and *The First Presidential Contest: The Election of 1796 and the Beginnings of American Democracy* (2013), a finalist for the 2014 George Washington Book Prize. As part of the Missouri Bicentennial Alliance, he helped create *The Struggle for Statehood* traveling exhibit, sponsored by the Missouri Humanities Council, that toured the state from 2019 to 2021.

Donald Ratcliffe is a senior research fellow at the Rothermere American Institute in Oxford, England. He has written numerous articles on the early republic, two monographs on early Ohio politics, and a double-prizewinning book, *The One-Party Presidential Contest: Adams, Jackson, and 1824's Five-Horse Race* (2015).

Andrew Shankman is a professor of history at Rutgers University, senior research associate at the McNeil Center for Early American Studies, and coeditor of the *Journal of the Early Republic*. His most recent book is *Original Intents: Hamilton, Jefferson, Madison, and the American Founding* (2017).

Anne Twitty is an associate professor of history at the University of Mississippi and a sixth-generation Missourian. Her first book was *Before Dred Scott: Slavery and Legal Culture in the American Confluence, 1787–1857* (2016), which examined a remarkable collection of nearly three hundred freedom suits filed in the St. Louis circuit court.

John R. Van Atta, who now lives in Northampton, Massachusetts, received his PhD in history from the University of Virginia in 1982. He has taught at Hiram College in Ohio and, for thirty-six years, at Brunswick School in Greenwich, Connecticut, where he held the Oaklawn Chair in American History until retiring in 2020. He is the author of *Securing the West: Politics, Public Lands, and the Fate of the Old Republic, 1785–1850* (2014); *Wolf by the Ears: The Missouri Crisis, 1819–1821* (2015); and *Charging Up San Juan Hill: Theodore Roosevelt and the Making of Imperial America* (2018).

David Waldstreicher is a distinguished professor of history at the Graduate Center of the City University of New York and author of *In the Midst of Perpetual Fetes: The Making of American Nationalism, 1776–1820* (1997); *Runaway America: Benjamin Franklin, Slavery, and the American Revolution* (2004); and *Slavery's Constitution: From Revolution to Ratification* (2009). Most recently, he has coedited, with Van Gosse, *Revolutions and Reconstructions: Black Politics in the Long Nineteenth Century (2020)*.

A Fire Bell in the Past: The Missouri Crisis at 200

Jeffrey L. Pasley

T HINGS RARELY GO as planned in the state of Missouri—that's why people have to keep showing us. This phenomenon began with the very process of becoming a state. What was normally a dry constitutional procedure spiraled instead into a three-year national crisis from which the old republic of the founders never truly recovered. The immediate stumbling block was Representative James Tallmadge Jr., who had narrowly won election from Poughkeepsie, New York, with the support of free African American and other antislavery voters. When the bill for Missouri statehood was brought to the House floor in mid-February 1819, Tallmadge introduced an amendment to prohibit the "further introduction of slavery" in the new state. Fellow New Yorker John W. Taylor, soon to be Speaker of the House, gave a passionate speech: the vote would "determine whether the high destinies" of all the lands westward to the Pacific Ocean would "be fulfilled, or whether we shall defeat them by permitting slavery, with all its blighting, baleful consequences, to inherit the land." Such proposals had occasionally been made before, without success or much hope of it. This time, the House passed the antislavery measure, eighty-seven to seventy-six, sending an electric shock through the country. A Georgia congressman warned that Tallmadge had "kindled a fire which all the waters of the ocean cannot put out, which seas of blood can only extinguish." The Senate refused to accept the Tallmadge Amendment; Congress adjourned with the question of Missouri statehood unresolved, and the Missouri Crisis was on.[1]

Its initial resolution in the Missouri Compromise of 1820 turned out to be, as Thomas Jefferson predicted, "a reprieve only, not a final sentence." It required a second compromise the following year to actually get Missouri into the Union and a bloody civil war to partially resolve the contradictions that the compromises created: "a geographical line, coinciding with a marked principle, moral and political," with Missouri on the wrong side. That line would indeed "never be obliterated" completely, not to this day (see the figure *Moral Map*). What Jefferson called "a fire bell in the night," the outbreak of political conflict over slavery in an expanding continental union, could not be unrung. To the extent that the Missouri Question occasioned the first national public debate on not only the future of slavery but also the possibility of Black people living as equal citizens of the republic, that bell continues to ring loudly all over the country right now. Neither the Missouri Compromises nor the deeper moral compromises they reflected have ever been adequate.[2]

Figure 1. Julius Rubens Ames, *Moral Map of the United States* (1847), in *The Legion of Liberty and Force of Truth, Containing the Thoughts, Words, and Deeds, of Some Prominent Apostles, Champions and Martyrs*, 10th ed. (New York: American Anti-Slavery Society).

Bad Bicentennial Minutes

This book, the first of two volumes, aims to explore the Missouri Crisis and the many reverberations and ramifications thereof. The volumes are offered as part of the University of Missouri and the Kinder Institute on Constitutional Democracy's contribution to the state's 2021 bicentennial commemoration. This particular celebration has faced serious obstacles, even setting aside the fact that it has ended up coinciding with a global pandemic. As bankable as foundings and bicentennials have become in the age of David McCullough, *Hamilton*, and *National Treasure*, the most popular ones have come with inspirational stories or nostalgic charm, along with characters and values modern sensibilities can get behind without distress. The founding of the state of Missouri is harder to disguise than Alexander Hamilton in terms of its negatives: as John Craig Hammond's opening chapter argues, it was about the eager westward expansion of slavery, full stop. While there were plenty of ambitious people "taking their shot" in early Missouri history, most of the well-known ones were on the wrong side of history, with goals too self-interested and methods too ruthless to be embraced in a twenty-first-century commemoration. Namely, they were working to restrict the ambit of liberty rather than expand it. As Jefferson City pastor Brian Kaylor recently pointed out in calling for the state to apologize for its role in perpetuating slavery, it would be wrong to expect Black Missourians "to throw confetti and eat birthday cake" on such an occasion, and based on the evidence so far, it would be equally mistaken to expect embarrassed and apathetic whites to flock to the idea either.[3]

Not that much confetti or cake is in the offing. At this writing, Missouri has mounted one of the quietest bicentennial celebrations in memory, with no gubernatorial commission until after the commemorations were already in progress and Governor Eric Greitens had fled office in a sex scandal. Such commemorative energy as seemed to exist went into an almost comically generic bicentennial license plate that did not so much whitewash Missouri history as dehydrate it.

In typical Show-Me State fashion, the lack of state leadership was partly replaced by do-it-yourself initiatives. The Missouri Humanities Council joined with the State Historical Society of Missouri, the Kinder Institute, and what eventually became a long list of other agencies to form a "Bicentennial Alliance" as an umbrella for their various separate activities. Without state funding or central direction, though, it attracted little attention. There was one major milestone achieved: under the indefatigable leadership of Gary Kremer, the State Historical Society of Missouri finally escaped from the

Figure 2. Bicentennial license plate, *Missouri 2021 Bicentennial*, State Historical Society of Missouri, https://missouri2021.org/bicentennial-license-plate/.

basement of the university library in 2019 and opened a fabulous new Center for Missouri Studies in downtown Columbia. Yet the timing of the opening was more of a happy coincidence enabled by the slow movement of the wheels of progress than an intentional bicentennial observance. It is still possible that the actual bicentennial year will have brought a groundswell of popular interest by the time this book is published. In November 2020, Greitens's replacement as governor, Mike Parson, was elected to a full term that promises to be more bicentennial-friendly if the COVID-19 pandemic abates. Check https://missouri2021.org/ for the latest news and the signatories of the Bicentennial Alliance.

What seems guaranteed is that there will be little introspection about the state's proslavery, land-grabbing origins unless scholars help provide it. At this writing, the most substantial official bicentennial observance so far was a monument commemorating the founding of Boone, Callaway, and Cole Counties dedicated just after the 2020 election, out on a popular local bike trail near Jefferson City. There was typical bland rhetoric about "pioneers" building the "crossroads of the nation," but no mention of slavery or race that managed to get in the papers.[4] This was a telling omission in terms of what it revealed about the local mind-set. The urge to avoid the thought of Missouri's unfree heritage remains strong perhaps especially here in the heart of what was the state's most intensive slaveholding region—later known as "Little Dixie" for its continued identification with the Old South deep into the twentieth century. Indeed, the migration of the seat of government upriver from St. Louis was a direct result of the proslavery, "antirestrictionist" forces' decisive victory in 1820, fueled by the land rush of slave-state settlers, onto unilaterally seized Indigenous land, as described by Robert Lee in chapter 2. The white settlers brought with them or purchased thousands of enslaved Black workers who had no choice about moving west to become pioneers or about doing all of the heaviest labor involved.[5]

To be sure, repressed shame over slavery has undoubtedly played a lesser role in Missouri's low-energy bicentennial than apathy, parsimony, and balkanization. Political power and cultural identity here are unusually divided among disparate regions that take little interest in each other: the proudly hillbilly Ozarks; two diverse urban areas that straddle other states and look different directions, Kansas City west and southwest toward the Plains and the Rockies and Texas, St. Louis northeast toward old rival Chicago and downriver along the "Creole Corridor" toward the Delta and New Orleans; and a giant swath of midwestern farmland that fills the rest of the space between Iowa, Kansas, Illinois, and the Missouri River. By contrast, the state did much more with the bicentennial of the Lewis and Clark Expedition, which had the advantage of a best-selling book to promote it and a story that could be recostumed as a multicultural triumph of the American spirit, with white southern men, African Americans, Indigenous people, and women all banding together in a "Corps of Discovery." To see the surviving evidence, and perhaps the limitations of tourism-driven history, visit downtown Kansas City and the waterfront of St. Charles, Missouri, and behold the bicentennial statues of William Clark's enslaved servant York, their famous fellow traveler Sacajawea (also enslaved), and even Clark's dog Seaman. One of the editors of this volume could also share the libretto of the Lewis and Clark bicentennial opera *Corps of Discovery*, commissioned by the University of Missouri, which he was once asked to fact-check as a young faculty member.[6]

There are advantages to a bad bicentennial: the substantive aspects of this one have largely been left to the historians, with no requirements to remove its thorns and provide a happy ending or a tidy lesson. On the level of local and regional heritage, the weak commemorative impulse has freed us to address the uncomfortable facts that made Missouri an important place historically. These begin with its physical and imperial geography. A climatically northern location with little plantation potential in terms of soils or growing season meant that antebellum Missouri never developed the cotton, tobacco, or sugar plantations where the fattest profits in the North American slave-labor economy were made. The lands that became Missouri nevertheless happened to lie in a zone where slavery had gained a strong foothold before the United States claimed possession of the region with the 1803 Louisiana Purchase and where slavery was preserved by international politics from the ideological forces that challenged the institution on the other side of the Mississippi. Before 1803, Missouri was a place where French, Natives, and "Americans" alike could go to get away from first the British Empire and then the United States and the Northwest Ordinance. Once under U.S. control, Missouri Territory attracted large numbers of migrants from the South, of a particularly aggressive and pragmatic type. Civic leaders in Illinois Territory, where slavery's status was murky (officially banned but tolerated in certain forms), were jealous of Missouri's superior appeal in the early days. U.S. territorial official Alexander Stuart sought a transfer from Illinois to Missouri in no small part because "if I go to Missouri I can take my slaves with me."[7]

This concatenation of circumstances set Missouri up to be the political, legal, and physical battleground on which the major issues and arguments of the sectional crisis were hashed out before they spread to the rest of the country. The troubles that began with the Missouri Crisis inspired extreme states' rights advocates across the South and encouraged respectable opinion to embrace a new defense of slavery as a positive good, as seen in John Van Atta's chapter and other places in this volume. The troubles hardly stopped there. In the 1850s, the outrageous racism and cynicism of the *Dred Scott* decision originated in efforts to shut down the St. Louis–area freedom suits that Anne Twitty's chapter analyzes, a loophole in the institution that yawned wider in Missouri because free territory was so near. Meanwhile, the violence and electoral fraud in "Bleeding Kansas" Territory was started by another generation of white Missourians defending slavery on yet another frontier, located directly in the path of their westward trajectory, before many of them enthusiastically joined in the worst guerrilla warfare ever seen on U.S. soil during the Civil War itself. Between the two sectional crises, Missouri spent decades as the vanguard of the western conquests that exacerbated the problem, the trailhead and supplier of materials and personnel to the overland trade, migration, and invasion routes to Mexico, California, and Oregon.[8]

There is, however, no need to make Missouri out to be uniquely or uniformly villainous. Slavery was probably at its peak importance in the state at the time of its founding. By 1860, Missouri had the second-lowest percentage of enslaved people in its population among the "slave states," 9.72 percent. Only Delaware had a lower one. In 1820, even the worst Missourians felt (however self-servingly) that they were acting in self-defense, and they had plenty of outside encouragement from around the South and Washington, DC. What's more, division and inconsistency played a major part in that which made Missouri what it was. Slavery found numerous active political and legal enemies in Missouri in addition to its aggressive defenders. At the same time, in St. Louis, especially, both enslaved and free African Americans were commonly able to move around (even via steamboat), work outside the slave owner's household (as long as the wages went there), defend their interests, and access the courts to a notable degree.[9]

A quintessential St. Louis scene was young William Wells Brown, later the first African American to publish a novel, picking up "what little learning I obtained" on the job at Elijah P. Lovejoy's antislavery newspaper, while enslaved, a few blocks from the site of a horrific early lynching. (Lovejoy was later murdered, but let the record show it happened in Illinois.) Brown pronounced Lovejoy "decidedly the best master I ever had," but also left a note in his autobiography for Missourians and Missouri historians tempted to consider slavery in the state a special case: "Though slavery is thought, by some, to be mild in Missouri, when compared with the cotton, sugar and rice growing States, yet no part of our slave-holding country, is more noted for the barbarity of its inhabitants."[10]

At any rate, commemorating a bad bicentennial allows us to present the true complexities of history to the public and, in the case of Missouri, to help bring, to those who wish to form one, a better understanding of a difficult place not overly prone to self-reflection. With the generous, broad-minded support and partnership of the Missouri Humanities Council, the University of Missouri's Kinder Institute on Constitutional Democracy was able to help mount a real historians' bicentennial, creating a warts-and-all traveling exhibit, *The Struggle for Statehood*, that was displayed in community museums all over the state from 2019 to 2021. The traveling exhibit was the brainchild of Missouri Humanities executive director Steve Belko, a prolific historian himself, and wrangled together by development associate Claire Bruntrager. It was written by a team that included Steve, public historian Brian Grubbs, MU graduate student Lawrence Celani, University of Virginia's Christa Dierksheide, and myself. Many of the ideas and research that went into my contributions to these volumes were developed for the exhibit and an accompanying Twitter account, @MO_Crisis200, as well as many years of teaching the History of Missouri survey class to hundreds of bemused and appalled Mizzou students.

As part of the same Missouri Humanities–funded program, the Kinder Institute also convened an international conference, "A Fire Bell in the Past: Re-assessing the Missouri Crisis at 200," at the University of Missouri on February 15–16, 2019, in conjunction with the bicentennial not of the state but of the Tallmadge Amendment that delayed its admission to the Union for two years. On what turned out to be the coldest and snowiest weekend of the winter, more than fifty scholars gathered to spend two days locked in intense conversation, in front of a surprisingly large public audience given the conditions outside. A number of attendees, including several authors and the coeditor of this volume, got to spend an extra day in Columbia thanks to the weather. Exciting keynote lectures were delivered by Stephen Aron of the University of California at Los Angeles and David Waldstreicher, whose brilliant remarks on John Quincy Adams form the basis of our final chapter. Kinder Institute coordinator Allison Smythe suffered mightily to organize the conference and produced its beautiful program and promotional materials. My colleagues on the Kinder Institute faculty Jay Sexton, Al Zuercher Reichardt, Daive Dunkley, and especially director Justin Dyer were all enthusiastic participants and supporters of the conference, along with many others around campus and the state. I would particularly like to acknowledge several members of the Missouri Regional Seminar on Early American History who braved the snow and cold to give papers or chair sessions: illustrious co-convener Kenneth Owen of the University of Illinois–Springfield, Lorri Glover of St. Louis University, Peter Kastor of Washington University in St. Louis, and Lily Santoro of Southeast Missouri State University. Robert Pierce Forbes made the trip all the way from Connecticut to do the same. Lieutenant Governor Mike Kehoe showed us the state did care after all by opening the proceedings. Thank you to these people and all of the other contributors and attendees for making the "Cricentennial" conference a great scholarly occasion.

Most of the essays in this volume and the next began as papers at the conference. Though there was room for only a fraction of the papers, I deeply appreciate the warm response to the conference and hope that these volumes fulfill its promise.

Jeffrey L. Pasley

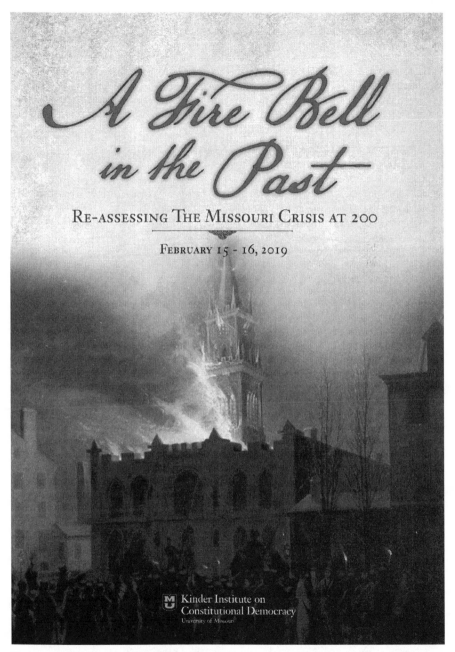

Figure 3. Conference program for "A Fire Bell in the Past: Re-assessing the Missouri Crisis at 200," February 15–16, 2019. Created by Allison Smythe.

Notes

1. *Annals of Congress*, 15th Cong., 2nd sess., 1166, 1170, 1170–79, 1203–5.

2. Thomas Jefferson to John Holmes, April 22, 1820, in Thomas Jefferson, *Writings*, ed. Merrill J. Peterson, Library of America (New York: Literary Classics of the United States, 1984), 1433–35. For a powerful recent effort to bring the legacy of Missouri's early history into the present, see Walter Johnson, *The Broken Heart of America: St. Louis and the Violent History of the United States* (New York: Basic Books, 2020).

3. Brian Kaylor, "Unfinished Business before Our Big Birthday Bash: Missouri Compromise Bicentennial Must Include an Official Apology for Slavery," *St. Louis Post-Dispatch*, March 12, 2020. By contrast, Alabama seems to have done much better, in terms of both the scope of the activities and the attention to slavery and its legacy. See Jay Reeves, "Alabama Tries to Bring Pain as Well as Pride to Bicentennial Celebration," *St. Louis Post-Dispatch*, April 1, 2019.

4. Makalah Hardy, "Bicentennial Marker Gets a Jump on Statehood Anniversary," *Columbia Missourian*, November 16, 2020, https://www.columbiamissourian.com/news/local/bicentennial-marker-gets-a-jump-on-statehood-anniversary/article_ab0a3b50-2845-11eb-975c-ff4c88232e8c.html; Jeff Haldiman, "Three Counties Celebrate 200 Years of History, Vision for Future," *Jefferson City News-Tribune*, November 16, 2020, https://www.newstribune.com/news/news/story/2020/nov/17/three-counties-celebrate-200-years-history-vision-future/849321/.

5. On mid-Missouri as "Little Dixie," see Robert Crisler, "Missouri's Little Dixie," *Missouri Historical Review* 42, no. 2 (1948): 130–39; Howard W. Marshall, *Folk Architecture in Little Dixie: A Regional Culture in Missouri* (Columbia: University of Missouri Press, 1981), 1–16; R. Douglas Hurt, *Agriculture and Slavery in Missouri's Little Dixie* (Columbia: University of Missouri Press, 1992); and Christopher Phillips, *Missouri's Confederate: Claiborne Fox Jackson and the Creation of Southern Identity in the Border West* (Columbia: University of Missouri Press, 2000), 23–52.

6. Stephen E. Ambrose, *Undaunted Courage: Meriwether Lewis, Thomas Jefferson, and the Opening of the American West* (New York: Simon & Schuster, 1996), repopularized Lewis and Clark for the millennial age. For a scholarly analysis of the celebrations, see Kris Fresonke and Mark Spence, eds., *Lewis & Clark: Legacies, Memories, and New Perspectives* (Berkeley: University of California Press, 2004). For the best-curated and most sober of the observances, see the companion book and catalog to the Smithsonian-sponsored exhibit that traveled from 2004 to 2006: Carolyn Gilman, *Lewis and Clark: Across the Divide* (Washington, DC: Smithsonian Books; St. Louis: Missouri Historical Society, 2003). We only wish that something a fraction as beautiful and elaborate could have been mounted for the Missouri state bicentennial.

7. Alexander Stuart to James Monroe, February 13, 1813, in Clarence E. Carter, ed., *The Territorial Papers of the United States*, 28 vols. (Washington, DC: U.S. Government Printing Office, 1934–75), 16:299.

8. Don E. Fehrenbacher, *The Dred Scott Case: Its Significance in American Law and Politics* (New York: Oxford University Press, 1978); Jonathan Earle and Diane Mutti Burke, eds., *Bleeding Kansas, Bleeding Missouri: The Long Civil War on the*

Border (Lawrence: University Press of Kansas, 2013); Gunja SenGupta, *For God and Mammon: Evangelicals and Entrepreneurs, Masters and Slaves in Territorial Kansas, 1854–1860* (Athens: University of Georgia Press, 1996); Michael Fellman, "Rehearsal for the Civil War: Antislavery and Proslavery at the Fighting Point, 1854–1856," in *Antislavery Reconsidered: New Perspectives on the Abolitionists,* ed. Lewis Perry and Michael Fellman, 287–307 (Baton Rouge: Louisiana State University Press, 1979); Michael Fellman, *Inside War: The Guerilla Conflict in Missouri during the American Civil War* (New York: Oxford University Press, 1989). For just a taste of Missouri's role in the conquest and exploitation of northern Mexico, the Plains, the Rockies, and the Pacific Coast, see Duane G. Meyer, "Missouri and the West," in *The Heritage of Missouri,* 3rd ed. (St. Louis: River City, 1988), 188–234; Anne F. Hyde, *Empires, Nations, and Families: A New History of the North American West, 1800–1860* (New York: Ecco, 2012); and Henry W. Berger, *St. Louis and Empire: 250 Years of Imperial Quest and Urban Crisis* (Carbondale: Southern Illinois University Press, 2015).

9. On the particularities of African American life in antebellum Missouri, see Diane Mutti Burke, *On Slavery's Border: Missouri's Small Slaveholding Households, 1815–1865* (Athens: University of Georgia Press, 2010), along with Judy Day and M. James Kedro, "Free Blacks in St. Louis: Antebellum Conditions, Emancipation, and the Postwar Era," *Bulletin of the Missouri Historical Society* 30, no. 2 (1974): 117–35; Harrison A. Trexler, *Slavery in Missouri, 1804–1865* (Baltimore: Johns Hopkins University, 1914); Hurt, *Agriculture and Slavery;* Thomas C. Buchanan, *Black Life on the Mississippi: Slaves, Free Blacks, and the Western Steamboat World* (Chapel Hill: University of North Carolina Press, 2004); Julie Winch, *The Clamorgans: One Family's History of Race in America* (New York: Hill and Wang, 2011); and Melton A. McLaurin, *Celia: A Slave* (Athens: University of Georgia Press, 1991). For prominent white foes of slavery in Missouri Territory at the time of the statehood application, see David Kaser, *Joseph Charless: Printer in the Western Country* (Philadelphia: University of Pennsylvania Press, 1963); Merton L. Dillon, *Benjamin Lundy and the Struggle for Negro Freedom* (Urbana: University of Illinois Press, 1966); and John Mason Peck, *Forty Years of Pioneer Life : Memoir of John Mason Peck, D.D.,* ed. Rufus Babcock (Philadelphia : American Baptist Publication Society, 1864).

10. William Wells Brown, *Illustrated Edition of the Life and Escape of Wm. Wells Brown from American Slavery Written by Himself* (London: C. Gilpin, 1851), 26.

A FIRE BELL IN THE PAST

INTRODUCTION

The Missouri Crisis as Early American History

Jeffrey L. Pasley and John Craig Hammond

> The great Missouri question is finally determined, and I cannot but
> think every true American has cause to blush for the reputation of his
> country. The period is probably very far distant when the effects of the
> monstrous principle of extending the miseries of slavery will be wit-
> nessed in a radical modification of our present form of government,
> or in the still more dreadful evil of a dissolution of our Union. But that
> the seeds of a fatal sectional dissention, to occur hereafter, are sown, I
> have no doubt—their expansion in their embryo growth will be gradual
> but sure—their ultimate maturity certain, and posterity will curse the
> day in which the proposed restriction on the admission of Missouri
> was rejected.
>
> —William Greene to Ethan Allen Brown, March 29, 1820

W HILE THE MISSOURI Crisis is treated in almost every narrative account of
the early American republic or the coming of the Civil War, those accounts
have tended to retell the same old stories for the same purposes. Over the
past century, professional historians have produced only a handful of studies on the Missouri Crisis itself, usually from the state or the congressional
point of view, or to serve the market for general readers on the Civil War.
Even more strangely, the tradition has actually been to minimize the events.
The still-standard study, Glover Moore's *The Missouri Controversy*, takes the
view that the dispute over Missouri was largely an "inside the beltway" (or,
perhaps, an "on the banks of Tiber Creek") affair that had little salience nationally, even if it did rehearse certain later debates and conflicts.[1]

Moore's downplaying suited the "revisionist" interpretation of the Civil
War that was dominant among U.S. historians through the 1960s. Revisionists
such as J. G. Randall and Avery Craven minimized the differences between

North and South, treated accounts of the horrors of slavery as exaggerated abolitionist propaganda (especially if the eyewitness testimony came from African Americans), and saw the sectional crisis and war as tragedies that better leadership could have prevented. It is easy to ridicule such ideas as "neo-Confederate" or worse today, but not so long ago Ivy League faculties were full of scholars who made these kinds of arguments. Even historians with more radical and iconoclastic approaches tended to diminish the significance of slavery and racism as causes of the conflict, with religion or northern capital as two preferred culprits. From the revisionist point of view, the import of the Missouri debates had been blown out of proportion (like most abolitionist complaints), and the Missouri Compromise was a wise solution that became a problem only when a "blundering generation" undid it later.[2]

Then there is a question of terminology, which carries much interpretive weight with it. Between 1819 and 1821, the "Missouri Question" was the most common label used in newspapers and correspondence. Later generations adopted more anodyne formulations like Moore's "controversy" or else collapsed the scale and importance of the events into its formal congressional result, the "Missouri Compromise," a decidedly inaccurate term given that there were at least two.[3] "Missouri Compromise" is the term that has found its way into textbooks and the modern-day public consciousness. It streamlines the larger crisis into a high-level political bargain involving the admission of Maine to balance the addition of the new slave state of Missouri.[4] As Donald Ratcliffe shows in chapter 6, the "balance" idea is a myth that has crept into popular interpretations of these events, simplifying them and taking some of the proslavery onus off Missouri and its advocates.

"Missouri Compromise" also takes popular politics out of the equation, mistaking the disorganization of the old parties in 1819–21 for a lack of democratic energy. Yet a wave of new scholarship on the political history of the early republic has come out since the turn of the twenty-first century. Drawing on neglected popular sources and the once-lost voting returns recovered by the American Antiquarian Society's New Nation Votes project, this newer political history has disproved the old idea that active political democracy in America emerged only with the Jacksonians of the 1830s. As the chapters in this volume amply demonstrate, voters and nonvoters, Black people and whites, men and women, expressed themselves and took action in the decade surrounding the Missouri Crisis. Politicians responded, to slavery among other issues, with or without the Federalist and Republican parties.[5]

Following what has become standard practice among historians of the early American republic, we have adopted the term "Missouri Crisis." This terminology may be unfamiliar to general readers and seem inflated to scholars less steeped in the topic than we are. It might be that the word "crisis" should be reserved for huge world-historical events that brought on some Kuhnian paradigm shift, the climactic resolution of a Marxian dialectic, or at least a major war. One might question whether the Missouri Crisis properly qualifies for such a loud noun in an early American historiographic landscape that is dotted with them, from the Stamp Act Crisis to the Nullification Crisis to the big one, the sectional crisis that ended in the Civil War.[6] We think the Missouri situation qualifies. When Jürgen Habermas sought to define a "social-scientifically useful concept of crisis" in his classic account, he began with Marx's idea of a crisis as the culmination of "contradictions" within a social system. This triggers a catastrophic event that the system in question may not have the resources to address or recover from. The antecedent to Marx's usage, Habermas claims, was medical: "the phase of an illness in which it is decided whether or not the organism's self-healing powers are sufficient for recovery," so that heroic intervention or death must follow. The most common usage in American newspapers in early 1819 was in relation to the worldwide financial collapse that came to be known as the Panic of 1819. In the American press, a widely circulated letter from Europe reported that the Paris markets had, "perhaps, never witnessed so serious a crisis" as the recent drop, and the president of the Bank of the United States asked for understanding about the "peculiar delicacy and difficulty" of the "crisis" in which he had just had to save his bank from failure by severely contracting the national credit.[7]

In that sense, like many of the crises to which historians and philosophers have referred, the federal Union's impasse over Missouri statehood is most properly considered a crisis whose full extent was averted. This potential cataclysm resulted from the sudden clash of two contradictory forces, one enmeshed in a culture, politics, and economy that believed it had turned away from slavery and all it represented, and the other too far embedded culturally, socially, politically, and economically in slavery to perceive any real alternatives to it. Even if we now see southern slavery and northern "free labor" as two sides of the same capitalist coin, nineteenth-century Americans regarded them as hegemonic, contradictory, and antagonistic. They perceived the controversy sparked by the question of Missouri statehood as a crisis, if not necessarily in capital letters.

In Missouri, the place and the issue, the sectional streams crossed. Northern ideas, capital, ambitions, and transportation systems reached out to connect with a territory that was geographically contiguous but largely southern and slavery oriented in its population. In Boston and Ohio, they complained that any New Englanders in Congress who voted for slavery in Missouri had contradicted the "sentiments of their constituents," "the principles of our [colonial] fore Fathers, and of those who achieved our independence," and that therefore "a new crisis [was] at hand." Out in Missouri Territory, Thomas Hart Benton's *St. Louis Enquirer* cited the "glorious declaration of independence" to the opposite effect, stating that Missouri's right to have whatever constitution and institutions its voters wanted was so absolute that it was "a question to be decided not by argument, but by physical force." Luckily, there was "no reason to fear such a crisis," a writer signed "Hampden" argued, as long as the U.S. constitutional system worked as he thought it should. In the broader political sense, however, the crisis had already arrived by revealing the completely different terms in which not just the Constitution but the whole project of an expanding federal Union was understood in different regions of the country.[8]

Overlooking Missouri

The constitutional questions arising from the Missouri Crisis are not the main topic of this volume.[9] Instead, our concerns are with the social, economic, political, geopolitical, and personal forces that created the crisis and were then shaped by it. A review of the literature on the politics of the Missouri Compromise reveals that the "Missouri Crisis" terminology came into use in the 1960s, at the moment when scholars began demonstrating that slavery and race occupied a central place in the history of the early American republic. As far as can be detected in standard databases, the first major modern deployment was Richard H. Brown's influential article "The Missouri Crisis, Slavery, and the Politics of Jacksonianism." By arguing that the protection of slavery—rather than the advancement of democracy—was the keystone of the Second Party System, Brown threw a grenade into the historical reputation of "Jacksonian Democracy." Brown showed that the *stated* purpose of Martin Van Buren's proposed alliance "between the planters of the South and the plain Republicans of the north," which became the Democratic Party, was to prevent any further possible outbreaks of "the clamour agt Southern Influence and African Slavery" that had sparked the Missouri debates.[10] As the upheavals of the 1960s crashed in on the evidently cloistered world of political historians, a new wave of seminal scholarship on slavery, social history, and radical movements challenged historians to consider that the lived experiences of Black people in slavery and freedom just might be "A Central Theme in American History," as the startlingly blunt title of an early historiographic essay incorporating Brown's thesis put it.[11]

But it was slow going. While superficially accepting the Brown thesis, mainstream political history took the wrong message from the rise of social history and devoted itself to the quantitative study of mass voting behavior. Prone to evangelizing about its methodologies by finding hidden secrets that the data revealed, this "new political history" threw the focus on voters' ethnic and religious identities—and away from ideologies and national issues—because broad ethnocultural identifiers correlated more readily with long-term voting patterns. These conclusions opened a significant gap between political historians and social historians even as both adopted social scientific methods. One of the authors in this volume, Donald Ratcliffe, was a rare holdout against this trend. His research on Ohio politics showed that voters' intense negative reactions to the proslavery outcome of the Missouri Compromise were a major driver in the formation of new parties there, turning voters away from "dealer in slaves" Henry Clay and toward John Quincy Adams.[12]

Not accidentally, Ratcliffe's 1973 *Journal of American History* article also seems to be the first occasion, along with William Freehling's piece "Slavery and the Founding Fathers" over at *American Historical Review*, in which articles in the top national history journals consciously adopted the term "Missouri Crisis." Freehling and especially Ratcliffe, channeling his Ohioans, used it just the way it appears in these volumes: as a traumatic political shock that revolutionized the way political leaders and their followers understood their nation and its possible future. Slavery and its consequences would have to be reckoned with or somehow put forever beyond reach.[13]

From the mid-1970s on, writing of the Missouri debates as a crisis was a bit of a calling card for historians who were building a radical critique about the role of slavery and race in American democracy and constitutionalism.[14] At the same time, there were many promising moves to emphasize the significance of slavery, race, and sectionalism during the era of the American Revolution and the early American republic. Led by David Brion Davis's thorny, comprehensive volumes on the problem of slavery in Western culture and the Age of Revolution, and the magisterial works of Winthrop Jordan and George Frederickson on anti-Black racism in early America, these works established the enduring importance of slavery, antislavery, and racism in early American history, and many of these works concluded with an evaluation of the meaning and significance of the Missouri Crisis.[15]

Historians who focused on the period after 1815 produced a body of literature that seemed just as promising with regard to understanding the significance of race, slavery, and the Missouri Crisis to early-nineteenth-century U.S. history. As historians rethought the post-1830 emergence of the sectional crises that initiated the long road to disunion, they located the origins of southern sectionalism in the fifteen-year period following the War of 1812. They also placed the defense of slavery at the heart of southern and national politics in the 1820s. At the same time, historians of the post-1830 abolitionist movements reached back to the 1820s and the Missouri Crisis as they searched for the origins of immediatism. Taken collectively, these works conceived of "the problem of slavery" broadly in revolutionary America and the early republic, using social, cultural, legal, and intellectual history in their efforts to understand the significance of slavery and sectional conflict from the Revolution through the 1820s. In doing so, they addressed a series of fundamental questions about the perpetuation of Black bondage, the solidification of white supremacy, the halting emergence of antislavery politics, and concerted efforts to create a political system that protected slavery and southern interests. In sum, by the late 1970s, these works presented historians a propitious moment for evaluating both the Missouri Crisis and the contentious decade of sectional, racial, and political upheaval that surrounded it.[16]

Historians largely failed to take up the offer. Most of Donald Ratcliffe's contemporaries in the "new political history," eager to maintain their subfield's traditional dominance by aggressively deploying then-trendy quantitative methods, went all the way down the rabbit hole of their ethnocultural interpretation. While producing some wonderfully rich, detailed, and accurate histories, the "new political historians" nevertheless seemed bent on proving, with science, that local tensions over immigrant culture, especially over alcohol and Bibles, were the primary movers of nineteenth-century U.S. politics, not slavery or the favorites of traditional political historians, economic issues like banking or the tariff. Social science also "proved" that the American party system did not even exist (at least in a fully developed and countable form) until the late 1830s. That left the Missouri Crisis and all the decades before it as the "lost Atlantis" of American politics. Ronald Formisano's five-hundred-page account of Massachusetts politics from the

1790s to the 1840s does not include a single mention of the Missouri Crisis, despite the fact that it literally split the commonwealth in two: the District of Maine's representatives embraced the protection of slavery in Missouri in order to secure congressional approval of their new state.[17]

Dissenting political historians who wrote from the perspective of labor and neo-progressive history rarely did much better. Through the theory of a transition to capitalism (the "Market Revolution") or by emphasizing the class-formation and social-control elements of the era's reform movements, these historians defended the relevance of class as a major category of political analysis and, in a backhanded way, shifted historians' focus back to the economic issues that dominated the older "Age of Jackson" historiography. For Market Revolution historians, slavery and antislavery were incidental to economic and cultural conflicts that pitted market capitalists and allied social reformers against subsistence agriculturalists, southern planters, and northern workingmen. The placement of the "common man" and white working class at center stage both dictated and depended on ignoring the politics of race and slavery except at key moments such as Jackson's stand against the Nullification Crisis. Otherwise, it would have been difficult for the coiner of the term "Market Revolution," Charles G. Sellers, to write with such sympathy for Andrew Jackson and the southern white farmers and northern white laborers who served as the shock troops of every invasion of Indigenous land and murderous antiabolitionist riot. Sellers did lay great stress on the period of the Missouri Crisis, but for him the inciting event was the Panic of 1819 and the ensuing economic depression.[18]

It was not that labor history was incapable of addressing race and slavery. A group of labor historians more or less created the field of "whiteness studies," but their purpose in doing so was to answer the classic question of left-oriented scholarship: Why was there no socialism or social revolution in the United States? Fuller, more accurate accounts of U.S. political history could not have been further from their concerns, so they either omitted the Missouri Crisis entirely or provided only passing references.[19]

Filling Out the Virtue Bracket: Slavery and the Founders

From the vantage point of 2021, neither the "new political history" nor the Market Revolution has been new or revolutionary for a long time. The editors and authors here mostly hail from the world of early American history, which has taken a surprisingly different and unrelated approach to political history that speaks volumes about the segmentation that plagues the wider field. Current patterns date back to the era of the U.S. Bicentennial, which brought forth a new efflorescence of scholarship on the so-called founders and their political thought. Historians of early America with a political bent became absorbed in debates over the intellectual influences of the American Revolution—"republican" or liberal—that tended to wall it off from later eras of history and from the insights of social history. Scholars of the re-publicanism school, such as Bernard Bailyn, Gordon Wood, and J. G. A. Pocock, began with the rather subversive project of relocating the ideas of the American Revolution away from their traditionally assumed basis in the liberalism of John Locke and other great Enlightenment thinkers to an "ideology" patched together from the writings of various radical and con-servative critics of British government. Yet the fact that their shift to the history of ideas came in reaction to the materialist progressive interpretation pioneered by Charles Beard put them on a collision course with the radical historians who influenced or were influenced by the upheavals of the 1960s. Criticized a bit unjustly by the radicals as out-of-touch reactionaries in the campus struggles of the late 1960s and early 1970s, members of the repub-lican school took to dismissive rhetoric that risked caricature of their own position; their response was received and remembered as "ideas matter," but social inequalities and diverse voices didn't.[20]

Thus, a methodological polarization that started out within the realm of political history, with neo-progressive historians such as Alfred Young and Gary Nash vying with the "republican synthesis" for the soul of the American Revolution, ended with a whole generation of younger and more self-consciously left-leaning historians rejecting political history altogether, as a retrograde enterprise. If serious historians were going to write about political struggles in early American history, it would be in the form of so-cial movements and subversive cultures, oppressed peoples resisting in their daily lives or through their cultural practices, or outside the formal political system of elections and legislation, in the streets, the woods, the churches, and the union halls. Many productive new lines of inquiry, and indeed whole new fields, were opened this way, some revolutionizing the canon of basic scholarship on early America. However, the sometimes artificial stance of re-jecting political history left the study of formal politics in the early American republic—the kind that might involve elections, legislation, or policy—a shallower, more backward-looking pond where the founders became bigger and bigger fish and issues of race and slavery became harder to discern even when they did touch the world of formal politics.[21]

These methodological divisions became yet more pronounced during the nation's conservative turn after 1980. The approach of the Constitution's bicentennial in 1987, and the rise of constitutional "originalism" as the official judicial philosophy of the Reagan and Bush administrations, conferred ever more prestige and money on the study of the founders. "Originalism" was even spearheaded by a legal organization that took its name from early American history, the Federalist Society. Other well-funded but less directly political conservative groups such as the Liberty Fund and the Gilder Lehrman Institute of American History invested in humanities scholarship and history education designed to fix attention on the thoughts and deeds of the American Revolution, the federal Constitution, and the "founders."[22]

This whole approach to early U.S. politics was almost designed to elevate and separate it from the long-term contours of American history: the economic developments, the geographic movements, and the contentions of its diverse peoples. One teaching of the republican school, especially as practiced by the second wave of scholars who adopted it, was that the past of the founding era "was a foreign country," dominated by eighteenth- or earlier-century concepts and practices. The politics that mattered to historians of this viewpoint was an elite world of great men "above party," free from the vicissitudes of popular public opinion, who conducted intellectual debates, pursued personal rivalries, and vied for honor and eternal "fame."[23] How that world changed was of little interest, except occasionally as an elegy lamenting the democratic barbarians who overran the gates or presented problems the aging founders were not equipped to solve. This was often the only way that social issues like race, class, or gender were ever addressed in these studies, if they were—as tragic exceptions or relatively minor impediments that revolutionary forces swept aside.[24]

A clear element of hero worship entered the picture as the new founder studies developed, and it became still more pronounced once historians grew tired of the republicanism versus liberalism debate, turning to "character" and "leadership" as their main subjects. Early American political history scholarship grew increasingly personality driven as historians chased founding-era best sellers in the vein of the *Greatest Generation*-style memorial tomes and misty-eyed presidential biographies that caught on with audiences in the 1990s. Popular author and John Adams biographer David McCullough became the face of early American history whether the academic historians liked it or not, though academia produced one of the most popular and influential celebratory visions of the era's politics in Joseph

Ellis's *Founding Brothers*. Ellis presented himself as a patriotic dispeller of the "radioactive cloud" that America haters on the Left and in the "scholarly community" had allegedly cast over the founders, bravely returning to political history for another best seller.[25]

Nothing in this tradition dealt easily or accurately with anything connected to the Missouri Crisis: slavery, the trans-Appalachian West, or even the nineteenth century. At most, the republican synthesis was able to probe the ideological uses of the concept of "slavery" in revolutionary discourse, and suggest the implications of that rhetoric, in terms that later historians have found overly sanguine. In a famous but now often-maligned passage, Bernard Bailyn argued that slavery was one of the colonial institutions unintentionally undermined by what he calls "the contagion of liberty," a view that many historians now think gives the Revolution too much credit and the power of enslavers not enough. That section is worth rereading, despite its limitations to the realm of political discourse alone. Bailyn actually locates the origins of American antislavery thought long before 1776, gives much of the impetus to Loyalists, and claims only that the institution "bore the marks ever after"—chiefly in the form of needing to justify itself. The passage was built on by Duncan Macleod in the only full book on slavery that the republican synthesis produced. Without getting anywhere near it chronologically, Macleod explained a dynamic we see clearly at work in the Missouri Crisis: an attack on slavery from northeastern restrictionists rooted in a stated commitment to "universal and natural rights" that evoked in response "a positive racism and an explicit denial of those rights."[26]

Later republicanism scholars did even worse with the topic of slavery, relegating it to a single chapter (out of nineteen) in the case of Gordon Wood's massive contribution to *The Oxford History of the United States* series. Wood's coverage was generous compared to the scattered pages in the competing giant synthesis of the 1790s by Stanley Elkins and Eric McKitrick, or zero in the standard account of the "Jeffersonian persuasion" by Lance Banning. It was partly a matter of periodizing in a way that silently embedded an interpretive decision not to address slavery. None of the major republicanism scholars except Steven Watts and Drew McCoy took much interest in anything past the point where Jefferson took office in 1801, except occasional nods to the War of 1812. Once the Missouri Crisis came along in their narratives, raising an unmistakably nineteenth-century issue, as it seemed to the republicanism school, it was time to tap out. Thus, the first two decades of the nineteenth century remain one of the least studied and most poorly understood periods in American history, even for the specialists![27]

When slavery finally did come for the founders, it was largely as a new twist on the moralistic celebrity history and competitive hero worship that animated "founders chic," with slavery treated primarily as a window on personal character rather than an economic institution, labor system, or social force. Ellis and McCullough had developed the art of selling whatever figure they were working on by contrasting their virtues with the vices of overrated colleagues, and slavery quickly became the most popular standard. As an added bonus, this standard allowed founders chic to celebrate the founders most suited to a conservative era in every other respect, such as political participation, religion, foreign policy, and finance: John Adams, Alexander Hamilton, Gouverneur Morris, and others.

Of course, a reckoning of the "founding fathers" with slavery was long overdue after so many years of downplaying or suppressing the subject in their hagiographies and house museums. High upon his pedestal of soaring rhetoric on liberty and equality, Thomas Jefferson—chief rival of Adams and Hamilton—became the main target. In the 1990s, prominent Jefferson scholars continued to regard his paternity of Sally Hemings's children as an unsubstantiated rumor, but science and historical research finally ran them down. Just as founders chic was taking off, Annette Gordon-Reed's definitive study of Jefferson and Hemings arrived around the same time as news of the DNA tests.[28]

In the early 2000s, the resolution of the Jefferson-Hemings debate turned founding-era political history into a kind of virtue bracket, pitting caricatured individuals and groups who allegedly remained steadfast opponents of slavery against the hypocrites who fastened the chains of slavery and racism on both the enslaved and the nation. Jefferson and his followers became the easy villains of this morality contest, which was fair enough on some levels. At the same time, scholars and popular authors sometimes strained their ingenuity trying to make their favorites into antislavery heroes: not just Ben Franklin and Alexander Hamilton, who were at least associated with elements of the antislavery movement despite their many ties to the institution, but also George Washington (one of Virginia's wealthiest planters), for prospectively freeing his slaves—after he and Martha were dead—and James Monroe, for his murky-to-sinister role in the Missouri Crisis.[29]

The search for heroes often led to questionable historical judgments and strange political bedfellows, with historians thinking almost like voters reacting to "negative reference groups." Having soured on the racist and hypocritical Jefferson, a disappointing advocate of universal human rights to say the least, historians who shared that commitment became enamored with

Jefferson's enemies, the avowed opponents of universal human rights. So the Federalist Party, the professed Christian conservatives of their day, received a makeover in the image of late-twentieth-century academic liberalism. Once castigated for their smug elitism, nativism, and authoritarianism, leading Federalists were recast as uniquely moral antislavery paternalists eager to use government to improve society. Historians thrilled as Alien and Sedition Act enforcer Timothy Pickering and libertine reactionary Gouverneur Morris snarked against slavery and the corrupting influence of planters, chin-stroked seriously over Federalist conspiracy theories about violent American "Jacobins," and made a humanitarian out of choleric realist John Adams for passively aiding rebellious slaves on Saint-Domingue as a war measure against France. One historian even imagined (rather wishfully) that Adams might have negotiated a "free-soil" Louisiana Purchase had he been president in 1803, thus precluding the Missouri Crisis entirely.[30]

The most politically grounded version of these arguments can be found in the work of intellectually ambitious Civil War–era historians who, with a certain vested interest in focusing all of U.S. history on their area of specialty, dug deeply and located the origins of disunion and war and racial oppression in the founding of the American republic. The most provocatively radical of the nineteenth-century abolitionists had done the same with their attacks on the Constitution as "an agreement with Hell." By 2000, historians such as Don Fehrenbacher, William Freehling, Leonard Richards, and especially the period-hopping Paul Finkelman had built what we might call the "founding slavers" thesis. Finkelman threw down the gauntlet at an infamous Monticello conference in 1992 and made himself a gadfly on the early American history conference circuit for many years thereafter. Adapting the abolitionist theory of the Slave Power, these historians posited a kind of proslavery deep state that had been operating since the Continental Congress and held particular sway over the Constitutional Convention and the Jefferson and Madison administrations. The Missouri Crisis loomed rather large in this narrative as a moment when the Slave Power bared its fangs, but these scholars evinced relatively little interest in the event in and of itself. Nor was any significance or detail attached to the decade of turmoil and trauma immediately surrounding it. Rather, the significance of the Missouri Crisis for these historians lay in what it demonstrated about the shortcomings of the founders and the Constitution and their connection to southern secession and the Civil War. We wonder whether the pained remarks of fearful old men such as Jefferson, far from the seats of power and everyday local politics, are really the most meaningful index to understanding the Missouri Crisis.[31]

While we quite agree that historians must hold America's feet to the fires of racism and slavery, the danger of "founding" interpretations and the moralizing that goes with them is the way they work against the sense of time, place, and contingency that makes history an indispensable discipline and state and local history worthwhile. Any politician, social scientist, or journalist can stereotype and totalize without qualms, based on a few shreds of evidence. Historians need to get down in the weeds and find the paths through them, preferably new ones. That is the approach we took in returning attention to the Missouri Crisis on the occasion of its bicentennial and in putting together these volumes.

The Way beyond the Founders:
Scholarship on Slavery in the Twenty-First Century

For many practitioners of founders chic, the decision to write about political history was a self-consciously reactionary or nostalgic choice (historiographically rather than politically in most cases) or a commercial calculation. The great dead white men still sold books. The present volume comes from a different place. One of the editors and one of the authors collaborated a couple of decades back on a collection like this called *Beyond the Founders*, highlighting then-younger scholars working on political history after a long period when that had become a rarity. The key move we were trying to make was writing political history that *drew on* the new subjects and methods and historiographies that had emerged since the 1960s, rather than ignoring them or trying to reclaim the lost primacy of political history.[32]

Vast new terrain had opened up in the study of early American history and all other fields, as previously neglected sources, new methodologies, and radically changed priorities expanded the range of whom and what historians could study and be taken seriously. From this movement came newly sympathetic histories of slavery, free labor, racism, the family, Christianity, social movements like abolitionism and feminism, and all the social and cultural groups who were not the wealthy white male stars of almost all political history. The only problem was that the practitioners of the new histories often saw their work as replacing political history with a "bottom-up" narrative of peoples and social movements that was bracing but not always fully convincing as a way to understand the early American republic as a whole or how it changed over time. The studied lack of interest in speaking even to relevant political events, whether at the local, state, sectional, or national level, started to look like avoidance or academic politics rather than methodological innovation. By the 1990s, historians working on the social and cultural history of race and slavery often felt free to eschew political events altogether.[33]

The first two decades of the twenty-first century dramatically changed that orientation. Facing the millennial swerve back into history that seemed to follow the end of the Cold War—the resurgence of nationalism, racial contention, and partisan polarization in the 1990s, followed by the 2000 election crisis, 9/11, and the endless ensuing real and cultural wars of the current century—historians of all stripes increasingly saw political practices, institutions, and language as more vital for historians to understand than ever. The idea that politics did not affect the real lives of ordinary Americans, or that an era could be understood when setting aside its political currents, seemed increasingly ridiculous. Yet any new "new political history" would need to rest on an updated, more open-ended, and inclusive basis, in terms of both method and interpretation.[34]

Beyond the Founders and the individual works of its eclectic collection of contributors and fellow travelers were just a start in that direction, and it is by no means clear that the profession has followed its lead in the past fifteen years. The forces of scholarly specialization and innovation—and cultural polarization, if we are being honest—have been a little too strong. The founders and the other traditional great figures remain with us, though a bit more likely to be demonized or put on stage than lionized in the traditional ways (still a place of overly high honor in our book). A counterpantheon has developed, often referred to as founders of one type or another, of abolitionists, reformers, first ladies, and Indigenous resistance leaders, a necessary corrective but hardly an intellectual advance. At the same time, history "from the bottom up" transitioned into an "anything but" approach to most of the old political narrative of American history: major events and topics were inverted in their meaning and point of view or globalized to the point that people and events within the United States became almost tangential. Under the banner of #VastEarlyAmerica, the mainstream of early American history embarked on a kind of scholarly colonization project that shifted much of the field's attention outside the anglophone settlements of the thirteen colonies into the Caribbean, Latin America, the Indigenous interior and coasts, and francophone colonies in all directions (including Le Pays des Illinois, which includes Missouri, with forays into the Pacific, Africa, and Asia).[35]

The preceding is offered as a description rather than a criticism and as a confession that political history has not always been able to keep up. What we have learned from all of this ferment is that those of us who choose to operate as U.S. political historians will have little credibility if we pretend that the high politics of elections, legislation, and diplomacy alone can give us a full and accurate picture of the American past, even of its past politics.

We try to do the opposite in the following pages. What we have found particularly relevant to the Missouri Crisis is the continually burgeoning and developing literature on slavery and abolition and the historical development of Black communities. This almost seems too obvious to say, but clearly it was not that obvious to earlier historians of the Missouri Crisis and early Missouri. Building on post-1960s advances in social history and adding some new ones of their own, twenty-first-century historians have gained a fuller understanding of how enslavement and slavery worked, how they changed, and how slavery and white supremacy were deeply woven into the fabric of American life, in all sections, and into the contours of the world economy. Everything about slavery in Missouri, the anything-for-money entrepreneurial frontier that practically gave birth to the Wild West and embodies it to this day in many ways (such as the lowest-in-the-nation cigarette tax and America's most dangerous recreational lake), fully confirms the links that recent literature has made between slavery and capitalism: morally speaking, commodifying human beings was little more than another side hustle in such an environment.[36]

To our surprise, the call for articles on the Missouri Crisis turned up a completely different side of the new history of slavery, emphasizing the resistance to its growing power. Resistance by enslaved people in their daily lives, as well as by escaping or rebelling (or conspiring to), had been a major theme of social and cultural history since the 1960s. Later historians surfaced much more of it, including previously little-known slave rebellions and conspiracies across the South, and they no longer limited their studies to the English-speaking mainland or the antebellum slave states. Racism and slavery and Black life in the northern half of the early republic became an increasing preoccupation, as historians worked to make sure that the "free" states no longer got a free pass.[37]

The newer work also discovered more conventionally political forms of resistance, though not always seen as such. Through new histories of northern free Black communities and abolitionists, historians saw the actual tortuous process by which slavery was rolled back, through the struggles of free Black people and escaped slaves themselves. The reality was that slavery lived on in the North, deep into the nineteenth century. Growing free Black communities became the bedrock of the antislavery movement, targets of white racist violence, and a constant bone of contention in local, state, and national politics as African Americans in the northern states fought against slavery and subordination at home, in the South, and across the larger Atlantic world. Attention to resistance by free and enslaved African Americans, and a heightened awareness of the Haitian Revolution's impact on the mainland, also helped historians understand the level of pressure under which slaveholders found themselves, even when slavery was an economic success. Woody Holton, Alan Taylor, and many others made powerful arguments for the role of the white fears of Black rebellion in driving key political events and decisions from the Revolution to the secession crisis. Fear helped explain the movement for the Constitution, the rise of Andrew Jackson, and, most of all, the lack of stronger action against the institution that at least some revolutionaries had so bitterly condemned. Not all of these arguments were consistent with one another, but all the studies effectively testified to the power of Black resistance to bend the arc of political history toward crisis, if not justice.[38]

Another example of political resistance to slavery was enslaved and free Black people seeking what justice they could in court, which historians found to be a surprisingly open and often effectual arena for individual emancipation. In particular, historians fastened on freedom suits, a phenomenon strongly associated with but not limited to Missouri and highlighted in a wave of new studies rooted in the recently recovered records of the St. Louis Circuit Court, including an excellent book by Anne Twitty, a contributor to this volume. Clearly, law and institutions did matter, and slave society in practice did not present quite the monolith that the rhetoric of the "slavery and capitalism" genre projected.[39] In a completely different vein, historians of the global or transnational turn in historical studies, of which #VastEarlyAmerica is a by-product, revealed new racist and proslavery dimensions of U.S. foreign policy and constitutionalism that recast the views of historians and the American public about some familiar events—for instance, showing how much of the War of 1812 served to defend and promote the institution of slavery.[40]

Perhaps most surprisingly and counterintuitively for those of us raised on the still-growing heroic story of William Lloyd Garrison, Frederick Douglass, Harriet Tubman, and the other stalwarts of antebellum radical abolitionism, the recent literature recovers the powerful role of the early republic's antislavery movement. We have learned that early abolitionism, formerly minimized as hopelessly conservative or limited to a few obsessive Quakers, had roots that ran far deeper and wider than previously imagined, stretching back before the American Revolution and as deeply associated with the mid-Atlantic region and its free Black communities as rarefied white intellectual circles in New England. The early antislavery movement featured the kind of interracial alliances more often associated with the antebellum years, while also enjoying notable successes such as the campaigns for gradual emancipation and the abolition of the slave trade that created the conditions for the Missouri Crisis.

The influence of the new literature on slavery and the antislavery movement also helped political history open its eyes, especially through the work of Matthew Mason, who demonstrated that slavery had always been an issue in American national politics, figuring constantly into congressional debates and major elections of the Federalist-Republican era in ways that gave the Missouri Crisis a dramatically new place in the narrative. Instead of "the overture to an operatic drama," as Daniel Walker Howe put the traditional view, the controversy over slavery in Missouri emerged in Mason's hands as the "commencement exercises" of a long-developing debate into a full-fledged problem. To put it another way, it was the fulcrum of the early nineteenth century rather than the start of it.[41]

Periodization is another unifying theme of *Beyond the Founders* that is amplified here. U.S. historians are notorious among non-U.S.-studying colleagues for the narrowly defined slices of history in which we specialize. Following the old "presidential synthesis" that gets constantly reinforced by the habits of present-day political analysis, historians of early American politics and social movements continue to operate according to strict boundaries set by headline events, with the Declaration of Independence, the Constitution, the "Revolution of 1800," the War of 1812, the election of Andrew Jackson, and the U.S.-Mexican War still acting as break points that few scholars cross except from a great height or global distance. The politics of the early American republic, whether centering slavery or not, was carefully broken up between the founding era, the "Jacksonian" period, and the antebellum rise of sectionalism. The Missouri Crisis always represented an anomaly in this scheme, a prelude to the Civil War in which the founders could make a cameo appearance and then shuffle off. Interweaving political history with the history of slavery and other aspects of social and cultural history allows for a more logical and less overdetermined flow of events, including periods that fit poorly into the usual schema, such as the tumultuous decade of upheaval, reform, conflict, and expansion that surrounded the Missouri Crisis.[42]

Time and place are the key problems in interpreting any major historical event, but also one of the most overlooked in the age of globalized scholarship. Slavery was an economic and political powerhouse, but not in the same way in all places at all times. This is where the slavery and capitalism literature, with its global ambitions, is not as helpful as it might be. We need to make sure we address the obvious question: Why was there a crisis over slavery in this time and place and not some other? How was it, and what does it mean, that Missouri was a problem in 1819 and not Kentucky, Tennessee, or Mississippi before it, all of which presented much the same set of issues twenty-five years earlier, arguably in a more combustible environment with the French and Haitian Revolutions in progress? Why was there no crisis over the Louisiana Purchase itself, with war in the air and disaffected vice presidents and northern sectionalists actively conspiring? Why was Missouri's statehood application the moment when the persistent undercurrent that the Union had previously navigated calmly became a boiling swell that nearly overwhelmed it?

Luckily, the specificities of time and place occupy a central theme in some of the newest studies of slavery and emancipation, politics and power. Although the field of early American history will probably always maintain its East Coast, colonial college viewpoint regardless of how much it globalizes or how high the oceans rise, recent historians have afforded the trans-Appalachian West a more central place in the history of the early American republic. Recent studies have delineated how political development created borders between slavery and freedom in western states and territories, but also how both the enslaved and their enslavers repeatedly blurred or violated those boundaries. Meanwhile, historians have shown, the complex struggles over enslavement and emancipation were still playing out farther east in the Ohio Valley, Virginia, the Carolinas, and elsewhere.[43]

The Missouri Crisis arose from a long era of war, state development, and territorial acquisition from the Revolutionary War to the War of 1812 and the many frontier conflicts before, during, and after them. These generated prolonged and widespread conflicts over slavery and emancipation because of the intensive use of state power through all of them, writ large and small, to keep enslaved men and women in slavery. War created spaces for slaves to flee and find unlikely allies, partly by disrupting old patterns of voting and thought among whites. Expansion invited conflicts over slavery in new states and territories while opening up additional spaces for slave flight and rebellion. Before 1819, these conflicts were diffused, disparate, and mostly localized. The Missouri Crisis changed that. More than merely a question about slavery in a would-be state, it concentrated and nationalized conflicts and tensions stretching across nearly half a century and covering nearly half a continent.[44]

The other major factor in the timing and impact of the Missouri Crisis, and one that demands much more analysis in some other volume, is the fact that it coincided with world capitalism's first major crash of the nineteenth century, the Panic of 1819. Economic vicissitudes fell with particular power and arbitrariness on enslaved people, who were treated as commodities and financial assets as well as laborers, with prices that rose and fell and physical locations that were forced to shift according to the needs of the markets. Economic booms and busts threw the lives of enslaved men and women into disarray, opening opportunities for self-emancipation for some, while dooming others to the "Georgia Trade" and life on a Deep South cotton plantation. Virginia kept itself afloat economically by exporting a major portion of its Black population south and west, to Georgia, Alabama, Missouri, and everywhere else enslaved workers were bought. In Missouri, the postpanic depression undoubtedly saw a number of them reexported farther south, with a corresponding human toll. Economic expansion, contraction, and stagnation also shaped middling white perceptions about the desirability of slavery in their communities and states while provoking new debates about permitting slavery where it was already prohibited or prohibiting it in places where it already existed.[45]

Previewing Volume 1

Over the past twenty years, historians have significantly revised our understandings of race, slavery, and emancipation in the decades surrounding the Missouri Crisis, in the early American republic proper, but also on the North American continent and in the Atlantic world. The chapters in this volume analyze the Missouri Crisis from all of those perspectives while developing several new ones. Both in this volume and in other works, recent scholarship reveals that political elites found themselves reacting to events and actors that forced slavery into local, state, regional, and national politics far more frequently than they initiated and directed them. Politically powerful icons such as John Quincy Adams appear in this literature and volume, as do important national-level institutions such as Congress and the presidency. However, they are joined by an expansive cast of individuals, groups, and institutions whose actions led to, shaped, and determined the outcomes of the Missouri Crisis in various ways.

John Craig Hammond examines how the struggles of diverse groups—the habitants, French-descended farmers who were longtime practitioners and dogged defenders of slavery in many forms; Native American warriors who kidnapped and murdered enslaved Africans; enslaved African Americans such as Peter, Ellen, Sylvia, and Martin, who fled just as word of passage of the Tallmadge Amendments reached St. Louis—made Missouri into a place where sovereignty, settlement, and state power were all subordinated to efforts to keep African Americans enslaved. Likewise, Robert Lee shows how intertribal conflicts in the Missouri Valley shaped the natural environment that enticed so many European colonizers to Missouri, while inadvertently laying the groundwork for a brazen act of Native dispossession by territorial governor William Clark. Sauk and Meskwaki, Little Osage, Iowa, and Missouri land uses and conflicts made the Boon's Lick region a settlers' paradise of game and fertile soil. Fecund game and soil attracted settlement by middling squatters and slaveholders, along with attention from federal officials such as William Clark.

Throughout these volumes, free and enslaved African Americans appear as the political actors they were. Sarah Gronningsater examines how James Tallmadge's lifelong interactions with enslaved men and women who struggled to secure freedom in the Hudson Valley influenced his decision to call for restricting slavery in the Missouri and Mississippi Valleys. As Gronningsater shows, it is difficult to imagine Tallmadge introducing restrictions on slavery in Missouri had he not come of age in Providence, Rhode Island, and the Hudson Valley of New York, sites of intense conflicts over enslavement and emancipation, conflicts in which African Americans played a central role. Similarly, David Gellman demonstrates how the antislavery activism of the Jay family of New York was entangled with its dependence on the enslaved bodies of numerous men and women, many of whom lived in some form of servitude to the family into the 1820s. As Gellman shows, the personal and political proved inextricable in the extended Jay household. Moving west to Missouri, Anne Twitty reveals how enslaved individuals like Winny used whatever legal and social tools they could access to free themselves from enslavement. In doing so, enslaved African Americans in Missouri won important legal protections that made the outcome of the Missouri Crisis less decidedly proslavery than it otherwise might have been. As Twitty concludes, "We cannot understand the Missouri Crisis without understanding the concomitant efforts of enslaved people to use issues of law and jurisdiction for their own benefit." Collectively, these chapters illustrate that, more than just the domain of sectional clashes in Congress, the Missouri Crisis and Compromises arose from the efforts of diverse groups and individuals who repeatedly forced conflicts between enslavement and emancipation into local, regional, and national politics. They did so not because they were committed abolitionists or zealous proslavery fire-eaters, but because slavery permeated so many aspects of everyday life in the United States, whether in the Hudson Valley or the Missouri Valley.

The Missouri Crisis was preeminently a political event, and political history pervades this volume. But the authors assembled here practice an expansive kind of political history. The editors, along with many of the contributors to this volume, came of age as historians in the midst of raging faculty battles over the propriety of social and cultural history versus political and intellectual history. Like other recent works, the chapters in this volume move beyond these methodological and disciplinary confines to seamlessly combine social, cultural, legal, intellectual, and political history. Christa Dierksheide provides a cultural and intellectual analysis of enslavers' moral desire to "ameliorate" slavery by "domesticating" it. Dierksheide weds this to a political analysis of laws designed to regulate the migration of free and enslaved people, a social history of migration, and a geopolitical analysis of conflicts over slavery and sovereignty on the broader North American continent. As Dierksheide also shows, the specter of slave rebellion loomed large in the minds of policy makers in Washington and in Missouri. Policy makers charged slaveholders with the responsibility for treating enslaved people humanely while simultaneously determining which enslaved people could enter Missouri; as Dierksheide concludes, state and federal power were both ever present and deliberately hidden. David Waldstreicher uses the tools of biography, social history, and cultural history to provide a deep reading of the life of John Quincy Adams, a Massachusetts Yankee who spent almost the entirety of his public life in the company of enslavers (and often in service to them). Waldstreicher's reading of Adams yields a rich argument that not only solves the conundrum of Adams's turn to antislavery politics but also shows how the Missouri Crisis revealed that slaveholders' interests had permeated nearly every aspect of politics and governance domestically within the United States and geopolitically across the North American continent and the Atlantic world. As Adams discovered, governing in the United States meant governing slavery, in one form or another, whether by commission, omission, or both.

At the core of the Missouri Crisis stood questions centering on electoral politics and policy, the customary concerns of political history. While the traditional subjects of political history permeate this volume, the authors push the historiography on politics and sectional conflict in important new directions. Donald Ratcliffe disentangles the Missouri Crisis (or Crises) and

Compromise (or Compromises) from the political myths built up around them in the nineteenth century and the historiographical paradigms that they served in the twentieth and twenty-first centuries. Like so many other historians, Ratcliffe places the Missouri Crisis somewhere toward the middle of a long conflict over slavery that stretches from the Revolution through the sectional crisis of the late 1850s. Ratcliffe, though, offers a decidedly iconoclastic reading of the Missouri Crisis. Defying recent historiographical trends that treat the United States—as nation, state, and nation-state—as overwhelmingly proslavery, Ratcliffe argues that the Missouri Compromise should be read, at least in part, "as a long-term antislavery triumph" that stemmed from and contributed to sectional conflict.

Feeding into Ratcliffe's argument, Jeffrey L. Pasley's chapter traces a distinctly nonlinear path of events and surprising set of circumstances that made this antislavery break possible. These included a surprise attack of democratic populism, in the middle of the so-called Era of Good Feelings, that wiped out the majority of Congress in response to an unpopular pay raise. The House of Representatives filled up with political novices, idealists, and misfits, many of them War of 1812 veterans indifferent to existing Washington orthodoxies and eager to make good on wartime rhetoric about liberty by curbing the future of slavery.

Ratcliffe's chapter is complemented well by John Van Atta's examination of the salience and persistence of sectional conflict, which gave rise to the Missouri Crisis, just as the Missouri Crisis would feed sectional crises over the ensuing decades. As Van Atta makes clear, southern white fears of northern antislavery words and deeds were not overblown. Running counter to historiographic trends that downplay the commitment of many northern whites to abolition while conflating the similarities between the increasingly free states of the North and the slave states of the South, Van Atta shows that southern white fears of growing northern white commitment to using state power to take action against slavery reflected a realistic understanding of the dynamics of political power. Southern whites understood that the moment they lost control of the state—whether at the local, state, or federal level—northern whites would move to use state power to restrict slavery in numerous ways, just as they had done over the previous four decades in their own states and locales. Indeed, a majority in the House of Representatives proposed to do what the federal government had never done before: impose a plan of gradual abolition on a territory-cum-state. Northern whites in the early nineteenth century were overwhelmingly racist and committed to white supremacy and Black subordination, to be sure. However, they were also eager to use state power to halt slavery's expansion forever as the first step toward forcing southern whites to consider seriously some plan of very gradual, very long-term abolition accompanied by removal.

The concluding chapter, by Andrew Shankman, extends this first of two volumes into the 1830s. Situating the Missouri Crisis in the "global 1820s," Shankman probes the sources and limits of northern white opposition to slavery while highlighting growing southern white intransigence toward any policy or program that weakened enslavers' hold on slavery. As Shankman indicates, the Missouri Crisis was hardly an aberration in either the United States or the broader history of the Western Hemisphere. The slave and free Black resistance that seemed ceaseless in the half century between the 1770s and the 1820s became particularly intense in the decade surrounding the Missouri Crisis. Enslavers in the United States feared that any measure that undercut their ability to use state power to keep slaves in slavery welcomed the dismantling of their slave societies, as had happened across the Caribbean and Latin America. As Shankman shows, U.S. enslavers' responses to the Missouri Crisis shaped everything from the development of political parties in the 1820s to the "Negrophobia" that became a core component of northern antislavery politics.

Overall, the chapters in this and its companion volume approach the Missouri Crisis on its own terms, rather than treating it as the inevitable outcome of a flawed founding or as a prequel to the sectional showdown that resulted in the Civil War. That seems as good a place as any to start the third century of assessing its legacy.

Notes

Epigraph. William Greene to Ethan Allen Brown, March 29, 1820, Ethan Allen Brown Papers, Ohio History Connection, Archives and Library, Columbus.

1. Monographs on the Missouri Crisis and Compromise include Floyd Calvin Shoemaker, *Missouri's Struggle for Statehood, 1804–1821* (Jefferson City, MO: Hugh Stephens, 1916); Glover Moore, *The Missouri Controversy, 1819–1821* (Lexington: University Press of Kentucky, 1953); Robert Pierce Forbes, *The Missouri Compromise and Its Aftermath: Slavery and the Meaning of America* (Chapel Hill: University of North Carolina Press, 2007); and John R. Van Atta, *Wolf by the Ears: The Missouri Crisis, 1819–1821* (Baltimore: Johns Hopkins University Press, 2015). Major works that take a longer-term or wider-angled view of the creation of the state of Missouri and thus lead up to an account of the Missouri Crisis include William E. Foley, *The Genesis of Missouri: From Wilderness Outpost to Statehood* (Columbia: University of Missouri Press, 1989); Stephen Aron, *American Confluence: The Missouri Frontier*

from Borderland to Border State (Bloomington: Indiana University Press, 2006); Matthew Mason, *Slavery and Politics in the Early American Republic* (Chapel Hill: University of North Carolina Press, 2006); and John Craig Hammond, *Slavery, Freedom, and Expansion in the Early American West* (Charlottesville: University of Virginia Press, 2007). For works on the politics of slavery from the Revolution through the Civil War that include important analyses of the Missouri Crisis, see William W. Freehling, *The Road to Disunion*, 2 vols. (New York: Oxford University Press, 1991–2007); and Don E. Fehrenbacher, *The Slaveholding Republic: An Account of the United States Government's Relations to Slavery* (New York: Oxford University Press, 2001) and *The Dred Scott Case: Its Significance in American Law and Politics* (New York: Oxford University Press, 1978).

2. J. G. Randall, "The Blundering Generation," *Mississippi Valley Historical Review* 27, no. 1 (1940): 3–28; Avery Craven, *The Coming of the Civil War* (Chicago: University of Chicago Press, 1957); Thomas J. Pressly, *Americans Interpret Their Civil War* (New York: Free Press, 1965).

3. For contemporary use of the term "Missouri Question," see John Craig Hammond, "President, Planter, Politician: James Monroe, the Missouri Crisis, and the Politics of Slavery," *Journal of American History* 105, no. 4 (2019): 843–67.

4. Kate Masur examines the second Missouri Compromise, which centered on the rights of free African Americans, in volume 2.

5. Jeffrey L. Pasley, Andrew W. Robertson, and David Waldstreicher, eds., *Beyond the Founders: New Approaches to the Political History of the Early American Republic* (Chapel Hill: University of North Carolina Press, 2004); Caroline F. Sloat, "A New Nation Votes and the Study of American Politics, 1789–1824," *Journal of the Early Republic* 33, no. 2 (2013): 183–86; Donald J. Ratcliffe, "The Right to Vote and the Rise of Democracy, 1787–1828," *Journal of the Early Republic* 33, no. 2 (2013): 219–54; Daniel Peart, *Era of Experimentation: American Political Practices in the Early Republic* (Charlottesville: University of Virginia Press, 2014).

6. For a strict use of "crisis" that would not include the events analyzed in this book, see Jay Sexton, *A Nation Forged by Crisis: A New American History* (New York: Basic Books, 2018).

7. Jürgen Habermas, *Legitimation Crisis*, trans. Thomas McCarthy (Boston: Beacon Press, 1975), 1–2. Newspaper quotations from "Commercial," *Baltimore Patriot*, January 23, 1819; and "Finance-National Economy. Bank of the United States," *American Watchman* (Wilmington, DE), January 2, 1819.

8. "From the Boston Yankee: SLAVERY," *Chillicothe (OH) Scioto Gazette*, July 2, 1819; "No. I. To the People of Missouri Territory," *St. Louis Enquirer*, April 7, 1819. For other contemporary uses of the term "crisis," see, for example, James J. Wilson to Joseph Bringhurst, February 21, 1820, folder 4, Bringhurst Family Papers, Delaware Historical Society, Wilmington; Jonathan Roberts to Mathew Roberts, Washington, DC, February 25, 1820, Jonathan Roberts Papers, coll. 0558, Historical Society of Pennsylvania; John Tyler to [Dr.] William Selden, February 12, 1820, Kiplinger Research Library, Historical Society of Washington, Washington, DC; and James Monroe to James Madison, February 5, 1820, James Madison Papers, Library of Congress.

9. For these issues, see William S. Belko, ed., *Contesting the Constitution: Congress Debates the Missouri Crisis, 1819–1821* (Columbia: University of Missouri Press, 2021).

10. Richard H. Brown, "The Missouri Crisis, Slavery, and the Politics of Jacksonianism," *South Atlantic Quarterly* 65, no. 1 (1965): 55–72. Quotation from Martin Van Buren to Thomas Ritchie, January 13, 1827, Martin Van Buren Papers, Library of Congress.

11. Robert Starobin, "The Negro: A Central Theme in American History," *Journal of Contemporary History* 3, no. 2 (1968): 37–53.

12. Donald J. Ratcliffe, "The Role of Voters and Issues in Party Formation: Ohio, 1824," *Journal of American History* 59, no. 4 (1973): 847–70. To trace out some of the debates over the "new political history," its take on slavery, and relations with social history, see Ronald P. Formisano, "Toward a Reorientation of Jacksonian Politics: A Review of the Literature, 1959–1975," *Journal of American History* 63, no. 1 (1976): 42–65; Richard B. Latner, "A New Look at Jacksonian Politics," *Journal of American History* 61, no. 4 (1975): 943–69; John M. McFaul, "Expediency vs. Morality: Jacksonian Politics and Slavery," *Journal of American History* 62, no. 1 (1975): 24–39; Sean Wilentz, "On Class and Politics in Jacksonian America," *Reviews in American History* 10, no. 4 (1982): 45–63.

13. William W. Freehling, "The Founding Fathers and Slavery," *American Historical Review* 77, no. 1 (1972): 81–93; Ratcliffe, "Role of Voters and Issues in Party Formation."

14. For other articles in major journals referencing the "Missouri Crisis," see Alexander Saxton, "Blackface Minstrelsy and Jacksonian Ideology," *American Quarterly* 27, no. 1 (1975): 3–28; Kenneth S. Greenberg, "Revolutionary Ideology and the Proslavery Argument: The Abolition of Slavery in Antebellum South Carolina," *Journal of Southern History* 42, no. 3 (1976): 365–84; Robert Kelley, "Ideology and Political Culture from Jefferson to Nixon," *American Historical Review* 82, no. 3 (1977): 531–62; Richard B. Latner, "The Nullification Crisis and Republican Subversion," *Journal of Southern History* 43, no. 1 (1977): 19–38; Kenneth M. Stampp, "The Concept of a Perpetual Union," *Journal of American History* 65, no. 1 (1978): 5–33; and David W. Blight, "Perceptions of Southern Intransigence and the Rise of Radical Antislavery Thought, 1816–1830," *Journal of the Early Republic* 3, no. 2 (1983): 139–63.

15. David Brion Davis, *The Problem of Slavery in the Age of Revolution, 1770–1823* (Ithaca, NY: Cornell University Press, 1975) and *The Problem of Slavery in Western Culture* (Ithaca, NY: Cornell University Press, 1966); Winthrop D. Jordan, *White over Black: American Attitudes towards the Negro, 1550–1812* (Chapel Hill: University of North Carolina Press, 1967); George M. Fredrickson, *The Black Image in the White Mind: The Debate on Afro-American Character and Destiny, 1817–1914* (New York: Oxford University Press, 1971); Leon Litwack, *North of Slavery: The Negro in the Free States, 1790–1860* (New York: Oxford University Press, 1960); Robert McColley, *Slavery and Jeffersonian Virginia* (Urbana: University of Illinois Press, 1964); Staughton Lynd, *Class Conflict, Slavery, and the United States Constitution* (Indianapolis: Bobbs-Merrill, 1967); Arthur Zilversmit, *The First Emancipation: The Abolition of*

Slavery in the North (Chicago: University of Chicago Press, 1967); James M. Banner, *To the Hartford Convention: The Federalists and the Origins of Party Politics in Massachusetts, 1789–1815* (New York: Alfred A. Knopf, 1970); Donald L. Robinson, *Slavery in the Structure of American Politics, 1765–1820* (New York: Harcourt Brace Jovanovich, 1971); Linda K. Kerber, *Federalists in Dissent: Imagery and Ideology in Jeffersonian America* (Ithaca, NY: Cornell University Press, 1970), 23–66; Duncan J. MacLeod, *Slavery, Race, and the American Revolution* (Cambridge: Cambridge University Press, 1974); William Wiecek, *The Sources of Antislavery Constitutionalism in America, 1760–1848* (Ithaca, NY: Cornell University Press, 1977); Edmund S. Morgan, "Slavery and Freedom: The American Paradox," *Journal of American History* 59, no. 1 (1972): 5–29; William Cohen, "Thomas Jefferson and the Problem of Slavery," *Journal of American History* 56, no. 3 (1969): 503–26; Freehling, "Founding Fathers and Slavery."

16. Brown, "Missouri Crisis, Slavery, and the Politics of Jacksonianism"; Norman K. Risjord, *The Old Republicans: Southern Conservatism in the Age of Jefferson* (New York: Columbia University Press, 1965); William W. Freehling, *Prelude to Civil War: The Nullification Crisis in South Carolina, 1816–1832* (New York: Harper & Row, 1966); Benjamin Quarles, *Black Abolitionists* (New York: Oxford University Press, 1969); Major L. Wilson, *Space, Time, and Freedom: The Quest for Nationalist and the Irrepressible Conflict, 1815–1861* (Westport, CT: Greenwood Press, 1974); J. Mills Thornton III, *Politics and Power in a Slave Society: Alabama, 1800–1860* (Baton Rouge: Louisiana State University Press, 1978).

17. William E. Gienapp, *Origins of the Republican Party, 1852–1856* (New York: Oxford University Press, 1987); William G. Shade, *Banks or No Banks: The Money Issue in Western Politics, 1832–1865* (Detroit: Wayne State University Press, 1972); Ronald P. Formisano, "Federalists and Republicans: Parties, Yes—System, No," in *The Evolution of American Electoral Systems*, ed. Paul Kleppner et al., 33–76 (Westport, CT: Greenwood Press, 1981); Formisano, "Deferential-Participant Politics: The Early Republic's Political Culture, 1789–1840," *American Political Science Review* 68, no. 2 (1974): 473–87; Formisano, *The Birth of Mass Political Parties: Michigan, 1827–1861* (Princeton, NJ: Princeton University Press, 1971); Formisano, *The Transformation of Political Culture: Massachusetts Parties, 1790s–1840s* (New York: Oxford University Press, 1983). The "lost Atlantis" phrase comes from Walter Dean Burnham, "The Turnout Problem," in *Elections American Style*, ed. A. James Reichley (Washington, DC: Brookings Institution, 1987), 10. Regarding the "First Party System," Formisano and company shoved aside a once highly regarded wave of less-quantitative studies that still have much value but only just touch on the slavery issue: Noble E. Cunningham Jr., *The Jeffersonian Republicans: The Formation of Party Organization, 1789–1801* (Chapel Hill: University of North Carolina Press for the Institute of Early American History and Culture, 1957) and *The Jeffersonian Republicans in Power: Party Operations, 1801–1809* (Chapel Hill: University of North Carolina Press for the Institute of Early American History and Culture, 1963); Paul Goodman, *The Democratic-Republicans of Massachusetts: Politics in a Young Republic* (Cambridge, MA: Harvard University Press, 1964); David Hackett Fischer, *The Revolution of American Conservatism: The Federalist Party in the Era of Jeffersonian Democracy*

(New York: Harper & Row, 1965); Risjord, *Old Republicans*; Carl E. Prince, *New Jersey's Jeffersonian Republicans: The Genesis of an Early Party Machine, 1789-1817* (Chapel Hill: University of North Carolina Press for the Institute of Early American History and Culture, 1967); Alfred F. Young, *The Democratic Republicans of New York: The Origins, 1763-1797* (Chapel Hill: University of North Carolina Press for the Institute of Early American History and Culture, 1967); and Kim T. Phillips, "William Duane, Philadelphia's Democratic Republicans, and the Origins of Modern Politics," *Pennsylvania Magazine of History and Biography* 101, no. 3 (1977): 365-87.

18. Wilentz, "On Class and Politics in Jacksonian America"; Paul E. Johnson, *A Shopkeeper's Millennium: Society and Revivals in Rochester, New York, 1815-1837* (New York: Hill & Wang, 1978); Charles Sellers, *The Market Revolution: Jacksonian America, 1815-1846* (New York: Oxford University Press, 1991); Harry L. Watson, *Liberty and Power: The Politics of Jacksonian America* (New York: Oxford University Press, 1990); Daniel Feller, *The Jacksonian Promise: America, 1815-1840* (Baltimore: Johns Hopkins University Press, 1995).

19. David R. Roediger, *The Wages of Whiteness: Race and the Making of the American Working Class* (New York: Verso, 1991); Alexander Saxton, *The Rise and Fall of the White Republic: Class, Politics, and Mass Culture in Nineteenth-Century America* (New York: Verso: 1990); Noel Ignatiev, *How the Irish Became White* (New York & London: Routledge, 1995).

20. On the rise and fall of "republican ideology" in early American historiography, see Robert E. Shalhope, "Toward a Republican Synthesis: The Emergence of an Understanding of Republicanism in American Historiography," *William and Mary Quarterly*, 3rd ser., 29, no. 1 (1972): 49-80; Shalhope, "Republicanism and Early American Historiography," *William and Mary Quarterly*, 3rd ser., 39, no. 2 (1982): 334-56; and Daniel T. Rodgers, "Republicanism: The Career of a Concept," *Journal of American History* 79, no. 1 (1992): 11-38.

21. For some paradigmatic examples of "neo-Prog" history, as one of the editors likes to call it, see Jesse Lemisch, "Jack Tar in the Streets: Merchant Seamen in the Politics of the Revolutionary America," *William and Mary Quarterly*, 3rd ser., 25, no. 3 (1968): 371-407; Lemisch, "The American Revolution Seen from the Bottom Up," in *Towards a New Past: Dissenting Essays in American History*, ed. Barton J. Bernstein, 3-45 (New York: Pantheon Books, 1968); Alfred F. Young, ed., *The American Revolution: Explorations in the History of American Radicalism* (DeKalb: Northern Illinois University Press, 1976); Gary B. Nash, *The Urban Crucible: Social Change, Political Consciousness, and the Origins of the American Revolution* (Cambridge, MA: Harvard University Press, 1979); David P. Szatmary, *Shays' Rebellion: The Making of an Agrarian Insurrection* (Amherst: University of Massachusetts Press, 1980); Alfred F. Young, "George Robert Twelves Hewes (1742-1840): A Boston Shoemaker and the Memory of the American Revolution," *William and Mary Quarterly*, 3rd ser., 38, no. 4 (1981): 561-623; Thomas P. Slaughter, *The Whiskey Rebellion: Frontier Epilogue to the American Revolution* (New York: Oxford University Press, 1986); Paul A. Gilje, *The Road to Mobocracy: Popular Disorder in New York City, 1763-1834* (Chapel Hill: University of North Carolina Press for the Institute of Early American History and Culture, 1987); Alfred F. Young, "The Framers of the Constitution and the 'Genius' of

the People," *Radical History Review* 42, no. 3 (1988): 8–18; Michael A. Bellesiles, *Revolutionary Outlaws: Ethan Allen and the Struggle for Independence on the Early American Frontier* (Charlottesville: University of Virginia Press, 1993); Alfred F. Young, *Beyond the American Revolution: Explorations in the History of American Radicalism* (DeKalb: Northern Illinois University Press, 1993); Terry Bouton, *Taming Democracy: "The People," the Founders, and the Troubled Ending of the American Revolution* (New York: Oxford University Press, 2007); Barbara Clark Smith, *The Freedoms We Lost: Consent and Resistance in Revolutionary America* (New York: New Press, 2010); and Alfred F. Young, Gary B. Nash, and Ray Raphael, eds., *Revolutionary Founders: Rebels, Radicals, and Reformers in the Making of the Nation* (New York: Alfred A. Knopf, 2011).

22. Amanda Hollis-Brusky, *Ideas with Consequences: The Federalist Society and the Conservative Counterrevolution* (reprint; New York: Oxford University Press, 2019); Steven M. Teles, *The Rise of the Conservative Legal Movement: The Battle for Control of the Law* (Princeton, NJ: Princeton University Press, 2010); Andrew Hartman, *A War for the Soul of America: A History of the Culture Wars* (Chicago: University Of Chicago Press, 2015).

23. For clear deployments of this theme, see Douglass Adair, *Fame and the Founding Fathers* (New York: W. W. Norton for the Institute of Early American History and Culture, 1974); Ralph Ketcham, *Presidents above Party: The First American Presidency, 1789–1829* (Chapel Hill: University of North Carolina Press for the Institute of Early American History and Culture, 1984); and, in a different but consonant form, Joanne B. Freeman, *Affairs of Honor: National Politics in the New Republic* (New Haven, CT: Yale University Press, 2001); and Andrew S. Trees, *The Founding Fathers and the Politics of Character* (Princeton, NJ: Princeton University Press, 2004).

24. The barbarians are especially present in the final third of Gordon S. Wood, *The Radicalism of the American Revolution* (New York: Alfred A. Knopf, 1992); and the elegiac tone in Drew R. McCoy, *The Last of the Fathers: James Madison & the Republican Legacy* (Cambridge: Cambridge University Press, 1989). Women had their own subgenre of the republicanism literature, of course, in the form of Mary Beth Norton, *Liberty's Daughters: The Revolutionary Experience of American Women, 1750–1800* (New York: HarperCollins, 1980); Linda K. Kerber, *Women of the Republic: Intellect and Ideology in Revolutionary America* (New York: W. W. Norton, 1986); and Jan Lewis, "The Republican Wife: Virtue and Seduction in the Early Republic," *William and Mary Quarterly*, 3rd ser., 44, no. 4 (1987): 689–721.

25. Some of the key titles included Joseph J. Ellis, *Passionate Sage: The Character and Legacy of John Adams* (New York: W. W. Norton, 1993); Stephen E. Ambrose, *Undaunted Courage: Meriwether Lewis, Thomas Jefferson, and the Opening of the American West* (New York: Simon & Schuster, 1996); Ellis, *American Sphinx: The Character of Thomas Jefferson* (New York: Alfred A. Knopf, 1997); Ellis, *Founding Brothers: The Revolutionary Generation* (New York: Alfred A. Knopf, 2001); David G. McCullough, *John Adams* (New York: Simon & Schuster, 2001); Walter Isaacson, *Benjamin Franklin: An American Life* (New York: Simon & Schuster, 2003); Ellis, *His Excellency George Washington* (New York: Alfred A. Knopf, 2004); and Ron

Chernow, *Alexander Hamilton* (New York: Penguin Press, 2004) and *1776* (New York: Simon & Schuster, 2005).

26. Bernard Bailyn, *Ideological Origins of the American Revolution*, enlarged ed. (Cambridge, MA: Belknap Press of Harvard University Press, 1992), 232–46; MacLeod, *Slavery, Race and the American Revolution*, 184.

27. Gordon Wood, *Empire for Liberty: A History of the Early Republic, 1789–1815* (New York: Oxford University Press, 2009); Stanley Elkins and Eric McKitrick, *The Age of Federalism* (New York: Oxford University Press, 1993); Drew R. McCoy, *The Elusive Republic: Political Economy in Jeffersonian America* (Chapel Hill: University of North Carolina Press, 1980); Lance Banning, *The Jeffersonian Persuasion: Evolution of a Party Ideology* (Ithaca, NY: Cornell University Press, 1978) and *The Sacred Fire of Liberty: James Madison and the Founding of the Federal Republic* (Ithaca, NY: Cornell University Press, 1998); Steven Watts, *The Republic Reborn: War and the Making of Liberal America, 1790–1820* (Baltimore: Johns Hopkins University Press, 1987). Liberal interpretations overlooked slavery as well. See, for example, Joyce Appleby, *Capitalism and a New Social Order: The Republican Vision in the 1790s* (New York: New York University Press, 1984) and *Inheriting the Revolution: The First Generation of Americans* (Cambridge, MA: Harvard University Press, 2000). To some degree, this reflects the relative absence of contention over the slavery issue from the major congressional and newspaper debates of the early 1790s. Both the Federalists and the Republicans included slaveholders among their national leaders, and initially there was general superficial agreement about the antislavery implications of the American and French Revolutions. Recent studies have shown that there was a great deal more antislavery political activity than appeared on the surface, as well as emerging differences of opinion over the proper response to the Haitian Revolution, but many of these emerged most clearly only after Jefferson became president and the New England Federalists his not-so-loyal opposition. During the 1796 presidential campaign, one of the few occasions when slavery came up as an issue was southern Federalist efforts to frighten southern voters over the slave rebellion that Jefferson and his alleged French Revolutionary ideas might inspire: Jeffrey L. Pasley, *The First Presidential Contest: 1796 and the Founding of American Democracy* (Lawrence: University Press of Kansas, 2013), 257–58, 259–61. In other words, Jefferson was treated as the antislavery candidate in the race. One quadrant of the republican synthesis where race and slavery did arise was in studies that focused on the Federalists after 1800, when many of them felt marginalized and sufficiently desperate to experiment with sectionalism and less compelled to modulate their tone or hide their antislavery views for fear of alienating southern voters. Indeed, the priority was alienating New England voters from Virginia presidents. See Kerber, *Federalists in Dissent*, 23–66; and William C. Dowling, *Literary Federalism in the Age of Jefferson: Joseph Dennie and the "Port Folio," 1801–1811* (Columbia: University of South Carolina Press, 1999), 16–19.

28. Noble E. Cunningham Jr., *In Pursuit of Reason: The Life of Thomas Jefferson* (New York: Ballantine Books, 1988); Virginius Dabney, *The Jefferson Scandals: A Rebuttal* (New York: Dodd, Mead, 1981); Annette Gordon-Reed, *Thomas Jefferson*

and Sally Hemings: An American Controversy (Charlottesville: University of Virginia Press, 1997); Gordon-Reed, *The Hemingses of Monticello: An American Family* (New York: W. W. Norton, 2009); Gordon-Reed, "Engaging Jefferson: Blacks and the Founding Father," *William and Mary Quarterly*, 3rd ser., 57, no. 1 (2000): 171–82; Gordon-Reed and Peter S. Onuf, *"Most Blessed of the Patriarchs": Thomas Jefferson and the Empire of the Imagination* (New York: Liveright, 2016).

29. Henry Wiencek, *An Imperfect God: George Washington, His Slaves, and the Creation of America* (New York: Farrar, Straus and Giroux, 2003); Roger G. Kennedy, *Mr. Jefferson's Lost Cause: Land, Farmers, and the Louisiana Purchase* (New York: Oxford University Press, 2003); Garry Wills, *"Negro President": Jefferson and the Slave Power* (Boston: Harcourt, 2003); Gary B. Nash and Graham Russell Gao Hodges, *Friends of Liberty: Thomas Jefferson, Tadeusz Kościuszko, and Agrippa Hull: A Tale of Three Patriots, Two Revolutions, and a Tragic Betrayal of Freedom in the New Nation* (New York: Basic Books, 2008); Henry Wiencek, *Master of the Mountain: Thomas Jefferson and His Slaves* (New York: Farrar, Straus and Giroux, 2012). For Monroe, see Forbes, *Missouri Compromise and Its Aftermath.* For one of the more original and thoughtful entries in this genre, seeking to complicate a supposed antislavery paragon rather than create a new hero or villain, see David Waldstreicher, *Runaway America: Benjamin Franklin, Slavery, and the American Revolution* (New York: Hill and Wang, 2004).

30. For the more traditional and better-grounded view of Federalists as conservatives, see Fischer, *Revolution of American Conservatism*; Richard H. Kohn, *Eagle and Sword: The Beginnings of the Military Establishment in America* (New York: Free Press, 1975); Johann N. Neem, "Freedom of Association in the Early Republic: The Republican Party, the Whiskey Rebellion, and the Philadelphia and New York Cordwainers' Cases," *Pennsylvania Magazine of History and Biography* 127, no. 3 (2003): 259–90; Paul Douglas Newman, "The Federalists' Cold War: The Fries Rebellion, National Security, and the State, 1787–1800," *Pennsylvania History* 67, no. 1 (2000): 63–104; Carl E. Prince, "The Passing of the Aristocracy: Jefferson's Removal of the Federalists, 1801–1805," *Journal of American History* 57, no. 3 (1970): 563–75; Prince, "The Federalist Party and Creation of a Court Press, 1789–1801," *Journalism Quarterly* 53, no. 2 (1976): 238–41; Prince, *The Federalists and the Origins of the U.S. Civil Service* (New York: New York University Press, 1977); Whitman H. Ridgway, "Fries in the Federalist Imagination: A Crisis of Republican Society," *Pennsylvania History* 67, no. 1 (2000): 141–60; Jonathan D. Sassi, *A Republic of Righteousness: The Public Christianity of the Post-Revolutionary New England Clergy* (New York: Oxford University Press, 2001); Lewis P. Simpson, ed., *The Federalist Literary Mind: Selections from the "Monthly Anthology and Boston Review, 1803–1811," Including Documents Relating to the Boston Athenaeum* (Baton Rouge: Louisiana State University Press, 1962); and Marshall Smelser, "The Jacobin Phrenzy: Federalism and the Menace of Liberty, Equality, and Fraternity," *Review of Politics* 13, no. 4 (1951): 457–82. For the new-model antislavery Federalists, see Kerber, *Federalists in Dissent*; Wills, *"Negro President"*; Doron Ben-Atar and Barbara B. Oberg, eds., *Federalists Reconsidered* (Charlottesville: University of Virginia Press, 1998); James Horn, Jan Ellen Lewis, and Peter S. Onuf, eds., *The Revolution of 1800: Democracy, Race, and the New Republic*

(Charlottesville: University of Virginia Press, 2002); Marc M. Arkin, "The Federalist Trope: Power and Passion in Abolitionist Rhetoric," *Journal of American History* 88, no. 1 (2001): 75–98; and Rachel Hope Cleves, *The Reign of Terror in America: Visions of Violence from Anti-Jacobinism to Antislavery* (New York: Cambridge University Press, 2009) and "'Hurtful to the State': The Political Morality of Federalist Antislavery," in *Contesting Slavery: The Politics of Bondage and Freedom in the New American Nation*, ed. John Craig Hammond and Matthew Mason, 207–26 (Charlottesville: University of Virginia Press, 2011). For the claim that John Adams might have negotiated a free-soil "Louisiana Purchase," see Douglas Egerton, "Empire for Liberty Reconsidered," in *Revolution of 1800*, ed. Horn, Lewis, and Onuf, 121–52. It may be significant that the new-model Federalists have not received full monographic or synthetic treatment. The whole interpretation depends quite heavily on imaginative projection and counterfactual speculation and works better as antipopulist cultural politics than political history. For a judicious evaluation of the limits and origins of Federalist antislavery, see Matthew Mason, "Federalists, Abolitionists, and the Problem of Influence," *American Nineteenth Century History* 10 (March 2009): 1–27. Alexander Hamilton became the ultimate beneficiary of this trend, with a best-selling biography and a hit musical that traded heavily on his limited antislavery credentials to transform the militaristic financier of previous interpretations, Wall Street's favorite founder, into an unlikely new liberal hero for the twenty-first century. See David Waldstreicher and Jeffrey L. Pasley, "*Hamilton* as Founders Chic: A Neo-Federalist, Antislavery, Usable Past?," in *Historians on "Hamilton": How a Blockbuster Musical Is Restaging America's Past*, ed. Renee C. Romano and Claire Bond Potter, 137–66 (New Brunswick, NJ: Rutgers University Press, 2018).

31. Leonard L. Richards, *The Slave Power: The Free North and Southern Domination, 1780–1860* (Baton Rouge: Louisiana State University Press, 2000); Fehrenbacher, *Slaveholding Republic*; Paul Finkelman, "Jefferson and Slavery: 'Treason against the Hopes of the World,'" in *Jeffersonian Legacies*, ed. Peter S. Onuf (Charlottesville: University of Virginia Press, 1993), 181–221; Finkelman, *Slavery and the Founders: Race and Liberty in the Age of Jefferson* (Armonk, NY: M. E. Sharpe, 1996); Freehling, *The Road to Disunion* and "The Founding Fathers, Conditional Antislavery, and the Nonradicalism of the American Revolution," in *The Reintegration of American History: Slavery and the Civil War* (New York: Oxford University Press, 1994), 12–33; William M. Wiecek, "'The Blessing of Liberty': Slavery in the American Constitutional Order," in *Slavery and Its Consequences: The Constitution, Equality, and Race*, ed. Robert A. Goldwin and Art Kaufman (Washington, DC: American Enterprise Institute for Public Policy Research, 1988); Gary B. Nash, *Race and Revolution* (Madison: University of Wisconsin Press, 1990); Robin L. Einhorn, *American Taxation, American Slavery* (Chicago: University of Chicago Press, 2006); Kennedy, *Mr. Jefferson's Lost Cause*; Egerton, "Empire for Liberty Reconsidered." For more ambiguous takes on the question of the founders and slavery, dealing with the issue seriously but not following the Garrisonian line quite as closely, see Earl M. Maltz, "The Idea of a Proslavery Constitution," *Journal of the Early Republic* 17, no. 1 (1997): 37–60; Ari Helo and Peter Onuf, "Jefferson, Morality, and the Problem of Slavery," *William and Mary Quarterly*, 3rd ser., 60, no. 3 (2003): 583–614; Peter S. Onuf, *Jefferson's Empire:*

The Language of American Nationhood (Charlottesville: University of Virginia Press, 2000); and David Waldstreicher, *Slavery's Constitution: From Revolution to Ratification* (New York: Hill & Wang, 2009).

32. Pasley, Robertson, and Waldstreicher, *Beyond the Founders*.

33. For social and cultural histories of slavery and African American life that omit or severely minimize the Missouri Crisis and the issues surrounding it, see Ira Berlin, *Generations of Captivity: A History of African-American Slaves* (Cambridge, MA: Harvard University Press, 2003); Joanne Pope Melish, *Disowning Slavery: Gradual Emancipation and "Race" in New England, 1780–1860* (Ithaca, NY: Cornell University Press, 1998); Sylvia Frey, *Water from the Rock: Black Resistance in a Revolutionary Age* (Princeton, NJ: Princeton University Press, 1991); Gary B. Nash and Jean R. Soderlund, *Freedom by Degrees: Emancipation in Pennsylvania and Its Aftermath* (New York: Oxford University Press, 1991); and Gary B. Nash, *Forging Freedom: The Formation of Philadelphia's Black Community, 1720–1840* (Cambridge: Cambridge University Press, 1991). For the parting of abolitionist studies and political history, see James Brewer Stewart, "Reconsidering Abolitionists in the Age of Fundamentalist Politics," *Journal of the Early Republic* 26, no. 1 (2006): 1–23.

34. For a sampling of this work that joined social and political history in innovative ways, emphasizing books and including some harbingers and influences, but excluding particular items cited prominently elsewhere in this introduction, see, in reverse chronological order, Billy Coleman, *Harnessing Harmony: Music, Power, and Politics in the United States, 1788–1865* (Chapel Hill: University of North Carolina Press, 2020); Laura Lohman, *Hail Columbia! American Music and Politics in the Early Nation* (New York: Oxford University Press, 2020); John L. Brooke, *"There Is a North": Fugitive Slaves, Political Crisis, and Cultural Transformation in the Coming of the Civil War* (Amherst: University of Massachusetts Press, 2019); Daniel Peart, *Lobbyists and the Making of US Tariff Policy, 1816–1861* (Baltimore: Johns Hopkins University Press, 2018); Kenneth Owen, *Political Community in Revolutionary Pennsylvania, 1774–1800* (Oxford: Oxford University Press, 2018); Daniel Peart and Adam I. P. Smith, eds., *Practicing Democracy: Popular Politics in the United States from the Constitution to the Civil War* (Charlottesville: University of Virginia Press, 2015); Patrick Griffin et al., eds., *Between Sovereignty and Anarchy: The Politics of Violence in the American Revolutionary Era* (Charlottesville: University of Virginia Press, 2015); Kirsten E. Wood, "'Join with Heart and Soul and Voice': Music, Harmony, and Politics in the Early American Republic," *American Historical Review* 119, no. 4 (2014): 1083–1116; Peart, *Era of Experimentation*; Pasley, *First Presidential Contest*; Seth Cotlar, *Tom Paine's America: The Rise and Fall of Transatlantic Radicalism in the Early Republic* (Charlottesville: University of Virginia Press, 2011); Ronald J. Zboray and Mary Saracino Zboray, *Voices without Votes: Women and Politics in Antebellum New England* (Durham, NH: University of New Hampshire Press; Hanover, NH: University Press of New England, 2010); John L. Brooke, *Columbia Rising: Civil Life on the Upper Hudson from the Revolution to the Age of Jackson* (Chapel Hill: University of North Carolina Press for the Omohundro Institute of Early American History and Culture, 2010); Carolyn Eastman, *A Nation of Speechifyers: Making an American Public After the Revolution* (Chicago: University

of Chicago Press, 2009); Johann N. Neem, *Creating a Nation of Joiners: Democracy and Civil Society in Early National Massachusetts* (Cambridge, MA: Harvard University Press, 2008); Catherine O'Donnell Kaplan, *Men of Letters in the Early Republic: Cultivating Forms of Citizenship* (Chapel Hill: University of North Carolina Press for the Omohundro Institute of Early American History and Culture, 2008); Rosemarie Zagarri, *Revolutionary Backlash: Women and Politics in the Early American Republic* (Philadelphia: University of Pennsylvania Press, 2007); Albrecht Koschnik, *"Let a Common Interest Bind Us Together": Associations, Partisanship, and Culture in Philadelphia, 1775–1840* (Charlottesville: University of Virginia Press, 2007); Todd Estes, *The Jay Treaty Debate, Public Opinion, and the Evolution of Early American Political Culture* (Amherst: University of Massachusetts Press, 2006); Meg Jacobs, William J. Novak, and Julian E. Zelizer, eds., *The Democratic Experiment: New Directions in American Political History* (Princeton, NJ: Princeton University Press, 2003); Max M. Edling, *A Revolution in Favor of Government: Origins of the U.S. Constitution and the Making of the American State* (New York: Oxford University Press, 2003); Horn, Lewis, and Onuf, *Revolution of 1800*; Kenneth R. Bowling and Donald R. Kennon, *The House and Senate in the 1790s: Petitioning, Lobbying, and Institutional Development* (Athens: Ohio University Press for the United States Capitol Historical Society, 2002); Sassi, *Republic of Righteousness*; Andrew W. Robertson, "'Look on This Picture . . . and on This!': Nationalism, Localism, and Partisan Images of Otherness in the United States, 1787–1820," *American Historical Review* 106, no. 4 (2001): 1263–80; Jeffrey L. Pasley, *"The Tyranny of Printers": Newspaper Politics in the Early American Republic* (Charlottesville: University of Virginia Press, 2001); Freeman, *Affairs of Honor*; Susan Branson, *These Fiery Frenchified Dames: Women and Political Culture in Early National Philadelphia* (Philadelphia: University of Pennsylvania Press, 2001); Reeve Huston, *Land and Freedom: Rural Society, Popular Protest, and Party Politics in Antebellum New York* (New York: Oxford University Press, 2000); Catherine Allgor, *Parlor Politics: In Which the Ladies of Washington Help Build a City and a Government* (Charlottesville: University of Virginia Press, 2000); Saul Cornell, *The Other Founders: Anti-Federalism and the Dissenting Tradition in America, 1788–1828* (Chapel Hill: University of North Carolina Press for the Omohundro Institute of Early American History and Culture, 1999); David Waldstreicher and Stephen R. Grossbart, "Abraham Bishop's Vocation; or, The Mediation of Jeffersonian Politics," *Journal of the Early Republic* 18, no. 4 (1998): 617–57; Elizabeth R. Varon, *We Mean to Be Counted: White Women and Politics in Antebellum Virginia* (Chapel Hill: University of North Carolina Press, 1998); Nancy Isenberg, *Sex and Citizenship in Antebellum America* (Chapel Hill: University of North Carolina Press, 1998); David Waldstreicher, *In the Midst of Perpetual Fetes: The Making of American Nationalism, 1776–1820* (Chapel Hill: University of North Carolina Press for the Omohundro Institute of Early American History and Culture, 1997); Simon P. Newman, *Parades and the Politics of the Street: Festive Culture in the Early American Republic* (Philadelphia: University of Pennsylvania Press, 1997); Michael Durey, *Transatlantic Radicals and the Early American Republic* (Lawrence: University Press of Kansas, 1997); John L. Brooke, "Ancient Lodges and Self-Created Societies: Voluntary Association and the Public Sphere in the Early Republic," in *Launching the "Extended Republic": The*

Federalist Era (Charlottesville: University of Virginia Press, 1996), 273–377; Alan Taylor, *William Cooper's Town: Power and Persuasion on the Frontier of the Early American Republic* (New York: Alfred A. Knopf, 1995); Andrew W. Robertson, *The Language of Democracy: Political Rhetoric in the United States and Britain, 1790–1900* (Ithaca, NY: Cornell University Press, 1995); Richard R. John, *Spreading the News: The American Postal System from Franklin to Morse* (Cambridge, MA: Harvard University Press, 1995); Sean Wilentz, "Artisan Republican Festivals and the Rise of Class Conflict in New York City, 1788–1837," in *Working-Class America: Essays on Labor, Community, and American Society*, ed. Michael Frisch and Daniel J. Walkowitz (Urbana: University of Illinois Press, 1983); and Jean H. Baker, *Affairs of Party: The Political Culture of Northern Democrats in the Mid-Nineteenth Century* (Ithaca, NY: Cornell University Press, 1983).

35. For introductions to #VastEarlyAmerica, see Karin Wulf, "Vast Early America: Three Simple Words for a Complex Reality," *Omohundro Institute of Early American History & Culture: Uncommon Sense* (blog), February 6, 2019, https://blog.oieahc.wm.edu/vast-early-america-three-simple-words/; and Jeffrey Ostler and Nancy Shoemaker, "Settler Colonialism in Early American History: Introduction," *William and Mary Quarterly* 76, no. 3 (2019): 361–68, as well as most recent issues of that journal. The trend it describes is much older than the hashtag, ironically seeming to date back particularly to the late Bernard Bailyn's Atlantic History seminar in the 1990s and beyond that to the old "imperial school" Bailyn was raised in, although the Atlantic has long since ceased to contain it. See, speculatively, Bernard Bailyn, *Atlantic History: Concept and Contours* (Cambridge, MA: Harvard University Press, 2005); and Bernard Bailyn and Philip D. Morgan, eds., *Strangers within the Realm: Cultural Margins of the First British Empire* (Chapel Hill: University of North Carolina Press for the Institute of Early American History and Culture, 1991).

36. For the current regnant interpretation of slavery as capitalism's most powerful and generative form, see Walter Johnson, *Soul by Soul: Life Inside the Antebellum Slave Market* (Cambridge, MA: Harvard University Press, 1999); Sven Beckert, *Empire of Cotton: A Global History* (New York: Vintage, 2014); Edward Baptist, *The Half Has Never Been Told: Slavery and the Making of American Capitalism* (New York: Basic Books, 2014); Calvin Schermerhorn, *The Business of Slavery and the Rise of American Capitalism, 1815–1860* (New Haven, CT: Yale University Press, 2015) and *Unrequited Toil: A History of United States Slavery* (New York: Cambridge University Press, 2018); and Sven Beckert and Seth Rockman, eds., *Slavery's Capitalism: A New History of American Economic Development* (Philadelphia: University of Pennsylvania Press, 2018). For this view, and the history of white supremacy as applied to Missouri and the rest of the Mississippi Valley, see Walter Johnson, *River of Dark Dreams: Slavery and Empire in the Cotton Kingdom* (Cambridge: Harvard University Press, 2013) and *The Broken Heart of America: St. Louis and the Violent History of the United States* (New York: Basic Books, 2020).

37. On the abolition of slavery in the North, see Nash, *Forging Freedom*; Nash and Soderlund, *Freedom by Degrees*; Shane White, *Somewhat More Independent: The End of Slavery in New York City, 1770–1810* (Athens: University of Georgia Press, 1991); Graham Russell Hodges, *Root and Branch: African Americans in New York*

& *East Jersey, 1613-1863* (Chapel Hill: University of North Carolina Press, 1999); Melish, *Disowning Slavery*; David N. Gellman, *Emancipating New York: The Politics of Slavery and Freedom, 1777-1827* (Baton Rouge: Louisiana State University Press, 2006); Beverly C. Tomek, *Colonization and Its Discontents: Emancipation, Emigration, and Antislavery in Antebellum Pennsylvania* (New York: New York University Press, 2010); Richard Newman and James Mueller, eds., *Antislavery and Abolition in Philadelphia: Emancipation and the Long Struggle for Racial Justice in the City of Brotherly Love* (Baton Rouge: Louisiana State University Press, 2011); and James J. Gigantino II, *The Ragged Road to Abolition: Slavery and Freedom in New Jersey, 1775-1865* (Philadelphia: University of Pennsylvania Press, 2014).

38. Jason T. Sharples, *The World That Fear Made: Slave Revolts and Conspiracy Scares in Early America* (Philadelphia: University of Pennsylvania Press, 2020); Matthew J. Clavin, *The Battle of Negro Fort: The Rise and Fall of a Fugitive Slave Community* (New York: New York University Press, 2019); S. Charles Bolton, *Fugitivism: Escaping Slavery in the Lower Mississippi Valley, 1820-1860* (Fayetteville: University of Arkansas Press, 2019); Richard Bell, *Stolen: Five Free Boys Kidnapped into Slavery and Their Astonishing Odyssey Home* (New York: 37 Ink, 2019); Vanessa M. Holden, "Generation, Resistance, and Survival: African-American Children and the Southampton Rebellion of 1831," *Slavery & Abolition* 38, no. 4 (2017): 673-96; Nicole Eustace and Fredrika J. Teute, eds., *Warring for America: Cultural Contests in the Era of 1812* (Chapel Hill: University of North Carolina Press, 2017); Nathaniel Millett, *The Maroons of Prospect Bluff and Their Quest for Freedom in the Atlantic World* (Gainesville: University Press of Florida, 2015); Matthew J. Clavin, *Aiming for Pensacola: Fugitive Slaves on the Atlantic and Southern Frontiers* (Cambridge, MA: Harvard University Press, 2015); D. A. Dunkley, *Agency of the Enslaved: Jamaica and the Culture of Freedom in the Atlantic World* (Lanham, MD: Lexington Books, 2012); Hammond and Mason, *Contesting Slavery*; Douglas R. Egerton, *Death or Liberty: Africans Americans and Revolutionary America* (New York: Oxford University Press, 2009) and *He Shall Go Out Free: The Lives of Denmark Vesey* (Lanham, MD: Rowman & Littlefield, 2004); Laurent Dubois, *A Colony of Citizens: Revolution and Slave Emancipation in the French Caribbean, 1787-1804* (Chapel Hill: University of North Carolina Press for the Omohundro Institute of Early American History and Culture, 2004); William G. Merkel, "To See Oneself as a Target of Justified Revolution: Thomas Jefferson and Gabriel's Uprising," *American Nineteenth Century History* 4, no. 2 (2003): 1-31; William A. Link, *Roots of Secession: Slavery and Politics in Antebellum Virginia* (Chapel Hill: University of North Carolina Press, 2003); Simon Newman, "The World Turned Upside Down: Revolutionary Politics, Fries' and Gabriel's Rebellions, and the Fears of the Federalists," *Pennsylvania History* 67, no. 1 (2000): 5-20; Woody Holton, *Forced Founders: Indians, Debtors, Slaves and the Making of the American Revolution in Virginia* (Chapel Hill: University of North Carolina Press for the Omohundro Institute of Early American History and Culture, 1999); James Sidbury, *Ploughshares into Swords: Race, Rebellion, and Identity in Gabriel's Virginia, 1730-1810* (Cambridge: Cambridge University Press, 1997); Peter P. Hinks, *To Awaken My Afflicted Brethren: David Walker and the Problem of Antebellum Slave Resistance* (University Park: Pennsylvania State University Press, 1997); Douglas R.

Egerton, *Gabriel's Rebellion: The Virginia Slave Conspiracies of 1800 & 1802* (Chapel Hill: University of North Carolina Press, 1993); Paul F. LaChance, "The Politics of Fear: French Louisianans and the Slave Trade, 1786–1809," *Plantation Society* 1, no. 2 (1979): 162–97; Steven A. Channing, *Crisis of Fear: Secession in South Carolina* (New York: W. W. Norton, 1974). On the influence of the Haitian Revolution in particular, see David P. Geggus, *The Impact of the Haitian Revolution in the Atlantic World* (Columbia: University of South Carolina Press, 2001); Laurent Dubois, *Avengers of the New World: The Story of the Haitian Revolution* (Cambridge, MA: Harvard University Press, 2004); Matthew J. Clavin, *Toussaint Louverture and the American Civil War: The Promise and Peril of a Second Haitian Revolution* (Philadelphia: University of Pennsylvania Press, 2011); Marlene L. Daut, "The 'Alpha and Omega' of Haitian Literature: Baron de Vastey and the U.S. Audience of Haitian Political Writing," *Comparative Literature* 64, no. 1 (2012): 49–72; Julia Gaffield, "Haiti and Jamaica in the Remaking of the Early Nineteenth-Century Atlantic World," *William and Mary Quarterly* 69, no. 3 (July 2012): 583–614; Ashli White, *Encountering Revolution: Haiti and the Making of the Early Republic* (Baltimore: Johns Hopkins University Press, 2012); Julia Gaffield, *Haitian Connections in the Atlantic World: Recognition after Revolution* (Chapel Hill: University of North Carolina Press, 2015); and James Alexander Dun, *Dangerous Neighbors: Making the Haitian Revolution in Early America* (Philadelphia: University of Pennsylvania Press, 2016).

39. Kelly M. Kennington, *In the Shadow of* Dred Scott: *St. Louis Freedom Suits and the Legal Culture of Slavery in Antebellum America* (Athens: University of Georgia Press, 2017); Anne Twitty, *Before* Dred Scott: *Slavery and Legal Culture in the American Confluence, 1787–1857* (New York: Cambridge University Press, 2016).

40. For the origins of the transnational turn in U.S. history, see Ian Tyrell, "American Exceptionalism in an Age of International History," *American Historical Review* 96, no. 4 (1991): 1031–55, 1068–71; and the special issue led off by David Thelen, "The Nation and Beyond: Transnational Perspectives on United States History," *Journal of American History* 86, no. 3 (1999): 965–75. As applied to early American history, key works include Eliga H. Gould, *Among the Powers of the Earth: The American Revolution and the Making of a New World Empire* (Cambridge, MA: Harvard University Press, 2014); and Eliga H. Gould and Peter S. Onuf, eds., *Empire and Nation: The American Revolution in the Atlantic World* (Baltimore: Johns Hopkins University Press, 2005), among many others. For reinterpretations of early U.S. foreign policy through its response to the Haitian Revolution, see Gordon S. Brown, *Toussaint's Clause: The Founding Fathers and the Haitian Revolution* (Jackson: University Press of Mississippi, 2005); and Ronald Angelo Johnson, *Diplomacy in Black and White: John Adams, Toussaint Louverture, and Their Atlantic World Alliance* (Athens: University of Georgia Press, 2014). On the War of 1812 and slavery, see Alan Taylor, *The Internal Enemy: Slavery and War in Virginia, 1772–1832* (New York: W. W. Norton, 2014); Gene Allen Smith, *The Slaves' Gamble: Choosing Sides in the War of 1812* (New York: St. Martin's, 2013); and Nathaniel Millett, "Slavery and the War of 1812," *Tennessee Historical Quarterly* 71, no. 3 (2012): 184–205.

41. Mason, *Slavery and Politics in the Early American Republic.* For works that argue for the relative success of the early antislavery movement, see Nicholas P. Wood,

Let the Oppressed Go Free: The Revolutionary Generation of American Abolitionists (Philadelphia: University of Pennsylvania Press, forthcoming, 2021); Paul J. Polgar, *Standard-Bearers of Equality: America's First Abolition Movement* (Chapel Hill: University of North Carolina Press for the Omohundro Institute of Early American History and Culture, 2019); Manisha Sinha, *The Slave's Cause: A History of Abolition* (New Haven, CT: Yale University Press, 2016), 4–194; and Merton Lynn Dillon, *Benjamin Lundy and the Struggle for Negro Freedom* (Urbana: University of Illinois Press, 1966). Following the traditional time line, but presenting a more than usually complete and upbeat take on the early decades, is Richard S. Newman, *The Transformation of American Abolitionism: Fighting Slavery in the Early Republic* (Chapel Hill: University of North Carolina Press, 2002), along with many other wonderful works by the same author. On colonization and the role of part of the putative antislavery movement in modernizing the institution and promoting white supremacy, see Christa Dierksheide, *Amelioration and Empire: Progress and Slavery in the Plantation Americas*, (Charlottesville: University of Virginia Press, 2014); Nicholas Guyatt, *Bind Us Apart: How Enlightened Americans Invented Racial Segregation* (New York: Basic Books, 2016); and Eric Burin, *Slavery and the Peculiar Solution: A History of the American Colonization Society* (Gainesville: University Press of Florida, 2005).

42. For a review of the literature on slavery and politics between 1770 and 1820 through the early 2010s, see John Craig Hammond, "Race, Slavery, Sectional Conflict, and National Politics, 1770–1820," in *The Routledge History of Nineteenth Century America*, ed. Jonathan Daniel Wells, 11–32 (New York and London: Routledge, 2017).

43. John Mack Faragher, "'More Motley than Mackinaw': From Ethnic Mixing to Ethnic Cleansing on the Frontier of the Lower Missouri, 1783–1833," in *Contact Points: American Frontiers from the Mohawk Valley to the Mississippi, 1750–1830*, ed. Andrew R. L. Cayton and Fredrika J. Teute, 304–26 (Chapel Hill: University of North Carolina Press for the Omohundro Institute of Early American History and Culture, 1998); Andrew R. L. Cayton, "'When Shall We Cease to Have Judases?': The Blount Conspiracy and the Limits of the 'Extended Republic,'" in *Launching the "Extended Republic": The Federalist Era*, ed. Ronald Hoffman and Peter J. Albert, 156–89 (Charlottesville: University of Virginia Press for the United States Capitol Historical Society, 1996); John Craig Hammond, "'The Most Free of the Free States': Politics, Slavery, Race, and Regional Identity in Early Ohio," *Ohio History* 121 (2014): 35–57; Suzanne Cooper Guasco, *Confronting Slavery: Edward Coles and the Rise of Antislavery Politics in Nineteenth Century America* (DeKalb: Northern Illinois University Press, 2013); Matthew Salafia, *Slavery's Borderland: Freedom and Bondage Along the Ohio River* (Philadelphia: University of Pennsylvania Press, 2013); Ryan A. Quintana, *Making a Slave State: Political Development in Early South Carolina* (Chapel Hill: University of North Carolina Press, 2018).

44. Gautham Rao, "The New Historiography of the Early Federal Government: Institutions, Contexts, and the Imperial State," *William and Mary Quarterly*, 3rd ser., 77, no. 1 (2020): 97–128; Andrew Shankman, "Toward a Social History of Federalism: The State and Capitalism to and from the American Revolution," *Journal of the Early Republic* 37, no. 4 (2017): 615–53; John Reda, *From Furs to Farms: The*

Transformation of the Mississippi Valley, 1762–1825 (DeKalb: Northern Illinois University Press, 2016); Dierksheide, *Amelioration and Empire*; Eberhard L. Faber, *Building the Land of Dreams: New Orleans and the Transformation of Early America* (Princeton, NJ: Princeton University Press, 2015); John Craig Hammond, "Slavery, Sovereignty, and Empires: North American Borderlands and the American Civil War, 1660–1860," *Journal of the Civil War Era* 4, no. 2 (2014): 264–98; Martin Öhman, "A Convergence of Crises: The Expansion of Slavery, Geopolitical Realignment, and Economic Depression in the Post-Napoleonic World," *Diplomatic History* 37, no. 3 (2013): 419–45; John Craig Hammond, "Slavery, Settlement, and Empire: The Expansion and Growth of Slavery in the Interior of the North American Continent, 1770–1820," *Journal of the Early Republic* 32, no. 2 (2012): 175–206; Peter J. Kastor, *The Nation's Crucible: The Louisiana Purchase and the Creation of America* (New Haven, CT: Yale University Press, 2004).

45. Sharon Ann Murphy, "Collateral Damage: The Impact of Foreclosure on Enslaved Lives during the Panic," *Journal of the Early Republic* 40, no. 4 (2020): 691–96; Andrew H. Browning, *The Panic of 1819: The First Great Depression* (Columbia: University of Missouri Press, 2019), 120–23, 240–50; Clyde A. Haulman, *Virginia and the Panic of 1819: The First Great Depression and the Commonwealth* (New York & London: Routledge, 2016).

PART I

BACKGROUND TO THE MISSOURI CRISIS,
1770–1820

1. The Centrality of Slavery

Enslavement and Settler Sovereignty in Missouri, 1770–1820

John Craig Hammond

W HITE MISSOURIANS DEMONSTRATED their strong commitment to enslaving others long before the Missouri Crisis. Indeed, European settlement
was inextricably tied to enslavement, captivity, and bondage in Missouri
during the half century stretching between initial European colonization in
the 1770s and the Missouri Crisis of 1820.[1] In the late 1770s, permanent
European settlements on the west bank of the Mississippi River had been
in place for only a short time. The mostly French-descended inhabitants
deemed the enslavement of Africans a precondition for establishing permanent settlements that would be integrated into the larger political economy
of the lower Mississippi Valley, imperial North America, and the Atlantic
world. Sensing an opportunity to use the resources of the Spanish state to
acquire enslaved Africans far away from the main routes of the Atlantic slave
trade, in 1777 the European inhabitants of Missouri petitioned the Spanish
Crown for assistance. The settlers asked "that the compassion of the King
should deign to provide them with negro slaves on credit, for whom they
may pay with the crops." Spanish officials obliged in assisting the French-
descended colonists in obtaining enslaved Africans from markets downriver
in New Orleans. From the 1770s through the 1790s, the population of enslaved Africans grew rapidly in Missouri, while white Missourians reclassi-
fied enslaved Native Americans as "negroes."[2]

By 1804, when American officials arrived to claim sovereignty over
Missouri per the terms of the Louisiana Purchase, perhaps 20 percent of
Missouri's non–Native American population was enslaved and classified
as "negro," and the European American settlements in Missouri straddled
the ill-defined line separating societies with slaves from slave societies.
Regardless of where exactly Missouri fell on the spectrum between slave
societies and societies with slaves, the most vocal and prominent white

Missourians insisted that the United States commit itself to keeping enslaved Africans in slavery. The "Committee of the Town of St. Louis," for example, demanded that the United States implement laws to "keep the slaves in their duty according to their class; in the respect they owe generally to all whites, and more expressly their masters." American officials obliged, and over the next fifteen years the population of enslaved Africans in Missouri grew: slowly at first, rapidly after 1815. By 1819, perhaps ten thousand of the sixty thousand non–Native Americans in Missouri were black and enslaved, and Missouri still bestrode the ambiguous line between a society with slaves (where gradual emancipation remained a distinct possibility) and a slave society (where gradual emancipation seemed unlikely). James Tallmadge sensed that the comparatively small number of slaves in Missouri welcomed some kind of gradual abolition plan. But the majority of politically active white Missourians rejected the Tallmadge Amendments out of hand; they rejected every proposal for some kind of gradual abolition program at the state level, threatened disunion should Congress insist on restrictions, and proceeded to elect strictly proslavery candidates to the Missouri Constitutional Convention. During the Missouri Crisis, many white Missourians insisted that they would "never become a member of the Union under the restriction relative to slavery." They meant it.[3]

The Missouri Crisis has rightfully come to occupy a central place in the historiography of slavery and politics in the early republic. Since 2006, seven monographs and numerous articles and book chapters have afforded the Missouri Crisis a central place in their narratives and analyses. Some have used the Missouri Crisis as the conclusion to an early epoch of the politics of slavery that began with the American Revolution and closed with the Missouri Compromise.[4] Others have found in the Missouri Crisis the genesis of a new form of national political parties committed to protecting slavery.[5] Still others have used the crisis as an inflection point to examine why southern whites adopted a proslavery ideology or why white northerners retreated from antislavery politics.[6] The chapters in this volume analyze the Missouri Crisis from all of those perspectives while developing several new ones.

Yet for all of the insights produced by scholarship old and new, historians have written far less about struggles between slaves and slaveholders, enslavement and emancipation, in prestatehood Missouri and the broader confluence region.[7] Major works examining the Missouri Crisis have focused far more on white people in the East arguing about Missouri slavery in the abstract than on white Missourians' efforts to create a slave society and African American challenges to their enslavement. The new history of slavery and capitalism should provide some redress to this oversight. Those works have been invaluable in uncovering the processes by which whites created plantation societies in the Deep South while examining the never-ending series of challenges to slavery, both internal and external.[8] Yet Missouri falls outside the model of a plantation society employed by the new historians of slavery and capitalism. As a result, these works overlook the processes by which settler colonists and imperial powers created new slave societies in the middle Mississippi Valley. This omission is striking given that the slave societies of the middle Mississippi Valley and the southern interior both originated in the Atlantic plantation complex's "second slavery," the period between the 1770s and the 1810s that resulted in the great growth and expansion of slavery from its eighteenth-century core in places such as Saint-Domingue, Jamaica, and the coastal colonies of British North America to once peripheral places such as Cuba, Puerto Rico, Trinidad, Louisiana, the southern interior, and the Ohio and Missouri Valleys.[9] Collectively, the new history of capitalism and slavery along with the robust literature on the Missouri Crisis overlooks the lives of free and enslaved African Americans in prestatehood Missouri and the processes by which whites created and maintained various systems of bondage and enslavement. Likewise, the meanings and significance of slavery and racial subordination to the white inhabitants of Missouri are almost entirely overlooked in the historiography of slavery and politics in the early republic and the new history of slavery and capitalism.[10] Why do we have a "Missouri Crisis" but no "Indiana Crisis" or "Alabama Crisis"? How and why was a slave society constructed in Missouri? How did the quotidian lives of enslaved people in Missouri differ from those in Mississippi? The best literature on the Missouri Crisis and the new history of capitalism has no good answers to those questions.

Between 1770 and 1820, in what would become the state of Missouri, slavery was central to processes of European settlement and development, conquest and colonialism, and governance and incorporation into the contested imperial worlds of North America. Slavery was less important to settlement and sovereignty in places such as Ohio and Indiana, between the 1790s and the 1810s, and in later periods such as the 1830s. That's why we have a Missouri Crisis, but no Ohio, Indiana, or Iowa Crisis. Slavery had long been tied to settlement and sovereignty in Illinois. That's why there were nearly Illinois Crises in 1818 and 1824. Slavery, settlement, and sovereignty were coterminous with each other in Mississippi, Alabama, and Louisiana long before the United States acquired those regions. There were brief "Natchez" and "Louisiana" Crises in 1798 and 1804 when the United States created territorial governments for these regions, but Congress quickly acceded to the demands of white enslavers in those territories. The situation with Missouri in 1819 would be different. European settlement and claims of sovereignty became inextricably tied to state support for slavery in Missouri between the 1770s and the Louisiana Purchase of 1803 and again between 1803 and 1819. White commitment to enslaving others ran so deep—whether in the 1770s, 1804, or 1819—that it is difficult to envision a feasible path to gradual abolition in Missouri short of the kind of massive war and rebellion that led to abolition during the U.S. Civil War. Slaveholders and would-be slaveholders in Missouri proved to be as defensive about their particular institution as their counterparts in Virginia, Mississippi, and Alabama. Whether in the 1770s, 1804, or 1819, for white Missourians imperial state power was to be deployed to keep slaves in slavery, not to facilitate their emancipation, immediate or gradual.[11]

And while white Missourians' firm commitment to slavery makes it difficult to envision a peaceful path to emancipation in Missouri, enslaved Native and African Americans challenged their bondage in numerous ways. Shifting jurisdictional and legal regimes combined with the diverse origins of enslaved Missourians to permit some African Americans to challenge the legality of their enslavement. Likewise, the unsettled, indeterminate structures of social, political, and economic life in the Missouri borderlands created spaces that slaves exploited to claim freedoms within slavery, even when they found themselves unable to flee or challenge the legality of their own personal enslavement. Missouri's borderland location and the inability of Missouri slaveholders to maintain widespread social, economic, and institutional commitments to keeping slaves in slavery afforded enslaved men and women continuous opportunities to blur and sometimes challenge the lines between slavery and freedom, emancipation and enslavement. At the same time, because Missouri never underwent the plantation revolutions that transformed places like Louisiana, and because Missouri never fully crossed the threshold that separated societies with slaves from slave societies, on three occasions between 1770 and 1820 lawmakers in Washington and Madrid tried to force white Missourians to adopt some kind of gradual abolition plan. In each case, Missouri's powerful class of slaveholders and would-be slaveholders fought off all such external efforts to effect such a move.

Slavery's initial expansion and then great growth in Missouri occurred in the four decades between the Seven Years' War and the Louisiana Purchase. Beginning in the 1760s, imperial conflicts led to the expansion of the

Caribbean plantation complex into the lower Mississippi Valley, as Spain and Britain used state support for slavery as an important tool of empire building. The establishment of plantation economies in the lower Mississippi Valley led, in turn, to the transformation and growth of slavery upriver in the Missouri and Ohio Valleys, where farmers and planters increasingly used enslaved Africans to produce food and stores for plantations downriver. In the process, Native American slavery ended—on paper, at least—as Native American slaves were transformed into African American slaves. In that forty-year span, African American slavery became central to economic, social, and political life in the imperial Ohio, Missouri, and Mississippi Valleys. By the time of the Louisiana Purchase at the start of the nineteenth century, these regions composed a distinct Mississippi Valley plantation complex that was part of a broader Atlantic world of empires, commerce, and slavery. Whether in New Orleans or Natchez, Ste. Genevieve or Shawneetown, Creole elites in the broader Mississippi Valley plantation complex made claims on imperial states as they sought to mobilize power locally so that they could enslave Africans and then keep them in slavery.[12]

In the early 1700s, the banks of the Mississippi in present-day Missouri constituted something of a middle ground between competing Native American nations. European settlers from the French Illinois Country—habitants—began migrating across the Mississippi River to mine lead and to trade for furs and salt with Osages from the Missouri and Arkansas Valleys in the 1720s. In the 1750s, trading and mining camps began to take the form of more permanent agricultural, fur-trading, and diplomatic settlements. The outcome of the Seven Years' War divided European claims along the Mississippi River, ceding the Ohio Valley to Britain and the Mississippi and Missouri Valleys to Spain. Seeking to integrate the region into Spain's new Mississippi Valley empire, Spanish officials used state support for slavery to encourage habitants to settle in Spanish Missouri and to cultivate their loyalties to the Spanish Crown. In the 1750s, the French Illinois Country—which encompassed the settlements on the west bank of the Mississippi—was oriented as much toward French Canada as it was toward Louisiana. Likewise, economic life in the scattered French villages comingled Native American slavery and the fur trade toward Canada, with African American slavery and the production of staples and stores for Louisiana. In the 1770s, Spanish officials used their shared Catholicism to lure across the river habitants now living under Protestant British rule. To incorporate those habitants into their new Mississippi Valley empire, Spanish officials also worked to shift the economic and geopolitical orientation of the Missouri Country from fur trading and the Great Lakes to agricultural production for Louisiana. Finally, Spanish officials sought to maintain peace with the numerous and powerful Indigenous nations who lived in the Mississippi Valley and along its many tributaries. Combined, these imperial imperatives would shape the transformation of slavery in Missouri from initial European settlement through the Louisiana Purchase.[13]

Bondage, captivity, and slavery of various kinds were more or less ubiquitous among the diverse peoples and polities of the North American continent in the eighteenth century. Spanish officials immediately learned—as would their successors—that European Americans in the middle Mississippi Valley saw the enslavement of others as inseparable from settlement. Spanish officials' first census of the Missouri settlements counted twenty-nine Native American slaves at the agricultural-oriented village at Ste. Genevieve and sixty-nine Native American slaves at the fur-trade-oriented village of St. Louis.[14] Fearful that the trade in Native American captives would incite wars and raids that they were ill-equipped to fight off, Spanish officials initially banned the enslavement of Native Americans.[15] But Spanish officials just as quickly learned that an outright prohibition on Native American enslavement so deeply clashed with the customs of the Illinois Country that any enforcement of the decree would undermine whatever authority Spain might be able to exercise over the habitants. Spanish officials instead opted to ban the further enslavement of Native Americans and to prohibit the trade in Native American captives. Such measures were of little effect. Habitants immediately defied the ban, as Spanish officials reported that "the inhabitants of St. Louis had engaged to buy Indians and had even advanced money. As a result, they had acquired fourteen." This would not be the last time that Spanish officials decreed that settlers were "not to buy any Indians henceforth nor subject them to slavery."[16]

Spanish officials seeking to promote agriculture and to curb Native American enslavement concluded that the chief obstacle to both was habitant insistence that they would engage in commercial agriculture only if they had access to African American slaves. As one official noted, "Everyone wants to be a merchant on account of the profits he could make in trading, while none can be expected from farming without" enslaved African Americans.[17] Spanish officials quickly resolved to use slavery as a tool of empire building and "proposed to the King that he furnish them negro slaves in order to develop more quickly the crops." Knowing that the settlers in Missouri would stall until the enslaved Africans arrived there, the officials recommended that "pending receipt of the Royal decision, they should make a start with these crops, in order to have sufficient seed."[18] But the promise of slaves was not good enough for the settlers. Six months later, the habitants were "all waiting for this aid before beginning" to produce flour, hemp, and other food and stores.[19] While it's unclear exactly what "aid" Spanish officials provided to the habitants, slavery and settlement in Missouri received a boost as habitants from Illinois crossed the Mississippi to flee British Protestantism and to collect on Spanish promises of land, tools, seed, and slaves.

By the 1780s, enslaved Native and African Americans accounted for somewhere between 20 and 30 percent of the population of the main European American settlements in Missouri. Whether the settlements could properly be classified as part of a slave society or not, settlers and Spanish officials found themselves confronting the central problem of all slave societies: keeping in slavery people who do not want to be slaves. Several factors allowed enslaved Missourians to claim for themselves considerable freedoms within slavery and sometimes to dash for freedom. Spain and the habitants might have imagined Missouri as their own, but the reality of the Spanish and habitant presence consisted of a few villages scattered along the Mississippi and Missouri Rivers. Nonexistent borders between habitant villages and Native American settlements created spaces for flight, as did the neutral grounds found in woods, prairies, and plains. The frontier exchange economy that prevailed in the French Illinois Country allowed enslaved Africans and Natives to claim numerous customary rights in the 1700s, including the right to travel between Native American and habitant settlements. As slavery crossed the river, as imperial regimes changed, and as economic life remained varied and required considerable mobility, slaves continuously claimed and exercised a host of customary privileges and freedoms within slavery, while others managed to flee.[20]

Enslaved Native American man Louis Mahas took advantage of all these circumstances to free himself. Originally "a slave of Monsieur Darpentigny" in Illinois, Mahas was sold to "an English merchant" after the transfer of sovereignty from France to Spain. Mahas "killed the said English merchant" with a "fatal blow," then "fled into the nations of this continent," where he found refuge with an unnamed Native American nation. After "being chased" away by Native Americans for unknown reasons, Mahas made his way to St. Louis. "For 6 or 7 years," Mahas "lived, at intervals, in this village and in the woods, committing a number of outrages, stealing, running off cattle, debauching slaves with liquor, and insulting citizens, even trying to shoot some one, committing all sorts of atrocities, threatening to take the scalps of French and Spanish." Louis Mahas lived in the netherworlds between slavery and freedom, Native American and Spanish sovereignty, all the while evading the imperial and local mechanisms of enslavement. St. Louis habitants eventually sought Mahas's capture, reenslavement, and sale out of the colony rather than his arrest, trial, and execution for murder. For Mahas, conflicts and competing sovereignties between imperial powers and Native American nations created opportunities for freedom. But as Mahas discovered, Native American nations treated individuals like Mahas opportunistically. Native American nations welcomed Mahas when it was advantageous for them; they expelled him when he became a liability. Mahas and fugitives like him, forced to live in the netherworlds between Native American and European American sovereignty, found "freedom" difficult to realize. Officials eventually captured Mahas. But for habitants and Spanish officials, the purpose of imperial state power was not so much to punish a murderer as it was to enforce boundaries between European and Native American sovereignties, especially as they concerned keeping people in a state of slavery and subordination. Officials sentenced him "to perpetual banishment from the country" and ordered him "to be sent below" to New Orleans, where he would be sold as a slave. But Mahas evaded Spanish authority one last time. While imprisoned in St. Louis, Mahas "made his escape" by "flinging off his shackles, and making a hole in the bottom of the wall, through which he passed out."[21]

The ordinances seeking to govern the behavior of enslaved African and Native Americans demonstrate that both groups claimed, exercised, and secured a considerable range of privileges. Ordinances issued in St. Louis in 1781 prohibited slaves from "hold[ing] any assembly at night," "leave[ing] their cabins at night," or "receiv[ing] in their cabin other slaves." Slaves were likewise not "allowed to dance, either by day or night, in the village or elsewhere." If Spanish Missouri was like most slave regimes, regulations governing slave behavior sought to clamp down on slave actions that were already widespread. In either case, enslaved African and Native Americans found a way around these new regulations. An ordinance issued only three days after the above noted that enslaved Native and African Americans had begun "to dress themselves in a barbarous fashion, adoring themselves with vermillion [red paint] and many feathers which render them unrecognizable, especially in the woods." Enslaved African and Native Americans now took to the woods, where they passed themselves off as free Native Americans.[22]

Other Native and African Americans took to the woods to escape slavery altogether, often with tragic consequences. Just as state-sanctioned violence was instrumental in keeping slaves in slavery, so too did enslaved men and women resort to violence to emancipate themselves. In 1798, an enslaved "mulatto" man, "Yssac," murdered "the woman, Josefa Beaugenoce, widow of Hunau," as part of his escape.[23] In November 1785, seven Native American men, one Native American woman, and several African American slaves fled to the woods. On the way out of St. Louis, they "robb[ed] their former masters of horses, guns, blankets and ammunition, taking with them several negro slaves, and from appearances setting on fire two or three places, with a view of destroying the village." Placing the resources of the imperial state at the disposal of enslavers, Spanish troops were dispatched to apprehend the runaways. In their haste, Spanish soldiers accidentally killed an enslaved man of African descent named Baptiste. Reinforcing the close connections between the Spanish imperial state, settler sovereignty, and slavery, Spanish authorities awarded to "Marie Therese Bourgeois . . . the sum of six hundred dollars of silver, value of my negro named Baptiste, who was killed in the expedition against the runaway Indians who belonged to different inhabitants of this village."[24]

In the 1790s, African American enslavement grew, overtaking and absorbing Native American slavery. The United States' Northwest Ordinance of 1787 banned slavery in Illinois, if only on paper. While American officials indicated that the ordinance did not apply to slaves present in 1787, the ordinance left uncertain the status of any slaves forced to migrate to Illinois after adoption of the ordinance. Rather than negotiating with a far-off government that seemed utterly unconcerned about upholding habitant titles to land and slaves, habitants fled across the river to "the Spanish side of the Mississippi."[25] Between 1787 and 1789, Spanish officials recorded 33 families and 293 individuals having migrated from Illinois to Missouri. Fourteen of the 33 families owned slaves; 106 of the 293 individuals recorded were slaves.[26]

A growing cadre of expatriated Americans joined them, readily pledging loyalty to the Spanish Crown for outsize land grants and access to the Mississippi River. The most famous expatriated American, Daniel Boone, entered Missouri with his wife, 6 children, and 10 slaves in 1799.[27] The expansion of plantation slavery downriver in New Orleans and the Natchez Country spurred the growth of slavery in Missouri. As New Orleans planters devoted increased resources to the production of cash crops such as cotton and sugar, they gave less attention to the production of staples, opening new markets for farmers, traders, and slaveholders in Missouri. Fleeing or bypassing uncertain land titles in Kentucky and prohibitions on slavery in Ohio, expatriated Americans continued to migrate to Spanish Missouri in the decade preceding the Louisiana Purchase.[28] Meanwhile, the enslaved African

American population of Missouri continued to grow as slaveholders and would-be slaveholders acquired slaves through small-scale exchanges with American merchants operating in the Ohio and Mississippi Valleys, through cross-river sales from Illinois into Missouri, and through natural increase.[29]

The growth of Missouri's enslaved African American population, the expansion of commercial agriculture, and Spanish prohibitions on Native American enslavement transformed the racial dimensions of slavery by the 1790s. As early as 1770, habitants had recorded the children of Native American mothers and African American fathers as "negro." The 1770 census of Ste. Genevieve thus lists "Louis," son of "Rose of the Pawnee nation," as a "negro."[30] The imperative for slaveholders to reracialize their slaves grew in the 1780s. A 1787 Spanish ordinance "strictly forbid any subject, of whatever rank or condition he may be, to make any Indian a slave, or to hold one as such, under any pretext whatsoever." The ordinance extended to fur traders and other "travelers who chanced to be in this province." The same ordinance also "ordained that the present owners of the said savage slaves shall not be allowed to get rid of those whom they have, in any manner whatsoever, except it be by giving them their freedom." As enslaved women gave birth, and as slaves were counted, purchased, sold, and traded, enslavers increasingly recorded Native American slaves and slaves of mixed African and Native American descent as "negroes."[31]

Native American slavery did not disappear so much as habitant slaveholders and imperial officials absorbed Native American slaves and slavery into African American slavery. In the 1770s and 1780s, Spanish officials had sought to abolish Native American enslavement. Habitant slaveholders defied Spanish regulations—likely with the connivance of Spanish officials—by simply transforming the mixed forms of Native American enslavement that had developed in the Illinois Country into African American enslavement. In the 1787 and 1791 censuses, Spanish official Francisco Cruzat used the terms "negro" and "*pardo*"—meaning colored—rather than the traditional categories of "negro" and "*esclavage*," "*sauvage*," or "*metis*" to record enslaved persons of Native American ancestry.[32] Spanish officials and settlers from the Illinois Country likely did much the same thing. Thus, of the twenty-nine "mulatto slaves" recorded by Spanish officials between 1787 and 1789 as having migrated from Illinois to Missouri, many were likely of partial Native American descent. In the midcontinent, Creole elites and imperial officials found it easy enough to reracialize enslaved people, aligning local practices with imperial dictates.[33]

By the early 1790s, merchants, farmers, and officials had successfully reoriented the settlements on the west bank of the Mississippi away from the Great Lakes region and toward the production of stores and food for plantations downriver. All of this was predicated on the enslavement of African-descended people and others now defined as "negro." By 1804, African American slaves—or, more precisely, enslaved people categorized as "negro"—accounted for one-fifth of Missouri's non-Indigenous population and nearly one-third of the population around the main settlements of St. Louis and St. Genevieve. Forty years of Spanish rule and support for slavery had transformed Missouri from a fur-trading outpost dependent on Native American bondage into an agriculturally oriented settlement, dependent on enslaved African Americans and thoroughly integrated into the transnational Mississippi Valley plantation complex and frontier.

By the eve of the Louisiana Purchase, the European-descended residents of Missouri had created a mostly self-governing multiethnic community within the larger Spanish empire. While cultural differences and clashing interests often divided the francophone and anglophone populations, they shared much in common. Both groups readily exchanged nominal professions of allegiance to the Spanish empire for nominal protection of their interests. But the main concern of both groups centered on maintaining peaceful and prosperous relations with Native Americans, keeping enslaved African Americans in slavery, securing land grants, and preserving access to markets via the Mississippi River. Spanish officials readily supported all four, solidifying further the loyalties of the European-descended population of Missouri. The Louisiana Purchase threatened to upset the precarious balance forged by settlers and Spanish officials, while enslaved African Americans stood ready to use the disruptions created by the transfer for their own purposes.

Immediately upon receiving word of the cession of Louisiana to the United States, white Missourians expressed apprehension about the future of slavery under U.S. rule. One U.S. official in the region advised Thomas Jefferson that most whites in Missouri remained "averse" to U.S. rule were it to be accompanied by "the liberation of their slaves (of which they have great numbers)." Other Americans familiar with Missouri sent similar letters eastward. Louisianans were "very much interested in obtaining an unlimited slavery," wrote one American official from the West. That interest left them "very much divided on the score of becoming American citizens . . . lest their slaves should be liberated." The "sooner their minds can be quieted on that subject the better." Meriwether Lewis wrote of a more menacing situation. Upon arriving in Missouri, Lewis found circulating "a report that the Americans would emancipate their slaves immediately on taking possession of the country." These concerns extended beyond the class of enslavers, encompassing Missouri's many would-be slaveholders. "There appears to be a general objection not only among the French, but even among the Americans not slaveholders," he continued, "to relinquish the right which they claim relative to slavery in its present unqualified form." As the letters sent eastward by Lewis and other U.S. officials confirmed, whatever differences divided anglophone and francophone settlers, both groups remained committed to using the mechanisms of state power to maintain slavery and prop up its beneficiaries.[34]

In 1803–4, the United States seemed dangerously abolitionist to white Missourians—with good reason. As of 1803, the United States reigned as the only imperial power in the Atlantic world or on the North American continent to permit the peaceful abolition of slavery and to prohibit its expansion. Massachusetts and New Hampshire had abolished slavery completely in the 1780s. By 1784 six northern states had taken legislative action providing for the gradual abolition of slavery. In 1799 and 1804, gradual abolition laws were adopted in New York and New Jersey, the northern states with the largest enslaved populations. In the trans-Appalachian West, the United States had twice passed the Northwest Ordinance along with its Article VI prohibition on slavery. Slaveholders proved unable to overturn the Article VI ban in Ohio in 1799 and 1804, when Ohio entered the Union with a constitution expressly adopting Article VI and prohibiting slavery. At the same time, slaveholders in Indiana and Illinois had failed to overturn Article VI there, despite more than a decade of efforts seeking congressional repeal or modification of the ban. Meanwhile, over the previous decade, habitants had fled across the river to escape the uncertainties of Article VI on slavery. White Missourians understandably expressed concern that U.S. rule would threaten slavery.[35]

The actions of enslaved Native and African Americans added to the uncertainties surrounding slavery under U.S. rule. A long-running family dispute over three enslaved sisters of mixed African and Native American descent gained new life with the arrival of U.S. sovereignty. Born in the 1740s, Marie Scypion was likely the daughter of an enslaved Native American mother and an enslaved African American father. Since the 1790s, her three daughters, Celeste, Catiche, and Marguerite, had been seeking to block their sale based on their maternal Native American ancestry. When their enslaver tried to sell them again in the spring of 1804, Celeste and Catiche filed judicial claims seeking emancipation. Amos Stoddard, the chief American official in the territory, blocked the sale until the matter could be heard by a U.S. court, but refused to emancipate the plaintiffs, leaving the status of the sisters undetermined. The Scypion sisters drew on overlapping Spanish and U.S. imperial structures for their own purposes, producing ambiguity concerning the uses of state power, ambiguity that was dreaded by slaveholding Creole elites everywhere: Would the powers of the imperial state favor enslavement or emancipation?[36]

The territorial ordinance Congress framed for Missouri heightened white concerns that the United States would implement some kind of gradual emancipation program in Missouri. For administrative purposes, the 1804 territorial act for Upper Louisiana appointed officials from the Indiana Territory to Missouri. Though the bill created two distinct territories, white Missourians suspected that this was a prelude to the extension of the Northwest Ordinance's Article VI across the river. They may have been correct. While debating the territorial ordinance for Missouri, Maryland senator Samuel Smith supported joining the two territories, saying, "I know that it will estop slavery there, and to that I agree."[37] In addition, the territorial ordinance for Missouri limited the migration of enslaved people into Missouri; only "a citizen of the United States, removing into said territory for actual settlement, and being at the time of such removal bona fide owner of such slave or slaves," could now bring slaves to Missouri.[38] Once the terms of the territorial ordinance reached Missouri in the summer of 1804, the "people" of Missouri became "very much agitated" in "regard to this district's being annexed to the Indiana Territory & the regulations which Congress might adopt relative to slavery."[39] American William Carr found nearly all white Missourians "apprehensive that slavery" would soon "be prohibited" under American rule. The greatest concerns came from small slaveholders who "were fearful lest those already in their possession would also be manumitted."[40] By midsummer, rumors swirled that Missouri's slaves "will be free before long."[41]

As anxiety about the status of slavery under American rule grew, Captain Amos Stoddard (the leading American official in Missouri) and Auguste Chouteau (Missouri's most prominent resident) intervened. In August 1804, Stoddard and Chouteau staged a public exchange to address the uncertainties surrounding slavery under American rule. The Connecticut-born

Stoddard was a harsh critic of slavery, but as the top American official in Missouri his primary concern was to oversee a peaceful transfer and to reconcile white Missourians to U.S. rule. Like every other U.S. official in the West, Stoddard was more committed to fulfilling his official duties than to freeing slaves. Stoddard and Chouteau readily engaged in the performative politics of empire, to the benefit of both. Chouteau played the role of the loyal supplicant, Stoddard the representative of benevolent imperial power. Both framed their exchange to quell white concerns about the future of slavery and to warn enslaved African Americans that the United States would not support emancipation.[42]

Chouteau mobilized local power within larger imperial structures by organizing "The Committee of the Town of St. Lewis," which operated as an informal government for St. Louis and its surrounding villages during the transition from Spanish to U.S. sovereignty. Under the auspices of "the Committee," Chouteau drew up a petition filled with requests rather than demands. The petitioners expressed commitment to U.S. rule but also voiced concerns about the recent "conduct of their slaves." Slaves acting on the uncertainty surrounding the transfer and rumors of abolition had made the white "inhabitants" of Missouri "uneasy and alarmed." "There exist amongst the Blacks a fermentation," the Committee warned, a fermentation exacerbated "by the report spread by some Whites, that they will be free before long." Alluding to the violent slave rebellion that had just concluded in January of that year with the creation of Haiti, the petitioners pleaded that the United States "preserve the New territory" of Missouri "from the horrors which different American colonies have lately experienced." Continuing, they reminded Stoddard that "in all countries where slavery exists there is a Code that establishes in a positive manner the Rights of the Masters, and the Duties of the slaves. There is also a Watchful policy, which prevents their nocturnal assemblies, that subject them to their labor." Under "the old French government and Spanish, the Black Code was our guide," they explained, asking Stoddard "to have it put in force" under U.S. rule. Only a strong slave code could "keep the slaves in their duty according to their class; in the respect they owe generally to all whites, and more expressly their masters." U.S. commitment to slavery would place slaves "again under the subordination which they were heretofore" and "insure the tranquility of a people who depends entirely on your viligency." Without strict slave codes, slaves would surely rebel, and Missouri would be reduced to "nothing but ruins," much like French Saint-Domingue.[43]

Stoddard readily played the part of benevolent imperial benefactor. Acknowledging white Missourians' concerns, he requested that they "suggest such rules and regulations as appear necessary to restrain the licentiousness of slaves, and to keep them more steadily to their duty." He assured them that "I will add my sanction to whatever may contribute" to Missouri's "peace and security" and concluded by admonishing "those Whites who have propagated among the slaves the hope of a speedy emancipation."[44] Furthering their performance, the following week the Committee presented to Stoddard "the regulations of police concerning the slaves," rules that would "ensure the rights of the masters." Like his Spanish predecessors, Stoddard used slavery as a tool of empire building. As Stoddard well knew, in the contested borderlands of imperial North America, imperial support for local slavery was a necessary precondition for establishing sovereignty. It was also a necessary precondition for keeping enslaved men and women in slavery.[45]

Having secured Stoddard's support for slavery, white Missourians now turned toward convincing the U.S. government to draft a new territorial ordinance for Missouri. Shortly after Chouteau's exchange with Stoddard, Chouteau created another representative body, likely with Stoddard's endorsement. Again demonstrating white Missourians' expectations of local self-government within larger imperial structures, Chouteau and the Committee put out a call for the settlements in Missouri to send representatives to St. Louis, where they would draft a petition to send to Washington. "The Representatives Elected by the Freemen of their Respective Districts" drafted a strongly worded "remonstrance and petition" that hinted at disunion while expressing four related concerns reflecting their experiences during forty years of Spanish sovereignty. White Missourians requested that officials be chosen from among their ranks and that they be fluent in both French and English. The petitioners also defended the often fraudulent land claims that many settlers had acquired over the previous decade and insisted that the United States maintain a military presence in Missouri sufficient to ward off raids by Native Americans. Finally, the petitioners warned that the 1804 territorial ordinance seemed "calculated . . . to create the presumption of a disposition in Congress to abolish slavery altogether" in Missouri. The petitioners demanded that the United States recognize their right "to the free possession of our slaves" along with "the right of importing" more. Under Spanish rule, white Missourians had received a large degree of self-government and autonomy within a larger imperial structure that protected their interests, provided them advantages over Native Americans, and supported subordination of enslaved African Americans. They expected nothing less from the United States.[46]

Imperial lawmakers in Washington obliged the demands of white Missourians—sort of. Until the Civil War, most territorial ordinances either extended the Northwest Ordinance's Article VI prohibition on slavery to a new territory or recognized slavery indirectly by exempting a territory from Article VI. But the 1805 territorial ordinance for Missouri is odd in that it makes no reference to slavery or Article VI, either directly or indirectly. A proposed version of the ordinance would have acknowledged slavery indirectly, by creating "a government in all respects similar to that now exercised in the Mississippi Territory." This proposed ordinance would have recognized slavery in Missouri by twice removing it from the Northwest Ordinance's Article VI. The final version of the 1805 territorial ordinance omitted all references to slavery. Under the 1805 ordinance, slavery existed legally in Missouri (which included all of the Louisiana Purchase outside of Louisiana) by force of local law and territorial statute, rather than by territorial ordinance, as was the case in other territories where slavery was permitted.[47] It is unknown if Congress purposely omitted any reference to slavery or Article VI in the 1805 territorial ordinance. Nonetheless, over the next fifteen years, some restrictionists—including Amos Stoddard—claimed that this omission was deliberate, intended to allow the U.S. government to prohibit slavery in Missouri if circumstances proved more favorable in the future.[48]

What were the intentions of the U.S. Congress in 1804 and 1805 when it came to slavery in Missouri? Imperial lawmakers in Washington initially underestimated the extent of the white population in Missouri, as well as the strength of their commitment to slavery. Thomas Jefferson, for example, thought the United States could easily swap out Missouri's European-descended population and replace them with Native Americans from east of the Mississippi. Operating on the same level of ignorance of white Missourians, northerners in Congress expected that the United States could simply extend some version of the Northwest Ordinance across the river with little controversy. Beyond that, Congress seemed to have no definite plans for slavery in Missouri outside an expectation that an Article VI for Missouri would operate in much the same way that it had in Illinois, Ohio, and Indiana since 1787. Slavery would be prohibited from new areas of settlement in Missouri and Upper Louisiana, the sale of slaves into Missouri would be prohibited, and slaveholders in Missouri would be permitted to keep slaves already in their possession. At some far-off date in the future, slavery would somehow wither away in Missouri, just as it was supposed to do in the Northwest Territory.

But whatever Congress's intentions in 1804 and 1805, it remains difficult to envision a process by which the United States—or any other imperial power—could have implemented and enforced these kinds of restrictions on slavery in Missouri. It is even more difficult to envision how any imperial power could have enforced some kind of gradual abolition plan in Missouri in the first decade of the 1800s while retaining any claims of sovereignty or dominion over European-descended peoples there. Any attempt to halt slavery's growth in Missouri had to contend with the colonial realities, imperial rivalries, and Atlantic markets that had shaped the place of slavery, settlement, and territoriality in the Missouri, Ohio, and Mississippi Valleys since the 1760s. In the four decades preceding the Louisiana Purchase, settlers and imperial states had made slavery inseparable from European sovereignty and territoriality. They had also made state support for slavery central to the processes of development and incorporation into the contested imperial worlds of the North American continent and the Atlantic world. U.S. officials—like their Spanish predecessors—believed that imperial rivalries, the weaknesses of imperial states in the Mississippi Valley, and the loose loyalties of white settler groups meant that they could govern settlers and local elites only by accommodating local interests.[49]

In Missouri, slavery bound together the disparate and diverse settler populations, and the necessity of state support for slavery was a policy on which those same settler groups could agree. Stoddard estimated that "more than four-fifths" of the white inhabitants agreed with the main concerns of the "remonstrances" regarding slavery and land.[50] Indeed, even before the United States began formally governing Missouri, its white inhabitants demanded that protections for slavery accompany the extension of American sovereignty. As for the authors of the "remonstrance," despite their hints at disunion, they did not intend to leave the United States and return to French or Spanish sovereignty. Rather, they hoped to frighten imperial lawmakers in Washington into rescinding the restrictions on slavery, recognizing land claims, and jettisoning plans to swap out Native American and European American populations across the Mississippi. From the 1760s through the 1810s, Native American and European American settler groups in the greater Mississippi Valley used threats of rebellion and secession—or promises of loyalty and fealty—to gain favor from imperial lawmakers in Philadelphia,

London, Paris, and Madrid. "The Representatives Elected by the Freemen of their Respective Districts" were simply doing what a multitude of groups in imperial North America had done for decades in order to maintain autonomy for themselves and supremacy over conquered and enslaved peoples as imperial sovereignty shifted.[51]

The authors of the "remonstrance" all but admitted to Stoddard that drafting and then presenting it in Washington was an unpleasant but necessary part of the performative politics of empire. Before departing for Washington with their "remonstrance and petition" in hand, the "representatives of the several districts" of Missouri issued a public letter of gratitude to Stoddard. Referring to the whole process as a "painful task," they thanked him for his "judicious, attentive & exemplary dispensation of Justice within this territory during your administration, and the readiness which you have always shown to contribute to the public good." They then asked that "genuine philanthropy—solid parts & unblemished Disinterestedness continue to characterize the governors" of territorial Missouri.[52] All they wished from the United States was the same kind of regards for their interests that Stoddard and his Spanish predecessors had shown them. The United States ultimately supported white Missourians' demands for slavery—not because the United States was an inherently proslavery empire, but because like every other imperial power in the Americas, lawmakers in the imperial center and officials on the ground believed that they had to yield to the demands of settlers and elites, especially on questions of slavery.[53]

From 1805 through 1819, American acquisition changed little in Missouri regarding empire, governance, and slavery. Prominent locals were appointed to offices and received government contracts. Town and village councils governed their particular locales as they saw fit. Land remained cheap and accessible due to the circulation of floating grants and warrants issued first by the Spanish and later by the United States. Native American nations in Missouri interacted with the U.S. government and merchants in ways that seemed best calculated to protect their interests. Local and territorial officials worked to keep slaves in slavery, and slavery continued its slow but steady growth. Enslaved African Americans continued to seek freedom from slavery when possible and greater freedoms within slavery when flight or freedom suits seemed unobtainable.

The political geography of slavery in the United States attracted or repelled certain groups of free migrants, shaping the peculiar characteristics of settler colonialism in Missouri. Wealthy slaveholders from the Atlantic states preferred settlement in the South Carolina piedmont and the Georgia upcountry, where cotton produced an increase in the enslaved population by more than two hundred thousand people, the greatest expansion of any slave regime on the North American continent between 1800 and 1820. Antislavery migrants from the northern and southern states, on the other hand, preferred settlement in the Northwest Territories covered by Article VI, especially Ohio and Indiana.[54] These circumstances kept small and would-be slaveholders out of Ohio, Indiana, and Illinois, but Kentucky and Tennessee had their own set of drawbacks. Land titles in both were tied up in a morass of lawsuits stemming from the haphazard and often fraudulent surveys and sales of land in the 1790s. Middling and would-be slaveholders therefore tended to bypass Kentucky, while ambitious Kentuckians who could not make it there headed off to Missouri. Just like their predecessors, the European Americans who made their way to Missouri after 1803 tied slavery to settlement, territoriality, and incorporation into the U.S. empire along with the burgeoning Mississippi Valley plantation complex. Those ties would only strengthen in the fifteen years separating the Louisiana Purchase and Missouri statehood.[55]

Virginia lawyer Joseph Pollard Jr. exemplified the kind of middle-class enslaver or would-be enslaver who migrated to Missouri. In 1811, Pollard made plans to head to Missouri with "5 members" of his "white" family, and "my black one of not more than 12 or 15 slaves." Pollard sought a residence in the town of St. Louis, along with "a little farm in the neighborhood." The farm was to be "sufficiently large to work 6 or 8" slaves. The remaining enslaved African Americans would be used at his residence in St. Louis, where he would run his "practice of law," while his son would practice "that of medicine."[56] Other migrants were less well-off. Benjamin Reeves had moved from Virginia to Kentucky as a teenager. By 1812, his ambitions had carried him to the Kentucky statehouse, but wealth still evaded him. The following year, he and his brother were seeking to rent slaves, "either publickly" from an annual slave-rental auction or "privately," for somewhere between $65 and $80 for the year. In 1818, Reeves and his growing family moved to Missouri. Two years later, the voters of Howard County sent him to the state constitutional convention. In 1824, he was elected Missouri's lieutenant governor. Ambitious middling and would-be enslavers could rise quickly in Missouri.[57]

Virginian native William C. Carr demonstrated the importance of chattel slavery to ambitious middling southern white men such as himself. Arriving in St. Louis in 1804, Carr became an attorney involved in all kinds of sales and lawsuits involving slaves and land. Within a year, he had purchased "a negro boy named Jack, aged about eleven years."[58] In 1807, he became engaged to "a little Yankee girl at Ste. Genevieve," Ann Marie Elliot, daughter of Dr. Aaron Elliot and brother-in-law to Moses Austin. Befitting the Carrs' rising status, William wrote to his brother in Kentucky asking that he procure "a negro woman suitable for the kitchen."[59] Carr's brother was unable to obtain the enslaved woman William desired, so he purchased a husband and wife accustomed to field work instead, hoping that William could convert them into house servants. Carr accepted his brother's offer, but lamented, "If they do not answer, upon experiment," as house servants, "they must be sold; not withstanding my abhorrence to that kind of traffic." If the husband and wife could not advance Carr's social status, they would improve his economic status. In either case, the Carrs could not imagine respectability or wealth in St. Louis without owning enslaved men and women.[60]

Enslaved men, women, and children were central to Carr's growing fortune in other ways. He speculated in land and enslaved people, using both as a form of liquid capital. In 1809, he purchased "two negro fellows" in the spring and "another" in the summer for "$333" with "1/3 part on credit for 12 months." Carr then "sold again" this slave "for one of those land warrants," valued at $640. He decided to keep the other slaves because he found them "very likely," expecting their value to increase.[61] The following summer, Carr acted as a slave-purchasing agent for John B. C. Lucas, a territorial official and expatriated Frenchman who arrived in St. Louis after spending two decades in western Pennsylvania. While visiting his brother in Lexington, Kentucky, Carr sought out enslaved people to purchase for Lucas. Carr "made every inquiry in my power on the subject of purchasing negroes in this country since my arrival," but had determined that he could not "purchase any tolerably good negro man for less than $500." Carr instead suggested that Lucas purchase an enslaved man "with his wife and two small children," which Carr believed "might be purchased much below their value." Extending his own expectations to Lucas, Carr counseled that while this particular enslaved family might fail to enhance Lucas's social status, Lucas could more than make up for it by improving his economic fortunes. It went without saying that in acting as Lucas's agent, Carr would increase his own fortunes as well.[62]

Ambitious middling migrants from the North quickly jettisoned whatever antislavery scruples they may have carried with them. Ann Marie Elliot and John B. C. Lucas became slaveholders immediately after arriving in Missouri, but no northern migrant took to slavery as quickly and as fervently as Vermont native Justus Post. Post graduated Middlebury College and then West Point in 1806. After serving in the U.S. Army during the War of 1812, Post moved to Missouri in 1815. By January 1816, he had purchased his first slave, a "negro woman, named Ellen, aged 23 years, a slave during the period of her natural life."[63] John Post intended to join his brother in Missouri, which prompted a warning from Justus that "there is one thing you must reconcile your mind to when you get in this region, that is the owning of slaves." Post had by then purchased "two negro women and three girls." He had "no negro men yet but will have so soon as I can get them. I shall try hard to get two this winter and as many next spring as I can."[64] The following month, Post purchased Peter, "a slave for and during the period of his natural life."[65] Post promised his brother that his slaves could "be sure of three things—victuals, clothes & work in abundance."[66]

As Post promised, the lives of enslaved men and women such as Peter and Ellen were filled with unrelenting physical labor; their lives were also filled with violence, forced separation from loved ones, and general uncertainty. Betty, a mother and enslaved woman, "had two children" around 1799. Betty's children were sold away from her when they were young to a "M. Cabanne." Cabanne then "swapped" the children with James McDaniel. A decade later, Betty's children became involved in a lawsuit between Cabanne and McDaniel after the enslaved children developed smallpox. Betty's life must have been difficult enough when she lost her two young children; it must have become unimaginably more so a decade later when she was asked to determine if two enslaved children who had just survived smallpox were her own. Whether due to time or the scars of smallpox, Betty "could not identify" the children as her own.[67]

Separation, movement, and uncertainty seemed endemic in the lives of many of Missouri's slaves. U.S. Indian agent George Sibley had purchased Betty, a "black servant girl," when he "was last in Georgetown." Betty left all that she knew behind her when she was forced to move from Washington to St. Louis with Sibley. After meeting Sibley's slave George in St. Louis, the party traveled on to Fort Osage, near present-day Kansas City. Along the way, Betty and George developed a relationship and "entered into partnership soon after they got to Fort Osage." Betty's newfound family was short-lived. Betty's pregnancy required her return to St. Louis, while George continued on as "cook and man servant" for Sibley, far away at Fort Osage.[68]

Travel and work sometimes proved deadly for enslaved men and women. Because slaves were often the most valuable and mobile pieces of property to be found in borderlands like Missouri, banditti, Native Americans, and rival white groups kidnapped slaves. In 1816, two enslaved men living around the Boon's Lick settlements were kidnapped by a group of Sak and Ioway warriors. The Native American warriors intended to sell or ransom the twice captives. But when the Boon's Lick militia made "pursuit," the warriors "killed the two negro men with a tomahawk."[69] Travel and work proved especially tragic for an enslaved man named Phill. In 1811, Phill was rented by his owners in Tennessee to mine operators in Missouri for a term of six months. Hoping to squeeze as much labor as possible out of the rented slaves, the renter worked the slaves at the mines until only "a few days before the time was out." Having to move quickly from the mines to Nashville before the six months were up, the slaves had to cover considerable distances, even though it was "especially cold & snowing hard." But as the three slaves approached Ste. Genevieve, "an overseer digging another mine, heard of their going" back to Nashville. The overseer "pursued them, overtook them at night after they had walked the whole day thro the snow." Phill "had already given out" due to his arduous walk, "but the overseer made him drink a good deal" to recover. The overseer then "swore" that Phill "should go back" to the mine "or die." Under threat of death, Phill began walking on that dark, cold, snowy night. He never made it: "He failed and was found dead."[70]

The exchange between Phill's owner and renter demonstrates the callowness and calculations of profit that structured the lives of so many enslaved men and women in Missouri. Phill's owner expressed no concern about the fact of Phill's death, though he seemed relieved that Phill died "just before 6mo. expired." Phill's renter would thus be responsible for Phill's full value. But the renter would offer only one-third of Phill's value. The renter agreed that the overseer's actions were "censurable," but he denied that he could "be charged with wantonly playing with life or designedly taking it away." The renter instead alleged that Phill "had by his inebriation hastened his death," which in any case was caused by the snow and cold. In sum, the renter alleged that "the death of Phill can only be considered an act of God." All that remained was to determine the financial value of chattel.[71]

Work, profits, and mobility could kill; they also provided opportunities. Enslaved man York was determined to live life on his own terms. His owner, William Clark, was nearly as determined to maintain York's subordination. Clark split up York's family, having York reside in Missouri while his wife and children lived in Louisville. York repeatedly expressed his desire to move to Louisville and "hire himself" out, with his wages going to Clark. Clark refused, partially because York was "serviceable to me at this place," but mostly because Clark was "determined not" to "gratify" York's efforts to define the terms of his enslavement.[72] Clark gave his brother directions to have York "sent to New Orleans and Sold, or hired out to some severe master," if he shirked his duties because he missed his wife and children.[73] Clark did not sell York, even after York extended his one-month stay in Louisville into five. But after York returned from Louisville, he became "insulate and sulky" because he missed his family. Clark "gave him a severe trouncing," undoubtedly with the help of others.[74] Later that year, Clark "confined York" to the "Caleboos." Clark's efforts broke York: as Clark reported to his brother, York "has for two or three weeks been the finest negro I ever had." But York's breaking proved only temporary. York forced Clark to yield barely a month later.[75] York would now work "as a hand" on "a boat to Wheeling." On his return, he could stay in Louisville, provided York could find someone to purchase or hire him. York's ability to reunite with his family was hard won, filled with violence, confinement, and suffering.[76]

Other slaves chose flight when desperation and opportunity met to produce advantageous circumstances. An enslaved man, Jeffrey, spoke "good French and English, and tolerably good Indian Potawatomie." In 1809, he fled, likely to Illinois, a place where his fluency in three languages would presumably help him in maintaining his freedom.[77] Just as word of the Tallmadge restrictions on slavery reached Missouri, four of enslaver Justus Post's slaves fled. Peter, Ellen, Sylvia, and Martin made their way to "the state of Illinois," which white Missourians increasingly suspected of harboring antislavery sentiments and runaway slaves.[78] Other fugitives stayed closer to home. Enslaved man Sam had spent "several months" evading capture by living in the woods around "turkey Hill and Rich Law." Sam was somehow returned to his owner, but two years later he once again fled. Fluent in "English" and "French also," this time Sam had presumably "procured a forged pass as a free Negro."[79] Passing himself as a free man might have been a more sound strategy to secure his freedom. Missouri law recognized that "many times slaves run away and lie hid and lurking in swamps, woods and other obscure places killing hogs and committing other injuries." Missouri law "empowered and required" officials to search out and apprehend "such out lying slave or slaves." As the extensive slave code published in 1818 demonstrates, on the eve of statehood Missouri had all of the workings of a slave society.[80]

♠

Although a slave society in all but name, what Missouri still lacked was enough slaves and slaveholders. As such, Missouri continued to straddle the line between a society with slaves and a slave society. Sensing as much,

James Tallmadge proposed that Missouri adopt the kind of gradual emancipation program that had nearly eradicated slavery from the northern states over the course of the previous fifty years while forestalling its growth in the Northwest Territories. What Tallmadge did not know, however, was that white Missourians had long tied slavery to sovereignty, settlement, and incorporation into a burgeoning Mississippi Valley plantation complex and to whatever larger imperial state it would become a part. In the end, the differences between slavery in Mississippi, Alabama, and Missouri might have been vast. But white Missourians shared with their counterparts in the Deep South an ideological commitment to creating and maintaining a slave society. For white Missourians, the purpose of an imperial state was to preserve self-government for citizens (European American males), while using the coercive violence of the imperial state against subjects and conquered peoples (Native and African Americans). In practice, in a place like Missouri that meant keeping slaves in slavery, acquiring Native American territory through violence or the threat thereof, and protecting invading settlers from Native American attacks. For the better part of a half century, white Missourians used imperial state power to establish territorial borders, control land and labor, define the meanings and practices of race, direct voluntary and involuntary migration, and uphold white autonomy and sovereignty.

In 1820, northern whites overwhelmingly agreed with their counterparts in Missouri that the purpose of imperial state power was to establish territorial borders, control land and labor, define the meanings and practices of race, direct voluntary and involuntary migration, and uphold white autonomy and sovereignty. In this case, however, state power would be used to halt slavery's growth, facilitate emancipation, and draw borders demarcating the limits of slavery. Just as their predecessors had done in the 1780s and in 1804, white Missourians would use a mix of threats and pleas to fight off efforts to interfere with slavery. But the outcome of this conflict would be different. By refusing to accept any restrictions on slavery, white Missourians forced Congress to take up the enormous and divisive question of slavery's place in an expanding continental empire. Northern and southern whites would now fight with each other over the uses of state power to resolve issues centering on the division of territory, the practices of race, the direction of voluntary and involuntary migration, and the meanings of sovereignty in an expanding union with continental ambitions.

Notes

Special thanks to T.J. Slancauskas for his assistance in transcribing many of the documents used in this chapter.

1. The land that became the state of Missouri was part of numerous different territories, possessed changing and often indeterminate borders, and had many different Native American and European names between the 1600s and statehood. In the late 1600s and early 1700s, Osage (Ni-u-kon-ska) and Missouri (Niúachi) Peoples inhabited the lower Missouri Valley. On the east bank of the Mississippi River lived a diverse group of Native Americans that included Kaskaskias, Cahokias, and Peorias. Many of these Native Americans were refugees who had fled Iroquois attacks in the Great Lakes region and the upper Ohio Valley. Collectively, these Native American nations formed the Illinois, a loose confederacy with no central or formal political structure. For much of the first half of the 1700s, the west bank of the Mississippi River that would become Missouri was largely uninhabited, something of a no-man's-land that kept peace between the Illinois on the east bank of the Mississippi River and the Osage and Missouri of the lower Missouri Valley.

In the early 1700s, French traders and missionaries who explored the whole of the Mississippi Valley named the region "Louisiana." Around the same time, a different group of French Canadians who established five villages on the east bank of the Mississippi River placed their settlements in *le pays des Illinois*, "the country of the Illinois." When habitants began crossing the Mississippi River to establish settlements such as Ste. Genevieve, they continued to place their settlements in the Illinois Country. At the same time, the French settlements on both sides of the Mississippi River were part of the French province of Louisiana. To distinguish the settlements in the middle Mississippi Valley from French settlements in the lower Mississippi Valley around New Orleans, French officials and habitants referred to the Middle Mississippi Valley as *la haute Louisiane*, "the High Louisiana," or "Upper Louisiana."

The 1763 Treaty of Paris divided Illinois Country along the Mississippi River, with Britain claiming the east bank and Spain claiming the west bank. In the 1760s, the terms "Spanish Yllinois" and Upper Louisiana continued to be used. St. Louis, in particular, was referred to as "St. Louis of the Yllinois" until the early 1800s. With the Louisiana Purchase of 1803, the United States named what would become the state of Louisiana "Orleans Territory." Everything within the Louisiana Purchase but outside of Orleans became part of the "District of Louisiana," and the region was colloquially referred to as Upper Louisiana. In 1805 Congress separated the District of Louisiana from the Indiana Territory and created a separate Upper Louisiana Territory. When the Orleans Territory became the state of Louisiana in 1811, Congress renamed Upper Louisiana Territory "Missouri Territory," which included much of present-day Arkansas. In 1819, when Missouri applied for statehood, Congress created a separate Arkansas territory.

For simplicity and clarity, we use the term "Missouri" throughout this volume. I also use the term "the confluence region" to refer to the region surrounding the confluence of the Missouri, Ohio, Illinois, and Kaskaskia Rivers with the Mississippi.

While peoples, nations, and empires drew borders that marked off various parts of the region as distinct, the inhabitants of the region often ignored borders in their day-to-day lives. For the term "American Confluence," see Stephen Aron, *American Confluence: The Missouri Frontier from Borderland to Border State* (Bloomington: Indiana University Press, 2006).

2. "Bernardo Galvez to Joseph Galvez, January 27, 1778," in *The Spanish Regime in Missouri*, ed. Louis Houck, 2 vols. (Chicago: R. R. Donnelley, 1908), 1:158–59. Missouri had any different names from the 1760s through 1819.

3. Committee of the Town of St. Lewis to Amos Stoddard, True Translation from the original, by authority, J. Rankin, August 4, 1804, Amos Stoddard Papers, Missouri History Museum Archives (MHMA), St. Louis; *Missouri Intelligencer* (Franklin), June 4, 1819. For the distinction between slave societies and societies with slaves, see Ira Berlin, *Many Thousands Gone: The First Two Centuries of Slavery in North America* (Cambridge, MA: Harvard University Press, 1998). In slave societies, anywhere from 20 percent to 80 percent of the population was enslaved. Slavery was the most important institution, and the distinction between slave and free, white and Black, was the most important personal status, more important than class, gender, religion, or ethnicity. All institutions and nonenslaved individuals in that society were required to maintain and uphold the enslavement of others and to empower the dominant enslaving class. Individuals or institutions opposed to slavery were either driven out, destroyed, or modified to make them compatible with the enslavement of a significant portion of the population. In societies with slaves, slavery and enslavement mattered, but so did many institutions, statuses, and relationships. In societies with slaves, few people—other than slaves and slave owners—cared much about keeping other people in slavery. In the United States, the states north of Maryland were societies with slaves, while the states south of Pennsylvania were mostly slave societies. In societies with slaves, such as Pennsylvania in the 1770s, Black and white abolitionists could build coalitions to pass gradual abolition legislation. In slave societies, such as Virginia, peaceful, gradual abolition was impossible. Missouri consistently straddled the ill-defined line between the two kinds of society, exhibiting characteristics of both. For a recent creative use of these concepts, see Van Gosse, "Patchwork Nation: Racial Orders and Disorder in the United States, 1790–1860," *Journal of the Early Republic* 40, no. 1 (2020): 45–81.

4. John Craig Hammond, "Race, Slavery, Sectional Conflict, and National Politics, 1770–1820," in *The Routledge History of Nineteenth Century America*, ed. Jonathan Daniel Wells (New York: Routledge, 2017), 11–32; Padraig Riley, *Slavery and the Democratic Conscience: Political Life in Jeffersonian America* (Philadelphia: University of Pennsylvania Press, 2015); George William Van Cleve, *A Slaveholders' Union: Slavery, Politics, and the Constitution in the Early American Republic* (Chicago: University of Chicago Press, 2010); John Craig Hammond, *Slavery, Freedom, and Expansion in the Early American West* (Charlottesville: University of Virginia Press, 2007); Matthew Mason, *Slavery and Politics in the Early American Republic* (Chapel Hill: University of North Carolina Press, 2006).

5. Robert Pierce Forbes, *The Missouri Compromise and Its Aftermath: Slavery and the Meaning of America* (Chapel Hill: University of North Carolina Press, 2007).

6. Nicholas P. Wood, "The Missouri Crisis and the 'Changed Object' of the American Colonization Society," in *New Directions in the Study of African American Recolonization*, ed. Beverly C. Tomek and Matthew J. Hetrick (Gainesville: University Press of Florida, 2017), 146–65; John R. Van Atta, *Wolf by the Ears: The Missouri Crisis, 1819–1821* (Baltimore: Johns Hopkins University Press, 2015); Matthew W. Hall, *Dividing the Union: Jesse Burgess Thomas and the Making of the Missouri Compromise* (Carbondale: Southern Illinois University Press, 2015); John Craig Hammond and Mathew Mason, eds., *Contesting Slavery: The Politics of Freedom and Bondage in the New American Nation* (Charlottesville: University of Virginia Press, 2011); Elizabeth R. Varon, *Disunion! The Coming of the American Civil War, 1789–1859* (Chapel Hill: University of North Carolina Press, 2010); Lacy K. Ford, *"Deliver Us from Evil": The Slavery Question in the Old South* (New York: Oxford University Press, 2009).

7. For exceptions, which examine the enslavement of African Americans in the middle Mississippi Valley or the confluence region, see M. Scott Heerman, *The Alchemy of Slavery: Human Bondage and Emancipation in the Illinois Country, 1730–1865* (Philadelphia: University of Pennsylvania Press, 2018); John Craig Hammond, "Slavery, Settlement, and Empire: The Expansion and Growth of Slavery in the Interior of the North American Continent, 1770–1820," *Journal of the Early Republic* 32, no. 2 (2012): 175–206; Patricia Cleary, *The World, the Flesh, and the Devil: A History of Colonial St. Louis* (Columbia: University of Missouri Press, 2011); Aron, *American Confluence*; and Hammond, *Slavery, Freedom, and Expansion*, 55–75.

8. Calvin Schermerhorn, *Unrequited Toil: A History of United States Slavery* (New York: Cambridge University Press, 2018); Sven Beckert and Seth Rockman, eds., *Slavery's Capitalism: A New History of American Economic Development* (Philadelphia: University of Pennsylvania Press, 2018); Calvin Schermerhorn, *The Business of Slavery and the Rise of American Capitalism, 1815–1860* (New Haven, CT: Yale University Press, 2015); Edward Baptist, *The Half Has Never Been Told: Slavery and the Making of American Capitalism* (New York: Basic Books, 2014); Sven Beckert, *Empire of Cotton: A Global History* (New York: Vintage Books, 2014); Walter Johnson, *River of Dark Dreams: Slavery and Empire in the Cotton Kingdom* (Cambridge, MA: Harvard University Press, 2013).

9. The term "second slavery" was coined by sociologist Dale W. Tomich in a series of articles reprinted as Dale W. Tomich, *Through the Prism of Slavery: Labor, Capital, and World Economy* (Lanham, MD: Rowman & Littlefield, 2004). For "second slavery" in the United States, see Anthony Kaye, "The Second Slavery: Modernity in the Nineteenth-Century South and the Atlantic World," *Journal of Southern History* 75, no. 3 (2009): 627–50.

10. For three recent works examining freedom suits filed by African Americans that focus mainly on the period after 1820, see Kelly M. Kennington, *In the Shadow of* Dred Scott: *St. Louis Freedom Suits and the Legal Culture of Slavery in Antebellum America* (Athens: University of Georgia Press, 2017); Anne Twitty, *Before* Dred Scott: *Slavery and Legal Culture in the American Confluence, 1787–1857* (New York: Cambridge University Press, 2016); and Lea VanderVelde, *Redemption Songs: Suing for Freedom before* Dred Scott (New York: Oxford University Press, 2014).

11. For the broader relationship between slavery and sovereignty, settlement and empire in imperial North America, see John Craig Hammond, "Slavery, Sovereignty, and Empires: North American Borderlands and the American Civil War, 1660–1860," *Journal of the Civil War Era* 4, no. 2 (2014): 264–98. For Natchez and Louisiana, see Hammond, *Slavery, Freedom, and Expansion*, 13–54.

12. Hammond, "Slavery, Settlement, and Empire."

13. For the systems of Native American enslavement, captivity, and bondage created by French settlers, Native American nations, and Native American captives, see Brett Rushforth, *Bonds of Alliance: Indigenous and Atlantic Slaveries in New France* (Chapel Hill: University of North Carolina Press, 2013). For Native American slavery more generally, see Christina Snyder, *Slavery in Indian Country: The Changing Face of Captivity in Early America* (Cambridge, MA: Harvard University Press, 2010). For the coexistence and transformation of Native American and African American slavery in Illinois and Missouri, and the relationship of each to commercial agriculture and the fur trade, see Robert Michael Morrissey, "*Le pays des Illinois* Finds Its Context: The Early History of Illinois in a Continental Perspective," *Journal of the Illinois State Historical Society* 111, nos. 1–2 (2018): 9–30; John Reda, *From Furs to Farms: The Transformation of the Mississippi Valley, 1762–1825* (DeKalb: Northern Illinois University Press, 2016), 14–41; Carl J. Ekberg and Sharon K. Person, *St. Louis Rising: The French Regime of Louis St. Ange de Bellerive* (Urbana: University of Illinois Press, 2015); Peter K. Johnson, "Ésclavage Rouge: The Nature and Influence of Indian Slavery in Colonial St. Louis," *Missouri Historical Review* 105, no. 1 (2010): 14–30; Carl J. Ekberg, *Stealing Indian Women: Native Slavery in the Illinois Country* (Urbana: University of Illinois Press, 2007); Aron, *American Confluence*, 39–68; and Heerman, *Alchemy of Slavery*, 17–81. In theory, habitants and officials associated Native American enslavement with the fur trade and African American enslavement with commercial agriculture. In practice, the two often mixed and proved indistinguishable.

14. "Indian Slaves at Ste. Genevieve, May 28, 1770" and "Declarations . . . Concerning Indian Slaves at St. Louis, July 12, 1770," in *Spain in the Mississippi Valley, 1765–1794*, ed. Lawrence Kinnaird, 3 vols. (Washington, DC: Government Printing Office, 1946–49), vol. 2, pt. 1, 167–71, 172–79. A 1766 Spanish census of Ste. Genevieve counted 228 enslaved African Americans, approximately 40 percent of the town's population.

15. "Proclamation of O'Reilly, December 7, 1769," in *Spain in the Mississippi Valley*, ed. Kinnaird, vol. 2, pt. 1, 126.

16. "Luis de Unzanga to Piernas, undated letter from 1770 or 1771," in *Spain in the Mississippi Valley*, ed. Kinnaird, vol. 2, pt. 1, 190–91. This particular order permitted habitants to keep but not purchase or sell Native American slaves.

17. "Fernando Leyba to Bernardo Galvez, January 13, 1779," in *Spain in the Mississippi Valley*, ed. Kinnaird, vol. 2, pt. 1, 314.

18. Bernardo de Galvez, "Special Instructions to Leyba," March 9, 1778, in *Spain in the Mississippi Valley*, ed. Kinnaird, vol. 2, pt. 1, 259. For the ways in which

imperial European powers used state support for slavery as a way of enhancing their claims of sovereignty, see Hammond, "Slavery, Sovereignty, and Empires."

19. "Fernando Leyba to Bernardo Galvez, Nov. 16, 1778," in *Spain in the Mississippi Valley*, ed. Kinnaird, vol. 2, pt. 1, 313. For the efforts of French settlers and Spanish officials to procure enslaved Africans to expand agricultural production in Missouri, see also "Franco Cruzat to Bernardo Galvez, Nov. 23, 1777," "Bernardo Galvez to Joseph Galvez, January 27, 1778," and "Joseph Galvez to Franc Cruzet, April 8, 1778," in *Spanish Regime in Missouri*, ed. Houck, 1:158–60.

20. Heerman, *Alchemy of Slavery*, 17–37; Aron, *American Confluence*.

21. Statement of Noel Langlois, January 1, 1779, Litigation Collection, 1773–1901, MHMA; "Trial of Louis Mahas, an Indian, December 31, 1778," in *Annals of St. Louis in Its Early Days under the French and Spanish Dominations*, ed. Frederic L. Billon (St. Louis: G. I. Jones, 1886), 156–58. For the various ways in which Native Americans interacted with enslaved African Americans, see Snyder, *Slavery in Indian Country*.

22. Local Ordinances for St. Louis and General Ordinance Published by Lieutenant Governor Don Francisco Cruzat, August 12 and 15, 1781, Louis Houck, Papers from Spain, Transcripts, MHMA.

23. "Documents Delivered to De Lassus by Trudeau [internal evidence shows that this is from 1798]," in *Spanish Regime in Missouri*, ed. Houck, 2:267.

24. "Killing of Baptiste, December 27, 1785," *Annals of St. Louis*, ed. Billon, 233–42.

25. "Memorial of Barthelemi Tardiveau, July 8, 1788," in *Kaskaskia Records, 1778–1790*, ed. Clarence W. Alvord (Springfield: Trustees of the Illinois State Historical Library, 1909), 488.

26. "Immigrants from the United States, into Missouri, December 1, 1787 through December 31, 1789," in *Spain in the Mississippi Valley*, ed. Kinnaird, vol. 3, pt. 2, 290.

27. Daniel Boone Petition to the Spanish Crown, November 9, 1799, Confirmed, March 1, 1806, box 1, Boone Family Papers, 1777–1930, MHMA.

28. For the migration of American slaveholders and would-be slaveholders to Spanish Missouri, see Meriwether Lewis to Thomas Jefferson, December 28, 1803, in *Letters of the Lewis and Clark Expedition with Related Documents, 1783–1854*, ed. Donald Jackson (Urbana: University of Illinois Press, 1962), 148–53; Thomas Jefferson, "Queries on Louisiana, 1803," Thomas Jefferson Papers (TJP), Library of Congress (LOC), Manuscript Reading Room, Washington, DC; Benjamin Stoddert, "Notes on Louisiana," June 3, 1803, TJP, LOC. For Spanish efforts to lure settlers from the American side of the Mississippi into Spanish Upper Louisiana, see Aron, *American Confluence*, 97–99.

29. Abyal Hunt to John Wesley Hunt, November 9, 1798, John Wesley Hunt Papers, Special Collections, Transylvania University, Lexington, KY; Francisco Cruzat, Sale of a Slave, 1786 (typescript copy), Slaves and Slavery Collection, box 1, folder 1, MHMA; Hammond, "Slavery, Settlement, and Empire."

30. "Indian Slaves at Ste. Genevieve, May 28, 1770," in *Spain in the Mississippi Valley*, ed. Kinnaird, vol. 2, pt. 1, 169.

31. Local Ordinances for St. Louis and General Ordinance, Published by Lieutenant Governor Don Francisco Cruzat, November 24, 1787, Louis Houck, Papers from Spain, Transcripts, MHMA.

32. A General Census of the Towns of St. Louis and Ste. Genevieve, 1787, and a census of St. Louis and its Districts, 1791, from the Archivo Nacional, Havana, transcribed and translated by Louis Houck, Census Collection, MHMA.

33. "Immigrants from the United States, into Missouri, December 1, 1787 through December 31, 1789," in *Spain in the Mississippi Valley*, ed. Kinnaird, vol. 3, pt. 2, 290. Claims of Native American ancestry would serve as the basis for several freedom suits in the early 1800s. See William E. Foley, "Slave Freedom Suits before *Dred Scott*: The Case of Marie Jean Scypion's Descendents," *Missouri Historical Review* 79, no. 1 (1984): 1–23; Kennington, *In the Shadow of* Dred Scott; Twitty, *Before* Dred Scott; and VanderVelde, *Redemption Songs*. For the processes by which slaveholders transformed slaves of mixed Native and African American ancestry into "negroes" in Illinois, see Heerman, *Alchemy of Slavery*, 17–37.

34. "Thomas T. Davis to Thomas Jefferson, November 5, 1803," in *The Territorial Papers of the United States*, ed. Clarence E. Carter, 28 vols. (Washington, DC: Government Printing Office, 1934–75), 13:7–8; "John Edgar to John Fowler, September 25, 1803," in *Territorial Papers*, ed. Carter, 13:5–7; "Thomas T. Davis to John Breckinridge, October 17, 1803," in *Territorial Papers*, ed. Carter, 7:124; "Meriwether Lewis to Jefferson, Dec. 28, 1803," in *Letters of the Lewis and Clark Expedition*, ed. Jackson, 153.

35. Hammond, *Slavery, Freedom, and Expansion*; Hammond, "Race, Slavery, Sectional Conflict, and National Politics."

36. Foley, "Slave Freedom Suits before *Dred Scott*"; VanderVelde, *Redemption Songs*, 39–56. The Scypion family freedom suit would drag on into the 1820s.

37. Everett S. Brown, ed., "The Senate Debate on the Breckinridge Bill for the Government of Louisiana, 1804," *American Historical Review* 22, no. 2 (1917): 360. It remains unclear whether Congress intended to apply Article VI to Missouri in some fashion. The main primary sources for the congressional debates have little to say about slavery in Missouri, excepting Maryland senator Samuel Smith's comment that he favored joining the two territories to stop slavery. In general, Congress devoted far more attention to Louisiana than Missouri when framing territorial ordinances in 1803 and 1804.

38. "An Act for the Organization of Orleans Territory and the Louisiana District, March 26, 1804," in *Territorial Papers*, ed. Carter, 9:209.

39. "The Remonstrance and Petition of the Representatives Elected by the Freemen of Their Respective Districts in the District of Louisiana," in *American State Papers: Documents, Legislative and Executive, of the Congress of the United States, from the First Session of the First to the Second Session of the Tenth Congress, Inclusive, Commencing March 3, 1789, and Ending March 3, 1809* (Washington, DC: Gales and Seaton, 1834), Class X, *Miscellaneous*, 1:401–4.

40. William Carr to John Breckinridge, July 4, 1804, in *Territorial Papers*, ed. Carter, 13:29–30.

41. Committee of the Town of St. Lewis to Amos Stoddard, True Translation from the original, by authority, J. Rankin, August 4, 1804, Stoddard Papers, MHMA.

42. For Stoddard's criticisms of slavery and his hope that the United States could somehow abolish it in Missouri, see Amos Stoddard, *Sketches, Historical and Descriptive, of Louisiana* (Philadelphia: Mathew Carey, 1812).

43. Committee of the Town of St. Lewis to Amos Stoddard, True Translation from the original, by authority, J. Rankin, August 4, 1804, Stoddard Papers, MHMA.

44. Amos Stoddard to Auguste Chouteau, Aug. 6, 1804, Stoddard Papers, MHMA.

45. Committee of the Town of St. Lewis to Amos Stoddard, True Translation P. Provenchere, August 11, 1804, Stoddard Papers, MHMA.

46. "Remonstrance and Petition of the Representatives," *American State Papers*, Class X, *Miscellaneous*, 1:401–4; Richard J. Waters and Richard Caulk (St. Louis) to the Citizens of Cape Girardeau, September 6, 1804, Louisiana Transfer Collection, MHMA; For the broader relationship between slavery, sovereignty, and empire in imperial North America, see Hammond, "Slavery, Sovereignty, and Empires."

47. "An Act for the Government of Louisiana Territory, March 3, 1805," "A Bill for the Government of the Territory of Louisiana, Feb. 7, 1805," in *Territorial Papers*, ed. Carter, 13:92–95, 87–89.

48. Amos Stoddard, *Sketches*; A Citizen of Ohio [Alexander Mitchell], *An Address to the Inhabitants of the Indiana Territory, on the Subject of Slavery* (Hamilton, OH, 1816); [Robert Walsh], *Free Remarks on the Spirit of the Federal Constitution, the Practice of the Federal Government, and the Obligations of the Union, Respecting the Exclusion of Slavery from the Territories and New States* (Philadelphia, 1819).

49. For suggestions that the United States could have enacted a Louisiana Purchase "under free-soil conditions" had lawmakers proved sufficiently committed to emancipation, see Douglas R. Egerton, "The Empire of Liberty Reconsidered," in *The Revolution of 1800: Democracy, Race, and the New Republic*, ed. James Horn, Jan Ellen Lewis, and Peter S. Onuf (Charlottesville: University of Virginia Press, 2002), 309–30.

50. Amos Stoddard to William C. C. Claiborne, May 19, 1804, Stoddard Papers, MHMA.

51. For the ways in which imperial rivalries in borderlands required that imperial officials yield to the demands of settlers and elites, see Peter J. Kastor, *The Nation's Crucible: The Louisiana Purchase and the Creation of America* (New Haven, CT: Yale University Press, 2004); and Jeremy Adelman and Stephen Aron, "From Borderlands to Borders: Empires, Nation-States, and the Peoples in between in North American History," *American Historical Review* 104, no. 3 (1999): 814–41.

52. Committee of the Town of St. Lewis to Amos Stoddard, September 30, 1804, Stoddard Papers, MHMA.

53. For U.S. officials and Missouri elites accommodating their interests and concerns in the period surrounding the Louisiana Purchase, see Aron, *American Confluence*, 115–27.

54. While few northern migrants headed to Illinois between 1800 and 1818, enough did to allow Illinois voters to reject efforts to repeal Article VI in 1818 and 1824. So few antislavery migrants went to Missouri, and slavery was so central to settlement and development, that the internal debate over slavery in 1820 and 1821 was overwhelmingly in favor of slavery. For Illinois, see Suzanne Cooper Guasco,

Confronting Slavery: Edward Coles and the Rise of Antislavery Politics in Nineteenth-Century America (DeKalb: Northern Illinois University Press, 2013). For the internal debates over slavery in the Missouri state constitution, see Hammond, *Slavery, Freedom, and Expansion*, 71–75.

55. Hammond, *Slavery, Freedom, and Expansion*; Hammond, "Slavery, Settlement, and Empire."

56. Joseph Pollard Jr. (Spotsylvania, VA) to William Clark, October 25, 1810, Clark Family Collection, box 11, William Clark Papers, 1789–1810, MHMA.

57. H[enry] G. Ewin [Nashville] to Benjamin H. Reeves [Frankfort, KY], January 3, 1813, C1013, Abiel Leonard Papers, 1782–1932, Correspondence Series, f. 22, State Historical Society of Missouri, Columbia.

58. Bill of Sale for Enslaved Child, Jack, Age 11, December 20, 1805, Carr-Papin Family Papers, 1776–1877, box 1, MHMA.

59. William C. Carr to Charles Carr, July 3, 1807, William C. Carr Papers, MHMA.

60. William C. Carr to Charles Carr, September 8, 1807, Carr Papers, MHMA.

61. William C. Carr to Charles Carr, August 25, 1809, Carr Papers, MHMA.

62. William C. Carr to John B.C. Lucas, July 7, 1810, Lucas Collection, MHMA.

63. Bill of Sale, Ellen, January 9, 1816, Justus Post Papers, 1807–21, MHMA.

64. Justus Post to John Post, October 7, 1817, Post Papers, MHMA.

65. Bill of Sale, Peter, November 17, 1817, Post Papers, MHMA.

66. Justus Post to John Post, October 7, 1817, Post Papers, MHMA.

67. James McDaniel vs. Juan P. Cabanne, Court Papers Concerning Swapping of Negroes, 1807, Lucas Collection, MHMA.

68. George Sibley to Samuel H. Sibley, September 25, 1813, Sibley Papers, MHMA.

69. Deposition of Martin Dorion, October 14, 1817, and Deposition of Maurice Blondeau, October 14, 1817, Indians Collection, MHMA; William Clark to George C. Sibley, August 6, 1816, Sibley Papers, MHMA; "A Subscriber," *Missouri Gazette* (St. Louis), June 22, 1816.

70. N. Wilson (Ste. Genevieve) to William B. Robertson (Near Nashville, TN), July 27, 1811, Slaves and Slavery Collection, MHMA.

71. N. Wilson to Robertson, July 27, 1811, Slaves and Slavery Collection, MHMA.

72. "William Clark to Jonathan Clark, November 9, 1808 [St. Louis]," in *Dear Brother: Letters of William Clark to Jonathan Clark*, ed. James J. Holmberg (New Haven, CT: Yale University Pres, 2002), 160.

73. "William Clark to Jonathan Clark, November 24, 1808," in *Dear Brother*, ed. Holmberg, 172.

74. "William Clark to Jonathan Clark, May 28, 1809," in *Dear Brother*, ed. Holmberg, 201.

75. "William Clark to Jonathan Clark, July 22, 1809," in *Dear Brother*, ed. Holmberg, 204.

76. "William Clark to Jonathan Clark, August 26, 1809," in *Dear Brother*, ed. Holmberg, 210.

77. "Forty Dollars Reward," *Missouri Gazette* (St. Louis), April 5, 1809.

78. "Two Hundred Dollars Reward," *Missouri Gazette* (St. Louis), January 25, 1809.

79. Rough Draft, Runaway Slave Poster for Sam, December 29, 1815, Lucas Collection, MHMA.

80. Henry S. Geyer, *A Digest of the Laws of Missouri Territory* . . . (St. Louis, 1818), 376. In 1809, St. Louis implemented its own ordinances regulating slaves. See "Police Regulations," "An Ordinance Regulating Patroles in the Town of St. Louis," and "An Ordinance Concerning Slaves in the Town of St. Louis," *Louisiana Gazette* (St. Louis), December 28, 1809.

2. The Boon's Lick Land Rush and the Coming of the Missouri Crisis

Robert Lee

On NOVEMBER 22, 1818, Missouri's territorial assembly began its petition for statehood with a wild exaggeration. The territory "contains at present a population little short of one hundred thousand souls," it exclaimed.[1] Missouri's combined free and enslaved population was actually closing in on sixty thousand, but the overstatement probably *felt* right. At that moment, Missouri's population was exploding at a rate never seen before or since. Between 1815 and 1818, central Missouri hosted one of the most intense growth spurts in American history. For a few years after the War of 1812, a settlement in central Missouri known as Boon's Lick appears to have become not just the fastest-growing region in Missouri but the fastest-growing region in the entire United States. The rush did not drive Missouri's population near one hundred thousand, but it did bring more than enough emigrants to justify statehood, inadvertently setting the stage for the Missouri Crisis. More surprisingly still, its underlying cause—a massive grab of Indigenous land orchestrated by William Clark—remains unincorporated into accounts of the origins of the crisis.

Most studies of the Missouri Crisis downplay demography by default, focusing instead on politics in Washington, DC. Even when looking westward, they tend to consider Missouri's decennial population increase overall, a scale on which it appears middling at best. Between 1810 and 1820, Missouri jumped from about twenty thousand to sixty-six thousand non-Indigenous inhabitants, a 236 percent increase that looks huge next to the national growth rate of 33 percent, but lagged among western territories and states. This rate ranked fourth out of the five trans-Appalachian territories that became states shortly after the War of 1812. In terms of raw population gains, Missouri ranked third in this group and was far behind states like Ohio, whose population rose by more than a quarter million between 1810

77

and 1820.[2] On the whole, Missouri's decennial growth toward statehood was noteworthy, but hardly unusual.

Historians of Missouri have added local color to this picture without altering its composition. On population, they invariably home in on Boon's Lick, a squatter community named for a saltworks in Howard County that began attracting droves of newcomers in 1815. Miles of wagon trains made the influx hard to miss by contemporaries, who left stunned accounts of the migration. Not unexpectedly, such accounts seldom attempted to gauge the movement's actual or relative size, making the changes it brought liable to the kind of hyperbole that appeared in the statehood petition. To their credit, historians have resisted such exaggeration but unintentionally generated a false synecdoche that can be just as misleading. Drawing on anecdotes about the rush without contextualizing them quantitatively, historians have miscast an outlier as an emblem. By generalizing descriptions of demographic growth specific to Boon's Lick—like John Mason Peck's impression that "it seemed as though Kentucky and Tennessee were breaking up and moving to the 'Far West'"—to describe emigration to Missouri or the trans-Appalachian West writ large, this localized rush has become representative of a western "great migration" after the War of 1812, an event that was impressive but not extreme.[3] Long portrayed as illustrative of an era of broad growth, the rush to Boon's Lick has come to depict Missouri's lunge toward statehood as a product of a significant but predictable migration, the westward movement taking its normal course.

On close inspection, the rush to Boon's Lick was anything but normal. Quantitative and spatial analysis reveals that even at a time of high mobility, this migration was atypically large and unpredictably intense. In fact, it appears that Boon's Lick was the most explosively growing settlement in the nation for a brief period after the War of 1812. After declaring central Missouri uninhabited by settlers in 1810, the census of 1820 found more people in Howard County—whose population was synonymous with the Boon's Lick settlement—than in 70 percent of U.S. counties. Propelled by a tidal wave of emigration from 1815 to 1818, Howard grew faster than all 761 of those counties. In this window, Missouri's population more than doubled from fewer than twenty-five thousand to more than fifty-five thousand, with over half that rise in Boon's Lick, which skyrocketed from about five hundred to more than eighteen thousand inhabitants. To grasp that leap's significance, consider that Howard County attracted more newcomers in 1817 and 1818 than seven of the nine California gold rush counties in the two years before the census of 1850.

At first glance, such phenomenal growth statistics might appear to be just a cartographic anomaly. The "mother of counties," Howard had an enormous footprint, but that fact has only obscured the rush's concentration in a relatively small area (see fig. 1). When onlookers marveled at the "avalanche" of newcomers, they were describing a migration condensed primarily in a stretch of central Missouri about fifty miles long by thirty miles wide, a balloon of population at the end of an emigrant road, tied off at the Boon's Lick saltworks north of the Missouri River.[4]

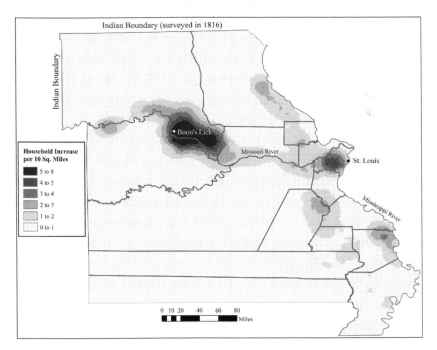

Figure 1. Settler population growth in Missouri Territory, 1810-20. This heat map visualizes the spatial imprint of the Boon's Lick land rush, using the acquisition of federal land patents to distribute population changes from the federal censuses of 1810 and 1820. Map shows 1820 county boundaries. *Sources*: Figures 8 and 9. Drawn by the author.

By 1820, nearly a third of Missouri's inhabitants and a quarter of its slaves lived in Boon's Lick, whose surging growth precipitated its statehood bid. Given the lopsided migration fueling Missouri's rise, there is little reason to suspect that if this settlement had not become a lodestar for emigrants, then the territory could have credibly petitioned for statehood before James Tallmadge Jr., whose abolition amendment touched off the Missouri Crisis debate, retired from Congress in 1819. Albeit unintended, that coincidence makes identifying how this growth spurt occurred vital to understanding the contingent origins of the crisis. Key preconditions included the end of the War of 1812 and central Missouri's celebrated natural advantages, but peace returned everywhere and boosterism was nearly as widespread. The prospect of obtaining titles to public lands formed a more direct trigger, with emigrants drawn by a "terrific excitement about getting land."[5] While public land was widely available after the war, emerging markets in first-rate land were limited, and none appeared more abruptly than the one at Boon's Lick, after an unusual and little-known seizure of Indian title in 1815.

Indigenous land expropriation goes virtually unmentioned in the literature on the Missouri Crisis, probably because it was ignored in congressional debates over Missouri's admission. But it was critical to Missouri's demographic growth and is centered in this account of the rise of Boon's Lick in the territorial era. The land market that trained settlers' imaginations on Boon's Lick emerged from an aggressive misinterpretation of an Osage treaty. In 1815, William Clark, Missouri's governor and Indian superintendent, unilaterally declared Indian title extinguished at Boon's Lick.[6] The move reversed long-established recognition of the area as Sauk, Meskwaki (Fox), and Iowa territory by arguing that the Osages had ceded this region to the United States in a vaguely worded 1808 treaty.[7] Contrived but effective, Clark's proclamation cranked the machinery for public land disposal into motion and opened an emigration floodgate, turning a small community clamoring for inclusion under the territory's government into a bustling destination for thousands of migrant families, many with slaves. Officials knew erasing Indian title would bring newcomers, but no one predicted one of the most intense land rushes in U.S. history would ensue, or that it would unwittingly set the stage for a national crisis over slavery's future.

The Boon's Lick Saltworks

Boon's Lick, sometimes spelled Boone's Lick or Boonslick, was the name of a salt spring north of the Missouri River about 150 miles from its confluence with the Mississippi. Nathan Boone—Daniel Boone's son—first visited the site in the winter of 1804–5 while hunting west of Upper Louisiana's settlements. He did not discover the spot, but he made it a landmark. In 1805, Nathan and his brother built a saltworks there with financial backing from James Morrison, a St. Charles–based trader. The partnership ended by 1811, but the famous name stuck. The site would be remembered for its salt-boiling operation and forgotten for being the hunting grounds of the Sauk, Meskwaki, and Iowa nations.[8]

Sauks and Meskwakis, in close cooperation with Iowas, took over what would become known as the Boon's Lick country north of the Missouri River in a war with the Osages in the eighteenth century. The conflict lasted decades but reached a tipping point in the 1790s with the expulsion of the Little Osages and Missourias from their villages not far upriver from where the saltworks would stand. As the Sauk chief Keokuk explained in 1824, his parents' generation had driven these enemies "across the troubled waters" to become "masters of the soil" above the turbid Missouri.[9] By the early nineteenth century, Boon's Lick lay on this war zone's still-dangerous fringe, used as a hunting ground by its Indigenous owners and trespassed on by poachers like the Boones.

U.S. officials who came to Upper Louisiana after the Louisiana Purchase acknowledged Sauk and Meskwaki possession north of the Missouri River. While camped near the ruins of the Little Osage and Missouria villages in 1804, Lewis and Clark—both future territorial governors and ex officio Indian superintendents—heard about this now-obscure conflict from their *engagés*. Meanwhile, in St. Louis, Sauk visitors explained to U.S. military officers that they had "conquered the lands on the Missouri River." Likewise, in November 1804, Governor William Henry Harrison would rely on Sauk and Meskwaki claims to obtain a Mississippi River–straddling land cession from them. That treaty later became infamous as the root cause of the Black Hawk War of 1832, but it remains largely forgotten for its role in central Missouri's demographic history. It established an Indian boundary north of the Missouri River whose breakdown after the War of 1812 would encourage mass migration to Boon's Lick.[10]

William Clark, who became Indian agent for the territory in 1807, knew this geography well. In 1810, he carefully laid the "Sac & Fox Boundary" on a map illustrating his expedition with Lewis (fig. 2). Through 1814, U.S. officials recognized the land west of this line, where Clark inscribed the "Boon's salt works" as Sauk, Meskwaki, and Iowa territory. Nothing about the recognition of this claim was unusual. As they had with the Haudenosaunee, and they would with the Lakota and Comanche, U.S. officials regularly recognized Indigenous conquests and often exploited those claims as a means to obtain cheap land cessions.

The saltworks operated under the auspice of Morrison's trade license and with the approbation of the territorial governor, but at its own risk. For the

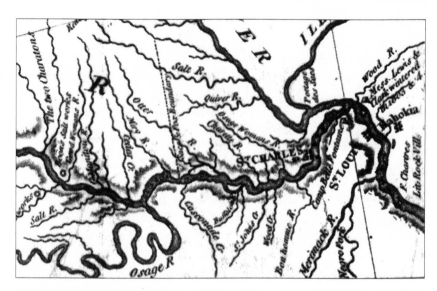

Figure 2. Clark map with Boon's Lick west of the Sauk and Meskwaki boundary, 1814 (original 1810). *A Map of Lewis and Clark's Track, across the Western Portion of North America* (1814). The detail depicts the Missouri River valley from St. Louis to the "Boons Salt works," which lies beyond the "Sac & Fox Boundary" of 1804. *Source*: Library of Congress Geography and Map Division, Washington, DC, https://www.loc.gov/item/79692907/.

first several years, there was no permanent settler occupation near the seasonal enterprise, which produced a lucrative commodity but became a target for raids, the first of which came in 1805. Governor James Wilkinson chastised Sauk and Meskwaki chiefs for the attack, but neither his bluster nor the raid had the desired effect. With the spring capable of producing $250 worth of salt a day, the Boones rebuilt. Eventually, though, ongoing theft of the cattle brought to feed the workers forced them out of business. "The works," Nathan recalled, "would have been profitable, but for the troubles & pilferings of the Indians."[11] By 1811, the Boones had sold their interests to Morrison. The works bearing their name survived two more major attacks—the last in 1816, when two slaves were kidnapped—and continued to operate long past the land rush.[12]

Although the saltworks was established as a seasonal operation rather than a permanent settlement, Morrison saw value in encouraging illegal emigration to the site. The first squatters intending to settle nearby hitched a ride on one of his keelboats. In the spring of 1808, Benjamin Cooper of Kentucky came with his family, built a cabin, and cleared a field near the works. Almost immediately, Governor Meriwether Lewis, who had succeeded Wilkinson, informed the Coopers they were on Indigenous land and ordered them downriver. The family complied, retreating to Loutre Island, just inside the Sauk and Meskwaki treaty line. They did so for their own safety, and not without reason. In the summer of 1808, a party of Sauks and Iowas killed two hunters while crossing the Missouri in search of Osages. The culprits surrendered themselves in St. Louis, but were later released because the encounter happened outside territorial jurisdiction, beyond the line "established by Treaty with the Sacs and Foxes."[13]

Ongoing intertribal hostilities along the Missouri, Osage raids on American settlements to its south, and the limited reach of U.S. authority into what Lewis derisively called the "hunting ranges of the 'Sovereign' savages" converged in the Osage treaty of 1808. Initially negotiated by Clark, then imposed via an ultimatum from Lewis, the treaty extinguished Osage title to a swath of territory between the Missouri and Arkansas Rivers. It also included an ambiguous clause that would play an outsize role in the demographic history of Missouri. In addition to the specific tract ceded between the Missouri and Arkansas Rivers, the Osages vaguely relinquished claim to "all lands situated northwardly of the river Missouri."[14] For the Osages, giving up a right to their enemies' land was an easy task. Hardly a novel maneuver, it helped net them a larger annuity. For Lewis, who prewrote the treaty, the measure was meant to mitigate intertribal warfare, not liquidate all Indigenous claims in the region. There was no suggestion until Clark's 1815 proclamation that the Osage cession of 1808 impinged on Indian title north of the river—quite the opposite. Governor Benjamin Howard, who succeeded Lewis, and Governor William Clark, who succeeded Howard, would continue to recognize Sauk, Meskwaki, and Iowa title even after a squatter colony launched the small-scale invasion that birthed the Boon's Lick settlement.

The Boon's Lick Settlement in Indian Country

That invasion began when the Coopers returned to the saltworks with more trespassers in 1810. George Sibley, the factor at Fort Osage, upriver from Boon's Lick, encountered six to eight of these "first families" that February. The group represented the forward guard of a small colony filled out by summer's end. One early history described the fledgling community as "a large portion" of twenty-five families, listing forty-two men and claiming that "the names we have given embrace nearly the entire number who emigrated to the colony with Colonel Benjamin Cooper."[15] Wives and children followed that summer. Only one family located south of the Missouri River on the Osage cession. The rest located north of the Missouri on the unceded Sauk, Meskwaki, and Iowa lands.

This region had qualities desirable to small farmers, especially those from the Upper South. In addition to salt springs and freshwater, the area had wooded hills and black loess soil suitable for tobacco and hemp cultivation. When traveler Henry Brackenridge passed through in 1811, Braxton Cooper had a job at the saltworks and an opinion that "the upland, back, is the most beautiful he ever beheld." The same year, John Bradbury saw squatter fields with fourteen-foot cornstalks. Many marveled at the supply of game, too. "The forests nearby were full of deer and bears and other wild animals," recalled Patsy Cox, who emigrated in 1812. "Had it not been for the Indians, it would have been a paradise," she concluded, unaware that this abundance was partly a by-product of intertribal warfare. With the Missouria and Little Osage villages gone, and seasonal parties passing through gingerly, early Boon's Lick was one of the conflict-induced game sinks that speckled the American West.[16]

By the time Governor Howard declared the Boon's Lick region "the finest, body of land I believe, in Louisiana" in mid-1812, roughly seventy-five more families had arrived. The fact that they were families, often extended ones, runs counter to the myth of the self-reliant American settler. The community was almost certainly mostly children. Nine-year-old Samuel Cole, for instance, came with his widowed mother and eight siblings. Patsy Cox likewise came as a "young girl." The most famous of the early Boon's Lick squatters— Christopher "Kit" Carson—had little memory of the early years because he arrived as an infant. Nor were these families desperate. Reports described them as "respectable, and some wealthy, for this country," with Brackenridge adding that "most of them have slaves."[17]

They came to reap the benefits of establishing themselves and their slaves on Indigenous lands that they hoped would be incorporated into the United States one day. Federal authorities rarely challenged such invasions, but the attempts were high-stakes bets whose attractiveness is easy to exaggerate. Between 1810 and 1815, the part of Missouri Territory that would get carved off into a state had only two sites with substantial squatting on unceded Indigenous lands. One was at Boon's Lick. The other was on a tract by the Mississippi, near Cape Girardeau, that Spanish authorities had granted to the Shawnees in 1793. By 1811, "several families" had invaded, leaving that area "much crowded" by the end of the War of 1812.[18] Their numbers are unclear, but these intruders could not have been much more, and were likely less, than in Boon's Lick, where the five hundred or so inhabitants represented about one in fifty families in the territory. This does not mean squatting was not rampant, only that it tended to take place closer to established settlements, on land ceded by tribal nations but not yet sold by the United States. Waiting until the risks diminished and the benefits looked nearer at hand, squatter families would start flocking to Boon's Lick only after the erasure of Indian title.

For those who came earlier, life beyond the territory's civil jurisdiction was not among the location's advantages. In 1812, the Boon's Lick squatters told Governor Howard that they had a "strong disposition to come under the laws, and regulations, of the Territory." Howard refused because they were in Indian country in violation of "the treaty, between the U: States, and the Sacs & Foxes." At the same time, he found an excuse to allow them to stay. Lacking a formal protest of their presence, he denied having a mandate to expel them. Going further, he advocated purchasing the area. The mixed response indicated that the Osage treaty of 1808 had not ended federal recognition of Indian title at Boon's Lick, even if Howard was loath to respect it. But it also left the squatters exposed. For every one of them, there were perhaps ten Sauks, Meskwakis, and Iowas who lived most of the year on the Mississippi and Des Moines Rivers but claimed the land south to the Missouri as their hunting grounds and made their presence known in the summer when they set up encampments in the vicinity.[19]

While the Sauks and Meskwakis never formally requested an eviction, they signaled their displeasure with raids that started in 1811. When Howard suggested evacuating, Sarshal Cooper insisted decamping would ruin them and asked for munitions instead, explaining that they had around three hundred men, women, boys, and girls willing to fight. Staying required sheltering in blockhouses as the raids intensified, making subsistence activities dangerous. In one widely circulated story, an unidentified Indigenous party gave chase to a group of settlers harvesting corn, who escaped only thanks to the wagon-driving skills of one of their slaves. Not all were so lucky, including Sarshal. In the most famous incident from the conflict, a Sauk allegedly killed him after wedging his rifle through a crack in the log walls of one of the blockhouses. Most of the raids, however, targeted property rather than people, as depositions documenting the losses reveal. Sauks, Meskwakis, and Iowas stole horses, slaughtered livestock, destroyed fields, and wrecked homes. Not surprisingly, the community's growth flatlined during the War of 1812.[20]

Although usually treated as simply the War of 1812 in Missouri, the Sauk chief Black Hawk did not recall these raids as either masterminded by the British or part of a pan-Indian resistance. Rather, he couched them as part of an ongoing defense of "our best hunting ground," an effort to secure the territory they had conquered in the eighteenth century. That campaign did not map neatly onto the chronology of the War of 1812, having begun with the assault on the saltworks in 1805 and continuing past 1815, but it did interact with that larger conflict in critical ways. The War of 1812 enabled the attacks on Boon's Lick to spike as intertribal alliances thickened. When it was over, the violence abated as peace drained the pool of Indigenous allies. In its wake, Sauk and Meskwaki differences over whether to accommodate or continue resisting U.S. encroachment became more pronounced, with leaders such as Keokuk pushing for the former and Black Hawk carrying on the latter. Meanwhile, the Iowas gravitated toward accommodation. In 1815, fourteen nations, including the Iowa and diplomatically inclined Sauk and Meskwaki bands, signed peace treaties at Portage des Sioux. The militant bands followed the next year after Clark threatened to mount a campaign to prevent them from hunting in Missouri. Sauks, Meskwakis, and Iowas would continue to pass through, hunt in, and raid the Boon's Lick settlement, but doing so became more dangerous and less frequent after the settlement's population surged past their own in 1817.[21]

The raids provided the squatters with fodder for a second appeal for annexation. By early 1814, shortly after William Clark became governor, the territorial assembly received a petition begging "to come within the bounds of the civil Authority of this Territory." Taking a new tack, the squatters admitted their trespass and asked for "the extinguishment of the Indian title." The assembly responded with a resolution in favor of a purchase that Clark forwarded to the secretary of state. Clark's letter outlined "lands Claimed by the Socks & Ioways" that he believed he could acquire by a treaty, if given permission to hold a council.[22] But his wartime request went nowhere.

It must have been frustrating, as Clark and other federal officials in Missouri already had their eyes on Boon's Lick. When Governor Howard advised purchasing the area, he argued that this part of Missouri "would be sooner settled after the lands are offer'd for sale." Clark echoed that sentiment when he advocated for a treaty in 1814, asserting that this region could support a larger population than anywhere else in the territory. That same year, William Rector, the federal surveyor for Missouri and Illinois, got a tip that Boon's Lick would sell quickly if Indian title were to be extinguished.[23] The next year, Clark made it happen.

The Proclamation of 1815

The consistency with which officials acknowledged Sauk, Meskwaki, and Iowa title to Boon's Lick between 1804 and 1814 makes what happened next look brazenly underhanded. On March 9, 1815, Clark issued a proclamation unilaterally declaring Sauk, Meskwaki, and Iowa possession invalid and announcing that this region already belonged to the United States. Without referencing his own representations to the contrary, Clark's proclamation asserted that the vague relinquishment of all Osage claims "northwardly" of the Missouri River in the treaty of 1808 actually constituted a precisely bounded land cession and that the tract it referred to, which encompassed Boon's Lick, had been part of the unsurveyed public domain of the United States for more than six years.

The proclamation's text was brief, geographically dense, and less than forthcoming about its full implications. It mainly delineated Clark's new interpretation of the northern Osage boundary, which followed a line 140 miles due north from the Missouri River opposite the mouth of the Kansas River (the present Kansas City area) and then turned southeast until it hit the Ohaha (Salt) River, a western tributary of the Mississippi, before continuing south to the Missouri River opposite the mouth of the Gasconade River. Although it did not note the fact explicitly, this tract ended at the exact spot where the Sauk and Meskwaki line of 1804 met the Missouri, ostensibly extending a continuous stretch of ceded land up the northern banks of the Missouri as far as the Kansas River. Boon's Lick lay roughly in the middle of this stretch (see fig. 3). The proclamation then asserted that the "pretentions of other nations of Indians to lands lying within these limits, being of very recent date are utterly unsupported." With the flick of a pen, and without explicitly naming either the Sauk, Meskwaki, or Iowa nations or Boon's Lick in the proclamation itself, Clark deposited what he knew were "some of the best lands in the Territory" into the U.S. public domain.[24]

Clark's rejection of Sauk, Meskwaki, and Iowa title had a discernible, if selectively applied, logic. When he declared their "pretensions" to possession of Boon's Lick too recent to respect, Clark was not denying that these nations had conquered lands north of the Missouri. Rather, he denied the legitimacy of that action, suddenly and without acknowledging that there had been a change of policy at all. Behind this new assertion lay an assumption that Indigenous nations living within the colonial domains of European powers (or their successors like the United States) could not legally engage in conquest. Or, in Clark's opaque language, they did not follow the "prescription

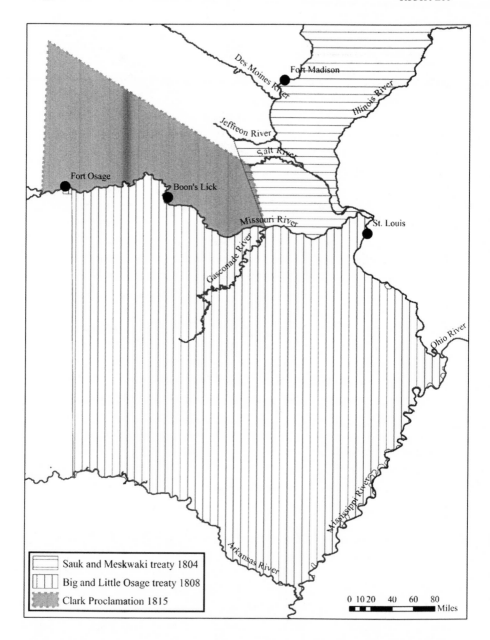

Figure 3. Indian land cessions in Missouri Territory, 1804-15. The Sauk and Meskwaki Treaty of 1804 and the Big and Little Osage Treaty of 1808 ceded most of modern-day Missouri. Clark's 1815 proclamation retroactively extended the boundary of the Osage cession of 1808. *Sources:* Treaty of 1804; Treaty of 1808; Proclamation of 1815. Drawn by the author.

of which the original Inhabitants of this country are accustomed to found their territorial claims." On the other hand, the proclamation held not only that the Big and Little Osages retained the right to transfer their "immemorially bounded" lands north of the Missouri to the United States, but that they had already done so in November 1808. All Clark had to do to turn the United States' vague acquisition "northwardly of the river Missouri" into a specific tract was identify the reach of the Osages' ancestral domain.[25]

How, then, did Clark ascertain those boundaries? This is a bit of a mystery, as the proclamation did not name its source. Still, its geography suggests that Clark relied on Auguste Chouteau, the longtime St. Louis resident, fur trader, and co-commissioner (with Clark and Governor Ninian Edwards of Illinois) for negotiating Indian peace treaties after the War of 1812. To advance the work of that commission, and undoubtedly his own interests, Chouteau penned a set of notes on historical Indian boundaries based on his personal knowledge. Gathered to deny Indigenous "claims by right of conquest," Chouteau outlined the area "northwardly of the river Missouri" ceded to the United States "on the 10th November 1808." That cession, Chouteau explained, included the old hunting grounds of the Little Osages and the Missourias, who, he contended, held them "with the consent of the Grande Ozages" (see fig. 4). The area Chouteau outlined corresponded to the one named in Clark's proclamation, with one notable difference of expression. Chouteau described its northern reach as the "dividing ridge" between the Missouri and Mississippi Rivers.[26] Clark called it a line from a point 140 miles north of the mouth of the Kansas River to the Ohaha (Salt) River, a different way of saying roughly the same thing.

Given Clark's reputation as a friend to tribal nations who tried in vain to temper settler aggression, an even bigger mystery appears to be why Clark issued this proclamation at all. To build up that reputation, historians have overlooked this proclamation and focused instead on a second one Clark issued in December 1815, one that pledged to protect Indian country from intruders. This second, better-known, proclamation ordered squatters in Indian country to vacate at once. It was aimed at the trespassers on the Shawnee lands near Cape Girardeau, whose Spanish grant Clark had a duty to recognize, at least on paper. On its face, this order, and the political price Clark paid for it, cast him as a tragic Jeffersonian philanthropist. But on the ground, there was no real enforcement, and not just regarding the Shawnees' grant. Within a few months of issuing the order, Clark got word of intruders on Quapaw lands on the Ouachita River. In response, he suggested holding

Figure 4. Chouteau's historical Indian boundaries north of the Missouri River, 1816. Detail of R. Paul, *A Map Exhibiting the Territorial Limits of Several Nations & Tribes of Indians Agreeably to the Notes of A. Chouteau*, showing the ancestral territory of the Little Osages and Missourias that Chouteau's notes (directly) and Clark's proclamation (indirectly) insisted was ceded to the United States by the Big and Little Osages in 1808. Boon's Lick was in the territory shown belonging to the Little Osages. *Source*: CMF884, Cartographic and Architectural Records, National Archives and Record Administration, College Park, MD.

a treaty to acquire the land, arguing it would be impractical to remove the squatters and undesirable given their improvements and wish to live under territorial jurisdiction. The reaction was consistent with his attempt to arrange a treaty to acquire Boon's Lick in 1814. When that earlier effort failed, it appears Clark deployed his March 1815 proclamation to appease the anxious squatters; punish the Sauks, Meskwakis, and Iowas for their raids; and claim a desirable region for the United States. His actions suggest his greatest fealty was not to a naively benevolent Indian policy but rather to the maintenance of federal authority in the dispossession and settlement process, whose pace and formalities often irked settlers but consistently favored their interests.[27]

News traveling west may explain the timing of the Osage boundary proclamation. In December 1814, word arrived in the United States that British and American peace commissioners at Ghent had agreed to an article—later numbered Article IX—requiring ending hostilities with tribes and restoring the Indian boundary to its position in 1811. By January 1815, the news reached St. Louis. The Treaty of Ghent itself arrived in Washington, DC, in February, and word quickly fanned out across the country. It reached Kaskaskia, Illinois, on March 8, putting it within a day's travel of St. Louis. The next day Clark issued his proclamation redrawing the Osage treaty line. That weekend he wrote to James Monroe to let him know he had learned the war had ended, and the *Missouri Gazette* published his proclamation side by side with an announcement of the signing of the Treaty of Ghent. Clark's move artfully sidestepped that peace treaty. By retracting recognition of Boon's Lick as Sauk, Meskwaki, and Iowa territory and declaring that the United States had actually purchased the land in 1808, it maneuvered around Article IX by routing the acquisition through a loophole in the normal treaty process required to extinguish Indian title, a process that would pause for several years while Clark and Chouteau led the Portage des Sioux peace commission tasked with reestablishing prewar Indian boundaries.[28]

When it came to the demographic development of Missouri, the how, why, and when of Clark's proclamation mattered less than the so what. Unlike Clark's order for intruders to vacate Indigenous lands, his aggressive reinterpretation of the Osage treaty of 1808 worked. It effectively erased Indian title to Boon's Lick, incorporated the settlement into the territory, and beckoned new migrants. The proclamation ended by annexing the region to St. Charles County. Soon after Missouri's assembly erected the settlement into its own county named after Governor Howard, who had died of an illness during a campaign against the Sauks and Meskwakis in 1814. Fusing Clark's and Chouteau's geographies, Howard County's original borders followed "the indian boundary line (as described in a proclamation of the governor, issued the ninth day of March 1815) northwardly one hundred and forty miles, thence eastward with the said line to the main dividing ridge of high ground between the rivers Mississippi and Missouri," before dipping below the Missouri River. Soon federal surveyors began crisscrossing central Missouri and newspapers began crowing about "Boone's Lick, now Howard County," marked out by "the Osage boundary line," where "lots will shortly be put in market."[29]

A Rush toward Statehood

Clark's proclamation accelerated Missouri's path to statehood. John G. Heath, whose slaves operated the Boon's Lick saltworks in the postwar period, was among the local observers who publicly marveled at the land rush that ensued. In 1816, Heath proudly told readers of the Washington, DC, *National Register* that he and his fellow settlers had entered "the first stage of our political existence, and expect to emerge from our darkness and obscurity very rapidly." George Sibley started predicting the same in 1817. "The Missouri territory will become an independent state in a few years without a doubt. Its population must be already great enough to entitle its admission to the union."[30] Their confidence came after seeing Boon's Lick become engulfed by emigrants. By the time the territorial assembly submitted its petition for statehood in November 1818, a few months before a land office opened in Howard County, one of the most intense land rushes in U.S. history was reaching a crescendo. By then, Howard County's share of Missouri's population had grown from less than 3 percent to more than 30 percent. Even in an era of high mobility, this kind of growth was extreme. When integrated with a quantitative reconstruction of the rush, it becomes apparent that observers like Heath and Sibley had witnessed the fastest-growing settlement in the United States.

There would have been no prospective land sales had Clark's proclamation not cranked the machinery of public land disposal into motion. After he issued his proclamation, surveyor William Rector sent a copy to the commissioner of the General Land Office, along with his impression that Boon's Lick "would immediately sell" if put to market.[31] He did not do so out of passing interest. As a bonded official, he risked financial ruin if the General Land Office rejected his surveying expenditures, and the land office would not authorize straying into Indian country. To put his plans to bring Boon's Lick to market on a sure footing, Rector waited until after the peace negotiations at Portage des Sioux in the summer of 1815. That council produced a treaty with the Osages that reconfirmed their 1808 treaty and silently rewrote history by folding in Clark's new interpretation of the cession. In its wake, Clark and Chouteau obtained Osage permission for Rector's men to run the line. The survey followed Clark's proclamation northward from the Missouri River and stopped after 100 miles. It then cut due east, striking the Des Moines River at a latitude parallel with Fort Madison on the Mississippi. The survey's path only partially matched Clark's proclamation, with the deviation realizing the northern boundary of the Sauk and Iowa treaty he had

proposed in 1814. Land north of the survey line that lay inside Clark's proclamation area would be repurchased decades later; land south of the survey
line not covered by either the proclamation or the Sauk and Meskwaki treaty
of 1804 was seized, following Chouteau's notes, as abandoned Illinois home-
lands (fig. 5). Rector did not locate this line by chance. According to his plat,
it conformed to Clark's and Chouteau's advice.[32]

Rector's boundary survey functioned as a lure for emigrants. It signaled
that first-rate lands within would soon come to market through the General
Land Office, which would hold auctions for sales on credit. "Boon's Lick
country no doubt is the richest considerable body of good land in the
territory. I think it very similar to the good lands of Kentucky," one of the
surveyors explained in a widely published letter. Newcomers could avoid
paying top dollar by getting in early. Squatters who made improvements
could keep choice parcels off the auction block by filing preemption claims,
allowing them to pay the federal minimum price. Emigrants could also turn

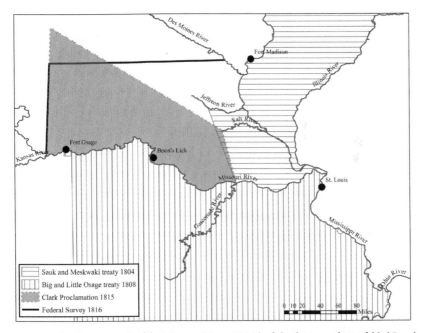

Figure 5. Federal survey north of the Missouri River, 1816. The federal survey of 1816 folded Boon's
Lick into the public domain of the United States. The line followed a path dictated by Clark and
Chouteau as it strayed from Clark's proclamation line. Sources: Treaty of 1804; Treaty of 1808; Proc-
lamation of 1815; John Gardiner and Thomas Streeter, Map of the Northern Part of Missouri (1818).
Drawn by the author.

to secondary markets in military bounty warrants and New Madrid scrip (issued to indemnify victims of the New Madrid earthquakes of 1811–12) that could be redeemed for land patents. All of these paths to market depended on the subdivision of the land for redistribution, which could start only after Indian title was acquired, which is why nationally circulated news items assured readers that this desirable country was in the U.S. public domain. "The Indian title has been extinguished," they reported, noting that military bounties and public land sales would follow. Emigrant guides touted Boon's Lick, like other desirable spots, as lands "yet purchased from the native savages." Private correspondents talked, too. One Ste. Genevieve dry-goods dealer told a friend in Kentucky that "Boon's Lick & settlement are one & the same thing," assured him he had little to fear from Indians, and predicted the imminent opening of a land office. Like the squatters who came before Clark's proclamation, those who followed came, as Rector put it, for "favors from Government" in the form of "Pre-emption rights, Donations, &c.," only in far-higher numbers.[33]

By late 1816, pressure to get Boon's Lick lands to market was intensifying. "The current of Emigration is so much directed to that quarter," Rector warned, "that Settlements will be formed notwithstanding the law forbids settlements on public lands." That current was anticipated, but its strength was not. With tens of millions of acres of unappropriated public domain land around the United States, no one could predict how many would come, where they would go, or how quickly they would arrive. So, when Boon's Lick actually started attracting "vast numbers" of families drawn by the "prospects of a speedy sale," Rector and many others took notice.[34]

Moved by the magnitude of the rush, shocked observers produced florid descriptions that would go on to color territorial histories of Missouri. To George Sibley, Howard County was "like enchantment," transformed by migrants who began arriving at rates "beyond all former example" in 1815 and 1816. By 1817, he said, "immense swarms of emigrants" were "constantly flocking to the country from all parts of the union." According to John Mason Peck's oft-quoted account: "Some families came in the spring of 1815; but in the winter, spring, summer, and autumn of 1816, they came like an avalanche. It seemed as though Kentucky and Tennessee were breaking up and moving to the 'Far West.' Caravan after caravan passed over the prairies of Illinois, crossing the 'great river' at St. Louis, all bound to the Boone's Lick." Timothy Flint recalled seeing the wagon trains pass through St. Charles for days on end. "Ask one of them whither he was moving," he recalled, "and the answer was, 'To Boon's Lick, to be sure." As the rush heated up, editors declared it *"astonishing* in what numbers the people are flocking to this country from every state, and of every description."[35]

The region particularly appealed to slaveholders and aspiring masters. Sibley, for one, favorably contrasted Missouri to Louisiana, as a region with slavery but without massive cotton plantations, where an upwardly mobile gentleman like himself might establish a household with "ten good sleek wellfed & wellclothed Blacks." Flint likewise commented approvingly on the "very pleasing and patriarchal scene" of slaves forced up the Boon's Lick trail. By 1820, there would be one enslaved person for every three free adults in the settlement. Not only did the land rush further entrench support for slavery in Missouri, but the growing number of slaves also further inflated the territory's constitutional population. By 1820, Boon's Lick was well on its way to becoming the new epicenter of slavery in Missouri, a development that would later earn the region a new nickname: "Little Dixie."[36]

The word that observers kept coming back to was "rapidity." But what did it mean for editors around the United States to spread reports that Boon's Lick was "increasing with an unusual rapidity"?[37] Historians have done little to situate these anecdotes quantitatively and muted the rush's extraordinary intensity as a result. If we cannot quite see through Flint's eyes, we can at least glimpse an outline of what he saw from population counts bent into growth curves. Observers in official and unofficial capacities produced a scattered record of estimates of total population, families, white males, and militia volunteers that can be normalized into comparable population estimates for ten of the twelve years from 1810 to 1821. Table 1 gathers these estimates. Figures 6 and 7 use them to interpolate the tidal wave of emigrants that crashed into Boon's Lick and track the region's skyrocketing share of Missouri's population. The rise illustrated by figure 6 parallels anecdotal accounts of the settlement's growth, illustrating how migration to Boon's Lick started in 1810, stalled during the War of 1812, and exploded after. When that increase is graphed as a portion of Missouri's total population, as figure 7 shows, it becomes clear how lopsided the territory's postwar growth spurt was. Migrants to Boon's Lick boosted the number of Missouri's inhabitants toward sixty thousand in 1818 and beyond the following year.

This quantitative view makes it possible to roughly gauge the flow of the "mountain torrent" Peck witnessed. At the time of Clark's proclamation in early 1815, when the Boon's Lick squatters were still in blockhouses, the settlement had perhaps six hundred inhabitants, likely fewer. Before the year's

Table 1. Boon's Lick settler population estimates, 1810-21

Date	Population estimate	Counts	Source type	Sources
February 1810	44[a]	8 families	letter	1
August 1810	139[a]	25 families	local histories	2; 3
August 1811	378[a]	average of 75 (April) and 60 (November) families	letter; journal	1; 4
June 1812	506[b]	average of 100 (June) families; 300 men/women/boys/girls (ca. midyear); and 112 militia volunteers (ca. midyear)	letter; letter; muster roll	5; 6; 2
October 1814	524[c]	116 militia volunteers	muster roll	7
November 1815	1,075[d]	525 white males	letter	8
August 1816	2,146[d]	1,050 white males	letter	8
September 1817	6,920[d]	3,386 white males	territorial census	9
May 1818	16,350[d]	8,000 males	newspaper	10
August 1820	20,385[e]	20,385 inhabitants	federal census	11
November 1821	21,255[f]	21,255 inhabitants	state census	12

Sources:

1. George C. Sibley to James G. Mask, March 29, 1817, in *The Emigrant's Guide to the Western and Southwestern States and Territories* (New York: Kirk and Mercein, 1818), by William Darby, 303.

2. *History of Chariton and Howard Counties, Missouri* (St. Louis: National Historical, 1883), 92-93, 95-98, 150-51.

3. *History of Howard and Cooper Counties* (St. Louis: National Historical, 1883), 93, 620.

4. Henry M. Brackenridge, "Journal of a Voyage Up the River Missouri, Performed in 1811, by H. M. Brackenridge," in *Early Western Travels, 1748-1846*, edited by Rueben Gold Thwaite (Cleveland, OH: Arthur H. Clark, 1904), 4:48.

5. Governor Howard to the Secretary of War in Clarence Edwin Carter, ed. and comp., *The Territorial Papers of the United States*, vol. 14, *The Territory of Louisiana-Missouri, 1806-1814* (Washington, DC: Government Printing Office, 1949), 568.

6. Walter B. Stevens, *Missouri: The Center State, 1821-1915* (Chicago: S. J. Clarke, 1915), 157.

7. War of 1812, Muster Roll, 1814, C1582, State Historical Society of Missouri, Columbia.

8. "To the Editor of the National Register," *National Register*, November 9, 1816, 163.

9. Floyd Shoemaker, *Missouri's Struggle for Statehood, 1804-1821* (Jefferson City, MO: Hugh Stephens, 1916), 328.

10. "Missouri," *Niles Weekly Register*, May 16, 1818, 208.

11. 1820 Federal Census, Minnesota Population Center, *National Historical Geographic Information System: Version 2.0* (Minneapolis: University of Minnesota, 2011).

12. I. MacDonald Demuth, *The History of Pettis County, Missouri* (1882), 26.

[a]Family count multiplied by 5.56 (that is, approximate U.S. family size in the years 1810-20). Based on a linear interpolation of family size between 1790 and 1850, the closest years for which figures are available.

[b]Men/women/boys/girls count divided by 0.61 (portion of total Boon's Lick white population over age nine in 1820 census); militia count divided by 0.25 (portion of total Boon's Lick white male population over age fifteen in 1820 census).

[c]Multiplies 1812 population estimate by 1.04 (ratio of 1812 militia count to 1814 militia count).

[d]Divides white male/males count by 0.49 (portion of total Boon's Lick population in 1820 census).

[e]Sum of Howard and Cooper Counties.

[f]Sum of Howard, Cooper, Boone, Chariton, Cole, Lillard, Ray, and Saline Counties.

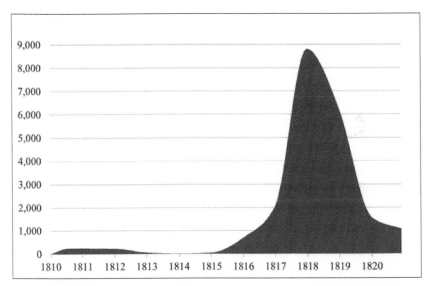

Figure 6. Annual settler population increase in Boon's Lick, 1810-21. Emigration to Boon's Lick spiked after the War of 1812, in the wake of Clark's proclamation in 1815 and the federal survey in 1816, which signaled land markets would soon open. The wave was peaking just as the Missouri Assembly petitioned for statehood in 1818. *Source*: Table 1. Growth curves interpolated by fitting counts to a one-way spline function.

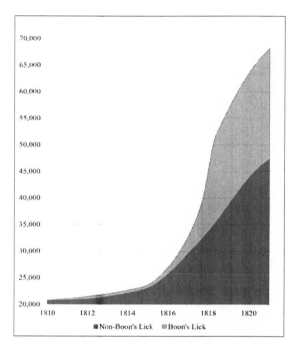

Figure 7. Total settler population in Missouri Territory, 1810-21. The wave of emigration to Boon's Lick lifted the Missouri Territory's population past sixty thousand in 1819, which made delaying statehood unlikely as the Missouri Crisis debates began. *Sources:* Table 1; federal censuses of 1810 and 1820; territorial censuses of 1814 and 1817 (white male counts assumed equal to 0.49 of total population estimate, based on census of 1820); state census of 1821. Growth curves interpolated by fitting counts to a one-way spline function.

end, when the territorial assembly set Howard County's boundaries, the population had nearly doubled, to more than eleven hundred. By late 1816, it nearly tripled, to around three thousand. During 1817, when Peck reported families streaming in from as far away as Virginia and the Carolinas, "not a few" from the mid-Atlantic states, and "a sprinkling" from New England and New York, the population more than tripled to about ten thousand and kept rising. By November 1818, when the Missouri Assembly sent its statehood petition declaring that the territory's population was "daily increasing with a rapidity almost unexampled," it nearly doubled again to more than eighteen thousand. Whereas about one in fifty Missouri households lived in Boon's Lick in early 1815, nearly one in three occupied the settlement by late 1818. This was the breakneck change lurking in descriptions, like Flint's, of the rush peaking that year, when the migrants "poured in a flood, the power and strength of which could only be adequately conceived by a person on the spot."[38]

In 1819, the growth rate began to taper, as the "pole-star of attraction" shifted to the Salt River country in Missouri and then into Illinois. By then, the Missouri Assembly had subdivided Howard County at the Missouri River, renaming the southern half Cooper County after Sarshal Cooper. In 1820, "Howard and Cooper Counties, embracing the country usually denominated *Boon's Lick* settlement," appeared in the federal census with more than twenty thousand of Missouri's sixty-six thousand residents, including twenty-seven hundred of its ten thousand slaves. Between the summers of 1820 and 1821, when Missouri entered the Union, the rush to Boon's Lick was finally dying down. By then, the Panic of 1819 was reaching the West, and public land sales on credit had become unavailable. That year, the region gained only about a thousand people, its brief spurt of exponential growth having collapsed to a far more typical level.[39]

Flint described the wave that peopled central Missouri in the run-up to statehood as fueled by a kind of irrational exuberance that suddenly made Boon's Lick more desirable than any other place in the country. He claimed to have seen a dozen such hot spots capture the "imaginations of the multitudes" during his lifetime, but he never talked about anywhere else in such shocked, land-hungry language. At the height of the Boon's Lick land rush, he recalled, "land claims, settlement-rights, preemption rights, unconfirmed claims, and New Madrid claims" were topics of daily conversation, "like the weather in other countries." Little of this conversation was polite. The frenzy generated allegations of claim jumping by speculators, denunciations of squatters as a "band of banditti," and acts of violence, including murder. Speculators in New Madrid scrip received the most hate for their efforts to claim squatter-occupied tracts. But the greatest threat to the prospects of the multitude entering Boon's Lick turned on preemption laws and Clark's proclamation.[40]

In late 1815, President James Madison issued a general order for squatters to vacate public lands across the United States. George Sibley worried that the order would deal a "crushing" blow to the Boon's Lick settlement. Fortunately for the squatters, the order proved toothless. It conflicted with a preemption law passed in 1814 that cleared a path to purchase for the incoming emigrants, but still left the rights of the minority who had migrated prior to Clark's proclamation uncertain. As Henry Carroll, the registrar of public lands put it as he prepared to open a land office in Boon's Lick, the earliest squatters had come when "Howard County was Indian Country," which excluded them from preemption privileges. The squatters pushed back with a memorial to Congress highlighting the catastrophic implications of Carroll's decision for *all* newcomers to the region. If Boon's Lick "was Indian Country then it is Indian Country now," they pointed out. "There has been no Treaty ceeding [sic] it to the United States since and it cannot be presumed, that the Government have proceeded unjustly to sell lands belonging to the Indians." William Clark likewise rallied to their cause, declaring Carroll's clear-eyed interpretation of events a "misconstruation [*sic*] in the view which has been taken of the subject." "Indian Title to the Lands North of the Missouri River," he insisted curtly, "was Extinguished by the Osage Treaty in 1808." In March 1819, a few weeks after James Tallmadge Jr. amended Missouri's statehood bill, Congress affirmed the original squatters' preemption rights in Boon's Lick. The following year, Henry Carroll was shot in the back over a land-title dispute.[41]

The violent storm of land jobbing permanently transformed the region. By 1820, a full two-thirds of the acres patented in Missouri would lay inside Howard County's original boundaries.[42] The significance of that figure is difficult to discern from the numbers alone, due to the large land area of Howard County and, by 1819, Howard and Cooper Counties. While these counties' populations were synonymous with the Boon's Lick settlement, their boundaries covered a third of what became the state of Missouri. Land records can help reconstruct the shape of the torrent. Figures 8 and 9 illustrate the growing geographic extent of non-Indigenous occupation of Missouri between 1810 and 1820. They estimate the number of rural households outside major towns based on county-level census counts and then distribute the number of households per county as points at the most desirable parcels, with parcel desirability determined by purchase order. Of course, there was not a perfect correspondence between purchases and occupation, which is part of what makes this approach useful. In many parts of the territory, public land was not yet for sale, but census counts make clear squatters were already there—this technique gestures at their most likely locations. In Boon's Lick, these maps help illustrate the concentration of the rush, which stretched far up the Missouri, but mainly fanned out from the saltworks in an area about fifty miles long by thirty miles wide, predominantly north of the Missouri on the lands deposited in the public domain by Clark's proclamation.

To appreciate the size and concentration of the rush makes it possible to begin putting it in a national context, one that suggests Boon's Lick was the most intensely growing settlement in the United States after the War of 1812. As the national population rose by 33 percent between 1810 and 1820, and Missouri's by 236 percent, Boon's Lick ballooned by more than 3,000 percent between early 1815 and late 1818. Even after Howard County's restriction to land north of the Missouri River in 1819, its population appeared in the census of 1820 with greater raw population gains than 97.6 percent of counties in the United States. To accomplish this, it

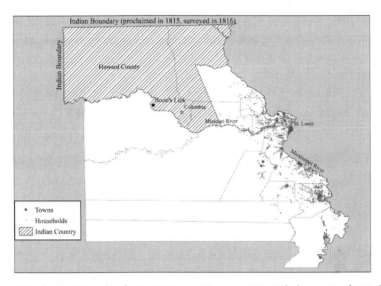

Figure 8. Settler population distribution in Missouri Territory, 1810. At the beginning of 1810, there was no permanent non-Indigenous settlement in Boon's Lick. *Source*: Household numbers based on federal census counts divided by the average household size for the decade (5.56). Locations based on General Land Office patent order within counties, with one family located per patent. Drawn by the author.

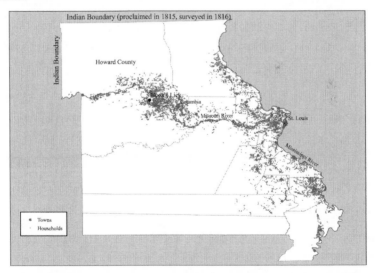

Figure 9. Settler population distribution in Missouri Territory, 1820. By 1820, nearly one in three non-Indigenous inhabitants of Missouri occupied the ballooning settlements around Boon's Lick. Map shows 1820 county boundaries. *Source*: Household numbers based on federal census counts divided by the average household size for the decade (5.56). Locations based on General Land Office patent order within counties, with one family located per patent. Drawn by the author.

had to grow at a faster rate than all 761 counties enumerated in the 1820 census. Howard's stunning debut in the federal census would occasionally be outmatched by similarly superlative cousins across the antebellum era, but not by much. The geographic core of Boon's Lick covered a smaller area than El Dorado County (the epicenter of the California gold rush), it filled with newcomers nearly as fast, and it attracted a larger percentage of the total population of the United States of its day.[43]

Only the emigrants came for land, not gold, and in that sense Boon's Lick had rivals, if not equals, after the War of 1812. Figure 10 shows zones of significant demographic growth in the United States between 1810 and 1820. It highlights areas of intense growth, that is, areas that simultaneously experienced large raw population gains and high growth rates, by identifying counties that added more inhabitants than the national average in absolute terms and then measuring how frequently those counties' populations doubled *after* reaching that threshold. The results highlight areas across the country that shared a common experience as emerging markets in expropriated Indigenous lands, though none of them appeared more suddenly than the one at Boon's Lick. Lands from the Holland Purchase of 1792, for instance, were still selling in western New York. An Illinois county carved out of the Sauk and Meskwaki cession of 1804 boomed from speculation in military bounties. Public land in Ohio acquired before the War of 1812, and newly secured after, sold briskly. Sections of Alabama ceded via the treaty of Fort Jackson in 1814 became a hotbed for the redemption of Yazoo scrip. The range of far-flung options strongly suggests that newcomers who chose Boon's Lick could not have been relied on to diffuse elsewhere in the Missouri Territory had Sauk, Meskwaki, and Iowa dispossession not suddenly made Howard County so desirable. There were too many other attractive areas in which to locate around the country. As a result, without the extraordinary population increase concentrated at Boon's Lick, Missouri's bid for statehood could have been delayed.

Ironically, it was the rush of predominantly proslavery emigrants to Boon's Lick that enabled Tallmadge to spark the debate that ignited the Missouri Crisis. Twelve hundred miles west of Washington, DC, the newcomers who spread out from the saltworks and spilled across and up the Missouri River were responsible for nearly half the territory's population growth between 1810 and 1820, with 97 percent of them arriving after Clark's proclamation. As the boom mounted in 1816, predictions that statehood was imminent "if the national legislature will give us a state with a population of 60, thousand"

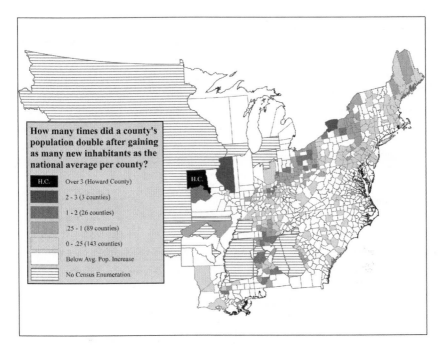

How many times did a county's population double after gaining as many new inhabitants as the national average per county?

H.C.   Over 3 (Howard County)

       2 - 3 (3 counties)

       1 - 2 (26 counties)

       .25 - 1 (89 counties)

       0 - .25 (143 counties)

       Below Avg. Pop. Increase

       No Census Enumeration

Figure 10. U.S. county growth rates after reaching average national population gain, 1810-20. Howard County, Missouri, whose population was synonymous with the Boon's Lick settlement, was the most intensely growing county in the United States between 1810 and 1820. Map shows 1820 county boundaries. *Source*: Federal censuses of 1810 and 1820. Drawn by the author.

began to appear. In 1817, the *Missouri Gazette* published a petition calling for statehood that claimed the territory's forty thousand inhabitants "entitle us to the privileges of a state government." This informal petition got little traction but presaged the more convincing version sent to Congress from the territorial assembly in 1818. The November 1818 petition, which led to the statehood bill that Tallmadge amended, began with the hyperbolic claim that the territory contained one hundred thousand inhabitants, an overblown figure that makes sense only when backlit by the exuberant talk swirling around Boon's Lick. No evidence suggests anyone took the exaggeration seriously. At the same time, however, the petition appended a territorial census from 1817 that persuasively showed the territory had "more than equal to the number of inhabitants heretofore required."[44] By late 1818, the rush had made a credible statehood bill possible earlier than might otherwise have been expected. And if an actionable statehood petition had been delayed even by a single congressional session, Tallmadge would have been out of office. To be sure, Missouri statehood would have been controversial without Tallmadge in the House. Just as certainly, the Missouri Crisis would have looked different without the Boon's Lick land rush.

When news broke of Tallmadge's gradual abolition amendment, the majority who "migrated thither under an expectation" that slavery would persist were angry, because it not only threatened their enslaved labor supply but would also hurt their land property values. In 1819, when David Manchester wrote to his sister about the emigrants "settling tolerably fast" and buying up land for two to twenty-six dollars per acre, he reported that the people "appear somewhat frustrated about the proceedings of Congress concerning our being admitted to the Union." William Lane was less circumspect. The army doctor was glad that "a majority of the good people are looking out for quarter-sections, & have their attention very much engrossed in that way: were it not for this circumstance, I think this Country would speedily be in an attitude, bordering on rebellion." One of the most widely distributed news items from the region in 1819 described a "mob at Boon's Lick" that viciously beat and threatened to kill a New Jersey couple "settled on the public lands" for speaking against admission with slavery.[45]

Driven by a "zeal to purchase," the unpredictably intense rush to Boon's Lick had set the stage for Missouri's push to join the Union. Counterintuitively, though, the significance of the territory's population growth registers most powerfully in its almost complete absence from the Missouri Crisis debates. Missouri's qualification on population grounds was barely mentioned because the growth of Boon's Lick turned it into a nonissue, lost in a sea of contention. A singular exception proves the rule: The numbers briefly became a point of discussion at one point when Rufus King—the most vocal opponent of the territory's admission as a slave state—said Missouri and Arkansas had just 11,300 inhabitants. William Smith of South Carolina pounced, showing off returns from an 1818 census indicating a population "of fifty-two thousand; and also, such evidence as ought not to be doubted, that there were ten thousand more not within the census taken, but were within the territory; amounting, in the whole number to a population of 62,000."[46] No one challenged Smith. Questions about Missouri's population were virtually unheard of in the debates, not because they did not matter but because the growth of Boon's Lick had rendered the point moot.

We can only ponder Smith's other "evidence as ought not to be doubted." It included a map of the territory "made from an actual servey [sic], ordered by the Government," which must have referred to the map of Rector's survey. Published in 1818 under the title *Map of the Northern Part of Missouri*, it showed the "Boon's Lick Settlement" in the Howard County Land District, outlined by the "Indian boundary." Smith's other evidence is more elusive. It might have been an 1818 report from *Niles Weekly Register* indicating Boon's Lick contained 8,000 white males (up from 3,386 in the territorial census of 1817). Or perhaps it was a copy of D. B. Warren's *A Statistical, Political, and Historical Account of the United States* (1819), showing Howard County's population had doubled in a span of nine months. It could have been excerpts from Samuel Brown's *Western Gazetteer* (1817), telling readers about the bustling settlement within the "Osage boundary line." It could have been any number of news clippings, like an 1819 article from the *Missouri Intelligencer and Boon's Lick Advertiser* reporting emigration that "almost exceeds belief" or notices in eastern papers expressing shock that someone had actually set up a printing press in the "wilds of Missouri" to churn out an ad-packed weekly "among a numerous population!"[47] Of course, it might have been something that did not mention Boon's Lick at all. Historians will never be able to say for sure what Smith showed his colleagues, but they can follow the link between the Boon's Lick land rush and the coming of the Missouri Crisis.

If the rush made Missouri's population a nonissue during the crisis debates, its connection to Indigenous dispossession seems to have been avoided by convention. At one point in the House, John W. Taylor of New York paused "to examine the policy of extending our settlements into the wilderness, with the astonishing rapidity which has marked their progress," before stopping himself: "This inquiry, although, intimately connected with the subject, would too much extend the range of discussion." At another, William Pinkney of Maryland could not resist wielding this silence on land expropriation like a cudgel. The United States, he explained, regularly deployed force and artifice to acquire lands from tribal nations to sell off, fill the treasury, and expand its empire: "Will you recur to those scenes of various iniquity for any other purpose than to regret and lament them? Will you pry into them with a view to shake and impair your rights of property and dominion?" Pinkney's questions were rhetorical, his outrage manufactured. He did not want those questions answered. He wanted slavery in Missouri, so he took to the floor to belittle his opponents' selective outrage at the violence underpinning Americans' property rights.[48]

Conclusion

Historians know how that debate ended. Slavery persisted in Missouri as part of an infamous compromise that proved a major turning point in U.S. history. We could know a lot more about how it started, especially the local conditions that made it possible. Looking backward and westward from Washington, DC, in 1819, it seems there was not just one unlikely presence in the House of Representatives that year; there were two. Tallmadge was one. A credible population-based statehood petition was the other. How it got there has less to do with the themes of sectionalism, slavery, and secession that have guided study of the Missouri Crisis than with contingencies of dispossession and demography conventionally excluded from that literature.

If historians of the crisis have not shown interest in Sauk, Meskwaki, and Iowa possession of central Missouri; the squatter invasion of 1810; Clark's proclamation of 1815; or the land rush that made Missouri, those who lived through these events were acutely aware. In the 1830s, the early Boon's Lick squatters got a stark reminder of where they had trespassed when the Treasury Department rejected their depredation claims from the War of 1812 because they had located in Indian country. In the 1820s, Sauk, Meskwaki, and Iowa delegations traveled to Washington, DC, to discuss the territory taken over by that settlement and ultimately signed treaties that relinquished their claims for a pittance. In 1820, shortly after Congress reached the Missouri Compromise, the editor of the recently founded newspaper at Boon's Lick ran an account of how the public land market had come to the "richest part of the State of Missouri" through William Clark's interpretation of an Osage treaty. It was written by Thomas Hart Benton, in support of Clark's bid to become the state's first governor. Attacked as an Indian lover, Clark lost the election but began to amass a reputation that would help keep his role in triggering the Boon's Lick land rush and feeding into the Missouri Crisis out of the history books. Two hundred years later, Benton's concluding question is still worth asking: "Is such an act as this to be forgotten at this time?"[49]

Notes

1. "Memorial and Resolutions of the Legislature of the Missouri Territory" (1818), in *Missouri's Struggle for Statehood, 1804–1821*, by Floyd Calvin Shoemaker (Jefferson City, MO: Hugh Stephens, 1916), 324.

2. Other new western states were Indiana (1816), Mississippi (1817), Illinois (1818), and Alabama (1819). Statistics from 1810 and 1820 censuses (and other federal censuses), Minnesota Population Center, *National Historical Geographic*

Information System: Version 2.0 (Minneapolis: University of Minnesota, 2011). On population as a factor in the lead-up to the Missouri Crisis, see Shoemaker, *Missouri's Struggle for Statehood*, 35, 42–43, 69–70; Glover Moore, *The Missouri Controversy, 1819–1821* (Lexington: University Press of Kentucky, 1953), 31–32; David D. March, "The Admission of Missouri," *Missouri Historical Review* 65, no. 4 (1971): 428n2; John Craig Hammond, *Slavery, Freedom, and Expansion in the Early American West* (Charlottesville: University of Virginia Press, 2007), 56–58, 62, 64; and John R. Van Atta, *Wolf by the Ears: The Missouri Crisis, 1819–1821* (Baltimore: Johns Hopkins University Press, 2015), 53–54. For a demographic study that examines how the Missouri Crisis affected the federal census, see Margo Anderson, "The Missouri Debates, Slavery and Statistics of Race: Demography in Service of Politics," *Annales de Démographie Historique*, no. 1 (February 2003): 23–38.

3. On the rush, see Hattie M. Anderson, "Missouri, 1804–1828: Peopling a Frontier State," *Missouri Historical Review* 31, no. 2 (1937): 150–80; Walter Schroeder, "Spread of Settlement in Howard County, Missouri, 1810–1859," *Missouri Historical Review* 63, no. 1 (1968): 1–37; Malcolm J. Rohrbough, *Trans-Appalachian Frontier: People, Societies, Institutions, 1775–1850* (Bloomington: Indiana University Press, 1978), 233–73; William E. Foley, *The Genesis of Missouri: From Wilderness Outpost to Statehood* (Columbia: University of Missouri Press, 1989), 238–68; R. Douglas Hurt, "Seeking Fortune in the Promised Land: Settling the Boon's Lick Country, 1808–1825," *Gateway Heritage* 13, no. 1 (1992): 4–19; Stephen Aron, *American Confluence: The Missouri Frontier from Borderland to Border State* (Bloomington: Indiana University Press, 2006), 149–85; and Lynn Morrow, "Boone's Lick in Western Expansion: James Mackay, the Boones, and the Morrisons," *Boone's Lick Heritage Quarterly* 13, nos. 3–4 (2014): 4–32. For use of Peck's quote, see John Mack Faragher, *Sugar Creek: Life on the Illinois Prairie* (New Haven, CT: Yale University Press, 1984), 49; Diane Mutti Burke, *On Slavery's Border: Missouri's Small-Slaveholding Households, 1815–1865* (Athens: University of Georgia Press, 2010), 24; and Christopher Phillips, *The Rivers Ran Backward: The Civil War and the Remaking of the American Middle Border* (New York: Oxford University Press, 2016), 50.

4. Censuses of 1810, 1820, 1850, Minnesota Population Center. Estimated increase for Howard County in 1817 and 1818 is roughly 15,000; see table 1 and figure 6. For Missouri's overall population, see figure 7. The California counties/population counts from 1850 are El Dorado (20,057), Calaveras (16,884), Yuba (9,673), Sacramento (9,087), Tuolumne (8,351), Mariposa (4,379), San Joaquin (3,647), Butte (3,574), and Sutter (3,444). John Mason Peck, *Forty Years of Pioneer Life: Memoir of John Mason Peck, D.D.*, ed. Rufus Babcock (Philadelphia, 1864), 146 ("avalanche").

5. Census of 1820, Minnesota Population Center; Peck, *Forty Years of Pioneer Life*, 146 ("terrific").

6. "A Proclamation by Governor Clark," [March 9, 1815], in *The Territorial Papers of the United States* (hereafter referred to as *Terr. Papers*), ed. Clarence E. Carter, 28 vols. (Washington, DC: Government Printing Office, 1934–75), 15:41.

7. A note on names: There are various spellings of the Sauk (Sac, Saque), Meskwaki (Fox, Mesquaki), and Iowa (Ioway) nations in the primary and secondary sources. Here I follow the English variants most commonly used by these nations today.

For names and links, see https://native-land.ca/. In quoted material I retain original spellings.

8. Nathan Boone, *My Father, Daniel Boone: The Draper Interviews with Nathan Boone*, ed. Neal O. Hammon (Lexington: University Press of Kentucky, 2013), 123, 126, 127; [Jesse Morrison interview], 86–89, Lyman Draper Manuscripts, Series C, vols. 16, 30, and 31; Series S, vol. 6, microfilm. For background, see Morrow, "Boone's Lick in Western Expansion," 4–32; and Robert T. Bray, "Boone's Lick Salt Works, 1805–33," *Missouri Archaeologist* 48 (1987): 1–66. In 1960, the Missouri park system acquired the spring and created the Boone's Lick State Historic Site. Visitors today can picnic near the old works and read placards that describe salt boiling, avoid referring to enslaved laborers, and omit that this was ever Sauk, Meskwaki, and Iowa land.

9. [Speech by Keokuk] in "Sock & Fox speaches made to the Secy of War," "Ratified Treaty No. 121: Documents Relating to the Negotiation of the Treaty of August 4, 1824, with the Sauk and Fox Indians," Documents Relating to the Negotiation of Ratified and Unratified Treaties with Various Indian Tribes, 1801–69, T494, Roll 1, National Archives and Records Administration, Washington, DC. On the conflict, see William T. Hagan, *The Sac and Fox Indians* (Norman: University of Oklahoma Press, 1958), 3–15; Michael Dickey, *The People of the River's Mouth: In Search of the Missouria Indians* (Columbia: University of Missouri Press, 2011), 85, 88, 102, 105–7; and Louis F. Burns, *A History of the Osage People* (Tuscaloosa: University of Alabama Press, 2004), 46–48, 122. On Indigenous boundary making, see Juliana Barr, "Geographies of Power: Mapping Indian Borders in the 'Borderlands' of the Early Southwest," *William and Mary Quarterly* 68, no. 1 (2011): 5–46.

10. *Journals of the Lewis and Clark Expedition*, June 15, 1804, https://lewisandclarkjournals.unl.edu/item/lc.jrn.1804-06-15; Amos Stoddard to Henry Dearborn, June 22, 1804, "Transfer of Upper Louisiana: Papers of Captain Amos Stoddard," *Glimpses of the Past* 2, no. 4 (1935): 114 ("conquered"); "Treaty with the Sauk and Foxes, 1804," in *Indian Affairs: Laws and Treaties*, ed. Charles J. Kappler, 7 vols. (Washington, DC: Government Printing Office, 1904–71), 2:75–76.

11. General Wilkinson to the Chiefs of the Sauk Nation, December 10, 1805, in *Terr. Papers*, 13:301; Boone, *My Father, Daniel Boone*, 126–27 ("profitable").

12. "A report upon the claims of certain citizens of the United States, who have lost property by Indian Depredations," 22nd Cong., 1st. sess., House Doc. No. 38, January 4, 1832, 97–104.

13. "Testimony of Col. Benjamin Cooper," Draper Manuscript 22S, Drapers Notes, Wisconsin Historical Society, MF reel 50; Governor Lewis to the President, August 27, 1809, in *Terr. Papers*, 14:294 ("established by Treaty"); William E. Foley, "Different Notions of Justice: The Case of the 1808 St. Louis Murder Trials," *Gateway Heritage* 9, no. 3 (1988–89): 2–13.

14. Governor Lewis to the President, August 27, 1809, in *Terr. Papers*, 14:295–96 ("hunting ranges"); "Treaty with the Osages," in *Indian Affairs*, ed. Kappler, 2:96 ("all lands").

15. George Sibley to James G. Mask, March 29, 1817, in William Darby, *The Emigrant's Guide to the Western and Southwestern States and Territories* (New York: Kirk

and Mercein, 1818), 303; *History of Howard and Cooper Counties, Missouri* (St. Louis: National Historical, 1883), 93–94, 150, 806 ("the names," "large portion").

16. Schroeder, "Spread of Settlement in Howard County," 2–7; Henry M. Brackenridge, *Journal of a Voyage up the Missouri River in 1811*, 2nd ed. (Baltimore, 1816), 48–49; John Bradbury, *Travels in the Interior of America, in the Years 1809, 1810, and 1811* (Liverpool, 1817), 195 ("upland"); Edith S. Burris, "Patsy the Pioneer," n.d., qt. 5, Miscellaneous Manuscripts, C2947, State Historical Society of Missouri (SHSM), Columbia ("forests"); Paul S. Martin and Christine R. Szuter, "War Zones and Game Sinks in Lewis and Clark's West," *Conservation Biology* 13, no. 1 (1999): 36–45; R. Douglas Hurt, *Agriculture and Slavery in Missouri's Little Dixie* (Columbia: University of Missouri Press, 1992), 1–50.

17. Governor Howard to the Secretary of War, June 14, 1812, in *Terr. Papers*, 14:567 ("finest," "respectable"); Brackenridge, *Journal of a Voyage*, 48 ("slaves"); *History of Howard and Cooper Counties, Missouri*, 164, 620; Burris, "Patsy the Pioneer," 1 ("young girl"). On family-centered settlement, see Honor Sachs, *Home Rule: Households, Manhood, and National Expansion on the Eighteenth-Century Kentucky Frontier* (New Haven, CT: Yale University Press, 2015); and Carolyn Earle Billingsley, *Communities of Kinship: Antebellum Families and the Settlement of the Cotton Frontier* (Athens: University of Georgia Press, 2004).

18. Governor Clark to the President, January 22, 1816, in *Terr. Papers*, 15:105; William Clark to the President, April 10, 1811, in *Terr. Papers*, 14:446 ("several families"); "Talks," in *American State Papers: Indian Affairs* (Washington, DC: Gales and Seaton, 1834), 2:11 ("much").

19. Governor Howard to the Secretary of War, June 14, 1812, in *Terr. Papers*, 14:568 (all quotes); "The State of the Indians of Missouri Territory from September 1817," Miscellaneous Manuscripts, M1628, SHSM.

20. Governor Howard to the Secretary of War, June 14, 1812, in *Terr. Papers*, 14:568; Walter B. Stevens, *Missouri: The Center State, 1821–1915* (Chicago: Clarke, 1915), 157 ("Fight"); Peck, *Forty Years of Pioneer Life*, 135–38; U.S. Congress, Senate, *Memorial of the State of Missouri and Documents in Relation to Indian Depredations upon the Citizens of That State*, 19th Cong., 1st sess., 1826.

21. Black Hawk, *Life of Black Hawk* (London: Richard James Kennett, 1836), 61 ("our best"); Patrick J. Jung, "Toward the Black Hawk War: The Sauk and Fox Indians and the War of 1812," *Michigan Historical Review* 38, no. 1 (2012): 27–52; David Bernstein, "'We Are Not Now as We Once Were': Iowa Indians' Political and Economic Adaptations during U.S. Incorporation," *Ethnohistory* 54, no. 4 (2007): 605–37; Roger L. Nichols, *Black Hawk and the Warrior's Path* (Arlington Heights, IL: Harlan Davidson, 1992); Anthony F. C. Wallace, "Prelude to Disaster: The Course of Indian-White Relations Which Led to the Black War of 1832," in *The Black Hawk War, 1831–1832*, ed. Ellen M. Whitney (Springfield: Illinois State Historical Library, 1970), 1–51.

22. Governor Clark to the Secretary of War, January 6, 1814, in *Terr. Papers*, 14:728 ("to come"); "Resolution of the Territorial Assembly," [January 17, 1814], in *Terr. Papers*, 14:731 ("beyond"); William Clark to James Monroe, January 23, 1814, Mary Louise Dalton Collection, 1812–1917, Missouri History Museum Archives (MHMA), St. Louis ("lands Claimed").

23. Governor Howard to the Secretary of War, June 14, 1812, in *Terr. Papers*, 14:568 ("would be"); William Clark to James Monroe, January 23, 1814, Dalton Collection, MHMA; William Russell to William Rector, April 20, 1814, in *Terr. Papers*, 14:752.

24. "A Proclamation by Governor Clark," [March 9, 1815], in *Terr. Papers*, 15:41 ("pretentions"); William Clark to James Monroe, January 23, 1814, Dalton Collection ("best lands").

25. "A Proclamation by Governor Clark," [March 9, 1815], in *Terr. Papers*, 15:41.

26. Grant Foreman, ed., "Notes of Auguste Chouteau on Boundaries of Various Indian Nations," *Glimpses of the Past* 7, nos. 9-12 (1940): 132, 138-39.

27. "A Proclamation," December 4, 1815, in *Terr. Papers*, 15:191-92; Governor Clark to the Secretary of War, September 30, 1816, in *Terr. Papers*, 15:177; Petition of Inhabitants of Missouri Territory, [ca. 1816], in *Terr. Papers*, 15:182. On Clark's reputation, see recent biographical treatments: Jay H. Buckley, *William Clark: Indian Diplomat* (Norman: University of Oklahoma Press, 2008); William E. Foley, *Wilderness Journey: The Life of William Clark* (Columbia: University of Missouri Press, 2006); and Landon Y. Jones, *William Clark and the Shaping of the West* (New York: Hill and Wang, 2005).

28. "The Negotiation," *National Intelligencer* (Washington, DC), December 3, 1814, 1-3; "Despatches—Concluded," *National Intelligencer*, December 6, 1814, 1-4; "The Negotiation," *Missouri Gazette* (St. Louis), January 7, 1815, 2-3; "The Negotiation," *Missouri Gazette*, January 7, 1815, 1-2; Governor Edward to the Secretary of War, March 8, 1815, in *Terr. Papers*, 17:145; "By William Clark," *Missouri Gazette*, March 11, 1815, 3; "Peace," *Missouri Gazette*, March 11, 1815, 3; William Clark to James Monroe, March 13, 1815, National Archives, RG 107: Letters Received by the War Department; Secretary of War to the Indian Commissioners, March 11, 1815, in *Terr. Papers*, 15:14.

29. "A Proclamation by Governor Clark," [March 9, 1815], *Terr. Papers*, 15:41; Henry Geyer, *A Digest of the Laws of Missouri Territory* (St. Louis, 1818), 134 ("the indian boundary"); John G. Heath, "To the Editor of the National Register," *National Register* 2, no. 11 (November 9, 1816): 162 ("Boone's Lick").

30. John G. Heath, "To the Editor of the National Register," *National Register* 2, no. 11 (November 9, 1816): 162; Sibley to Mask, 29 March 1817, in Darby, *Emigrant's Guide*, 305 ("admission").

31. William Rector to Josiah Meigs, April 17, 1815, in *Terr. Papers*, 15:31 ("surveyed and offered").

32. William Rector to William Clark, Ninian Edwards, and Auguste Chouteau, July 12, 1816, and William Rector to Josiah Meigs, July 22, 1816, and August 12, 1816, in *Letters Received by the Commissioner of the General Land Office from the Surveyor General, 1813-25*, M1323, Roll 1 (hereafter referred to as "Letters and Surveying Contracts"); William Clark to George Sibley, August 6, 1816, George Sibley Papers, MHMA; Indian Commissioners to the Secretary of War, November 11, 1816, in *Terr. Papers*, 15:202.

33. "From the Missouri Gazette," *New-York Herald*, December 25, 1816, 3 ("Boon's Lick Country no doubt"); "Soldiers' Bounty Lands," *Niles' Weekly Register* 12, no. 6 (April 5, 1817), 82 ("Indian title"); Darby, *Emigrant's Guide*, 137 ("yet purchased");

James Clemens Jr. to Isachar Pawling, October 4, 1816, in *Glimpses of the Past* 3, nos. 7–9 (1936): 135–37 ("one & the same"); William Rector to Josiah Meigs, November 25, 1816, in *Terr. Papers*, 15:210 ("favors").

34. William Rector to Josiah Meigs, November 25, 1816, in *Terr. Papers*, 15:210 ("current"); William Rector to Josiah Meigs, July 7, 1817, "Letters and Surveying Contracts Received by the General Land Office from the Surveyor General for Illinois, Missouri, and Arkansas, 1813–32," "Letters and Surveying Contracts" ("vast numbers").

35. George Sibley to James G. Mask, March 29, 1817, in Darby, *Emigrant's Guide*, 302–3 ("enchantment," "immense"); Peck, *Forty Years of Pioneer Life*, 146 ("some families"); Timothy Flint, *Recollections of the Last Ten Years* (Boston, 1826), 201–3 ("Ask"); "From Fort Osage, in the Missouri Territory," *Baltimore Patriot*, October 17, 1816, 2 (*"astonishing"*; emphasis in the original).

36. "Soldiers' Bounty Lands," *Niles' Weekly Register* 12, no. 6 (1817): 82; Sibley to Sibley, September 25, 1813, George Sibley Papers, 5 ("Ten good"); Flint, *Recollections*, 201 ("a very"). There were 8,177 free adults, 2,726 slaves; see Census of 1820, Minnesota Population Center.

37. "Cincinnati, Nov. 8," *Suffolk County Recorder* (Sag Harbor, NY), November 30, 1816, 3.

38. Peck, *Forty Years of Pioneer Life*, 146 ("not a few," "sprinkling"); "Memorial and Resolutions" (1818), in *Missouri's Struggle for Statehood*, by Shoemaker, 324 ("daily increasing"); Flint, *Recollections*, 201–3 ("poured").

39. Flint, *Recollections*, 199 ("pole-star"); "Petition to Congress by Citizens of the Territory of Missouri," March 14, 1820, in *Terr. Papers*, 15:594 ("country usually"); Charles Carroll to Josiah Miegs, March 11, 1820, in *Terr. Papers*, 15:594.

40. Flint, *Recollections*, 202–3 ("imaginations," "land claims"); John Scott to Thomas A. Smith, July 26, 1818, folder 15, Thomas Adams Smith Papers [1029], SHSM ("banditti"); Schroeder, "Spread of Settlement in Howard County," 10–13.

41. James Madison Presidential Proclamation, December 12, 1815, Founders Online, https://founders.archives.gov/documents/Madison/99-01-02-4796; Mary S. Easton Sibley to Rufus Easton, February 11, 1816, George Sibley Papers, ("crushing"); Henry Carroll to Josiah Meigs, October 15, 1818, in *Terr. Papers*, 15:441 ("Howard County"); "Memorial to Congress by the Territorial Assembly," *Terr. Papers*, 15:504 ("was Indian Country then"); William Clark to Thomas A. Smith, folder 16, Smith Papers [1029], SHSM; Schroeder, "Spread of Settlement in Howard County," 10–11; "Petition of the Inhabitants of Howard Land District," September 14, 1819, in *Terr. Papers*, 15:556–61; Charles Carroll to Josiah Meigs, March 11, 1820, in *Terr. Papers*, 15:594.

42. Two-thirds based on 335,784 of 496,073 acres patented in Missouri. See Bureau Land Management, Eastern States Office, www.glorecords.blm.gov.

43. See note 4.

44. See table 1 and figure 6. Rufus Easton to the Secretary of War, December 31, 1816, in *Terr. Papers*, 15:223 ("if the national"); "A Petition," *Missouri Gazette* (St. Louis), October 23, 1817, 2 ("entitle us"); "Memorial and Resolutions," reprinted in Shoemaker, *Missouri's Struggle for Statehood*, 324, 326 ("daily increasing," "more than equal").

45. Flint, *Recollections*, 198 ("zeal to purchase"); *Annals of Congress*, House of Representatives, 15th Cong., 2nd sess., 1171–72 ("migrated thither"); David Manchester to Lydia Manchester, April 19, 1819, C2064, SHSM ("settling tolerably"); William Carr Lane to Mary Lane, April 2, 1819, "Letters of William Carr Lane, 1819–1831," *Glimpses of the Past* 7, nos. 7–9 (1940): 60 ("a majority"); "Mob at Boon's Lick," *Palladium of Liberty* (Warrenton, VA), October 29, 1819, 3 ("mob," "settled").

46. *Annals of Congress*, Senate, 16th Cong., 1st sess., 375, 379 ("of fifty-two").

47. *Annals of Congress*, Senate, 16th Cong., 1st sess., 375, 379 ("evidence"); John Gardiner and Thomas Streeter, *Map of the Northern Part of Missouri* (1818), St. Louis Mercantile Library at the University of Missouri–St. Louis, https://dl.mospace.umsystem.edu/umsl/islandora/object/umsl%3A66218; *Niles' Weekly Register* (Missouri) 2, no. 12 (1818), 208; D. B. Warren, *A Statistical, Political, and Historical Account of the United States* (Edinburgh, 1819), 146; Samuel R. Brown, *The Western Gazetteer* (Auburn, NY: H. C. Southwick, 1817), 192 ("Osage"); *Franklin Intelligencer and Boon's Lick Advertiser*, November 19, 1819 ("almost exceeds"); "Missouri Intelligencer," *Alexandria (VA) Gazette*, July 3, 1819 ("wilds").

48. *Annals of Congress*, House of Representatives, 15th Cong., 2nd sess., 1171–72 ("to examine"); *Annals of Congress*, Senate, 16th Cong., 1st sess., 401–2 ("force").

49. "A report on the claims of certain citizens of the United States, who have lost property by Indian Depredations," 81, 105; "Sock & Fox speaches made to the Secy of War" under "Ratified Treaty No. 121: Documents Relating to the Negotiation of the Treaty of August 4, 1824, with the Sauk and Fox Indians," Documents Related to Treaties 1801 to 1869, T494, roll 1; "Brief Notice Respecting Governor Clark," *Missouri Intelligencer* (Franklin), August 26, 1820 ("richest," "forgotten").

3. Slavery, War, and Democracy

The Winding Road to the Missouri Crisis

Jeffrey L. Pasley

DESPITE THE DEEP roots of slavery in the American West, and the relative frequency with which the peculiar institution had already troubled the United States over its early years, the Missouri Crisis still came as a shock to most of its participants. While Missouri Territory was hardly considered a trouble-free location, either locally or nationally, few realized that the incipient new state on the Missouri River was on a collision course with some of the most powerful geopolitical and ideological trends at work in the early American republic: westward migration, the antislavery movement, democratization, and the economic renaissance of slavery that came with expansion. Even fewer took into account the contingencies that might develop out of local politics in far-flung parts of the nation, where political conflict proceeded apace even as the national parties seemed to demobilize during the "Era of Good Feelings," or the difficulties that might arise from the sketchy, stylized knowledge that participants in Washington debates had about other regions they would be legislating for or defending against. Serious conflicts and misunderstandings lay just out of sight. What follows is an attempt, mostly in narrative form, to trace the winding road and unexpected turns that led Missouri Territory and the United States to their 1819 impasse on the way to Missouri statehood.

In some ways, the eventual stoppage was nothing new, because for many years Missouri Territory's "struggle for statehood" had been more of a bureaucratic crawl. Though in the hands of the United States since 1804, the territory progressed with unusual slowness through the various stages leading to self-government, feet dragging on both ends of the transaction. The French residents of Upper Louisiana felt they would have more influence under the familiar French colonial system of dealing with appointed magistrates than they would after the Anglo-American system of voting and juries was installed. Not a few of them moved across the Mississippi after 1763 or 1776 to get away from such annoyances. Their reluctance suited the authorities in Washington, too. According to territorial delegate Rufus Easton, official policy before the end of the War of 1812 had been "not only to discourage, but to prevent the extension of settlements west of the Mississippi and north of the State of Louisiana." Jefferson thought "the best use" that the United States could make of the west bank was to postpone creating states there for some time. Instead, he planned to aggressively acquire the lands of the remaining eastern Indians and send *them* on a westward movement, keeping the white population more compactly settled on the east side until space ran out. Easton wrote home from Congress in the spring of 1816 that opinion at the seat of government had finally changed on this matter. Only then was Missouri last promoted to the third and final stage of territorial government, and soon the petitions and expectations were flowing.[1]

The change of heart may partly have been Easton's, because democratic processes were now lumbering into action back in Missouri. John Scott of Ste. Genevieve had just announced a run against Easton in the St. Louis newspapers, declaring himself "anxious to see our territory freed from the shackles of colonial dependence." Scott's platform called for Missouri to take every means necessary to "hasten its progress" to statehood, encourage emigration, and facilitate the selling of public land to settlers. He voiced key complaints of various groups of constituents: the old French elite, the new American entrepreneurs, and the backcountry settlers, condemning the forcible of ejection of squatters from public land and the "useless monopoly" that the federal government exercised over the Indian trade as well as the restraints on the other traditional local industries, salt making and lead mining. Not much happened on statehood until after the Scott-Easton election, which Easton initially appeared to have won by seven votes—until Scott personally retrieved the ballots from the then far-western Missouri River hamlet of Cote Sans Dessein and went ahead by twenty-three. That set up a minidrama involving several future principals in the Missouri Crisis. Territorial governor William Clark declared Scott the winner, but Easton, a native of Litchfield, Connecticut, followed Scott to Washington, DC, and contested the election, both rivals testifying before the congressional investigating committee and speaking on the floor of the House. The committee, chaired by northern Democratic-Republican leader John W. Taylor, issued a report that favored Easton, in response to which Thomas M. Nelson of Virginia moved successfully to declare the seat vacant. Then Scott and Easton returned home and staged one of the most vicious rematches in Missouri political history, complete with rioting soldiers and multiple murders. Scott came out on top and led the Missouri side of the statehood process throughout.[2]

The first concrete step toward statehood was congressional approval of an "enabling bill" authorizing the citizens of the territory to write a constitution. This part looked to be a snap. The recently concluded War of 1812 had secured a host of lands in the trans-Appalachian West for European American settlement, and they had so far been rapidly incorporated into the federal Union. Congress voted statehood for Indiana in March 1816, for Mississippi in February 1817, and for Illinois (with well below the previously required population of 40,000) just before Missouri's bid was submitted in 1818. The Illinois process took place so quickly, a little more than a year from initiation to completion, that it drew the label "instant statehood" from a later historian. Statehood for the eastern half of Mississippi Territory, called Alabama, sailed through with little controversy on its way to approval without a recorded roll-call vote.[3]

The main holdup for Missouri seemed to be convincing skeptical easterners that the west bank of the Mississippi was actually ready for full membership "in the great American family." The fact that the former frontier outpost "appears to have sprung into importance as if by magic" was mentioned back east in a tone of skepticism. The *New York Evening Post* quipped that if St. Louis really was as big and rich as reported, it should at least pave its streets. The vague population figures seemed to shift radically and draw on mysterious sources. The 1817 legislature commissioned a territorial census that showed 19,218 white males, but it did not surface until a year later, by which time state leaders were claiming "a population little short of one hundred thousand souls." An initial petition went out unsigned through the *Western Emigrant* newspaper, to the bitter detractions of the rival *Missouri Gazette*, ruing the loss of its decadelong monopoly of the territorial market.[4]

Slavery was not mentioned in any of the commentary on Missouri's statehood potential or the contested election case against John Scott, but the possibility that questions about slavery in the West it was a silent factor in Missouri's slow progress should not be discounted. Possibly there was a reason that the 1817 territorial census, so belatedly shared by Scott, enumerated only white males. Back in DC after his bloody "reelection," and finally the official territorial delegate, Scott chaired a committee that reported a resolution authorizing Missourians to write a constitution and introduced it on the House floor on April 3, where it remained unconsidered when the session ended two weeks later. The next day, Representative Arthur Livermore of

New Hampshire proposed what might have been an epochal constitutional amendment had it not been immediately killed, without a roll call: "No person shall be held to service or labor as a slave, nor shall slavery be tolerated in any State hereafter admitted into the Union." A yawning official silence greeted this move, but the amendment was widely reprinted in newspapers around the country as part of the congressional proceedings, often under the headline "Abolition of Slavery." As far as can be determined from the extant record, few seemed to take this radical suggestion seriously or connect it with the Missouri bill, at least not in public.[5]

At last, just before the new session of Congress began, in November 1818, Missouri's territorial legislature sent an official memorial to Congress, signed by the legislative leaders with a census attached, albeit the old one. Citing Congress's past "wise and generous policy" of advancing populated territories promptly to statehood, the legislature expressed the hope that "they need only pray to be incorporated in the Union and to show that it is not only possible but convenient and proper . . . to have their prayer answered."[6] In December, Speaker Henry Clay duly presented the Missouri territorial legislature's memorial to the House, recommending that it be used to frame the required enabling bill to admit Missouri "into the Union on an equal footing with the original States," as the expansionist U.S. mode of adding new lands had prescribed since the first new states, Vermont and Kentucky, entered in the 1790s. As far as anyone in the territory—or even in the Monroe administration—seemed to know, Missouri statehood would now be a matter of working out the exact details of the boundaries, the subject on which the statehood memorial and enabling bill spent most of their space. It turned out to be far less simple than that.[7]

An Emerging Dichotomy: Slave Country versus Free States

While the migrant population and local public opinion in Missouri Territory was more diverse than its leaders liked to admit, there was no real question on the ground about slavery's place in the nascent state. As John Craig Hammond shows in chapter 1 of this volume, slavery was a long-established, uncontroversial, and growing practice in the Ohio, Missouri, and middle Mississippi Valleys. Slavery, captivity, bondage, and various forms of unfreedom had been practiced by every group of residents in the region—Indigenous, French, Spanish, and Anglophone—as part of warfare and trade going back to before Europeans even arrived in present Missouri. The bondage and enslavement of captives played a central role in commerce, culture, and diplomacy between and among Indigenous nations and European traders. Beginning in the mid-1700s, French, Spanish, and U.S. imperial officials provided material, institutional, and legal support for the enslavement of African Americans and the maintenance of white supremacy and racial subordination. The French habitants of Louisiana were promised in 1764 that their property rights would be protected when the region was transferred to Spain, and received firm guarantees from the United States and France in Article III of the 1803 Louisiana Purchase treaty, a point that advocates of slavery in Missouri made over and over during the debates of 1818–21.[8]

New arrivals from the United States trickled in by Spanish invitation from the time of the American Revolution, then in larger numbers after 1803, and a mass migration after 1815. The slaveholders of the Upper South needed an outlet for a burgeoning population of enslaved men and women whom they refused to emancipate but could not profitably exploit in the crowded, exhausted tobacco lands of Virginia, Maryland, and, increasingly, Kentucky. The best-capitalized slaveholders relocated to lucrative cotton and sugar-growing areas, first in South Carolina and Georgia, then in the new states of Louisiana, Alabama, and Mississippi. Missouri was a bargain option, with an active secondary market in shady Spanish land grants, land warrants issued to soldiers, and congressionally issued earthquake-relief certificates that lowered the cost of its already low land prices. So enticed, many small-scale and aspiring slaveholders decided to take a plunge on it. As George Sibley, longtime Indian agent in the Missouri Valley, noted in 1817, "The increase in population, wealth, and improvement of all kinds in this territory within the past year is immense." Slaveholders and would-be slaveholders from the United States eagerly expanded and racially codified the existing French and Indian slave system, accelerating its move toward the binary U.S. model of exclusively enslaving people considered to be of African descent.[9]

What white Missourians had not counted on was just how rapidly American politics, culture, and society were evolving to their north and east, especially regarding slavery. The egalitarian rhetoric of the American Revolution and British attacks on the hypocrisy of American slave owners fighting for liberty and equality—as well as British attempts to exploit that hypocrisy by offering freedom to slaves who joined their side (in some cases their ranks) during the Wars of Independence and 1812—had placed slavery under great pressure in places where it was economically less important. The New England states and Pennsylvania either abolished or began phasing out human bondage during and after the American Revolution, often by means of lawsuits brought by enslaved people who pointed out the ideological contradictions between slavery and the stated ideals of the American cause as outlined in the Declaration of Independence and state constitutions. Of course, the federal Constitution protected slavery on many levels, especially with the infamous three-fifths clause that partially counted the enslaved population for purposes of representation, but also in its strict protections for property and requirements that fugitive slaves be returned to their owners and that states respect each other's laws. Yet in deference to the feelings of the American Revolution's liberal admirers abroad and a significant body of public opinion at home, the framers of the Constitution omitted the peculiar institution by name. They also opened the door to regulation by setting a date for a possible ban on the further importation of enslaved Africans, 1808, that became a greater and greater certainty with time. The mid-Atlantic states of New York and New Jersey, where a more significant portion of labor force was enslaved than elsewhere in the North, passed gradual emancipation laws in 1799 and 1804, respectively. Those states' abolition laws were exceedingly gradual and conservative, with no slaves freed immediately and those born in slavery required to serve their masters until they reached age twenty-five (or older). Nevertheless, by the 1810s, the end of slavery was the clear trend in the northern half of the country, composed of those states soon to be known as the free ones.[10]

Most significant for the Missouri Crisis, the 1787 ordinance organizing the public domain north and west of the Ohio River banned slavery there for both practical and ideological reasons. While the Northwest Ordinance was promulgated with little comment or immediate effect on slavery, as David Brion Davis put it, "the ideological consequences of creating free soil" were immense, if mainly as a precedent and as advertising for the future. The Confederation Congress needed the revenue expected from an impending land sale to the New England–based Ohio Company of Associates. The Ohio Company's lobbyist, Rev. Manasseh Cutler, is often credited with writing the ordinance's antislavery provision; he knew that slave country was unlikely to sell to Yankee farmers, and the comparative advantage of "free" territory in attracting migrants and industry would only grow over time. "The creation and expansion of a free-soil world," writes Davis, "however accommodating in certain respects, invited increasingly invidious comparisons between antithetical and seemingly irreconcilable social systems."[11] Those divisions had become pronounced by the time of the Missouri Crisis. Peripatetic Yankee Josiah Meigs had traveled widely across the United States from his Connecticut birthplace. After his republicanism proved too strong for Yale in the 1790s, he left and, in 1801, would serve as the first acting president of the University of Georgia. Meigs grew openly contemptuous of Georgian planters, leading him in 1811 to begin work as the surveyor general of the United States. At a July 4 celebration held in Cincinnati in 1813, he toasted "the Mississippi, father of the rivers: May the rains and dews of Heaven, never fertilize the fields which he drains, if they are occupied by slaves." In the six years between his toast and the crisis, the scientifically observant Meigs traveled widely between the Northwest Territories and Missouri, prompting his conclusion that "the character of the Free & the Slave States, will, however always be distinguishable."[12]

Along with and beyond these localized phaseouts, a serious antislavery movement was growing and gaining significant purchase over political opinion in northern states, driving the new gradual emancipation laws and advocating for further measures. In Pennsylvania, Quakers and a growing community of free Black people led a small but influential antislavery movement that seriously roiled the early days of the new federal government with petitions to regulate the slave trade, most famously an open letter from Benjamin Franklin in 1790 that asked Congress to "remov[e] this inconsistency from the character of the American people." Black and white abolitionists, particularly from the middle states, repeatedly petitioned Congress to take some kind of action against slavery in the 1790s, and nary a congressional session passed without debates about slavery disturbing the waters in one form or another. Meanwhile, a growing array of organizations and activists worked to undermine slavery, from the Pennsylvania Abolition Society that sponsored the petitions and other legal challenges to slavery to the quieter charitable activities of the New York Manumission Society that included Alexander Hamilton and John Jay among its founding members.[13]

Though overshadowed by other issues like public finance, the French Revolution, foreign policy toward Britain and France, and the rights of political dissent, antislavery themes also crept into the partisan politics of the early American republic. Jay and Hamilton were associated with the Federalist Party in politics, and while the Federalists were a national party that repeatedly put forward South Carolina slaveholders as presidential candidates, their base was in maritime New England. There, antislavery sentiment, Christian contempt for southern morals, and regional chauvinism ran strong. The three-fifths clause had been a source of bitterness for New England Federalists since its adoption, and these feelings naturally became much more harsh once it emerged that northern candidates, and the Federalists, were at a disadvantage in presidential elections, especially after John Adams became the first incumbent president not to be reelected in 1800–1801. During the 1800 presidential campaign and thereafter, with sincere conviction but also political defensiveness, Federalists intermittently but increasingly took shots at slavery when criticizing Thomas Jefferson and the Democratic-Republicans, hitting on both the hypocrisy of alleged democrats who held people in bondage and the unfairness of "slave votes" counting in the Electoral College (though they never complained about child and female "votes" counted at *full* value).[14] Not to be outdone, many Democratic-Republicans in the northern states developed their own forms of antislavery politics from the 1790s through the 1810s, though their antislavery actions frequently fell victim to their political dependence on southern slaveholders like Thomas Jefferson.[15]

For a time, the revolutionary fallout was strong enough that even some of the future slave states seemed to be joining in with the drift away from slavery. In general, Upper South slaveholders of the postrevolutionary era readily agreed with the larger revolutionary consensus about the evils of slavery. Virginia, Kentucky, and several other states considered emancipation laws but stopped far short of enacting them, instead making it easier for owners to voluntarily manumit their slaves and developing new legal codes and management systems designed to "ameliorate" slavery as a labor system and make it more humane, efficient, and sustainable.[16]

The contradictory impulses at work in these changes added fuel to the Missouri Crisis in multiple, conflicting ways. Increased manumission meant that the free Black populations of places like Pennsylvania and New York grew rapidly, and many of them became strident antislavery activists who joined abolition societies, lobbied officials, helped escaped and freed slaves, and voted for antislavery politicians, a phenomenon addressed by Sarah Gronningsater in chapter 7 of this volume and in a seminal *William and Mary Quarterly* article.[17] Meanwhile, Upper South slaveholders looked west with highly variable eyes. Virginian Edward Coles, family friend of Jefferson and Madison, famously moved to Illinois and freed his slaves on the way there, becoming a major force for keeping Illinois in the free column. Most other southern slaveholders, however, looked to places such as Kentucky, Tennessee, and Missouri as places where they could re-create the familiar racial and labor systems of their native Chesapeake.[18]

At the same time, ameliorationist ideas found their way into the legal codes and constitutions of many of the new western states where slavery was allowed. Enslaved men and women used these laws to gain access to and protection from the courts in their efforts to resist enslavement. The "freedom suits" Anne Twitty examines in chapter 8 were just one manifestation of enslaved men and women using the law to seek emancipation for themselves and their families. The most predominant approach to the West among Upper South slaveholders, however, was the most self-serving one, that of seeing the more spread-out and allegedly ameliorated conditions of slavery out west as both a golden opportunity to make money from their human property and a salve for whatever pangs of conscience might be weighing on them. Missouri's cooler climate and the lack of large plantations there made it an especially ripe environment for the cultivation of that form of self-deception and the further fantasy—promoted by Jefferson and many other Virginians, Marylanders, Kentuckians, and Missourians—that the "diffusion" of the enslaved population across the continent would prevent it from growing and solve many of the problems they associated with it.[19]

The most popular form of antislavery among whites, by far, was colonization, rooted in the fearful, racist notion that the only safe approach to mass emancipation was removing formerly enslaved workers from the vicinity of their former owners, and most other whites, by sending them to Africa or some other distant location. Colonization played a key role in the plans and expectations of northern restrictionists. By early 1820, James Tallmadge's proposal to place restrictions on slavery in Missouri had morphed into a wider demand among northern restrictionists to prohibit forever the "extension of slavery in all states and territories hereafter admitted to the Union." Most white northern restrictionists expected that halting slavery's expansion in Missouri and elsewhere was the first step toward some kind of long-term, gradual abolition that would be coupled with forced removal of emancipated African Americans. Though highly debatable as to its motives and goals and much criticized even in its day, colonization was an important stage in the politics of slavery because it signaled wide acceptance of two key antislavery propositions: the long-term incompatibility of slavery with American ideals of liberty and the inevitability of Black resistance to enslavement.[20]

Enslaved people constantly tried to escape their enslavers and sought manumission for themselves and family members. They also increasingly seemed to be turning to armed rebellion. The successful Black revolution and failed French counterrevolution in Haiti weighed heavily on white minds since the 1790s. By the early 1800s, homegrown rebellions seemed to lurk everywhere. A major revolt had taken place on U.S. soil in southern Louisiana in 1811, while the "Negro Fort" in Spanish Florida served as a beacon for runaway slaves, disaffected Native Americans, and alleged British saboteurs until the U.S. Army destroyed it in 1818. Elsewhere, a number of other major uprisings seemed to have been narrowly averted, most notably Gabriel's Rebellion in Virginia in 1801, which had sparked debates over colonization and forced removal in the Virginia Legislature. The American Colonization Society (ACS), founded in 1817, was famously fronted by prominent Upper South political figures, including former president James Madison, Henry Clay, and Francis Scott Key. Their fears and sentiments were widely shared, albeit with differential effects as whites looked west. Upper South slaveholders dreamed of selling off or diffusing the enslaved Black population among a larger white one to better control it; northerners often envisaged the western frontier as an entirely white society, from which Indigenous people would be cleared and Black people never allowed to go.[21]

There has been a long American tradition of debating the relationship between slavery and capitalism: whether slavery helped or hindered economic growth sectionally and nationally, whether it was a feudal holdover antithetical to capitalist ideas and practices or the ultimate expression of them, and so on. In many respects, this debate began in earnest in the press and on the floor of Congress during the Missouri Crisis. In the antebellum North, the former conviction became gospel among abolitionist and doughfaces alike, used to justify aggressive action against slavery, on the one hand, or none, on the other, with the idea that progress would soon sweep slavery away in any case. Historians now reject this notion, with the capitalist interpretation of slavery controversially pioneered by economic historians Robert Fogel and Stanley Engerman fully ascendant at this writing, in a more angry and politicized key.[22]

The ruthless, grasping entrepreneurialism and bourgeois practicality on display in chapters 1 and 2 by John Craig Hammond and Robert Lee, respectively, make it clear that "slavery's capitalism" was hard at work in Missouri Territory long before it applied for statehood. St. Louis was known as "Paincourt"—literally "short loaf"—in French times because of a single-minded focus there on conducting commerce over growing its own food, and even in the agricultural settlement of Ste. Genevieve the habitants used African and Native slave labor to make wheat and flour they could sell to New Orleans and the French Caribbean rather than producing sufficient food for themselves. Lee shows that the central Boone's Lick region of Missouri became one of the fastest-growing places in history for a short period because of an especially audacious act of surreptitious commodification, territorial governor William Clark's quiet, deliberate misinterpretation of an 1808 treaty with the Osage to appropriate for Missouri a huge swath of Sauk, Meskwaki, and Ioway lands north of the Missouri River. The local penchant for capitalism became even clearer once the Panic of 1819 dispelled the initial land bonanza, and Boone's Lick settlers turned to other lines of business, opening trade with Mexico by foot and mule over the Santa

Fe Trail and creating a patent medicine empire, Dr. Sappington's Anti-Fever Pills, to name just two examples.[23]

Regardless of the local ethos, however, Missouri's statehood bid stood athwart the fork of a widening gap between two different regional paths. Missouri's men on the make happened to have their small capital or hopes of it tied up in slavery, like their forebears in Virginia, Kentucky, and North Carolina. To the east and north, the decline of slavery coincided chronologically with the beginning of those regions' rapid urban and market growth. While Gulf Coast cotton lands were still largely in Indigenous hands and threatened by multiple European powers, shipping and flour milling boomed to supply both sides of the Napoleonic War years, and then Jefferson's Embargo kick-started the beginnings of the New England textile industry. To facilitate the expansion of commercial agriculture, huge investments were made in road- and bridge-building projects, financed by those then novel and controversial devices the corporation and the bank, which sprouted by the hundreds, especially in Pennsylvania and New York. The booming cities of New York and Greater Philadelphia both passed one hundred thousand in population. To be sure, the slave ports of Charleston and New Orleans were booming, too, but in their cases as adjuncts of a slavery-based agricultural economy that would lag even further behind the North in developing a diversified economy once the monolithic cotton economy took off.[24]

Most crucially for understanding the politics of the Missouri Crisis, by the 1810s the Northeast seemed as though it was on the verge of pulling ahead of the South in spreading its economy, culture, and politics across the West, thanks to the lure of the Northwest Ordinance and the transport and credit links that were being built. Ohio was already a populous place at the time the Erie Canal was under construction and about to firmly connect Illinois and Indiana to New York City and the Atlantic economy via the Hudson River and the Great Lakes. Migrants from the East and later from abroad came more much rapidly across the northern tier of states than they would lands farther south. What mattered politically was that the Old Northwest was filling with free families in which every person was fully counted for representation, creating a northern advantage in the population-based House of Representatives, an imbalance that was going to get only worse. After the 1820 census, the slave state share would be down to 38 percent of the seats, and by then the Missouri fight had made it clear that this made a huge difference. The emergence of the Old Northwest and its eastern connections as the "Free States" in the course of the Missouri Crisis would increasingly exacerbate the disparity as time went on.[25]

War of 1812 Overture

All of these trends were brought into focus and pushed into politics by the impact of the War of 1812, an event with much more far-reaching implications for the politics of slavery than historians typically acknowledge.

First, the Second War for American Independence opened the way for the North-South political cleavages and national debates over slavery by destroying the Federalists as a national party. The party of John Adams, John Jay, and Alexander Hamilton had first brought slavery and racism into the political picture, gingerly and not very successfully, as one way to alienate voters from Thomas Jefferson during the presidential elections of 1796 and 1800. They did so chiefly through embarrassing quotations from Thomas Jefferson's one book, *Notes on the State of Virginia*, in which Jefferson had both eloquently denounced slavery and engaged in some racist pseudo-scientific speculation about the biological capacities of both Africans and Native Americans. Post-1800, now in opposition and with the Sally Hemings scandal out in public thanks to a disgruntled Jefferson supporter, Federalists doubled down on the strategy of defending their northeastern base by fomenting antipathy for all things Virginian and Jeffersonian, including not just slavery-related issues that actually did disturb many northern voters, but also westward expansion, religious toleration, reduced military spending, and other aspects of the Jefferson regime that were widely popular. Jefferson won reelection by a landslide in 1804, and the Federalists sank to their lowest ebb, losing power even in Massachusetts.[26]

Then Thomas Jefferson's decision to implement his progressive foreign policy ideas about "peaceable coercion" put the Federalist strategy temporarily back on track. Trying to stay at peace and pressure warring Britain and France to respect American neutral commerce in 1807, Jefferson proposed an embargo suspending all commerce with foreign nations. This extreme step wrought economic devastation down east and allowed Federalists to make a political comeback, winning back lost seats in statehouses and Congress in New England and certain other stronghold locations such as rural southeastern Pennsylvania.[27]

To be clear, despite their antislavery rhetoric, Federalists almost never offered actual proposals to deal with slavery itself—they were far too reverent toward property rights—usually restricting themselves to talking points and private charity. This lent partial credence to the Democratic-Republican charge that any talk about slavery in a political context, even if couched in philanthropic and moralistic language, represented a grab for power rather than a call for justice. This was why conspiracy theories about the Tallmadge

Amendment—that "the Missouri question covers designs 'dark and deep'" for a northern party or a Rufus King presidency—were popular in Missouri and could even gain endorsements from some antislavery northerners.[28] But it was not merely that. New England rather than the South was the Bible Belt of the early American republic and the self-conscious avatar of the Protestant work ethic. It was a place where "SLAVERY" was sincerely regarded as "that abomination in the sight of GOD, that foul reproach to a Christian nation . . . fastened upon this land . . . for the mere selfish gratification of those who are too indolent to labour," wrote former Connecticut senator Theodore Dwight, editor of the influential *Daily Advertiser* of New York. Some arch-Federalists like Dwight and Timothy Pickering really did dream of a new northern-only party or even a separate Northern Confederacy. They hoped to leverage both their fellow Yankees' disgust for the South and the Virginia Dynasty's proved indifference toward the economic interests of their region as the basis of their project.[29]

The burdens imposed by the first years of the war were like the Embargo in falling much more heavily on those in New England and New York than elsewhere, strengthening the sectional tendencies among the Federalists that would eventually bring them to grief. With the war going badly to the point that northern governors and mayors and militia commanders were sometimes disobeying U.S. government orders, a group of Federalists called for a convention of northern states at Hartford in 1814 that became notorious, especially in Democratic political circles. The Hartford Convention never considered secession, but it did propose state rights'–oriented constitutional reforms and congressional apportionment by free population only, thus tossing out the three-fifths clause. Taking shots at two other factors that New England leaders felt reduced their influence in national politics, the Hartford Convention also proposed requiring a supermajority to admit new states, intended to slow down the westward migration of political power within the Union, and a ban on naturalized immigrants ever again serving in Congress or other federal offices. This was a dig at the immigrant population New England Federalists felt was overwhelming their political influence as much as "slave representation" and depopulation did and a reminder of their fervent support for the alien parts of the Alien and Sedition Acts. (Of course, if the New England Federalists thought "wild Irishmen" were a problem in Philadelphia, they hadn't seen anything yet, decades before the potato famine, in their own still homogeneous region.)[30]

All of this looked terrible when, in an unexpected twist, General Andrew Jackson and his troops, largely militia, won a miraculous victory at the battle of New Orleans in January 1815 against a larger and more seasoned force of British regulars. The fight famously took place two weeks after the signing of the Treaty of Ghent, but, even so, news of the rout of the British by American land and naval forces politically transformed a failed, unpopular war into America's greatest national triumph since Yorktown. Even the Federalist *New York Evening Post* doubted "whether the English history furnishes one instance of a more complete discomfiture, a more disgraceful defeat." The Federalist name was now mud, if not traitorous, in most of the country. The party withered away to the point that the remaining Federalist leaders readily embraced the presidency of James Monroe, once among the most hated of Virginia Republicans, in the so-called Era of Good Feelings. Indeed, the phrase was coined by one of the Federalists' most stalwart partisan newspapers, the now thoroughly chastened *Columbian Centinel* of Boston.[31]

Some other vehicle was needed for Federalist politicians, voters, and ideas. It turned out that, once separated from Federalist elitism, nativism, and possible disloyalty, their critique of slavery and the South found more and more willing ears among their former northern enemies. This was a necessary ingredient of the Missouri Crisis, because while former Federalists were on board with the proposed western slavery ban, the people who brought the ban forward and passed it through the House of Representatives were northern Democratic-Republicans, led by two New Yorkers, James Tallmadge Jr. and John W. Taylor. Sixty-two of the eighty-seven votes that initially passed the Tallmadge Amendment came from the Democratic-Republican side, including half of New England's "yea" votes and five-sixths of those from the mid-Atlantic states.[32]

Ideologically, Democratic-Republicans had much more riding on the outcome of the War of 1812 than Federalists did, even if not so steep a political downside. "General" James Tallmadge "commanded a company of home guards in defense of New York," and at least eighteen of his antislavery amendment's other supporters were War of 1812 veterans, the vast majority of them newly elected after the war. With the revised ending to the conflict, they gladly accepted the whole effort as a victory, despite the disappointing results of most of the eastern battles. One major reason was that from the vantage point of westward expansion, the crux of Jeffersonian Republican hopes for an endless future empire of liberty, New Orleans was just the capstone of a very real strategic victory.[33]

On the eve of the war, much of both the Northwest and Southwest Territories and the state of Tennessee was still unceded or contested Indian land. The so-called civilized tribes of the South such as the Creek, Cherokee, and Choctaw were growing in population, as well as in their capacity to stay put. Meanwhile, north of the Ohio, Tecumseh and his brother Tenskwatawa, the Prophet, were building what threatened to be a frontier-wide Indigenous resistance movement and attracting the outside support from the British that was crucial to sustaining such an enterprise. Then the War of 1812 in the West turned it all around. Future presidents William Henry Harrison and Andrew Jackson destroyed the major centers of resistance at the battles of Tippecanoe and Horseshoe Bend, respectively, then followed up by embarrassing the British forces sent to intervene, Harrison at Moraviantown in Canada and Jackson at New Orleans.

A new strategic situation was at hand. Before 1815, the Indigenous peoples of North America had often been able to stand their ground at the periphery of competing empires with relative ease by playing European powers against the other and assuming key roles in the local imperial economy as they did in the French version of the St. Louis fur trade. Holding off the populous anglophone settlements long-term, or mounting prolonged military campaigns against them, was another matter, requiring a European power to supply it. With the exception of some clandestine, officially disavowed British activities in Spanish Florida (ruthlessly crushed by Jackson in his 1818 campaign against the Seminoles), significant outside assistance to Indigenous groups resisting U.S. encroachment would never materialize again.[34]

Despite its distance from the primary battlefields, the Missouri Territory was affected quite strongly by the War of 1812 and the larger frontier situation it addressed. In the long lead-up to the war, white migration and the land-acquisition process slowed down in this far outpost. Since long before the official start of the war, Missouri settlers had been gripped in a largely cold war with the region's Indigenous peoples that brought only occasional violence but inflicted enough casualties and terrifying experiences to be long remembered. Usually, the conflicts came from random encounters with sojourning Ioway, Sauk, and Meskwaki war and hunting parties rather than their Osage neighbors, who were tied down through the 1808 treaty that created the Indian "factory" at Fort Osage some ninety miles west of the Boone's Lick country. Local whites did not tend to make those kinds of distinctions. The area's pioneer squatters spent months at a time "forted up" behind stockade walls, afraid to move around the country and sometimes unable to shoot at Natives, regardless of their feelings, because of military orders or the house being so completely surrounded that it would have been suicidal. The first operations of government in Cooper County, including the early meetings of the county and circuit courts, took place in the fortified camp of Hannah Cole, a widow in her fifties with nine children whose home site overlooked a stretch of the Missouri River where they expected invaders to appear at any moment. Water was piped in through a hollow log, and the mood was desperate enough for the Coles to rob some passing French fur traders of their weapons. The real threat turned out to come from the lawyers visiting Hannah Cole's fort for court, some of whom connived to fleece her of the land rights to the town of Boonville after the war was over.[35]

Missourians were certain that their fortunes were firmly tied to the 1812-era Indian wars even if they never fully flared in their vicinity. A St. Charles Fourth of July celebration saluted "the brave & patriotic citizens of our territory, who in times of war and danger shielded our frontier from the horrors of savage hostility" and should therefore "flourish in prosperity on the soil which they have valiantly defended." St. Louis greeted the news of the battle of New Orleans with particular jubilation—cannons fired and houses illuminated—because at that particular moment, the Sauk and Meskwaki were as active in Missouri as they had ever been, and much closer to town. Led by Black Hawk, the local Indigenous resistance killed scores of white settlers, at first in advance of the expected British invasion up the Mississippi and then by simply taking the opportunity of the federal and territorial government's paralysis in the wake of the Treaty of Ghent, which awkwardly forbade hostilities with British-allied Natives. The tensions settled down by the summer of 1815, but they left Missourians feeling watchful and vengeful toward Natives in general, especially if they were "aided by a foreign foe." They thrilled to the reports of the Seminole campaign and lifted their glasses to Jackson, "the scourge of Indians, the avenger of Spanish outrage."[36]

So it was that the War of 1812 became an important factor in making the mass-scale westward movement of North American settler colonialism possible, much more so than events more heavily associated with it, like the Louisiana Purchase. In each area where the Indigenous military threat had continued to exist, the end of it seemed to open the settlement floodgates, as a tide of migrants (both free and forced), in the hundreds of thousands, streamed west to the fertile central lands of Indiana, Illinois, Tennessee, Georgia, Alabama, and Mississippi, as well as across the big river into Missouri.[37]

"The Eyes and the Hopes of Weeping Admiring Nations Are upon Thee": Postwar Qualms about Slavery's Destiny

If the emigrants to Missouri were making personal and financial investments in the future of the American West, other parts of the nation were getting culturally and emotionally invested. Even for those with no need or ambition

to move west, the promise and pressure of the birthing of all these new societies carried a heavy psychological weight, especially once the Mississippi
was breached. A wide variety of charitable concerns and movements sprang
up to found churches, schools, colleges, and other cultural institutions, with
the thought that if this new West was the future, the early models might set
the patterns for the rest of the continent. The American Home Missionary
Association was the earliest and most influential of these reforming institutions. There also was a vogue for planned utopian communities to go with
the thousands of for-profit town-building ventures. Missions and planned
communities were not new thoughts in the Anglo-American world, but they
struck Americans with particular intensity after the War of 1812.[38]

There was also great concern for what the West and the future should
not be, especially in the climes of Federalist New England where religious
leaders worried about depopulation and only recently stopped trying to prevent westward migration. The new societies should not be allowed to lapse
into savagery, westward-turning Federalist divines like Jedidiah Morse and
Lyman Beecher thought; neither should the opportunistic Catholic Church
be allowed to propagate there in a Christian void. (The anti-Catholicism of
many New Englanders at the time was about on par with their antislavery
feelings, if not greater.) A more broadly based concern was ensuring that
the new societies be not only Protestant but white. A major goal of the
American Colonization Society, one of the first of the new charitable concerns to be founded, was keeping the Black population of the new West as
low as possible. The creation of a Black colony west of the Mississippi had
been considered, but this notion conflicted with the idea of diffusing the
enslaved population over the continent, so Africa was chosen as the place
where manumitted slaves should be resettled.[39]

The fact was that while the most rapacious whites salivated over the
money to be made in the newly opened cotton and sugar lands, the War of
1812 made slavery seem more problematic and dangerous than ever in the
eyes of many others. "That species of property sir has been very injurious
to the Southern states," warned a western Virginia militia officer to James
Monroe. The Chesapeake-adjacent areas of Virginia and Maryland, home to
the country's largest enslaved population, had proved pathetically vulnerable to invasion; the British had been able to turn slavery to their advantage
much more effectively than they had during the Revolutionary War. As Lord
Dunmore had in the first British war with the United States, British commanders offered freedom to slaves who joined them and found thousands
of takers who provided vital support and extra manpower to the stretched

invading forces. Many slaveholders came to realize much more concretely that their own workers were potentially "worse than an open enemy in the heart of their country." It was no accident that the urgent need to manumit, "diffuse," or colonize away much of the enslaved population swept through the Chesapeake planter community after the war. The contradiction between American principle and practice regarding slavery had become not just mortifying but a security risk.[40]

The northern Democratic-Republicans who instigated the Missouri Crisis shared some of these fears, but the War of 1812 registered most powerfully for them as a vindication of two decades of overheated but passionately sincere rhetoric about America as the vessel of liberty, equality, republicanism, and the rights of man against British aristocracy and tyranny.[41] While many of these staunch antiaristocrats were ready to embrace some "New School" approaches to public finance and economic development, the ideologues and veterans of the so-called Second War of Independence were on high alert for anything the might seem to besmirch or undermine their vindication. Their patriotic pride, tied closely to their liberal humanist ideals and enlightened self-image, had smarted under the barbs of the Federalists and of British politicians, journalists, and diplomats whose thoughts they could read about in the newspapers. Americans had proved the republic could survive, but many northern Democratic-Republicans also wanted to make sure that they did not look like liars.

The immediate postwar era saw a wave of new books and pamphlets indicting American slavery, often in terms of its ideological hypocrisy. One of the most striking and relevant to this discussion was Dr. Jesse Torrey's *A Portraiture of Domestic Slavery, in the United States*, which drew its examples from the author's experiences in the Washington, DC, area during the war and provided blood-curdling illustrations to go with them: a woman eerily floating as she leaps out of a third-story window on F Street to escape transfer to a plantation in Georgia, or a boy frozen to death in a Maryland cornfield, his eyes pecked out by birds, after hiding too long to escape slave traders. "Blessed, infatuated Columbia! the eyes and the hopes of weeping admiring nations are upon thee!" Torrey imagined poetizing while passing by the U.S. Capitol. "Suffer not the lamp of public liberty to be smothered and extinguished by the gloomy shroud of private slavery!"[42]

James Tallmadge, recently elected to Congress, echoed these sentiments in a less poetic vein. From the beginning of his congressional crusade against the extension of slavery, which actually began in November 1818 with some tough questions about the protection of existing slave owners in Illinois's proposed constitution, Tallmadge specifically cited the need to silence the "odious aspersion[s]" of foreign critics, especially in Britain, by removing the basis of their charges of hypocrisy. In a speech whose transcript was evidently too incendiary to include in the *Annals of Congress*, Tallmadge "hoped we would no longer leave it in the power of the world to say that while we held the torch of freedom in one hand, we brandished the slave-driver's whip in another." In his mind and those of many others, slavery was a relic of aristocratic barbarism that had no place in the future republic for which War of 1812 veterans had fought.[43]

On the eve of Missouri's statehood application, apprehension was growing across the northern half of the country that this hypocrisy was actually getting worse rather than better. With the war over and western demand for slave laborers booming, there was a rash of horrifying incidents that demonstrated the growth of the domestic slave trade and the way it was driving evasions of the Atlantic slave-trade ban, the gradual emancipation laws, and the basic civil liberties and human rights of Black people. Much like the tales in Torrey's book but greatly multiplied, there were widely circulated reports of free African Americans attempting suicide or escape after being sold and of slave owners cashing out people scheduled for emancipation by selling them to traders. Supporters of the mid-Atlantic states' program of gradual abolition were galled to learn of their fellow citizens making the intended Black beneficiaries "slaves for life" out of state and cast around for means of stopping the "illegal traffic in People of color." At the request of the New Jersey state legislature, Senator James J. Wilson introduced a bill to bar the interstate sale of slaves from states where the institution was now illegal. Wilson was a longtime critic of slavery who was also the owner of Trenton's *True American*, the state's leading Democratic-Republican newspaper since just after Jefferson was inaugurated; in 1819, Wilson would be one of the Senate's most vocal supporters of the Tallmadge Amendment.[44]

Much worse, and seemingly more common, was organized kidnapping of free or soon-to-be free Black people, a longtime issue that metastasized after the war. The new western demand and negligible overseas supply of enslaved labor meant there was suddenly too much money to be made for avaricious and unscrupulous whites to pass up. As depicted in the newspapers, and later corroborated by historians, a proslavery crime wave of "Reverse Underground Railroad" activity swept the mid-Atlantic region, enough to lead liberal politicians and concerned clergy to propose concerted measures and new laws to curb "the increased activity of the lawless violators of domestic enjoyment within our borders."[45] For instance, in July 1817, the schooner *Creole* was discovered by police in New York Harbor with ten to twelve Black men, women, and children confined aboard, ready to sail in the night for Darien, Georgia. "We cannot sufficiently express our abhorrence at this abominable practice, disgraceful to our country, to humanity and principle," responded the *National Advocate*, a paper edited by Mordecai M. Noah, another enthusiast for the War of 1812. He would soon be famous for his hit patriotic play about the war, *She Would Be a Soldier; or, The Plains of Chippewa*.[46]

It was not that northern Democratic-Republicans had suddenly become radical antiracists while cheerleading for the advance of settler colonialism. The idea of kidnapping rings, like chains, manacles, whips, and cropped ears, just offended their sense of America as a modern society and a progressive force in the world. Another Republican literary favorite, poet Selleck Osborne's *American Watchman* newspaper, applied a bit of historical imagination to this feeling: "We are realizing in our own country—this retreat of civil and religious liberty—this asylum of the oppressed of other nations—the scenes of those barbarous ages when the husbandmen went armed to his labours in the field, conscious that he was liable every moment to the attacks of the manstealer, who lay in wait to seize the unsuspicious and the unprotected."[47]

Southerners with slaves of their own to sell and some sense of decency and political optics sometimes joined in with proposals to reduce the volume of the slave trade and curb its most abusive and illegal forms; proslavery firebrand John Randolph of Roanoke even chaired a congressional investigation of the DC slave trade. Yet in the end, concerned northerners learned, most southerners were too solicitous about the economic cost of escapes and their own property rights to countenance real action against the kidnapping problem. On the contrary, southerners thought fugitive slaves already had too much protection. In December 1817, a committee led by James Pindall of Virginia reported a bill to make slave catchers virtually immune from any out-of-state court and force alleged fugitives to prove they were free only after being forcibly transported to some faraway jurisdiction. The collapse of this measure in the House turned out to be an unheralded precursor of the Tallmadge Amendment vote.[48]

"Hurl Them from Their Seats": Congress Tries to Get Paid but Democracy Crashes the Party

While long-term trends and contradicting forces did much to produce the Missouri Crisis, there was also a good deal of happenstance in its precise timing. Circumstances with relatively little direct relation to slavery had created a political situation in which old Federalists and young northern Republicans were both more willing and able to take some concrete action on the slavery problem.

As many historians have argued over the years, the "Era of Good Feelings" was a misnomer from most angles other than James Monroe's. The old Federalist-Republican party division had ceased to function in Congress and presidential elections, it was true, but that was much more of a bug than a feature, blocking the expression of a great deal of political ferment and potential democratic energy. From the top reaching out, there was a bitter rivalry inside the cabinet and outside of it over who would succeed Monroe, leading to networks of John Quincy Adams, William Crawford, John C. Calhoun, and Henry Clay supporters beginning to coalesce around the country and seek out issues. From the bottom, there was a slow-burning yet distinct movement toward more democratic voting procedures, especially in New England and the West, as it became increasingly difficult to justify according political rights on the traditional basis of wealth. All the new western states came into the Union with universal white male suffrage, and by 1821 all of the eastern states north of Maryland had adopted that system, except for Rhode Island. The royal charter that Connecticut still used as its constitution had finally fallen in 1818, along with its established church.[49] Finally, while it did not make much difference for a while, a larger and larger percentage of states were switching over permanently to choosing their presidential electors by popular vote, with Massachusetts, Connecticut, New Jersey, Virginia, and North Carolina making the change between 1812 and 1820.[50]

In this environment, new political conflicts were developing in many states and localities from the rapid social and economic changes of the war and postwar era. For instance, the movement for religious toleration in New England went beyond Connecticut, taxation, and voting. In New Hampshire, the battle extended to higher education, with the newly Democratic-Republican state government and a board of trustees dominated by Federalist Congregational clergy fighting over control of the publicly chartered Dartmouth College. John Marshall's Supreme Court declared it private in an epochal decision issued two weeks before the passage of the Tallmadge Amendment.[51] In Pennsylvania, a number of old-school Democratic-Republican ideologues, literally known as the "Old School" in Philadelphia, fought back furiously against new public policy departures on economic development and public finance, notably a huge expansion in the number of banks and other private corporations being created, often through political connections and under the control of corrupt or incompetent managers. Similar or even worse disputes over banking developed in Missouri, Kentucky, and many other places with the approach and unfolding of the Panic of 1819. Missouri's first constitution would limit the state to one banking corporation at any given time to avoid further troubles of this nature.[52]

Another force for political conflict was the many rank-and-file politicians who had built up the Democratic-Republican majority as local party activists, especially by running and filling the pages of the partisan newspapers so central to politics in the era, They took umbrage over their own exclusion from court circles in Washington, DC. There, "a residential elite" of bureaucrats, elected officials, and their families had been presiding more or less continuously since Jefferson took office in 1801, despite the myriad embarrassments of the Madison years. The government was losing touch with public opinion as a result, many local political activists believed. As restrictionist stalwart John Sloane of Ohio observed, "certain democrats who have grown up under the care of Madison's and Monroe's Administration are too much the creatures of courtly power to be depended of" to do the right thing regarding slavery. Their close dependence on the administration had made them as aristocratic as Roger Griswold, he said, a Connecticut Federalist congressman whose contempt for Democrats had been legendary since the day he beat Vermont representative Matthew Lyon with a cane on the floor of the House for talking smack about him. To put a bow on the growing antiaristocratic mood, the Fourteenth Congress, elected during the war and full of self-pitying "statesmen" who complained about the expense of living a properly genteel life in remote Washington, DC, gave themselves a lavish pay raise, converting their $6 per diem to a $1,500 annual salary (and considering higher figures), thus doubling or tripling their compensation, depending on who was counting.[53]

The political world spontaneously combusted upon learning this news, with newspapers, town meetings, grand juries, Fourth of July celebrations, state legislatures, and individual citizens rushing to condemn Congress for such "terrible squinting at aristocracy" at a time when Americans were still recovering from the war economically and being asked to take on additional taxes and public debt. A concerned group of Democratic-Republicans meeting at the Lake George Coffee-House issued a mock Declaration of Independence: "We hold these truths to be inconvertible" that the new compensation law was unconstitutional, unnecessary, and extremely impolitic with an election coming up. A newspaper poet pictured congressmen blowing their $6 a day "gallanting ladies—Riding in coaches, drinking wine/Dressing and going out to dine." Equality to such politicians, the poet thought, was

> A theme that answers mighty well
>> To harp on at elections;
> But when elected, very soon,
> You'll find those harpers change their tune.

Federalists and Republicans alike joined in the uproar while occasionally debating which side's congressional aristocrats were more responsible.[54]

Many of the pay-raise critics linked the issue explicitly to their frustration with the practice of using congressional or legislative caucuses to make nominations, long under heavy fire in Pennsylvania and other states. While there was no groundswell of opinion against President James Monroe himself, the closed process by which he got named a candidate, by meeting of the Democratic-Republican members of Congress that many did not attend, was deeply unpopular. National party competition may have lost the thread in the late 1810s, but the outbreak over the "Salary Bill" inspired a serious democratic awakening that puzzled and threatened many in the expensive environs of Washington, DC. The Federalist *Alexandria (VA) Gazette* lamented that public opinion was being grievously misled, "subservient to the influence of unprincipled partizans, brought to bear upon them in every shape which practised demagogues know how to assume, whether of newspaper essay or paragraph, or of oration from the hustings, the oak stump, the court-house, the church, or the tavern meeting."[55]

Most important for the Missouri Crisis, the pay-raise issue seemed to bring new and unpredictable voices into the political discourse. "It has not only pointed the pens of some of our ablest writers," marveled Washington's *National Intelligencer*, house organ of the residential elite, "but has inspired those with eloquence who never spoke before." The *Intelligencer* would have preferred such unwelcome voices kept quiet. "It cannot be correct that the Representatives of the People should be stinted" to less pay than their salaried clerks and doorkeepers, the editors lamented on behalf of their D.C. politician readers.[56]

Despite the disbelief in official Washington, the uproar quickly gathered into the first-ever rush to throw the congressional bums out. In Putnam County, Georgia, the citizenry shot and burned effigies of congressmen who voted for the Compensation Act, but most other places stuck to words and the electoral process. If public servants went against "the opinions and wishes of their Constituents," declared a town meeting in Stillwater, New York, John W. Taylor's neck of the woods, "then it becomes the *duty* of the Citizens to hurl them from their seats, and commit the care of their Civil Rights to more worthy Servants." Taking that logic to its conclusion, a county nominating meeting in West Chester, Pennsylvania, resolved that self-compensators had "forfeited the confidence of their Republican Brethren" and hence were off the team. Numerous members who had voted for the Compensation Act were forced to recant and promise to sin no more, including the man generally regarded as the political chieftain of Baltimore, General Samuel Smith, a merchant and shipowner known to have most of Mobtown's dockside muscle at his back. General William Henry Harrison had been recruited to run in a special election out in Ohio during the fall of 1816 and still had to take the pledge despite being fresh from frontier military glory. Young Tippecanoe promised to lead the repeal himself if no one else did. Many congressmen simply resigned, as editors and town meetings demanded. Only 54 percent of the Fourteenth Congress even sought reelection, down from 66 percent the previous election. The real shock was the success rate of their reelection campaigns, which dropped from 88 percent during the Fourteenth Congress elections to 56 percent after the pay raise.[57]

In the face of all this ferment, the immediate postwar elections produced the largest turnover in congressional history, with 63 percent of the House of Representatives and 50 percent of the Senate newly elected when the Fifteenth Congress assembled. New York returned only seven members of its twenty-seven-man House delegation, Pennsylvania only ten of twenty-three, Massachusetts only seven of twenty. Ohio turned over completely, except for the just-arrived Harrison. From Monticello, Thomas Jefferson pronounced the 1816 congressional elections "the most signal display which has ever been seen of the exercise by the people of the controul they have retained over the proceedings of their delegates." It was a happy "proof of the innate good sense, the vigilance, and the determination of the people to act for themselves," Jefferson told Albert Gallatin. Perhaps Jefferson had not yet considered everything the people themselves might want done, such as about slavery.[58]

The change was actually most striking in places Jefferson knew little about, like northern New England, where the New Hampshire and Vermont delegations, six each in those days, turned over wholesale and swung from Federalist to Democratic-Republican. While this only made the Republican supermajority even more overpowering, it also silently shifted its center of gravity north with consequences that emerged slowly once the Fifteenth Congress gathered. To go with the new Pennsylvanians and New Yorkers, the House majority had taken on board some New Englanders shaped by political and ideological battles with the Federalists that had continued to be closely fought there throughout the Jefferson and Madison years. The swing was as sharp as it was in northern New England partly because of the region's multimember districts, but also because of the strong efforts Democratic-Republicans made there.

As entrenched as it was in its New England stronghold, the Federalist Party did not simply wither away; it had to be crushed. Jefferson supporters made inroads in New England after the "Revolution of 1800," but more at the state than at the congressional level, and these gains were largely rolled back during the Embargo and war. More important, the "Standing Order" was still largely intact at the end of the war, with state-supported Congregational churches and heavily Federalist social and cultural institutions that considered Democratic-Republicans unwashed and unworthy and the late war sinful. Hence, in New Hampshire and Vermont and much of Massachusetts, and just after that in other parts of New England, 1816 was a moment to try to complete unfinished business.[59]

Coming so soon as after the embarrassments of the Hartford Convention, the congressional pay raise presented a golden opportunity to bring all of the issues of the past fifteen to twenty-five years down in a large mallet on the Federalists' heads. This was done most aggressively in New Hampshire, under the populist leadership of Levi Woodbury and hard-faced printer Isaac Hill of Concord's *New Hampshire Patriot*, both future leading Jacksonians. Working against the total lack of voter interest in the nonexistent presidential race, Hill's 1835 campaign biographer wrote, "Each party proposed its strongest men, and every editor entered zealously into the contest."

Hill loosed an avalanche of print that framed the 1816 contest as the ultimate Federalist-Republican showdown. On the front page of the *Patriot* just before the election, he put an emblem of the American eagle in the left-hand column and the British Crown on the right, with the motto "Vigilance and Liberty, Economy, and National Prosperity" under the first and "Expensive Government and Royalty, Enervation and Slavery" under the latter. Further copy above and below large versions of the tickets, probably intended for use at the polls, connected the issues all the way back to the Alien and Sedition Acts of 1798 and the debates over the French

Revolution, then through the War of 1812, and forward to the current battle over religious pluralism and public secular control of higher education.

BEHOLD YOUR CANDIDATES!

WHO WISHES FOR moderate salaries, no unnecessary Taxes, no shackles to freedom, no arbitrary restraints on the rights of con- science, manful resistance to all foreign encroachments, a flourish- ing Treasury, "free trade and no im- pressments," will, on Monday next, vote for the **REPUBLICAN TICKET**.

BUT WHO WISHES FOR exorbitant salaries, "PERPETUAL Direct Taxes," a sedition law to abridge the liberty of speech and of the press, a "law religion" that shall compel all denominations to support the "standing order," submission to foreign insults; a continually accumulating national debt—in fine a government with all the tinsel and trappings of monarchy, will vote for such **2500 DOLLAR MEN**, as [the Federalist incumbents].[60]

While all of this was probably more extreme than what went on in most places during the 1816 congressional campaign, at least as publicly recorded, Hill saw it as part of a national movement he could spin as the triumph of Democratic-Republicanism. He headlined an election news roundup *"FEDERALISM SINKS AS THE COUNTRY RISES!"* pointing out the sur- prise pickup of one seat in Delaware, the complete turnover in Vermont, and good prospects—only some of which panned out—in Maryland, Connecticut, New Jersey, and Rhode Island.[61] The 1816 campaign obvious- ly took very different forms in other locations, like Kentucky and North Carolina, where the established churches were long gone and the Federalists were more bugbear than ruling party. Pennsylvania was tied up in complex factionalism, with Democratic-Republicans divided over banking, a gover- nor's race, and many other matters. Led by a newly resurgent Philadelphia *Aurora*, the old Jeffersonian warhorse newspaper that originally inspired the Alien and Sedition Acts, Pennsylvanians were also engaged in the early stages of a long death struggle over caucus nominations, at the state level and nationally, that dovetailed well with the pay-raise rebellion and added to both the fallen incumbent head count and the vote for the Tallmadge Amendment, to the which the Keystone State contributed twenty. Yet what- ever miscellaneous parts the 1816 congressional elections were made of, the results were unmistakable, even if they struck some sophisticates as the "disgraceful" result of "a people laboring under a political phrenitis . . . inflamed beyond the use of their sober discretion."[62]

Politically, the nature of the resulting shift at the congressional level was quite opaque at the time. The Compensation Act and the nominating caucus were among the few partisan issues discussed in common from state to state, and those were out of date before the Fifteenth Congress even assembled (which was not until December 1817, according to the practice of that time). The Fourteenth Congress guiltily reversed the salary grab as lame ducks. All that seemed certain was that the new Congress would never live up the "commanding genius" and "vigorous eloquence" of the rejected one and that the "federal and democratic scuffles" of the past would be off the table. In retrospect, it seems obvious that something new was coming.[63]

Humans of the Fifteenth Congress

A question that has been asked surprisingly seldom about the Missouri Crisis is who exactly set it off in the first place, other than James Tallmadge himself. The available biographical information on the candidates elected in the 1816 electoral cataclysm is scanty and scattered. Reading through what does exist on the House members who ended up voting against slavery in Missouri, one begins to perceive, as few did at the time, that a load of loose cannons was rolling toward Washington. There were 108 new members, many of them remarkably unsteeped in or insusceptible to the unspoken customs and gentlemen's agreements of the capital—and quite prepared to ignore them. A shockingly low number of them would be back two years later. While slavery was largely not discussed in the 1816 congressional campaigns, the sheer political devastation cleared the way temporarily for new voting patterns that made action against it possible. When the Fifteenth Congress convened in December 1817, the new occupants of the Capitol displayed an inclination to disregard the limitations of the Hamilton-Jefferson era and implement aspects of the popular will or personal conviction that had previously been blocked, repressed, or ignored.[64]

From New Hampshire, Hill had recruited a slate of candidates who, like many Democratic-Republicans in Federalist New England, stand out in the records as square pegs who were looked down on by the state's "Standing Order" for lack of some traditional qualification or smelling of free thought, but were unafraid to stare back. The slate was headed by the scholarly Salma Hale. Hale had trained in the printing trade and published a highly regarded and nationally read newspaper called the *Political Observatory* in Walpole, New Hampshire, that tangled with Protestant Federalist intolerance up close. Then he studied and practiced law, but made more of name for himself writing history, penning one of the first successful U.S. history textbooks. Hale was also one of the Democratic-Republican infidels Governor William Plumer had so provocatively appointed to the Dartmouth College board. Plumer and Hill did not consider this an insult to the college; the New Hampshire *Patriot* compared young Hale to Benjamin Franklin, eminently qualified for the position despite his suspect origins and opinions.

Starting work on his history while still in Congress, Salma Hale decided to consult Jefferson about it at Monticello between sessions, presidential home visits being a done thing in the early nineteenth century. The two bonded over shared liberal religious ideas. Jefferson was pleased to learn that his theological letters were eagerly read in New England, where they had been collected and published without his knowledge. "The consequence," Hale thought, would "be the dissemination of liberal principles, and a victory not distant over bigotry & fanaticism." Hale does not directly mention slavery in his notes and letters, yet he found Virginia a sad place despite his lovely and encouraging visit with Jefferson and came away not regretting "my lot was cast in New Hampshire."[65]

Further down the slate in terms of vote getting were two judges who had been reorganized out of their jobs by an earlier Federalist state assembly and still sniffed at generations later: Clifton Clagett, with "no brilliant powers of mind," they said, and Arthur Livermore, a former Federalist deemed to be "not entirely safe" by many of his legal colleagues. Livermore had been regarded as a Federalist earlier in the very year of his election, in fact, and his race drew strong opposition from within his new party, in the form of a special electioneering paper, the *People's Advocate*. This publication carried no ads or news and commentary on any subject other than what an untrustworthy man and unprofessional judge Arthur Livermore was, along with similar material about fellow candidate John F. Parrott. "Judge Livermore" was depicted as a difficult, unfiltered character with no figs to given for anyone else's opinion of his conduct. The *People's Advocate* reported that he had once recessed court for three weeks midcase, announcing that he needed to go home and oversee the digging of a well.

Livermore showed this tendency in a better cause almost as soon as the Fifteenth Congress opened, jumping on the Pindall fugitive slave bill mentioned above in impressively frank terms. He derided its total failure to ensure "the safety of those colored people who resided in the States where slavery was known only by name," such as his small but existent number of Black constituents. (His allegedly thick colleague Clagett actually delivered the most legally devastating takedown of that same bill.) Later, as we have already seen, Livermore tried to start the Missouri Crisis early with his radical proposal for a constitutional amendment banning slavery in any new state.[66]

The 1816 elections seemed to have produced a host of such unpredictable spirits. Massachusetts sent Walter Folger Jr., Quaker polymath of Nantucket, a lawyer like most politicians but better known as a clockmaker, mathematician, surveyor, and inventor. Folger's contribution to wartime self-sufficiency was to go around wearing the ultimate act of home manufacture. "At one time, when he went to the General Court, all his clothing was made from cloth manufactured in his establishment by his own family," marveled his obituary.[67]

One of the minor northern stars of the Missouri debates was the would-be intellectual bon vivant Timothy Fuller, father and mentor of the great Transcendental feminist thinker and journalist Margaret Fuller. Fuller père would have been an archetypical member of the Harvard Federalist lawyer-literati set except for not quite fitting in with them and thus ending up a Democratic-Republican. Fuller did his law studies with Levi Lincoln of Worcester, who served as attorney general under Thomas Jefferson and undertook to politically convert New England. Lincoln's son Enoch was yet another brand-new congressman in 1817 and a veteran of his family's Worcester newspaper, the *National Aegis*.[68]

In Vermont, the 1816 elections were held under near-famine conditions caused by the "year without a summer," when it snowed a foot in June, destroyed the crops, and sent thousands of Vermonters fleeing west, where they did not expect to find slavery. (Obviously, this weather pattern affected the whole world, but try it in the Green Mountains.) The most frequent speaker in Vermont's new Democratic-Republican delegation was Charles Rich, a sheep farmer and the son of a Universalist pastor from Shoreham. Universalists believed that all were saved, no matter what, and Rich joined Arthur Livermore and Clagett in taking apart the Pindall fugitive slave bill. This sparked a legislative interest in Black citizenship that would eventually lead to Rich overseeing the first U.S. Census schedule to require counting the free Black population.[69]

Among those following in Rich's wake were "Colonel" Orsamus Cook Merrill of Bennington. Merrill was a printer at the *Vermont Gazette* who had married a local judge's daughter, worked for his father-in-law's court, and served as an officer in the War of 1812. His congressional career was cut short by a contested election arising from Vermont's version of the caucus dispute. Colonel Merrill was anticaucus but not as good at politics as his silver-tongued competitor Rollin C. Mallary, and found himself forced to make a sudden, cold, sad trip home in the middle of the Missouri debates.[70]

Also from Vermont came the reluctant pioneer Samuel C. Crafts, a Harvard graduate who faced numerous economic and personal challenges as a leading citizen of the failing far-northern town of Craftsbury. In 1802, Crafts traveled roughly four thousand miles by canoe to scope out lands in the Yazoo country in present-day Mississippi, seeking the possibility of a warmer and more lucrative life for his family; he traveled much of the way with French botanist André Michaux. In the end, Crafts was either too poor or too principled to invest in slave country. By 1817, Congressman-elect Crafts remained in dire enough straits that the paltry post–Compensation Act repeal per diem still looked like a financial windfall, or so he told his depressed wife, Eunice, back in Vermont. Faced with the Missouri Question, it seems that whatever Crafts had seen down south in the Yazoo lands had stuck with him. Samuel explained from sunny Washington that he would rather be with Eunice and the children, but under the circumstances (in the middle of the Missouri debates and votes), "if I can do any good to my country, or aid in preventing any evil from befalling it, I shall according to my best judgement, do my duty."[71]

In Washington, these New Englanders and other northerners found each other, lived and rode together, compared notes, and aligned themselves with one another. Timothy Fuller nervously but very successfully gave an "ingenious speech of considerable length," his first, against the same draconian fugitive slave bill that got so many of the others on their feet. Arthur Livermore introduced himself afterward "and expressed his approbation and satisfaction in the most flattering terms," Fuller remarked in his diary. The northerners bonded over the *National Intelligencer*'s tendency to heavily redact or vaguely summarize speeches that went beyond the Virginia-adjacent views on slavery that served as the capital's conventional wisdom. Fuller was one of "many able speakers" of an antislavery bent who found that the *Intelligencer* "prudently suppresses them—on the subject of the slave law." Gales and Seaton, the publishers of both the *Intelligencer* and the *Annals of Congress*, must have taken notice when the House majority who controlled their income began to express the views they had previously kept out of the papers.[72]

We should not give the impression that the potential for new and un-blocked thinking and action in the Fifteenth Congress was somehow limited to New England. After all, the largest sources of both congressional freshmen and Tallmadge Amendment votes were Pennsylvania and New York. There were also at least two angry Republican newspaper editors who got themselves elected straight from the press in those states, though by very different vectors. John Canfield Spencer was a young lawyer of distinguished background, the son of New York Supreme Court justice Ambrose Spencer. The younger Spencer held down the offices of postmaster and assistant attorney general at Canandaigua, New York, but was also the purported editor of the *Ontario Messenger*.[73] Thomas J. Rogers of the Easton, Pennsylvania, *Northampton Farmer* was an Irish-born printer who had learned his trade in the rough-and-tumble of Philadelphia's party newspaper business and then worked in early Washington, DC, as a journeyman at the *National Intelligencer*. "Like many young printers of the era, Rogers eventually found a moribund newspaper to take over in an area where his party needed assistance, in his case the Lehigh Valley back home in Pennsylvania; he founded the *Northampton Farmer* at Easton in the empty shell of a Federalist sheet called the *American Eagle*. Also like many others Thomas J. Rogers realized his political ambitions better than his economic ones." Like many others in his position, Thomas J. Rogers achieved his political ambitions better than his economic ones. Subsidizing his newspaper with income from holding minor offices, government printing contracts, and selling books to the public schools, Rogers became a feared political force in the locality and the state, promoting populist candidates and party nominations by delegate convention rather than caucuses of officeholders. The elevation of a printer, Irishman, and tough partisan was bitterly resented by the established local families, especially once Rogers made his queue-jumping ascent to Congress after the war, via special election. He was as controversial figure within his own party as he was with the Federalists.[74]

Another militia officer, Rogers was a prime example of a northern Democratic-Republican politician who joined enthusiasm for the War of 1812 with restrictionist leanings on slavery. Rogers and his newspaper stridently defended the war along with the trade embargos and sanctions that led up to it, despite heavy opposition from the local flour milling and exporting interests. In the process, he formed a close alliance with Pennsylvania senator Jonathan Roberts, a Quaker who received national attention in 1811–12 for abandoning his creed's pacifist ways and arguing that "open war" was better than submission to "absolute recolonization" by the British. In the

Fifteenth Congress, Roberts and Rogers teamed up against the expansion of slavery, horrified as northerners and patriotic Americans that southerners could claim to own human beings "as a matter of right."[75]

The southernmost restrictionist to be elected to the Fifteenth Congress came from the declining slave state of Delaware. Sliding in thirteen votes ahead of his nearest competitor, Willard Hall was a refugee from Federalist New England who had sometimes raised hackles down in Delaware by showing the good side of his Yankee ways, especially an interest in fashioning a more progressive, developed society. He would go on to found Delaware's public school system, and according to his thorough eulogist, "The subject of American slavery engaged his earnest reflections before it had the country at large." It was already a major source of conflict in Federalist Delaware, which became an epicenter of kidnapping and other slavery-related crimes after the 1808 close of the slave trade. In 1812, as Delaware secretary of state, Hall helped handle a kidnapping case involving four free Black people whom one Henry Brereton assaulted and tried to carry off into slavery; Hall issued a $200 reward. Though invited to Delaware by Federalist James A. Bayard, Hall ended up a Democratic-Republican, possibly because in the universe of the Delmarva peninsula, the Federalists tended to be the party of the planters. Hall became the longtime president of the Delaware Colonization Society. Unfortunately, he may also have supported Delaware's 1811 ban on free Black migration into the state, not uncommonly a secondary plank of "antislavery" thought in the period of the Missouri Crisis, even among the restrictionists.[76]

Let us stress that it would be wrong to make all the newly elected members of the Fifteenth Congress into paragons of twenty-first-century political virtue. The children of the Compensation Act did provide the bulk of the restrictionist vote (at least fifty-three of the eighty-seven yeas at the peak of Tallmadge's support). Yet plenty of southern incumbents had also been pushed out, and *their* replacements were listening to *their* constituents when they defended slavery and proposed measures to protect it. Even most of the restrictionists would no longer qualify for college-dorm naming rights or campus statues because of colonizationism and other racist ideas to which many of them subscribed.

Then too, one point of wide agreement among the new members (notably excluding Timothy Fuller) was rapidly commodifying and incorporate captured Indigenous lands into the United States. New western states were quickly created and confiscatory treaties approved in lands targeted by settlers and entrepreneurs from all the overcrowded regions of the East, whatever the latitude. Most of the new congressional recruits cheered not only the wartime exploits of Andrew Jackson but also his postwar adventures as overbearing commissioner to the Indians and territorial governor of Florida, turning back the efforts of established House leader Henry Clay to have Congress disavow and censure Jackson's illegal foray against the Seminoles and their Spanish and British allies in Florida. James Tallmadge arrived in the new Congress late, via a special election in 1817. In January 1819, he gave a widely reported and praised speech defending Jackson, earning accolades from many southerners and doughfaces who would soon think about him differently.[77]

Tallmadge's next move after the pro-Jackson speech was to launch the Missouri Crisis. He was backed by fifty-nine other newly arrived northern House members, unbound by party restraints and ready to make good on their past liberal rhetoric, along with Federalists looking to renew the old war on Virginia politics under new banners. The newly elected members provided the Tallmadge Amendment's exact margin of victory in the House, eleven votes, with the older guard tying at twenty-seven each. Democracy was in play against the future of slavery, and it was the job of those who wanted to protect their unjust investments (or avoid the consequences of not doing so) to either shut it down or redirect it.[78]

Notes

1. William E. Foley, "The American Territorial System: Missouri's Experience," *Missouri Historical Review* 65, no. 4 (1971): 403–26; Easton circular, April 27, 1816, in *Circular Letters of Congressmen to Their Constituents, 1789–1829*, ed. Noble E. Cunningham Jr., 3 vols. (Chapel Hill: University of North Carolina Press for the Institute of Early American History and Culture, 1978), 2:990–91; Thomas Jefferson to John C. Breckinridge, August 12, 1803, in *Writings*, by Thomas Jefferson, ed. Merrill D. Peterson, Library of America (New York: Literary Classics of the United States, 1984), 1136–39. On Jefferson's policy toward Native peoples, see Anthony F. C. Wallace, *Jefferson and the Indians: The Tragic Fate of the First Americans* (Cambridge, MA: Belknap Press of Harvard University Press, 1999), among many others.

2. Floyd Calvin Shoemaker, *Missouri's Struggle for Statehood, 1804–1821* (Jefferson City, MO: Hugh Stephens, 1916), 42–43; "(Circular.) To the Citizens of Missouri Territory" & "A Voter," *Missouri Gazette* (St. Louis), March 30, September 21, 1816; William E. Foley, *The Genesis of Missouri: From Wilderness Outpost to Statehood* (Columbia: University of Missouri Press, 1989), 288–90; Lawrence O. Christensen et al., eds., *Dictionary of Missouri Biography* (Columbia: University of Missouri Press, 1999), 271–72, 683. On the contested election, see Walter Lowrie and Walter

F. Franklin, eds., *American State Papers: Documents, Legislative and Executive of the Congress of the United States*, Miscellaneous (Washington, DC: Gales and Seaton, 1834), 2:408–11, 414–15.

3. Robert P. Howard, *Illinois: A History of the Prairie State* (Grand Rapids, MI: W. B. Eerdmans, 1972), 98–105.

4. Shoemaker, *Struggle for Statehood*, 40–43, 324–28; *Missouri Gazette* (St. Louis), July 10, 1818, October 25, 1817; "Missouri Territory," *Lancaster (PA) Journal*, July 6, 1818; "Prosperity of St. Louis," *New York Evening Post*, November 25, 1817; *New England Palladium* (Boston), June 30, 1818. On St. Louis's *Missouri Gazette*, see David Kaser, *Joseph Charless: Printer in the Western Country* (Philadelphia: University of Pennsylvania Press, 1963).

5. John Scott, *Memorial and Resolutions of the Legislature of the Missouri Territory, and a Copy of the Census of the Fall of 1817, Amounting to 19,218 Males* (Washington, DC: Gales and Seaton, 1819); *Annals of Congress*, 15th Cong., 1st sess., House, April 3, 1818, 1672, and April 4, 1818, 1675–76; John Craig Hammond, *Slavery, Freedom, and Expansion in the Early American West* (Charlottesville: University of Virginia Press, 2007), 153. For headlined reprintings of the Livermore amendment, see *Middlesex Gazette* (Concord, MA), April 18, 1818; *Providence (RI) Gazette*, April 18, 1818; *Concord (NH) Gazette*, April 28, 1818; *Dartmouth Gazette* (Hanover, NH), April 22, 1818; and *Bangor (ME) Weekly Register*, April 23, 1818.

6. Memorials reprinted in Shoemaker, *Struggle for Statehood*, 321–26.

7. *Senate Journal*, 15th Cong., 1st sess.; *Annals of Congress, 15th Cong., 2nd sess., House, Dec. 18, 1818, 418*.

8. Stephen Aron, *American Confluence: The Missouri Frontier from Borderland to Border State* (Bloomington: Indiana University Press, 2006), 106–85; Carl J. Ekberg, *Stealing Indian Women: Native Slavery in the Illinois Country* (Urbana: University of Illinois Press, 2010); Christina Snyder, *Slavery in Indian Country: The Changing Face of Captivity in Early America* (Cambridge, MA: Harvard University Press, 2010); Peter K. Johnson, "Ésclavage Rouge: The Nature and Influence of Indian Slavery in Colonial St. Louis," *Missouri Historical Review* 105, no. 1 (2010): 14–30; Patricia Cleary, *The World, the Flesh, and the Devil: A History of Colonial St. Louis* (Columbia: University of Missouri Press, 2011); John Craig Hammond, "Slavery, Settlement, and Empire: The Expansion and Growth of Slavery in the Interior of the North American Continent, 1770–1820," *Journal of the Early Republic* 32, no. 2 (2012): 175–206; Brett Rushforth, *Bonds of Alliance: Indigenous and Atlantic Slaveries in New France* (Chapel Hill: University of North Carolina Press, 2014); Carl J. Ekberg and Sharon K. Person, *St. Louis Rising: The French Regime of Louis St. Ange de Bellerive* (Urbana: University of Illinois Press, 2015). On the facts of the transfers and the later citations of them, see the king's letter, translated, reprinted and quoted by locals, in Alcée Fortier, A History of Louisiana (New York: Goupil & Co. of Paris; Manzi, Joyant & Co., successors, 1904,), 1:148-150, 165, 179; and Shoemaker, Struggle for Statehood, 9-14.

9. George Sibley to Samuel Hopkins Sibley, July 10, 1817, Sibley Papers, Missouri History Museum, Archives, St. Louis; Hammond, *Slavery, Freedom, and Expansion*.

10. For summaries of these matters, see Van Gosse, "Patchwork Nation: Racial Orders and Disorder in the United States, 1790–1860," *Journal of the Early Republic* 40, no. 1 (2020): 45–81; John Craig Hammond, "Race, Slavery, Sectional Conflict, and National Politics, 1770–1820," in *The Routledge History of Nineteenth Century America*, ed. Jonathan Daniel Wells, 11–32 (New York: Routledge, 2017); and Manisha Sinha, *The Slave's Cause: A History of Abolition* (New Haven, CT: Yale University Press, 2016), 34–85. We make no effort to adjudicate the heated debate over the precise relationships between slavery, emancipation, and the Revolution, only that it set different regions of the nation on separate paths regarding slavery and that the would-be state of Missouri found itself athwart those differences.

11. David Brion Davis, "The Significance of Excluding Slavery from the Old Northwest in 1787," *Indiana Magazine of History* 84, no. 1 (1988): 75–89; Paul Finkelman, "Slavery and the Northwest Ordinance: A Study in Ambiguity," *Journal of the Early Republic* 6, no. 4 (1986): 343–70; R. Douglas Hurt, "Historians and the Northwest Ordinance," *Western Historical Quarterly* 20, no. 3 (1989): 261–80; Peter S. Onuf, *Statehood and Union: A History of the Northwest Ordinance*, Midwestern History and Culture (Bloomington: Indiana University Press, 1992); John Craig Hammond, "'The Most Free of the Free States': Politics, Slavery, Race, and Regional Identity in Early Ohio," *Ohio History* 121 (2014): 35–57; Suzanne Cooper Guasco, *Confronting Slavery: Edward Coles and the Rise of Antislavery Politics in Nineteenth Century America* (DeKalb: Northern Illinois University Press, 2013); Matthew Salafia, *Slavery's Borderland: Freedom and Bondage Along the Ohio River* (Philadelphia: University of Pennsylvania Press, 2013); Stanley Harrold, *Border War: Fighting over Slavery before the Civil War* (Chapel Hill: University of North Carolina Press, 2010).

12. *Western Spy* (Cincinnati), July 10, 1813; Josiah Meigs to Henry Eddy, September 25, 1819, MSS Alpha Meigs, Chicago History Museum, Archives. John Craig Hammond contributed this paragraph.

13. Nicholas P. Wood, *Let the Oppressed Go Free: The Revolutionary Generation of American Abolitionists, 1758–1808* (Philadelphia: University of Pennsylvania Press, 2021); Paul J. Polgar, *Standard-Bearers of Equality: America's First Abolition Movement* (Chapel Hill: University of North Carolina Press, 2019); David N. Gellman, *Emancipating New York: The Politics of Slavery and Freedom, 1777–1827* (Baton Rouge: Louisiana State University Press, 2006). Quotation from Annals of Congress, 1st Cong., 2d sess. House, February 12, 1790, 1239-1240.

14. A full political history of the Federalist Party has yet to be written, but this paragraph draws especially on Matthew Mason, *Slavery and Politics in the Early American Republic* (Chapel Hill: University of North Carolina Press, 2006), chaps. 1–2. See also Linda K. Kerber, *Federalists in Dissent: Imagery and Ideology in Jeffersonian America* (Ithaca, NY: Cornell University Press, 1970); James M. Banner Jr., *To the Hartford Convention: The Federalists and the Origins of Party Politics in Massachusetts* (New York: Alfred A. Knopf, 1970); Doron Ben-Atar and Barbara B. Oberg, eds., *Federalists Reconsidered* (Charlottesville: University Press of Virginia, 1998); James H. Broussard, *The Southern Federalists, 1800–1816* (Baton Rouge: Louisiana State University Press, 1978); Rachel Hope Cleves, "'Hurtful to the State':

The Political Morality of Federalist Antislavery," in *Contesting Slavery: The Politics of Bondage and Freedom in the New American Nation*, ed. John Craig Hammond and Matthew Mason, 207–26 (Charlottesville: University of Virginia Press, 2011); Manning J. Dauer, *The Adams Federalists*, 2nd ed. (Baltimore: Johns Hopkins University Press, 1968); John Kyle Day, "The Federalist Press and Slavery in the Age of Jefferson," *Historian* 65, no. 6 (2003): 1303–29; Stanley Elkins and Eric McKitrick, *The Age of Federalism* (New York and Oxford: Oxford University Press, 1993); David Hackett Fischer, *The Revolution of American Conservatism: The Federalist Party in the Era of Jeffersonian Democracy* (New York: Harper & Row, 1965); Marshall Foletta, *Coming to Terms with Democracy: Federalist Intellectuals and the Shaping of an American Culture* (Charlottesville: University Press of Virginia, 2001); Matthew Mason, "Federalists, Abolitionists, and the Problem of Influence," *American Nineteenth Century History* 10 (March 2009): 1–27.

15. Padraig Riley, *Slavery and the Democratic Conscience: Political Life in Jeffersonian America* (Philadelphia: University of Pennsylvania Press, 2015); Hammond and Mason, *Contesting Slavery*.

16. Honor Sachs, *Home Rule: Households, Manhood, and National Expansion on the Eighteenth-Century Kentucky Frontier* (New Haven: Yale University Press, 2015); Christa Dierksheide, *Amelioration and Empire: Progress and Slavery in the Plantation Americas* (Charlottesville: University of Virginia Press, 2014); Woody Holton, *Forced Founders: Indians, Debtors, Slaves, and the Making of the American Revolution in Virginia* (Chapel Hill: University of North Carolina Press, 1999); Robin L. Einhorn, *American Taxation, American Slavery* (Chicago: University of Virginia Press, 2006); Eva Sheppard Wolf, *Race and Liberty in the New Nation: Emancipation in Virginia from the Revolution to Nat Turner's Rebellion* (Baton Rouge: Louisiana State University Press, 2006); Michael A. McDonnell, *The Politics of War: Race, Class, and Conflict in Revolutionary Virginia* (Chapel Hill: University of North Carolina Press, 2007).

17. Sarah L. H. Gronningsater, "'Expressly Recognized by Our Election Laws': Certificates of Freedom and the Multiple Fates of Black Citizenship in the Early Republic," *William and Mary Quarterly* 75, no. 3 (2018): 465–506; Polgar, *Standard-Bearers of Equality*; Wood, *Let the Oppressed Go Free*. For a bracing and detailed new take on the role of Black voters in the antislavery politics of the early American republic, often allied with vengeful Federalists and other Yankee moralists in the forgotten corners of New England, New York, and Pennsylvania, see the just-published major work by Van Gosse, *The First Reconstruction: Black Politics in America from the Revolution to the Civil War* (Chapel Hill: University of North Carolina Press, 2021).

18. Guasco, *Confronting Slavery*; Hammond, *Slavery, Freedom, and Expansion*; Sachs, *Home Rule*.

19. A number of scholars have recently delved into the freedom suits, based on recently recovered St. Louis court records. See, among others, Lea VanderVelde, *Redemption Songs: Suing for Freedom before* Dred Scott (New York: Oxford University Press, 2014); Kelly M. Kennington, *In the Shadow of* Dred Scott: *St. Louis Freedom Suits and the Legal Culture of Slavery in Antebellum America* (Athens: University of Georgia Press, 2019); and the best of these studies, Anne Twitty, *Before* Dred Scott: *Slavery and Legal Culture in the American Confluence, 1787–1857* (New York:

Cambridge University Press, 2016), which Twitty's chapter on this volume extends with new research and analysis. For "amelioration," see Dierksheide, *Amelioration and Empire*.

20. John Craig Hammond, "President, Planter, Politician: James Monroe, the Missouri Crisis, and the Politics of Slavery," *Journal of American History* 105 (March 2019): 843–67; Beverly C. Tomek and Matthew J. Hetrick, *New Directions in the Study of African American Recolonization* (Gainesville: University Press of Florida, 2017); Eric Burin, *Slavery and the Peculiar Solution: A History of the American Colonization Society* (Gainesville: University Press of Florida, 2008).

21. On Black resistance in the early American republic, see Calvin Schermerhorn, *Unrequited Toil: A History of United States Slavery* (New York: Cambridge University Press, 2018), 47–73; Gerald Horne, *The Counter-Revolution of 1776: Slave Resistance and the Origins of the United States of America* (New York: New York University Press, 2014); and Sinha, *Slave's Cause*. On the influence of the Haitian Revolution and fears of rebellion on the racial politics of the mainland, an especially crowded field in recent years, see David P. Geggus, *The Impact of the Haitian Revolution in the Atlantic World* (Columbia: University of South Carolina Press, 2001); Matthew J. Clavin, *Toussaint Louverture and the American Civil War: The Promise and Peril of a Second Haitian Revolution* (Philadelphia: University of Pennsylvania Press, 2011); Julia Gaffield, "Haiti and Jamaica in the Remaking of the Early Nineteenth-Century Atlantic World," *William and Mary Quarterly* 69, no. 3 (2012): 583–614; Ashli White, *Encountering Revolution: Haiti and the Making of the Early Republic* (Baltimore: Johns Hopkins University Press, 2012); James Alexander Dun, *Dangerous Neighbors: Making the Haitian Revolution in Early America* (Philadelphia: University of Pennsylvania Press, 2016); and Matthew J. Clavin, *The Battle of Negro Fort: The Rise and Fall of a Fugitive Slave Community* (New York: New York University, 2019).

22. Schermerhorn, *Unrequited Toil*; Sven Beckert and Seth Rockman, eds., *Slavery's Capitalism: A New History of American Economic Development* (Philadelphia: University of Pennsylvania Press, 2018); Calvin Schermerhorn, *The Business of Slavery and the Rise of American Capitalism, 1815–1860* (New Haven, CT: Yale University Press, 2015); Edward E. Baptist, *The Half Has Never Been Told: Slavery and the Making of American Capitalism* (New York: Basic Books, 2014); Sven Beckert, *Empire of Cotton: A Global History* (New York: Alfred A. Knopf, 2014); Walter Johnson, *River of Dark Dreams: Slavery and Empire in the Cotton Kingdom* (Cambridge, MA: Belknap Press of Harvard University Press, 2013). For a contrarian argument about the significance of free soil, see Eva Sheppard Wolf, "Early Free-Labor Thought and the Contest over Slavery in the Early Republic," in *Contesting Slavery*, ed. Hammond and Mason, 32–48.

23. On the commercial origins of the region that become Missouri, see Jay Gitlin, *Bourgeois Frontier: French Towns, French Traders, and American Expansion* (New Haven, CT: Yale University Press, 2010); Carl J. Ekberg, *French Roots in the Illinois Country: The Mississippi Frontier in Colonial Times* (Urbana: University of Illinois Press, 1998); and William E. Foley and C. David Rice, *The First Chouteaus: River Barons of Early St. Louis* (Urbana: University of Illinois Press, 1983). On the aggressive

and multivalent entrepreneurial pursuits of the Boone's Lick region, named after its origins in an illegally sited salt-making business that used enslaved workers, see R. Douglas Hurt, *Nathan Boone and the American Frontier* (Columbia: University of Missouri Press, 1998); Jonas Viles, "Old Franklin: A Frontier Town of the Twenties," *Mississippi Valley Historical Review* 9, no. 4 (1923): 269–82; Lynn Morrow, "Dr. John Sappington: Southern Patriarch in the New West," *Missouri Historical Review* 90, no. 1 (1995): 38–60; David Dary, *The Santa Fe Trail: Its History, Legends, and Lore* (Lawrence: University Press of Kansas, 2012); William E. Unrau, *Indians, Alcohol, and the Roads to Taos and Santa Fe* (Lawrence: University Press of Kansas, 2013); Jeff Bremer, *A Store Almost in Sight: The Economic Transformation of Missouri from the Louisiana Purchase to the Civil War* (Iowa City: University of Iowa Press, 2014); and William Patrick O'Brien, *Merchants of Independence: International Trade on the Santa Fe Trail, 1827–1860* (Kirksville, MO: Truman State University Press, 2014).

24. Stanley L. Engerman, "Slavery and Its Consequences for the South," in *The Cambridge Economic History of the United States*, vol. 2, *The Long Nineteenth Century*, ed. Stanley L. Engerman and Robert E. Gallman, 329–66 (Cambridge: Cambridge University Press, 2000); Stanley L. Engerman and Kenneth L. Sokoloff, "Technology and Industrialization, 1790–1814," in *Cambridge Economic History of the United States*, ed. Engerman and Gallman, 2:367–401; George Rogers Taylor, *The Transportation Revolution, 1815–1860*, Economic History of the United States (New York: Harper & Row, 1968), 3–14; John Majewski, "The Political Impact of Great Commercial Cities: State Investment in Antebellum Pennsylvania and Virginia," *Journal of Interdisciplinary History* 28, no. 1 (1997): 1–26.

25. Davis, "Significance of Excluding Slavery"; John J. Binder, "The Transportation Revolution and Antebellum Sectional Disagreement," *Social Science History* 35, no. 1 (2011): 19–57. For the House apportionment figures, see U.S. Census Bureau, "Apportionment of the House of Representatives," 1990, table 3. For "Free States" as a proper name, see "Slavery," *New York Daily Advertiser*, March 7, 1820.

26. Jeffrey L. Pasley, *The First Presidential Contest: 1796 and the Founding of American Democracy* (Lawrence: University Press of Kansas, 2013), chap. 6; Charles O. Lerche Jr., "Jefferson and the Election of 1800: A Case Study in the Political Smear," *William and Mary Quarterly*, 3rd ser., 5 (1948): 467–91; Jeffrey L. Pasley, *"The Tyranny of Printers": Newspaper Politics in the Early American Republic* (Charlottesville: University Press of Virginia, 2001), chap. 10; Kerber, *Federalists in Dissent*, chap. 2.

27. Philip J. Lampi, "The Federalist Party Resurgence, 1808–1816: Evidence from the New Nation Votes Database," *Journal of the Early Republic* 33, no. 2 (2013): 255–81; Louis Martin Sears, *Jefferson and the Embargo* (reprint; New York: Octagon Books, 1966); Jeffrey A. Frankel, "The 1807–1809 Embargo against Great Britain," *Journal of Economic History* 42, no. 2 (1982): 291–308.

28. "From the Hartford Times, Feb. 20," *St. Louis Enquirer*, April 12, 1820. A balanced assessment of the New York senator suspected in Missouri as the archmastermind of Federalist sectional plots can be found in Joseph L. Arbena, "Politics or Principle? Rufus King and the Opposition to Slavery, 1785–1825," *Essex Institute*

Historical Collections 101, no. 1 (1965): 56–77. The primacy of politics over morality in Federalist antislavery agitation is a running theme throughout Mason, *Slavery and Politics*.

29. L. Douglas Good, "Theodore Dwight: Federalist Propagandist," *Connecticut Historical Society Bulletin* 39, no. 3 (1974): 87–96; Robert J. Imholt, "Timothy Dwight, Federalist Pope of Connecticut," *New England Quarterly* 73, no. 3 (2000): 386–411; Mark D. Kaplanoff, "Religion and Righteousness: A Study of Federalist Rhetoric in the New Hampshire Election of 1800," *Historical New Hampshire* 23 (1968): 3–20; Kevin M. Gannon, "Escaping 'Mr. Jefferson's Plan of Destruction': New England Federalists and the Idea of a Northern Confederacy, 1803–1804," *Journal of the Early Republic* 21 (2001): 413–44. Quote from "Slavery," *New York Daily Advertiser*, March 7, 1820.

30. Mason, *Slavery and Politics*, 42–74; Donald R. Hickey, *The War of 1812: A Forgotten Conflict* (Urbana: University of Illinois Press, 1990), 255–80; Banner, *To the Hartford Convention*; "Amendments to the Constitution Proposed by the Hartford Convention, 1814," Avalon Project: Documents in Law, History, and Diplomacy, Yale Law School, Lillian Goldman Law Library, https://avalon.law.yale.edu/19th_century/hartconv.asp; Edward C. Carter II, "A 'Wild Irishman' under Every Federalist's Bed: Naturalization in Philadelphia, 1789–1806," *Pennsylvania Magazine of History and Biography* 94, no. 3 (1970): 331–46.

31. *Connecticut Courant* (Hartford), February 21, 1815; *Columbian Centinel* (Boston), July 12, 1817; Hickey, *The War of 1812*, 307–9; George Dangerfield, *The Era of Good Feelings* (Chicago: I. R. Dee, 1989); Shaw Livermore Jr., *The Twilight of Federalism: The Disintegration of the Federalist Party, 1815–30* (Princeton, NJ: Princeton University Press, 1962); Joseph F. Stoltz, "'It Taught Our Enemies a Lesson': The Battle of New Orleans and the Republican Destruction of the Federalist Party," *Tennessee Historical Quarterly* 71, no. 2 (2012): 112–27; Troy Bickham, *The Weight of Vengeance: The United States, the British Empire, and the War of 1812* (Oxford: Oxford University Press, 2012), 266–69.

32. On the Republican origins of the Tallmadge Amendment and thus the "Missouri Question," see Riley, *Slavery and the Democratic Conscience*, 199–228; and Hammond, *Slavery, Freedom, and Expansion*, 150–68. For the initial Tallmadge Amendment vote, see the roll-call page for House vote 89, February 16, 1819, https://voteview.com/rollcall/RH0150089 (from *House Journal*, 13:272–73), at the University of California at Los Angeles's Voteview web site, which can reorder congressional votes by state, party, seniority and other variables. Voteview was developed for the political science research explained in Keith T. Poole and Howard Rosenthal, *Congress: A Political-Economic History of Roll Call Voting* (New York: Oxford University Press, 2000). University of Missouri PhD student Jessica Johnson helped compile data on the vote from this and other sources.

33. Quote from Bruce A. Ragsdale and Kathryn Allamong Jacob, eds., *Biographical Directory of the United States Congress, 1774–1989*, Bicentennial Edition (Washington, DC: U.S. Government Printing Office, 1989), 1910. Despite going through its own recent bicentennial, the War of 1812 still does not get its due as a massive

turning point in American history, but we found much to recommend in Nathaniel Millett, "Slavery and the War of 1812," *Tennessee Historical Quarterly* 71, no. 3 (2012): 184–205. Besides those already cited, the works this account draws on include Richard White, *The Middle Ground: Indians, Empires, and Republics in the Great Lakes Region, 1650–1815* (Cambridge, U.K.: Cambridge University Press, 1991); Gregory Evans Dowd, *A Spirited Resistance: The North American Indian Struggle for Unity, 1745–1815* (Baltimore: Johns Hopkins University Press, 1992); J. Leitch Wright Jr., *Britain and the American Frontier, 1783–1815* (Athens: University of Georgia Press, 1975); R. David Edmunds, *The Shawnee Prophet* (Lincoln: University of Nebraska Press, 1983); R. David Edmunds, *Tecumseh and the Quest for Indian Leadership* (New York: HarperCollins, 1984); Bickham, *Weight of Vengeance*; Frank Lawrence Owsley Jr., *Struggle for the Gulf Borderlands: The Creek War and the Battle of New Orleans, 1812–1815* (Gainesville: University Presses of Florida, 1981); Robert M. Owens, *Mr. Jefferson's Hammer: William Henry Harrison and the Origins of American Indian Policy* (Norman: University of Oklahoma Press, 2007); and Reginald Horsman, *The Frontier in the Formative Years, 1783–1815* (Albuquerque: University of New Mexico Press, 1975).

34. On the "First Seminole War," see J. Leitch Wright Jr., *Creeks and Seminoles: The Destruction and Regeneration of the Muscogulge People* (Lincoln: University of Nebraska Press, 1986); David S. Heidler and Jeanne T. Heidler, *Old Hickory's War: Andrew Jackson and the Quest for Empire* (Mechanicsburg, PA: Stackpole Books, 1996); Deborah A. Rosen, *Border Law: The First Seminole War and American Nationhood* (Cambridge, MA: Harvard University Press, 2015); Clavin, *Battle of Negro Fort*; and Nathaniel Millett, "The Radicalism of the First Seminole War and Its Consequences," in *Warring for America: Cultural Contests in the Era of 1812*, ed. Nicole Eustace and Fredrika J. Teute, 164–202 (Chapel Hill: University of North Carolina Press, 2017).

35. Kate L. Gregg, "The War of 1812 on the Missouri Frontier," *Missouri Historical Review* 33, no. 2 (1938–39): 3–22, 184–202, 326–48; O. P. Williams, *History of Howard and Cooper Counties, Missouri* (St. Louis: National Historical Co., 1883), 116, 165–66, 617–28; Christensen et al., *Dictionary of Missouri Biography*, 198.

36. *Missouri Gazette* (St. Louis), "Hail Columbia!!!," February 18, 1815; St. Charles toasts, July 10, 1818; "Public Lands, No. II," April 28, 1819. On the late burst of fighting at the end of war, see Gregg, "Missouri in the War of 1812," 340–48.

37. Robert Lee, "Accounting for Conquest: The Price of the Louisiana Purchase of Indian Country," *Journal of American History* 104, no. 4 (2017): 921–42.

38. A wonderfully eloquent and incisive old article on this theme is Arthur E. Bestor, "Patent-Office Models of the Good Society: Some Relationships between Social Reform and Westward Expansion," *American Historical Review* 58, no. 3 (1953): 505–26. On community planning in the trans-Appalachian west, see John W. Reps, *Town Planning in Frontier America* (Columbia: University of Missouri Press, 1980); Arthur Bestor, *Backwoods Utopias: The Sectarian Origins and the Owenite Phase of Communitarian Socialism in America, 1663–1829* (Philadelphia: University of Pennsylvania Press, 1970); and Richard C. Wade, *The Urban Frontier: Pioneer Life in Early Pittsburgh, Cincinnati, Lexington, Louisville, and St. Louis* (Chicago: University of Chicago Press, 1967), among many others.

39. For accounts of the New England westward migration, and some of the efforts to control and guide it, see Stewart H. Holbrook, *The Yankee Exodus: An Account of the Migration from New England* (New York: Macmillan, 1960); Gerald McFarland, *A Scattered People: An American Family Moves West* (New York: Pantheon, 1985); and Ray Allen Billington, *The Protestant Crusade, 1800–1860: A Study of the Origins of American Nativism* (Chicago: Quadrangle Books, 1964). For the ACS, see Burin, *Slavery and the Peculiar Solution*; and Tomek and Hetrick, *New Directions*.

40. John Stokely to James Monroe, February 20, 1815, M179, Roll 31, Miscellaneous Letters of the Department of State, 1789–1906, Letters Received, Record Group 59, General Records of the Department of State, National Archives (reference courtesy of John Craig Hammond); Millett, "Slavery and the War of 1812"; Hammond, "President, Planter, Politician"; Alan Taylor, *The Internal Enemy: Slavery and War in Virginia, 1772–1832* (New York: W. W. Norton, 2014); Gene Allen Smith, *The Slaves' Gamble: Choosing Sides in the War of 1812* (New York: St. Martin's, 2013).

41. Historians once agreed that an outpouring of nationalism followed the War of 1812. However, Alan Taylor, in "Dual Nationalisms: Legacies of the War of 1812," in *What So Proudly We Hailed: Essays on the Contemporary Meaning of the War of 1812*, ed. Pietro S. Nivola and Peter J. Kastor (Washington, DC: Brookings Institution Press, 2012), and *Internal Enemy*, 395–98, argues that nationalism was confined mainly to the North and the West.

42. Jesse Torrey, *A Portraiture of Domestic Slavery, in the United States* (Philadelphia: published by the author; John Bioren, 1817), 36–40; Rev. George Bourne to A. B. Davidson, August 10, 1815, "Negro Slavery, and Presbyterians in Virginia," in *The Philanthropist; or, Repository for Hints and Suggestions Calculated to Promote the Comfort and Happiness of Man* (London, 1816), 6:338–40; Thomas D. Morris, *Free Men All: The Personal Liberty Laws of the North, 1780–1861* (reprint; Clark, NJ: Lawbook Exchange, 2001), 33–34; Mason, *Slavery and Politics*, 131–45. On the war as a test of republican ideology, see Roger H. Brown, *The Republic in Peril: 1812* (New York: W. W. Norton, 1971); and Drew R. McCoy, *The Elusive Republic: Political Economy in Jeffersonian America* (New York: W. W. Norton, 1982). For northern Republicans' defense of the Tallmadge Amendments as a vindication of republican government and ideology, see Hammond, *Slavery, Freedom, and Expansion*, 150–68.

43. Tallmadge's speech reported in "From Our Correspondent at Washington," *Alexandria (VA) Gazette*, November 25, 1818. It does not appear in the reports of debates in the *Annals of Congress*, which were largely copied from the pages of the semiofficial administration spokespaper, the *National Intelligencer*. On the Illinois "French slavery" that Tallmadge was complaining about, see M. Scott Heerman, "In a State of Slavery: Black Servitude in Illinois, 1800–1830," *Early American Studies* 14, no. 1 (2016): 114–39.

44. Mason, *Slavery and Politics*, 130–45; Hammond, *Slavery, Freedom, and Expansion*, 152–54; James J. Gigantino II, *The Ragged Road to Abolition: Slavery and Freedom in New Jersey, 1775–1865* (Philadelphia: University of Pennsylvania Press, 2014), 155–67; Carl E. Prince, "James J. Wilson: Party Leader, 1801–1824," *Proceedings of the New Jersey Historical Society* 83 (January 1965): 24–39; Pasley, *"Tyranny of*

Printers," 320–29. Quote from "Negro Trading and Kidnapping," *Trenton (NJ) Federalist* (reprinting *True American*), September 14, 1818.

45. Richard Bell, *Stolen: Five Free Boys Kidnapped into Slavery and Their Astonishing Odyssey Home* (New York: 37 Ink, 2019), 1–9; Polgar, *Standard-Bearers of Equality*, 280–86; Gigantino, *Ragged Road*, 167–70.

46. "Kidnapping," *National Advocate*, June 28, 1817; *Orange County Patriot* (Goshen, NY), July 4, 1817. On Noah, see Jonathan D. Sarna, *Jacksonian Jew: The Two Worlds of Mordecai Noah* (New York: Holmes & Meier, 1981).

47. "Woolman," *American Watchman* (Wilmington, DE), January 1, 1817. On Osborn, see Willa G. Cramton, "Selleck Osborn: A Republican Editor in Wilmington, Delaware, 1816–1822," *Delaware History* 12 (April 1967): 198–217; Selleck Osborn, *Poems, Moral, Sentimental, and Satirical* (Boston: John P. Orcutt, 1823).

48. Nicholas Wood, "John Randolph of Roanoke and the Politics of Slavery in the Early Republic," *Virginia Magazine of History and Biography* 120, no. 2 (2012): 106–43; Morris, *Free Men All*, 33–41.

49. For just a taste of some of the conflicts, see George Dangerfield, *The Awakening of American Nationalism, 1815–1828*, New American Nation Series (New York: Harper & Row, 1965); Richard J. Purcell, *Connecticut in Transition, 1775–1818* (Middletown, CT: Wesleyan University Press, 1963); and Alan W. Brownsword, "The Constitution of 1818 and Political Afterthoughts, 1800–1840," *Connecticut Historical Society Bulletin* 30, no. 1 (1963): 1–10.

50. Charles O. Paullin, *Atlas of the Historical Geography of the United States*, ed. John K. Wright (Washington, DC, and New York: Carnegie Institution of Washington and the American Geographical Society of New York, 1932), 89; Alexander Keyssar, *The Right to Vote: The Contested History of Democracy in the United States* (New York: Basic Books, 2000), tables A3 and A5.

51. Donald B. Cole, *Jacksonian Democracy in New Hampshire, 1800–1851* (Cambridge, MA: Harvard University Press, 1970), 30–41; John S. Whitehead, *The Separation of College and State: Columbia, Dartmouth, Harvard, and Yale, 1776–1876* (New Haven, CT: Yale University Press, 1973); Eldon L. Johnson, "The Dartmouth College Case: The Neglected Educational Meaning," *Journal of the Early Republic* 3, no. 1 (1983): 45–67; Francis N. Stites, *Private Interest & Public Gain: The Dartmouth College Case, 1819* (Amherst: University of Massachusetts Press, 1972).

52. Kim T. Phillips, "Democrats of the Old School in the Era of Good Feelings," *Pennsylvania Magazine of History and Biography* 95 (July 1971): 363–68; Charles Sellers, *The Market Revolution: Jacksonian America, 1815–1846* (New York: Oxford University Press, 1991), 34–136; Andrew Shankman, *Crucible of American Democracy: The Struggle to Fuse Egalitarianism and Capitalism in Jeffersonian Pennsylvania* (Lawrence: University Press of Kansas, 2004); C. Edward Skeen, *1816: America Rising* (Lexington: University Press of Kentucky, 2003); Andrew H. Browning, *The Panic of 1819: The First Great Depression* (Columbia: University of Missouri Press, 2019); Donald B. Cole, *A Jackson Man: Amos Kendall and the Rise of American*

Democracy, Southern Biography Series (Baton Rouge: Louisiana State University Press, 2004), chaps. 4–7; Daniel Peart, *Era of Experimentation: American Political Practices in the Early Republic* (Charlottesville : University of Virginia Press, 2014).

53. John Sloane to Benjamin Tappan, March 29, 1820, Benjamin Tappan Papers, Library of Congress (quote courtesy of John Craig Hammond); Catherine Allgor, *Parlor Politics: In Which the Ladies of Washington Help Build a City and a Government* (Charlottesville: University Press of Virginia, 2000); Aleine Austin, *Matthew Lyon: "New Man" of the Democratic Revolution, 1749–1822* (University Park: Pennsylvania State University Press, 1981). On the Fourteenth Congress and the Compensation Act imbroglio, see Sellers, *Market Revolution*, 69–81; Pasley, *"Tyranny of Printers,"* 359–61; Edward K. Spann, "John W. Taylor, the Reluctant Partisan, 1784–1854" (PhD diss., New York University, 1957), 133–36; and especially C. Edward Skeen, "Vox Populi, Vox Dei: The Compensation Act of 1816 and the Rise of Popular Politics," *Journal of the Early Republic* 6 (1986): 253–74.

54. "Protest," *North-Carolina Star* (Raleigh), May 17, 1816; "To the Members of Congress, Who Voted for the SALARY BILL," reprinted in *American Watchman* (Wilmington, DE), August 28, 1816; "Short Questions and Plain Answers," *Poughkeepsie (NY) Journal*, April 24, 1816.

55. *True American* (Trenton, NJ), reprinted in *Vermont Gazette* (Bennington), September 17, 1816; "Voice of Warren County," "Excitability," and "Compensation of Congress," *Columbian* (New York), June 22, October 4 and 16, 1816; "New Brooms Sweep Clean," *Alexandria (VA) Gazette*, November 29, 1817; Skeen, "Vox Populi," 260–61. On the controversy over nominations by caucus, see Douglas E. Bowers, "From Caucus to Convention in Pennsylvania Politics, 1790–1830," *Pennsylvania History: A Journal of Mid-Atlantic Studies* 56, no. 4 (1989): 276–98; and Moisei Ostrogorski, "The Rise and Fall of the Nominating Caucus, Legislative and Congressional," *American Historical Review* 5, no. 2 (1899): 253–83.

56. *National Intelligencer and Washington Advertiser*, June 13, 1816.

57. "Compensation Bill," *Columbian* (New York), June 14, 1816; "From the Albany Register: VOICE OF THE PEOPLE," *Lancaster (PA) Intelligencer*, October 19, 1816; Chester County meeting, *Lancaster (PA) Intelligencer*, August 17, 1816; Michael J. Dubin, *United States Congressional Elections, 1788–1997: The Official Results* (Jefferson, NC: McFarland, 1998), 56, 62.

58. Spann, "John W. Taylor," 133–34; "Fifteenth Congress," *Niles' Weekly Register* 13 (December 20, 1817): 264–65; Skeen, "Vox Populi"; Thomas Jefferson to Albert Gallatin, May 18, 1816, and [before June 6, 1817], Founders Online, https://founders.archives.gov/documents/Jefferson/03-10-02-0036 & https://founders.archives.gov/documents/Jefferson/03-11-02-0341.

59. This moment in New England's history is not very well covered in the historical literature, with the grand exception of Cole, *Jacksonian Democracy in New Hampshire*, chap. 2. National political history in the United States is always best understood by aggregating state and local political histories as our system does, yet few historians bother with this sometimes bewildering task. See also Livermore,

Twilight of Federalism, 27–87, for the era from the viewpoint of the most depressed Federalists.

60. Cyrus Parker Bradley, *Biography of Isaac Hill, of New-Hampshire* (Concord, NH: J. F. Brown, 1835), 45–46; *New Hampshire Patriot* (Concord), October 1, 15, 22, 29 (quoted), November 2, 12, 1816; Cole, *Jacksonian Democracy in New Hampshire*, 29–31.

61. *New Hampshire Patriot* (Concord), October 15, 1816.

62. Sanford W. Higginbotham, *The Keystone in the Democratic Arch: Pennsylvania Politics, 1800–1816* (Harrisburg: Pennsylvania Historical and Museum Commission, 1952), 308–23; Philip Shriver Klein, *Pennsylvania Politics, 1817–1832: A Game without Rules* (Philadelphia: Historical Society of Pennsylvania, 1940), 42–96; "New Brooms Sweep Clean," *Alexandria (VA) Gazette*, November 29, 1817.

63. "Fifteenth Congress," *Niles' Weekly Register* 13 (December 20, 1817): 264–65; Skeen, "Vox Populi"; "New Brooms Sweep Clean," *Alexandria (VA) Gazette*, November 29, 1817.

64. Skeen, "Vox Populi"; Sellers, *Market Revolution*, 104–7; Pasley, *"Tyranny of Printers,"* 361–63. Facts and statistics on the Fifteenth Congress can be found in Dubin, *United States Congressional Elections*, 58–63, upgraded with the author's own tabulations.

65. Salma Hale to Thomas Jefferson, July 13, 1818, Hale to Arthur Livermore, May 16, 1818, Hale to William Plumer, May 8, 1818, and Hale's notes on his visit to Monticello [after 1818], available at "Salma Hale's Visit to Monticello," Founders Online, https://founders.archives.gov/ancestor/TSJN-03-13-02-0015; "Salma Hale Papers," *Proceedings of the Massachusetts Historical Society* 46 (1912): 401–9; Robert Safford Hale and George Rogers Howell, *Genealogy of Descendants of Thomas Hale of Walton, England, and of Newbury, Mass.* (Albany, NY: Weed, Parsons, 1889), 367–69.

66. Charles Henry Bell, *The Bench and Bar of New Hampshire* (Boston: Houghton Mifflin, 1893), 71–72, 55–58; *Concord (NH) Gazette*, September 17, 1816; *People's Advocate* (Portsmouth (NH), October 5, 29, 1816.

67. William Coleman Folger, *Memoir of the Late Hon. Walter Folger* (New Bedford, MA: Fessenden & Baker, 1874); William Edward Gardner, *The Clock That Talks and What It Tells; A Portrait Story of the Maker: Hon. Walter Folger, Jr., Astronomer, Mathematician, Navigator, Lawyer, Judge, Legislator, Congressman, Philosopher, but He Called Himself: Clock and Watchmaker* (Nantucket, MA: Whaling Museum, 1954).

68. Leona Rostenberg, ed., "Diary of Timothy Fuller: In Congress, January 12–March 15, 1818," *New England Quarterly* 12, no. 3 (1939): 521–29; Charles Capper, *Margaret Fuller: An American Romantic Life* (New York: Oxford University Press, 1992), 1:8–15.

69. Josiah F. Goodhue, *History of the Town of Shoreham, Vermont: From the Date of Its Charter, October 8th, 1761, to the Present Time*, History of Shoreham (Middlebury, VT: A. H. Copeland, 1861), 61–64, 125–28; Walter Hill Crockett, *Vermont: The Green Mountain State* (New York: Century History, 1921), 3:134–40; Morris, *Free Men All*, 33–41; Margo Anderson, "The Missouri Debates, Slavery and Statistics of

Race: Demography in Service of Politics," *Annales de Demographie Historique*, no. 1 (February 2003): 23–38.

70. J. Kevin Graffagnino, "'I Saw the Ruin All Around' and 'A Comical Spot You May Depend': Orsamus C. Merrill, Rollin C. Mallary and the Disputed Election of 1818," *Vermont History* 49, no. 3 (1981): 159–68.

71. Rostenberg, "Diary of Timothy Fuller," 523; Mary Ellen Hessel, "The Quiet Virtues of Samuel Chandler Crafts," *Vermont History* 30 (October 1962): 259–90; François André Michaux, *Travels to the Westward of the Allegany Mountains, in the States of the Ohio, Kentucky, and Tennessee, in the Year 1802* (London: printed for R. Phillips, 1805), 34–50.

72. Rostenberg, "Diary of Timothy Fuller," 521–29; Riley, *Slavery and the Democratic Conscience*, 221. For Fuller's nonspeech as recorded, see *Annals of Congress*, 15th Cong. 1st sess., House, January 28, 1818, 828.

73. "Printers, Editors, and Publishers in the U.S. Congress, 1789-1861," 2001–7, http://pasleybrothers.com/newspols/congress.htm; Milton W. Hamilton, *The Country Printer: New York State, 1785-1830*, 2nd ed. (New York: Columbia University Press, 1964), 111.

74. William J. Heller, *History of Northampton County [Pennsylvania] and the Grand Valley of the Lehigh* (New York: American Historical Society, 1920), 1:290–91; Jeffrey L. Pasley, "From Print Shop to Congress and Back: Easton's Thomas J. Rogers and the Rise of Newspaper Politics," in *Backcountry Crucibles: The Lehigh Valley from Settlement to Steel*, ed. Jean R. Soderlund and Catherine S. Parzynski, 227–54 (Bethlehem, PA: Lehigh University Press, 2008).

75. Riley, *Slavery and the Democratic Conscience*, 175–77, 180, 196, 222–23; Pasley, *Tyranny of Printers*, 329–41; Raymond W. Champagne and Thomas J. Rueter, "Jonathan Roberts and the 'War Hawk' Congress of 1811–1812," *Pennsylvania Magazine of History and Biography* 104, no. 4 (1980): 434–49.

76. Daniel M. Bates, *Memorial Address on the Life and Character of Willard Hall* (Wilmington: Historical Society of Delaware, 1879), 47 (quote); John A. Munroe, *Federalist Delaware, 1775-1815* (New Brunswick, NJ: Rutgers University Press, 1954), 215–20; *American Watchman* (Wilmington, DE), May 16, 1812. Thanks to ace undergraduate historian Owen Pasley for his research assistance in the matter of Willard Hall.

77. Riley, *Slavery and the Democratic Conscience*, 204–8.

78. Calculated using the roll-call page for House vote 89, February 16, 1819, ordered by seniority, https://voteview.com/rollcall/RH0150089.

PART II

STATE, SECTIONAL, AND POLITICAL POWER
IN THE MISSOURI CRISIS

4. Border Control

Slavery, Diffusion, and State Formation in the Era of the Missouri Crisis

Christa Dierksheide

In 1813, SETTLERS in the Missouri Territory had already identified the "peculiar" kind of slavery that would later be codified in the state's 1820 constitution. George Sibley, an Indian agent appointed as the factor at Fort Osage, distinguished between the droves of slaves who populated the vast cotton and sugar plantations of Lower Louisiana and the minority slave population who labored on smaller farms in Missouri. For Sibley, the "great number of Slaves" owned by a white minority on the banks of the lower Mississippi River was a ticking time bomb. These gangs of bondspeople, he warned, were merely waiting for a "safe opportunity to cut the throats of their masters." But in Missouri, Sibley declared, "we have but few slaves," who were "all well fed & clothed & kindly treated." The result, he mused, holding up his own slave, George, as an example, was that enslaved people were more "faithful, industrious and attentive" in Missouri. While slave-grown hemp and tobacco might not "amass great wealth" in Missouri, Sibley asserted that there were clear advantages to not being a sugar baron. In his telling, a domesticated slave regime and a minority slave population rendered life as a slave owner in Missouri "easy, comfortable and happy." Seven years later, when Missouri legislators met at the Mansion House hotel in St. Louis to draft the state's first constitution in only thirty-eight days, Sibley's observations were translated into law, granting the new general assembly the authority to "oblige the owners of slaves to treat them with humanity." At the same time, legislators were also empowered to regulate slave immigration into the state.[1]

Sibley's treatise—echoed by many other Missouri slaveholders—as well as the state constitution of 1820 suggest that the most pressing issue among white Missourians was not whether slavery would be a permitted in the territory and later state, but how to create security for slavery in a volatile borderland on the western periphery of the United States. For many lawmakers and slave owners in the early nineteenth century, an important part of the answer was a domesticated slave regime. Domestication—the inclusion, and subsequent invisibility, of slaves within masters' households—was an effort to mitigate slavery's violent edge and transform captives from "foreign" threats to U.S. white supremacy into "happy" and submissive members of plantation "families." It also meant changing what had been a British, French, or Spanish system into a national "peculiar institution" within the postcolonial United States. To these ends, owners of enslaved men and women reasoned that improving the material conditions of slavery—allotting slaves adequate shelter, food, and clothing as well as abstaining from corporal punishment— would make them less likely to revolt. Moreover, the implementation of supposedly humanitarian principles on farms and plantations by individuals diverted attention from the power allocated to the Missouri legislature to ensure that a particular kind of slave system was created within Missouri's borders. But in reality, the general assembly—like the federal government before it—was given broad powers to exert control over immigration. From 1820, the Missouri legislature maintained the power to regulate the Black persons who entered its borders, barring those "types" of enslaved or free Black people whom it considered likely to incite rebellion. As such, even before slaves arrived with their owners to labor at farms and plantations under the so-called benevolent regimes of planters, the state would have managed the lion's share of the domestication project by keeping rebellious or "foreign" slaves outside of Missouri. Thus, the "improvement" that slaveholders imagined themselves deploying on individual landholdings was in fact facilitated by state and federal power that remained largely invisible to them.[2]

The creation of a domesticated slave regime in Missouri dovetailed with other federal—and later state—government projects aimed at including the newly acquired Northwest, Mississippi, and Louisiana Territories within the American federal Union. One U.S. official in Louisiana neatly summarized the aims of the federal government in areas largely populated by Spanish and French settlers and Native tribes: "The American population must be increased" so as to "overbalance that of every other description of persons. The character, the manners, the language of the country must become American if we wish the government to be such." To accomplish this goal, federal officials attempted to impose population control in the new territories, aiming to channel settlers into specific areas to increase population density. Because the U.S. state lacked a strong military, it developed innovative ways of controlling and directing settlement, seeing densely populated areas as the key to security and defense, especially in southwestern borderlands. Soon after the Louisiana Purchase of 1803, President Thomas Jefferson outlined his vision for settlement on both sides of the Mississippi River. "The best use we can make of the country for some time," Jefferson wrote of Louisiana, would be to "give" it to eastern Native American tribes in order to incentivize "removal," thus allowing white settlers "the means of filling up the Eastern side" of the Mississippi. But, Jefferson promised, "when we shall be full on this side"—the East—"we may lay off a range of States on the Western bank from the head to the mouth, and so, range after range, advancing compactly as we multiply." In the 1790s and early 1800s, both Federalists and Republicans hewed to the same playbook in incorporating America's 1783 borders: federal policies designed to mobilize and direct the movement of settlers in order to enable an otherwise "weak" state to assert sovereignty over vast swaths of territory. The intended result was the increased capacity of the American state to impose coercive power over unstable regions while also creating increasingly domesticated populations suitable for future admission into the federal Union.[3]

Although the federal government wanted to use its power to create "compact" white settlements, it sought to exert control over African Americans to achieve the opposite outcome: dispersing their numbers across the Union's newly immense geographic space. The state's goal of domestication hinged on its ability to engineer racial geography, not just in the West but also in the East. The specter of the slave rebellion in Saint-Domingue in 1791 and the creation of the independent Haitian Republic in 1804 created a visceral link between slave demography and violence. In the minds of many U.S. planters and lawmakers, Black majority areas, such as the Caribbean sugar islands, Lowcountry rice plantations, and Louisiana sugar estates, created an ideal environment for conspiracies and revolts. In the West, without the imposition of federal power to control settlement, policy makers worried that settlers in new southern territories—especially former French Louisiana—might simply replicate (or preserve) Black majority areas and become incubators of slave violence and instability. But federal oversight of slavery in the West also gave the state an opening to regulate it in the East. From the 1790s, planters and politicians in eastern slave states, particularly Virginia, feared that a rapidly rising, self-reproducing slave population would soon render whites a vulnerable minority. In Virginia, for example, the enslaved population skyrocketed in the last decade of the eighteenth century—from 292,627 in 1790 to 346,671 in 1800. This surging population meant that slaves increasingly appeared to be an "internal enemy" to planters, as historian Alan Taylor has suggested. Meanwhile, Thomas Jefferson hoped that slave owners, fearing the "bloody process of St. Domingo," would preemptively "repatriate" their human chattel to Africa in order to avoid slaughter and destruction at the hands of rebellious slaves. But instead, the acquisition of the Mississippi and Louisiana Territories at this time offered an alternative solution—diffusion of slaves west under the oversight of the federal government. As one Virginian wrote to James Monroe, diffusion would prevent whites in eastern states from being "dammed up in a land of slaves." Although Upper South slave populations were substantial, lawmakers reasoned that large new landholdings in Mississippi and Louisiana would allow "room enough" to disperse slave populations.[4]

Diffusing slavery westward as a potential solution to eastern slave demographics and instability and violence in the West has not attracted much scholarly attention. Often dismissed as an impractical pipe dream or a proslavery sham, diffusion has been deemed an insincere or insignificant solution to the "problem" of slavery in the early republic. Part of historians' issue with diffusion stems from the fact that it doesn't seem to sit squarely in either the proslavery or the antislavery camp. This is true—many Upper South slave owners and congressional leaders embraced diffusion as a step toward abolition, particularly between 1790 and 1810. On the other hand, a large number of politicians and slave masters endorsed diffusion as a means of extending and perpetuating slavery in both the East and the West. Like African colonization, diffusion was elastic enough to garner appeal from a wide range of Americans—especially in the North and Upper South—precisely because it could result in two different outcomes: abolition or slavery's expansion and amelioration. Antislavery diffusion, advocated by northern Federalists and Upper South Republicans, was premised on the idea that a static slave population (at least after abolition of the Atlantic slave trade in 1808) should be spread out, thus alleviating the threat of race war and turning the tide of public opinion toward antislavery. On the other hand, proslavery diffusion, advocated by many Deep South Republicans, was rooted in the assumption that a self-regenerating slave population could be directed westward, thus solving the issue of rising slave populations in the Upper South while also supplying captive laborers to eager planters in the new Louisiana and Mississippi Territories. But the key to diffusion wasn't its murky proslavery or antislavery outcome, but rather its emphasis on *who* diffused slaves westward. According to contemporaries, diffusion was *not* synonymous with the internal slave trade; it was characterized by a master bringing his own slave property into new territories or states.[5] Historian Adam Rothman has suggested that the dichotomy between the internal slave trade and diffusion was a false one, since it depended on a "proslavery worldview that distinguished between slave selling and slaveholding." But this distinction was untenable, since it "evaded a basic reality of chattel slavery—that slaveholding required slave selling." As a result, Rothman asserts, the distinction collapsed, and by 1820 the internal slave trade was firmly "domesticated" and included within a national slave regime. Yet many state and federal lawmakers were much more concerned about the security risk posed by the internal slave trade than by its challenge to the "proslavery argument." Diffusion generated broad appeal because it necessitated regulating slave migration by federal or state governments as a means to create and impose borders—and reduce security threats—in contested borderland regions.[6]

Adopted as federal policy in Mississippi and Louisiana, diffusion was far from a pipe dream. It offered a compelling and pragmatic strategy to regulate slave populations and control borders in the territories. Seeking to copy this policy, new legislatures in the South and West integrated what had been federal law into their new state constitutions between 1790 and 1840. While historians have often evaluated these constitutional provisions as "antislavery" or "proslavery," these laws instead reflected slaveholders' desire to control slavery at the state level. Indeed, after admission to the Union, several states adopted their own population-control measures, empowering legislatures to regulate what kind of settlers—including what kind of slaves—crossed their borders. Beginning in 1792, legislatures in Kentucky, Mississippi, Alabama, and Missouri all passed new constitutions that sought to encourage the immigration of individual slaveholders and their human chattel while prohibiting slave dealers, rebellious slaves, and foreign slaves from entering their states. Moreover, all of these legislatures maintained the authority to "compel" those slave owners admitted for settlement to treat their bondspeople with "humanity." The state assemblies' power to regulate and ameliorate slavery was a state-level corollary to the domestication project begun at the federal level in the territories decades before.[7] Though historians' analyses of the Missouri Crisis have largely focused on sectional politics in Congress or the pro- and antirestrictionism unleashed in the North and South after 1819, this chapter frames the issue differently. It argues that the challenge facing white Missourians was not whether slavery would exist in the new state, but *what kind* of slavery would exist there. Seeking to avoid slave revolts and other destabilizing violence, planters and lawmakers envisioned a domesticated slave regime in Missouri that bore little resemblance to the labor system found on Deep South cotton and sugar plantations or free-labor farms in the Northwest. To accomplish this goal, Missouri elites adapted and retooled the federal policy of "diffusion" to the state level. After Missouri entered the federal Union in 1820, proslavery Missourians endorsed constitutionally sanctioned border-control policies that would regulate the diffusion of slaves into the state.[8]

Missouri's plan to heavily regulate what kind of enslaved people—and how many—passed through the state's borders after 1820 originated decades earlier. Beginning in the 1790s, the federal government embraced various diffusion policies in new western territories in an attempt to control—and even weaken—slave populations. Still, the diffusion policies were only one part of the main goal—and challenge—for Congress: how to secure the Mississippi and Louisiana Territories and bring them more squarely under U.S. influence and control. Given that these new western outposts were highly unstable areas predominantly peopled by French, Spanish, and British settlers, under near-constant threats of violence from hostile Indian tribes or rebellious slaves, highly coveted by rival European imperial powers, and subject to would-be western secessionists like Aaron Burr, lawmakers from both political parties asserted that stability was paramount. To secure the region from threats from without—and within—congressional leaders sought to craft laws that would facilitate the migration of thousands of U.S. farmers, traders, and planters to the Gulf Coast and the Missouri River valley. The creation and defense of newly implemented U.S. borders depended not on the presence of a strong army but on the dense population of "domesticated" settlers.[9]

Diffusion also appealed to congressional leaders because it satisfied both proslavery and antislavery agendas, at least until the 1810s. Proslavery lawmakers supported the extension of slavery westward as well as its permanent presence in the new plantation societies of the Gulf South. The only debate among these proslavery partisans was how much—if any—federal oversight was needed for the immigration of settlers and slaves into the Louisiana and Mississippi Territories. But diffusion also appealed to politicians who hoped to end slavery gradually. While expanding slavery to end it appeared paradoxical, Jefferson explained the logic. Spreading out the population of slaves across the "empty space" of the West would replicate demographic conditions found in postrevolutionary New England where a series of gradual abolition laws had been enacted after the American Revolution. As Jefferson declared to British reformer Richard Price in 1785, "Northward of the Chesapeak," there "being but few slaves," the masters can "easily disencumber themselves of them, and emancipation is put into such a train that in a few years there will be no slaves Northward of Maryland." With fewer slaves in Mississippi and Louisiana and the threat of slave revolt reduced, Jefferson and other antislavery diffusionists predicted that masters would consent to free their slaves. But the logic behind an antislavery outcome of diffusion rested on the assumption that the U.S. slave population would remain static—particularly after Congress outlawed the transatlantic slave trade in 1808.[10]

Still, pro- or antislavery outcomes were less important than imposing U.S. sovereignty in the territories. During congressional debates over the organization of the Mississippi Territory in the 1790s, lawmakers sought to transform a violent borderland into a domesticated federal territory. While Spain ceded land above Spanish Florida to the United States through the Treaty of San Lorenzo in 1795, it was up to congressional leaders to impose sovereignty over a region bounded by the Mississippi and Chattahoochee Rivers to the west and east, the thirty-first parallel to the south, and the confluence of the Yazoo and Mississippi to the south. This was no easy task, given that France, Britain, and Spain had all issued competing land grants in the region, Native peoples there were hostile to U.S. expansion, and Spanish officials in West Florida and Louisiana posed a security threat to the new territory. Still, many lawmakers viewed federally regulated diffusion as a means to stabilize and secure the area. A few dissenters, led by Republican Albert Gallatin of Pennsylvania, Federalist George Thacher of Massachusetts, and Republican Joseph Varnum of Massachusetts, rallied for an outright ban on slavery in the new territory, arguing that it was a moral evil that violated natural rights. But diffusionists countered that their plan was actually more moral, since it would result in greater security for whites in addition to slaves' amelioration. Virginia Republicans, including William Giles and John Nicholas, supported the spread of slavery from the Old Dominion to Mississippi. "If slaves of the Southern States were permitted to go into the Western country, by lessening the number in those States, and spreading them over a large surface of country, there would be a great probability in ameliorating their condition, which could never be done whilst they were crowded together as they now are," Giles asserted. But even if Republicans and Federalists supported the introduction of slaves into Mississippi, they also advocated stringent regulations. In the end, Congress passed legislation that prohibited the introduction of enslaved people who originated from "foreign" territories—such as New Spain or the French Caribbean. Anyone who violated the law would be fined and their slaves manumitted. The hope was that this restriction would cordon off Mississippi from potentially incendiary foreign influences as well as lay a foundation for a more domesticated slave regime.[11]

After the Louisiana Purchase of 1803, congressional leaders again debated the efficacy of diffusion in the enormous new territory west of the Mississippi River. With U.S. control of the former French colony tenuous at best, policy makers hoped to deploy the state's regulatory power to prevent slave rebellions from being unleashed there. John Watkins, the mayor of New Orleans, lamented the weakness of the U.S. military "scattered over such an extensive country." Under normal circumstances, Watkins opposed strong military force, but in sparsely settled Louisiana, he decreed that "we are in a country of Slaves," with a sizable free Black population augmenting the threat. In the absence of military protection, the only way to lessen that danger was to increase the white population, Watkins argued, or outlaw the importation of fresh captives from Africa or the Caribbean. As Kentucky Republican John Breckinridge warned, "Unless we mean to aid the destruction of our Southern states, by laying the foundation for another St. Domingo," then the importation of "foreign" slaves into Louisiana must be banned. The fear of slave revolts was so great that congressional leaders—including southern lawmakers—also voted against the domestic slave trade, seeking to prevent slave dealers from selling human beings to eager Louisiana buyers. James Hilhouse, a Federalist senator from Connecticut, proposed an antislavery diffusion plan: any adult slave carried by an American into Louisiana would be emancipated after one year, with younger slaves receiving their freedom when they came of age. Hilhouse's motion, reminiscent of the gradual emancipation codified in the Northwest Ordinance more than a decade earlier, was defeated by senators from both parties. Instead, a majority of lawmakers supported a "bona fide" settler restriction of the diffusion of slavery into Louisiana. Under this proposal—the most important innovation of the debates—slaves could be introduced into Louisiana only by their owners. The finalized version of the law allowed a "citizen of the United States, removing into said Territory for actual settlement, and being, at the time of such removal, *bona fide* owner of such slave or slaves." The "bona fide" law introduced a typology into federal policy. The ideal settler in Louisiana was not a Spaniard or a Frenchman or a slave seller, but rather a white slave-owning American. Federal regulation of immigration into Louisiana would, congressional leaders hoped, result in the introduction of thousands of "bone fide" settlers who would domesticate the new Louisiana Territory and harden borders between the United States, Native peoples, and the Spanish Empire.[12]

But the congressional attempt to regulate the diffusion of slaves into Louisiana ultimately failed. Facing an onslaught of petitions from proslavery

American and French settlers, particularly from New Orleans, Congress soon caved and repealed its earlier prescriptions for the territory. Still, it seemed plausible to some federal lawmakers that Upper Louisiana, which was attached to the Indiana Territory in 1804 and claimed considerable landholdings too far north to cultivate either sugar or cotton, might not need slavery. Moreover, a slave rebellion in the Orleans Territory in 1811 and the outbreak of war with Britain in 1812 underscored the security threat posed by slavery in the western borderlands, prompting several congressional leaders to propose bills that would bar slaves from Upper Louisiana. Yet migrants to Upper Louisiana resisted calls to restrict slavery, fearing that such proposals gestured toward gradual abolition. Settlers were particularly anxious about Congress's decision to annex Upper Louisiana to Indiana, a territory where slavery was prohibited. Even if Upper Louisiana was not cotton country, slavery, land speculation, and settlement were already firmly intertwined in a vast swath of land that stretched from the Mississippi River north to Canada and west to the Rockies. In 1809, land hunter William Carr reported from St. Louis that the "day is now close at hand when a fortune may be made by the purchase of lands on Louisiana." Carr was keen to buy cheap, newly available federal lands that could be had for anything from fifty cents to two dollars per acre. To do this, he "bought two negro fellows," one of which he sold again "directly for one of those land warrants issued by the late Secretary of War to the followers of Lewis & Clark for 320 acres each." As Carr's transaction suggests, slaves were not simply being brought to Upper Louisiana to cultivate recently settled land; they were also brought there in order to be sold or exchanged for land as part of a "brisk change of property." Indeed, according to Carr, the "introduction of the American government here" brought "into circulation a considerable quantity of cash" that increased the "commerce of the country," including land and slave sales. In Carr's telling, slavery was an important part of the commercial enterprise that would domesticate Upper Louisiana and bind it more tightly to the federal Union. Upper Louisiana migrants demanded that Congress allow them to retain slaves already in the territory and the ability to import new ones, though they accepted a ban on the international slave trade. Virtually powerless to enforce any restriction of slavery in the West, Congress had little choice but to comply with settlers' demands.[13]

In 1812, when Upper Louisiana advanced to the second stage of territorial government, slavery went unmentioned in the territorial ordinance. Indeed, from 1805 until Missouri statehood in 1820, slavery continued to exist in the territory "only by force of local law and territorial statute." And as Missouri moved closer to statehood, surveyors, speculators, settlers, and slavery poured into the territory, largely without restriction, between 1812 and 1820. The result was a huge population spike, from just over twenty thousand settlers in 1810 to nearly sixty-seven thousand settlers in 1820. A large proportion of these settlers were drawn to the Boon's Lick region along the Missouri River, and many who flocked there did so with their slaves in tow. The draw of cheap and unencumbered property created a "rage for speculating" in Missouri and a chaotic land grab. The speed with which Missouri was settled was unparalleled when compared with lands in another slaveholding federal territory: Mississippi. As late as 1817, when Mississippi was admitted as a new state, surveyors complained that the "settlements are scattered here and there" in an "irregular and unlicensed system." Violence and unrest were commonplace in an area dominated by smugglers, squatters, rumors of falsified land claims, news of foreign intrigues, and the presence of Chickasaw and Choctaw peoples who resisted federal removal. One official doubted that Mississippi could draw enough settlers to allow it to compete with—or become equal to—"the largest sized of the northern, middle, and western States." In contrast, Missouri had attracted a flood of settlers and their slaves, though it may have done so too quickly. By the time Missouri petitioned for statehood, its settlers were struggling to protect themselves— and their slaves—from hostile Indian attacks. Sauk Indians, seeking to resist the tide of white settlers, embarked on slave-stealing expeditions. In 1816, Martin Dorian and Mairice Blondeau testified that "Indians of the Winebago [sic] nation" stole two enslaved men settlers in the Boon's Lick region "with the purpose of carrying them off." When a local militia of "ranchers" gave chase, the Indians "killed said negromen with a tomahawk." Hostile Native tribes, slave stealing, and slave mobility all pointed to the chaos of settlement and the dangers of slavery in the borderlands of Missouri.[14]

Between 1815 and 1819, a picture emerged: tens of thousands of migrants entered the Missouri Territory, keen to purchase land and maintain slaves. An emigrant from New York, Charles Carroll noted that the Missouri River valley "perhaps embraces the finest body of rich land in any country." A "judicious selection" of cheap Missouri lands that went for two dollars per acre, Carroll reckoned, would "double y'r investment every five years." But available federal land was not the only draw for settlers—the navigable Missouri River and the proximity to the commercial hubs of St. Louis and New Orleans made the territory that much more appealing. As a result, the "country is populating rapidly with a respectable yeomanry from Kentucky, Vir'a, M'd, Ten'see & N. Carolina," he added. Although proslavery sentiment increased as this "yeomanry" moved into the territory with their slaves, skeptics questioned the efficacy of slavery there. Some observers wondered how Missouri would survive as a slaveholding state in such close proximity to the sugar barons and cotton kings of the Gulf Coast. George Sibley believed that the restriction of slavery would make Missouri the "happiest state in the West," rather than a "mere colony of the Southern States." Moreover, Missouri held little appeal to migrants who wanted to plant cotton. Recent Virginian transplant Joseph Gill planned to move to Texas or Arkansas because "I would by far prefer a warm country" where "we can raise cotton." Other Missourians opposed "any more negroes being brought to this country" because they competed with—and undermined—free labor in Missouri. "I am a farmer and get my living by the sweat of my brow and I expect my Children to get theirs the same way," settler David Murphy wrote, adding that "I am a friend of the Industrious and honest poor man." Still, by the time of the Missouri Crisis, the attitude of most migrants in Missouri was firmly proslavery. The "vast majority of voters," George Tompkins, a future justice of the Missouri Supreme Court, declared from "Little Dixie," supported the preservation of slavery in Missouri. He warned that "no man will be elected" unless "he declare himself for slavery & perhaps it will require a property in slaves to qualify him in the eyes of the people." But even proslavery Missourians understood the continued security risk that slavery posed to a fledgling state.[15]

Until the Missouri Crisis, diffusion accommodated a range of political interests—those who wanted to see slavery expanded and entrenched and those who wanted to abolish it. But because the Missouri Question fundamentally altered the slavery issue, transforming it from a problem in the West to a crisis that carved a "geographical line" between North and South, so too did diffusion take on a decidedly different—and more proslavery—valence. By 1820, Jefferson was perhaps one of the few remaining exponents of antislavery diffusion. Spreading slaves into Missouri in the midst of the crisis, he asserted, meant that slaves' "happiness will be increased, & the burthen of their future liberation lightened by bringing a greater number of shoulders under it." But the Marquis de Lafayette privately questioned Jefferson's logic and suggested, "By Spreading the prejudices, habits, and Calculations of planters over a larger Surface You Rather Encrease the difficulties of final liberation." As Lafayette astutely noted, antislavery diffusion appeared implausible in the West by 1819 for a number of reasons. The first was the alleviation of geopolitical threats—the potential for violence and volatility that had framed the debates about the Mississippi and Louisiana Territories was largely absent from the Missouri Question. But the threat of slave rebellion was only increasing in the East. The swell in slave populations effectively rendered restrictionism a dead letter among southerners. Some planters, like Jefferson and James Madison, had predicted that ending the transatlantic slave trade would reduce slave numbers, thus paving the way for abolition. "Mr. Madison thought, we all thought," that Congress's ban of the commerce would give "slavery its death-blow, or the blow at least under which the institution could only linger a few years," Jefferson declared just before his death. But, he conceded in hindsight, instead of slavery's "rapid decline," he and other Virginians witnessed "it taking root deeper than ever." In fact, in the decade preceding the Missouri Crisis, the slave population increased from 392,518 to 425,153 in Virginia and from 196,365 to 251,783 in South Carolina. Despite these factors, northern Federalists proposed restricting slavery to the eastern states. When James Tallmadge of New York proposed a ban on the introduction of slavery in Missouri and a gradual emancipation of enslaved children, his argument echoed the Northwest Ordinance and Hilhouse's earlier plan for the Louisiana Territory. In short, Tallmadge was essentially applying what had been a congressional policy for population restriction or management in federal territories to the state level. Unsurprisingly, Missourians and other slave-state settlers were up in arms over Tallmadge's amendment, asserting that the new state of Missouri, rather than the federal government, now had the power to determine if and how slaves were diffused within its borders.[16]

Missourians' continued emphasis on the introduction of slaveholding settlers—rather than slaves—into the territory-cum-state during the Missouri Crisis was telling. As one Missourian declared in a letter to Thomas Ritchie's *Richmond (VA) Enquirer*, the "only thing we have to fear is that migration from the Southern states will be checked." In place of whites and their slaves streaming into the state from Kentucky and Virginia, Missouri might instead be peopled by antislavery northerners. "Emigration from the New England states will increase," wrote one proslavery supporter, "under hope of gaining supremacy in this country." Missourians fumed, believing that an inundation of antislavery northerners in a state populated with mostly proslavery southerners would be a recipe for disharmony—and perhaps disunion. But what was so critical about the prodiffusion language being deployed by planters, farmers, and state politicians was the emphasis on the *type* of settler who would enter Missouri. To be sure, they constructed a binary of settlers *with* slaves or settlers *without* slaves, but in no case did Missourians suggest that they favored the spread of slaves to their state through the internal slave trade. Instead, echoing the "bone fide" provision enacted as federal law when Missouri was part of the Louisiana Territory, Missourians supported the introduction of slaves accompanied by their masters, shying away from the unregulated introduction of bondspeople by slave traders. They supported the admission of slaves "domesticated" by— and supposedly attached to—their masters as part and parcel of the creation of a domesticated slave regime in Missouri. At the time of the debates over Missouri statehood, no large-scale slave rebellion had come to pass in the confluence region, and slaveholders aimed to keep it that way.[17]

Historians have emphasized the centrality of the internal slave trade to the expansion of slavery to the south and west, calculating that approximately 1 million men, women, and children were forcibly transported from the Upper South to Deep South slave marts between 1820 and 1860. Michael Tadman has characterized Missouri as a net "importing" state, concluding that most slaves arrived in Missouri with slave dealers rather than owners. There are many references to slave coffles arriving in Missouri from the Upper South in the antebellum era. In 1849, for example, the *Liberty Tribune* reported that 25 "plough boys and hemp breakers" as well as "nurses, house girls and seamstresses . . . cooks, washers, and ironers" had arrived "from Virginia, under the best discipline, bought with care, sound and healthy, and titles good." But historian Diane Mutti Burke believes that the evidence offered in slave narratives and pension claims "strongly suggest[s] that most slaves accompanied their owners westward rather than being brought through the interstate slave trade." Many experiences of the enslaved mirrored that of Dolly Hughes, a woman brought to Missouri by her master from the Upper South in 1836. Hughes, like her parents, siblings, and extended family members, was originally owned by Thomas Jefferson and lived at his five-thousand-acre Monticello plantation. But after Jefferson's death in 1826, Hughes and 140 other enslaved people were forced onto the auction block. Hughes's father, who had served as Jefferson's hostler and gardener and had even dug the grave of the former U.S. president, was freed informally by Jefferson's daughter. Nevertheless, Hughes's father witnessed his wife and children—including Dolly—sold at the 1827 dispersal sale. Nine years after being bought by a Virginia planter named Samuel Henley, Dolly Hughes was forcibly taken to Missouri with her children, one son named after her father. Hughes would not spend long in Missouri—she died there only two years later. Although she emigrated to Missouri with her master rather than in a slave coffle, her story is no less tragic, no less riven by the coercion, violence, and separation so endemic to the antebellum American slave system. But critically, Hughes *did* appear different from captives who arrived via the slave trade to white Missourians. Because she had grown up and lived in a "family" of two Virginia patriarchs—first Jefferson's and then Henley's—Hughes seemed to be exactly the type of domesticated, nonrebellious slave that Missourians desired within their borders.[18]

In order to ensure that settlers like Samuel Henley and slaves like Dolly Hughes would be the future of Missouri's slave regime—rather than free Black people or slave rebels—Missourians gave the new state government the authority to regulate the importation of slaves after 1820. In the midst of the uproar created over the Tallmadge Amendment and the subsequent federal debates over Missouri's admission to the Union, state legislators were eager to create a new state constitution that would impose order by creating—and controlling—the state's new borders. Border control was a legitimate exercise of state power, especially if used to control the flow of slaves. But jurisdiction over slavery in Missouri remained a precarious issue, since whites imagined their slaves as *both* valuable property *and* potential insurrectionists. Thus, the new state constitution addressed both. To protect slaveholders' human property from state interference, Missouri lawmakers agreed that the legislature could not free masters' human property. As the clause would later read, the general assembly held no power to pass laws that would manumit "slaves without the consent of their owners, or without paying them, before emancipation, a full equivalent for such slaves so emancipated." But the next section focused on slaves not as property but as potential disruptors—and destroyers—of Missouri society. Echoing the federal regulation of Mississippi and Louisiana territorial borders as well as the slave immigration restrictions codified in other new state constitutions, the Missouri legislature sought to "prohibit the introduction into this state" of any slave who posed a security risk. The Missouri General Assembly classified four types of "dangerous" African Americans in the new state constitution: slaves who "may have committed any high crime in any other state or territory," slaves who were introduced "for the purpose of speculation, or as an article of trade or merchandise," slaves "imported from any foreign country into the United States," and "free negroes and mulattoes." The constitution provided the general assembly with the power to determine whether migrant slaves could be categorized as any of the four threatening "types" as well as the authority to bar them from entering Missouri. But the exercise of state power would be visible only in what—or who—it kept out at the border, thereby allowing those slave owners who successfully passed into Missouri nearly total control over the "government" of their slaves. Yet few Missourians realized that it was state and federal laws—rather than individual slaveholders—that facilitated control over slave bodies and their "improvement" on farms and plantations.[19]

The general assembly was constitutionally sanctioned not just to tighten the borders but also to shape Missouri's slave society. Cribbing from the Louisiana territorial law, Missouri legislators stipulated that they could not "prevent bona fide emigrants to this state, or actual settlers therein, from bringing from any of the United States, or from any of their territories, such persons as may there be deemed to be slaves." Keen to copy the domesticated slave regime that federal legislators had tried to create within the Louisiana Territory, Missouri lawmakers concluded that the safest way slaves could enter Missouri was in the company of their owners. Moreover, the state constitution also allowed the government expanded jurisdiction over the master-slave relationship. In a controversial clause that was thrice debated during the 1820 constitutional convention in St. Louis, delegates voted twenty-one to eight to "oblige the owners of slaves to treat them with humanity, and to abstain from all injuries to them extending to life or limb." Alexander Stewart of St. Louis County made the initial proposal at the convention, but the "subject" was first debated by a smaller committee and then tabled for further discussion. Finally, the bill passed. Lawmakers later included language stipulating that any "person who shall maliciously deprive of life or dismember a slave, shall suffer" the same "punishment" as if "it were committed on a free white person." Crucially, these clauses demonstrated that legislators did not think that it was only slaves who could undermine a domesticated slave regime in Missouri. Masters, particularly cruel ones who exercised no "humanity," might incite slaves to rebel, run away, or further destabilize society. Encouraging masters to properly feed and clothe their slaves and avoid excessive corporal punishment was a pragmatic policy designed to alleviate violence that might jeopardize Missouri's survival. The legislature's incorporation of the federal "bona fide" settler law into the state constitution, as well as its new authority to police masters' cruelty and inhumanity, highlighted the importance of domestication to Missouri statehood.[20]

Asserting the state's power to regulate slavery in Missouri was far from exceptional. Indeed, Missouri's constitution copied—in some cases verbatim—previous state constitutions that also sought to regulate and domesticate slavery. Repeating what other state constitutions had asserted both legitimized Missouri statehood and underscored the centrality of domestication to state formation in the South and West. Though accounts in letters and newspapers emphasized the agency of individual slaveholders in entering and later settling in these new states, it was the state governments that controlled this diffusion of settlers and slaves. Kentucky's state constitution of 1792 was the first to empower its legislature to regulate the state's borders in order to provide security for slavery. To insulate the state from slave rebellions, Kentucky lawmakers could prevent slaves from entering the state as "merchandise" or from a "foreign country." Legislators were also given "full power to pass such laws as may be necessary, to oblige the owners of slaves to treat them with humanity, to provide for them necessary clothing and provisions, to abstain from all injuries to them extending to life or limb." In the constitutions ratified by the two new states carved from the Mississippi Territory—Mississippi in 1817 and Alabama in 1819—the same language appears, word for word. Missouri also copied Kentucky's language, but added several more clauses cribbed directly from the Louisiana territorial law to restrict slavery more stringently at its borders.[21]

By several measures, border control and domestication were successful projects in Missouri. First, no slave conspiracy or large-scale slave rebellion ever gripped the state. The 1806 Gabriel Prosser slave conspiracy in Virginia, the 1811 German Coast Uprising in the Territory of Orleans, the Negro Fort insurrection in West Florida, the 1822 Denmark Vesey slave conspiracy in South Carolina, and the 1831 Nat Turner revolt in Virginia appeared to confirm slave owners' fear that a large-scale slave rebellion might be unleashed in the South, destroying whites and their property. But that no such rebellion occurred in Missouri seemed to endorse the efficacy of state control of the diffusion of slavery, while also facilitating the unparalleled emigration of whites, especially to the region known as "Boon's Lick." Second, Missouri's slave population remained a small minority proportion of the total population between statehood and the Civil War. By 1860, Missouri slaves composed only 9.72 percent of the state population and were confined mainly to counties stretching along the Missouri Valley. This statistic differed from the other slave states that had incorporated border-control policies into their constitutions. By the outbreak of the Civil War, the cotton states held majorities or near majorities of their populations in bondage—slaves composed 45.12 percent of Alabama's population and 55.18 of Mississippi's while only 19.51 percent of Kentucky's. Moreover, few Missouri slaveholders held large numbers of slaves at a time when large populations of enslaved people also seemed to jeopardize security and foment rebellion. Of 24,320 Missouri slaveholders in 1860, only 4 owned more than 100 slaves, and the vast majority—17,349—held between 1 and 5 people in bondage. Most of these slaveholders and their human chattel lived on farms rather than on plantations and practiced diversified agriculture, cultivating tobacco, hemp, and corn and tending livestock. In the absence of the production of a single lucrative cash crop—like sugar in Louisiana, rice in Lowcountry South Carolina and Georgia, and cotton in the "Old Southwest"—in Missouri a "small-scale" slave system emerged during the antebellum era. Like their counterparts in Upper South states such as Virginia and Maryland, Missouri slave owners put their bondspeople to work as seasonal agricultural laborers, domestic servants, and artisans. Slave owners also frequently leased "excess" laborers out around the state, leading to a robust hiring market and statewide slave trade that was devastating for the enslaved. The success of Missouri's domestication project—at least on paper—and its apparently distinctive slave society became central to whites' notion that bondage was "milder" in Missouri when compared with the cotton South. Because Missourians owned few slaves and managed farms rather than plantations, whites reasoned, slavery was not nearly as coercive and violent as it was elsewhere in the South. Indeed, as George Sibley had pointed out, it was precisely *because* Missouri contained "few slaves" that they could be "well fed & clothed & kindly treated."[22]

Of course, enslaved people in Missouri would be hard-pressed to reconcile this view with the brutality that they experienced. The overwhelming majority of slave memoirs and interviews from the antebellum period highlight a slave regime every bit as horrific as that in any other slave state. Missouri slaves' testimony shows that though humane treatment toward captives may have been codified in the state constitution in 1820, legislators appear never to have enforced it. William Wells Brown entered Missouri under the "bona fide" law—he accompanied his master with his mother and siblings from Lexington, Kentucky. His owner, a physician by training, established a farm outside of St. Charles that produced tobacco and hemp and employed an overseer to direct his field hands. Punishment, Brown detailed, was frequent and debilitating. Tardiness for work meant ten lashes with the "negro whip," which "was about three feet long, with the butt-end filled with lead, and the lash, six or seven feet in length, made of cow hide, with platted wire on the end of it." Brown once witnessed his mother's violent punishment at the hands of the overseer. "I could hear every crack of the whip, and every groan and cry of my mother," he related, and "cold chills ran over me, and I wept out loud." But Brown and his mother also endured abuse at the hands of other white Missourians when they were leased out to other masters. Brown's most sadistic temporary master, a hotel keeper named John Colburn, was not only an "inveterate hater of the negro" but also "from one of the free states." While enduring Colburn's constant cruelty, Brown received news that "caused me great unhappiness." His owner had sold his mother and all his siblings, retaining only Brown. After taking stock of his situation, as well as that of other slaves who were burned, maimed, and killed around him, Brown concluded that "no part of our slave-holding country is more noted for the barbarity of its inhabitants than St. Louis." Although some whites reported that slavery was "mild in Missouri, when compared with the cotton, sugar and rice growing states," Brown declared that nothing could be further from the truth.[23]

Missouri lawmakers sought to use the new state constitution of 1820 as a legal technology to control slavery and create borders, much as the federal government had done in the Louisiana and Mississippi Territories. Constitutional clauses restricting certain slaves and free Black people made it clear what Missouri didn't want—a robust domestic slave trade bringing thousands of foreign-born and rebellious slaves into the state. In order to avoid the security threats that whites imagined were created by large populations of free Black people and majority slave populations, the state legislature claimed broad powers to head off these individuals before they even had a chance to set foot in Missouri. This border-control policy grew out of necessity: Missouri, like the federal government, could not count on a strong military to police slavery within its borders. In fact, though the general assembly was given some ability to monitor the "humanity" of Missouri slaveholders, in practice it left the business of "governing" slavery largely up to individual masters. This approach allowed masters to imagine themselves as the ultimate protectors—and domesticators—of slavery rather than the state government.[24]

Slave states' use of constitutional clauses to control—or exclude—certain populations facilitated the emergence of varying types of slave societies across the South and West in the era of the Missouri Crisis. When exerting control over state borders, local lawmakers and slaveholders were given tremendous power to shape the nature of their slave society at the state level—to determine whether a state became a slave importer or slave exporter or whether it became a "slave society" or a "society with slaves." The states examined in this chapter underscore this point: though all embraced similar constitutional provisions to control slavery, Missouri and Kentucky became "societies with slaves," while Alabama and Mississippi became "slave societies." Jefferson's belief that the 36°30' parallel implemented as part of the Missouri Compromise would draw a permanent "line" between "slave" and "free" states obfuscates the divisions and differences *between* slave states. Eager to maintain security for white settlers and prevent slave revolts, slaveholders and lawmakers were eager to draw lines of their own making—between themselves and "other" neighboring states or territories.[25]

Notes

1. George Sibley to Samuel Sibley, September 25, 1813, Sibley Papers, Missouri Historical Society, St. Louis; John Craig Hammond, *Slavery, Freedom, and Expansion in the Early American West* (Charlottesville: University of Virginia Press, 2007), 59; Andrew C. Isenberg, "The Market Revolution in the Borderlands: George Champlin Sibley in Missouri and New Mexico, 1808–1826," *Journal of the Early Republic* 21, no. 3 (2001): 445–65.

2. John Craig Hammond, "Slavery, Sovereignty, and Empires: North American Borderlands and the American Civil War, 1660–1860," *Journal of the Civil War Era* 4, no. 2 (2014): 264–98; Willie Lee Rose, *Slavery and Freedom* (New York: Oxford University Press, 1982); Christa Dierksheide, *Amelioration and Empire: Progress and Slavery in the Plantation Americas, 1770–1840* (Charlottesville: University of Virginia Press, 2014); Peter S. Onuf, "The Empire of Liberty: Land of the Free and Home of the Slave," chap. 9 in *The World of the Revolutionary American Republic: Land, Labor, and the Conflict for a Continent*, ed. Andrew Shankman (New York: Routledge, 2014); Brian Balogh, *A Government Out of Sight: The Mystery of National Authority in Nineteenth-Century America* (New York: Cambridge University Press, 2007).

3. John Watkins to John Graham, September 6, 1805, in *The Territorial Papers of the United States*, ed. Clarence E. Carter (Washington, DC: Government Printing Office, 1934–75), 9:504; Thomas Jefferson to John Breckinridge, August 12, 1803, Founders Online, https://founders.archives.gov/documents/Jefferson/01-41-02-0139; Paul Frymer, *Building an American Empire: The Era of Territorial and Political Expansion* (Princeton, NJ: Princeton University Press, 2017), 72–127.

4. Hammond, "Slavery, Sovereignty, and Empires"; U.S. Census, 1790, 1800; Alan Taylor, *The Internal Enemy: Slavery and War in Virginia, 1772–1832* (New York: W. W. Norton, 2013); Jefferson to Edward Coles, August 25, 1814, Founders Online, https://founders.archives.gov/documents/Jefferson/03-07-02-0439; Peter S. Onuf, *Jefferson's Empire: the Language of American Nationhood* (Charlottesville: University of Virginia Press, 2000), 150–51; Dierksheide, *Amelioration and Empire*, 44–45; Spencer Roane to James Monroe, February 16, 1820, in "Letters of Spencer Roane, 1788–1822," *Bulletin of the New York Public Library* 10 (1906): 174–75.

5. On diffusion, see Adam Rothman, *Slave Country: American Expansion and the Origins of the Deep South* (Cambridge, MA: Harvard University Press, 2005), 22–27, 213; Hammond, *Slavery, Freedom, and Expansion*, 165–66; Onuf, *Jefferson's Empire*, 185–87; William W. Freehling, *The Road to Disunion*, vol. 1, *Secessionists at Bay, 1776–1854* (New York: Oxford University Press, 1990), 150–57; Drew R. McCoy, *The Last of the Fathers: James Madison and the Republican Legacy* (New York: Cambridge University Press, 1989), 253–322; Dierksheide, *Amelioration and Empire*, 45–47. On

proslavery and antislavery diffusion, see Christa Dierksheide, "'Taking Root Deeper and Deeper': Jeffersonians and Slavery," chap. 11 in *Jeffersonians in Power: The Rhetoric of Opposition Meets the Realities of Governing*, ed. Joanne B. Freeman and Johann N. Neem (Charlottesville: University of Virginia Press, 2019).

6. Adam Rothman, "The Domestication of the Domestic Slave Trade," in *The Chattel Principle: Internal Slave Trades in the Americas*, ed. Walter Johnson (New Haven, CT: Yale University Press, 2005), 32–33.

7. Frymer, *Building an American Empire*, chap. 3; Paul E. Herron, "Slavery and Freedom in American State Constitutional Development," *Journal of Policy History* 27, no. 2 (2015): 301–36.

8. See the introduction to this volume.

9. Frymer, *Building an American Empire*, chap. 3; Hammond, "Slavery, Sovereignty, and Empires"; Jeremy Adelman and Stephen Aron, "From Borderlands to Borders: Empires, Nation-States, and the Peoples in Between in North American History," *American Historical Review* 104, no. 3 (1999): 814–41.

10. Dierksheide, "'Taking Root Deeper and Deeper'"; Thomas Jefferson to Richard Price, August 7, 1785, Founders Online, https://founders.archives.gov/documents/Jefferson/01-08-02-0280; Thomas Jefferson to John Holmes, April 22, 1820, Founders Online, https://founders.archives.gov/documents/Jefferson/98-01-02-1234.

11. William H. Bergmann, *The American National State and the Early West* (New York: Cambridge University Press, 2012); John R. Van Atta, *Securing the West: Politics, Public Lands, and the Fate of the Old Republic* (Baltimore: Johns Hopkins University Press, 2014); *Annals of Congress*, 42 vols. (Washington, DC: Gales and Seaton, 1834–56), 5th Cong., 2nd sess., 8:1306–10; Rothman, *Slave Country*, 22–27, 213.

12. John Watkins, *Territorial Papers*, 9:503; Everett S. Brown, ed., "The Senate Debate on the Breckinridge Bill for the Government of Louisiana, 1804," *American Historical Review* 22, no. 2 (1917): 349, 354; *Annals of Congress*, 8th Cong., 1st sess., 244; George William Van Cleve, *A Slaveholders' Union: Slavery, Politics, and the Constitution in the Early American Republic* (Chicago: University of Chicago Press, 2010), 218–19; Hammond, *Slavery, Freedom, and Expansion*, 37, 44–45.

13. Hammond, *Slavery, Freedom, and Expansion*, 51–54; Freehling, *Road to Disunion*, 141–42; William C. Carr to Charles Carr, August 25, 1809, William C. Carr Papers, Missouri Historical Society, St. Louis.

14. Hammond, *Slavery, Freedom, and Expansion*, 57–58, 64; Committee Report: Statehood for Mississippi, January 17, 1817, in *Territorial Papers*, 5:20; Thomas L. McKenney to the Acting Secretary of War, February 26, 1817, in *Territorial Papers*, 18:46–53; Frymer, *Building an American Empire*, 90–91; Deposition of Martin Dorion, October 14, 1817, Indians Collection, Missouri Historical Society, St. Louis; Deposition of Maurice Blondeau, October 14, 1817, Indians Collection.

15. Charles Carroll to Nathaniel Rochester, December 15, 1818, Rochester Family Papers, Library of Virginia, Richmond; Charles Carroll to Col. Rochester, February 22, 1819, Library of Virginia, Richmond; [?] to John Holmes, February 26, 1817, John Holmes Papers, New York Public Library; Joseph Gill to Josiah Browder, August 26, 1822, Isham Browder Papers, Virginia Historical Society, Richmond; David Murphy to Independent Electors of the County of St. Genevieve, April 30, 1820,

GLC01450.600.58, Murphy Family Papers; George Tompkins to George C. Sibley, July 20, 1819, Sibley Papers, Missouri Historical Society, St. Louis.

16. Hammond, *Slavery, Freedom, and Expansion*, 150–68; Onuf, *Jefferson's Empire*, 185–87; Dierksheide, "'Taking Root Deeper and Deeper'"; T. J. to John Holmes, April 22, 1820, Founders Online, http://founders.archives.gov/documents/Jefferson/98-01-02-1234; T. J. to Charles Pinckney, September 30, 1820, Founders Online, http://founders.archives.gov/documents/Jefferson/03-07-02-0439; T. J. to John Holmes, April 22, 1820, Founders Online, http://founders.archives.gov/documents/Jefferson/98-01-02-1234; Thomas Jefferson to Marie-Joseph-Paul-Yves-Roch-Gilbert du Motier, Marquis de Lafayette, December 26, 1820, Founders Online, https://founders.archives.gov/documents/Jefferson/98-01-02-1708; Marie-Joseph-Paul-Yves-Roch-Gilbert du Motier, Marquis de Lafayette to Thomas Jefferson, July 1, 1821, Founders Online, https://founders.archives.gov/documents/Jefferson/98-01-02-2151; Marie-Joseph-Paul-Yves-Roch-Gilbert du Motier, Marquis de Lafayette to Thomas Jefferson, June 1, 1822, Founders Online, https://founders.archives.gov/documents/Jefferson/98-01-02-2841; U.S. Census, 1810, 1820; Daniel Pierce Thompson, "A Talk with Jefferson," *Harper's New Monthly Magazine* 26 (May 1863): 833–35.

17. "To the Editor, Letters from St. Louis," *Richmond (VA) Enquirer*, May 14, 21, 1819; *Missouri Intelligencer* (St. Louis), July 9, 1819; Hammond, *Slavery, Freedom, and Expansion*, 64–71; Rothman, "Domesticating the Domestic Slave Trade."

18. Michael Tadman, *Speculators and Slaves: Masters, Traders, and Slaves in the Old South* (Madison: University of Wisconsin Press, 1989), 11–46; Robert Gudmestad, *A Troublesome Commerce: The Transformation of the Interstate Slave Trade* (Baton Rouge: Louisiana State University Press, 2003), 18–20; Steven Deyle, *Carry Me Back: The Domestic Slave Trade in American Life* (New York: Oxford University Press, 2005), 45, 74–76; Edward Baptist, *Creating an Old South: Middle Florida's Frontier before the Civil War* (Chapel Hill: University of North Carolina Press, 2002), 60–87; Diane Mutti Burke, *On Slavery's Border: Missouri's Small Slaveholding Households, 1815–1865* (Athens: University of Georgia Press, 2010), 38–39; *Liberty (MO) Tribune*, February 9, 1849; Lucia Stanton, *"Those Who Labor for My Happiness": Slavery at Thomas Jefferson's Monticello* (Charlottesville: University of Virginia Press, 2012).

19. Hammond, "Slavery, Sovereignty, and Empires"; Missouri State Constitution, 1820, Article III, Section 26; Herron, "Slavery and Freedom"; Freehling, *Road to Disunion*, 147; Isidor Loeb, *Constitutions and Constitutional Conventions in Missouri* (Columbia: State Historical Society of Missouri, 1920), 7–11; George Sibley to Samuel Sibley, September 25, 1813, Sibley Papers.

20. Missouri Constitution, 1820, Article III, Sections 26, 27, 28; *Journal of the House of Representatives of the State of Missouri, at the First Session of the First General Assembly; Begun and Held in the Town of St. Louis . . .* (St. Louis: Edward Charles, 1822); Herron, "Slavery and Freedom."

21. *Journal of the House of Representatives of the State of Missouri . . .*; Herron, "Slavery and Freedom"; Kentucky Constitution, 1792, Article I, Sections 5 and 10, Article II, Section 2, and Article VI, Section 1; Joan Wells Coward, *Kentucky in the*

New Republic: The Process of Constitution Making (Lexington: University Press of Kentucky, 1979).

22. U.S. Census, 1860; Mutti Burke, *On Slavery's Border*, 17–51. See also Robert Lee's essay in this volume.

23. William Wells Brown, *Narrative of William W. Brown: An American Slave* (London: Charles Gilpin, 1849), 13–26; Mutti Burke, *On Slavery's Border*, 13–14, 125–26, 179–80, 193–94.

24. Missouri Constitution, 1820; Hammond, "Slavery, Sovereignty, and Empires"; Adelman and Aron, "From Borderlands to Borders"; Balogh, *Government Out of Sight*; Onuf, "Home of the Free and Land of the Slave."

25. See John Craig Hammond's essay in this volume. Ira Berlin, *Many Thousands Gone: The First Two Centuries of Slavery in North America* (Cambridge, MA: Belknap Press of Harvard University Press, 1998); Thomas Jefferson to William Short, April 13, 1820, Founders Online, https://founders.archives.gov/documents/Jefferson/98-01-02-1218.

5. "At War with their Equal Rights"

The Missouri Crisis in Southern Eyes

John R. Van Atta

RECENT SCHOLARSHIP ON the Missouri Crisis has asserted, rightly, that earlier historians underplayed the antislavery buildup to the controversy and underestimated popular pressures in the free states that influenced it. Before, we did not fully gauge the breadth and depth of antislavery (and, one should add, antisouthern) feeling in the North. The same has been true of our assessment of the southern response to the Tallmadge Amendment—a genuine fear of advancing northern despotism, as evidenced all through the struggle and showing not only in Congress, and not just in Missouri and Virginia, but around most of the South. From that perspective, the famous crisis of 1819–21—*the* great early-republic confrontation over the future of slaveholding in America—turns out to have been as much about the preservation of self-governance and the assertion of "equal rights" as it was the expansion of slavery.[1]

In years past, as well, we have concentrated more on the *internal* political workings of the Missouri Crisis, including the debate itself, congressional deal making, the implications for party development, and so forth, than on the *external* cultural forces that gave the issue such gravity from the start. Hence the need to inspect not only the operation of Congress and events in Washington but also reactions at the grassroots level of the country—in towns, hotels, coffeehouses, and taverns; in printers' offices, churches, county seats, and lecture halls—public forums all over, a broader "public sphere" than historians have generally considered for this subject.[2]

From this external viewpoint, one sees that southern newspapers took, and circulated one to another, a consistent line from the start of the crisis. It was that designing, moralistic politicians in the North meant to subjugate Missourians, and white southerners in general, under a hostile and increasingly aggressive antislavery majority. Southern congressmen and senators said the same in Washington, reflecting as much as influencing what their constituents believed back home. The Tallmadge Amendment, requiring that slavery be marked for extinction in Missouri, assumed congressional power not only to shape territorial government *prior* to statehood but also to impose a broad social and economic agenda within new states *afterward* as well. Beyond just that—and central to the controversy—New York representative James Tallmadge and his antislavery allies wanted restriction like that proposed for Missouri to become standard for *all* further new states west of the Mississippi. To adopt such an agenda might indeed threaten the ultimate demise of the slaveholding South by preventing its further westward expansion as well as threatening its concept of state sovereignty.

To southern statesmen and newspaper commentators alike, the amendment carried more comprehensive and radically statist implications than it might seem today: "a wider scope of operation than, on the *face* of it, would be supposed," said the *National Intelligencer* soon after Tallmadge introduced it on February 13, 1819—a condition for admission to the Union beyond simply a "republican" form of government. It was, the *Intelligencer* noted, the "first instance of such a restriction being imposed on the new states," as opposed to new territories—or, as Virginian-turned-Missourian Nathaniel Beverley Tucker declared a few months later, an "assumption of power, never before attempted or assumed." To see the Missouri issue through white southerners' eyes, as it appeared at home as well as in Congress, is to understand why it represented such a "crisis" to them in the first place.[3]

From the South's outlook, the Missouri Crisis related to principles that dated from the beginning of the republic. In addition to the fundamental themes of liberty and equality, the American Revolution had asserted the right of newly independent states to govern themselves, meaning they would control their own internal affairs and their property rights, including those of slaveholders. White southern leaders, then and in years to come, would refer to this arrangement as "state sovereignty," which they viewed as a fundamental part of their revolutionary heritage, granted both to them and, on an equal basis, to all additional states to follow. They would brook no northern challenge on that point. Meanwhile, antislavery northerners tried what they could to stymie the westward expansion of slavery, beginning with a provision to that effect in the Northwest Ordinance of 1787, which applied to an extensive area north of the Ohio River while implicitly conceding the region south of that to slaveholding.[4]

During and after the Revolution, state-by-state gradual emancipation had progressed in the northeastern states, whose economies had not depended as heavily on slave labor as did the plantation South. Over the same period, new states continued to enter the Union, including the slave states of Kentucky (1792), Tennessee (1796), Louisiana (1812), Mississippi (1817), and, during the Missouri Crisis, Alabama (1819)—all regarded as equal in footing to the original states with full control over matters of their internal governance. Prior to Tallmadge's challenge to the conditions of Missouri's admission in 1819, southerners in Congress and Missouri Territory leaders had every reason to regard this equality of status as normal. To deny its admission on that basis would have dared Missourians to break away from the American republic, potentially drawing the surrounding area into a proslavery economic sphere of its own.[5]

Despite gradual emancipation programs in the North and the federal government's ending of the legal slave-import trade in 1808, slavery had also expanded more rapidly in the United States by 1820 than anyone, including southern whites, had expected. Slave importing had continued in defiance of federal law, while the domestic reproduction of slaves boomed. Even in the northern "free" states, more than nineteen thousand slaves still remained, awaiting the day of their mandated release or that of their children. Of those, somewhere between ten and eleven thousand still lived in Tallmadge's New York, where the gradual emancipation statute of 1799 had been amended in 1817 to promise "the final and total abolition" of slavery as of July 4, 1827, applying equally to the enslaved born after and before 1799. Interestingly, the Missouri Territory in 1819 had about the same number of enslaved Black people as slave owners in the Empire State still held—a point that Tallmadge and other "restrictionists" hardly could have missed.[6]

For a time, however, it looked as if Illinois, not Missouri, might become the great test case in Congress over further slavery expansion. Slaveholding former southerners led the movement for Illinois statehood in 1818. Most settlers who lived in the southern part of the Illinois Country had come from the slave states, like many who migrated across the river onto Missouri lands after the War of 1812. Hoping to emulate the economic pattern of the South, some came with small numbers of slaves. Despite the Northwest Ordinance, many believed that Illinois might still protect slaveholding, whatever Congress would soon decide on the matter.[7]

In the fall of 1818, the House of Representatives in Washington took up Speaker Henry Clay's resolution to admit Illinois as the twenty-first state under a proposed state constitution that prohibited new slaves but allowed those already there, along with preserving a race-based indentured-servant system that held Black people under indefinite "contract." The most ardent spokesman against this arrangement proved to be none other than James Tallmadge. Southerners, including frontier lawyers Richard Clough Anderson of Louisville and George Poindexter of Natchez, insisted that Illinois had "virtually" conformed with all requirements of the 1787 ordinance, just as had Ohio and Indiana in years before. Tallmadge retorted that a congressional obligation to prohibit slavery in Illinois constituted a solemn promise—"a tie not to be broken." That spurred William Henry Harrison, once a Virginian and now of Ohio, to claim that no earlier provisions could have stripped the people of Illinois of their "sovereign authority"—code language for southern rights, not to be violated. Only a few congressmen from New England and other northeastern states joined the protest against the admission of Illinois—the vote was 34 opposed and 117 in favor. Following Senate approval, President James Monroe, another Virginian, signed Illinois into statehood on December 3, 1818. Significantly, the two newly elected U.S. senators for Illinois, Ninian Edwards and Jesse B. Thomas—both Maryland born and proslavery—would side with the South, taking the antirestrictionist and, later, the procompromise side on the Missouri Question.[8]

▲

The Missouri Territory, however, presented a different case altogether. No congressional ordinance had ever discouraged slavery there or anywhere west of the Mississippi River. Between 1763 and 1800, the population of the lower Mississippi Valley had exploded, roughly a fifth of it enslaved. As it had for Kentucky and Tennessee, Congress admitted the new states of the lower-Mississippi region, not so much allowing slavery there as accommodating the system already well established—full-blown "slave societies" as opposed to "societies with slaves."[9] By 1804, the Missouri Country already hosted a small but thriving frontier commerce, with French, British, and even Native American inhabitants relying on their Black people in fur trapping, mining, and trade. The 1787 prohibition of slavery in the Northwest Territory had also driven additional French slaveholders and other proslavery settlers over to the west side of the Mississippi.[10]

The 1803 Louisiana Purchase Treaty, in addition to securing the property-holding rights of French slave owners, had also promised that "the inhabitants of the ceded territory shall be incorporated in the Union of the United States and admitted as soon as possible according to the principles of the federal

Constitution to the enjoyment" of all the "rights, advantages and immunities of citizens of the United States." Antirestrictionists during the Missouri controversy would point to that treaty provision as guaranteeing Missouri's admission and on terms of its own choosing. In any case, southerners in Congress had long contended that slavery west of the Mississippi could not be reversed. Settlers crossing the Mississippi River would be "governed by their interest, not the law," as Georgia senator James Jackson defiantly put it in 1804. Tacitly accepting that principle, Congress the following year split the Louisiana Territory into two separate parts, saying nothing on provisions of the purchase treaty or the restricting of slavery. Over the next decade and a half, it seemed increasingly likely to many northerners that unless federal lawmakers found some way to change the course of slavery expansion, the entire trans-Mississippi West might evolve into a region antithetical to free laborers, thus forever unwelcoming to them and their descendants.[11]

During that same period, an increasingly radicalized antislavery movement throughout the Northeast, as far south as Maryland, had accelerated efforts to end the practice in America. In its extremism, abolitionist rhetoric had ratcheted up several notches from that of the late eighteenth century. These changes outside of the nation's capital went together with the widespread assumption that migrants from the free-labor states indeed would not settle in areas open to slavery, as historically they had not. James Forten, a Pennsylvania free Black person who had agitated in 1799 for Congress to abolish the slave trade, concluded in 1813 that the "unprejudiced must pronounce any act tending to deprive a free man of his right, freedom and immunities, as not only cruel in the extreme, but decidedly unconstitutional." John Kendrick's 1817 pamphlet *Horrors of Slavery* demanded immediate emancipation, predicting that a southern institution so "impolitic, antirepublican, unchristian, and highly criminal" as slavery could end only by widespread violence. George Bourne, an English-born radical Presbyterian minister, not only denounced slavery but often threw slave owners out of his congregations. "Christians!" he exclaimed in 1816. "How long will you tacitly or openly sanction or actually engage in a system which includes every practicable iniquity?" Among other demands, abolitionists now insisted that Congress employ its powers over territorial development and new-state admission for the moral improvement of the republic.[12]

Grassroots action against slavery heightened even in parts of the Upper South. As one indication, the *Baltimore Patriot* on January 3, 1820, while the Missouri Crisis raged, advised readers interested in signing a certain restrictionist memorial that they might do so at any of several bookstores, hotels, or taverns in the city, a coffeehouse, the mayor's office, or the office of the *Federal Gazette*—all places of significant political interest. Before that, antislavery Methodist camp meetings, and other expressions of the Second Great Awakening, had stirred fears of slave unrest in the southern states and would in Missouri as well. One such preacher in August 1818 found himself arrested in Maryland for "feloniously counselling, conspiring and attempting with certain negroes to raise an insurrection and rebellion in the state."[13]

If the Tallmadge Amendment reflected the rising antislavery passion in the Northeast, as well as in Tallmadge's own New York, it also asserted a view of federal government power that, in proslavery southern eyes, went significantly beyond the establishing of banks, protective tariffs, and internal improvements—"a spirit of fanaticism dangerous to the constitutional rights of the slave holding states," judged one southern congressman privately. The ferocious defensive response it provoked from southern members of Congress revealed concerns reaching far deeper for whites in the slave states than just Missouri's fate. In the House chamber, Georgia's Thomas W. Cobb, replying to Tallmadge, questioned whether the New Yorker and his antislavery crowd even understood the trouble they now invited, the traditional boundaries between North and South they were endangering. "Did they foresee no evil consequences likely to result, if the measure were adopted?" Cobb inquired. "Could they suppose that the southern states would submit with patience to a measure, the effect of which would be to exclude them from all enjoyment of the vast region purchased by the United States beyond the Mississippi, and which belonged equally to them as to the northern states?" The amendment would deprive Missouri "of one branch of sovereignty not surrendered by any other state in the Union, not even those beyond the Ohio." Further, "in what clause or section" of the Constitution was such federal power "expressly given" or open to inference?[14]

Cobb's February 1819 resistance and that of other southerners in Congress mirrored the readiness of their constituents around the South and in Missouri Territory to agree with it. Some historians have noted that the anticonsolidation language that elite southerners employed resonated not only with fellow slaveholders but also with southern white yeomen—and potential northern sympathizers, too. As for slavery, some of those back home might admit "its *moral impropriety*," said Cobb, yet there remained "a vast difference between moral impropriety and political sovereignty." A heavy element of southern honor entered here, too. In an elite-dominated culture claiming to be one of honor, such as that of the southern states, it was especially humiliating for a "gentleman" to endure the kind of "unmasking" or "pressing of the lie" about slavery and slaveholders that Tallmadge and others now seemed to want. By those cultural rules, to allow any serious insult to go unchallenged was to accept degradation akin to that of a slave. More used to ruling than being ruled (and fearful of the latter), Cobb on behalf of the southern planter class thus interpreted the Missouri issue as an aggression not just on slavery and slave-state sovereignty but also on *them* personally and their cultural identity. As many white southerners saw it, they now faced a comprehensive northern attack on the entire structure of their society, on their concept of manhood and the roots of their self-respect, on their dream of future expansion, and even on their right to govern themselves.[15]

Along with all that, the contest for control in Congress between slave states and free states figured to some extent in the Missouri fight—again, not just in Washington but among politically attuned observers back home as well. In 1789, North and South had been close to even in population and wealth, with three-fifths of the slaves counting for House representation and electoral votes. But over the next thirty years, economic development in the North had given the northern states a significant advantage. By 1819, a free-state majority of 105 to 81 dominated the House. Southern influence in Congress had declined steadily. In 1790, 49 southern House seats stood against 57 northern; twenty years later, it was 79–107; and after 1820, they numbered 89–124. That placed critical importance on the Senate. There, the number of slave-state members remained equal to the free-state members, as Alabama's admission would make twenty-two of the former against twenty-two of the latter. Still, southerners held at least a temporary edge, as they could find support on slavery-related issues from the two Illinois senators along with a few northern "doughfaces" (northern men who, for one reason or another, voted with the South). But to restrict slavery from spreading further into Missouri, and other new states thereafter, could eventually shift power in the Senate against the South and promise *more* free states to come until the two-thirds majority needed to pass an abolition amendment, and the three-quarters of states to ratify, became a frightening possibility for the South. With that aggressive antisouthern supermajority, not only slavery but everything that depended on it—planter-class authority, white control over the Black race, and much more.[16]

In addition, both the Republican Tallmadge and fellow New Yorker Rufus King, on the Federalist side, wanted another crack at the three-fifths-clause

dispute of 1787. That constitutional provision had since that time been another vital source of southern strength in national politics, along with Senate
influence and, for now, control of the executive branch. The three-fifths provision mattered in competitive presidential elections and close congressional
votes. It had elected Jefferson in 1800 and kept the "Virginia Dynasty" in
power, which many antislavery northeasterners, not just Federalists, also
resented. Did the clause actually apply for new states west of the Mississippi,
given that the framers of the federal Constitution had not expected such
further expansion and had made no rules for it? Virginia's Philip Pendleton
Barbour would answer that if the three-fifths compromise in 1787 did not
apply to the new states, then how could the other compromises of that time,
such as proportional representation in the House and the two U.S. senators
per state?[17]

In contrast with the first responders like Cobb, some southern members,
along with House Speaker Henry Clay from Kentucky, thought the whole
debate superfluous and overblown. Even if Congress *could* require intrusive
details of government for a new state, beyond just its being "republican" in
form, that power would be "nugatory," argued Clay. The same stood tech-
nically true for Illinois, where the question of its converting into a slave
state still remained very much in play. Once admitted to the Union, Clay
believed, any state had the right to amend its constitution and govern itself
accordingly. But in Missouri's case, that argument did not quite work: Once
the unprecedented terms that Tallmadge proposed were carried out, would
enough proslavery sentiment still remain in Missouri to facilitate its conversion back? The Speaker, of course, wanted to mollify southern congressmen
who now felt betrayed by antislavery northerners, but he also believed that
the Constitution protected slavery. Besides, he needed votes in Congress to
pass further protective-tariff, internal-improvement, and land-policy bills
that would later constitute the "American System" and, he hoped, carry him
to the presidency.[18]

So, as the debate unfolded further, the rhetoric intensified. The antislavery
side ignored the question of state sovereignty in favor of their overarching
moral vision as applying for the future of western society and, with that,
for the nation. Southerners disputed that vision, of course, but in so doing
revealed their own deep anxieties about the plantation world they so boasted. The "destiny of millions," all the way to the "Western ocean," hung in
the balance, announced Tallmadge's antislavery New York colleague John
W. Taylor. Others followed Taylor's lead. According to New Hampshire

abolitionist lawyer Arthur Livermore, the Constitution did not specifically *impose* slavery, but it did establish liberty. "Let us no longer tell idle tales about the gradual abolition of slavery," Livermore declared. In response, Edward Colston of Virginia warned that Livermore's inflammatory words could not be contained within Congress. When the slaves heard this kind of talk, as all knew they would, it might "excite a servile war," endangering the very lives of southern whites. Northerners responsible for such a breach of southern security, said Colston, deserved "no better fate" than that of Arbuthnot and Armbrister, the two British subjects whom southern hero Andrew Jackson had executed in Spanish Florida during the 1818 Seminole Campaign. Sensitive to Colston's complaint, Tallmadge later denied having meant any violation: "I would in no manner intermeddle with the slave-holding states, nor attempt manumission in any of the original States in the Union." This danger of sparking servile war, he backtracked, was why he had not advocated prohibition of slavery in Alabama Territory. The "safety of the white population" was paramount. But this long-standing courtesy to white southerners of guarding their safety or their vital institutions also ceased at the banks of the Mississippi, Tallmadge now professed. It did not apply regarding "a newly acquired territory, never contemplated in the formation of our government."[19]

From a constitutional perspective, Virginia's Philip Barbour (a future U.S. Supreme Court justice) insisted that the document could not be read as giving Congress power to impose such terms on the admission of Missouri. To do so would be to encroach on the sovereignty of Missouri and, by extension, on all future states admitted into the Union. A man of consistent principle, always on the antinationalist, strict-constructionist side of post–War of 1812 economic questions, Barbour opposed also the national bank, protective tariffs, and federal funding for improvements. State sovereignty, he believed, provided the bulwark against overreaching federal authority. Aside from that, everyone knew that in Barbour's Virginia, with its long-declining economy, the sale of excess slaves southward and westward had become more prosperous than tobacco growing. Even so, Barbour thought that slaveholders could ameliorate the institution. He combined his notion of white paternalism toward the slaves with a sincere aversion to an over-powering nation-state. Most slave owners, he said, treated their slaves "as the most valuable, as the most favored property" and with a sympathy that binds "one man to another, though that other may be our inferior." Virginia slave owners who transplanted to Missouri had taken their slaves along not only because their labor was "peculiarly necessary," he contended, but also because their vaunted sense of honor and supposed obligation to their slave property could not permit otherwise.[20]

On February 16, 1819, after the Committee of the Whole voted seventy-nine to sixty-seven to include the Tallmadge Amendment in the bill, Missouri territorial delegate John Scott's turn came to storm into the northern restrictionists. To impose this "unconstitutional inhibition" on Missouri raised the memory of the American Revolution, threatening new states with a new order of oppression, "when the General Government" would "dictate to them on questions of internal policy," Scott thundered. Tallmadge, embracing the extreme, responded: "If a dissolution of the Union must take place, let it be so! If civil war, which gentlemen so much threaten, must come, I can only say, let it come!" To extend the three-fifths clause to slave states beyond the Mississippi, Tallmadge further insisted, "would be unjust in its operations, unequal in its results, and a violation of original intentions." By that time, many southern congressmen had grown tired of having their "republicanism" questioned and their honor disparaged. Cobb had stated his position as opposite Tallmadge's, equally uncompromising and demanding a withdrawal of the amendment, lest it kindle "a fire that all the waters of the ocean cannot put out, which seas of blood can only extinguish."[21]

By the end of the Fifteenth Congress, on March 4, 1819, the stalled Missouri bill stood "lost between the Senate and the House of Representatives on the question of slavery," as a letter to Thomas Hart Benton's *St. Louis Enquirer* sadly concluded. Missouri territorial government would continue; statehood could wait, perhaps indefinitely. Meanwhile, adding insult to Missourians' injury, Alabama's admission to the Union went forward, as expected, without restriction on slavery. The *Enquirer* contributor worried that "some timid people, thinking Congress omnipotent . . . will sell off their property at a sacrifice, and remove away." Emigration of slaveholding families would dry up, while that from New England would increase "under the hope of gaining supremacy in this country." With that prospect on the horizon, would Missouri accept restriction as dictated in Washington? "No! never!" the anonymous writer cried, "and those who suppose her capable of such pusillanimous submission" had much underestimated the majority of Missourians.[22]

♠

Looking at popular pressures that mounted on federal lawmakers in the months that followed, we may dismiss any notion of the crisis being confined to Washington politics. While the Panic of 1819 spread financial worry everywhere during that same period, many ordinary Americans, regardless of section, nonetheless cared deeply about the political destiny of their republic. Southerners, moreover, did not remain "blissfully unaware of the fact that they were engaged in a mighty sectional contest," as historian Glover Moore once stated. They well recognized what they were up against, and they, too, registered their opinions in all likely venues.[23]

Apart from reporting the galleries and lobbies of Congress never to have been "more crowded," newspaper editors noted the public concern that swept through the white South as well as other regions of the country. The *New-Hampshire Sentinel* cited reports in early June 1819 that the "fate" of the Missouri bill had produced "great excitement in the territory proposed for admission, and in the slave-holding States generally." That remained true throughout the Missouri Crisis. Learning in December 1819 from the *New-York Evening Post* that no question had "more agitated the feelings of the Southern section of the Union, or will eventually more excite those of the Northern," Thomas Ritchie's *Richmond Enquirer* urged Virginians to elevate the "tone" of their reaction all the more. After adoption of the 36°30' agreement, the editor of the *Monticello Republican*, in southern Mississippi, still devoted half of his April 1, 1820, front page to an early January letter reprinted from the *Columbia (SC) Telescope*: "The crisis is awful, and big with consequences fatal to the peace and safety of the southern states, and the states formed from the country acquired by the purchase of Louisiana as well as Missouri, and other portions of empire lying westward." Southern indignation flamed anew the following year, during the fight over Missouri's exclusion of free Black people in its proposed constitution. In Tennessee, the *Nashville Gazette* noted in March 1821 that "the dissolution of the union, is as openly spoken of in Congress Hall, as in private conversation or the public prints." If Missouri were to fall "by those whose aim is to gratify the views of ambition," the *Gazette* added, "*she will not fall alone.*"[24]

In an apt summary of the prevailing white southern view, the *Georgia Journal*, reprinting a February 25, 1819, column from the *Richmond Enquirer*, told its readers that "certain Eastern members" of the House of Representatives had pursued with the citizens of Missouri a course of action "at war with their equal rights, as well as the public faith of the nation." By that time, the debate in the Fifteenth Congress had reached an impasse, "a struggle of Eastern prejudice against southern principles." That opinion, too, resonated around the South, despite approval of the compromise the following year. In March 1820, the editor of the *Newbern (NC) Sentinel*, also reprinting another, treated his readers to the same essential conviction:

"There is a vital point connected with this subject; it is the integrity of our constitution, which nothing should bend or impair. . . . I do not believe that Congress possess a constitutional right to shackle the sovereignty of any State." The April 19, 1820, issue of the *Louisiana Advertiser* of New Orleans agreed, adding that the northerners "most prominent in urging shackles upon Missouri, have been influenced rather by love of political power over our *whites* than *humanity* for our blacks."[25]

Was not all this talk of oppressive authority and "equal rights"—so ironic for a society rooted in slaveholding—really just a sectionalist smoke screen to disguise southerners' actual motive in protecting slavery? In part, of course, it *was*, just as similar arguments are still used to mask the unadulterated racism of some whites today. But for 1820, it would be a mistake to underestimate the depth—indeed the history—of white southern fear that northern radicals would take away their freedoms and make *them* the slaves, just as British tyrants had once tried. The "equality" they meant referred mainly to the sovereignty of states, based on the assumption of their equal footing within the Union. If a growing northern majority could deny that now to Missouri, might still larger antislavery majorities later take it away from the southern states as well?[26]

In one telling example, Samuel B. T. Caldwell's antislavery *Genius of Liberty*, in Leesburg, Virginia, stood as strongly against federal consolidation as it did against slaveholding. "Averse as we are to slavery," wrote Caldwell for November 2, 1819, "we do not think that the restrictions attempted to be imposed, in this instance, . . . were strictly constitutional or could be binding on Missouri after it became a state." A few months later, Caldwell elaborated that the issue had been "greatly mistaken by many" as an "abstract question of *morality*," but instead it was "that of a constitutional right" of Missouri to membership "on the *same terms* as other states." Agreeing that many had mistaken the crisis, an anonymous March 4, 1820, commentator in the *St. Louis Enquirer* went still further, referring to the "designs of the *north*" as being easy enough to discern, never mind the compromise then being passed in Congress. "New York is making *rapid strides* towards that power which is to give law to the Union," the writer warned, "and the control over the great country west of the Mississippi, is no small part of her plan." If antislavery men in Washington could "*demand* a constitutional abolition of slavery in the state," could they not equally insist that "all free negroes and mulattos may migrate to the proposed state," vote in elections, serve as witnesses and jurors, hold "offices of trust," become senators and representatives, and "intermarry with the whites of Missouri"? Would the next step be to limit the amount of land a man could own, require Missourians to vote for "the *great men* of New York for president," demand support for a "general emancipation of all the slaves of the Union," decree that "no bank except a branch of the bank of the United States shall be established in Missouri," or insist that its senators and representatives in Congress "be chosen exclusively from the *honorable class* of emigrants from New England, New York and Pennsylvania"?[27]

Along with matters of self-government, the prospect of "diffusing" slavery westward also lay at stake for the South. In February 1820, the *Georgia Journal* reprinted a column from the *National Intelligencer* insisting that northern newspapers had generally mischaracterized the Missouri controversy as involving an "*extension of slavery*, that is, the multiplication of slaves," whereas the question actually concerned "only the *diffusion* or the *concentration* of slaves now in the country." Among "enlightened" late-eighteenth-century slaveholders, including Thomas Jefferson, the idea of "diffusion" at first had been that slavery and the slaves themselves could be "ameliorated," that is, improved morally, by abolishing first the slave-import trade and then refining the institution as it expanded. Slaves might be prepared sufficiently for freedom and then for emancipation and expatriation abroad. In a way, this concept of ameliorating slavery came down to a reluctant confession: that slaveholding was by nature a ruinous practice that southerners needed to reform and then eradicate for the good of all. Famously, Jefferson had given the classic statement of this in *Notes on the State of Virginia* (1785), his concern focusing less on what slavery did to Black people and more on its negative impact on the behavior of white southerners. Apart from that, for Chesapeake slave owners living on depleted soil and eager to unload excess bondsmen, the argument held the attraction of profitable sales of experienced slaves to settlers in the new states, where fresh land provided for new farms and plantations. Between 1790 and 1820, Maryland sold roughly 75,000 slaves to other parts of the South; Virginia sold another 140,000. The economic downturn of 1819 had heightened the urgency of selling westward the excess of slaves, while the rising value of slaves who remained in the East satisfied owners as well. The logic of diffusion, whatever its persuasiveness on other grounds, appealed well enough to Upper South planters for financial reasons alone.[28]

By the early nineteenth century, however, slaveholders who worried about the volatility of slavery also identified their personal safety with a westward draining of the slave population. If slave states could not disperse westward this dangerously growing number of potential insurrectionists, argued the *Richmond Enquirer* on February 25, 1819, "more slaves are kept here, and their condition is not ameliorated as fast as the natural course of events would direct." As a result, "you do not lessen the evil of slavery; but you make it bear more heavily upon a smaller space." The *Charleston (SC) City Gazette* would have "rejoiced" over the Tallmadge Amendment, it declared on February 26, if its effect in Missouri could have been to "diminish the number of slaves in the United States or improve their condition," but in reality it would only "concentrate that description of population." Answering the restrictionists, Barbour mirrored these views in Congress, arguing similarly that spreading slavery over a greater surface would reduce the threat of slave insurrection and encourage the eastern slave master to be "more tender in his treatment to his dependents."[29]

By the time of the Missouri Crisis, slaveholders in the Southeast lived in a plantation world of alarmingly high numbers of Black people compared to whites. The slave population in the South Atlantic states had grown dramatically in the early decades of the 1800s, from roughly 684,000 in 1800, to 863,000 in 1810, to 1,038,000 in 1820. The numbers of slaves had exploded by similar percentages in the southwestern states, from about 17,000 to 97,000 to 229,000 during the same period. But somehow the numbers of enslaved men and women in the southwestern Cotton Belt seemed less daunting than in the older South. Whether they owned slaves or not, southeastern white families lived in palpable fear of slave insurrection, justified soon enough by news in 1822 of Denmark Vesey's failed plot in Charleston and, later, when Nat Turner's rebellion of 1831 rocked Virginia. By 1820, the dreaded "fire bell in the night" might as easily denote a sudden slave uprising as any other emergency. The Missouri debate, as Edward Colston had predicted, seemed only to worsen the danger—and, with that, white fears. Slave owners in New York and New Jersey, where Black-to-white ratios remained much lower than in the South, could end the institution perhaps with less worry about racial adjustment afterward. By contrast, white Virginians, South Carolinians, or Georgians thought twice about liberating their "internal enemy" with no more confidence than the colonization movement offered them.[30]

In spite of these dangers, most southern planters by 1820 could still not imagine a better economic milieu than their own. They rejected the free-labor model then forming in the North—farming, commerce, and manufacturing operating more or less in balance. For southerners, after all, the War of 1812 had guaranteed a bright future for King Cotton, largely thanks to Jackson's armies at Horseshoe Bend and New Orleans. A dynamic new political economy of slavery advanced up the Mississippi and westward, reflecting forces at work since the 1790s as well as wartime gains. Eli Whitney's cotton gin had arrived in the lower Mississippi region by 1795, transforming both the production of cotton and the demand for slaves. The global market promised that short-staple cotton would be *the* plantation crop for decades to come. Cotton production had tripled since 1815, while its prices skyrocketed from seventeen cents a pound in 1814 to nearly thirty cents in 1817, promising a lucrative future despite the Panic of 1819. The climate of the Deep South along with the shortage of white workers, further, seemed to make slavery necessary. Economic and social realities reinforced that conclusion: landless whites would demand high wages, resent harsh supervision, object to doing "slave work," and eventually venture westward themselves.[31]

During the Missouri Crisis, an Alabama editor reprinted a column from the *Savannah Republican* that summarized the labor dilemma that he thought even the most well-meaning slaveholders faced, given the limitations of their situation and of their vision. Many people in the North had come to view slavery "as the curse of our country—the portentous cloud that threatens to blast, wherever it extends, every bud of virtue." But how, the writer asked, were slaves in the South to be emancipated? Would "the northern people, in case we consent to give them up, bear an equal proportion of this loss of property, as in justice they ought?" Would they annually send their proportion of laborers "to cultivate our swamp lands and rice fields, or shall we let them lay waste[?]" And what were southern whites to do with these former chattels, "turn them loose on society?" Northerners, however reform intentioned, stood unwilling to receive them, and no one could raise the money needed to colonize them to Africa. Notwithstanding the alternative of diffusion, "The fact is we have no other alternative than to retain them amongst us, and alleviate and make their condition as comfortable as we can compatible with our own safety."[32]

As if the Missouri issue had not been troubling enough for politically conscious southern whites, just three days after the congressional session ended in March 1819, the Supreme Court generated another wave of anti-federal reaction with its *McCulloch v. Maryland* ruling, which declared the Second Bank of the United States to be constitutional and exempt from state taxation. Much of the early blame for the panic, especially in economically distressed parts of the South and West, had settled upon the bank and its president, William Jones, whose financial mismanagement had weakened the institution. But the broader problem, as more southern pundits than ever now said, was the "implied powers" doctrine and the deep-seated fear of "consolidation"—concentrated federal power—that went with it. John Taylor of Caroline made the point in three books he wrote between 1820 and 1824, especially his *New Views of the Constitution* (1823). The bank decision also enraged others of the "Old Republican" faction in Virginia, including Ritchie, Spencer Roane, and William Brockenbrough of Richmond—leaders of the strict-constructionist "Richmond Junto," a small group of vintage 1798 Jeffersonians who feared a resurgence of the Federalist Party. In Ritchie's *Richmond Enquirer*, beginning on March 30, 1819, one of the "Junto," signing as "Amphictyon," condemned Chief Justice John Marshall's aggressively nationalist stance in *McCulloch*. Would not such a constitutional interpretation empower Congress to fund roads and canals wherever it pleased, incorporate companies and other organizations under federal authority, and even found churches—all under the pretext of "implied powers"? Roane, more famously, under the pseudonym "Hampden," also railed against federal "consolidation" and further lamented the growing of congressional power. And now, too, southern leaders easily understood all the same warnings as applying with no less force to Missouri.[33]

Soon afterward, the Virginia House of Delegates, also reflecting the "Old Republican" view, weighed in with a set of resolutions supporting Missouri's cause. The author, Briscoe Baldwin, a Staunton attorney, emphasized the inviolability of the states, including all newly admitted ones. Congressionally imposed restrictions, if adopted, would offend "the sovereign character" of the Missouri people, now forming their own constitution and government. Success of the Tallmadge Amendment would mean not only forcing a hostile will on Missourians but also "the exclusion of the inestimable right to alter the same hereafter as those people may deem necessary for their prosperity and happiness." Beyond just the Missouri Question, here was a "most serious and portentous danger to the sovereign rights reserved to the states; alarming as it respects the future liberties of the people; and tending immediately to weaken the strong cement . . . of our happy union." Independent of the legislature, another anonymous contributor in the *Richmond Enquirer* of May 21, 1819, provided a more personal—and compelling—statement of Virginia indignation: "If we should unfortunately fail in support of our principle, the certain effect will be to make all the territory west of the Mississippi, and north of latitude 36, a Yankee country, governed by the sniveling, sanctimonious doctrines in politics and religion which, as a Virginian, I early learned to abhor." Several months later, the *Weekly Messenger*'s subscribers around Russellville, Kentucky, read that their legislature, long kindred to Virginia's, would adopt James Johnson's resolutions instructing its U.S. senators to oppose the northern restrictionists on grounds that they meant to undercut state sovereignty, "bind" the Missouri Territory "in perpetual vassalage, and reduce it to the condition of a province" forever dependent on Congress for its rights.[34]

Out west in Missouri, meanwhile, practically everyone now agreed that if other western states could enter the Union on terms of their own choosing, then they should too. One public meeting after another in Missouri doubted that Congress had any constitutional right to restrict their slavery. Some cited the 1803 treaty with France as leaving slavery for them alone to determine. Others, including Thomas Hart Benton, maintained that northeasterners had always wished to cripple the West, as he would say again ten years later as a U.S. senator during the Webster-Hayne debate.[35]

Talk of revolution spread as well. In May 1819, "A ST. LOUIS MECHANIC" condemned the "eastern aristocrats" now in control of the "domineering, unprincipled party" in the House of Representatives who allegedly had made Missouri's admission part of their larger tyrannical scheme to achieve "a consolidated government" in Washington. "The day is approaching," the writer exhorted, "when the people of Missouri will show to their enemies that they not only know their rights, but also, if occasion requires, they have still enough of 1776 left, to fight for them." Likewise, a dinner in Franklin, Missouri, that same month included a toast to those who would "defend their rights," including slave owning, "even at the expense of blood." Later on, readers of the *Charleston (SC) City Gazette* probably applauded the report in their newspaper of a dinner in St. Louis featuring a toast to the people of Missouri: "Willing to contend for their just rights with moderation; ready to defend them at the point of the bayonet." In the meantime, recent Missouri settlers dug in their heels, while new ones showed up to join the fight. The *Richmond Enquirer*, in December 1819, printed a letter from one who had migrated from South Carolina: "For my part, I am determined to put everything to hazard upon the question; for I am not disposed to go farther south, still less to relinquish the advantages of this most commanding section of country." That same month, a St. Louis correspondent noted some thirty to fifty wagons crossing the Mississippi daily, carrying four or five hundred white settlers, mostly from Kentucky, Tennessee, Virginia, and states farther south, along with "great numbers of slaves." They came, assuming "that congress has no power to impose the agitated restriction, and that the people of Missouri will never adopt it."[36]

Apart from all that, some Missouri slaveholders took matters of sovereignty into their own hands. According to the newspapers, the few Missourians who actually opposed slavery had been pressured either to change their minds or to keep quiet. One example: the experience of Humphrey Smith, a New Jersey native who had brought his family as squatters on federal land near Boon's Lick. He openly condemned slavery and vowed to do all he could in the cause of freedom. Then, one night, an armed proslavery mob approached his house, pulled Smith out of bed, beat him up, "abused" his wife "in a shocking manner," and declared they would "kill or drive out of the country" any man who spoke against slaveholding. When auction time came, one of that rabble made sure to outbid Smith, costing him both his claim and the improvements he had made on it. In another case, a group of antislavery Methodists putatively attempted in September 1819 to hold a camp meeting in Cape Girardeau County, only to find "a mob of slaveholders" appearing among them, driving away the preachers and dispersing the followers. Reports of such lawless behavior in Missouri, mostly on the part of proslavery people, could not have registered favorably with restrictionists in Congress or softened their resolve to bring order and moral reform to the place.[37]

As for that small minority of antislavery Missourians, it seemed many of them, too, opposed congressional interference in business they regarded as properly Missouri's own. A June 1819 citizens' meeting at the St. Louis home of Elisha Patterson, for example, condemned slaveholding as contrary to "the laws of nature" and one of the country's "greatest evils." Yet the same group viewed "with jealousy any attempt made in congress to usurp from us, any right with which we may be legally vested by any treaty of cession, or guaranteed to us by the constitution of the United States."[38]

As part of a long story of western resistance to eastern authority, the threat of an independent Missouri should have been regarded seriously. Some easterners indeed took it so. Economic nationalist Mathew Carey, for one, cautioned that Missouri and other parts of the West, if "thrown out of the attraction of the present sphere," might well "revolve in another system" and find their "liberty, security, and prosperity . . . without the aid of the United States." In that case, the *Philadelphia Union* reminded, good-bye to the coveted fur trade of the region; its salt springs and its lead mines "sufficient to furnish all America"; its proximity for roads stretching to Washington, New Orleans, and Louisville; and its natural port of entry at St. Louis. Southerners, too, considered the economic consequences of losing the Missouri Territory. As South Carolinian John C. Calhoun later noted, "All saw that if Missouri was not admitted, she would remain an independent State on the west bank of the Mississippi, and would become the nucleus of a new confederation of States extending over the whole of Louisiana."[39]

In January 1820, all hopes for compromise during the Sixteenth Congress shifted to the Senate. There, the Missouri bill emerged from the Senate Judiciary Committee *without* the restrictionist provision. Antislavery northerners, including Pennsylvania's Jonathan Roberts, did their best to restore it. With that, the possibility of disunion seemed to grow. "From the present appearances the fate of the application for admission will be the same as last year," the *Missouri Gazette* glumly predicted. Southerners widely praised sectionalist diehards on their side. At the same time, the pressure to compromise mounted on southern moderates—men such as Virginia's senator James Barbour, older brother of Philip. As he explained to James Madison privately, the elder Barbour feared that Congress might admit Maine (newly broken off from Massachusetts) but not Missouri, and "the whole territory to the west of the Mississippi will be taken from us." A further political disaster for Jeffersonian Republicans might follow: that Federalist senator Rufus King or New York's DeWitt Clinton, a Federalist sympathizer, "will most probably be the next President."[40]

While avoiding that outcome, some in the Southwest still resented the proposed 36°30' line as a further antislavery limiting of their expansionist hopes. Secretary of State John Quincy Adams's 1819 treaty with Spain (though still unratified) already seemed to have done so by placing the Louisiana Purchase boundary eastward to exclude Texas. The compromisers' "views are in conformity with those of Mr. ADAMS in surrendering to the Spaniards, so much valuable territory *south of this projected line*, in order to bring our limits as near as possible to the Mississippi," cried the *Kentucky Reporter* on January 12, 1820. With the compromise nearly finalized that March, another of its columnists deplored an apparent pro-eastern bias of the agreement: "Thus it seems, with *restriction* on the one side, and *cessions* to Spain on the other, there is a limit to the growth of the west." As in New Yorker John Jay's unratified Jay-Gardoqui agreement in 1786, the second writer implied, Secretary Adams's work "would desolate the country to check our progress south west, and congress would forbid our migration north; he would cede to Spain more territory than she asked, and create an unnatural barrier between us and our Spanish neighbors."[41]

In any case, had the Missouri bill come to him in March 1820 without a compromise and including the Tallmadge Amendment, President Monroe would have had no choice but to veto it. His fellow Virginia planters would never have forgiven him otherwise, and his support elsewhere depended on pleasing moderates in the party, regardless of section. When Monroe took over the presidency in 1817, his main political objective had been reconciliation among conflicting factions and sections after the War of 1812. Following a goodwill tour of the Northeast at that time, Monroe had written, happily, "I have seen enough to satisfy me, that the great mass of our fellow-citizens, in the Eastern States are as firmly attached to the union and to republican gov[t]. as I have always believ'd or could desire them to be." In his first annual message of December that year, he proclaimed: "Local jealousies are rapidly yielding to more generous, enlarged and enlightened views of national policy." For the all-important cabinet post of secretary of state, he had chosen Adams, of Massachusetts, partly for that reason. Had his presidency marked the end of partisan spirit in American politics, it would have fulfilled a major intention of his most admired predecessor, George Washington, as stated in the Farewell Address of 1796.[42]

Involved here too, of course, was Monroe's own view of Missouri's rights, again politically influenced. Like Clay and others who opposed the Tallmadge Amendment, he wanted the states themselves to determine whether they would have slavery. Looking at Article IV, Section 3, of the Constitution, he considered the power of Congress over the admission of new states to be vastly different from its power over territorial development. "I never doubted the right of Congress, to make such a regulation in [the] territories," Monroe privately told Jefferson in May 1820. But to assume federal control over the internal affairs of a state was another matter. Apart from that, he indicated to his Virginia friends (perhaps because they wanted to believe it) that ambitious northeastern Federalists stood behind the whole matter. "The object of those, who brought it forward," he had said to Jefferson earlier, "was undoubtedly to acquire power, & the expedient well adapted to the end, as it enlisted in their service, the best feelings, of all that portion of our Union, in which slavery does not exist, & who are unacquainted with the condition of their Southern brethren." The northeastern restrictionists like Rufus King, he further added, really did want to inhibit the growth of the West by blocking the addition of slave states indebted to Republican policy makers for their very existence. Monroe also recalled the Jay-Gardoqui negotiations of 1786, where Federalists had offered to accept a closing of the Mississippi to American commerce for twenty-five years. "The dismemberment of the Union by the Allegheny Mountains, was then believed to be their object," he asserted, and while "a new arrangement of powers, is more particularly sought on this occasion, yet it is believ'd, that the anticipation of even that result, would not deter its Authors from the pursuit of it."[43]

Even after the Missouri Crisis had shaken what some historians have dubbed his "Era of Good Feelings," Monroe felt relieved. If the compromise had prevented a revival of the Federalist Party, it had even more forestalled a breakup of his own party along sectional lines. "Surely our government may get on and prosper without the existence of [opposing] parties," the president would tell James Madison in 1822. "I have always considered their existence as the curse of the country," he added, again endorsing Washington's increasingly archaic belief. The challenge, Monroe said, was to succeed in "the experiment whether there is sufficient virtue in the people to support our free republican system of government." By then, it looked as if the Missouri Compromise had bought that "experiment" further time to prove successful—or not.[44]

When news of the March 1820 passage of the Missouri bill without restriction arrived in St. Louis, it landed, said those on the scene, with "the ringing of bells, the firing of cannon, and the joyful congratulations of the citizens." At the War Department in Washington, Secretary John C. Calhoun indulged in cautious optimism. In August 1820, he wrote his Maryland friend Virgil Maxcy that the only real danger now threatening the republic would be an erroneous perception in the slaveholding states that the North actually meant to undermine their property in slaves. "Should so dangerous a mode of believing once take root, no one can calculate the consequences; and it will be found, that a reagitation of the Missouri question will tend strongly to excite such a belief." But as Calhoun implied, other southerners remained unconvinced that such a perception had been far wrong. Earlier, in May, the *Louisiana Advertiser* in New Orleans, for one, still questioned northern intentions: "Even the most intemperate advocates of Restriction will be convinced of the danger of *agitating* such a question. . . . Slavery among us has been as fully considered as it is possible it ever should be, and it is idle to discuss it further. . . . We cannot come to any *new resolve* upon it, and it can be stirred only from *invidious* motives." When, why, or whether that further "stirring" would occur, neither Calhoun nor anyone else could then predict.[45]

♠

Yet southerners could rest easy for a while. They got the better of the deal even if not all thought so at the time. "The Southern people are complaining," John Eaton of Tennessee observed to Andrew Jackson on March 11, 1820, "but they ought not, for it [the compromise] has preserved peace[,] dissipated angry feelings, and dispelled appearances which seemed dark and horrible and threat[en]ing to the interest and harmony of the nation." From a southern standpoint, the compromise had honored state sovereignty; the antislavery part of it affected only territorial development, as earlier in the Northwest Ordinance, and not the right of new states to govern themselves. In Virginia, where the "Old Republican" faction of the Jeffersonian Republican Party would go on flourishing, much of that "complaining" would continue. Beyond that, slave owners throughout the South would sharpen their state-sovereignty argument over the course of the 1820s, asserting local and state control as it served their interests. As for the newest slave state, the *Alexandria (VA) Gazette* concluded on August 14, 1821, after *all* controversy had abated, that "the fate of Missouri is now fairly put into her own hands, the extension of slavery, which she so eagerly sought for, has been unconditionally obtained: a solemn pledge was required and has been given, that the rights of citizens of any of the states shall not be contravened, and the Federal constitution duly observed."[46]

Granted, the antislavery side received the largest territorial share of the Louisiana Purchase, all of it north of 36°30′, minus Missouri itself. But most southerners recognized the free-soil part as lying well above the traditional Ohio River dividing line between the so-called slave and free states. Few regarded that region as promising for plantation-style agriculture anyway— or likely to be settled soon. Still, the compromise line would establish a more sectionalized division between "North" and "South," free states and slave, than had existed before, making more likely the eventual taking of Texas and areas beyond. "If we are cooped up on the north, we must have elbow room to the west," the *Richmond Enquirer* adumbrated.[47] All things considered, the South and Missourians got what they wanted most: a victory of state self-determination and, with that, a temporary repulsing of antislavery nation-building designs for the trans-Mississippi West. The fate of the institution in the slave states remained a uniquely southern concern, off limits to northern abolitionists. With that, southerners could go on accepting union with a North that they largely did not trust.

Looking back, as slavery expanded westward, southern leaders, along with their politically attuned constituents, tried all the more to protect the right to hold slave property. Meanwhile, their antislavery attackers condemned an institution that now weighed more heavily on *their* consciences than on those of slave owners. This deadlock produced widespread anxiety that the country might break into two or more distinct and conflicting political entities. Antislavery ideas in themselves may not have motivated many people far beyond their lamenting the suffering that slaveholders perpetrated. But when opponents of slavery could argue persuasively that the labor system of the South and the values that underlay it directly threatened their personal lives, economic interests, and hopes for the future, then belief could more quickly convert into advocacy and action. The same held true as well on the slaveholding side, especially when southerners (and Missourians) sensed more working against them than just basic disagreement over politics and economic practices.[48]

In matters of "equal rights," sovereignty, and self-identity, as southern white leaders construed them all, the Missouri Crisis revealed the power that slavery and its side effects had gained over American nation building. By that time, so many Americans, in all parts of the country, had invested so much in a future of westward expansion that serious talk of *whose* West it would be mattered heavily. The question of what kind of society and labor system would develop there, along with the political implications that might result, had energized public opinion all around.

Notes

1. For the antislavery buildup to the controversy, see Matthew Mason, *Slavery and Politics in the Early Republic* (Chapel Hill: University of North Carolina Press, 2006); and on slavery expansion, John Craig Hammond, *Slavery, Freedom, and Expansion in the Early American West* (Charlottesville: University of Virginia Press, 2007). Regarding antisouthern attitudes, see Leonard L. Richards, *The Slave Power: The Free North and Southern Domination, 1780–1860* (Baton Rouge: Louisiana State University Press, 2000); and Susan-Mary Grant, *North over South: Northern Nationalism and American Identity in the Antebellum Era* (Lawrence: University Press of Kansas, 2000). For southern perspectives, see Robert E. Bonner, *Mastering America: Southern Slaveholders and the Crisis of American Nationhood* (Cambridge: Cambridge University Press, 2009).

2. The classic monograph on the Missouri Crisis is Glover Moore, *The Missouri Controversy, 1819–1821* (Lexington: University Press of Kentucky, 1953). Robert P. Forbes, *The Missouri Compromise and Its Aftermath: Slavery and the Meaning of America* (Chapel Hill: University of North Carolina Press, 2007), offers an extensive revisionist study. See also Peter B. Knupfer, *The Union as It Is: Constitutional Unionism and Sectional Compromise, 1787–1861* (Chapel Hill: University of North Carolina Press, 1991); and Gary J. Kornblith's brief *Slavery and Sectional Strife in the Early American Republic, 1776–1821* (Lanham, MD: Rowman and Littlefield, 2010). For

my own view, see John R. Van Atta, *Wolf by the Ears: The Missouri Crisis, 1819–1821* (Baltimore: Johns Hopkins University Press, 2015).

3. *National Intelligencer*, quoted in the *Mercantile Advertiser* (New York), February 19, 1819; Tucker, "From the *St. Louis Enquirer*," reprinted in *Weekly Messenger* (Russellville, KY), May 21, 1819. See also the Tallmadge Amendment report in the *Commercial Advertiser* (New York), February 16, 1819.

4. Don E. Fehrenbacher, *The Slaveholding Republic: An Account of the United States Government's Relations to Slavery* (New York: Oxford University Press, 2001), 26–28; Kornblith, *Slavery and Sectional Strife*, 30–31; David Waldstreicher, *Slavery's Constitution: From Revolution to Ratification* (New York: Hill and Wang, 2009), 88.

5. Regarding gradual emancipation in the North, see Joanne Pope Melish, *Disowning Slavery: Gradual Emancipation and "Race" in New England, 1780–1860* (Ithaca, NY: Cornell University Press, 1998); and David N. Gellman, *Emancipating New York: The Politics of Slavery and Freedom, 1877–1827* (Baton Rouge: Louisiana State University Press, 2006). On the "equal footing" doctrine, see Gary Lawson and Guy Seidman, *The Constitution of Empire: Territorial Expansion and American Legal History* (New Haven, CT: Yale University Press, 2004), 73–75, 79–81.

6. On the changes in New York, see Gellman, *Emancipating New York*, chap. 8.

7. See Nicole Etcheson, *The Emerging Midwest: Upland Southerners and the Political Culture of the Old Northwest, 1787–1861* (Bloomington: Indiana University Press, 1996); and Jeremy Adelman and Stephen Aron, "From Borderlands to Borders: Empires, Nation-States, and the Peoples in between in North American History," *American Historical Review* 104, no. 3 (1999): 814–23.

8. For the Illinois debate, see *Annals of Congress*, House, 15th Cong., 2nd sess., 296–98, 305–11. For the vote, see p. 311. For the Illinois senators' votes on the Missouri question, see Moore, *Missouri Controversy*, 55, 108, 144, 158.

9. On the distinction between "slave societies" and "societies with slaves," see Ira Berlin, *Many Thousands Gone: The First Two Centuries of Slavery in North America* (Cambridge, MA: Belknap Press of Harvard University Press, 1998), 8–9, 7–13, 22, 98, 105–8.

10. On early-nineteenth-century development of the Missouri region, see Stephen Aron, *American Confluence: The Missouri Frontier from Borderland to Border State* (Bloomington: Indiana University Press, 2006), 151–52; Paul C. Nagel, *Missouri: A History* (Lawrence: University Press of Kansas, 1977), 30–32; and John Craig Hammond, "Slavery, Settlement, and Empire: The Expansion and Growth of Slavery in the Interior of the North American Continent, 1770–1820," *Journal of the Early Republic* 32, no. 2 (2012): 175–206.

11. "Louisiana Purchase Treaty, April 30, 1803," General Records of the U.S. Government, Record Group 11, National Archives, https://www.ourdocuments.gov/doc.php?flash=false&doc=18&page=transcript; Jackson quoted in William Plumer, *Memorandum of Proceedings in the United States Senate, 1803–1807*, ed. Everett Somerville Brown (New York: Macmillan, 1923), 115–16. See also Lawson and Seidman, *Constitution of Empire*, 73–78; and Kornblith, *Slavery and Sectional Strife*, 46–47. On free-labor fears, see Joshua Michael Zeitz, "The Missouri Compromise

Reconsidered: Rhetoric and the Emergence of the Free Labor Synthesis," *Journal of the Early Republic* 20, no. 3 (2000): 447–85; and George William Van Cleve, *A Slaveholders' Union: Slavery, Politics, and the Constitution in the Early American Republic* (Chicago: University of Chicago Press, 2010), 231–37.

12. See, for example, "SLAVERY," *Albany (NY) Gazette*, September 1, 1817; "HORRORS OF SLAVERY," *Columbian Centinel* (Boston), November 12, 1817; James Forten, "Letters from a Man of Colour on a Late Bill before the Senate of Pennsylvania," in *American Antislavery Writings: Colonial Beginnings to Emancipation*, ed. James G. Basker (New York: Library of America, 2012), 211–15, quote on 215; and George Bourne, "The Book and Slavery Irreconcilable," in *American Antislavery Writings*, ed. Basker, 216–18, quote on 218. On Kendrick, see Richard S. Newman, *The Transformation of American Abolitionism: Fighting Slavery in the Early Republic* (Chapel Hill: University of North Carolina Press, 2002), 108–9. Regarding the antislavery media, see Trish Loughran, *The Republic in Print: Print Culture in the Age of U.S. Nation Building, 1770–1870* (New York: Columbia University Press, 2007), chap. 6.

13. "MEMORIAL ON THE MISSOURI QUESTION," *Baltimore Patriot and Mercantile Advertiser*, January 3, 1820; "Hideous Persecution of the Methodists," *Easton (MD) Gazette, and Eastern Shore Intelligencer*, December 6, 1819.

14. *St. Louis Enquirer*, April 29, 1820; "Remarks of Mr. Cobb, of Georgia," *City of Washington Gazette*, March 27, 1819.

15. Cobb, *City of Washington Gazette*, March 27, 1819. On "unmasking," see Kenneth S. Greenberg, *Honor & Slavery* (Princeton, NJ: Princeton University Press, 1996), 25–27. See generally Bertram Wyatt-Brown, *Southern Honor: Ethics and Behavior in the Old South* (New York: Oxford University Press, 1982); and Alan Taylor, *Thomas Jefferson's Education* (New York: W. W. Norton, 2019), 69–100, esp. 76–79. Regarding the language of the southern political elite, see Bonner, *Mastering America*, xix.

16. William W. Freehling, *The Road to Disunion*, vol. 1, *Secessionists at Bay, 1776–1854* (New York: Oxford University Press, 1990), 146–48; Richards, *Slave Power*, 44–46.

17. Richards, *Slave Power*, 44–46; Knupfer, *Union as It Is*, 96. See Barbour's speech of February 10, 1820, *Annals of Congress*, House, 16th Cong., 1st sess., 1218–42, esp. 1231–32. On earlier Federalist dissatisfaction, see James M. Banner Jr., *To the Hartford Convention: The Federalists and the Origins of Party Politics in Massachusetts, 1789–1815* (New York: Alfred A. Knopf, 1970).

18. "Remarks on Tallmadge Amendment," February 15, 1819, in *The Papers of Henry Clay*, ed. James F. Hopkins et al., 10 vols. (Lexington: University Press of Kentucky, 1959–92), 2:670. On the compatibility of slavery and the "American System," see Andrew Shankman, "Neither Infinite Wretchedness nor Positive Good: Mathew Carey and Henry Clay on Political Economy and Slavery during the Long 1820s," in *Contesting Slavery: The Politics of Bondage and Freedom in the New American Nation*, ed. John Craig Hammond and Matthew Mason (Charlottesville: University of Virginia Press, 2011), 247–66.

19. Taylor, *Annals of Congress*, House, 15th Cong., 2nd sess., 1170–79, esp. 1170, 1174; Livermore, 1191–93, esp. 1193; reference to Colston's words, 1205; Tallmadge, 1203–14, esp. 1203. On southern anxiety, see Bonner, *Mastering America*, 15–23; and, generally, Alan Taylor, *The Internal Enemy: Slavery and War in Virginia, 1772–1832* (New York: W. W. Norton, 2013).

20. Barbour, *Annals of Congress*, House, 15th Cong., 2nd sess., 1184–91, esp. 1188. On Virginia's decline, see Susan Dunn, *Dominion of Memories: Jefferson, Madison, and the Decline of Virginia* (New York: Basic Books, 2007). For Philip P. Barbour and family, see William S. Belko, *Philip Pendleton Barbour in Jacksonian America: An Old Republican in King Andrew's Court* (Tuscaloosa: University of Alabama Press, 2016); and Charles D. Lowery, *James Barbour: A Jeffersonian Republican* (Tuscaloosa: University of Alabama Press, 1984).

21. Scott, *Annals of Congress*, 15th Cong., 2nd sess., 1195–1203, esp. 1201–2; Tallmadge, 1203–14, esp. 1204; reference to Cobb's words, 1214.

22. Letter to the editor, *St. Louis Enquirer*, March 31, 1819.

23. For interpretation of the "crisis" as Washington based, see Moore, *Missouri Controversy*, 65, 170, 218–19, 342. The "blissfully unaware" statement appears on p. 218. On grassroots pressure, see Donald Ratcliffe, *The One-Party Presidential Contest: Adams, Jackson, and 1824's Five-Horse Race* (Lawrence: University Press of Kansas, 2015), 10–11, 30–31.

24. *National Intelligencer*, reprinted in *American Beacon* (Norfolk, VA), January 22, 1820; *New-Hampshire Sentinel* (Keene, NH), June 5, 1819; "MISSOURI QUESTION," *Richmond (VA) Enquirer*, December 3, 1819; "Extract of a Letter to the Editor of the Columbia, S.C. *Telescope*," reprinted in the *Monticello (MS) Republican*, April 1, 1820; *Nashville (TN) Gazette*, March 3, 1821.

25. "State of Missouri," *Georgia Journal* (Milledgeville), March 16, 1819 (see also "STATE OF MISSOURI," *Richmond (VA) Enquirer*, February 25, 1819; "MISSOURI QUESTION," *Newbern [sic] (NC) Sentinel*, March 11, 1820; "MISSOURI," *Louisiana Advertiser* (New Orleans), April 19, 1820.

26. As one of many widely circulated expressions of this historical comparison, Beverley Tucker reportedly told a grand jury, meeting in St. Louis on April 5, 1819, that the attempt of Congress to restrict "the formation of a constitution and form of state government for ourselves" represented a greater "usurpation of power, over our unalienable rights and privileges as a free people . . . as any other power or body politic whatever since our emancipation from British tyranny and oppression." "From the *St. Louis Enquirer*," in *Weekly Messenger* (Russellville, KY), May 21, 1819.

27. "MISSOURI QUESTION," *Genius of Liberty* (Leesburg, VA), November 2, 1819, and January 18, 1820; "MISSOURI QUESTION," *St. Louis Enquirer*, March 4, 1820.

28. *National Intelligencer*, reprinted in the *Georgia Journal* (Milledgeville), February, 15, 1820; Lacy K. Ford, *Deliver Us from Evil: The Slavery Question in the Old South* (New York: Oxford University Press, 2009), 74–76; Van Cleve, *Slaveholders' Union*, 232–36, esp. 235. On the idea of "diffusion," see Christa Dierksheide, "'The Great Improvement and Civilization of That Race': Jefferson and the 'Amelioration'

of Slavery, ca. 1770–1826," *Early American Studies* 6, no. 1 (2008): 165–97; and Dierksheide, *Amelioration and Empire: Progress and Slavery in the Plantation Americas* (Charlottesville: University of Virginia Press, 2014). For Jefferson's statement, see Query XVIII, "Notes on the State of Virginia," in *The Portable Thomas Jefferson*, ed. Merrill D. Peterson (New York: Viking Press, 1975), 214.

29. "STATE OF MISSOURI," *Richmond (VA) Enquirer*, February 25, 1819; *City Gazette* (Charleston, SC), February 26, 1819; Philip P. Barbour, *Annals of Congress*, House, 16th Cong., 1st sess., 1391.

30. Freehling, *The Road to Disunion*, 151–52. For statistics on slave population growth, see Songho Ha, *The Rise and Fall of the American System: Nationalism and the Development of the American Economy, 1790–1837* (London: Pickering and Chatto, 2009), 58. On the fear of slave insurrection, see Taylor, *Thomas Jefferson's Education*, 202–3; and, generally, Taylor, *Internal Enemy*.

31. Adam Rothman, *Slave Country: American Expansion and the Origins of the Deep South* (Cambridge, MA: Harvard University Press, 2005), 170–71, 177; Christopher Clark, *Social Change in America: From the Revolution through the Civil War* (Chicago: Ivan R. Dee, 2006), 123–27, esp. 125. On the northern free-labor vision, see Clark, *Social Change in America*, 16, 138–41, 152, 158, 173–74, 227–28.

32. *Savannah Republican*, reprinted in *Halcyon* (St. Stephens, AL), March 27, 1820.

33. "Amphictyon" [William Brockenbrough], *Richmond (VA) Enquirer*, March 30–April 2, 1819, reprinted in *John Marshall's Defense of McCulloch v. Maryland*, ed. Gerald Gunther (Stanford, CA: Stanford University Press, 1969), 71. See the discussion of "Hampden" in John L. Larson, *Internal Improvement: National Public Works and the Promise of Popular Government in the Early United States* (Chapel Hill: University of North Carolina Press, 2001), 132–33. See also Don E. Fehrenbacher, *The South and Three Sectional Crises* (Baton Rouge: Louisiana State University Press, 1980), 19–20. For John Taylor of Caroline, see especially *New Views of the Constitution of the United States* (Washington, DC: Way and Gideon, 1823) and *Construction Construed, and Constitutions Vindicated* (Richmond, VA: Shepherd & Pollard, 1820). See also Bonner, *Mastering America*, 44–47. On the southern anti-consolidation tradition, see Saul Cornell, *The Other Founders: Anti-Federalism and the Dissenting Tradition in America, 1788–1828* (Chapel Hill: University of North Carolina Press, 1999).

34. *Preamble and Resolutions Offered by Mr. Baldwin, to the House of Delegates, on the Missouri Question* (Richmond, 1819); *Richmond Enquirer* quoted in the *Edwardsville (IL) Spectator*, June 26, 1819; *Weekly Messenger* (Russellville, KY), January 11, 1820.

35. See Thomas Hart Benton, *Thirty Years' View; or, A History of the Working of the American Government for Thirty Years, from 1820 to 1850*, 2 vols. (New York: D. Appleton, 1879), 1:5. For Benton's views in the Webster-Hayne debate, see John R. Van Atta, *Securing the West: Politics, Public Lands, and the Fate of the Old Republic, 1785–1850* (Baltimore: Johns Hopkins University Press, 2014), chap. 5.

36. "A ST. LOUIS MECHANIC," *St. Louis Enquirer*, May 19, 1819; Resident of Franklin, Missouri, quoted in Hammond, *Slavery, Freedom, and Expansion*, 55; *City*

Gazette (Charleston, SC), August 15, 1821; "FROM MISSOURI," *Richmond (VA) Enquirer*, December 11, 1819; "The Emigration," *Farmers' Repository* (Charles Town, VA), December 1, 1819; *Carolina Centinel* (New Bern, NC), December 25, 1819.

37. "MOB AT BOON'S LICK," *Edwardsville (IL) Spectator* (Edwardsville, IL), August 28, 1819, reprinted in the *Alexandria (VA) Herald*, October 7, 1819; "MOB IN MISSOURI," *Farmers' Repository* (Charles Town, VA), November 24, 1819.

38. From the *Missouri Gazette* (St. Louis), June 23, 1819, reprinted in the *Edwardsville (IL) Spectator*, June 16, 1819.

39. [Mathew Carey], *Considerations on the Impropriety and Expediency of Renewing the Missouri Question* (Philadelphia, 1820), 35, 65, 66–67, 68–69; *Philadelphia Union*, reprinted in *Baltimore Patriot and Mercantile Advertiser*, August 14, 1819; "Remarks on the Missouri Compromise," July 26, 1848, in *The Papers of John C. Calhoun*, ed. Robert L. Meriwether et al., 28 vols. (Columbia: University of South Carolina Press, 1959–2003), 25:630–33, quote on 632.

40. "STATE OF THE MISSOURI QUESTION," *Missouri Gazette* (St. Louis), reprinted in the *Arkansas Weekly Gazette* (Little Rock), March 4, 1820; James Barbour to Madison, February 10, 1820, in *The Papers of James Madison: Retirement Series*, ed. David B. Mattern, 2 vols. to date (Charlottesville: University of Virginia Press, 2009–), 2:8–9 (for Madison's response, see 10–11). See also Moore, *Missouri Controversy*, 92–93, 97–98.

41. "THE MISSOURI QUESTION," *Kentucky Reporter* (Lexington), January 12 and March 1, 1820. Following direction from the Monroe administration, Adams had yielded Texas in order to get Florida from Spain. See Samuel Flagg Bemis, *John Quincy Adams and the Foundations of American Foreign Policy* (New York: Alfred A. Knopf, 1950), 339–40; and George Dangerfield, *The Era of Good Feelings* (New York: Harcourt Brace, 1952), 152, 156.

42. Monroe to Thomas Jefferson, July 27, 1817, in *The Writings of James Monroe*, ed. Stanislaus Murray Hamilton, 7 vols. (New York: G. P. Putnam's Sons, 1902), 6:26–29, quote on 27; "First Annual Message," in *Messages and Papers of the Presidents*, comp. James D. Richardson, 10 vols. (Washington, DC: Government Printing Office, 1896), 2:11–20, esp. 12. A good alternative interpretation on Monroe is John Craig Hammond, "President, Planter, Politician: James Monroe, the Missouri Crisis, and the Politics of Slavery," *Journal of American History* 105, no. 4 (2019): 843–67.

43. Monroe to Thomas Jefferson, May [no date], 1820, in *Writings of James Monroe*, ed. Hamilton, 6:119–23, quote on 123; Monroe to Jefferson, February 7, 1820, 113–15, quote on 114.

44. Monroe to James Madison, May 10, 1822, in *Writings of James Monroe*, ed. Hamilton, 284–91, quotes on 289, 291.

45. *Alexandria (VA) Gazette*, April 29, 1820; Calhoun to Virgil Maxcy, August 12, 1820, in *Papers of John C. Calhoun*, ed. Meriwether, 5:327–28, quote on 327; "MISSOURI QUESTION," *Louisiana Advertiser* (New Orleans), May 6, 1820.

46. Eaton to Jackson, March 11, 1820, Andrew Jackson Papers: Series 1, General Correspondence and Related Items, 1775–1885, Manuscript Division, Library of Congress; "MISSOURI ADMITTED—*at Last!*" *Alexandria (VA) Gazette*, August 14, 1821; Bonner, *Mastering America*, 41, 50.

47. Ritchie quoted in Richard H. Brown, "The Missouri Crisis, Slavery, and the Politics of Jacksonianism," *South Atlantic Quarterly* 65 (Winter 1966): 55–72, esp. 60–61.

48. Matthew Mason, "Necessary but Not Sufficient: Revolutionary Ideology and Antislavery Action in the Early Republic," in *Contesting Slavery*, ed. Hammond and Mason, 11–31.

6. The Surprising Politics of the Missouri Compromise
Antislavery Doughfaces, Maine, and the Myth of Sectional Balance
Donald Ratcliffe

SOME THINGS IN American history have become so familiar that everyone takes them for granted. One of the most obvious is the Missouri Compromise of 1820, which—as we all know—consisted of three elements: the admission of Missouri as a state without any restriction on slavery, the admission of Maine as a free state to maintain the traditional balance between slave and free states, and the prohibition of slavery north of a line drawn across the Louisiana Purchase west of Missouri at 36°30'. Yet is that all true? Are you sure? Are you really, really sure? (Relax: only the stuff about Maine is wrong.) Do these terms represent the whole compromise, or were there other issues involved, some of them settled, perhaps tacitly, outside Congress? Do we fully understand what happened and why? After all, there has been no detailed monograph since Glover Moore's *Missouri Controversy* in 1951, and most subsequent studies have either ignored the political detail or described the process rather than explained convincingly how compromise was achieved.[1]

Ultimately, the difficulty of enacting a compromise arose not because it was hard to find a compromise formula, but because the structure of Congress gave control of one house to each antagonistic standpoint. How could any measure conciliating northern antislavery pass the proslavery Senate, or any measure that established slavery in Missouri without restriction ever pass the Northern-dominated House of Representatives? Some modern historians have stressed the role of northern doughfaces, arguing that the Missouri Compromise was a defeat for freedom that prepared the way for northern Jacksonian Democrats to become the racist tools of the slave South, thus confirming political control by the "Slave Power" for the next forty years.[2] Yet is there not an even stronger case for seeing the compromise as a long-term antislavery triumph? That possibility would explain why a cobbled-together congressional hotchpot came to be seen as a compact between the sections, and why its repeal in 1854 amounted to the irresponsible destruction of an essential pillar of the Union.

So much seemed at stake in these postwar years. The position of the United States in the world was still uncertain after 1815, as Europe tried to recover from the cataclysms of recent times; international boundaries and national identities were still undefined, and economic recovery remained in doubt. Slavery, however, thrived, as European demand for American produce revived. In the United States the visceral dislike of slavery generated during the Revolution became more anxious as northerners sensed that liberty was not necessarily going to triumph. Despite the qualified abolition of slavery within the North before 1808, slavery still advanced elsewhere in the Union, doubling the nation's slave population in twenty-five years and rapidly increasing the territory that it commanded both economically and politically. Slavery was moving beyond the geographical bounds within which it had been tolerated since 1783, crossing the Mississippi and raising the question of where its influence would end. The nation's borders were still undetermined in 1818–19 and had not been firmly settled by the time of the 1820 compromise. It was not only uncertain whether the area west of the Mississippi would be slave or free; it wasn't even clear what economic activities might succeed there or even at what cost the title to the land might be wrested from resident Indian nations. The future moral and political character of the republic depended on what happened in the massive lands of the Louisiana Purchase, and many felt that the United States could not in good conscience—at the time when Latin American countries were seeking their freedom—abort the principle of liberty in any new republics that arose within its own bounds. Boldness and imagination were needed in the midst of uncertainty, as men on both sides recognized that critical choices would have to be made that would have a long-term influence on the future of the republic. Southerners showed an ever-clearer determination to defend slavery's interests—and by 1820 many northerners were insisting that slavery must be prohibited not merely in Missouri but throughout the whole of the trans-Mississippi West.[3]

Since 1815 controversies had arisen about several other irksome issues that helped to breed and then exacerbate the political crisis. Conflicts involving fugitive slaves, illegal slave imports, and the future of slavery in the Old Northwest repeatedly troubled congressional and state politics. As the crisis over Missouri intensified, feelings on each side became more, not less, recalcitrant. The South clung together in defense of the states as guarantors of slavery but divided between East and West over the virtues of federal power.

The North too had apparent weaknesses derived from internal partisan and regional differences, but attempts to exploit them failed to undermine the overwhelming popular commitment to the cause of restricting slavery.

The fact that the sections were not clearly distinguished at this time ensured that maintaining a numerical balance between slave and free states had never been a serious concern before 1819. The issue of Maine's statehood did not open the way to compromise but rather made things worse, and the conference committee that devised the final settlement duly disentangled Maine from Missouri. In the end, Maine was merely another complicating side issue akin to fugitive slaves and illegal imports. Arguably, what in the last resort proved critical was the decision of a handful of northerners to break the deadlock between the proslavery Senate and the antislavery House by voting for the admission of Missouri without any restriction on slavery. This apparent victory for proslavery came about not because of weak-kneed or racist "doughfaces," but because some antislavery men believed that it was more important to gain the exclusion of slavery from the Far Northwest beyond and above Missouri than to persist, as their constituents demanded, in the immediate object of restricting slavery within Missouri itself. They suffered immediate retribution at the polls, but their foresight was acknowledged when thirty-four years later southern radicals insisted that the safety of slavery in the United States depended on repealing the Missouri Compromise.[4]

The Context of Antagonism

The crisis that Congress faced in 1819–20 involved a broad range of issues that arose from the expansion of slavery within a young republic devoted to liberty. Gaining intensity since 1815, these minor conflicts not only help to explain why the question of Missouri statehood instantly raised such deeply held sectional differences of opinion; during the crisis of 1819–20 they continued to ferment in the background, intensifying the central problem Congress faced and potentially complicating the process of finding a compromise.

The economic revival of the South following the pacification of 1815 quickly revealed that the demand for slaves had not been dampened by the official closing of slave importation from abroad. Slave traders now began to hunt out new, illicit sources of supply, most conspicuously by kidnapping northern free Black people. In the mid-Atlantic states, including Delaware and Maryland, efforts were made to obstruct the transportation of Black people to the South, including, southerners claimed, recaptured fugitives who were being legitimately returned to their owners under the 1793 Fugitive Slave Act. By January 1818 southern congressmen were demanding a new law to make rendition easier: in particular, they wanted the judicial decision on whether an apprehended Black person was truly a runaway to be transferred from judges in the state of capture to judges in the claimant's own state—in other words, from a free state to a slave state. The House divided on the issue mainly along sectional lines, but eighteen northern congressmen were willing to vote in favor as long as all Black people moved across state boundaries had their details registered in the state from which they were being moved. Not surprisingly, the Senate refused to accept the registration clause, and the bill fell between the two houses.[5]

This debate proved a portent of the Missouri Crisis: demands for immediate emancipation were advertised within Congress in 1818, and some southerners now responded that slavery was a positive good. However, during the controversies of 1819–21, the South remained silent on the fugitive-slave issue, while other arguments swirled around. But when the main crisis was over, the South raised the issue again in March 1822, producing a House bill that one Ohio congressman said was calculated "to excite afresh those angry feelings which are hardly yet subsided." This new fugitive-slave bill was defeated, sixty-one to forty, and southerners would not renew their efforts under this head for another twenty years. But the brief rancorous dispute of 1822 revealed how far silence on the issue had contributed to making the compromises of 1819–21.[6]

The mismatch between the supply and demand for slaves also encouraged the illegal revival of slave importation from abroad. The brazen smuggling of slaves, notably through Spanish Florida, increased after 1815 until, according to some reports, it numbered about fourteen thousand in 1818. Some of these slave imports were intercepted by the authorities, but recapture merely reraised the issue that had aroused great bitterness in 1807: What should happen to Africans who were recaptured in the process of being illegally imported? The South had insisted that they be handed over to the state in which they were recaptured, allowing the state to dispose of them as it wished. After 1815 northerners increasingly objected that this meant selling them as slaves—in other words, importing them in flagrant violation of the 1807 prohibition—but the South still objected to handing them over to a federal government that might simply free them.[7]

Potentially, this confrontation could have seriously embittered the initial debate over Missouri that arose in February 1819 after James Tallmadge of New York introduced his famous amendment designed to restrict slavery in the new state. However, the impasse was solved in March by passing a further Slave Trade Act that provided for more effective naval patrolling, ordered that rescued Africans be handed over to the federal government, and gave the president an appropriation to send them back to Africa. The young American Colonization Society immediately offered to help and used the appropriation to found an African homeland, which in 1821 became Liberia. This solution, as President Monroe recognized, was of dubious constitutionality but helped to simplify the immediate crisis over Missouri; no doubt, the recent rapid growth in the domestic market for slaves from the Upper South helped to appease the situation. Furthermore, Congress agreed on tougher enforcement of the importation ban in May 1820 when it declared the smuggling of slaves to be piracy and a capital offence. According to W. E. B. DuBois, this lethal toughening of the 1807 law "may be regarded as the last of the Missouri Compromise measures."[8]

Such arguments over slavery were especially sensitive for the South because the federal census of 1810 had shown that population growth in the North was outstripping that in the South. The growing antislavery sensibilities of the new northern majority in the House of Representatives inevitably brought home the need for the slave states to strengthen their political defenses in the Senate. Southern sympathizers endeavored to legalize slavery in the new states of the Old Northwest, arguing that the Northwest Ordinance's prohibition of slavery could not apply after statehood. Local public opinion quickly defeated their efforts in Indiana and Ohio, but in Illinois influential men were determined to persist in the attempt. The territory made a bid for statehood in 1818 with a constitution that nominally banned slavery but was criticized by Tallmadge for having insufficient safeguards against its subsequent legalization. Congress accepted Illinois in December 1818 partly because, though its constitution allowed Black people to be held in indentured servitude, it also provided for the children of such people to be freed at the age of twenty-one for men and eighteen for women. Similarly, the continued use of slave labor at the federal saltworks near Shawneetown was to be banned after 1825. But there were also provisions in the state constitution that ensured that the new state would have to reconsider the status of slavery before 1825, and this opportunity to reverse the effect of the Northwest Ordinance lingered in the background through 1819–21, not to be settled until the famous state referendum on slavery in 1824. On broadcasting that referendum result, Hezekiah Niles would remark that if Illinois had adopted slavery, it would have raised "a question of much more dangerous tendency" than the Missouri controversy itself.[9]

Over the Old Southwest, by contrast, most northern antislavery men were more relaxed. Admittedly, some of them had earlier opposed the introduction the slavery into the Mississippi Territory in 1798 and the Louisiana Purchase in 1804, and in 1819 John Quincy Adams expected an attempt to ban slavery in Florida. Yet such efforts were usually overwhelmed by the belief that other considerations trumped antislavery principle. The states of the Old South were not held responsible for the existence of slavery in their midst and were considered to have earned the right to sympathetic treatment by their contribution to the revolutionary struggle—and that included the territories they claimed between the Appalachians and the Mississippi. National security necessitated the acceptance of slavery in newly acquired Louisiana in 1812 and Florida in 1819–21, especially as securing American sovereignty along the Gulf Coast and up the lower Mississippi Valley meant containing the powerful external pressures that had forced on slavery expansion in the region in the previous thirty years. Even Tallmadge had no desire to interfere with slavery in regions that were surrounded by slave states, for fear of starting a servile war; he therefore did not advocate the prohibition of slavery in the Alabama Territory. Some northern congressmen questioned the admission of Alabama as a state in December 1819 but enough accepted that slavery could not be excluded from an area in the Deep South that already possessed a large number of slaves. Alabama was admitted, at that critical moment, on its own merits without concern for the balance of sectional power. Even in 1819–21 many northerners continued to acquiesce in the expansion of slavery in parts of the nation where slavery had had a legal existence in 1783.[10]

New slave territory west of the Mississippi and north of Louisiana could not expect the same treatment. This area had not participated in the Revolution and therefore, it was argued, could not expect the allowances and privileges made to regions subordinate to the original states that had large slave populations. Thus, when Missouri and Arkansas applied in 1818 to be admitted as a state and a territory of the United States, Tallmadge and his New York colleague John W. Taylor proposed that the admission of further slaves should be banned and the *post-nati* children of existing slaves be freed on reaching the age of twenty-five. In the case of Arkansas, the House divided evenly, eighty-eight to eighty-eight, and only Speaker Henry Clay's casting vote allowed the territory's organization in March 1819 without restriction. The vote was so close only because five northerners who favored imposing these restrictions on Missouri thought that the new territory lay too far south for slavery to be excluded.[11]

None of this applied to Missouri, which lay in the path of the wave of nonslaveholding farmers that was sweeping through the Old Northwest. Thus, it was scarcely surprising that northerners should claim Missouri for what would later be called Free Soil, even though it already contained ten thousand slaves. The conditions that Tallmadge proposed imposing on the would-be state in February 1819 required no more than northern states had repeatedly imposed on themselves since the Revolution—an end to importation and gradual emancipation for the *post-nati*. No suggestion was made that any slaves already in Missouri should be emancipated. To most antislavery northerners, these were reasonable and necessary proposals if slavery were ever to be voluntarily abolished, and the in-built northern majority in the House of Representatives passed the Tallmadge Amendment by a healthy margin.

Southern spokesmen responded almost immediately with threats of violent consequences, somewhat unnecessarily since the South could resist these proposals through its control of the Senate. Following the admission of Illinois in December 1818, there were eleven free states and ten slave, but the Illinois senators consistently voted with the South on slavery issues. Delaware had slaves but was often considered a free state;[12] as a consequence, its senators often divided or abstained, but they were more than balanced elsewhere by a handful of northern men with southern principles. The admission of Alabama in December 1819, though ostensibly providing sectional balance, actually consolidated a distinct southern advantage in the Senate. Thus, the South could be confident of frustrating the demands of the House's antislavery majority, creating the stalemate between two fixed majorities.

The Power of Antislavery

The prospect for compromise was much enhanced by the fact that northern and southern sectional identities, and their geographical range, were not as yet clearly defined. Admittedly, some recent historians have seen the Missouri Crisis as resulting from the sense of sectional identity that the free states had developed over the previous twenty years. With its disproportionate growth in population, they claim, the North in 1819–20 aggressively tried to ensure that its own newly crystallizing free-labor ambitions for the nation's future development were not impeded by the challenge of an expanding slave society.[13] Such views, however, put the evolution of a clear sense of *northern* sectionalism at far too early a date, as the politics of the years immediately following the crisis make clear.[14] In 1820 antisouthern resentments varied within the northern states by region and party. In Atlantic areas some remembered how the federal government had ignored their commercial interests between 1807 and 1815, while westerners resented southeastern obstruction of schemes for federally financed internal improvements. Northeastern Federalists objected in particular to the political advantage the South gained from the Constitution's three-fifths rule. A sense of the practical superiority of a free-labor economy was developing, especially among Jeffersonian Democrats in the older states, as seaboard farmers, speculators, and artisans increasingly looked toward opportunities in the New West.[15] But the binding thread of commitment within the North remained the antislavery sentiment inherited from the Revolution, which gained a greater voice after the War of 1812, especially in the mid-Atlantic states. Its power had been demonstrated in New York when the first total emancipation act was passed in 1817, and hopes that emancipation would spread to the South were encouraged by the foundation of the American Colonization Society. But such anticipations were dashed as it became clear that not only were most southerners committed to retaining their peculiar institution, but they also insisted on advancing ever-greater claims for its protection. What would, above all, inflame antislavery men in 1820 was the inflation of the South's traditional claim that slavery be respected where it already existed into the broad assertion that slavery had a *right* under the Constitution to equal treatment in newly acquired virgin territories.[16]

Undeniably, there was an element of "negrophobia" (as Clay termed it) within this northern concern about slavery's expansion. Besides strong disapproval of slavery on moral, social, and economic grounds, many white northerners possessed a sense that the West must be a homeland for free white labor and not be spoiled by the polluting influence of slavery, which would make the West "the receptacle of a class of population dangerous to many portions of the Country."[17] This fear that the new region would be spoiled if a "slave [or servile] population" were allowed into it was deeply ambiguous: Was the objection to the sort of people who became slaves or to the debasing effects that slavery had on its victims? This was an age when the Enlightenment's emphasis on environmental and social impacts on human character was being replaced by a renewed sensitivity to supposedly inherent biological characteristics, and northern opposition to a slave Missouri embraced both extremes of that continuum. That variety of view also explains why some men who were ideologically opposed to slavery could support measures that actually reinforced it and led to its extension, even while most northerners fiercely opposed the admission of Missouri.[18]

So strong was this popular sentiment that the antislavery commitment of northern politicians tended to be reinforced whenever they met with their constituents. As early as the congressional elections of 1818, a few northern representatives who had voted for the fugitive-slave bill were stung by their constituents. We are often told that Illinois was virtually a slave state at this time, and certainly its U.S. senators (who were elected by a state legislature dominated by Virginian factions) voted steadily with the South. But it also had a single congressman who was popularly elected in a statewide ballot. In his brief term the incumbent, John McLean, had voted with the South on slavery issues; in the August 1819 election campaign this offense was hung round his neck by his opponent, Daniel Pope Cook, himself from Virginia. Winning 58 percent of the vote, Cook spoke up in Congress as a vocal antislavery man, arguing powerfully for restriction. His consistent stance helped secure his reelection in 1820, 1822, and 1824. He also took a prominent antislavery role in the referendum campaign that in 1824 destroyed hopes of making slavery openly legal in Illinois and then campaigned in the presidential election for John Quincy Adams as the sole nonslaveholding candidate. Though the districting of the state in that election gave Adams only one presidential elector out of the state's three, Adams actually won a plurality of the statewide popular vote, confirming the strength of grassroots antislavery in Illinois.[19]

Similarly, in 1819 some other northern representatives found themselves under pressure at home after voting against gradual emancipation in Missouri and for the unrestricted creation of Arkansas as a territory. The firm statement of restrictionist views on the admission of Missouri by the spate of crowded public meetings in the North in 1819–20 as well as the passage of resolutions and instructions by state legislatures were designed, according to a St. Louis newspaper, to "lash into the ranks" those members who had not voted with them in the previous session.[20] As the next session started, the old Federalist Philemon Beecher was warned by his law partner back home in Ohio to take a more openly anti-Missouri stance: the recent controversy in Ohio over revising the state constitution, so risking the reintroduction of slavery, had "aroused [the people], and no detail of the question will now pass them unheeded." Other returning representatives who firmed up their position included, in the Senate, the venerable Massachusetts Federalist Harrison Gray Otis and the partisan Pennsylvania Democrat Jonathan Roberts.[21]

Despite the growing expression of anti-Missouri opinions within the North, restrictionists had no problem with the idea of finding a compromise that might conciliate all sides. Even the doomed Tallmadge Amendment of 1819 allowed slavery to survive for a generation in Missouri, and in the early days of the next Congress some northern state legislatures were advising their representatives in Washington to drop its second clause, which favored the gradual emancipation of the *post-nati*. Tallmadge had withdrawn from Congress in 1819, but his successor as de facto antislavery leader, John W. Taylor, began the new session by offering a deal. He persuaded the House to establish a compromise committee chaired by himself and then in committee he proposed a bill "to secure to proprietors of slaves now in Missouri, the right of property in them and their posterity for ever, and to prohibit the further introduction of slaves into Missouri, and all the territory west of the Mississippi." The committee rejected this ambitious proposal, and before December was out the House had discharged the committee. Then in January Taylor offered an amendment to the Missouri bill that would prohibit the future existence of slavery in the new state on the condition that "the provision shall not be construed to alter the condition or civil rights of any person now held to service or labor in the said Territory." In the Senate the Quaker Jonathan Roberts proposed a similar amendment, banning only the "further introduction" of slavery, which attracted the support of sixteen out of twenty-two free-state senators. Thus, in January 1820 northern restrictionists in Washington were specifically offering, as a deliberate compromise gesture, to guarantee the future property rights of Missouri's slaveholders in existing slaves and their progeny in return for a prohibition on the further introduction of slavery.[22]

From the start, however, southern representatives in Congress reacted to proposed restrictions on Missouri, of any kind, as though they faced a deadly threat. According to the *St. Louis Enquirer*, if the North imposed a restriction, "lighted torches will be put into the hands of slaves to rouse their sleeping masters from their beds amid the flames of their houses and the cries of their slaughtered children."[23] In Congress southerners replied not so much by defending slavery as by arguing the question of constitutional authority. Restriction, they insisted, threatened both the right of new states to enter the Union as equals and the constitutional guarantee that the federal government could take no action that threatened slavery in the southern states. After all, if a state couldn't choose slavery for itself at the moment of statehood, when could it choose? On this principle the South stood solid in defense of its domestic institutions, demonstrating in 1819 a long-term commitment to the institution that had never previously been so obvious or so unapologetic. Even when antislavery men in the House moderated their demands in January 1820, southerners remained adamant. Of course, the House's call for an end to the further importation of slaves into Missouri would probably have led to full abolition in the long run as the proportion of slaves in the population fell, but that was not what the South complained of at the time: what they feared throughout was federal interference and the weakening of constitutional safeguards for southern slavery—and on that principle, there could be no compromise.[24]

The Territorial Solution

From the beginning of the controversy, people on both sides had recognized that, overall, a simple compromise was possible. In late February 1819, a Philadelphia newspaper reported, "It would almost seem as if an understanding prevailed [in Congress] that a line of demarcation should take place in the west" between slave and free areas. A week earlier Louis McLane, Delaware's antirestrictionist congressman, had proposed a line west of the Mississippi "north of which slavery shall not be tolerated," an idea, he said, that had the approval of several southern and western congressmen. Two days thereafter, in the Arkansas debate, John W. Taylor himself proposed drawing such a line at 36°30', continuing the agreed southern boundary of Missouri. Such proposals found little support at that time, partly because many antislavery men still looked for total success.[25]

But if a compromise might be based on a division of the Louisiana Purchase into slave and free territory, just what would they be dividing? What lay on either side of the line? Northward, the boundary with British North America had long been in doubt: in negotiations with Britain since 1812, the proposed boundary west of the Great Lakes had, on different occasions, been drawn westward from points as southerly as the future Chicago and on one occasion up the Missouri River from St. Louis. Only in October 1818 did Britain agree to a much more northerly boundary, along the forty-ninth parallel as far as the Rockies plus joint occupancy of the Oregon Country, thus opening for the United States a potentially huge North by Northwest, presumably destined for nonslave settlement.

As for the southern boundary with Spain, President Monroe's administration recognized that it must not be too greedy in the negotiations of 1818–19. If the United States gained too much land suitable for slave-grown staple crops, an internal territorial compromise would be more difficult. It was essential to acquire the strategically important Florida as soon as possible, but what about Texas? All the indications were that Spain would be willing to concede much of eastern Texas, but the cabinet pressed Secretary of State John Quincy Adams to not even ask for it. Thus, the Transcontinental Treaty agreed in February 1819 (and immediately ratified by the Senate) limited the new Southwest south of Missouri to the future Arkansas and Oklahoma. This offered an important framework for a sectional compromise, though the Spanish king's refusal to ratify the treaty meant that the whole boundary settlement remained in doubt. As a result, through the Missouri controversy Washington would remain troubled by a threat of war arising from the crisis created by Spain's rebellious American colonies.[26]

The potential limitation on slavery's expansion toward the Southwest made it easier for northern leaders to contemplate making concessions to the South. As chair of the House compromise committee created in December 1819, Taylor once more suggested a partition of the territory west of Missouri, this time offering a number of possible lines, ranging from the higher reaches of the Missouri River to a line drawn west of St. Louis. All such proposals were rejected by the House select committee, which was promptly discharged.[27] But in the Senate the southern forces began to take the idea seriously.

Many southern representatives saw the value of the distinction between the rights of states and the legal subordination to the federal government of the organized territories. In 1819–20, unlike thirty years later, they accepted that the federal government's absolute control of the territories enabled Congress to forbid the introduction of slaves and make rules governing their legal position. Hence, in January 1820 the widely respected southern leader William Lowndes had proposed his own line in Taylor's select committee, with slavery prohibited north of the line; President Monroe thought some such proposal might offer a compromise that principled New England Democratic-Republicans could accept.[28] By February 5 Congressman William Plumer of New Hampshire reported that such a compromise was "much talked of in the Senate and by many in our House—The opponents of restriction see that they are likely not to succeed, & many of them are willing to give up the rest of the territories, if we will allow of Slavery in Missouri & Arcansaw." After the deal had passed in March, Plumer added that "the slave-holders . . . came with the greatest reluctance even to the compromise . . . but they were compelled to surrender this, or lose the whole."[29]

On February 16 Senator Jesse B. Thomas of Illinois moved the famous amendment forbidding slavery in the upper part of the Far West north of 36°30'. Whereas other proposals had drawn the line farther north, a majority in the Senate agreed, thirty-four to ten, to transform the Senate's bill admitting Missouri without any restriction into an offer that the North could not refuse, by adopting the most southerly line proposed by the antislavery forces. Moreover, the proviso said such prohibition would be "forever," thus controlling the action of the state that succeeded the territory, which, as Monroe pointed out, created great difficulty for the constitutionally principled.[30] The most prominent southern leaders were aghast. So why then did so many southern senators join with the antislavery minority to make the generous territorial offer that the Senate decided on in mid-February 1820?

Southern Divisions

The various votes in Congress relating to 36°30' revealed that a clear cleavage existed within the South. The nation as a whole was riven by sectional divisions after 1818, and not all of them divided South from North; the distinction between East and West mattered just as much in the so-called Era of Good Feelings. The South Atlantic states had supported the nationalistic policies pursued under Jefferson and Madison, but after 1816 many of their leaders—especially in the more Atlantic-oriented counties—began to have strong reservations about the direction of the federal government. They believed it too eager to expand federal economic power, too willing to adopt Federalist and even Hamiltonian principles. The small group of Old Republicans who had criticized the drift away from old party values since 1801 were now increasingly joined by those who believed that policies like federal internal improvements penalized older areas of the Southeast. With the onset of the panic of 1819, such projects could be seen as part of the dangerous new world of banks and debts and falling agricultural prices that John Taylor of Caroline continued to warn against.[31] The obvious conclusion was to recall the federal government, and especially the Supreme Court, to the Old Republican standard of states' rights and strict construction. The most immediate threat came from Congress's attempt to interfere with slavery in Missouri, for behind it lurked a potential federal threat to slavery in Virginia, which held nearly one-third of the nation's slaves and had felt the menace of this "internal enemy" during the recent war against Britain.[32] The consequent "revival of the spirit and principles of 1799" not only in Richmond but in many parts of the South Atlantic area ensured that most seaboard politicians were "strongly opposed to any compromise with constitutional principle" where slavery was concerned. As the venerable Nathaniel Macon of North Carolina warned, "To compromise is to acknowledge the right of Congress to interfere and to legislate on the subject" of slavery.[33]

By contrast, the southwestern states not only possessed fewer slaves but also had good experiences of the federal government: defense against the Indians and the British, the purchase of Indian land, subsidized territorial government, and land grants and educational support for the territories and states with federal lands. And the Southwest wanted more, notably the removal of the remaining Indian tribes west of the Mississippi—a hope that was not to be frustrated until the Cherokee and Creek decided to stand fast in 1822—and national schemes of internal improvements that could speed western development.

Moreover, the panic of 1819 made the western states as a whole desperate for federal assistance for those in debt for public land. The older states might be sympathetic, but first they wanted to prevent a recurrence of high indebtedness by ending the existing credit system for public land sales, which many in the newer states thought helped sales and underwrote land prices. In 1820 a new land act lowered the price of public lands but removed the credit facility; this represented a triumph for the Southeast over resistance from the southwestern representatives. On development issues the westerners could find allies at the margins of the southeastern states—in the border states, the western counties, and among former South Carolina war hawks like Lowndes and Secretary of War John C. Calhoun.[34] Thus, it was no accident that southern approval for the territorial compromise of 1820 came from those who looked toward the federal government as their ally against the more localistic and economy-minded politicians of the seaboard areas of the South and especially Virginia.

On the face of it, these southern supporters of the 36°30' territorial concession imposed a bad deal on the South. The area south of the line could accommodate only two possible future slave states, and already the federal government had begun persuading Indian tribes in the southeastern states to move west and settle in that general area, thus taking up lands open to slavery. By contrast, the North won for Free Soil a massive area nowadays covered by at least ten states. So why did the southern nationalists accept such a smaller share?

The answer has to be their low opinion of the economic prospects for this new area north and west of Missouri. Though this was not widely voiced during the congressional debates and many hailed the fertility of the Upper West, the idea was already common that the Great Plains, where no trees grew, constituted an area where productive agriculture could not be sustained. This perception had been supported by Zebulon Pike, who had explored the central plains in 1806–7 and declared them likely to become as "celebrated as the sandy deserts of Africa."[35] The various schemes in the 1820s for removing Indian tribes west of the Mississippi assumed that they would be taking up land that white men would not be interested in farming, while no land north of 36°30' had yet been bought from the Indians and its settlement seemed far distant. In any case, southern senators would be able to block or delay future treaties with Indians in the Far Northwest and so, as Senator Charles Tait of Alabama anticipated, ensure that the concession was "mostly nominal."[36]

In effect, the Southwest, in accepting 36°30', was giving up lands that many thought it could never use for slavery anyway, while the area now dedicated to Free Soil would not convert into more than a few states, and that was far in the future. Those who disagreed, like St. George Tucker, claimed they had given up "the fairest and largest part of the Western territory," but for South Atlantic politicians it scarcely mattered what the lands north of 36°30' were like: for them, the central issue remained the future constitutional protections of slavery. They remained absolutely adamant on this principle, even after the Senate had voted to offer the 36°30' concession to the House.[37]

The Difficulties of Compromise

For the North, there was no contradiction between sincere antislavery and the belief that some sort of compromise was necessary. Despite the failure of earlier proposals, knowledgeable observers still believed that a division of the West could yet solve the problem. However, as the session wore on, northern attitudes sharpened, and the House's votes toward the end of February suggested that a majority of its members would not accept the unrestricted admission of Missouri at any price the South could offer. Equally, the Senate rejected "by increasing majorities" all propositions for restriction.[38]

One reason for antislavery intransigence was the growing tide of support from northern state legislatures and local meetings in the constituencies; another was the growing tone of moral commitment among northern spokesmen. When Rufus King first spoke on Missouri early in 1819, he emphasized the political danger of allowing slave interests to increase their power in Congress. When, newly reelected, he returned to the subject in two speeches in February 1820, he delivered the most crushing condemnation of slavery yet uttered on the floor of Congress. Several observers remarked that King had changed the terms of the debate and infused an element of moral absolutism into the controversy that had not previously been there. According to the Speaker of the Virginia House of Delegates, King's language meant that the North "would sound the tocsin of freedom to every negro of the South, and we may live to see the tragical events of St. Domingo repeated in our own land."[39] King's rhetoric not only was echoed by the Federalist minority but also found forceful and coherent expression from Democratic-Republicans. As southern threats reached new heights, the House had begun to express a sort of antislavery that was unwilling to consider the concession of immutable principles.[40]

The sharp polarization of sectional attitudes over slavery helped undermine the position of those trying to find some weakness in the Northern restrictionist majority on the Missouri question. Efforts to blame the controversy on a "Federalist plot" held promise because old party loyalties remained strong among the electorate, especially as the 1820 presidential election approached. Yet in practice such rhetoric operated more to strengthen Southern unanimity for sectional defense than to weaken the North's overwhelming consensus on Missouri. In the North the cry gained some leverage later on, but in 1820 it did not shake Northern unity, despite the prominence of Federalists like Rufus King and John Sergeant in the anti-Missouri assault. The campaign for restriction was led primarily by Democratic-Republicans, while some prominent Federalists were distinctly dilatory in supporting anti-Missourism. In any event, in most northern states there was little chance that the Federalists could carry an election for national office in the face of organized Republican opposition, as northern congressmen repeatedly told the House.[41] Only in parts of New England was there a sufficient fear of Federalism to make some Republican spokesmen change their mind on the policy of restriction: New Hampshire senator John Parrott's warnings apparently had a great effect on the state's delegation in Washington and on the party press back home, yet New Hampshire's congressmen in practice proved solid supporters of the anti-Missouri cause.[42] The restrictionist campaign swept up a broad bipartisan body of support, and those party leaders like Martin Van Buren of New York who feared a Federalist revival chose to ride the antislavery tidal wave and wait for it to subside. Only in the aftermath of the crisis, in 1821–22, did Van Buren begin to call for a revival of the Democratic-Republican Party nationally as a means of promoting sectional reconciliation.[43]

Even the effort to bribe New England support by linking the admission of free Maine with a slave Missouri failed to divide the North. If anything, as the Maine doughface John Holmes acknowledged, this "improper" maneuver "increased the excitement and widened the breach" between the houses.[44] In June 1819 the Massachusetts General Court had agreed to allow its District of Maine to apply for statehood as long as Congress acted by March 4, 1820. When the district applied in December 1819, leading southerners grasped at an opportunity to "coerce where they cannot convince," and the Senate linked the two applications for statehood in the same bill. President Monroe approved the idea of using Maine to force northerners to see sense, but foresaw that linking the two states in one bill would only alienate and make them less accommodating.[45] When the Senate included the linkage in the "compromise" package it sent to the House on February 18, the whole proposed bill was "instantly rejected . . . as being a procedure unprecedented, and an unwarrantable attempt on the part of the Senate to force the House to a compliance with their own views."[46] The votes (93–72 and 102–68) on February 22 showed that many who usually voted on the southern side had voted with their antislavery colleagues, and the 36°30' proposal, though inherently attractive to the North, won little support in the House as long as it was tied up with Maine. Even the representatives from Maine voted against the linking, insisting that statehood must not be bought by a sacrifice of principle. The same day they presented a joint formal appeal to Congress to deal with the two states separately and process Maine's statehood rapidly. After that, all but two of the seven Massachusetts congressmen who represented Maine districts continued to vote steadily against a slave Missouri, although that risked leaving Maine's future in the hands of a resentful Senate.[47]

But a still more serious difficulty stood in the way of the Senate proposal. Northern public opinion had hardened and was now adamantly committed against the unrestricted admission of Missouri; most northern congressmen had no doubt their political survival was at risk if they voted for it. The argument that slavery in Missouri was the price that had to be paid for the gains of 36°30' cut little ice: 36°30' was a long-term and distant policy triumph, of little immediate appeal, especially as the Upper West could not convincingly be extolled for promised riches that no one knew existed. Not surprisingly, those who favored compromise spoke of "these fair and fertile regions"; those opposed spoke of "a prairie, resembling the Steppes of Tartary, without wood or water."[48]

Even if the land was worth having, some said the South's concession was meaningless. Even if the danger of the South blocking Indian land cessions in the Senate was disregarded, the current example of Illinois threw in doubt the basic assumption behind the 36°30' proposal, namely, that the rules governing the territorial stage would determine the future. Illinois's sole congressman, Daniel Cook, refused to give up trying to place restrictions on Missouri because, he said, regardless of what happened in the territorial stage, the South could still try to create a slave state at the point of statehood. He asked if southern members accepted that the word "forever" in the proposal meant the prohibition would be binding on future states created in the restricted area. As he said it, he turned to the respected southern leader and proponent of compromise William Lowndes, who was sitting close by. According to the reporter, "Here Mr. Lowndes smiled and shook his head." In that sad smile lay the future civil war.[49]

Throughout February the House debated a revised amendment to the Missouri bill proposed by Taylor on January 26. This represented a toughening up of the antislavery position: although it specifically stated that its provisions "shall not be construed to alter the condition or civil rights of any person now held to service or labor in the said territory," it required Missouri to accept not only no further introduction of slaves but also the emancipation of the future children of current slaves *at birth*.[50] This amendment commenced the principal House debate on the Missouri bill, though there was little discussion of its specific provisions and argument focused once more on the desirability of allowing slavery into the new lands west of the Mississippi and the constitutionality of restricting it. Once more the debate was marked by threats of disunion on one side and assertions on the other that slavery contradicted the eternal republican principles on which the Union was founded. Twice in this period the House rejected the proposal for a complete prohibition of slavery north of 36°30', because the majority still wanted to include restrictions on Missouri. Doughface Henry Storrs suggested that "honest zeal in its excess of ardour . . . , pride of opinion or the expectation of political or parliamentary triumph" led the restrictionist cause to believe it could still achieve a total victory. On March 1, the House passed its own antislavery Missouri bill, including the new hard-line Taylor Amendment, by margins of between eight and eleven votes on the three final ballots; no southerner voted for it, and only nine northerners (of the one hundred voting) opposed.[51]

Yet already, amid this apparent impasse, the crisis was being resolved. The previous day, February 29, the two houses had agreed to discuss their differences over Maine through a conference committee. On March 2, the committee reported, recommending the Senate drop its blocking of Maine's admission and the House drop its restrictions on slavery in Missouri in return for the 36°30' proviso. That same day, the House reversed itself and accepted the deal—narrowly (90–87) in favor of Missouri's unrestricted admission and overwhelmingly (134–42) in favor of 36°30'. But first it had debated for three hours whether it should vote on the two issues *before* the Senate had given a pledge to pass the Maine bill; if the House acted first, it would do so under the implicit threat that the Senate might yet reject Maine. Had the Senate acted first, some later claimed, "many more" members who approved the principle but objected to the Senate's implied threat over Maine would have been willing to vote "in favor of the compromise."[52]

So why the sudden shift, in a mere twenty-four hours, in the balance of power? Why did northern antislavery forces that for two years had retained control of the House of Representatives suddenly lose control on March 2 and a majority of congressmen vote for the admission of Missouri without any restriction on slavery?

President and Doughface

One modern line of explanation has emphasized President Monroe's role in securing congressional acceptance of the compromise. Recently, however, John Craig Hammond has demonstrated that Monroe was a consistent supporter of the Virginia slaveholding interest, whose overriding concern in 1820 was to prevent federal restrictions on slavery. The political necessity of doing so became obvious when Virginia's legislators made it clear in February that their support for his reelection depended on his unyielding defense of slavery's right to expand. Yet at the same time Monroe became convinced that the growing power of northern antislavery sentiment was making it difficult for New England Republicans to support southern rights, and so some territorial concession had to be made to enable them to hang on. Whether his aim was to preserve the Union and advance antislavery or to defend southern rights by appeasing northern allies makes little difference to the basic fact that by mid-February he backed compromise: once the final deal had passed Congress, he worked to reconcile Virginia to the 36°30' concession and, despite personal doubts, guided the cabinet toward agreeing that the agreed compromise did not breach the U.S. Constitution. On March 6 he signed the bill enacting it.[53]

But had Monroe gone further and used the influence and patronage of the executive to buy the support of northerners for the unrestricted admission of Missouri? In January he told Secretary of State John Quincy Adams that he was confident a compromise could be passed, which made Adams wonder whether there was an "underplot" under way, which until that moment he had (uncharacteristically) not even suspected. Some historians have pointed to indications that such a maneuver was happening, but they remain no more than that—indications, innuendoes, and suspicions. Admittedly, Congressman Plumer wrote of "the influence of the Palace" strengthening the pressure for compromise in late February, and spoke of bargaining between "southern and western members & the members from Maine." But Monroe himself described his efforts as nothing more than engaging in "a mere understanding between those who wished to save the union." Above all, there is no clear evidence that *in 1820* executive patronage influenced the votes of the critical northern congressmen who at last made possible the admission of Missouri as a slave state.[54]

The Speaker of the House was probably better placed than the president to encourage the passage of a settlement. Henry Clay has been rightly credited with exercising his office so as to place moderates on key committees, ensure that their proposals were not disadvantaged procedurally, and defend them against destructive motions. Yet his main contribution as the "Great Pacificator" came in the following session, after he had left the Speaker's chair in November 1820: as a plain congressman, he "almost single handedly" prevented the crisis over Missouri's racist constitution from disrupting the final count in the presidential election; and then, according to one northern representative, "nothing but the exertions of Mr Clay" secured a majority for the new state's final admission in March 1821. In the 1818–19 session Clay had scarcely been an obvious proponent of compromise, with his eloquent speeches in opposition to the restriction of slavery and his casting vote in favor of making Arkansas a slave territory. His main contributions to compromise *in 1820* were to turn his eloquence, late in the day, in favor of restricting slavery in the territories north of 36°30', to appoint the House members of the conference committee, and then, by an almost unprecedented piece of sharp practice, to prevent John Randolph from moving a reconsideration of the final decisive House vote. He was indeed rumored to have used his private influence to win over individual congressmen, but he later repeatedly denied that he had been responsible for the compromise of 1820.[55]

The Missouri Enabling Act passed without any mention of slavery on March 2, 1820, because fourteen northern congressmen voted with the South and four others absented themselves from the vote. As a result, a House that for two years had, for the most part, shown a ten-vote antislavery majority suddenly voted ninety to eighty-seven in favor of the new slave state. These eighteen so-called doughfaces have been repeatedly analyzed to discover what distinguished them. Almost all were Democratic-Republicans, which makes it possible that they were influenced by fear of a resurgent Federalism; certainly, most appear to have been disciples of a states' rights view that insisted Congress had no right to place limitations on a sovereign state at the moment of its creation. Monroe himself ascribed the final compromise to "the patriotic devotion of several members in the non slave holding States, who preferr'd the sacrifice of themselves at home, to a violation of the obvious principles of the Constitution, & the risk of the Union."[56]

Others were committed protectionists led by the Pittsburgh ironmaster Henry Baldwin, who wished to avoid turning southern representatives against high tariffs as a matter of sectional identity. Fifteen of the eighteen northern congressmen who helped to admit Missouri were high-tariff men, but the ploy failed because most of the South was already hostile to protectionism; in any case, most protectionists voted in favor of slavery's restriction.[57] Yet all such attempts to find common characteristics among the doughfaces as a whole miss an important point: many of them had been voting consistently with the South from the early days of the crisis without affecting northern control of the House.

In effect, some had been "doughfaces" long before the term became common in 1820. Back in January 1818, five of the fourteen northern congressmen who voted to admit Missouri in March 1820 had voted with the South in favor of the abortive fugitive-slave bill. In February 1819, five of them had voted against both clauses of the Tallmadge Amendment, another had voted against the second clause, while a seventh was absent; all seven had then voted for a slave Arkansas.[58] In other words, these men had always been counted as a fixed part of the antirestriction minority in the House, and their vote on March 2 to admit a slave Missouri was no surprise. To reverse the regular anti-Missouri majority, they had to be joined by men who had not only been counted as firm members of that majority but also voted for the previous day's hard-line Taylor bill, with its demand that the *post-nati* in Missouri be emancipated at birth. In fact, four such antislavery men joined them, while four like-minded representatives somehow missed this vote. What can explain this critical shift by a handful of men who were otherwise regarded as committed and principled opponents of slavery?

Table 1. Northern Doughface Congressmen of 1820

Fourteen Northern Congressmen voted to admit Missouri without restriction on slavery:

Six of them voted the proslavery line in both 1818–19 and 1819–20

Joseph Bloomfield	New Jersey (at large)
John Holmes	Massachusetts (Maine district)
Mark Hill	Massachusetts (Maine district)
Jonathan Mason	Massachusetts (Boston)
Henry B. Shaw	Massachusetts
Henry Storrs	New York

One abstained in 1818–19 but supported slavery in Missouri in 1820

Henry Baldwin	Pennsylvania (Pittsburgh)

Three new members in December 1819 voted the proslavery line through 1820

Samuel A. Foot	Connecticut
David Fullerton	Pennsylvania
Henry Meigs	New York (City)

Four voted the antislavery line in 1819–20 except for the critical vote on Missouri

Samuel Eddy	Rhode Island (at large)
Charles Kinsey	New Jersey (at large)
Bernard Smith	New Jersey (at large)
James Stevens	Connecticut

Four Northern Congressmen Abstained:

Four voted the antislavery line in 1820 but missed the critical vote on Missouri

Leonard Case	New York
Henry Edwards	Connecticut (slipped out to eat!)
Hermanus Peck	New York (consistent absentee–ill health?)
Caleb Tompkins	New York

The Antislavery Alternative

After the critical vote, northern antislavery men condemned the doughfaces as cowardly tools of the slave interest. The usually balanced and thoughtful William Plumer of New Hampshire reported that southern and western threats of disunion and civil strife had "fairly frightened our weak-minded members" into abandoning the anti-Missouri cause. "About ten members," he reported, ". . . after having voted with us through all the previous stages of the business flinched at last & gave way when the real 'tug of war' came." But, he then added, "though we have lost Missouri, we have imposed the restriction on the territories—and this is in my opinion a great point gained—It is infinitely worth more than all the trouble it has cost us, the time we have spent, & the unkind feelings which have been excited."[59]

The final compromise not only banned slavery in the Far Northwest but also reduced the size of the new slave state. Initially, the boundaries proposed for Missouri had been excessive, including what would become three tiers of counties in Iowa, two tiers in Kansas, plus small parts of Oklahoma and even Arkansas. Taylor in December 1819 attempted to limit the new state to south of the Missouri River, but that was a step too far, especially as the Missouri Valley already had many slaves growing hemp for rope making. But then the House had worked to bring the proposed state within bounds, and the revised boundaries were contained in the House's Missouri bill approved (except for the hard-line Taylor amendment) by both the Senate and the conference committee.[60] Given that the fact of statehood was more important than sheer size, the South had little objection to accepting a Missouri cut down to a size closer to that of antebellum Virginia. No wonder both Tallmadge and Taylor of New York thought the overall result of the compromise was an antislavery victory: "We have gained all that was possible, if not all that was desired."[61]

Evidently, the decision to trade a slave Missouri for the prohibition of slavery elsewhere did not necessarily reflect a sympathy with slavery or cowardice in the face of southern threats. Of course, some expressions of antislavery sentiment by doughfaces may have been politically motivated. John Holmes, the "doughface of doughfaces" who above all stressed his concern to defend Maine's interests, described slavery as "a most afflicting, a most dangerous evil" and in October 1819 voted to defend Black suffrage in the Maine constitutional convention, but he was still denounced even in Maine as "the unblushing advocate of domestic slavery" and despised as "the merest sycophant, and hollow-hearted man." And when Congressman Henry Meigs

from New York City proposed that the public lands be used to fund emancipation and colonization, Adams thought it was intended "to serve him as
an apology to his constituents for voting against the [Missouri] restriction."[62]

But however dubious the sincerity of some long-term doughfaces,
there can be little doubt of the antislavery commitment of others. Joseph
Bloomfield had long been president of the New Jersey Abolition Society.
Samuel Foot of Connecticut insisted that "no man detests slavery more than
I do. . . . [N]o gentleman would go further to prevent . . . the expansion of
the evil, if I could believe Congress possesses the power."[63] The most striking
example was Henry Storrs of New York, the sole self-proclaimed Federalist
among the doughfaces, a man who expressed his determination to advance
the cause of human liberty in his many speeches, initiatives, and votes in the
House. Throughout the debate, as he said later, "the prohibition and extinction of slavery, as a moral and political curse to any nation, was the chief
object to be attained." Rufus King thought he and Storrs were "of one mind"
and was distressed that Storrs in the end "fought under the black flag." But,
in fact, Storrs had always said that Congress lacked the constitutional power
to impose restrictions on a new state, he feared disunion, and he steadfastly
voted for the unrestricted admission of Missouri. Like Foot, he persistently
brought up the 36°30' proposal, even in the face of almost solid hostility in
the House. Though he had throughout made no secret of his voting intentions, Storrs recognized that he would face political punishment at the polls
in 1820. But what incensed him was not the loss of his seat, but the "atrocious
calumny" voiced during the 1820 election that he was "the *friend or advocate
of slavery*" instead of one of its most active opponents in the House.[64]

These men, along with some of the last-minute doughfaces, can be numbered among the strong antislavery men in both houses who looked toward
bigger game than the mere exclusion of slavery from Missouri. At the beginning of the session, they hoped to acquire the whole of the Louisiana Purchase
for freedom, with the exception of Louisiana and possibly Arkansas, but they
realized that gains would be difficult in the face of southern intransigence.
However, they saw that this crisis created an opportunity—that might never
come again—to persuade the South to concede land for freedom. This was
just the moment when the South's eagerness to secure a slave Missouri gave
the North the political leverage to make a major antislavery advance by prohibiting slavery through the major part of the Louisiana Purchase.

Indeed, this was the best way to secure a restriction of slavery's growth.
Suppose Congress passed Missouri admission with Taylor's restrictions on

slavery: How could they oblige Missouri to accept the terms? Would they, southerners repeatedly asked, use force?[65] If so, where would they find the men—from the South and West? Missouri's threat to leave the Union and become an independent state may have been scarcely credible, given its land-locked position and dependence on outside markets and supplies, but some feared it might become a magnet for migrants and states that were unhappy within the Union. Or it could simply walk away from statehood (as Iowa did much later) until its population grew to a size that could not be ignored, or it could enact a state constitution, declare itself a state, and await acceptance by Washington. If any of those things happened, the North would have no leverage over slavery anywhere in the West; far better to accept 36°30' now, while the offer was on the table. As Storrs said later, "To have sacrificed to slavery the whole country covered by this restriction, when it was imprac-tical to have accomplished a more extensive prohibition, would have been wantonly to have sported with the most sacred obligations of moral duty and patriotism. To have rejected this restriction, even limited as it was, would have fixed a deep and odious stigma on the character of the country."[66]

So too thought Ohio's new senator, war hero William A. Trimble, who was a firm opponent of slavery but grieved to see the degree of sectional ill will the Missouri controversy aroused. In this, the most dangerous crisis Congress had faced, he believed, an outright victory to either party would be fatal to the republic, and so "some concession on our part will be necessary to reestablish harmony between the North and South." But he also wished to limit slavery's expansion and recognized that it would be difficult to do so in other territories without agreeing to admit Missouri without restriction. By mid-February he thought "moderate men on both sides appear to desire" the territorial compromise that had been mooted, and he was privately gratified when in the end Congress endorsed the deal. But he did not have to vote for a slave Missouri himself because its passage was inevitable in the Senate, however he voted.[67]

Northern representatives in the House were placed in a very different posi-tion. Public opinion had made the issue of slavery in Missouri the touchstone of political soundness, and Lord help any congressman who voted in favor. The hardening of opinion at home made it politically difficult for a northern congressman to vote for Missouri's unrestricted admission, even if without it the chance to block slavery north of 36°30' would be lost. By the end of January, according to Plumer's venerable father back in New Hampshire, it had become "political suicide" for any free-state representative "to tolerate slavery beyond its present limit."[68] Yet someone had to vote with the South on Missouri in order to achieve a moral antislavery triumph comparable with Article 6 of the Northwest Ordinance—and do so while trusting in the Senate's good faith over Maine.

A key figure was Charles Kinsey of New Jersey. As a lame-duck congressman in 1819, he had voted to impose the Tallmadge Amendment in Missouri but not Arkansas. After returning to the House on February 16, 1820, he voted solidly for the Taylor amendment to the Missouri bill and—like the other last-minute doughfaces—opposed Storrs's proposal to treat the territorial restrictions on slavery as purely advisory for new states.[69] Then on March 2 he voted to admit Missouri without restriction—the only congressman to vote for Tallmadge in 1819 and for Missouri the next year. His decision has often been explained by his interest in "our mouldering, sinking, ruined manufactures" and has been linked with Baldwin's strategy of conciliating the South in order to promote tariff reform.[70] The evidence seems slim, compared with Kinsey's own words explaining his vote to the House. Having served on the conference committee, he argued for peace and the restoration of normal political conditions to help the people escape from their current economic plight. But he also argued that the North could now secure a great victory, because "our Southern brethren . . . have agreed to fix an irrevocable boundary beyond which slavery shall never pass," and in so doing had conceded nine-tenths of the Louisiana Purchase to freedom. He felt the proposed settlement had to be seized for the sake of the Union, even though "my constituents may differ with me in opinion."[71] Along with New Jersey's other two doughfaces, he was refused renomination in 1820 by the state Democratic nominating convention, despite their antislavery credentials and their pleas, in his colleague Bernard Smith's words, that "a compromise was *necessary* to prevent a dissolution of the Union."[72]

Similarly, Samuel Eddy of Rhode Island had shown his antislavery convictions, voting steadily with John W. Taylor and disapproving only his suggestion early in January that slaves already in the Missouri Territory, and their offspring, could remain slaves. A month after voting for unrestricted statehood for Missouri, Eddy insisted that his "views of slavery are not at all altered, either morally or politically considered. Neither do I question the right of Congress to impose conditions on the admission of new States from acquired territory." But he thought that the compromise laid before the House by the conference committee operated "to restrict, not extend slavery." If the Senate was determined not to accept either Maine or Missouri with a restriction on the latter, "what then was the best course to be pursued to effect the object of a mere abolition man?"

> Before the compromise, slavery was permitted in all the U.S. territory west of the Mississippi. To refuse the compromise, therefore, was to permit slavery still to continue in all this territory. It was to lose all and gain nothing. To accept the compromise was to limit it to the new State of Missouri, and the territory south of [36°30']. The territory therefore within which slavery is permitted is a small space, compared with the whole territory from which it is excluded. Considering the prohibition of slavery as the only object, I insist that the compromise has effected more than could have been effected in any other way.

Eddy would be the only last-minute doughface to win renomination by his party and popular reelection over an opponent critical of his Missouri vote—and he survived long enough to once again put sectional principle above party pressure when in the House election of February 1825 he helped to make the "northern candidate" president.[73]

The four turncoats of March 1820 did not stand alone. After the House had approved the compromise, the egregious Virginian John Randolph tried to have the vote reconsidered in order to flush out the northerners who had skipped the vote.[74] After much parliamentary maneuvering, the House refused his motion by a vote that suggested some northern members were either pleased that a measure they had voted against had passed or were so relieved by the settlement that they were unwilling to reverse it. Randolph was probably right when he claimed that, had the South wanted three more northern votes, they could have had them, and if necessary three more after that, from "these men, whose conscience, and morality, and religion, extend to 36°30' north latitude." He described them as "doughfaces" who were frightened at the prospect of southern resistance and the breakup of the Union. But the probability is that if other northern congressmen had not been so frightened of their own constituents, the number of antislavery doughfaces would have been far larger.[75]

Confirmation

Many northerners were so shocked by the compromise of 1820 that they looked for ways to reverse Missouri's admission as a slave state. When Missouri drew up a state constitution that excluded "free Negroes" and "mulattoes" from the new state, they provided their foes with grounds to keep Missouri out of the Union, since many legal experts, North and South, believed the clause to be a violation of the U.S. Constitution's guarantee of reciprocal civil rights. The subsequent debate produced "more violence" of language and manner from southerners than even in the preceding session.[76] So the crisis moved into a third congressional session but with the central issue transmuted from slavery to race. The form of words that finally finessed the grounds of dispute diminished free Black people by implying that they had no rights that the white man was bound to respect, just as its decision to accept Missouri's constitution confirmed the compromise of March 1820.

Although passions were raised to new heights during the session, the sectional blocs in each house began to lose their hard-line commitment under pressure to confirm the previous year's settlement. In the Senate, many southerners thought the explanatory proviso finessing the troublesome clause in Missouri's constitution contradicted earlier statements of principle, but in the end all except Randolph reluctantly voted for it.[77] In the House, the antislavery bloc lost its unity, as some could see that "the people at large had become tired of the subject, & wished to see the controversy closed without further delay." According to Plumer, "At least thirty of those who last year voted for restriction [in Missouri] have given up that ground, as either settled last year, or no longer holding out any prospect of success." Nine hard-line anti-Missourians of 1820 in the end voted to accept the state's constitution, demonstrating that it was easier to split northern congressmen off from the antisouthern bloc in 1821 over racial justice than it had been the year before over slavery.[78] The critical swing votes came mainly from middle-state Democrats, including four New York Bucktails, possibly influenced by Van Buren. In the case of three from Pennsylvania, the president used Nicholas Biddle as an intermediary to persuade them to accept Missouri's constitution. Significantly, those three then justified their vote as ensuring that the gains of the 1820 compromise were not lost; by confirming that deal, they insisted their acceptance of Missouri was a blow against slavery.[79]

Yet the decision also reflected the immediate consequences of the previous year's compromise. Between the two congressional sessions that met in 1820, Missouri had turned itself into "a free and independent republic," with its own constitution, general assembly, and state government, and had elected U.S. senators and a congressman. Southerners in Congress could therefore argue that it was already a sovereign state beyond Congress's control. That claim complicated the final count of Electoral College votes in Congress in February, as extreme southern patriots argued Missouri had fulfilled

Congress's terms and must be included in the count to decide the presidential election. In the end, the result was declared to be the same whether Missouri's vote was counted or not, but the incident highlighted that Missouri had become a force to be reckoned with. In the process, Congressman William Brown of Kentucky proposed that the 36°30' provision should be repealed if the North continued to block the new state's admission.[80]

By 1821 various strands were coming together to confirm the settlement. The news that Spain had at last ratified the 1819 Adams-Onís Treaty arrived the day before the critical vote to admit Missouri, so that members knew that Florida would be acquired as slave territory and the western boundary of the United States would exclude Texas. Two days later, the bill relieving those in debt for public lands completed its passage of both houses, with majority support from all sections. These settlements of 1821 underwrote the easing of the sense of national crisis, and finding solutions for the economic depression became the central popular concern. By 1822 the revival of party consciousness in the northern and border states helped to restore politics as usual and focus arguments on conflicts within as much as between states. However, the sectional sensitivities exacerbated by the Missouri Crisis could not safely be ignored in the early 1820s. In New York even the overwhelming political dominance established locally by Van Buren's doughfaced Albany Regency in 1820–21 could not be converted into electoral support in the forthcoming presidential election for the obvious "Virginia" candidate, William H. Crawford of Georgia, and the regency's attempt to manipulate the state's vote provoked a popular uprising that temporarily destroyed its political control of the state.[81]

Throughout the crisis the contest had been between the "empires" of slavery and freedom rather than North and South. Both sections were divided between Atlantic-oriented and internally oriented districts, as voting on economic issues demonstrated; in May 1820 the Baldwin tariff narrowly failed in the Senate, with half the members from New England voting against in both houses.[82] Such cleavages had influenced the outcome of the struggle over Missouri and continued thereafter to mute tensions between North and South. The impending presidential election would reveal that while southern seaboard areas were concerned primarily about constitutional defenses and limited government, newer and potentially developing parts of the South wished to secure favorable federal economic policies and voted for whichever nationalist candidate best suited their local circumstances. Missouri itself did not become "southern" as a result of being admitted as a slave state; rather, for more than a decade it supported policies that were identified as northern and western—federal internal improvements and even protective tariffs in 1824 and 1828. As for the North, antislavery sentiment quickly ceased to be a major driving force behind political action, except among Quakers and the "Universal Yankee Nation" in New England and its westward extensions. Not until the administration of John Quincy Adams did the combination of slavery, tariff, and Indian issues force all elements of the South together into a coherent political force united behind Andrew Jackson, and not until 1826 did some northern Jacksonians in Congress begin to act as essential supports of the slave South.[83]

The everyday obscuring of North-South rivalries behind other issues meant that there was no tradition before 1819 of admitting states in pairs in order to balance the Senate. Though both sections were concerned about the future balance of power, no two states seeking admission had ever previously been combined in one bill. When the Senate tried to impose this practice on the House in 1820, it backfired and made compromise more difficult; in the end, the separation of Maine and Missouri meant that the former would be admitted to statehood seventeen months before the latter. There was some talk at the time of insisting on joint admission in future, but between 1822 and 1844 the only two territories promoted to statehood—Michigan (1836) and Arkansas (1837)—succeeded in different sessions. In 1845 two slave states were admitted (Florida and Texas) and were not balanced by free states until 1846 (Iowa) and 1848 (Wisconsin), even though sectional tensions were becoming more acute in those years. The balancing of slave and free states in the Senate is apparently no more than a historical illusion created retrospectively by generalizing the particular sectional sensitivities of 1819–21 across the whole antebellum period.[84]

Like the Compromise of 1850, that of March 1820 did not pass Congress as a coherent totality. It passed the House on separate votes, as disparate agreements between different groups of southern and northern members. Even so, almost immediately some commentators insisted the outcome must be regarded as a sectional compact, to be revered as much as the Constitution itself.[85] By 1849, according to Stephen A. Douglas (no less), the compromise had come to be "canonized in the hearts of the American people as a sacred thing which no ruthless hand would ever be reckless enough to disturb." Why? Because, in Salmon P. Chase's words of 1854, it had "consecrated to freedom by statute and compact" an "immense region, well-watered and fertile . . . and larger . . . than all the existing free states including California."

This was a moral and practical gain more than commensurate with the Northwest Ordinance of 1787.[86]

Contemporaries had appreciated in 1820 that the preservation of that achievement depended on preventing further territorial expansion from undermining the delicate geopolitical balance upon which the 1820 settlement was based. President Monroe warned Jefferson in May 1820 that any "further acquisition of territory to the West and South involves difficulties, of an internal nature, which menace the Union itself."[87] Mainly for that reason, successive U.S. governments eschewed territorial expansion for the next twenty years, spurning even independent Texas until the days of Tyler and Polk. What followed after 1846 revealed just what a dangerous hazard the men of 1820 had run, and how significant their antislavery achievement.

In the immediate aftermath of the Missouri Crisis, many believed that the South had won, but in reality the outcome reveals a greater victory for the North. Besides the prohibition on slavery in the northern Louisiana Purchase, the 1807 abolition of slave importation had been strengthened, a solution found for the problem of rescued contrabands, and the international slave trade condemned as piracy. It was followed in 1822 by the congressional rejection of a tougher fugitive-slave law and in 1824 by the popular decision of frontier voters to prevent the legalization of slavery in Illinois. Thus, the further extension of slavery into the New West was rebuked and the effectiveness of territorial prohibitions demonstrated. No one could—or should—underestimate the power of northern antislavery sentiment in the years around 1820.

Notes

This essay is based on a "bicentennial lecture" given by the author at the Rothermere American Institute, University of Oxford, on May 31, 2019. He wishes to acknowledge the valuable comments made both then and later by Nicholas Cole, Daniel Feller, Joanne Freeman, Daniel Walker Howe, John Craig Hammond, Raymond Lavertue, Kay Wright Lewis, Grace Mallon, Jeffrey Pasley, Daniel Peart, Stephen Symchych, Peter Thompson, and Sean Wilentz. I am also indebted to a stimulating master's thesis written under my supervision by David Paul Robinson, *The Missouri Compromise Revisited* (University of Durham, UK, 1990), though our main conclusions differ.

1. Glover Moore, *The Missouri Controversy, 1819–1821* (Lexington: University Press of Kentucky, 1953). The most valuable recent treatments are Robert Pierce Forbes's provocative *The Missouri Compromise and Its Aftermath: Slavery and the Meaning of America* (Chapel Hill: University of North Carolina Press, 2007); John Van Atta's interesting but overly generalized *Wolf by the Ears: The Missouri Crisis, 1819–1821* (Baltimore: Johns Hopkins University Press, 2015); and Matthew W. Hall's thorough *Dividing the Union: Jesse Burgess Thomas and the Making of the*

Missouri Compromise (Carbondale: Southern Illinois University Press, 2016), 117–94, which is, however, unreliable on party identities.

2. For example, Richard H. Brown, "The Missouri Crisis, Slavery, and the Politics of Jacksonianism," *South Atlantic Quarterly* 65 (1966): 55–72; Forbes, *Missouri Compromise*; Leonard L. Richards, *The Slave Power: the Free North and Southern Domination, 1780–1860* (Baton Rouge: Louisiana State University Press, 2000), 83–89, 106.

3. John Craig Hammond, "President, Planter, Politician: James Monroe, the Missouri Crisis, and the Politics of Slavery," *Journal of American History* 105, no. 4 (2019): 843–67, esp. 846–51; Martin Öhman, "A Convergence of Crises: The Expansion of Slavery, Geopolitical Realignment, and Economic Depression in the Post-Napoleonic World," *Diplomatic History* 37, no. 3 (2013): 419–45, which discusses the context in stimulating fashion but without examining the process of making the Missouri Compromise.

4. Besides the works cited in these notes, this chapter draws heavily on William W. Freehling, *The Road to Disunion*, vol. 1, *Secessionists at Bay, 1776–1854* (New York: Oxford University Press, 1990); Don E. Fehrenbacher, *The Slaveholding Republic: An Account of the United States Government's Relations to Slavery* (New York: Oxford University Press, 2001); Matthew Mason, *Slavery and Politics in the Early American Republic* (Chapel Hill: University of North Carolina Press, 2006); John Craig Hammond, *Slavery, Freedom and Expansion in the Early American West* (Charlottesville: University of Virginia Press, 2007); and Padraig Riley, *Slavery and the Democratic Conscience: Political Life in Jeffersonian America* (Philadelphia: University of Pennsylvania Press, 2016).

5. Donald Ratcliffe, "The Decline of Antislavery Politics, 1815–1840," in *Contesting Slavery: The Politics of Bondage and Freedom in the New American Nation*, ed. John Craig Hammond and Matthew Mason (Charlottesville: University of Virginia Press, 2011), 267–90, esp. 270.

6. "Congress," *Niles' Weekly Register* (Baltimore) 23 (1822), supp. to vol. 22, 65–66.

7. Moore, *Missouri Controversy*, 50; Hazel Akehurst, "Sectional Crises and the Fate of Africans Illegally Imported into the United States, 1806–1860," *American Nineteenth Century History* 9, no. 2 (2008): 97–122, esp. 103.

8. W. E. B. DuBois, *The Suppression of the African Slave Trade to the United States, 1638–1870* (1896; reprint, Baton Rouge: Louisiana State University Press, 1969), 121–22.

9. "Important," *Niles' Weekly Register* 26 (August 28, 1824): 426–27. See also Paul Finkelman, *Slavery and the Founders: Race and Liberty in the Age of Jefferson* (Armonk, NY: M. E. Sharpe, 1996), esp. 34–79; Hall, *Dividing the Union*, 94–111.

10. Tallmadge, February 16, 1819, in *Annals of the Congress of the United States* (Washington, DC: Gales and Seaton, 1858), 15th Cong., 2nd sess., 1203; Forbes, *Missouri Compromise*, 46. For the pressures in the Gulf before 1815, see John Craig Hammond, "Slavery, Settlement, and Empire: The Expansion and Growth of Slavery in the Interior of the North American Continent, 1770–1820," *Journal of the Early Republic* 32, no. 2 (2012): 175–206.

11. William R. Johnson, "Prelude to the Missouri Compromise: A New York Congressman's Effort to Exclude Slavery from Arkansas Territory," *New York Historical Society Quarterly* 48, no. 1 (1964): 31–50.

12. For example, Jonathan Roberts to Mathew Roberts, February 16, 1820, Jonathan Roberts Papers, Historical Society of Pennsylvania, Philadelphia; Henry R. Storrs, *To the Electors of the Sixteenth Congressional District in the State of New-York*, Washington, DC, January 30, 1821, pamphlet at the American Antiquarian Society, 17.

13. George William Van Cleve, *A Slaveholders' Union: Slavery, Politics and the Constitution in the Early American Republic* (Chicago: University of Chicago Press, 2010), 232–35, 257–65; Van Atta, *Wolf by the Ears*, 61–89.

14. Donald Ratcliffe, *The One-Party Presidential Contest: Adams, Jackson, and 1824's Five-Horse Race* (2015; reprint, Lawrence: University Press of Kansas, 2021).

15. Joshua Michael Zeitz, "The Missouri Compromise Reconsidered: Rhetoric and the Emergence of the Free Labor Synthesis," *Journal of the Early Republic* 20, no. 3 (2000): 447–85, esp. 470–85.

16. Sean Wilentz, *No Property in Man: Slavery and Antislavery at the Nation's Founding* (Cambridge, MA: Harvard University Press, 2018), 152–205.

17. Storrs, *To the Electors*, 12; Van Cleve, *Slaveholders' Union*, 258–65.

18. Zeitz, "Missouri Compromise Reconsidered," 455–71.

19. Hall, *Dividing the Union*, 114–16; Suzanne Cooper Guasco, *Confronting Slavery: Edward Coles and the Rise of Antislavery Politics in Nineteenth-Century America* (DeKalb: Northern Illinois University Press, 2013), 89–91; Ratcliffe, *One-Party Presidential Contest*, 181–83.

20. *St. Louis Enquirer*, January 26, 1820, quoted in Frank H. Hodder, "Side Lights on the Missouri Compromise," *Annual Report of the American Historical Association for 1909* (Washington, DC, 1911), 154.

21. Thomas Ewing to Philemon Beecher, January 1, 1820, Thomas Ewing Family Papers, Library of Congress; Forbes, *Missouri Compromise*, 75–77. For Otis, see Rufus King to William King, March 23, 1819, Mark Langdon Hill to William King, February 9, 1820, Business and Political Correspondence, William King Papers, Collection 165, Maine Historical Society, Portland (I owe this reference to the kindness of Craig Hammond). For Roberts's shifting political course, see his letters, 1819–21, Roberts Papers; and Forbes, *Missouri Compromise*, 75–81.

22. Letter of January 1, 1820, in *New-York Evening Post*, quoted in Storrs, *To the Electors*, 5–6; *Annals*, 16:1, 119, 359, 802, 947, 1540.

23. *St. Louis Enquirer*, March 29, 1820, in Hodder, "Side Lights," 154–55.

24. John Van Atta, "'At War with Their Equal Rights': The Missouri Crisis in Southern Eyes," in this volume.

25. *Franklin Gazette* (Philadelphia), February 24, 1819, in Moore, *Missouri Controversy*, 60, also 64; Hall, *Dividing the Union*, 130.

26. James E. Lewis Jr., *The American Union and the Problem of Neighborhood: The United States and the Collapse of the Spanish Empire, 1783–1829* (Chapel Hill: University of North Carolina Press, 1998), 126–54.

27. Storrs, *To the Electors*, 5–6.

28. Storrs, *To the Electors*, 5–6; Monroe to George Hay, January 10, 1820, in Noble E. Cunningham, *The Presidency of James Monroe* (Lawrence: University Press of Kansas, 1996), 96.

29. William Plumer Jr. to his father, February 5, March 4, 1820, in *The Missouri Compromises and Presidential Politics, 1820–1825, from the Letters of William Plumer, Jr.*, ed. Everett S. Brown (St. Louis: Missouri Historical Society, 1926), 6, 15, 14–15n.

30. Monroe to Jefferson, February 19, 1820, in *The Writings of James Monroe*, ed. Stanislaus Murray Hamilton (New York: G. P. Putnam's Sons, 1898–1903), 6:115.

31. John Lauritz Larson, *Internal Improvement: National Public Works and the Promise of Popular Government in the Early United States* (Chapel Hill: University of North Carolina Press, 2001), 137–38; Norman K. Risjord, *The Old Republicans: Southern Conservatism in the Age of Jefferson* (New York: Columbia University Press, 1965); Duncan McLeod, "The Triple Crisis," in *The Growth of Federal Power in American History*, ed. Rhodri Jeffreys-Jones and Bruce Collins (Edinburgh: Scottish Academic Press, 1983), 13–24.

32. Richard E. Ellis, *Aggressive Nationalism: McCulloch v. Maryland and the Foundation of Federal Authority in the Young Republic* (New York: Oxford University Press, 2007), esp. 111–42; Alan Taylor, *The Internal Enemy: Slavery and War in Virginia, 1772–1832* (New York: W. W. Norton, 2013), esp. 389–417.

33. Spencer Roane to James Barbour, December 29, 1819, and Andrew Stevenson to Barbour, February 16, 1820, in "Missouri Compromise: Letters to James Barbour, Senator of Virginia in the Congress of the United States," ed. Lyon G. Tyler, *William and Mary Quarterly Magazine*, ser. 1, 10 (July 1901): 5–24, esp. 7, 13; Nathaniel Macon to Bolling Hall, February 13, 1820, in Hugh C. Bailey, "Alabama Political Leaders and the Missouri Compromise," *Alabama Review* 9 (1956): 126.

34. Daniel Feller, *The Public Lands in Jacksonian Politics* (Madison: University of Wisconsin Press, 1984), 27–36; Larson, *Internal Improvement*, 143–45.

35. Donald Jackson, ed., *The Journals of Zebulon Montgomery Pike*, 2 vols. (Norman: University of Oklahoma Press, 1966), 2:27. The term the "Great American Desert" would not become common until after the publication in 1823 of the Long expedition report. See Maxine Benson, ed., *From Pittsburgh to the Rocky Mountains: Major Stephen Long's Expedition, 1819–1820* (Golden, CO: Fulcrum, 1988), v–x.

36. Charles Tait to John Williams Walker, March 23, May 20, 1820, in Bailey, "Alabama Political Leaders," 131.

37. Henry St. George Tucker to James Barbour, February 11, 1820, in "Missouri Compromise," ed. Tyler, 31.

38. Storrs, *To the Electors*, 11–12.

39. Linn Banks to Barbour, February 20, 1820, in "Missouri Compromise," ed. Tyler, 21. For King's impact, see *Missouri Compromises*, ed. Brown, 9; Donald Robinson, *Slavery in the Structure of American Politics, 1765–1820* (New York: W. W. Norton, 1971), 415–16; and Van Cleve, *Slaveholders' Union*, 252–57.

40. For the Democratic-Republican majority among the restrictionists, see Major L. Wilson, *Space, Time, and Freedom: The Quest for Nationality and the Irrepressible Conflict, 1815–1861* (Westport, CT: Greenwood Press, 1974), 22–48; and Sean Wilentz, "Jeffersonian Democracy and the Origins of Political Antislavery in the United States: The Missouri Crisis Revisited," *Journal of the Historical Society* 4, no. 2 (2004): 375–401, esp. 387–89.

41. *Annals*, 16:1, 1482. See especially Plumer's speech of February 21, 1820, *Annals*, 16:1, 1412–40. The idea that Federalists were behind the restrictionist movement is rebutted in Shaw Livermore Jr., *The Twilight of Federalism: The Disintegration of the Federalist Party, 1815–1830* (Princeton, NJ: Princeton University Press, 1962), 88–95; and Wilentz, "Jeffersonian Democracy," 398–99.

42. Plumer to his father, February 26, 1820, in *Missouri Compromises*, ed. Brown, 12–13; Moore, *Missouri Controversy*, 156n, 186–88.

43. John C. Fitzpatrick, ed., *The Autobiography of Martin Van Buren* (1918; reprint, New York: Da Capo Press, 1973), 1:99–100.

44. Ronald F. Banks, *Maine Becomes a State: The Movement to Separate Maine from Massachusetts, 1785–1820* (Middletown, CT: Wesleyan University Press, 1970), 358.

45. Quotation from *Cleaveland (OH) Herald*, February 15, 1820; Monroe to Barbour, February 3, 1820, in "Missouri Compromise," ed. Tyler, 9. See also Hammond, "President, Planter, Politician," 857–61.

46. Samuel Eddy, "An Appeal to the Freemen of Rhode Island," *Providence (RI) Patriot, Columbian Phenix* [*sic*], August 12, 1820; Storrs, *To the Electors*, 7–9.

47. "District of Maine," *Niles' Weekly Register* 18 (March 4, 1820), 7; *Annals*, 16:1, 1450; Banks, *Maine Becomes a State*, 184–88.

48. Storrs, *To the Electors*, 13; Rufus King to J. A. King, March 4, 1820, in *The Life and Correspondence of Rufus King*, ed. Charles R. King (New York: G. P. Putnam's Sons, 1900), 6:289.

49. Daniel P. Cook, *Speech of Mr. Cook, of Illinois, on the Restriction of Slavery in Missouri. Delivered in the House of Representatives of the United States, February 4, 1820*, pamphlet at Western Reserve Historical Society, Cleveland; *Annals*, 16:1, 1091–14, esp. 1110–11.

50. *Annals*, 16:1: 1412, 1558 (emphasis added).

51. Storrs, *To the Electors*, 12–13; *Annals*, 16:1, 1565–73.

52. Samuel Eddy to Dr. Wheaton, March 10, 1820, and Eddy to Moses Brown, April 4, 1820, in *Providence (RI) Patriot*, August 26, July 29, 1820; *Annals*, 16:1, 1576–78, 1586–87; "Congress," *Niles' Weekly Register* 18 (March 11, 1820), 26, 29. The large majority for 36°30' demonstrated that only the tie-up with Maine had prevented an earlier expression of northern support in the House.

53. Hammond, "President, Planter, Politician," 843–67; Charles D. Lowery, *James Barbour: A Jeffersonian Republican* (Tuscaloosa: University of Alabama Press, 1984), 119–27. The case for Monroe is presented in Harry Ammon, *James Monroe: The Quest for National Identity* (Charlottesville: University Press of Virginia, 1990), 450–55; Cunningham, *James Monroe*, 93–104; Forbes, *Missouri Compromise*, 69–118; and Daniel Walker Howe, *What Hath God Wrought: The Transformation of America, 1815–1848* (New York: Oxford University Press, 2007), 151–52.

54. Charles Francis Adams, ed., *Memoirs of John Quincy Adams* (Philadelphia: J. B. Lippincott, 1874–77), 4:499 (January 8, 1820); Plumer to his father, February 26, 1820, in *Missouri Compromises*, ed. Brown, 13; Monroe, in Forbes, *Missouri Compromise*, 93. Some historians (Ammon, *James Monroe*, 367–68; Forbes, *Missouri Compromise*, 65, 69–73) seem to find proof of a subtly concealed plot in the fact that there is no surviving evidence of it! Cf. Van Cleve, *Slaveholders' Union*, 349–50.

55. Plumer to his father, February 26, 1821, in *Missouri Compromises*, ed. Brown, 43; Thomas Hart Benton, *Thirty Years' View: A History of the Working of the American Government for Thirty Years, from 1820 to 1850* (New York, 1859), 1:10; Alfred Lightfoot, "Henry Clay and the Missouri Question, 1819–1821," *Missouri Historical Review* 61, no. 2 (1967): 143–65, esp. 144, 160. Clay's speeches were not recorded, but their content has been commonly inferred from the comments of subsequent speakers.

56. Monroe to Jefferson, May 1820, in *Writings of Monroe*, ed. Hamilton, 6:121–22. Matthew Mason's insightful "The Maine and Missouri Crisis: Competing Priorities and Northern Slavery Politics in the Early Republic," *Journal of the Early Republic* 33, no. 4 (2013): 675–700, stresses the localism of the doughfaces. Their constitutional views are expounded in Van Cleve, *Slaveholders' Union*, 245–48.

57. Livermore, *Twilight of Federalism*, 91–92 (where the figures are slightly different); Moore, *Missouri Controversy*, 211–12.

58. *Annals*, 15, 2:252, 274, 1214–15.

59. Plumer to his father, March 4, 1820, in *Missouri Compromises*, ed. Brown, 14.

60. Storrs, *To the Electors*, 5–7, 25–26. See also the map in Matthew W. Hall, "Richard Symmes Thomas, Unwavering Conservative in the Early Missouri Judiciary," *Missouri Historical Review* 110 (2016): 277.

61. Tallmadge to Taylor, March 2, Taylor to his wife, March 3, 1820, in Forbes, *Missouri Compromise*, 99.

62. *Portland Gazette*, March 14–May 30, 1820, in Richards, *Slave Power*, 88; Banks, *Maine Becomes a State*, 354–61 (quote on 357); King, *Rufus King*, 6:328–30; Adams, *Memoirs*, 4:518. For Holmes, see Mason, "Maine and Missouri Crisis," 679–98.

63. Moore, *Missouri Controversy*, 212; *Annals*, 16:1, 940, 942, 949, 1171–72 (quotation), 1456–1457.

64. Storrs, *To the Electors*, 17, 1; King, *Rufus King*, 6:286, 291.

65. *Annals*, 16:1, 1518–26.

66. Storrs, *To the Electors*, 16.

67. William A. Trimble to Governor Brown, December 28, 1819, January 28, 29, 1820, Ethan Allen Brown Papers, Ohio Historical Connection, Columbus; William A. Trimble to Allen Trimble, February 12, 21, 1820, Allen Trimble Papers, Western Reserve Historical Society, Cleveland. The same is true of other principled antislavery senators—like Jonathan Roberts and Walter Lowrie of Pennsylvania—who shifted to a compromise position without affecting the outcome in the Senate. Forbes, *Missouri Compromise*, 77–85, 101; Van Cleve, *Slaveholders' Union*, 239–40.

68. William Plumer Sr. to his son, January 31, 1820, in Wilentz, "Jeffersonian Democracy," 380.

69. *Annals*, 15:2, 1214–15, 16:1, 1564–67.

70. *Annals*, 15:2, 1582.

71. *Annals*, 15:2, 1410, 16:1, 1578–83.

72. Moore, *Missouri Controversy*, 105 (quotation), 213.

73. Samuel Eddy to Moses Brown, April 4, 1820, in *Providence (RI) Patriot*, July 29, 1820. See also Eddy, "To the Freemen of Rhode-Island," August 12, "Congressional

Election," August 19, November 4, 1820; Moore, *Missouri Controversy*, 215–16. For Eddy's role in the House election of 1825, see Ratcliffe, *One-Party Presidential Contest*, 248, 252–53. The fourth last-minute doughface, James Stevens (CT), insisted to the House that he was a lifelong opponent of slavery, still wanted a ban on slave migration into Missouri, but valued the preservation of the Union above all else and so voted to admit Missouri without restriction. *Annals*, 16:1, 1583–86.

74. Four congressmen who had voted for the Taylor bill, on at least one ballot, on February 29, were absent from the critical vote on Missouri. Two from New York were thought vulnerable to party pressure: Leonard Case and Caleb Tompkins, the vice president's brother. A third, Hermanus Peck (NY), voted only occasionally throughout the session and is thought to have been troubled with illness. Henry W. Edwards (CT) had not eaten all day and unfortunately guessed the wrong moment to nip out for a bite; the explanation was accepted by his local party and constituents.

75. Moore, *Missouri Controversy*, 102–4; Forbes, *Missouri Compromise*, 98.

76. Plumer to his father, December 9, 1820, January 13, 1821, in *Missouri Compromises*, ed. Brown, 22, 25–26.

77. Plumer to his father, February 26, 1821, in *Missouri Compromises*, ed. Brown, 43; Hodder, "Side Lights," 159. The Delaware delegation abstained in both houses.

78. Plumer to his father, February 22, 25, 1821, in *Missouri Compromises*, ed. Brown, 29–30, 39–40; *Annals*, 16:2, 1238–39.

79. Forbes, *Missouri Compromise*, 123–25. There is more evidence of successful party and presidential pressure in 1821 than a year earlier.

80. Hodder, "Side Lights," 156; Hall, "Richard Symmes Thomas," 288–89; Bailey, "Alabama Political Leaders," 133; Forbes, *Missouri Compromise*, 117.

81. Ratcliffe, *One-Party Presidential Contest*, 40–45, 75–82, 216–28. For the revival of old-party politics, see Donald Ratcliffe, "Popular Preferences in the Presidential Election of 1824," *Journal of the Early Republic* 34, no. 1 (2014): 45–77, esp. 47–51, 71–74.

82. Moore, *Missouri Controversy*, 321–28.

83. Ratcliffe, *One-Party Presidential Contest*; Donald Ratcliffe, "The Nullification Crisis, Southern Discontents, and the American Political Process," *American Nineteenth Century History* 1, no. 2 (2000): 1–30. For Missouri's votes, see Larson, *Internal Improvement*, 145–46, 181–83; and Edward Stanwood, *American Tariff Controversies in the Nineteenth Century*, 2 vols. (Boston: Houghton Mifflin, 1903), 1:239, 283–88.

84. Cf. Richards, *Slave Power*, 48.

85. "The Slave Question," *Niles' Weekly Register* 18 (March 11, 1820), 26.

86. Douglas, speech at Springfield, October 23, 1849, in *The Impending Conflict, 1848–1861*, by David M. Potter (New York: Harper & Row, 1976), 156n; Chase, "The Appeal of the Independent Democrats," January 1854, in *The Life and Public Services of Salmon Portland Chase*, by J. W. Schuckers (New York: D. Appleton, 1874), 141–42.

87. Hamilton, *Writings of Monroe*, 6:123.

PART III

THE PERSONAL AND THE POLITICAL
IN THE MISSOURI CRISIS

7. James Tallmadge Jr. and the Personal Politics of Antislavery

Sarah L. H. Gronningsater

Twenty-one years before Representative James Tallmadge Jr. launched the Missouri Crisis with his controversial antislavery amendment in Congress, he was an ambitious young college student selected to deliver a commencement address. A rural New Yorker by birth, Tallmadge had left home for his studies and matriculated at Rhode Island College, an institution with Baptist roots, in Providence. His September 1798 graduation speech confronted the problems and politics of slavery in the nation at large.[1]

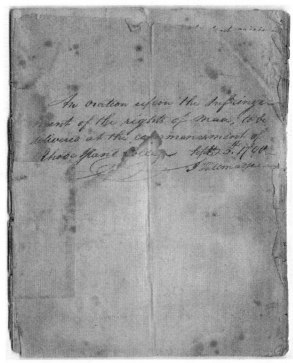

Figure 1. James Tallmadge Jr., "An Oration upon the Infringement of the Rights of Man, to be delivered at the Commencement of Rhode Island College, Sept. 5, 1798." Student essays and orations, 1786–1983, MS-1N-C1, John Hay Library, Brown University.

"The present," Tallmadge told the audience gathered in the Baptist Meetinghouse near campus, "is an important crisis in our political career." He was troubled by "errors committed by members of these United States." More specifically, he worried about "the *slave trade*," which was "repugnant to the laws both of God and humanity and an unjust and inhuman traffic of *human beings*."[2] In fourteen pages of text, Tallmadge offered arguments that would become axiomatic among future generations of abolitionists: "The declaration of American independence admitted that man was free and independent; that all were blessed with equal rights and privileges." Moreover, "Africans" were "justly entitled" to "the produce of their labor." In his conclusion, he channeled Thomas Jefferson's *Notes on the State of Virginia*: "Ought we not then to expect a day of retribution—A day when Justice will be universally dispensed" when "blacks be freed from the rapacious talons of relentless avarice." Unlike Jefferson, Tallmadge could imagine including freed slaves in the national polity. "Let us plead for mercy," he said, "while we endeavor that [a] universal emancipation take place. Then will our present slaves have a country to love and defend . . . alongside all true Americans."[3]

Although much has been written about the Missouri Crisis, our standard accounts do not devote much space to considering who Tallmadge was before he arrived in Congress or how he approached questions of slavery and emancipation in his own life. Political historians pay ample attention to what the middle-aged Tallmadge said in 1819 during congressional debates over his amendment, but not to the world he inhabited up until that point. Tallmadge's commencement speech, for instance, has rarely been cited, much less analyzed as a revealing piece of his biography. Glover Moore, whose 1953 monograph devotes more consideration to Tallmadge than most, says little about his personal life and nothing about his encounters with slavery in his own household or in the neighborhoods where he went to school and practiced as a lawyer. Moore's book serves as the main biographical authority on Tallmadge for most recent scholars, who, after sketching the basic outlines of Tallmadge's political career, tend to move quickly to the main events in the national capital between 1819 and 1821.[4]

But Tallmadge's famous political moment was deeply informed by his daily and personal life in the Hudson River Valley of New York, where he lived for decades, and in Providence, where he attended college. A new strand of scholarship in early-nineteenth-century political history reinforces the value of recognizing this point—that is, of drawing connections between what was happening at home and what was happening in Washington. Rosemarie Zagarri and Padraig Riley, among others, have urged historians to consider what congressmen cared about in addition to politics in the early 1800s. Zagarri notes that "a companionate notion of marriage, an increasing sensitivity to family responsibilities, and the emergence of a new masculine ideal had a pronounced role in influencing" congressmen's relationships to their political careers. Riley observes that northern congressmen born between the 1760s and 1780s were "deeply involved in constructing the private sphere of the home" and that both men and women from northern political families routinely moved "back and forth across an emerging public/private divide."[5] Zagarri's and Riley's insistence that we think about early republican congressmen's private selves, and take seriously the importance of their relationships back home, inspires a fresh look at Tallmadge and his role in the Missouri Crisis. While Tallmadge's politics in 1819 were no doubt influenced by partisan motives, constituent views, the quest for power, and the desire for patronage, his personal experiences and household relationships—including with his own family's slaves—affected his views and commitments, his way of understanding the world and trying to change it. In this respect, he was little different from other minor lawmakers, whose early, personal, and internal lives tend to receive less obsessive attention than those of founding fathers, presidents, and famous senators.[6]

Exploring Tallmadge's biography anew—with special attention to his encounters with slavery and emancipation, both in theory and in practice—reveals how closely the personal and the political were intertwined in his career and sense of self. To this end, we should think of Tallmadge's relationship with "home" in expansive ways. His connections to and memories of home included his early education, his regular communication with family, and his personal interactions with enslaved people. Indeed, we should recognize how many northern politicians in Tallmadge's orbit, including ones well-known for antislavery views, in fact held slaves—and also, quite often, emancipated them or saw their peers emancipating them. These experiences shaped their political convictions, their policy decisions, and their emotional investment in the actions they took while in office.[7]

In short, there is insight to be gained by examining what was happening politically and materially all around Tallmadge, at the local level, during the late 1700s and early 1800s. The laws and processes of slavery and emancipation were a routine part of everyday life in the Hudson River Valley, as well as in various locations across the northeastern states, including Providence. Tallmadge was not especially remarkable in his views on slavery and abolition; he was, in fact, a typical type of well-born northern citizen and voter who knew that it was feasible for a government to require that masters, in a gradual fashion, free their slaves. When Tallmadge looked at Missouri in 1819, he saw a territory that straddled the line between a society with slaves and a slave society—a region that looked similar to where he grew up. In truth, there were important distinctions between the two places, but it is not hard to see why Tallmadge saw antislavery potential in Missouri. He knew that with state support, slavery could be slowly abolished. He aimed to do for Missouri what had been accomplished in New York.[8]

It is tempting to want historical actors to do things, especially famous things—like launch a national crisis—for simple or clear reasons. There is no question that Tallmadge expressed antislavery sentiments throughout his life, from his student days into old age. But he was rarely on the radical edge of abolitionism. Tallmadge was a moderate on slavery, keen to see the system disappear over the long term (unlike many proslavery members of Congress), but also amenable to letting slavery stay in place where it was in some instances, for what he perceived as practical reasons. He took it for granted that men like him would shape and guide the process, not enslaved people themselves. While we can't transport ourselves directly into Tallmadge's 1819 Missouri Crisis brain, we can learn a great deal about how he saw the world, and his role in it, by immersing ourselves in the homes, classrooms, churches, offices, and towns where he was shaped. He kept some of his collegiate idealism with him throughout his life, but he lived up to his youthful principles better at some times than others.[9]

Born in 1778, James Tallmadge Jr. was raised in the rural town of Stanford, Dutchess County, on the east side of the Hudson River in New York. His father, Colonel James Tallmadge, was a successful blacksmith, farmer, and local politician who served honorably in the Revolutionary War. His mother, Ann (née Sutherland), was a devout Baptist with good penmanship, lively ideas about politics and religion, and a deep commitment to her family. Like many families of English descent in the area, the Tallmadges had roots in New England. Both James Sr. and Ann's father were originally from Connecticut. These "Yankee" migrants, who most often worshiped in Congregational or Baptist churches, were sometimes slave owners, but they tended, over time, to be less wedded to the institution than their Dutch- and German-descended "Yorker" neighbors, who worshiped in long-standing Reformed churches. The New York Tallmadges, for their part, were members of burgeoning Baptist churches. The young James Jr. grew up with slave owners on both sides of his family—his father and his maternal grandfather owned human beings in Dutchess County—but these same relatives also showed antislavery leanings.[10]

In addition to seeing slaves working in his parents' and grandparents' homes, the young James observed enslaved men, women, and children laboring all around him in the county's growing villages, along the busy Hudson River, and in the region's rich farmland. In 1790, one in seven families in the valley owned slaves; in the river towns of Ulster County, across the Hudson from the Tallmadges, the number was closer to one in three families.[11] It may not have been the tobacco South, but the future congressman knew what agricultural slavery in a rural area looked like. The Hudson Valley of Tallmadge's youth—where slavery played a vital role in commercial agriculture and many white households held fast to their human property well into the nineteenth century—was not, on the surface, that different from Missouri Territory in 1819.[12]

An important distinction, however, between New York in the late 1700s and Missouri in the 1810s was that New York was home to an embattled but effective political antislavery movement. Tallmadge saw his own father play a part in this history. In 1785, the elder James was elected to the state assembly, where he found himself part of an ongoing legislative debate over gradual abolition. Early in the session, Tallmadge Sr. voted in favor of a proposal to craft a law that would free all slaves born in New York since July 4, 1776, as well as "all that may hereafter be born." As the bill was watered down by proslavery opponents in the ensuing weeks, he continued to vote in favor of proposals to free children born to enslaved mothers after they served a long term of indentured servitude—an almost identical proposal to what his son would propose for Missouri in 1819. The New York Legislature failed to enact a gradual abolition bill in 1785, but it did pass a law that outlawed transporting slaves into the state for sale—another feature of James Jr.'s 1819 amendment—and liberalized manumission rules, making it easier for masters to free slaves voluntarily.[13]

James Sr. served only one term in the state legislature, but he continued to encounter antislavery laws in his roles as town supervisor and as justice of the peace in Stanford.[14] One of his duties, as justice of the peace, was to certify manumission documents for freed slaves. In April 1794, for example, he officially approved the manumission of a slave who had been owned by David Sutherland, his father-in-law. In his will, Sutherland "set free my negro girl, Dinah, as the law directs." Sutherland's family respected his wishes by ensuring the manumission was executed properly within days of the

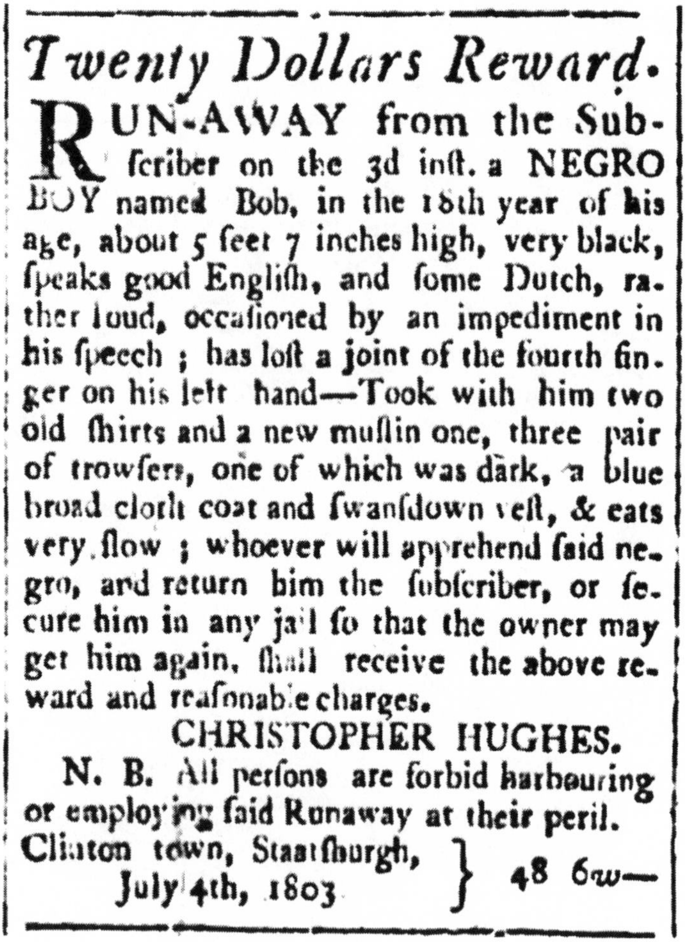

Twenty Dollars Reward.

RUN-AWAY from the Subscriber on the 3d inst. a NEGRO BOY named Bob, in the 18th year of his age, about 5 feet 7 inches high, very black, speaks good English, and some Dutch, rather loud, occasioned by an impediment in his speech ; has lost a joint of the fourth finger on his left hand—Took with him two old shirts and a new muslin one, three pair of trowsers, one of which was dark, a blue broad cloth coat and swansdown vest, & eats very slow ; whoever will apprehend said negro, and return him the subscriber, or secure him in any jail so that the owner may get him again, shall receive the above reward and reasonable charges.

CHRISTOPHER HUGHES.

N. B. All persons are forbid harbouring or employing said Runaway at their peril.

Clinton town, Staatsburgh,
July 4th, 1803   } 48 6w—

Figure 2. Runaway ad from the *Poughkeepsie Journal*, August 9, 1803.

death. James Jr., who was twelve years old at the time, thus witnessed the day-to-day effects of state antislavery laws as implemented by his own family and knew that his family members had made explicit antislavery decisions. It is highly likely that Dinah herself would not have chosen to remain enslaved up until Sutherland's demise, but her newfound freedom was no doubt meaningful for her, and her owner's decision would have formed part of the family history that his grandson, the future congressman, took with him into adulthood.[15]

Tallmadge Jr. entered his teenage years during New York's most public and lengthy debates over gradual abolition. Between 1790 and 1799, state legislators debated bills on four separate occasions.[16] The Hudson Valley, in particular, was home to an electorate whose passions ran hot on both sides. There were, for example, energetic abolitionist Quakers in the eastern section of Dutchess County whose votes helped the local electorate send a number of vocal antislavery lawmakers to Albany in the 1780s and '90s.[17] By contrast, the Yorkers were known for their antagonism to abolition politics. Added to the mix were the steady flow of Yankee migrants, who continued to move into the region. Politicians spoke knowingly of these divisions. In 1792, when John Jay made his first run for governor, a number of his allies fretted about his antislavery reputation. One fellow Federalist in Columbia County wrote that "the chief objection against Mr. Jay here is that he is for freeing the Negroes. It takes with some stiff-necked Dutchmen, though the most liberal are not swayed by it. In Canaan and Hillsdale [home to Yankee migrants] such a Sentiment would promote Mr. Jay's election."[18] Jay lost the election to the incumbent George Clinton, but he won a rematch in 1795, around the time that Tallmadge arrived at Rhode Island College.

When Tallmadge left home for Providence, he entered a jurisdiction where gradual abolition was already under way. In 1784, Rhode Island had passed a law granting freedom to children born of enslaved mothers, while also requiring that the children work as servants until eighteen, if female, and twenty-one, if male. The law did not free any living slaves.[19] Because this abolition process was a slow one, and because Providence had long been home to a sizable population of slaves—6 percent of the population in the mid-eighteenth century—there is no question that Tallmadge saw enslaved people and free Black servants at work as he moved around the New England city.[20]

Given his general interest in government, Tallmadge must have been aware of the politics of slavery in Rhode Island. There were vocal abolitionist Quakers, Congregationalists, and Baptists in the Providence area who promoted the state's antislavery laws and tried to ensure they were enforced. Many of these men were members of the Providence Abolition Society, founded in 1789. The society worked particularly hard lobbying against the foreign slave trade—a rancorous issue in Rhode Island because wealthy merchants in Providence, Bristol, and Newport were deeply involved in the business of shipping slaves in and out of Atlantic ports. Local masters, meanwhile, were irked by the society's influence on resident slaves and servants and by slaves' and servants' resistance to their bondage. In October 1796, when Tallmadge was an underclassman, a group of "householders" published a satirical notice in the *Providence Gazette* offering a "Five Hundred Dollar Award" to any person who would restore their servant girls' obedience: "Was mislaid, or taken away by Mistake (soon after the Formation of the Abolition Society) from the SERVANT GIRLS of this Town, all Inclination to do any Kind of Work." The following day, "A Friend to the Afflicted" wrote that the "Abolition Society should be abolished."[21] That same month, the *Gazette* published a notice that "a Negro WOMAN, named Jenny, about 25 years of Age" had escaped her master with her infant son.[22] These on-the-ground dynamics of slavery and resistance were matched by controversies and debates in the state's political sphere. As one citizen wrote to the *Gazette* in 1798, a week before Tallmadge's graduation, battles over the slave trade had "set many of our best citizens at variance."[23]

Rhode Island College itself was connected, via its leaders, to these political dynamics. The school's first president, Baptist minister James Manning, was a member of the Abolition Society; so was his immediate successor, interim president David Howell. Howell, also a Baptist, was a well-established public figure; he had been a delegate to the Continental Congress and a state supreme court justice. In the 1790s, he taught law at the college, while also serving as president of the Abolition Society. Thomas Arnold, the society's secretary, was a graduate of the college and the brother of one of the college's overseers.[24] Moses Brown, Rhode Island's most prominent abolitionist and a Quaker convert, also had strong ties to the university—and took part in a nasty and well-known dispute over the slave trade with his proslavery brother John Brown during the years Tallmadge was a student. Indeed, the college, like much of the North, was a place where one was apt to find both proslavery and antislavery elites. The institution at this time was small—enrolling eighty to one hundred students—and there is little doubt that Tallmadge was exposed to the ideas of these influential men on both sides of the slavery question in the years leading up to his commencement speech.[25]

There are hints that Tallmadge was thinking about national politics and antislavery ideas before he crafted his commencement address. In early 1798, Tallmadge was one of five students on a committee tasked with writing President John Adams a supportive letter in the wake of the XYZ Affair, a diplomatic confrontation between the United States and France sparked by three French diplomats' attempt to bribe American emissaries during a period of tension between the two nations. With telling undergraduate passion, the committee wrote: "With indignation we learn the humiliating conditions demanded of us by France, and trust they will never be complied with, while a drop of the American blood remains unshed." Adams wrote a kind reply, in which he praised the students' "generous indignation."[26] That same year, as Tallmadge was preparing to graduate, he was required to produce a number of "theses" upon which he was to be examined. He was among several students to write about slavery. Rhodolphus Williams, for example, titled one of his papers "No One Is Born a Slave Because Everyone Is Born with All His Original Rights." William P. Maxwell's argued that "ignorance accompanies slavery and is introduced by it." Tallmadge's contribution was "All Men Are by Nature Equal."[27] Both the letter to Adams and the students' essays suggest that Tallmadge was intrigued by national affairs and engaged with the moral questions of slavery in college.

By his own account, Tallmadge took his graduation speech seriously. In the spring of 1798, he wrote to a classmate about how nervous he was to learn who would be chosen to speak at commencement. He thought about "the allotment of our parts" with excitement, and he wasn't alone: "I am not the only son . . . whose tranquility of mind is interrupted by the contemplation of that fatal morning in which our parts are to be pronounced. . . . Anxious for advancement our class appear like a drove of deacons. All are attentive to their books, all are anxious to gain favor." A few weeks later, Tallmadge wrote the same friend, apparently with relief, reporting his assigned place on the program. One of their mutual friends, however, was angry with the list: "Maxwell is high, talked with [Rhode Island College President] Maxcy and at length told him it was a damned partial distribution, in a rage he went off to Newport."[28] The students' strong feelings suggest the degree to which this moment formed a part of their developing adult identities.

Tallmadge's commencement speech was important to him, and he chose to speak about the horrors of slavery and his desire for an inclusive emancipation. He accused Americans who supported slavery with failing the ideals of the Revolution, criticizing those "who were once willing to pour forth their blood in defense of rights violated by a *two-penny tea tax*" but did not speak out against "stealing, selling, and carrying men into the most insupportable servitude." He argued that the "enemies of liberty" used "colour" as an excuse for their sins. "But the opinion that one man is inferior to another upon account of his colour," Tallmadge explained, "is an opinion which the dictates of nature command us to reject. It is an opinion which will never be admitted by any except those who are prompted by avarice." He ended the speech with his hope that "all true Americans," including "blacks," would together clasp "the standard of liberty."[29]

Tallmadge was apparently pleased with his performance. After arriving home in Dutchess County a few weeks later, he wrote to a friend that he had stopped at Yale College on his way south to New York. He thought the rival college's speeches paled in comparison to his alma mater's. "The students," Tallmadge wrote, "speak formally and likewise theatrically. Their compositions were very poor, scarcely equal to our Sophomore productions. The [attendance] at Commencement was not more than one quarter as large as ours."[30] Tallmadge seems to have embarked on his postcollegiate career with a confident spring in his step.

Within months of Tallmadge's arrival home, New York's legislature finally passed a gradual abolition law, which in its basic outline looked similar to Rhode Island's. No adult slaves would be freed, but children born to enslaved mothers would gain freedom after lengthy terms as bound servants (until age twenty-five for females, twenty-eight for males). This 1799 law, approved by Governor Jay, maintained existing rules against the import and export of slaves for sale.[31]

Meanwhile, Tallmadge began to study law and work as a private secretary for former governor George Clinton, whose daughter Elizabeth would soon marry James's older brother, Matthias. Clinton came from a Hudson Valley slave-owning family from Orange County and was married to Cornelia Tappen, the daughter of a Dutch-descended slave-owning family in Ulster County. Clinton's constituency included many of his slave-owning neighbors, who tended to vote Republican and were wary of antislavery Federalists like Jay. These very voters helped put Clinton back in the governor's seat in 1801. Tallmadge thus spent the early years of his career working for an elite slaveholder who opposed abolitionist politics. At the same time, New York had managed to pass a gradual abolition law. Clinton, a towering figure in the state, had done virtually nothing to support abolition, but he did not spend his political energies raging against it, either, once the program was enacted. Both Clinton and Tallmadge, in other words, knew that antislavery sentiment had firmly entered influential segments of New York politics.[32]

Tallmadge was admitted to the bar in 1802 and settled down in Poughkeepsie, the seat of Dutchess County. He opened a law practice and remained close with his affectionate parents, who moved to Poughkeepsie as well. It appears, in fact, that the young bachelor James lived with his mother and father. While living at home, he began to serve various roles in local politics.[33] In 1804, he was appointed county surrogate. He was president of the village fire company. Over the next decade, Tallmadge married a second cousin named Laura (she was born a Connecticut Yankee, just like Tallmadge's father), started a family with her in a house near his parents, remained engaged in local affairs, and commanded a regiment during the War of 1812. Although Tallmadge didn't see much action in the war, he was often referred to as "General Tallmadge" because of his militia appointment.[34]

Tallmadge's law papers have not survived in collected form, but it is clear from newspaper notices and published reports that he and his partner, George Bloom, worked regularly on real estate, business, and commercial cases.[35] Unlike a number of other well-known New York antislavery politicians and lawyers, Tallmadge was not a member of the New-York Manumission Society—the state's equivalent of the Providence Abolition Society—which was based eighty miles away in New York City. It is unclear if Tallmadge represented any slaves or free Black people in court. He did assist owners in manumitting their slaves. In 1801, for example, Tallmadge swore before a master in chancery that he "did see Theodorus Bailey execute" a "written instrument" manumitting a "negro man slave named Jack." Bailey was Tallmadge's brother-in-law.[36]

Even if Tallmadge's legal work did not put him in regular contact with slave cases, he was undoubtedly aware that there were slave owners in the Hudson Valley who wanted to keep their slaves, that other owners were willing to free their slaves and abide by the state's gradual abolition laws, and that enslaved men and women themselves wanted liberty. The *Poughkeepsie Journal* is filled with such evidence. On a typical page in an 1807 edition of the paper, for example, on the left is a notice of a public auction of a foreclosed property; this particular case had been prosecuted by none other than Tallmadge and Bloom. On the right are two runaway ads for a "NEGRO MAN, named TOM" and "a NEGRO MAN, named Peter," as well as an advertisement selling a "A Strong healthy and industrious Black Woman."[37] The visual juxtaposition speaks volumes. Both slavery and Black people's desire for freedom could be found everywhere in the Hudson Valley. Tallmadge's law practice was literally and figuratively next door to these transactions in human beings and their quests for self-liberation.

At some point before or during 1810, Tallmadge became the owner of two slaves. Evidence suggests that these two people were a man, named Sam, and a woman, named Hannah, who had previously been owned by Tallmadge's father. It is possible that James's parents sold or gave him Sam and Hannah around the time he was married, perhaps in order to help James and Laura bottom of the falls, containing four acres of land or thereabouts, together with and including the said Creek and lands covered by the waters thereof as far as the said lot extends: and all the mills and buildings thereon erected and being, with the waters, water courses and mill seats to the same premises belonging or in any wise appertaining as the same have been heretofore reputed, known, occupied, possessed and enjoyed. Together with all and singular the rights, members, privileges and hereditaments unto the above described premises belonging, or in any wise appertaining upon condition, that if the said Hickey Bates his heirs, executors, or administrators, shall well and truly pay or cause to be paid to the said Reyneir Suydam, his certain attorney, executors, administrators, or assigns the just sum of eleven hundred and eighty three dollars, according to the condition of a certain bond bearing even date with the above said indenture of mortgage with the lawful interest thereof on or before the last day of May one thousand seven hundred and ninety nine, then the said indenture of mortgage to be void : And whereas the said Reyneir Suydam, did, on the twenty third day of August in the year one thousand eight hundred and four, for a valuable consideration, sell, assign, transfer and set over unto the subscriber, his heirs and assigns forever, the said indenture of mortgage, and bond abovementioned, and all monies due and to grow due thereon : And whereas the said sum of money, secured by the said bond and mortgage, has not been paid, [to the said mortgagee, nor to the said assignee, according to the condition of the said mortgage ; now therefore, public notice is hereby given, according to the act of the legislature of this state, entitled " an act concerning mortgages," passed April 6, 1801, and in pursuance of a power contained in the said mortgage, that the above described premises will be sold at public auction at Cunningham's Hotel, in the village of Poughkeepsie, on Friday the eighteenth day of December next, and conveyance executed to the purchaser by

GEORGE CLINTON.

TALLMADGE & BLOOM, Atts.

Poughkeepsie, June 10th, 1807.

FOR SALE.

A STRONG, healthy and industrious Black Woman, who understands all kinds of house work.—She is about 26 years of age. Enquire of the Printer.

July 14, 1807.   47—4w.

Ninety Dollars Reward.

FIFTY DOLLARS REWARD,

RUNAWAY on Monday the Twenty Fifth of May last, from the subscriber, a NEGRO MAN, named TOM, about Twenty Five or Twenty Six years old had on when he went away, a round blue jacket, swansdown vest, a homespun striped trowsers, a felt hat—he is about five feet nine or ten inches high, bends in his walk, he is cross ey'd, has a scar on one side of his head, speaks Dutch and broken English. Whoever will apprehend said NEGRO, and lodge him in any jail, shall receive the above reward and all reasonable charges.—Information to be given to GERARD S. SLOAN, Poughkeepsie, Dutchess County—JACOB DAYTON, New-Paltz, Ulster County, or to the subscriber near Ecker's Ferry, Marlborough, Ulster County.

CORNBURY DAYTON.

July 14, 1807.

FORTY DOLLARS REWARD.

RUNAWAY from the Subscriber about the first of August, eighteen hundred six, a NEGRO MAN named PETER, about five feet six inches high, speaks good English and Dutch, plays on the Violin, and is about thirty five years of age. The above reward will be given to any person who will apprehend the said NEGRO and return him to his master, or secure him in any jail and give information to his master, to GERARD S. SLOAN, Esq. in the Village of Poughkeepsie, or to CORNELY DAYTON, Marlborough.

DANIEL COE.

Fishkill, July 14, 1807.   37—3m.

N. B. It is supposed that the foregoing runaways have gone in the same direction, and will probably be found together.

Figure 3. Runaway ads from the *Poughkeepsie Journal*, July 29, 1807.

establish their own household. In the 1810s, Hannah was still performing regular work for James's parents, which is not entirely surprising given how intertwined daily life was for the three generations of Tallmadges. In 1813, for example, Ann wrote a letter to her older son Matthias mentioning that James and Laura had just come over for a visit with their toddler son, John James, who was "anxiously waiting" at her table for a "rice puden" that Hannah was making.[38]

We know that Tallmadge Jr. owned two slaves by 1810 because they appear in the Village of Poughkeepsie U.S. Census records under his name. In a fascinating twist, Tallmadge himself worked as the local Census taker. Not only did he mark down his own slave ownership, but he did the same for all of his neighbors. He went household to household to determine whether his neighbors owned slaves or supervised "other free persons, except Indians, not taxed." In this latter category, he wrote down the number of free Black workers and free-born Black servant children whose labor was regulated by the 1799 abolition law. James Sr. listed one of these "other free people" in his household. (This may have been a woman named Judith, who appears in family letters as a domestic laborer working alongside Hannah.) In his role as Census taker, Tallmadge Jr. encountered the slow and variegated unraveling of slavery in homes surrounding his own.[39]

It may seem surprising that a man who held antislavery views would also hold slaves. But Tallmadge was hardly alone in this respect. Some members of the New-York Manumission Society also owned slaves, including jurist, politician, and founding father Egbert Benson, who practiced law in both Poughkeepsie and New York City.[40] Many of these "antislavery slaveholders" inherited slaves or, at times, purchased slaves whom they later freed after terms of service. Sometimes these labor contracts—or conditional manumissions—were brokered at the request of the slaves themselves, who hoped to use the transfer to a new owner as a means to escape a particularly cruel master or to move closer to family.[41] The point here is not to exonerate Tallmadge or other antislavery slaveholders from the sin of holding human beings as property, but to illuminate how the personal politics of antislavery dovetailed with the public politics of antislavery. These antislavery politicians were likely more confident about the feasibility and the righteousness of gradual abolition laws because they had put themselves through similar manumission processes, either by advocating for laws that would affect their own slaveholding wealth or by overseeing manumissions in their own households even when the laws did not apply to their specific slaves.

The year 1817 was an important period in Tallmadge's antislavery career and consciousness. First, in March, the New York Legislature passed a significant new abolition law. The "Act Relative to Slaves and Servants" declared that in 1827 all remaining slaves in the state would be freed.[42] As conservative as this measure was in some respects—a decade is a long time, and children born to enslaved mothers in the meanwhile were still subject to bound servitude—the law was unique in American history. No state legislature had ever passed a law that freed living adult slaves. Nor was this law a mere token measure; ten thousand enslaved men and women lived in New York in 1817.[43]

Predictably, the 1817 law put wind in the sails of the state's antislavery movement. In an editorial republished across New York, the president of the Manumission Society, Cadwallader D. Colden (himself a future U.S. congressman), said the act "would vindicate and adorn the character of the state."[44] Papers throughout the Hudson Valley reported on the law's progress in the legislature, from Governor Daniel Tompkins's request for "the total abolition of slavery in this State after the year 1817," to the efforts of antislavery lobbyists, to various legislative committee reports.[45] After the bill passed, editors highlighted that the "final and total abolition of slavery" would occur on July 4, 1827. The *New-York Daily Advertiser* expressed hope that "the same political spirit will travel southward and produce . . . the same benign effects." In the city of Hudson, forty miles upriver from Poughkeepsie, a Federalist editor printed a letter from "Humanity" that praised "every member of the Legislature" who voted for the bill and predicted their future place in heaven.[46] These are the sort of articles and opinions that Tallmadge was reading during the winter and spring of 1817.

The second important event to occur in 1817 was a special election in Tallmadge's congressional district. Tallmadge decided to run. He was nominated by the Clintonian faction of the state's Republican Party in March 1817, and in May he won the seat.[47]

Then, in the fall of 1817, immediately before Tallmadge began his first weeks in Congress, he made a personal decision about slavery. He freed his two slaves, Sam and Hannah, who were now both in their thirties. These were almost certainly the two enslaved adults cited on the 1810 Census under his name.[48]

Historians dream of knowing more about people like Sam and Hannah, whose voices more often than not are entirely left out of the archive. We have only hints of their experiences. Mere days after Hannah was freed, Tallmadge's mother, Ann, wrote her children that "Hannah has left us and we have hired a white woman in the kitchen [for] 3 dollars a month." Although some freed people stayed with their former owners and worked for wages, Hannah did not. Did she leave in order to live elsewhere with family? Did that family include Sam, who was perhaps her husband? Or her brother? Or chosen kin? In 1818, James Sr. noted in a letter that "Hannah and Sam" had visited his son and daughter-in-law.[49] There are additional clues about Sam. At the height of the Missouri Crisis, he was in Poughkeepsie, the head of his own household. The Census notes that he lived with two boys under the age of fourteen and two women between ages twenty-six and forty-four. Was one of these women Hannah? Were the children theirs? Or nieces and nephews? Was this a family now united under their own roof? Sam, who used the last name Harris, was interested in politics. With the help of Nathanial P. Tallmadge—James Jr.'s cousin and new law partner—Harris acquired a

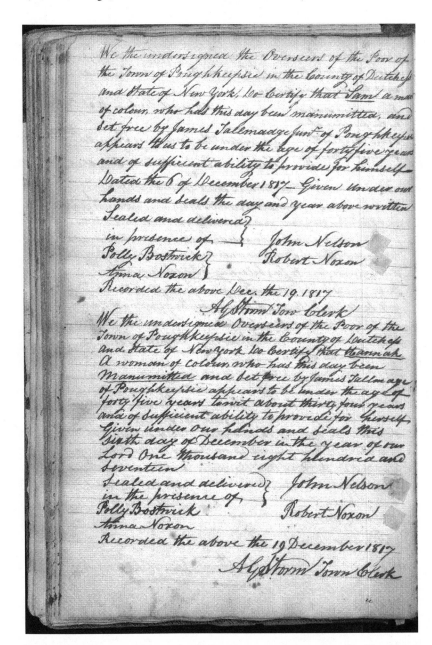

Figure 4. Sam's and Hannah's December 6, 1817 manumission papers. Records of Poughkeep-sie Precinct: 1769–1831—Roads: 1788–1842, Local History Room, Adriance Memorial Library, Poughkeepsie, NY.

certificate of freedom, a legal document that allowed him to vote as a free Black man. It is tempting to wonder if Harris ever cast a vote for his former master when he ran for office in the late 1810s and 1820s. On the one hand, Tallmadge had kept Harris in slavery; on the other, Tallmadge was often more committed to antislavery legislation and principles than the men he ran against.[50]

Why Tallmadge chose late 1817 as the moment to free Sam Harris and Hannah is hard to know precisely. It was not out of character for his family or his social circle. The state legislature had just moved decisively against slavery. Perhaps Sam Harris and Hannah had been pressing Tallmadge for a long time to put his antislavery sentiments into action. Regardless of the exact reason for his timing, it is clear that Tallmadge went off to Congress considering himself, at a personal level, a liberator of slaves.

Tallmadge took two major stands against slavery during his one term in Congress. In November 1818, he opposed the entry of Illinois into the Union because of its proposed constitution's proslavery features. In Tallmadge's view, the 1787 Northwest Ordinance explicitly forbade the further introduction of slavery into the territory, and Illinois's draft constitution contained features that cheated this prohibition. Illinois's proposed constitution included protections that allowed masters to hold on to existing slaves and servants through a grandfather clause. Another clause allowed for out-of-state slaves to work at an Illinois salt mine. Tallmadge tried to prevent Illinois's admission unless these slavery-friendly features were removed. Although he failed to muster a majority to his side, the nature of the debate gives some hints as to why he was willing to risk introducing his Missouri amendment several weeks later. Representative George Poindexter of Mississippi, in explaining his opposition to Tallmadge's motion, argued that the Illinois constitution was fine as it was, because it honored the antislavery spirit of the Northwest Ordinance while providing security for existing property in slaves; it was a fair compromise, in his view. This southern acceptance of Illinois's ambivalent antislavery constitution may have signaled to Tallmadge that perhaps a number of southerners would agree to a similarly conservative but nonetheless meaningful abolition plan for Missouri. Moreover, thirty-three northern antislavery congressmen joined Tallmadge in rejecting the Illinois constitution as it was. Tallmadge likely came away from this skirmish with a sense that a decent bloc of northern congressmen were ready to pursue substantial antislavery policies, while a useful minority of moderate southerners might be persuaded to agree to gradual abolition in Missouri, a territory that, like Illinois, was not home to a long tradition of plantation agriculture.[51]

In February 1819, Tallmadge threw down the gauntlet on Missouri, introducing his famous amendment to the Missouri statehood-enabling bill. His plan drew from both the Northwest Ordinance and New York's abolition laws. It proposed "that the further introduction of slavery or involuntary servitude be prohibited, except for the punishment of crimes, whereof the party shall have been fully convicted; and that all children born within the said State, after the admission thereof into the Union, shall be free at the age of twenty-five years."[52] At the time, Missouri was home to ten thousand slaves, the same number of slaves in New York when its legislature passed its 1817 abolition act. There had, in fact, been twenty thousand slaves in New York when the state passed its first significant abolition law back in 1799.[53] If New York could do it, so could Missouri.

Some of the best historians of the Missouri Crisis have noted that it is not entirely clear why it was Tallmadge, specifically, who introduced the amendment or why he felt compelled to do so.[54] There are, however, some clues—if not outright answers—in a range of seldom-cited primary sources.

Personal family letters, for instance, shed light on how Tallmadge's relatives reacted to his actions in Congress. Their responses to Tallmadge's bold stand do, at the very least, offer additional hints about how slavery may have been discussed in his household and how Tallmadge understood his personal purpose as a lawmaker. The correspondence sent among Tallmadge, his siblings, and his parents suggests that they remained a close and supportive family throughout his congressional term.[55]

In general, Tallmadge's parents urged their son to stick close to his Christian religion and not to worry about those who disagreed with him. An incident that occurred just before the Missouri Crisis began provides an example. By this time, James's elderly father had difficulty using a pen, but the old man made the effort to write his son a long letter during the national controversy over General Andrew Jackson's aggressive actions in Florida during the Seminole War. (Suffice it to say that Jackson had made some highly questionable and possibly unconstitutional decisions.) Both father and son believed Jackson deserved vindication because he had served the nation's interests. James Sr. wrote James Jr. in early January 1819: "You must not lose sight that you are legislating for a great nation whose decisions may be a president [sic] for ages to come. I hope the God of all grace may give you wisdom to act as a wise legislator and to give your vote without prejudice or passion."[56] Soon after receiving this letter, Tallmadge Jr. defended Jackson in a rousing two-part speech. His family, he knew, would be proud.[57]

But disaster struck before Tallmadge could celebrate his speech. James and Laura's seven-year-old son, John James, had died while staying with his maternal grandparents in Warren, Connecticut. According to Louisa Adams, Secretary of State John Quincy Adams's wife, Tallmadge heard the devastating news while on the floor of the Capitol. "Somebody," she wrote her husband, "had the *cruelty* to inform him that the news had just arrived of the death of one of his children, which overcame him, so much he could of course not go on with his speech."[58] Devastated, James and Laura returned home from Washington, but James didn't stay long, traveling back to Congress to resume "his official duty," as his mother, Ann, explained in a family letter. The death of John James was a "very heavy affliction," and Ann worried about her son going back alone at such a time. Laura wrote to her sympathetic brother and sister-in-law that when James had been "preparing for his Jackson speech" in recent days, "how much was he stimulated by the hope of one day hearing that boy repeat it." James seems to have had both his legacy and his family's good opinion in mind throughout the Fifteenth Congress.[59]

We can only speculate how or if it mattered that the man who proposed gradual abolition in Missouri was also a father in the midst of intense grief. In the deep winter of 1819, during his last weeks in office, Tallmadge could have just stayed home in the Hudson Valley, rather than return to Washington, at the end of the Fifteenth Congress.[60] Perhaps he felt he had to return because he knew what he wanted to do about Missouri. Perhaps his grief gave him a numb sort of courage to press forward with his determination to make antislavery progress on the national stage. It is possible to imagine that things could have gone very differently.

Mere days after returning to Congress, Tallmadge introduced his Missouri amendment. A public letter that Congressman John W. Taylor published twenty-eight years later, in 1847, provides further insight into Tallmadge's preparation for the moment and his reasons for thinking that his amendment was both just and constitutional. Taylor was a career legislator from Saratoga Springs, farther north up the Hudson River from Tallmadge's home district. Taylor backed Tallmadge's amendment throughout the Missouri Crisis, and the two men were friends. Taylor's retrospective account reveals some of the planning behind Tallmadge's famous moment.

Taylor's 1847 letter, published during the height of the Mexican-American War—which he viewed as an illegal Slave Power boondoggle—began on a telling note. Before addressing the details of the Missouri Crisis, Taylor explained that he had commenced his "professional life by rescuing from slavery a free man, emancipated by the New York law, in consequence of his master" breaking the state's antiexport rule. Thus, like Tallmadge, Taylor had arrived in Congress in 1819 with an antislavery conception of self. Taylor continued his story: "One day, early in February, 1819, Gen. James Tallmadge, then of Poughkeepsie . . . was sitting with me in the room of the committee of elections. . . . We discoursed of the petition of Missouri to become a State, then before the House, of its noble rivers, fertile soil, and position by the side of the Northwest Territory, and to which would, doubtless, have been applied the free ordinance of 1787, had Missouri then belonged to the Union." Tallmadge and Taylor knew that Missouri hoped to be "the empire State of the West." The two congressmen felt that the principles of the Northwest Ordinance, in combination with the methods adopted in New York—the original "Empire State"—could fairly and constitutionally be applied to Missouri. Thus, on "Saturday, Feb. 13th, the Missouri bill being reached, Gen. Tallmadge, as agreed, moved the restriction."[61]

At the time, Tallmadge's amendment was not received kindly by southerners and doughface northerners. Many antislavery northerners, however, rallied to Tallmadge's side. Fierce debate occurred on the floor of the House, with both sides rehearsing arguments, phrases, and threats that would echo throughout the many nineteenth-century disputes to come.

Tallmadge defended his amendment in a speech that summoned three of his selves: passionate undergraduate, gradualist emancipator, and practical politician. He insisted that he had no desire to "intermeddle" with slavery in the existing states. He added that he would not ask for abolition in Alabama Territory, because Alabama was surrounded by slaveholding states; it would be dangerous and unwise to create a free state in that region. "While we deprecate and mourn over the evil of slavery," he explained, "good morals require us to wish its abolition under circumstances consistent with the safety of the white population." But the newly acquired territory on the far banks of the Mississippi—Missouri—was different. Abolition was both possible and desirable there. He professed himself shocked by the "harsh" and "unfriendly" violence heaped upon his amendment by proslavery opponents. He had expected more "moderation" from them. He was unwilling to back down on his antislavery proposal. His constituents back home all hated slavery, too (an exaggeration, perhaps, but not entirely untrue). At the end of his speech, throwing caution to the wind, Tallmadge seemed to find his inner twenty-year-old: "If a dissolution of the Union must take place, let it be so!

If civil war, which gentleman so much threaten, must come, I can only say, let it come!" His devotion was "to the service of my country—to the freedom of man."[62]

The Tallmadge Amendment passed the House by a hair. Northern congressmen supported the measure eighty to fourteen, and the southerners opposed it sixty-four to two. The Senate subsequently rejected the amendment, and Congress adjourned with the amendment's fate hanging in the balance.[63]

Some historians of the crisis have noted that restrictionist northerners, including Tallmadge himself, seemed genuinely taken aback by the depth and tone of southern proslavery opposition to the amendment. Their surprise is explained, in part, by the fact that some elite southerners for a long time had been willing to condemn slavery in the abstract or frame it as a "necessary evil." It also seemed that northerners did not quite understand how much slavery had grown in the previous two decades. Furthermore, there is no indication that Tallmadge really knew much about Missouri Territory or the extent of proslavery sentiments on the ground there. Dutchess County newspapers in the 1810s rarely even printed the word "Missouri," much less explained how much of the territory's population boom stemmed from migrant southern slaveholders and aspiring slaveholders. While Missouri did indeed share a long border with mostly free Illinois, much of the territory's economy and many of its white residents were closely tied to the slave states to its south and east.[64]

Moreover, if we take seriously the local worlds that men like Taylor and Tallmadge came from, it may be fair to say that some northerners' surprise stemmed from their own experiences with gradual abolition; they had come to see it as a feasible option and imagined that others, even southerners, might have come to see it as feasible, too.[65]

Back home in Poughkeepsie, Tallmadge's mother approved of her son's controversial amendment. She wrote to James and his brother Matthias a couple of weeks after the close of the Fifteenth Congress: "James' speech for Jackson is published in all the republican papers at the North and now his speeches on slavery follow, we feel gratified with his performance, especially as we believe him on the side of truth and justice."[66] Tallmadge, who had already decided not to run for another term, must have felt some solace in the fact that he would return home to a loving and approving family.

And it wasn't just Tallmadge's family members who approved. So did the state's abolitionists and Black citizens. Black New Yorkers, cognizant of congressional events and their constitutional import, supported the state's antislavery politicians during the Missouri Crisis. In 1819, when Tallmadge came home from Congress and ran for state senate in the state's Southern District, his friends were optimistic that he would win. In a private letter, one supporter wrote that Tallmadge would "get the Quaker votes—the Manumission Society and the People of Color will generally support him—and he will get a number of Federalist Votes."[67] (Was Sam Harris, Tallmadge's former slave, one of these supportive voters?) The local press likewise observed Black voters' enthusiasm. In New York City, Black men held public meetings rallying support for both Tallmadge and gubernatorial candidate DeWitt Clinton, who had taken a rather opportunistic antislavery approach to the Missouri controversies. One Clintonian paper noted that "*numerous and respectable*" Black men viewed "JAMES TALLMADGE, *jun.* as the enlightened and humane advocate of their race."[68] In the end, Clinton won his statewide race, but Tallmadge lost his local bid to two (anti-Clintonian) Bucktail Republicans. No doubt exhausted from personal pain and political setbacks, Tallmadge returned to his law practice.

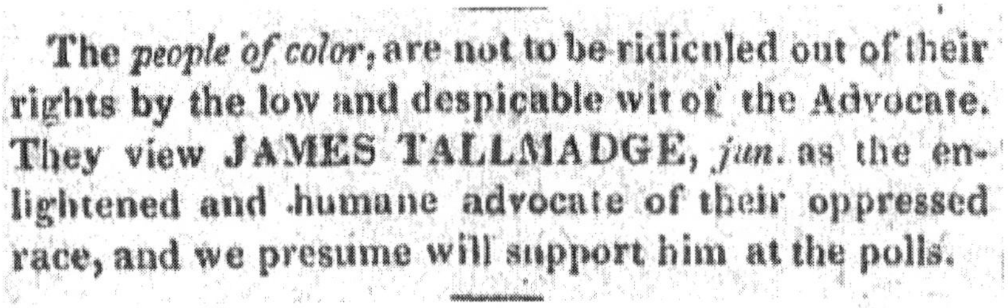

The *people of color*, are not to be ridiculed out of their rights by the low and despicable wit of the Advocate. They view JAMES TALLMADGE, *jun.* as the enlightened and humane advocate of their oppressed race, and we presume will support him at the polls.

Figure 5. Clipping from the *New-York Columbian*, April 22, 1819.

Although no longer in Congress in the fall of 1819, Tallmadge kept in touch with John Taylor, who remained a crucial force on the antislavery side of the Missouri debate. In early 1820, when the success of the Tallmadge Amendment was still possible, Tallmadge wrote to Taylor asking him to "accept the thanks of a sincere friend for your perseverance, talents and devotion to the course of your nation and of suffering human nature." He closed his letter by noting that his wife, Laura, "tenders to you her acknowledgment for your exertions and success on the Missouri question—in which she has taken great interest—your speech is an inmate of her room and parts of it she has committed" to memory.[69]

Several months later, Tallmadge wrote Taylor again: "The Missouri Bill[:] I look to it with fearful anxiety. It is *our child* and with me a darling favourite.

But I fear an ill-fated offspring—yet I fondly hope its birth may have produced moral effects which will eventually redeem our beloved country from
disgrace and danger."[70]

For Tallmadge, proposing gradual abolition in Missouri may have been a
"political" or a "policy" move. But his political and policy preferences were
clearly wrapped up with aspects of his self-concept and his emotional commitments. It is worth considering that a college student who in 1798 wrote a
speech whose opening line was about "political crisis"—a speech focused on
the moral and practical reasons for slave emancipation—found himself, two
decades later, starting a political crisis over the fate of slavery in the nation.
It is noteworthy that his family members, to whom he was close, supported
his course of action. It is important, too, to know that Tallmadge's older relatives had taken antislavery actions in their own lives. It is, moreover, relevant
that he made the decision to free his own slaves before entering Congress;
perhaps this personal choice meant that he brought a little extra determination and confidence to his political actions during the Missouri Crisis. Of
course, it would be fascinating to know how Hannah and Sam Harris may
have influenced Tallmadge's particular antislavery convictions. We don't
have the luxury of reading their words—they didn't have the opportunity to
write college graduation speeches—but we do know that their presence in
Tallmadge's life affected his understanding of what slavery was and affected
what he understood to be possible for a slave owner to do.

This exploration of Tallmadge's personal life, alongside a richer understanding of what was happening on the ground in New York State, helps us
further evaluate recent historiographical arguments about early national antislavery politics and northerners' motivations during the Missouri Crisis. This
work has emphasized the degree to which the Missouri Crisis didn't come out
of nowhere—that antislavery actors, including enslaved and free Black people
themselves, were busy and motivated in the early republic.[71] Although this
period was once coined "the neglected period of anti-slavery in America," it is
safe to say that this period is now far from ignored, at least among scholars.[72]
In addition, while older work on the Missouri Crisis often emphasizes the
claim that prorestriction northerners were fueled by political and economic
interests rather than any strong concern about the horrors experienced by
actual slaves, some scholars have become more comfortable giving weight to
northerners' genuinely abolitionist feelings and policy preferences.[73]

It is clear that, in Tallmadge's case, personal antislavery sentiment was
real. That personal sentiment doesn't make him an abolitionist saint—he
was content to keep his own slaves in bondage until 1817 and willing to let

slavery in Alabama stay as it was for the "safety" of white people in the area. But knowing that his antislavery feelings were fervent and of long standing helps us better understand the political action he is most famous for, as well as the wider context in which he and his legislative allies were operating. Due to the efforts of both white and Black New Yorkers, Tallmadge lived in a world where slavery was slowly being vanquished. It didn't seem so strange to Tallmadge and many of his fellow northerners to suggest this process could happen elsewhere.

Politicians in the early republic made all sorts of decisions for reasons of power and politics. But at least some of the time, what they did as lawmakers was deeply connected to their sense of selves, to the values and the practices that their parents made familiar to them, to the future men they imagined themselves to be at their college graduations, and to their experiences from home. It's not that historians, overall, don't know that—but we certainly have the capacity to go further in integrating formal political histories with social, emotional, and biographical histories of family and everyday life. James Tallmadge Jr. reminds us that we gain something when we put it all together.

Notes

For their generous help and/or feedback on this chapter, I thank Chinyere Achebe, John Brooke, Celia Dunlop, VanJessica Gladney, Sarah Barringer Gordon, Michael Groth, John Craig Hammond, Scott Heerman, Sophia Lee, Jane Manners, Michael McManus, Jeffrey Pasley, Seth Rockman, Francis Russo, Kathie Spiers, Kira Thompson, Kevin Vrevich, and the Penn Law School Legal History Writers Bloc(k). As usual, Dutchess County Historian William Tatum went above and beyond the call of duty.

1. James Tallmadge Jr., "An Oration upon the Infringement of the Rights of Man, to Be Delivered at the Commencement of Rhode Island College, Sept. 5, 1798," student essays and orations, 1786–1983, MS-1N-C1, John Hay Library, Brown University, Providence, RI. In 1804, Rhode Island College was renamed Brown University.

2. Tallmadge, "Oration upon the Infringement," 1–2; "Providence, September 15," *Providence Gazette*, September 15, 1798.

3. Tallmadge, "Oration upon the Infringement," 2–3, 13–14; Thomas Jefferson, *Notes on the State of Virginia* (Boston, 1801 [1787]), 241–44, 204. Jefferson and Tallmadge were not alone in predicting God's wrath for the sin of slaveholding. See David Brion Davis, *The Problem of Slavery in the Age of Revolution* (Ithaca, NY: Cornell University Press, 1975), esp. chaps. 6–7.

4. Glover Moore, *The Missouri Controversy, 1819–1821* (Lexington: University Press of Kentucky, 1953), 34–41. Seth Rockman is one of the few scholars to cite Tallmadge's graduation speech. Rockman, "Slavery and Abolition along the Blackstone," in *Landscape of Industry: An Industrial History of the Blackstone Valley* (Lebanon, NH: University Press of New England, 2009), 110–31.

5. Rosemarie Zagarri, "The Family Factor: Congressmen, Turnover, and the Burden of Public Service in the Early Republic," *Journal of the Early Republic* 33, no. 2 (2013): 285; Padraig Riley, "The Lonely Congressmen: Gender and Politics in Early Washington, D.C.," *Journal of the Early Republic* 34, no. 2 (2014): 247–49. Both articles draw from scholars of women's history and gender studies. See also Rachel Hope Cleves, *The Reign of Terror in America: Visions of Violence from Anti-Jacobinism to Antislavery* (New York: Cambridge University Press, 2009); Fredrika J. Teute, "Roman Matron on the Banks of Tiber Creek: Margaret Bayard Smith and the Politicization of Spheres in the Nation's Capital" and Jan Lewis, "Politics and the Ambivalence of the Private Sphere: Women in Early Washington, D.C.," in *A Republic for the Ages: The United States Capitol and the Political Culture of the Early Republic*, ed. Donald R. Kennon (Charlottesville: University of Virginia Press, 1999), 89–121, 122–51.

6. On moving beyond the founding fathers, see Jeffrey L. Pasley, Andrew W. Robertson, and David Waldstreicher, eds., *Beyond the Founders: New Approaches to the Political History of the Early Republic* (Chapel Hill: University of North Carolina Press, 2004); and John Craig Hammond, "Race, Slavery, Sectional Conflict, and National Politics, 1770–1820," in *The Routledge History of Nineteenth-Century America*, ed. Jonathan Daniel Wells (London: Routledge, 2016), 11–32.

7. See also David Gellman's chapter in this volume.

8. On the political, cultural, and demographic differences between Missouri and New York, despite the similar number of slaves living in each place, compare Robert Lee, "The Boon's Lick Land Rush and the Coming of the Missouri Crisis," and James Craig Hammond, "The Centrality of Slavery: Settlement, Enslavement, and Middle Class Slaveholders in Missouri, 1770–1820," in this volume with John L. Brooke, *Columbia Rising: Civil Life on the Upper Hudson from the Revolution to the Age of Jackson* (Chapel Hill: University of North Carolina Press, 2010), and Sarah L. H. Gronningsater, "'Expressly Recognized by Our Election Laws': Certificates of Freedom and the Multiple Fates of Black Citizenship in the Early Republic," *William and Mary Quarterly* 75, no. 3 (2018): 465–506. Placing Tallmadge in the context of recent work on northern emancipation makes the Missouri Crisis more intelligible. See Ira Berlin and Leslie M. Harris, eds., *Slavery in New York* (New York: New Press, 2005); Christy Mikel Clark-Pujara, "Slavery, Emancipation and Black Freedom in Rhode Island, 1652–1842" (PhD diss., University of Iowa, 2009); David N. Gellman, *Emancipating New York: The Politics of Slavery and Freedom, 1777–1827* (Baton Rouge: Louisiana State University Press, 2006); James J. Gigantino II, *The Ragged Road to Abolition: Slavery and Freedom in New Jersey, 1775–1865* (Philadelphia: University of Pennsylvania Press, 2014); John Craig Hammond and Matthew Mason, eds., *Contesting Slavery: The Politics of Bondage and Freedom in the New American Nation* (Charlottesville: University of Virginia Press, 2011); Paul J. Polgar, *Standard Bearers of Equality: America's First Abolition Movement* (Chapel Hill: University of North Carolina Press, 2019); Gloria McCahon Whiting, "Emancipation without the Courts or Constitution: The Case of Revolutionary Massachusetts," *Slavery & Abolition* 41, no. 3 (2019): 548–78; and Nicholas P. Wood, "A 'Class of Citizens': The Earliest Black Petitioners to Congress and Their Quaker Allies," *William and Mary Quarterly* 74, no. 1 (2017): 109–44.

9. For examples of Tallmadge's continued antislavery commitment after the Missouri Crisis, see Nathaniel Hazeltine Carter and William Leete Stone, *Reports of the Proceedings and Debates of the Convention of 1821 . . . Amending the Constitution of the State of New-York* (Albany, 1821), 167, 202, 485–87, but also 354–65; James King and James Tallmadge Jr. to D. Turnbull, March 1, 1841, Foreign Office, Series 84, Records of the Slave Trade and African Departments, vol. 356, 340, National Archives, Kew, England; James Tallmadge Jr. to John Jay, January 22 (?), 1847, Jay Family Papers, 1828–1943, Rare Book and Manuscript Library, Columbia University, New York.

10. Arthur White Talmadge, *The Talmadge, Tallmadge, and Talmage Genealogy* (New York: Grafton Press, 1909), 82; Ann Tallmadge's letters in the Matthias B. Tallmadge Papers, New-York Historical Society; "Notice," *Poughkeepsie Political Barometer*, June 7, 1809; Frank Hasbrouck, *History of Dutchess County, New York* (Poughkeepsie, NY: S. A. Matthieu, 1909), 253; "Old Baptist Burying Ground," *Poughkeepsie Daily Eagle*, December 25, 1911; "Records of the First Baptist Church of Poughkeepsie, NY," *Dutchess* (December 1976) pp. 9–16; J. Wilson Poucher and Helen Wilkinson Reynolds, *Old Gravestones of Dutchess County* (Poughkeepsie: n.p., 1924), 338; Edmund Platt, *The "Eagle"'s History of Poughkeepsie: From the Earliest Settlements, 1683 to 1905* (Poughkeepsie, NY: Platt & Platt, 1905), 312. On ethnoreligious identity and commitment to slavery, see Brooke, *Columbia Rising*, 264–79; "Census of Slaves, 1755," in *Documentary History of the State of New-York*, by E. B. O'Callaghan (Albany, NY: Weed, Parsons, 1850), 3:503. Tallmadge Jr. bought a burial plot from the Dutch Reformed Church of Poughkeepsie before the local Baptist cemetery was built in 1812, but according to surviving records, neither he nor any Tallmadge was ever a member. Platt, *History of Poughkeepsie*, 311; Celia Dunlop (office administrator, Poughkeepsie Reformed Church), e-mail to the author, June 29, 2020. I cannot find baptism records for any of James Jr.'s children (five of the six died young), which suggests he was, at the least, a semifaithful Baptist himself. He and his wife, Laura, were eventually buried in New York City's Marble Cemetery. James's brother-in-law Dr. Stephen Gano (married to Polly Tallmadge) was the well-known pastor of Providence's First Baptist Church, where James gave his 1798 graduation speech. James's brother, federal judge Matthias Tallmadge, was involved in building the Baptist church nationally. On Matthias, as well as the Baptists' inconsistent antislavery views in the early republic, see Michael Thomas Justus, "Ties That Bind? Baptists and the First Church System in America, 1784–1830" (PhD diss., University of Florida, 1993); William G. McLoughlin, *New England Dissent, 1630–1833: The Baptists and the Separation of Church and State*, vol. 2 (Cambridge, MA: Harvard University Press, 1971), chap. 39. On the family's slave owning, see David Southerland [*sic*] and James Talmage [*sic*], both in Washington, Dutchess County, NY, 1790 Federal Census, Ancestry.com; Stanford was incorporated in 1793 on land from the Town of Washington.

11. Shane White, "Slavery in New York State in the Early Republic," *Australasian Journal of American Studies* 14, no. 2 (1995): 5, 7; Shane White, *Somewhat More Independent: The End of Slavery in New York City, 1770–1810* (Athens: University of Georgia Press, 1991), 17.

12. On the conservative nature of Hudson Valley slaveholding, see Michael Groth, *Slavery and Freedom in the Mid-Hudson Valley* (Albany: State University of New York Press, 2017), esp. 50–54.

13. *Journal of the Assembly of the State of New-York* (New York, 1785), 14, 53, 64; *New York Laws*, 8th sess. (1785), chap. 67.

14. *Public Papers of George Clinton* (Albany, 1902), 6:577; James H. Smith, *History of Dutchess County, New York* (Syracuse, NY: D. Mason, 1882), 1:291; Stanford Town Records (Records of Road Work, 1794–1842), microfilm, Stanford Historical Society, Bangall, NY.

15. Douglas Merritt, ed., *Sutherland Records* (New York: Tobias A. Wright, 1918), 17; Manumission of Dinah, April 29, 1794, Stanford Town Records. David Sutherland's second slave, Roger, was extremely old at the time of Sutherland's death; the will instructed that Roger "be maintained by my sons free, upon equal expense." The sons appear to have followed their father's wishes in supporting Roger. *Sutherland Records*, 17–18, 24.

16. Sarah L. H. Gronningsater, "Born Free in the Master's House: Children and Gradual Emancipation in the Early American North," in *Child Slavery before and after Emancipation: An Argument for Child-Centered Slavery Studies*, ed. Anna Mae Duane (New York: Cambridge University Press, 2017), 123–24.

17. Edmund Prior to James Pemberton, February 26, March 3, 10, 1784, Pemberton Family Papers, 1641–1880, Historical Society of Pennsylvania, Philadelphia; *Journal of the Senate of the State of New-York* (New York, 1784), 38, 45, 54; Gellman, *Emancipating New York*, 161; *Journal of the Assembly of the State of New-York* (New York, 1796), 27, 51.

18. Francis Silvester to Henry Van Schaack, March 27, 1792, Van Schaack Family Papers, Special Collections, Columbia University Library, New York. Margaret Washington's *Sojourner Truth's America* (Urbana: University of Illinois Press, 2009) is particularly strong in its exploration of Truth's life among Dutch-descended slaveholders in the Hudson River Valley.

19. "An Act Authorizing the Manumission of Negroes, Mulattoes and Others, and for the Gradual Abolition of Slavery" (February 1784), in *Records of the State of Rhode Island and Providence Plantations in New England*, vol. 10, *1784 to 1792* (Providence, 1865), 7–8. See also "An Act Repealing Part of . . . 'An Act Authorizing the Manumission of Negroes . . .'" (1785), in *Records of the State of Rhode Island*, 10:132–33.

20. Clark-Pujara, "Slavery, Emancipation and Black Freedom," 56, 101, 119.

21. "Five Hundred Dollar Reward," *Providence Gazette*, October 15, 1796; "To the Editors of the *Providence Gazette*," *Providence Gazette*, October 29, 1796.

22. "Ran Away from the Subscriber," *Providence Gazette*, October 22, 1796.

23. "To the Electors of the State of Rhode-Island," *Providence Gazette*, August 25, 1798.

24. Reuben Aldridge Guild, *History of Brown University* (Providence, 1867), 14, 257, 348; "Wednesday Last Being the University Commencement," *Newport (RI) Mercury*, September 12, 1774.

25. J. Stanley Lemons, "Rhode Island and the Slave Trade," *Rhode Island History* 60, no. 4 (2002): 95–104; James F. Reilly, "The Providence Abolition Society," *Rhode*

Island History 21, no. 2 (1962): 33–48; *Encyclopedia Brunoniana*, s.v., "David Howell" and "Enrollment," http://www.brown.edu/Administration/News_Bureau/Databases/Encyclopedia/; "Meeting of the Baptist Society," *Providence Gazette*, September 1, 1798; *Slavery and Justice: Report of the Brown University Steering Committee on Slavery and Justice* (Providence, 2006). The report is filled with useful primary evidence, but it misdates John Tallmadge Jr.'s commencement speech as 1790. Kevin Vrevich's work explores the battles over the slave trade in Providence, including the clashes between the Browns. Tallmadge gave his commencement speech the year after John Brown had been prosecuted in federal court for violating the 1794 Slave Trade Act and mere days after Brown was elected to the U.S. Congress, where he tried to repeal slave-trade legislation. When Tallmadge, in his speech, said he knew the slave trade was "concordant to the feelings of some," those "some" were not abstract individuals; they were local merchants like John Brown. Vrevich, "The Inner Light of Radical Abolitionism: Greater Rhode Island and the Emergence of Racial Justice" (PhD diss., Ohio State University, 2019), 77–83; Tallmadge, "Oration upon the Infringement," 3.

26. "Address from the Students of Rhode-Island College to the President of the United States" and "Answer: To the Students of Rhode-Island College," *Spectator* (New York), June 6, 1798.

27. "Theses 1798," student essays and orations, 1786–1983, Brown University Archives, Providence, RI. On eighteenth-century collegiate education and commencement exercises, see Joe W. Kraus, "The Development of a Curriculum in the Early American Colleges," *History of Education Quarterly* 1, no. 2 (1961): 64–76; Phyllis Vine, "The Social Function of Eighteenth-Century Higher Education," *History of Education Quarterly* 16, no. 4 (1976): 409–24.

28. James Tallmadge Jr. to William E. Green, letters dated March 2 and March 23, 1798, in *Memories of Brown: Traditions and Recollections Gathered from Many Sources*, ed. Robert Perkins Brown et al., 27–28 (Providence: Brown Alumni Magazine, 1909).

29. Tallmadge, "Oration upon the Infringement," 13–15.

30. Tallmadge Jr. to Green, September 17, 1798, in *Memories of Brown*, Brown et al., 31.

31. *New York Laws*, 8th sess. (1785), chap. 68; *New York Laws*, 11th sess. (1788), chap. 40; *New York Laws*, 22nd sess. (1799), chap. 62.

32. In 1790, Clinton owned eight slaves. George Clinton, Esq., New York City East Ward, 1790 U.S. Census. Both the Clintons and the Tappens still owned slaves during the time that Tallmadge worked for Clinton. George Clinton, New York Ward 4, 1800 U.S. Census; Harry Yosphe, "Record of Slave Manumissions in New York during the Colonial and Early National Periods," *Journal of Negro History* (January 1941): 80; Peter Tappen, Kingston, Ulster Country, 1800 U.S. Census. Historians often write that Clinton was a member of the New-York Manumission Society (a state antislavery organization). Despite extensive effort, I have not been able to find evidence of this claim in any primary source, nor do any of the secondary sources I have read cite primary sources that corroborate his membership. See, for example, John Kaminski, *George Clinton: Yeoman Politician of the New Republic* (Madison, WI: Madison House, 1993), 193, which cites Alfred F. Young's *The Democratic Republicans of*

New York (Chapel Hill: University of North Carolina, 1967), 253, which cites Sidney Pomerantz, *New York, an American City, 1783–1803: A Study of Urban Life* (New York: Columbia University Press, 1938), 221. These are fantastic books, but the chase through the footnotes does not lead to any clear evidence of Clinton in the New-York Manumission Society. I agree with Paul Finkelman's assessment that Clinton had little to no interest in antislavery. Finkelman, *Slavery and the Founders: Race and Liberty in the Age of Jefferson* (Armonk, NY: M. E. Sharpe, 2001), 119.

33. Ann Tallmadge to Elizabeth Tallmadge, March 15, 1808, and Ann Tallmadge to Elizabeth and Matthias Tallmadge, February 9 and March 14, 1810, Tallmadge Papers.

34. John D. Gindele, "The Public Career of James Tallmadge," *Dutchess County Historical Society Yearbook*, pts. 1–2 (1960 and 1961); "Village Notice," *Poughkeepsie Journal*, June 8, 1808; Isaac Huntting, *History of Little Nine Partners* (Amenia, NY: Charles Walsh, 1897), 384. James and Laura married in Warren Connecticut's Congregational Church in January 1810 (Warren was her hometown). Connecticut Church Records: State Library Index, Warren, Church of Christ, 1756–1931, 97, Connecticut State Library, Hartford.

35. "Default Has Been Made," *Political Barometer*, January 17, 1810; "Loan Offices," *Poughkeepsie Journal*, May 26, 1813; "Notice," *Poughkeepsie Journal*, March 9, 1814; William Johnson, *Reports of Cases Argued and Determined in the Court of Judicature . . . in the State of New-York, 1816–1817* (Albany, 1818), 238.

36. Manumission of Jack, Records of Poughkeepsie Precinct: 1769–1831—Roads: 1788–1842, 49, Local History Room, Adriance Memorial Library, Poughkeepsie, NY.

37. *Poughkeepsie Journal*, July 29, 1807. For a similar juxtaposition, see *Poughkeepsie Journal*, August 19, 1818.

38. The earliest mention of Hannah I have been able to find is in a letter from Ann to Matthias in 1808. Ann reported that "Hannah is cleaning the upper part of the hous [*sic*]." Anna Tallmadge to Matthias and Elizabeth Tallmadge, April 19, 1808, Tallmadge Papers. See also Ann's letter from 1815, in which she mentions Sam thinking that a letter for her was for James Jr. Ann Tallmadge to Matthias Tallmadge, July 19, 1815, Tallmadge Papers. Ann signed her name both "Ann" and "Anna."

39. J. Talmadge Jr., Poughkeepsie, Dutchess County, NY, 1810 U.S. Census, Ancentry.com; J. Talmadge, Poughkeepsie, Dutchess County, NY, 1810 U.S. Census, Ancestry.com. Colonel Tallmadge's 1818 will makes no mention of slaves, either. Dutchess County Wills, vol. E, November 1814–September 1819, 282–84, Ancestry.com. For Tallmadge Jr. as census taker, see 1810 Federal Census for Village of Poughkeepsie, p. 312. For Judith as a household worker, see Ann Tallmadge to Elizabeth Tallmadge, March 15, 1808, and Ann Tallmadge to Elizabeth and Matthias Tallmadge, April 19, 1808, Tallmadge Papers.

40. In 1790, Egbert Benson manumitted a man named Francis in Poughkeepsie. Records of Poughkeepsie Precinct, 24.

41. Register of Manumissions of Slaves, Records of the New-York Manumission Society, New-York Historical Society; Register of Slaves Manumitted, Slavery Collection, 1700–1817, Museum of the City of New York. In 1821, Tallmadge's law

partner, George Bloom, manumitted one of his slaves. Manumission of Sarah Johnson, Records of Poughkeepsie Precinct, 121.

42. *New York Laws*, 40th sess. (1817), chap. 137.

43. Several scholars claim that Tallmadge worked on New York's 1817 abolition law before he went to Congress. I am confident that he didn't work on this or any other state antislavery law. Tallmadge did not run for, or serve in, the state legislature before going to Congress, nor is there any evidence that he was part of an antislavery lobbying group. The 1817 governor's seat and legislature were in Bucktail hands, and Tallmadge throughout this period was in the rival Clintonian camp. I've tried to find the original source that backs the dubious claim, but it's a journey through footnotes that don't lead to any primary source evidence. The earliest appearance of the claim seems to be William W. Freehling, *Road to Disunion*, vol. 1, *Secessionists at Bay* (Oxford: Oxford University Press, 1990), 144. Sean Wilentz, John R. Van Atta, and Daniel Walker Howe repeat (and cite) Freehling's claim. Wilentz, *The Rise of American Democracy: Jefferson to Lincoln* (New York: W. W. Norton, 2005), 222–23; Wilentz, "Jeffersonian Democracy and the Origins of Political Antislavery in the United States: The Missouri Crisis Revisited," *Journal of the Historical Society* 4, no. 3 (2004): 378; Van Atta, *Wolf by the Ears: The Missouri Crisis, 1819–1821* (Baltimore: Johns Hopkins University Press, 2015), 19; Howe, *What Hath God Wrought: The Transformation of America, 1815–1848* (New York: Oxford University Press, 2007), 147.

44. Cadwallader D. Colden, "To the Citizens of the State of New-York," *New-York Evening Post*, January 2, 1817. Colden's editorial in favor of the 1817 law was reprinted in the *New-York Herald, Albany Advertiser, Commercial Advertiser, National Advocate, New-York Spectator, Ulster Plebian, Northern Post*, and likely additional papers.

45. "Gov. Tompkins Has Sent a Message," *Poughkeepsie Journal*, February 5, 1817; "Governor's Message," *Ulster Plebian*, February 8, 1817; "Legislature of New-York," *Poughkeepsie Journal*, February 12, 1817; "The Friends of the Abolition of Slavery," *Albany Register*, February 18, 1817, and *Albany Advertiser*, February 19, 1817; "Petitions, Etc.," *Albany Advertiser*, February 18, 1817; "Abolition of Slavery," *Independent American*, March 19, 1817; "The Bill Relative to Slaves," *Ulster Plebian*, March 29, 1817.

46. "Abolition of Slavery in the State of New-York," *Northern Whig*, April 8, 1817; "Abolition of Slavery in the State of New-York," *Northern Post*, April 10, 1817; "The Legislature of this state," *New-York Daily Advertiser*, April 9, 1817. Humanity, "Abolition of Slavery and Imprisonment for Debt," *Ulster Plebian*, February 22, 1817. See also "Abolition of Slavery," *Suffolk County Recorder*, February 15, 1817; and "Report," *Albany Gazette*, April 25, 1817.

47. "Election Results," *Poughkeepsie Journal*, May 7, 1817. For a critical take on the Clintonian patronage network in the state (including a reference to James), see "Clintonian Republicanism," *Political Barometer*, April 24, 1811. Tallmadge broke with the Clintonians after his term in Congress.

48. On December 6, the Poughkeepsie Overseers of the Poor agreed that Hannah, aged thirty-four, and Sam, a "man of colour" under forty-five, both slaves of James

Tallmadge Jr., were eligible for manumission. Records of Poughkeepsie Precinct, 99. See also Sam Harris's certificate of freedom from April 25, 1821, in Record of Roads, 1756–88, film 285, Dutchess County Clerk's Office, Poughkeepsie, NY.

49. Ann Tallmadge to Elizabeth and Matthias Tallmadge, December 14, 1817, and John Tallmadge Sr. to Matthias Tallmadge, January 26, 1818, Tallmadge Papers. I have no wish to romanticize the Tallmadges' relationships with their slaves, but it is clear that the family felt they had personal relationships with the Black people in their households. A particularly revealing example concerns Ann's relationship with Susan Wright, a woman born enslaved in Elizabeth Clinton Tallmadge's childhood home. Wright would visit Poughkeepsie with Elizabeth and Matthias, and in 1810, according to her own narrative, she attended the Tallmadges' Baptist Church and "upon declaration of faith was unanimously accepted by them, and . . . baptized by Mr. Wayland their pastor and admitted a member of the church." Ann was delighted; in her letters to Eliza and Matthias, she sometimes closed with lines like "tell Suck [a nickname for Susan] I think much of her." Ann Tallmadge to Elizabeth Tallmadge, March 14, 1810, Tallmadge Papers. See also Ann to Matthias Tallmadge, May 31, 1815. Susan Wright's short, undated narrative of her life and baptism is in the Tallmadge Papers. See also "Records of the First Baptist Church of Poughkeepsie, NY," 9.

50. Samuel Harris, Poughkeepsie, Dutchess County, New York, 1820 U.S. Census; Sam Harris's certificate of freedom, Record of Roads. On Black voters, antislavery politics, and certificates of freedom, see Gronningsater, "'Expressly Recognized by Our Election Laws.'"

51. Constitution of the State of Illinois, 1818, http://www.idaillinois.org/cdm/ref /collection/isl2/id/167; Annals of Congress, 15th Cong., 2nd sess., 305–11; John Craig Hammond, "'Uncontrollable Necessity': The Local Politics, Geopolitics, and Sectional Politics of Slavery Expansion," in Contesting Slavery, ed. Hammond and Mason, 150–51.

52. Annals of Congress, 15th Cong., 2nd sess., 1170.

53. Susan B. Carter et al., Historical Statistics of the United States: Earliest Times to the Present (New York: Cambridge University Press, 2006), Series Eg1-59.

54. Moore, Missouri Controversy, 38–39; Wilentz, Rise of American Democracy, 378; Leonard L. Richards, The Slave Power: The Free North and Southern Domination, 1780–1860 (Baton Rouge: Louisiana State University Press, 2000), 53. Robert Pierce Forbes attributes Tallmadge's motives to his identity as a "devout Christian and staunch republican," in The Missouri Compromise and Its Aftermath: Slavery and the Meaning of America (Chapel Hill: University of North Carolina Press, 2007), 36. I don't think Forbes is wrong, but I think we can be a bit more specific. (Many in Congress considered themselves devout Christians and staunch republicans, but that didn't prompt them to take proactive antislavery stands like Tallmadge did.) It is also worth noting—as Moore did long ago—that Tallmadge had already decided not to run for another term in Congress. Perhaps he felt he had nothing to lose. Moore, Missouri Controversy, 37.

55. Moore writes that the Tallmadge Papers "throw almost no light" on the Missouri Crisis (Missouri Controversy, 37n18). This is true if one is looking for specific

commentary on Tallmadge Jr.'s maneuverings in Congress. But, as my discussion in this chapter suggests, we can learn quite a lot from these letters. One only wishes that more of Laura's and James's letters, specifically, had survived.

56. James Tallmadge to James Tallmadge Jr., January 7, 1819, Tallmadge Papers. On Jackson's invasion of Florida, see Wilentz, *Rise of American Democracy*, 172–75; and Howe, *What Hath God Wrought*, 98–107.

57. *Speech of the Honorable James Tallmadge, Jr. of Duchess County . . . on the Seminole War* (New York, 1819). See also James Tallmadge to James Tallmadge Jr. and Matthias Tallmadge, March 20, 1819, Tallmadge Papers.

58. Louisa Adams to John Adams, January 23, 1819, Adams Family Papers, Massachusetts Historical Society, Boston.

59. Ann Tallmadge to James Tallmadge Jr. and Matthias Tallmadge, February 3, 1819, Laura Tallmadge to Elizabeth Clinton Tallmadge and Matthias Tallmadge, February 21, 1819, Tallmadge Papers. James was also quite physically sick when he returned to Washington.

60. Wilentz notes, for example, that thirteen southern congressmen were absent when Tallmadge proposed his amendment. It was two weeks before the end of the session, and some members went home early. Wilentz, "Jeffersonian Democracy and Antislavery," 397.

61. "Interesting Letter," *Cleveland Herald*, June 1, 1847.

62. *Annals of Congress*, 15th Cong., 2nd sess., 1203–4.

63. *Annals of Congress*, 15th Cong., 2nd sess., 1214–16.

64. Lee, "Boon's Lick Land Rush"; Hammond, "Centrality of Slavery."

65. Forbes, *Missouri Compromise*, 38, 41, 43. Wilentz notes that many restrictionists came from mid-Atlantic states (where gradual abolition affected the largest number of masters and slaves). Wilentz, *Rise of American Democracy*, 225.

66. Ann Tallmadge to James Tallmadge Jr. and Matthias Tallmadge, March 29, 1819, Tallmadge Papers.

67. Theodorus Bailey to Matthias B. Tallmadge, April 27, 1819, Tallmadge Papers. Further research might reveal additional linkages between Tallmadge's politics/prospects for election and Quaker members of his constituency. Due to the Covid-19 pandemic, I was unable investigate the Creek/Stanford, Poughkeepsie, or Nine Partners meeting records for the years in question, but previous research in Quaker records from the late 1700s suggests that Dutchess County Quakers were especially committed to antislavery. Oblong Monthly Meeting, Men's Minutes, 1757–1788, Records of New York Yearly Meeting of Friends (microform), Milstein Division, New York Public Library; New York Yearly Meeting, Minutes, 1746–1800 (microfilm), Friends Historical Library, Swarthmore College, Swarthmore, PA.

68. "No Novelty," *Columbian*, April 26, 1819; *Columbian*, April 22, 1819. See also "Mr. Tallmadge's Speech," *Columbian*, April 1, 1819; "Buck-tail Hostility to Blacks," *Columbian*, April 20, 1820; *NA*, April 21, 1819; and "People of Color," *Columbian*, April 26, 1819. On Clinton, see Forbes, *Missouri Compromise*, 86–91.

69. James Tallmadge Jr. to John W. Taylor, September 14, 1819, John W. Taylor Papers, New-York Historical Society.

70. James Tallmadge Jr. to John W. Taylor, December 4, 1820, Taylor Papers.

71. The following two literature reviews are excellent: Michael E. Wood, "What Twenty-First-Century Historians Have Said about the Causes of Disunion: A Civil War Sesquicentennial Review of Recent Literature," *Journal of American History* 99, no. 2 (2012): 415–39; Corey Brooks, "Reconsidering Politics in the Study of American Abolitionists," *Journal of the Civil War Era* 8, no. 2 (2018): 291–317.

72. Alice Dana Adams, *The Neglected Period of Anti-slavery in America, 1808–1831* (Boston: Ginn, 1908).

73. Richard H. Brown, "The Missouri Crisis, Slavery and the Politics of Jacksonianism," *South Atlantic Quarterly* 65 (1966): 55–72; Moore, *Missouri Controversy*; Duane Diamond Mercer, "The Tallmadge Amendment and Missouri Controversy: A Problem in Motivation" (master's thesis, Montana State University, 1963); and Freehling, *Road to Disunion*, are examples of older works that underemphasize antislavery politics as a major force. More recently, George Van Cleve has described the controversy as "at base a recurrence of sectional tensions that had existed since the postrevolutionary period but had previously been suppressed by the creation of the federal constitutional structure and by very rapid national expansion"; it was a "balance-of-power" conflict about "long-term national political control." Van Cleve, *A Slaveholder's Union: Slavery, Politics, and the Constitution in the Early American Republic* (Chicago: University of Chicago Press, 2010), 227, 241–42, 225. Van Cleve's footnotes give a nice overview of historiographical trends (345–46). Contrast Van Cleve with Matthew Mason, *Slavery and Politics in the Early American Republic* (Chapel Hill: University of North Carolina Press, 2006), 179–80 (emphasizing northern "anxieties about slavery's infringements on their liberties" and "horror of the internal slave trade and kidnapping of free blacks"); and John Craig Hammond, *Slavery, Freedom, and Expansion in the Early American West* (Charlottesville: University of Virginia Press, 2007), 151 ("to northern restrictionists, precedent, the nation's founding principles, and the Constitution all created a potent antislavery past which demanded that Congress work to halt slavery's expansion as an important step toward gradually abolishing the institution"). For other scholars rethinking the intellectual and political context of the crisis, see Joshua Michael Zeitz, "The Missouri Compromise Reconsidered: Antislavery Rhetoric and the Emergence of the Free Labor Synthesis," *Journal of the Early Republic* 20, no. 3 (2000): 447–85; and Wilentz, "Jeffersonian Democracy." For my take on how Black men's antislavery politics and voting affected the Missouri Crisis, see Gronningsater, "Expressly Recognized by Our Election Laws." Matthew Mason's article on Missouri and Maine inspires my own thinking in this chapter; he urges scholars to zoom back and forth between local and national political circumstances. Mason, "The Maine and Missouri Crisis: Competing Priorities and Northern Slavery Politics in the Early Republic," *Journal of the Early Republic* 33, no. 4 (2013): 675–700.

8. Litigating Freedom during the Missouri Crisis

Anne Twitty

In OCTOBER 1817, white residents of Missouri sent the first of many petitions to Congress, seeking the territory's admission to the Union as a state. Eight months later, one of those residents, a Black woman from the small community of St. Ferdinand named Winny, who had spent all of her nearly forty years as a slave, filed a very different petition, a petition that initiated a freedom suit against her master, Phebe Whitesides. Over the next few years, as white Missourians sought statehood, Winny sought her freedom.[1]

White Missourians' efforts resulted in a national controversy that served, as an aging Thomas Jefferson proclaimed, "like a fire bell in the night," a harbinger of the sectional conflict over slavery that would ultimately culminate in the deaths of 750,000 Americans and the freedom of another 4 million. Though less sweeping, the consequences of *Winny v. Whitesides* (1824) were profound in their own way. Winny's victory, first in the St. Louis circuit court, and, later, in the Missouri Supreme Court, laid the groundwork for hundreds of other freedom suits in the state. Arguably the most doctrinally significant decision of its kind, *Winny v. Whitesides* established the "once free, always free" doctrine, which entitled those who had been held as slaves on free soil but later returned to slave territories or states to their freedom.[2] Until the Missouri Supreme Court reversed itself in *Scott v. Emerson* (1852), the precedent created by *Winny v. Whitesides* was used by scores if not hundreds of Missouri slaves to obtain their own freedom through the courts.[3]

Though the literature on both the Missouri Crisis and the freedom suits filed in the St. Louis circuit court is substantial and growing, none has sought to connect them. The overwhelming majority of the scholarship on the coming of Missouri statehood has examined only the events that unfolded in the halls of Congress. Older volumes on the Missouri Crisis that have considered the event from the perspective of Missouri, meanwhile, fixated on the high politics of the state, with little mention of slavery as anything other than a source of political controversy.[4] Newer work that considers how the economic and social realities of slaveholding shaped the views and strategies of local decision makers nevertheless remains focused on white politicians rather than enslaved people.[5] Scholarship on the St. Louis freedom suits, meanwhile, including my own past work, has either ignored the Missouri Crisis entirely or treated it only in passing, as an event largely external to—and unaffected by—the often intensely local events it seeks to describe.[6] The relationship between these cases and formal politics has been largely unexplored; to the extent formal politics are discussed in this scholarship, the focus has been significantly later, less committed to the analysis of political events *as* political events, and more narrowly centered on developments in Missouri that led, for instance, to the rise of registration requirements for free people of color and judicial elections that remade the Missouri Supreme Court. Even the *Dred Scott* decision, which sits squarely at the intersection of freedom suits and politics, has been treated as an almost entirely legal development by scholars of Missouri freedom suits. In short, historians have written about the politics of slavery without slaves or focused on freedom suits without much attending to the politics of slavery.

Putting them in the same frame, however, by examining Winny's experience litigating freedom during the drive for statehood, enriches our understanding of both. To be sure, neither Winny's efforts in court nor the outcome of her case can be wholly explained by reference to the political controversy swirling around her. Winny's story has a lot, but also, simultaneously, very little, to do with the Missouri Crisis. This is, in some sense, a story about the gap between these two events. But if we cannot explain Winny's case as a reaction to the Missouri Crisis, we also cannot understand it without understanding the crisis as the context. Likewise, we cannot understand the Missouri Crisis without understanding the concomitant efforts of enslaved people to use issues of law and jurisdiction for their own benefit.

Once we join Winny's struggle with the struggle for Missouri statehood, we perhaps begin to see both differently. Though most of the literature has painted the resolution to the crisis as an unambiguous triumph for proslavery forces, conceptualizing the emancipatory outcome of *Winny v. Whitesides* as one of its legacies reveals a different, more complicated picture. If we take the long view and consider all the enslaved people who used the precedent Winny's case created to gain their freedom, what is often called the Missouri Compromise appears to have been far more of a compromise than is traditionally assumed. Missouri statehood marked a triumph for proslavery forces, to be sure, but not before a handful of Missouri's enslaved people and their white allies wrung some meaningful antislavery concessions.

▲

Winny was likely born in Virginia, sometime between 1778 and 1780, but like so many enslaved people after the Revolution, she was repeatedly relocated in the years that followed.[7] Little is known about her earliest years, which were probably spent in Amelia and Nottoway Counties, just west of Petersburg. But in 1789, while she was still a child, the man who claimed her, Edward Jackson, died.[8] A slaveholder's death often portended great changes for enslaved people, as wills or probate proceedings dictated new masters within the same family or sale to neighbors or traders. Jackson's will legally conveyed Winny to Jackson's daughter Phebe Whitesides. But the will, it seems, merely reiterated an arrangement that was already in place before Jackson's death: by the time the old man died, Winny had already been transferred to Whitesides with a "deed of gift" and had been or was about to be taken from her home in Virginia.[9] It was the first of many moves. By the early 1790s, Winny; Whitesides; Whitesides's husband, John; and at least some of the Whitesides children resided in North Carolina.[10] Within a few years, they all relocated to Kentucky, only to move again shortly thereafter to a site just east of St. Louis in the Northwest Territory.[11] By crossing the Ohio River, Winny and the Whitesideses entered a region where slavery was supposedly banned by the Northwest Ordinance, but the reality was far murkier. Slavery continued to be widespread in the region, and the Whitesideses' decision to bring their slaves with them onto this supposedly free soil was hardly unusual. Lingering fears that the ordinance might eventually be enforced, however, convinced many slaveholders to relocate farther west to the Louisiana Territory, where slavery was legal.[12] Whether such concerns motivated the Whitesideses or not, they remained in the Northwest Territory for only a few years, until perhaps 1796, when they crossed the Mississippi River into Missouri.[13]

After almost a decade on the move, Winny's journey into Spanish Missouri apparently turned out to be her last. In 1798, two years after they arrived, Phebe Whitesides's husband, John, obtained a grant of six hundred arpents of land in the northern part of present-day St. Louis County, near St. Ferdinand, and seemingly resolved to go no farther.[14] Winny and the Whitesideses settled just outside a newly formed community with a population of fewer than two hundred people.[15] Originally settled by French *habitants* of Illinois who made their way across the Mississippi River, St. Ferdinand remained a largely French town throughout the Spanish regime and into the nineteenth century, but Winny and the Whitesideses joined a growing cohort of American transplants to the area when they arrived in the mid-1790s.[16] The white settlers in and around the village, both French and American, embraced slavery.[17]

For Winny, the move to St. Ferdinand was a turning point. It marked the beginning of a new permanent residence and the start of a new phase in her life, one that would continue unbroken for the next two decades. In the years that followed her relocation to the Louisiana Territory, Winny gave birth to at least two children, sons Jerry and Daniel. Many more would follow.[18]

If the experience of pregnancy and childbirth in her new home became a constant for Winny, however, a good deal else in her life continued to be tumultuous. John Whitesides died in 1803, and his death led to a string of changes. In the ten years that followed, Phebe Whitesides married twice, first George Wallis and later Fielding Pruitt, developments that presumably introduced two new masters into the lives of Winny and her children.[19] When Whitesides's last marriage ended in separation in 1813, moreover, she seemingly conveyed all of her property, including Winny and Winny's children, then six in number, to her own children.[20]

The dissolution of Phebe Whitesides's household threatened the dissolution of Winny's family. Though Winny and her children all remained in what had become St. Louis County after 1813, they apparently no longer lived under one roof. Phebe Whitesides's son Thomas seems to have inherited both Winny's eldest son, Jerry, and her eldest daughter, Jenny. But while Thomas held on to Jerry, he quickly sold Jenny to a neighbor and distant relation in 1814. Jenny was perhaps later transferred to that man's son.[21] Winny's next-oldest son, Daniel, meanwhile, was given to Whitesides's son John, while Winny's daughters Nancy, Lydia, and Sarah were conveyed to three of Whitesides's daughters.[22] Over the next few years, who, exactly, claimed Winny, and the children she continued to birth, remains unclear. It seems as though Winny and her youngest children may have remained in Whitesides's possession even if Whitesides no longer held legal title to them.[23] During this period Winny may have been hired out, but even if she wasn't, the arrangement hardly offered stability: once Whitesides separated from her last husband, she "quit housekeeping" and began moving between her own children's households, residing "sometimes with one of her children and sometimes with another."[24] Whether she continued to live with Whitesides or not, Winny probably bounced from residence to residence.

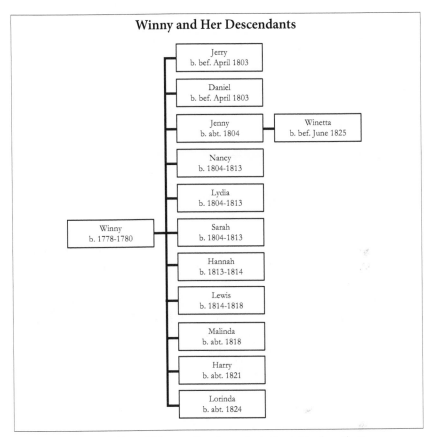

Figure 1. Chart of Winny and her descendants. Created by the author.

Keeping her family in St. Louis County must have been Winny's constant concern. She almost certainly worried that it was only a matter of time before at least one of her children was sold away from her or one of the many Whitesides heirs relocated to a different part of the territory or country, taking their property—her children—with them. That, after all, had most likely been her own experience as a child when she was given to Phebe Whitesides. These fears may have taken more concrete form around 1817, as Reuben Mitchell Hatton, who, along with his wife, Anne Whitesides Hatton, had inherited Winny's daughter Sarah, made plans to move up the Missouri River to the Boon's Lick region in central Missouri, more than a hundred miles farther west.[25]

Meanwhile, all around her, other enslaved people were responding to their bondage by stealing themselves. In doing so, some, no doubt, hoped to reestablish bonds with friends and family they'd been taken from, others sought to avoid the physical abuse so many slaveholders doled out, and still others were motivated by the basic desire to snatch a semblance of autonomy over their lives. Many used the instability and displacement occasioned by the widespread use of the hiring-out system to escape. A man named Juba who had been sent by his St. Louis master, explorer William Clark, to work near St. Ferdinand took off in June 1815 and apparently managed to evade recapture for a year before he was eventually found; packed off to Lexington, Kentucky; and sold.[26] Around the same time, the enslaved woman Lucy, who was occasionally sent to labor at a farm a few miles from the Whitesideses, did likewise. The following year, she did it again and was subsequently sent to the St. Louis jail until her master returned to the area.[27] Others escaped directly from their masters. On Daniel Bissell's nearby Franklinville Farm plantation, two different enslaved men escaped in successive years. Joseph Blake, who no doubt longed to be reunited with the loved ones in Kentucky he'd been separated from just a few months before, ran away in March 1816. Less than a year later, Frederick Sams of Georgia, who "had some marks of the whip on his back," followed suit.[28] While Blake and Sams absconded from Franklinville Farm, however, another enslaved man headed that way. Lewis, who had been sold away from his former master in Ste. Genevieve, left his new master in St. Louis in December 1816 and apparently set off for "the neighborhood of Bissell's plantation, where he ha[d] been seen."[29]

When he lit out for the St. Ferdinand area, Lewis may have been making his way north or seeking the aid of a sizable enslaved community—but he may also have been hoping, with reason, to find white allies. Several years before, a handful of St. Ferdinand's erstwhile Methodists, under the guidance of the Reverend John Clark, had affiliated with the antislavery Baptist "Friends to Humanity" sect. Like all such Friends to Humanity, Clark called on his flock to help bring slavery to an end. His most devout followers were members of John Patterson's large family, who held a significant amount of land and hosted religious meetings at their homes just north of St. Ferdinand.[30] Although the Friends to Humanity stopped short of viewing slaveholding as a "sin per se," generally refused to interfere with the legal or political rights of slaveholders, and, like Clark, often embraced colonization, they also took concrete steps to end the institution. Members were encouraged, for instance, to purchase and then manumit enslaved people.[31] Desperate runaways may have hoped that these white congregants would aid in their escape.

While there is no evidence that the Patterson family or their coreligionists facilitated the flight of those like Lewis, their antislavery sentiments would have been well known in their community, which, while growing, remained small. Because Missouri's individual territorial census returns for 1814, 1816, 1818, and 1820 were nearly all destroyed, population information about St. Ferdinand, specifically, is not available during this period.[32] But it seems that by 1820, the town itself would have contained roughly 250 people. The broader township in which it sat, while larger, nevertheless likely would have included only slightly more than 2,000 people.[33] Among those, the Pattersons were not only one of the first American families to settle in the area, but likely one of the most numerous as well.[34]

By the fall of 1817, in any case, as Winny and other enslaved people in the region struggled with the enduring problem of how to navigate and potentially escape their bondage, white Missourians were increasingly taking up a new challenge—turning Missouri Territory into a state. In October 1817, newspapers in St. Louis began publishing copies of statehood petitions.[35] Evidence suggests that the white men in Winny's orbit probably didn't have direct knowledge of these petitions—or the opportunity to sign them—but even if they didn't get the chance to see or add their names to such documents, they certainly would have read or heard about them from others.[36] Stories reported by the local press about the first statehood petitions and the conversations those stories generated no doubt reached Winny as well.

Gauging Winny's reaction to such news is a challenge. If the *Missouri Gazette*, which declared that it "highly approve[d]" of the "sentiments and expressions" contained in the petitions, was any guide, white Missourians seem to have greeted the development with enthusiasm.[37] But there's little to suggest that Winny—and the rest of Missouri's enslaved population—necessarily felt the same. It's possible that Winny and those like her may have viewed statehood as wholly irrelevant to their circumstances. Because nothing in the first statehood petitions raised the issue of slavery, and the stories that appeared about them did not seem to either, the territory's enslaved population—like its white population—may have concluded that admission to the Union would have no significant consequences for the institution. But a more expansive examination of Winny's own life experiences, and the information she gathered as she made her way across the United States, suggests that she understood the importance of the new legal regime statehood would usher in whether the first petitions mentioned slavery or not—and would have been keenly interested in and likely apprehensive about any such

developments. After all, Winny knew her bondage was the product of a series of legal instruments made possible by an assortment of laws passed in
a variety of different jurisdictions. One legal instrument, a deed of gift, had
made her Phebe Whitesides's slave when she was just a girl. Another legal
instrument, in the form of a will, had reaffirmed her transfer. Still another
legal instrument, this time a contract, had dispersed her children among
a variety of masters spread across several different households. These legal
instruments were given power and authority by statutes that upheld the legality of slavery and deemed Winny and her children movable property. In
her nearly forty years, moreover, Winny had lived in three states and two
territories that were part of both the United States and New Spain. In less
than a year, she would use her knowledge about how the laws in one of these
jurisdictions—the Northwest Territory—differed from the laws in the others as a basis for her freedom suit in the St. Louis circuit court. Statehood
raised the possibility of new legal instruments and new laws and promised
yet another legal regime. Given Winny's frame of reference, it is difficult to
imagine that she could have remained entirely indifferent to or ignorant of
the stakes that statehood raised for herself and her family. And such changes,
for enslaved people, only occasionally meant changes for the better.

If Winny followed and fretted over what statehood might mean for her
and her children as Missouri's petitions made their way to Congress in the
early months of 1818, however, her attention likely would have been subsequently diverted by events much closer to home after two men who were
being held as slaves in her small community initiated legal proceedings to
establish their freedom.[38] Jack and Arch, the two plaintiffs, complained that
they remained in bondage despite the fact that their former master, Eusebius
Hubbard, had set them free. In August 1817, they asserted, just before white
Missourians began agitating for statehood, the elderly Hubbard had signed
two documents stating that, after his death, Jack was to be freed immediately
and Arch was to be freed after an additional period of service to Hubbard's
daughter.[39] Once the old man died in March 1818, however, Jack was not
released from bondage, and both Jack and Arch were transferred to some
of Hubbard's male heirs, who had already conveyed their interest in the
two men to another local resident before Hubbard's death.[40] By May 1818,
Arch had sought a writ of habeas corpus from the St. Louis circuit court.[41] A
month later, both Jack and Arch petitioned for their freedom.[42]

Given that Winny began collecting evidence in what would become her
own freedom suit almost simultaneously, it seems that Jack's and Arch's efforts apparently affected her deeply. In June 1818, as Jack and Arch filed their

petitions, Winny presented the St. Louis circuit court with an affidavit from a white neighbor attesting to her past residence in the Illinois Territory. Such evidence had been used as grounds for freedom suits in other jurisdictions.[43] Then, at some point that summer, Winny followed Jack's and Arch's lead. She, too, sued for her freedom.[44]

Indeed, a closer examination reveals that this string of events was hardly a coincidence. Winny and Phebe Whitesides appear to have been close, in almost every conceivable sense, to Jack, Arch, and the white family who had claimed them. The two enslaved men had lived in the area for more than a dozen years, and their former master, Eusebius Hubbard, perhaps even longer than that, which made all three of them, like Winny and Whitesides, some of the very first American inhabitants in the region.[45] Hubbard, and presumably also Jack and Arch, meanwhile, lived in close proximity to Winny and Whitesides. Hubbard, at the very least, was among the St. Ferdinand residents who petitioned for a post office in his final months, and he owned property both a short ten miles east of the Whitesideses along the Mississippi River and northwest of them in what had once been the St. Charles district as well.[46] Family and friendship ties also knit Hubbard and Whitesides together. Hubbard was related to Whitesides through marriage—his wife was the widow of Whitesides's husband's uncle—and both Hubbard and Whitesides shared long-standing and deep connections to the Patterson family.[47]

These ties to the Pattersons appear to have been pivotal to the development of the freedom suits initiated by Jack, Arch, and Winny. In Jack's and Arch's cases, the key figure was Eusebius Hubbard's son-in-law John Patterson.[48] A devoted member of the antislavery "Friends to Humanity" Baptist sect, Patterson appears to have been guided by his faith. It seems likely that it was Patterson's commitment to such principles, and his efforts to convince—or coerce—his elderly father-in-law into living them out, that led Hubbard to endorse legal instruments in August 1817 designed to free Jack immediately and Arch eventually upon Hubbard's death. Indeed, Patterson and his minister, John Clark, were two of the witnesses to this document, while the third, Amy Jamison James, was yet another member of the Friends to Humanity and a relation to both Hubbard and Patterson.[49] After the old man died at Patterson's house, moreover, it may have been Patterson himself who helped guide Jack and Arch to file suit when they were claimed by some of Hubbard's other heirs. At the very least, he stepped forward on Jack's and Arch's behalf to attest to the authenticity of Hubbard's deed of emancipation.[50]

Winny's freedom suit, meanwhile, seems to have been midwifed by yet another member of the Patterson family. Although Frances Collard was a

Patterson by neither birth nor marriage, she was part of their extended family nevertheless: by the summer of 1818 her daughter Assenath had been
the wife of John Patterson's son William for nearly a decade.[51] Collard's ties
to Winny and Phebe Whitesides were lengthier still. All three had lived in
the Northwest Territory, near Whitesides Station, during the 1790s, and
when Collard followed Winny and Whitesides across the Mississippi River
into Missouri Territory, she settled near them and resumed an acquaintance. Whether they had ever been friendly or not, at some point Collard
and Whitesides argued about Winny's continued status as a slave. In this
argument, Collard almost certainly asserted that Winny was entitled to her
freedom because she had not been indentured while she was held in the
Northwest Territory. Whitesides responded that Winny needn't have been
indentured because she was a minor at the time.[52] When, exactly, this dispute took place is hard to determine, as are Collard's precise motives in chal-
lenging Whitesides. But clearly both women had developed a sophisticated
understanding of the Northwest Ordinance—sophisticated enough that they
could offer their own rival interpretations of its requirements.[53] Even more
important, Collard's willingness to give voice to her interpretation either
alerted Winny to such reasoning in the first place or, at the very least, enabled Winny to identify a sympathetic white witness who might be willing
to help her claim her freedom.

In the months that followed, as statehood agitation temporarily quieted,
news of the freedom suits filed by Jack, Arch, and Winny must have riveted
many in their small community. Although it's unclear exactly why, Arch's
case apparently didn't go any further, even though he continued living in the
county.[54] The most likely explanation seems to be that he decided to abandon
prosecution. Perhaps he was punished or threatened with sale after filing
suit. Maybe the defendant in his case promised to set him free eventually if
he dropped his case. Or it could be that Arch concluded that he was unlikely
to succeed. Given that his former master's will had promised him freedom
only after he served the old man's daughter for an additional fifteen years,
it was never clear what kind of legal argument he would have been able to
advance to secure his freedom immediately. His suit may have been filed to
forestall his conveyance to a different set of heirs who had no intention of
ever emancipating him, an intention they manifested by promptly transfer-
ring him to a third party, apparently as a slave for life.[55] Winny also seems to
have faced a temporary setback: for reasons that were never stated, her initial
suit was dismissed.[56] Jack, however, pressed on.

Despite uncertain prospects, they may have each concluded that it was better to have taken matters into their own hands—even if they failed in the attempt—than it was to expect their circumstances to improve without intervention. All around them, after all, other enslaved people—some with deep

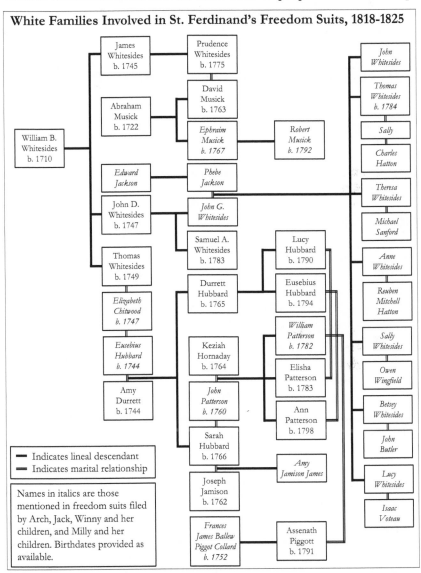

White Families Involved in St. Ferdinand's Freedom Suits, 1818-1825

■ Indicates lineal descendant
▬ Indicates marital relationship

Names in italics are those mentioned in freedom suits filed by Arch, Jack, Winny and her children, and Milly and her children. Birthdates provided as available.

Figure 2. Chart of white families involved in St. Ferdinand's freedom suits, 1818–25. Created by the author.

roots in the region and seemingly close ties to their masters—were being carted away. In September 1818, Steve, who lived on Stephen Hempstead's nearby farm, was sold, unceremoniously and seemingly without warning, to a man who took him to the Red River. He was accompanied by Hagga, another slave he sometimes worked alongside. Steve's sale, in particular, probably came as a shock. Hempstead had worked side by side with Steve for many years, described Steve's labors incessantly in his diary, and seems to have placed Steve in a position of authority on his farm, often referring to the efforts of "Steve & team." But that long-standing and seemingly intimate connection didn't protect Steve from being sold down the river.[57] For the enslaved people in the neighborhood, his sale served as yet another reminder that their relationships—to their masters, to their friends and family, and to the region—were tenuous and easily rent. Steve's fate was not inevitable, but if it befell him, it could befall any of them too. Given this constant threat, taking a chance on the courts, assuming one had the basis and opportunity to file suit, perhaps lost some of its terror.

When the push for statehood resumed in the fall of 1818, a jumble of events raised the stakes not only for those who had filed suit in St. Ferdinand, but also for Missouri's entrance to the Union. In October, as opposing counsel in Jack's case made plans to travel to Kentucky to collect depositions, Phebe Whitesides's son Thomas, who claimed Winny's son Jerry, died at age thirty-four.[58] Because Thomas died intestate, and the settlement of estates generally took several years, Jerry entered an extended state of limbo. The following month, meanwhile, Missouri's territorial legislature adopted a memorial to Congress calling for statehood.[59] Like the petitions before it, this memorial said nothing about slavery, but a few weeks later Congress itself was starting to signal that aspiring states that failed to curtail the spread of the institution might face trouble in their attempts to enter the Union. In late November, Representative James A. Tallmadge of New York took to the House floor in an effort to block the admission of Illinois because its constitution not only permitted slavery in a portion of the would-be state until 1825, but also sanctioned indenture contracts that legalized a form of bondage that was similar to slavery. Although Tallmadge primarily framed his objections to Illinois's admission around the claim that its proposed constitution violated the Northwest Ordinance, he also railed against the expansion of slavery more generally. His resolution to prevent its entrance into the Union was soundly rejected—Illinois was admitted as the twenty-first state in early December—but the challenge Tallmadge had thrown down was a harbinger of things to come.[60]

As fall gave way to winter, both situations reached a fever pitch. In mid-December, Winny appears to have refiled her suit—but this time she did so alongside at least nine of her children. Winny's eldest daughter, Jenny, who had been sold, sued her new master, but the rest of Winny's older children—Jerry, Daniel, Nancy, Lydia, and Sarah—named different Whitesides heirs as defendants. Meanwhile, Winny's younger children—Hannah, Malinda, and Lewis—all of whom had been born in the preceding five years and had likely remained in Winny's care, sued Phebe Whitesides, just as Winny did.[61] A few days later, in the nation's capital, the Missouri legislature's memorial calling for statehood was presented to Congress by the Speaker of the House.[62] In mid-February 1819, the Committee of the Whole took up a bill authorizing Missouri's entrance into the Union, but Representative James A. Tallmadge, who had recently attempted to block the admission of Illinois because its constitution didn't go far enough to root out slavery, stepped forth to offer two amendments that would ultimately upend any hope that the Missouri Territory would be added quietly or quickly. The first amendment called for a ban on the further importation of slaves to Missouri. The second insisted upon the creation of a gradual emancipation scheme that declared the children of all enslaved women born after statehood free at twenty-five. Although the House narrowly adopted Tallmadge's amendments on two occasions, they met with defeat in the Senate. Having turned the question of Missouri's admission to the Union into a debate over slavery's westward expansion, and with no clear path forward, the Fifteenth Congress adjourned shortly thereafter.

The Tallmadge Amendments transformed Missouri statehood into a referendum on slavery, but even before the news reached them, it must have seemed to those in St. Ferdinand that the institution was already being tested. Enslaved people in the area routinely ran away from their masters. The Friends to Humanity thundered against slavery in their services and sought out opportunities to bear witness to their faith. And their own small community had generated a dozen freedom suits in less than a year. Meanwhile, just days after the Tallmadge Amendments were introduced—but before word had arrived back in Missouri—a nearby slaveholder noted in his diary that two of his slaves, married couple George and Lucy, "got uneasy and Said they were free." What exactly their claim to freedom was based on, and whether their assertion had been inspired in any way by the actions of Jack, Arch, Winny, and Winny's children, is impossible to determine, but their master certainly took the threat seriously: he responded by taking them into St. Louis "to be sold." A little more than a month later, just as the first stories about the Tallmadge Amendments were appearing in local newspapers, "George & Lucy his wife went in the Steam Boat for Orleans."[63]

Word of the Tallmadge Amendments finally arrived in the St. Louis area about a month after they had been introduced and, in short order, inaugurated a lively debate. Initial reports in the *Missouri Gazette* and the *St. Louis Enquirer* did not editorialize, but by late March both papers were giving voice to the views of both their editors and their readers.[64]

Anti-Tallmadge sentiment ran high. In a lengthy letter to the *Gazette*, which ran alongside an advertisement announcing "Negroes for Sale," "A Citizen of Missouri" not only declared the Tallmadge Amendments "strange and unusual," but also warned that they raised the possibility that "the inhabitants of this territory shall *themselves* be slaves to the other states."[65] The *Enquirer* likewise lamented the effect the Tallmadge Amendments would have on the territory, despite assuring readers that "there seems to be no ground whatever for apprehending the passage of the bill." In any case, it asserted, "the people of the United States would have witnessed a specimen of Missouri feeling in the indignant contempt with which [Missourians] would have trampled the odious restriction under their feet" if the restrictions had been adopted by Congress.[66]

Most of the criticism of the Tallmadge Amendments printed in the St. Louis press was pitched in abstract constitutional terms, but there is no doubt that both the future of slavery more broadly and the continued enslavement of Jack, Winny, and Winny's children specifically weighed on the author of some of the most pointed critiques. From his home outside St. Ferdinand, Nathaniel Beverley Tucker issued a slew of anti-Tallmadge editorials carried by the *Missouri Gazette* under the pseudonym "Hampden." Tucker's five letters, which appeared between April and June, were a dense and almost exhaustive defense of the notion that the Tallmadge Amendments vastly exceeded congressional authority.[67] But such efforts were in addition to Tucker's formal duties as judge of the northern district of the circuit court of Missouri, where he had presided over all of the freedom suits filed in his small community, as well as those in nearby St. Louis, since February 1818. Tucker was the son of famed antislavery jurist St. George Tucker, but his own views on the institution appear to have been more closely aligned with those of his eccentric half-brother John Randolph, who would gain renown the following year thundering about northern "doughfaces" in Congress during his own battle against the Tallmadge Amendments. In the preceding months, Tucker had played an ambiguous role in the freedom suits filed in his court, all of which, with the exception of Arch's case, were still pending.[68] But he clearly understood that enslaved people in his district were seeking their freedom and that he would have an outsize ability to shape their fate. While we may never know whether presiding over these cases helped convince Tucker to become such a vocal opponent of the Tallmadge Amendments, the connection between the two developments is at least worth considering. If the relationship between the St. Ferdinand freedom suits and Tucker's editorials for the *Missouri Gazette* is difficult to parse, however, the effect his writings had on public opinion about the Tallmadge Amendments was far less complicated. His efforts were sufficient enough that he could, and did, brag to John C. Calhoun twenty-five years later that he was "believed to have exercised a decisive influence on the minds of the People of Missouri."[69]

Though fewer in number, supporters of the Tallmadge Amendments also aired their views—and proved far more likely than their opponents to identify slavery as the central issue at hand. Letters from those who supported the restriction of slavery in the territory were published only by the *Missouri Gazette*, which increasingly came to be seen as a prorestriction newspaper as a result. Their foremost antislavery correspondent was "A Farmer of St. Charles County." In a series of letters that started to appear in April, he ably defended his restrictionist position, repeatedly invoking the preamble to the Declaration of Independence and relentlessly deriding the hypocrisy of slaveholders. He claimed, moreover, to speak for many. "In my neighborhood, and as far as my acquaintance extends," he asserted, "the people with scarce one exception, declare that they wish to have no more slaves brought in to the territory."[70] His claim may have been overstated, but the letters written by a handful of other correspondents to the *Missouri Gazette*, one of whom also authored several missives, suggest that he was hardly alone, either.[71]

In addition to voicing their positions on the Tallmadge Amendments in the local press, those in the St. Louis area also assembled grand juries that delivered presentments detailing public opinion. The judge in the St. Ferdinand freedom suits, Nathaniel Beverley Tucker, also played an active role in these proceedings. In April, he presided over two different grand juries assembled in St. Louis that condemned Congress's efforts to restrict slavery in Missouri and may have even drafted their pronouncements.[72] The first assiduously avoided any discussion of slavery and instead railed against what it called "an unconstitutional and unwarrantable usurpation of power."[73] But the second acknowledged that the controversy over the Tallmadge Amendments was not limited to an abstract debate over whether Congress had the constitutional authority to dictate the terms upon which states could enter the Union. The future of slavery, the second pronouncement admitted, hung in the balance. The grand jury warned of a slippery slope that would lead Congress to eventually "make war upon" slaveholding states and advanced the notion that it would be "unfriendly to the slaves themselves" to confine them "to the *planting* regions of the south."[74] To be sure, this second grand jury did not attempt a defense of slavery per se, but its arguments were undoubtedly designed to stall any efforts to confront or contain the institution.[75]

It seems highly unlikely that this controversy escaped the attention of the freedom suit plaintiffs from St. Ferdinand. Indeed, available evidence suggests that the debate over the Tallmadge Amendments was swirling all around them. They certainly had some access, in any case, to the news and editorials that appeared in the local papers. Although Phebe Whitesides, Winny's master, was illiterate, both of Whitesides's sons had learned to read and write.[76] When Thomas Whitesides died, in fact, he owned a Bible, six volumes written by Methodist theologian John William Fletcher, and four other unspecified books.[77] It is also apparent that the *Missouri Gazette* was widely read within their circles. In 1818, the paper boasted nearly a thousand subscribers, including Jack's new master, Barnabas Harris, and David Musick, a neighbor and relation to the Whitesides family who had become the administrator of Thomas Whiteside's estate and whose nephew Robert was the defendant in the case filed by Winny's daughter Jenny just a few months earlier.[78] Among readers of the *Gazette*, moreover, it may have even become plain that the anti-Tallmadge correspondent "Hampden" was really Nathaniel Beverley Tucker, a fact that surely would have been discussed among the various freedom suit defendants.[79] Finally, at least two of the men who participated in the first grand jury to meet in St. Louis had close ties to St. Ferdinand and no doubt would have spoken about their experiences. James Richardson claimed a considerable amount of property near the town. Eli Musick, another relation of David and Robert, also lived in the area.[80]

As the response to the Tallmadge Amendments intensified, the St. Ferdinand freedom suits were making steady progress—and increasing in number. By the time the St. Louis circuit court began its March term, all but one of the defendants in cases filed by Winny and her children had been served with notice of their suits.[81] And although Jack's latest master, and the defendant in his case, died with seemingly little warning in March, the administrator of the dead man's estate carried on in his stead with little to no interruption.[82] In April, the court received and certified the deed that supposedly entitled Jack to his freedom, as well as depositions taken for the defense in Kentucky and St. Louis.[83] Later that month, moreover, three additional enslaved people living near St. Ferdinand filed freedom suits. Milly, who also filed on behalf of her two children, Elizabeth and Bob, was a relative newcomer to the small community. Otherwise, her life story bore broad similarities to those of Jack and Winny. Milly had once lived in Kentucky and had spent a considerable amount of time in the Northwest Territory. She also appears to have been encouraged to file suit by a member of the Patterson family: the petition she filed to initiate proceedings was attested to by William Patterson, John Patterson's son and Frances Collard's son-in-law.[84] The addition of Milly and her children's cases brought the total number of freedom suit plaintiffs in St. Ferdinand to fifteen.

In this charged local environment, something still more remarkable occurred: in late spring the only known prorestriction public gathering in the entire territory during the Missouri Crisis took place in St. Ferdinand. At this meeting, held June 5, 1819, almost exactly a year after Jack, Arch, and Winny had initiated their freedom suits, residents of their community unanimously adopted a series of antislavery resolutions. While participants rejected the notion that Congress had the right to place conditions on Missouri's entrance into the Union, they declared that the Tallmadge Amendments met with their "full approbation." Slavery, they continued, was "contrary to the term freedom" and "the laws of nature," "one of the greatest evils" of the day, and a practice whose persistence would bring "just censure, as well as the judgment of a just, but *angry God.*" In order to ensure their voices were heard, their resolutions were sent to, and subsequently published by, the *Missouri Gazette.*[85]

A member of the Patterson family, yet again, appears to have taken the lead in these proceedings. Although two men with no discernible ties to the clan were elected president and secretary, the meeting itself was held in the home of Elisha Patterson. Elisha, who lived northwest of St. Ferdinand adjacent to his brother William, had only recently obtained the property from his father, John.[86] Like other members of the Patterson family, Elisha appears to have been a devout follower of the Reverend John Clark, who encouraged the faithful to work toward emancipation.[87] As a close relation and near neighbor, Elisha must have known about the central role played by his father—and Clark—in Arch's and Jack's suits, as well as the actions taken by his brother William and William's mother-in-law, Frances Collard, to facilitate both Milly's and Winny's suits. Having seen his family members' efforts on behalf of some of the enslaved people of Missouri Territory, perhaps he leaped at the opportunity to advance their cause in his own way.

This prorestriction gathering of some of St. Ferdinand's white residents must have buoyed the hopes of those who were suing for their freedom. Perhaps, as a result, these plaintiffs began to imagine that slavery was on its way out in Missouri. At the very least, such an assembly likely convinced them that they had allies beyond the Patterson family. And given that many freedom suit plaintiffs walked away from their cases when the deprivations they suffered as a result—beatings, threats of sale, and, sometimes, lengthy confinements in the county jail—got to be too much, it's not unreasonable to conclude that these proceedings could have helped convince those in St. Ferdinand who were suing for their freedom to stay the course.

Whatever encouragement the meeting at Elisha Patterson's house may have given the town's freedom suit plaintiffs, however, it must have been tempered by the response it generated. It did not, for instance, initiate a wellspring of additional support for the Tallmadge Amendments. Indeed, the prorestriction gathering in St. Ferdinand appears to have been the high-water mark of such efforts during the Missouri crisis. No other communities in the territory went on record to back the Tallmadge Amendments. Indeed, in central Missouri, George Tompkins, who had been elected to his second term in the territorial legislature just a year before, suggested that antislavery commitments were exceptionally rare—and unwelcome. Not only did he tell a friend in July 1819 that, by his estimation, "nine tenths of the people of Howard & Cooper [Counties] are in favor of slavery," but he also gloomily predicted the death of his own future prospects on account of his antislavery leanings. "My political career," he wrote, "is ended: for some time after I had declared my sentiments against slavery some who had honored me or pretended to honor me with their friendship seemed to look on me with horror."[88] Back in St. Louis and its environs, meanwhile, just one additional prorestriction editorial appeared in the *Missouri Gazette* that year, and the St. Ferdinand meeting seems to have elicited something of a backlash.[89] When a very different group of the town's residents met to celebrate Independence Day, for instance, they took pains to enthusiastically endorse statehood without restriction, toasting that Missouri "be admitted into the Union on an equal footing with the original States, or not received in any other way."[90] After news of the St. Ferdinand meeting spread, moreover, first across the Mississippi River to Illinois and then to Massachusetts, New York, Rhode Island, Washington, D.C., Maine, Connecticut, New Hampshire, and Virginia, the *St. Louis Enquirer* worked to minimize its significance, disparaging the prorestriction gathering as wholly unrepresentative.[91] "What was called a 'meeting' in St. Ferdinand," it alleged, "consisted of six or eight individuals, and no more." Supposedly in an effort to expose the gathering's paltry attendance—or perhaps merely in an attempt to intimidate those who had participated—the newspaper then promised to publish the names of those who participated if they could be obtained.[92]

Far worse, two of the St. Ferdinand freedom suits came to an end shortly thereafter, albeit in very different ways. In August 1819, the defendant in Milly's suit asserted that Milly had absconded from his custody several weeks earlier. Given the fact that she left her children and a promising freedom suit behind, however, it seems far more likely that she had been intentionally run off, removed from the jurisdiction to prevent her case from going any further. Her attorney kept the suit alive for the better part of a year, but eventually had it withdrawn.[93] There is no indication that Milly ever returned to St. Ferdinand—or her children.[94] Shortly after Milly was reported missing, Jack's case finally went to trial, where the defendant convinced twelve jurors that the manumission deed Jack had obtained from Eusebius Hubbard was no good because the old man had conveyed Jack to his heirs long beforehand. Although Jack's attorney made two motions for a new trial, both were overruled. Jack, the court declared, would "take nothing" from his suit.[95]

While the freedom suits filed by Winny and her children moved forward as summer gave way to fall, it seemed increasingly obvious that white public opinion in Missouri had solidified against the Tallmadge Amendments. Very little agitation at all—and next to none that was prorestriction—appears to have taken place in and around St. Louis in the last several months of the year, while the *Missouri Gazette* was forced to fend off allegations that it supported emancipation. Grand jury pronouncements as well as resolutions adopted by and toasts drunk at public gatherings in the area seem to have ceased, and editorials and letters to the editor appear to have almost stopped entirely after July.[96]

Despite the ascendancy of antirestriction views in Missouri, however, the territory's fate was still very much in question when the Sixteenth Congress convened in December. In the preceding months, as protest had faded in Missouri, residents of northern states had banded together to insist upon the adoption of the Tallmadge Amendments. Their representatives arrived in the nation's capital bent on preventing Missouri from entering the Union as a slave state.

Nevertheless, Congress finally agreed to admit Missouri without the Tallmadge Amendments a few months later, thereby bringing the second, but not the last, phase of the Missouri Crisis to a close. As a result, the territory could write a constitution that prohibited the further introduction of slaves and established a gradual emancipation scheme if it wished, but neither would be a precondition for statehood. Given the tenor of the conversation in Missouri over the previous year, of course, the territory seemed highly unlikely to commit to either policy.

News that the president had signed an "enabling act" permitting Missouri to draft a constitution and form a state government was received warmly by many of St. Louis's white residents when it eventually reached them in late March 1820. In order to express their "satisfaction," the *Missouri Gazette* reported, they gathered not long thereafter one evening in the city's streets and homes. By way of celebration, "the town was generally and splendidly illuminated" and several transparencies were projected. One of the most arresting, the *Gazette* declared, was an image "representing a slave in great spirits, rejoicing at the permission granted by Congress to bring slaves into so fine a country as Missouri."[97] For the white residents delighting in the knowledge that Missouri would soon enter the Union, it seemed plain that statehood and slavery went hand in hand—and that slavery in Missouri would be more benign than it was in many other parts of the nation.

Winny and her children probably greeted such news differently. It remains to be seen whether any of them might have been hired out to work in the city when the festivities surrounding the announcement that an "enabling act" had been adopted took place. If they had been, perhaps, like many white St. Louisans, they would have agreed that a transparency showing "a slave in great spirits" was indeed captivating, but almost certainly not for the same reasons. And it's difficult to imagine that they met news of statehood with jubilation given the failure of the Tallmadge Amendments. Whether they thought Missouri a "fine country" or not, surely they didn't celebrate the impending addition of another slave state to the Union or the further spread of slavery in the trans-Mississippi West.

Whatever long-term ramifications Winny and her children perceived as a result of the territory's admission to the Union, the changes statehood would work on Missouri's court system were likely of even more immediate importance to them. At best, the transition from federal to state courts seemed likely to result in delays and new, potentially hostile, personnel in the courts. At worst, it might upend their cases by foreclosing the very possibility that proceedings like theirs could continue. As one historian of frontier law noted, "Once a territory became a state, it had complete power to make and unmake its own laws, and to do exactly as it (or its electorate) liked."[98] The 1807 law that permitted freedom suits, for instance, was the product of a territorial government that was soon to be dissolved. A new state government could refuse to reauthorize the statute or alter it in any way.[99] Winny and her children would have to wait and see.

They didn't have to wait long. White Missourians wasted little time in drafting a new governing document. Despite the apparent unpopularity of the Tallmadge Amendments in the territory as a whole, several prorestriction candidates stood for election to the subsequent constitutional convention. Some had close ties to St. Ferdinand or the freedom suits the town had produced. St. Ferdinand resident Robert Simpson declared slavery an "evil" and a "supreme curse" and pledged to oppose the further introduction of slaves even though he also announced that he was unwilling to interfere with the institution as it already existed in Missouri.[100] Winny and her children may have greeted news of his candidacy enthusiastically, but the candidacy of another restrictionist in their orbit, Rufus Pettibone, must have given them pause: as the Whitesides family attorney, Pettibone had been working to keep Winny and her children enslaved.[101] His candidacy was perhaps a pointed reminder that prorestriction sentiment could be readily advocated alongside a personal investment in slavery. In the actual event, however, neither of these men nor any other prorestriction candidates were ultimately elected. As a result, the constitutional convention that met in St. Louis in June 1820 drafted an unambiguously proslavery constitution. The document they produced was apparently modeled after the constitution of Alabama and commanded the general assembly to adopt a number of measures designed to regulate slavery.[102] In July 1820 it was adopted.

Despite Winny and her children's possible fears, the freedom suits they filed seem to have been largely unaffected by the dissolution of Missouri's territorial laws and government. The general assembly did not move to prohibit freedom suits. And although it acted quickly to reorganize the courts, in the new state's third district circuit court it simply appointed a former judge of the northern district of the circuit court of Missouri Territory. By December 1820 it was clear that the cases of Winny and her children would be heard by Nathaniel Beverley Tucker, the same man who had presided over nearly every interaction they'd had at law since they had filed their petitions.[103]

Both Missouri's white residents and Winny and her children, however, faced a few additional delays in reaching their respective goals. Congressional objections to a portion of Missouri's newly approved constitution led to renewed strife in the nation's capital. But eventually, in August 1821, Missouri officially entered the Union as the twenty-fourth state. Winny and her children would have to continue to wait another several months to achieve their aims. Remarkably, in February 1822, Nathaniel Beverley Tucker, a man who had perhaps done more than any other Missouri resident to defeat the Tallmadge Amendments, directed the jury in Winny's and her children's suits that the Northwest Ordinance "did in law set the said Winne free" if the jury believed the Whitesideses brought Winny to Illinois "with intent to make the territory the home of themselves and of the said Winne." Then Tucker went further. "Winne," he declared, "was entitled to damages . . . on the same principles that any other plaintiff might recover in an action of false imprisonment."[104] Tucker, it seems, was willing to recognize Congress's authority to regulate slavery in the Northwest Territory—just not its authority to dictate the terms of Missouri's admission to the Union. Whatever Tucker's reasons, the jury subsequently declared Winny and her children free—and awarded Winny, and several of her children, damages.[105]

Although both struggles seemed at an end, the battle wasn't quite over for Winny and her children. They spent the next couple of years ensuring that the verdict in their favor was honored. In the meantime, Phebe Whitesides died, and Winny and her youngest children were conveyed to Rufus Pettibone, Whitesides's attorney. Pettibone, who had run, unsuccessfully, as an antirestriction candidate to Missouri's constitutional convention, had presumably received Winny and her children as a form of payment for legal services—perhaps with the understanding that no other compensation would be forthcoming. Pettibone had been appointed to serve on the Missouri Supreme Court in 1823, and perhaps expected that his colleagues would overturn the verdict in Winny's and her children's suits when they came before the court the following year.[106] Any such assumptions, however, were misplaced. In November 1824, the Missouri Supreme Court upheld the original verdict in a landmark decision by George Tompkins. Tompkins, who had predicted that his antislavery commitments would end his political future, had found refuge in the courts. In *Winny v. Whitesides* (1824), he established the "once free, always free" doctrine, which held that enslaved people brought to free soil jurisdictions were entitled to freedom, even if they returned to a slave state or territory. It would be repeatedly invoked by freedom suit plaintiffs, often successfully, in the quarter century that followed.

Even after their triumph in Missouri's highest court, in fact, legal challenges remained for Winny and her family. In the year that followed, Winny, some of her children, and, for the first time, one of her grandchildren headed back to the St. Louis circuit court to fight off one last effort to enslave them and compel the defendants in their suits to pay up. Not until November 1826 was their freedom confirmed by a second jury.[107]

♠

Winny and her children succeeded in their bid for freedom, while many other enslaved people around her—those who sued alongside them as well as
those who attempted to escape—failed. The vagaries and contingencies that
explain such divergent outcomes caution us against reading too much into
her success. That said, it would also be a mistake to discount their triumph
and the broader patterns it illustrated.

By the traditional telling, the Missouri Crisis—especially in Missouri—
was a crushing victory for slavery. *Winny v. Whitesides* complicates this
narrative, however, in important ways. Not only were Winny and her
children set free, but her case also established one of the most important
emancipatory precedents in antebellum America. But even more than this,
Winny v. Whitesides reveals the various compromises proslavery forces
seemed compelled to make. Thanks to the actions of freedom suit plaintiffs
like Winny and her children, the self-liberatory struggles of other nearby
enslaved people, and the local antislavery activism of the Pattersons and
others, the settlement of the Missouri Crisis on the ground was perhaps less
decisively proslavery than existing literature suggests. Nathaniel Beverley
Tucker may have succeeded in thwarting the Tallmadge Amendments, for
instance, but he was forced to contend with eloquent opposing voices during
the crisis and perhaps bowed to such pressure in instructing Winny's and
her children's jury as he did—an act that led to a steady stream of additional
freedom suits in the years to follow. George Tompkins may have accurately
observed, in the midst of the crisis, that his antislavery views doomed his
political prospects, but his subsequent appointment to Missouri's high court
suggested that there was still a place for someone like him, and the emancipatory decisions he would issue, both in the new state and for decades to
come. The traditional narrative of the Missouri Crisis suggests an unambiguous victory for slavery, but as the outcome of *Winny v. Whitesides* reminds
us, that victory was neither complete nor final. Until *Scott v. Emerson*, more
than thirty years after the crisis ended, Missouri's constitutional protections
for slavery coexisted alongside hundreds of individual legal challenges to the
institution—challenges *Winny v. Whitesides* unleashed.

Notes

1. *Missouri Gazette* (St. Louis), October 11, 1817; *Winny v. Phebe Whitesides (alias
Pruitt)*, April 1821, case no. 190, St. Louis Circuit Court Historical Records Project, Circuit Court Case Files, Office of the Circuit Clerk, City of St. Louis, http://
digital.wustl.edu/legalencodingproject/ (hereafter referred to as SLCCHRP). The

date attached to Winny's suit suggests that it was filed in 1821, but documents in the case file itself make plain that it began in 1818. For other works that examine *Winny v. Whitesides*, see Robert Moore Jr., "A Ray of Hope, Extinguished: Slave Suits for Freedom," *Gateway Heritage* 14, no. 3 (1993–94): 4–15; David Thomas Konig, "The Long Road to *Dred Scott*: Personhood and the Rule of Law in the Trial Court Records of St. Louis Slave Freedom Suits," *UMKC Law Review* 75, no. 1 (2006): 53–79; Lea VanderVelde, *Redemption Songs: Suing for Freedom before Dred Scott* (New York: Oxford University Press, 2014); Anne Twitty, *Before* Dred Scott: *Slavery and Legal Culture in the American Confluence, 1787–1857* (New York: Cambridge University Press, 2016); Kelly M. Kennington, *In the Shadow of* Dred Scott: *St. Louis Freedom Suits and the Legal Culture of Slavery in Antebellum America* (Athens: University of Georgia Press, 2017).

2. For more on the decision in *Winny v. Whitesides*, see Don E. Fehrenbacher, *The Dred Scott Case: Its Significance in American Law and Politics* (New York: Oxford University Press, 1978), 262; Paul Finkelman, *An Imperfect Union: Slavery, Federalism, and Comity* (Chapel Hill: University of North Carolina Press, 1981), 217–28; and VanderVelde, *Redemption Songs*, 57–65.

3. *Winny v. Whitesides*, I Mo. 473 (1824). In the St. Louis circuit court, of a total 241 known freedom suit plaintiffs, 127 asserted, like Winny, that their residence on free soil entitled them to freedom, and another 30 claimed that their mother's or grandmother's residence on free soil entitled them to their freedom. Of these, at least 44 who claimed residence on free soil, including Winny, were freed, and 22 of the descendants of women who'd resided on free soil, including all of Winny's children and her granddaughter Winetta, were freed. Although there is no comprehensive study of freedom suits filed in other parts of the state, cases appealed to the Missouri Supreme Court make plain that freedom suits based on free-soil residence did originate in other areas, so it stands to reason that there are many more such cases, to say nothing of the enslaved people who used the precedent created in Winny's case as a bargaining chip to force their masters to negotiate an end to their enslavement without having to file suit. For more information about these cases, see Twitty, *Before* Dred Scott; and Kennington, *In the Shadow of* Dred Scott.

4. Floyd Calvin Shoemaker, *Missouri's Struggle for Statehood, 1804–1821* (Jefferson City, MO: Hugh Stephens, 1916); Glover Moore, *The Missouri Controversy, 1819–1821* (Lexington: University Press of Kentucky, 1953), chap. 8.

5. John Craig Hammond, *Slavery, Freedom, and Expansion in the Early American West* (Charlottesville: University of Virginia Press, 2007), chap. 4.

6. Neither Roy Moore Jr.'s nor David Konig's article discuss the Missouri Crisis at all, while recent books, including Lea VanderVelde's, my own, and Kelly Kennington's, reference it only fleetingly. Moore, "Ray of Hope, Extinguished"; Konig, "Long Road to *Dred Scott*"; VanderVelde, *Redemption Songs*, 17; Twitty, *Before* Dred Scott, 44, 233, 241; Kennington, *In the Shadow of* Dred Scott, 21, 171, 256.

7. *Winny, a free woman of color v. Rufus Pettibone, et al.*, July 1825, case no. 12, SLCCHRP, 25. The sale and forced migration of enslaved people in the decades after the Revolution has been a subject of a great deal of scholarly attention; among many

others, see Ira Berlin, *Many Thousands Gone: The First Two Centuries of Slavery in North America* (Cambridge, MA: Harvard University Press, 1998), pt. 3; Walter Johnson, *Soul by Soul: Life Inside the Antebellum Slave Market* (Cambridge, MA: Harvard University Press, 1999); Alan Taylor, *The Internal Enemy: Slavery and War in Virginia, 1772–1832* (New York: W. W. Norton, 2013); and Calvin Schermerhorn, *The Business of Slavery and the Rise of American Capitalism, 1815–1860* (New Haven, CT: Yale University Press, 2015).

8. Will of Edward Jackson, Nottoway County, VA, Will Book 1, 1789–1802, 76–78; Betty Smith Meischen, *From Jamestown to Texas: A History of Some Early Pioneers of Austin County, the Colonial Capitol of Texas* (Lincoln, NE: iUniverse, 2002), 443. The Jackson family seems to have lived in the same location for the entire period between Winny's birth and Edward Jackson's death, and there are reasons to suspect that Winny had been born Jackson's slave and remained with him thereafter. Most significantly, the names Winny later gave her own children are suggestive of familial connections between Winny and the other enslaved people Jackson claimed. There were two or three adult enslaved women listed in Jackson's will, for instance, who would have been old enough to have been Winny's mother, and one of them, Hannah, shares a name with one of Winny's daughters. Winny also gave two of her other children (Jerry and Lydia) the same names as other enslaved children (Jeremiah and Liddy) listed in Jackson's will. Perhaps these were her siblings. That said, Winny's mother could have died or been sold before Jackson's will was recorded, Winny could have been purchased by Jackson at some earlier date, and Winny may not have been related to any of the others Jackson's will distributed.

9. Will of Edward Jackson, Nottoway County, VA, Will Book 1, 1789–1802, 77; Inventory and Appraisal for the Estate of Edward Jackson, Nottoway County, VA, Will Book 1, 86–87. Jackson's will states that Phebe Whitesides had already been given a deed of gift for Winny, and Winny does not appear alongside other enslaved people who were appraised in Jackson's estate on February 20, 1793. Edward Jackson is also identified as Whitesides's father in *Nancy, a free girl of color v. Issac Voteau*, April 1821, case no. 193, SLCCHRP, 6.

10. For references to the time Winny spent in "Carolina," see *Winny v. Whitesides* (1821), SLCCHRP, 27.

11. *Winny v. Whitesides* (1821), SLCCHRP, 33; *Winny, a free woman of color v. Whitesides, Phoebe*, box 134, folder 11, Supreme Court of Missouri Historical Records, Missouri State Archives, Jefferson City, 26; "Petition of Winny, a free woman of color, to the St. Louis Circuit Court, May 16, 1825," Identifier D01695, Slaves and Slavery Collection, 1772–1950, Missouri Historical Society, St. Louis (hereafter referred to as MHS), 1.

12. For more about the pressure slaveholders in the Northwest Territory felt to relocate to Missouri, see Stephen A. Aron, *American Confluence: The Missouri Frontier from Borderland to Border State* (Bloomington: Indiana University Press, 2006), 79; M. Scott Heerman, *The Alchemy of Slavery: Human Bondage and Emancipation in the Illinois Country, 1730–1865* (Philadelphia: University of Pennsylvania Press, 2018), 77–78.

13. "Petition of Winny, a free woman of color, to the St. Louis Circuit Court, May 16, 1825," MHS, 1; *Winny v. Whitesides* (1821), SLCCHRP, 1.

14. Walter Lowrie and Walter S. Franklin, eds., *American State Papers: Documents, Legislative and Executive, of the Congress of the United States from the Second Session of the Eleventh to the Third Session of the Thirteenth Congress* (Washington, DC: Gales and Seaton, 1834), 538.

15. Louis Houck, *The Spanish Regime in Missouri* (Chicago: R. R. Donnelly, 1909), 1:324–25. The census taken by the Spanish in 1794–95 suggests that the population of St. Ferdinand at the time was 157, but does not include any enslaved people, which suggests undercounting given the ubiquity of the institution in the region.

16. Gilbert J. Garraghan, *Saint Ferdinand de Florissant: The Story of an Ancient Parish* (Chicago: Loyola University Press, 1923), 13–14, 61.

17. There is no census from the 1790s that enumerates enslaved people in the area, but burial and baptismal records from the Catholic Church founded in St. Ferdinand in 1790 reveal that enslaved people were held by French residents before the Louisiana Purchase, and many of the earliest American residents brought slaves with them to the region. See, for example, U.S., French Catholic Church Records (Drouin Collection), 1695–1954, Florissant, MO, s.v. "Louis Esclave," "Enfan Esclave," "de Fremeoie Esclave," AncestryLibrary.com; Garraghan, *Saint Ferdinand de Florissant*, 47n35, 54; Houck, *Spanish Regime in Missouri*, 1:xxi.

18. When John Whitesides died, an inventory of his estate dated March 19, 1803, listed an unnamed "Negroe Woman" and two unnamed "Negroe" boys—Winny and her sons Jerry and Daniel. Records do not provide information about the paternity of Winny's children. Given that Winny's children were never referred to as anything other than "negro" or "black," however, it seems likely that their father or fathers were also Black. There were no enslaved Black men claimed by the Whitesides family at this or any subsequent time, but there were certainly both enslaved and free Black men living in and around St. Ferdinand during this period. Probate Estate File of John Whiteside, St. Louis (1803), case no. 122, Missouri Judicial Records Database, https://www.sos.mo.gov/archives (hereafter referred to as MJRD), 12–13.

19. Oscar W. Collett, *Index to Instruments Affecting Real Estate Recorded in the Office of Recorder of Deeds, in the County of St. Louis, Mo., Grantors*, vol. 1, pt. 3, *N–Z* (St. Louis: R. & T. A. Ennis, 1874), 1083; Lowrie and Franklin, *American State Papers*, 689. Little can be determined about George Wallis or Wallace, including when he married Phebe Whitesides or when he may have died. A man by that name can be found, however, prosecuting and defending suits in the St. Louis circuit court between 1805 and 1808. Fielding or Fields Pruitt or Pruit or Prewitt was perhaps a native Virginian born in 1750 who lived in South Carolina, Kentucky, and Illinois Territory before his marriage to Phebe Whitesides. Between 1809 and 1814, he too was involved in St. Louis circuit court cases. Neither man seems to have been among the earliest American settlers of the Louisiana Territory who claimed land before the Louisiana Purchase. For more information about Fielding Pruitt, see Richard A. Prewitt, *Prewitt-Pruitt Records of Illinois* (Des Moines, IA: R. S. Prewitt, 1997), 2.

20. *Winny v. Whitesides* (1821), SLCCHRP, 23; Probate Estate File of John Whiteside, St. Louis (1803), case no. 122, MJRD, 7, 10. An inventory of John Whitesides's

estate dated May 15, 1813, list Winny's children as Jerry, Daniel, Jane (Jenny), Nancy, Lydia, and Sally (Sarah).

21. Probate Estate File of Thomas Whiteside/Whitsetts, St. Louis (1818), case no. 309, MJRD, 45, 55; Lowrie and Franklin, *American State Papers*, 706; U.S., Indexed Early Land Ownership and Township Plats, 1785–1898, Earliest Township and Range Public Land Survey, s.v. "Ephraim Musick," AncestryLibrary.com. Jerry was listed as part of Thomas Whitesides's estate when Whitesides died in 1818. His probate papers also include a claim against his estate from Ephraim Musick, who asserted that he bought Jenny from Whitesides and Owen Wingfield, the husband of Thomas's sister Sally, in February 1814 for $300 when Jenny was ten years old. Musick claimed that he took possession of Jenny "immediately after the execution of said bill of sale." Musick was the brother-in-law of Prudence Whitesides Musick, John Whiteside's cousin, and he held property in northern St. Louis County in township 46N, 5E, that was immediately southwest of the Whitesides's township, 47N, 6E. At some point, Musick seems to have given or sold Jenny to his son Robert, whom Jenny later named as the defendant in her freedom suit, even though, in Musick's claim against Thomas Whiteside's estate, he asserted that Jenny was in his possession—rather than his son's—from 1814 until 1821.

22. *Winny v. Pettibone, et al.* (1825), SLCCHRP, 3; Lowrie and Franklin, *American State Papers*, 1083. Nancy was apparently conveyed to Isaac Voteau, Lucy Whitesides's husband, while Lydia was conveyed to John Butler, Elizabeth or Betsey Whitesides's husband, and Sarah was conveyed to Reuben Mitchell Hatton (referred to as Michael Hatton in some court proceedings), Anne Whitesides's husband. The names of the Whitesides daughters appear in the case Winny filed against Rufus Pettibone in 1825 and in land records. There were two additional Whitesides daughters, Theresa, who was married to Michael Sandford, and Sally, who was married to Owen Wingfield. Both of them appear in these documents, but it's not clear whether they ever had possession of Winny or any of her children.

23. When Winny sued for her freedom in June 1818, she named Phebe Whitesides as defendant, and her three youngest children, Hannah, Lewis, and Malinda, did likewise when they filed suit several months later. *Winny v. Whitesides* (1821), SLCCHRP; *Hannah, a free girl of color v. Phebe Whitesides*, April 1821, case no. 197, SLCCHRP; *Lewis, a free boy of color v. Phebe Whitesides*, April 1821, case no. 199, SLCCHRP; *Malinda, a free girl of color v. Phebe Whitesides*, April 1821, case no. 198, SLCCHRP.

24. *Winny v. Whitesides* (1821) SLCCHRP, 23.

25. It's not clear when, exactly, Reuben Mitchell Hatton relocated to Boone County, Missouri, but his father, Reuben Hatton, emigrated in 1817 or 1818, and his children seem to have accompanied him or followed shortly thereafter. *History of Boone County, Missouri* (St. Louis: Western Historical, 1882), 981, 1032; W. S. Woodard, *Annals of Methodism in Missouri* (Columbia, MO: E. W. Stephens, 1893), 137.

26. The first advertisement promising a reward for the return of Juba, who belonged to explorer William Clark, was placed in the *Missouri Gazette*, July 22, 1815. This ad reappeared on at least eighteen additional occasions over the course of the following year. Information about Juba's eventual fate can be found in Landon Y.

Jones, *William Clark and the Shaping of the West* (New York: Hill and Wang, 2009), 285.

27. Dana O. Jensen, ed., "I at Home, by Stephen Hempstead, Sr., Part 2," *Missouri Historical Bulletin* 13 (April 1957): 295, 304.

28. *Missouri Gazette*, March 30, 1816; *Missouri Gazette*, February 8, 1817.

29. *Missouri Gazette*, January 4, 1817.

30. Allen Mueller, "Lucy and Elisha Patterson Farmstead," National Register of Historic Places Application, Florissant, MO, June 14, 2004, 60; Peggy Kruse, *Old Jamestown across the Ages: Highlights and Stories of Old Jamestown, Missouri* (n.p.: n.p., 2017), 86–87; Woodard, *Annals of Methodism in Missouri*, 25.

31. John Mason Peck, *"Father Clark"; or, The Pioneer Preacher: Sketches and Incidents of Rev. John Clark, by an Old Pioneer* (New York: Sheldon, Lamport & Blakeman, 1855), 157 and chap. 13 generally. For more information about other members of the "Friends to Humanity" who participated in freedom suits filed in the St. Louis circuit court, see Twitty, *Before* Dred Scott, chap. 7.

32. Although territorial censuses were taken in Missouri in 1814, 1816, 1818, and 1820, only the manuscript returns for Ste. Genevieve in 1818 have survived. "Territorial Censuses (1752–1819) and Tax Lists (1814–1821)," Missouri Secretary of State's Office, https://s1.sos.mo.gov/records/archives/census/pages/territorial.

33. While population figures are not available for St. Ferdinand in 1820, one can use the data available from the 1830 census—which showed a population of 341 in St. Ferdinand and a population of 2,911 in the larger St. Ferdinand township of which St. Ferdinand was a part—to project backward. It's clear that between 1820 and 1830, St. Louis County grew by 40.6 percent and the city of St. Louis grew by 27.3 percent. If one assumes the same growth-rate range for St. Ferdinand and St. Ferdinand Township, the 1820 population of St. Ferdinand should have been between 243 and 268 and the 1820 population of St. Ferdinand County should have been between 2,071 to 2,287. Information about the population of St. Louis County and city between 1820 and 1830 was derived from U.S. Department of the Interior, Bureau of the Census, *Fourth Census of the United States, 1820* (Washington, DC: Gales & Seaton, 1821), 159; U.S. Department of the Interior, Bureau of the Census, *Fifth Census of the United States, 1830* (Washington, DC: Duff Green, 1832), 41; and James Neal Primm, *Lion of the Valley: St. Louis, Missouri, 1764–1980*, 3rd ed. (Columbia: University of Missouri Press, 1998), 104, 132. Information about the population of St. Ferdinand (which was referred to as Florissant by 1830) and St. Ferdinand township was calculated from U.S. Department of the Interior, Bureau of the Census, "Populations Schedules of the Fifth Census of the United States, 1830, Missouri, St. Ferdinand Township" (Manuscript Microcopy M-19, roll 72). Because I believe the census taker made errors in his tabulations, my totals differ from his.

34. John Patterson supposedly had twelve children with his first wife. After she died, he married a widow with twelve children, and together they had one more child. William Lyman Thomas, *History of St. Louis County, Missouri* (St. Louis: S. J. Clarke, 1911), 315–16.

35. *Missouri Gazette*, October 11, 1817; *Missouri Gazette*, October 25, 1817. The *Missouri Gazette*'s first reporting on the subject referenced an article previously published by its rival, the St. Louis *Western Emigrant*, which is no longer extant.

36. When newspapers in St. Louis first reported on these petitions in early October, the editor of the only surviving article about them explained that he had neither learned "from whence it originated" nor "seen it in circulation for signature," which suggests that these petitions were not disseminated in the St. Louis area. Signatories on the only two copies of these petitions that survived, moreover, hailed from Washington County, more than fifty miles southwest of St. Louis.

37. *Missouri Gazette*, October 11, 1817.

38. On the receipt of the first statehood petitions in Congress between January and March 1818, see Shoemaker, *Missouri's Struggle for Statehood*, 38.

39. *Arch, a black man v. Barnabas Harris*, October 1818 [case number unavailable], SLCCHRP, 5; *Jack, a free man v. Barnabas Harris*, October 1818, case no. 111, SLCCHRP, 3, 21–22. A copy of the document that would have freed Jack upon Eusebius Hubbard's death is included in his case file. Arch's case file only refers to the existence of such a document, but a copy of that document is held by the Missouri History Museum, St. Louis. Arch was apparently supposed to serve Hubbard's daughter for an additional fifteen years. See Kennington, *In the Shadow of Dred Scott*, 17, 219n5.

40. *Jack v. Harris* (1818), SLCCHRP, 1. Eusebius Hubbard's heirs, Thomas Ballew, John Proctor, and George Hubbard, sold Jack and Arch to Barnabas Harris on March 2, 1818, five days before Hubbard died.

41. The petition in Arch's case is dated June 9, 1818, but another document in his case file indicates he was brought before the court on a writ of habeas corpus on May 6, 1818. *Arch v. Harris* (1818), SLCCHRP, 7.

42. Jack's petition, like Arch's, was filed June 9, 1818. *Jack v. Harris* (1818), SLCCHRP, 37.

43. The affidavit of Frances Collard was sworn on June 8, 1818, the day before Arch and Jack filed their petitions. *Winny v. Whitesides* (1821), SLCCHRP, 1. Although Winny's freedom suit would eventually establish, in Missouri, the precedent for granting freedom to those who had been held as slaves on the supposedly free soil of the Northwest Territory, such grounds had already been successfully used by Peter and Queen McNelly and then a woman named Peggy in the Northwest Territory to obtain legal recognition of their freedom. See VanderVelde, *Redemption Songs*, 23–36; and Jacob Piatt Dunn, *Indiana: A Redemption from Slavery* (Boston: Houghton Mifflin, 1890), 238.

44. Winny's original petition is undated, but another document in her case file makes plain that she sued for her freedom during the June 1818 term of the St. Louis circuit court. *Winny v. Whitesides* (1821), SLCCHRP, 9.

45. *Jack v. Harris*, SLCCHRP, 3–4. Arch and Jack had been in Missouri Territory since at least 1805, but may have been there much longer. When their master, Eusebius Hubbard, a Kentucky native, sought a Spanish land grant on January 1, 1803, in any case, he claimed to have already lived there "for some time," and perhaps

Arch and Jack had been there too. See *Public Documents Printed by the Senate of the United States, First Session of the Twenty-Fourth Congress* (Washington, DC: Gales and Seaton, 1836), 2:346–47.

46. Elizabeth Chitwood Whitesides Bond conveyed land in the Louisiana and later Missouri Territory, the vast majority of which fell in Township 48N, 5E, to Eusebius Hubbard when they married in 1805. Clarence Edward Carter, ed., *The Territorial Papers of the United States* (Washington, DC: Government Printing Office, 1951), 15:352–54; Lowrie and Franklin, *American State Papers*, 629, 692; U.S., Indexed Early Land Ownership and Township Plats, 1785–1898, Township and Range Public Land Survey of 1853, s.v. "Jsabella Chiteosod," AncestryLibrary.com; *Jack v. Harris* (1818), SLCCHRP, 4.

47. The connection between Phebe Whiteside's husband, John, and the rest of the Whitesides family in Missouri and Illinois was difficult to establish. *History of Boone County, Missouri*, however, which identified one of Phebe and John Whitesides's daughters as the niece of General Samuel A. Whitesides, establishes a clear family connection. Eusebius Hubbard's second wife, Elizabeth Chitwood Whitesides Bond, had previously been married to Thomas Whitesides, who was John Whitesides's uncle. *History of Boone County, Missouri*, 1031; *Jack v. Harris* (1818), SLCCHRP, 4; "Memorial Page for Thomas Whitesides (1748–1795)," https://www.findagrave.com/memorial/67471192/thomas-whiteside.

48. John Patterson married Eusebius Hubbard's widowed daughter Sarah Hubbard Jamison after his first wife died, but these families were still further intertwined: two of John Patterson's children from his first marriage married two of Eusebius Hubbard's grandchildren. Those were marriages, first, between Elisha Patterson and Lucy Hubbard, and, second, between Ann Patterson and Eusebius Hubbard. Lucy and Eusebius Hubbard were both children of the elder Eusebius Hubbard's son Durrett Hubbard. See Mueller, "Lucy and Elisha Patterson Farmstead," 59; Thomas, *History of St. Louis County*, 47, 87, 315–16; and "Memorial Page for John Patterson (1760–1839)," https://www.findagrave.com/memorial/16840289/john-patterson.

49. Amy Jamison James was Eusebius Hubbard's granddaughter and John Patterson's stepdaughter. She was one of the charter members of Reverend John Clark's Cold Water church. *Jack v. Harris* (1818), SLCCHRP, 21; "Memorial Page for John Patterson (1760–1839)," https://www.findagrave.com/memorial/16840289/john-patterson; Woodard, *Annals of Methodism in Missouri*, 25.

50. *Jack v. Harris* (1818), SLCCHRP, 21–22.

51. William Patterson, who was the son of John Patterson, married Assenath Piggott, daughter of Frances James Ballew Piggott Collard, in 1808. Carl William Veale, *The Patterson-Piggott Family of St. Louis County, Missouri* (Los Angeles: n.p., 1947), 1.

52. *Winny v. Whitesides* (1821), SLCCHRP, 1. Frances Collard's entire account of this dispute is that "the said Phebe Whitesides insisted in argument with this affiant that the said Winny could not be free inasmuch as she was under age when brought away." It is unclear what specific statute the two women were arguing about, but a similar law appears to have been invoked in another freedom suit that was later filed by a different woman held in bondage in St. Ferdinand. It seems that Whitesides interpreted this law to mean that enslaved people under the age of fifteen did not have

to be indentured. See *Milly, a free woman v. Mathias Rose*, August 1819, case no. 20, SLCCHRP, 6–9.

53. There were a handful of individuals around Whitesides Station who were indenturing slaves in the 1790s and plenty of reason to believe that the Whitesides were intimately familiar with the practice. A William Musick, for instance, no doubt some relation to the Ephraim Musick who purchased Winny's daughter Jenny in 1814, indentured two slaves, Phebe and George, in 1794 in St. Clair County. When and why the practice of indenturing became commonplace seems incredibly murky, but indenturing was one way of coping with the anxiety and uncertainty newcomers to the Northwest Territory evinced around the legality of importing slaves—the anxiety and uncertainty was widespread after the passage of the Northwest Ordinance. Phebe to William Musick, 1794, and George to William Musick, 1794, Illinois State Archives, Illinois Servitude and Emancipation Records (1722–1863), https://www.ilsos.gov/isa/servemansrch.jsp; Paul Finkelman, "Slavery and the Northwest Ordinance," 365–68; Hammond, *Slavery, Freedom, and Expansion*, chap. 6; Twitty, *Before Dred Scott*, chap. 1; Heerman, *Alchemy of Slavery*, chap. 4.

54. Arch was still alive and living in St. Louis County when Barnabas Harris died sometime the following year, as he was included in the inventory of Harris's estate. Harris's probate records appear under an alternate spelling of his first name. Probate Estate File of Barnibas Harris, St. Louis (1819), case no. 322, MJRD, 80.

55. The March 1818 document that conveyed both Jack and Arch from some of Eusebius Hubbard's male heirs to Barnabas Harris makes no mention of the fact that Hubbard's will would have freed them both, either immediately or eventually. *Jack v. Harris* (1818), SLCCHRP, 1.

56. *Winny v. Whitesides* (1821), SLCCHRP, 9; Kennington, *In the Shadow of Dred Scott*, 238n106.

57. For entry on Steve's sale, see Dana O. Jensen, ed., "I at Home, by Stephen Hempstead, Sr., Part 3," *Missouri Historical Bulletin* 14 (October 1957): 91. For entries on "Steve & team" or "Steve and team," see pt. 2, 295, 310, 311; and pt. 3, 73, 74, 76, 78, 79, 81.

58. *Jack v. Harris* (1818), SLCCHRP, 15. Although no death date was provided in Thomas Whitesides's probate records, the first inventory of his estate occurred on October 24, 1818. An estimate of Whitesides's age appears in Winny's later suit against Rufus Pettibone. Probate Estate File of Thomas Whiteside/Whitsetts (1818), MJRD, 44; *Winny v. Pettibone, et al.* (1825), SLCCHRP, 25.

59. Shoemaker, *Missouri's Struggle for Statehood*, 41.

60. *Annals of Congress*, 15th Cong., 2nd sess., 1:305–11. See also Hammond, *Slavery, Freedom, and Expansion*, 122–23; and Sean Wilentz, *No Property in Man: Slavery and Antislavery at the Nation's Founding* (Cambridge, MA: Harvard University Press, 2018), 188.

61. *Jenny, a free girl v. Robert Musick*, April 1821, case no. 194, SLCCHRP; *Jerry, a free man of color v. Charles Hatton*, April 1821, case no. 195, SLCCHRP; *Daniel, a free man v. John Whitesides*, April 1821, case no. 196, SLCCHRP; *Nancy v. Voteau* (1821), SLCCHRP; *Lydia, a free girl v. John Butler*, April 1821, case no. 192, SLCCHRP; *Sarah, a free girl v. Michael Hatton*, April 1821, case no. 191, SLCCHRP; *Hannah v.*

Whitesides (1821), SLCCHRP; *Lewis v. Whitesides* (1821), SLCCHRP; *Malinda v. Whitesides* (1821), SLCCHRP; *Winny v. Whitesides* (1821), SLCCHRP, 7, 11, 13–14. Two undated documents in Winny's case file imply that yet another child, named Bob, joined in her suit against Phebe Whitesides, but he does not appear in any other documents related to this case. Such limited references suggest either an error or the child's death early in the proceedings. *Winny v. Whitesides* (1821), SLCCHRP, 11–12, 30.

62. Shoemaker, *Missouri's Struggle for Statehood*, 55.

63. Dana O. Jensen, ed., "I at Home, by Stephen Hempstead, Sr., Part 4," *Missouri Historical Bulletin* 14 (April 1958): 274–75.

64. The *Missouri Gazette* and the *St. Louis Enquirer* reported on the Tallmadge Amendment for the first time on March 17, 1819—both of them citing the *National Intelligencer* as their source.

65. *Missouri Gazette*, March 24, 1819 (emphasis added).

66. *St. Louis Enquirer*, March 31, 1819.

67. *Missouri Gazette*, April 7, 21, 28, May 5, June 16, 1819.

68. Because most freedom suits at the local level were decided by juries, and circuit court judges did not issue formal opinions, it can be hard to discern their motives or even sometimes the effect they had on the outcome of cases. Judges did make decisions about the admissibility of evidence and the instructions that would be given to juries, but such decisions are often difficult to interpret.

69. *Annual Report of the American Historical Association for the Year 1929* (Washington, DC: Government Printing Office, 1930), 259. For more information about Nathaniel Beverley Tucker's role in the Missouri crisis, see Robert J. Brugger, *Beverley Tucker: Heart over Head in the Old South* (Baltimore: Johns Hopkins University Press, 1978), chap. 3; and John Francis McDermott, "Nathaniel Beverley Tucker in Missouri," *William and Mary Quarterly* 20, no. 4 (1940): 504–7.

70. *Missouri Gazette*, April 7, 1819. Other letters from "A Farmer of St. Charles County" appeared in the *Missouri Gazette* on April 21, May 5 and 18, and June 9 and 30, 1819. See also Shoemaker, *Missouri's Struggle for Statehood*, 106–07.

71. These other prorestriction letter writers included "Corrector" on April 28, 1819; "Pacificus" on May 12, 19, 26, and June 2, 1819; "An American" on May 26, 1819; and "Cato" on June 16, 1819.

72. Brugger, *Beverley Tucker*, 53.

73. *Missouri Gazette*, April 14, 1819.

74. *Missouri Gazette*, May 12, 1819 (emphasis in the original).

75. For more information on the grand juries that met in St. Louis and the rest of Missouri Territory in 1819, see Shoemaker, *Missouri's Struggle for Statehood*, 96–99.

76. Phebe Whitesides signed a variety of documents with her mark. Thomas Whitesides and John Whitesides, on the other hand, signed legal documents with their names. See Probate Estate File of John Whiteside (1803), MJRD, 10; *Winny v. Whitesides* (1821), SLCCHRP, 14.

77. Probate Estate File of Thomas Whiteside/Whitsetts (1818), MJRD, 44.

78. *Missouri Gazette*, October 20, 1818; Probate Estate File of Thomas Whiteside/Whitsetts (1818), MJRD, 94; Probate Estate File of Barnibas Harris (1819), MJRD,

105. There are not similar receipts for the *St. Louis Enquirer* in these probate files, which perhaps suggests that the *Missouri Gazette* was the preferred paper in St. Ferdinand.

79. Brugger, *Beverley Tucker*, 55.

80. James Richardson held two large noncontiguous plots in Township 46N, 5E (one in his own name of 599.51 acres, the other "under St. Cyr" of 771.79 acres). He also held another plot ("under Joseph Calais," of 340.28 acres) in Township 47N, 6E, immediately south of the St. Ferdinand commons. Eli Musick, the son of David's sister Terrell and Robert's cousin, held two contiguous plots near the center of Township 46N, 5E (one of 640 acres, the other of 255.51 acres). Township 46N, 5E, was to the immediate southwest of the township where St. Ferdinand was located. U.S., Indexed Early Land Ownership and Township Plats, 1785–1898, Earliest Township and Range Public Land Survey, s.v. "James Richardson" and "Ely Musick," AncestryLibrary.com; William Terrell Lewis, *Genealogy of the Lewis Family in America* (Louisville, KY: Courier-Journal Job Printing, 1893), 188.

81. The only defendant who was not served was Reuben Mitchell Hatton, the defendant in Sarah's case, whom the sheriff had not found. *Sarah v. Hatton* (1821), SLCCHRP, 2.

82. *St. Louis Enquirer*, April 7, 1819; *Jack v. Harris* (1818), SLCCHRP, 25.

83. *Jack v. Harris* (1818), SLCCHRP, 23, 18, 27–28.

84. *Milly v. Rose* (1819), SLCCHRP, 1–2, 6–9. Milly's case file suggests that she was born about 1789, making her about a decade younger than Winny. According to her petition, when Milly was sixteen her master took her to Indiana Territory and indentured her for a term of seventy years. At some point, she seems to have moved into the Illinois Territory, where she remained until about 1817, when her master relocated her once again, this time to St. Ferdinand. When she filed suit, Milly's daughter Elizabeth or Eliza was four and her son Bob was two. Her case file gives no indication about how or why the Pattersons came to be involved in her freedom suit. See also Twitty, *Before* Dred Scott, 35n19.

85. *Missouri Gazette*, June 23, 1819 (emphasis in the original). This gathering was held on June 5, 1819. For the claim that this was the only prorestriction public meeting, see Shoemaker, *Missouri's Struggle for Statehood*, 87.

86. Major Peter Bowler was chosen as president and Green DeWitt was selected as secretary. There are no other named participants or an estimated attendance. *Missouri Gazette*, June 23, 1819; Mueller, "Lucy and Elisha Patterson Farmstead," 65; Shoemaker, *Missouri's Struggle for Statehood*, 88.

87. Mueller, "Lucy and Elisha Patterson Farmstead," 60.

88. George Tompkins (Franklin, Mo.) to (George C. Sibley) July 30, 1819, A1510, box 1, George Champlain Sibley Papers, Missouri Historical Society, St. Louis.

89. On the timing of most agitation over the Tallmadge Amendments in St. Louis and Missouri generally, see Shoemaker, *Missouri's Struggle for Statehood*, chap. 3.

90. *St. Louis Enquirer*, July 21, 1819. There were two dozen other toasts—none of which invoked statehood—mentioned in this account, but the one quoted here was the only one drunk standing, a move that signaled its overwhelming support. It also tied one other toast, to the navy, for the greatest number of cheers.

91. *Edwardsville (IL) Spectator*, June 26, 1819; *Boston Patriot & Daily Mercantile Advertiser*, July 23, 1819; *Independent Chronicle and Boston Patriot*, July 24, 1819; *Mercantile Advisor* (New York), July 30, 1819; *Rhode-Island American* (Providence), July 30, 1819; *City of Washington Gazette*, August 2, 1819; *Portland (ME) Gazette*, August 3, 1819; *Hartford (CT) Times*, August 3, 1819; *New Hampshire Sentinel* (Keene), August 7, 1819; *Alexandria (VA) Herald*, August 9, 1819.

92. *St. Louis Enquirer*, September 8, 1819.

93. *Milly v. Rose* (1819), SLCCHRP, 11; Missouri State Archives–St. Louis, St. Louis Circuit Court Record Book no. 2, April 17, 1820, 111.

94. Milly disappears from the historical record after her suit was withdrawn. Her children appear to have remained with the defendant in her case. In the 1830 Census, Mathias Rose claimed four slaves, including one male and one female between the ages of ten and twenty-three. In 1830, Milly's daughter Elizabeth or Eliza would have been about fifteen and her son Bob about thirteen. The other two slaves Rose claimed were both under ten. U.S. Census Office, Fifth Census, 1830, St. Ferdinand, St. Louis County, s.v. "Mathias Rose," AncestryLibrary.com.

95. *Jack v. Harris* (1818), SLCCHRP, 31, 33–34; Missouri State Archives–St. Louis, St. Louis Circuit Court Record Book no. 1, August 23 and 24, 1819, 470, 482; Missouri State Archives–St. Louis, St. Louis Circuit Court Record Book no. 2, January 7, 1820, 27.

96. Shoemaker, *Missouri's Struggle for Statehood*, 94–97, 99–104.

97. *Missouri Gazette*, April 5, 1820. For more information on the use of illumination and transparencies as a form of celebration in eighteenth- and nineteenth-century Europe and the United States, see Shannon Selin, "Celebrating with Light: Illuminations and Transparencies," Imagining the Bounds of History, https://shannonselin.com/2016/10/illuminations-transparencies.

98. Lawrence Friedman, *A History of American Law*, 3rd ed. (New York: Simon and Schuster, 2005), 112. See also Stuart A. Banner, *Legal Systems in Conflict: Property and Sovereignty in Missouri, 1750–1860* (Norman: University of Oklahoma Press, 2000).

99. For more information about the 1807 territorial statute that sanctioned freedom suits, see Twitty, *Before* Dred Scott, 10.

100. Robert Simpson, who held a variety of positions in St. Louis County, is generally remembered as a resident of St. Louis, and was counted in the city's middle ward there in 1830, but a decade before that he listed St. Ferdinand as his residence in his candidate position statement. Simpson was a slaveholder by 1830, but it is not clear whether he claimed any slaves when he stood for election to the state's constitutional convention. Walter Barlow Steven, *St. Louis, the Fourth City, 1764–1904* (St. Louis: S. J. Clarke, 1909), 1:995; U.S. Census Office, Fifth Census, 1830, St. Louis, Middle Ward, St. Louis County, s.v. "Robert Timpson," AncestryLibrary.com; *Missouri Gazette*, April 5 and 12, 1820.

101. Although he declared himself a restrictionist in his candidate position statement, Rufus Pettibone, unlike Robert Simpson, made no broader statements about slavery. *Missouri Gazette*, April 12, 1820.

102. Shoemaker, *Missouri's Struggle for Statehood*, 129–31, 224–25.

103. When Winny and her children began their suits, the northern district of the circuit court of Missouri Territory was presided over by Nathaniel Beverley Tucker. Tucker continued in this role until the end of February 1820, when he resigned and was replaced by Alexander Gray. Tucker regained what was essentially his former seat in December 1820. Frederic Louis Billon, *Annals of St. Louis in Its Territorial Days, from 1804 to 1821* (St. Louis: Nixon-Jones, 1888), 278–79; McDermott, "Nathaniel Beverley Tucker," 504, 506.

104. *Winny v. Whitesides* (1821), SLCCHRP, 27–28.

105. Missouri State Archives–St. Louis, St. Louis Circuit Court Record Book no. 3, February 12, 1822, 77–80.

106. Phebe Whitesides died sometime before April 29, 1823, when her son John attested that she had died intestate. When, exactly, Winny and her children were conveyed to Rufus Pettibone is difficult to establish. By the time Winny's appeal was heard by the Missouri Supreme Court in November 1824, however, Pettibone, who had joined the high court the previous year, apparently claimed at least partial ownership over Winny and her children and consequently recused himself. In the suits Winny and three of her children filed after the Missouri Supreme Court ruling, moreover, Pettibone is the first named defendant. Probate Estate File of Phoebe Pruit, St. Louis (1823), case no. 594, MJRD, 2; William Van Ness Bay, *Reminiscences of the Bench and Bar of Missouri* (St. Louis: F. H. Thomas, 1878), 100; VanderVelde, *Redemption Songs*, 226n30.

107. *Winny v. Pettibone, et al.* (1825), SLCCHRP; *Lorinda, a free girl of color v. Rufus Pettibone, et al.*, July 1825, case no. 11, SLCCHRP; *Malinda, a free girl of color v. Rufus Pettibone, et al.*, July 1825, case no. 13, SLCCHRP; *Harry, a free boy of color v. Rufus Pettibone, et al.*, July 1825, case no. 14, SLCCHRP; *Jenny, a free woman of color v. Ephraim Musick*, et al., July 1825, case no. 15, SLCCHRP; *Winetta, a free girl of color v. Ephraim Musick, et al.*, July 1825, case no. 16, SLCCHRP.

9. Sharing the Founders' Flame

John Jay, Missouri, and Memory

David N. Gellman

"THIS MOMENTOUS QUESTION, like a fire bell in the night, awakened and filled me with terror," wrote Thomas Jefferson as he contemplated the political crisis touched off by Missouri's application in 1819 for admission to the Union. The patriarch of Monticello feared that the "self-government and happiness" forged by the revolutionary generation was "to be thrown away by the unwise and unworthy passions of their sons." The former U.S. president worried that partisan northern obstruction of Missouri's entrance as a slave state would rend the nation.[1]

John Jay heard the crisis bells too, but sought to safeguard a different version of the founders' legacy. Breaking his long public silence on national political affairs, John Jay released a letter criticizing slavery's spread as a violation of the American Revolution's enduring principles. Jay's place in the first rank of American Revolutionary figures was indisputable. Appointed by George Washington as the inaugural chief justice of the U.S. Supreme Court, the New Yorker negotiated two of the nation's foundational treaties with Great Britain. He served as a president and secretary for foreign affairs in the Continental Congress, as well as two terms as governor of New York. Along with James Madison and Alexander Hamilton, he also authored some of the Federalist Papers. If his founding-father bona fides were slightly less substantial than Jefferson's, few others still alive in 1819 shared a similar revolutionary stature.[2]

John Jay did not regard the "passions" of his sons against the extension of slavery to Missouri as either "unwise" or "unworthy." Peter Augustus Jay, lawyer, sometimes politician, and recent president of the New-York Manumission Society, continued to carry the family's political and antislavery banner by addressing a large meeting in New York City opposing the addition of a new slave state. William Jay, now a county judge and reformer

321

living in his father's Westchester County house, also frankly, if more privately, assessed the danger to the nation.[3] The political flames in Congress incit-
ed moral resolve rather than terror in John, Peter Augustus, and William Jay,
three men who represented the past, present, and future of the family's antislavery activism. John Jay and his sons viewed a strong congressional stand
against Missouri's admission as a slave state as wholly consistent with the
nation's foundational principles. But they went further still. The country's
founding principles, members of this founding family concluded, required
working toward slavery's gradual end throughout the nation.

This chapter examines the origins and reverberations of the Jay family's
response to the Missouri Question. The Jays drew, consciously and un-
consciously, on particular elements of the family's slaveholding, manumission, and abolitionist practices in formulating their response to the crisis.
Opposition to Missouri's admission as a slave state expressed not only an
interpretation of revolutionary principles but also a further articulation of
reform commitments, based at least in part on interactions with enslaved
people who served the extended Jay family. As New York's gradual emancipation process ground on, enslaved members of Jay-headed households
asserted their desire for freedom and a sense of the consideration owed them
by their white masters. In the years prior to the Missouri Crisis, John Jay
freed the last of his slaves, while the state of New York passed a law fix-
ing a date to formally complete the process of gradual emancipation. The
Missouri Crisis also informed Peter Augustus Jay's fight for Black voting
rights and against colonization. On the subject of slavery, the Jays literally
and figuratively came from a different place than Thomas Jefferson—as their
response to the crisis illustrated.

Examining the intergenerational reverberations of the Missouri Crisis in
the Jay family provides intergenerational biographical specificity to *longue
dureé* approaches to abolitionism and sectional strife.[4] The overlapping experiences of the Jay family with one another and with their slaves demonstrate
how northern opposition to the extension of slavery, particularly for New
Yorkers like the Jays, projected outward onto the continent an emancipation
process that was still under way not just in laws but within families.[5] More
specifically, the Jays demonstrate the ways in which abolitionist politics and
identities did not emerge in neat generational sequences akin to the passing
of a baton in a relay race.[6] The overlap in antislavery lives in the Jay family
and, presumably others, was substantial; parents and children influenced
one another, with opportunities to stimulate bolder, more progressive political sensibilities and engaging in subtle, respectful critique.

Long after the founding generation finally passed, descendants could re-shape, repurpose, and reinforce antislavery legacies to address subsequent sectional crises. The Missouri Crisis itself fostered divergent views on the founders' commitment to abolition decades after congressional compromise resolved the question of Missouri's statehood. Despite John Jay's public stance during the crisis against the extension of slavery, the nature of his abolitionist legacy remained contested. Apologists for slavery did not simply concede to John Jay's abolitionist offspring the right to interpret the found-ers' legacy. Voices hostile to or skeptical of radical abolitionism advanced an alternative biography of John Jay, discounting the significance of the nation-alist founding father's late-life call in the midst of sectional crisis that slavery be set on the road to extinction. At the end of his own life, William sought to keep his father not only out of Thomas Jefferson's camp but also out of Roger Taney's.

In the Jay family's antislavery history, the Missouri Crisis stands at the center point of an arc that stretches from the founding to the eve of the Civil War. From the 1830s to his death in 1858, William Jay assumed a vital role in the immediate abolition movement. The Missouri Crisis prompted some of his earliest recorded antislavery thoughts. The Missouri contest thus played a role in extending the legacy of one of the nation's most influential and longest-running abolitionist families. The alarm bells ringing in John Jay's Bedford, New York, proved, in a way, to be as consequential as those in Thomas Jefferson's Monticello, Virginia.[7]

John Jay's well-publicized intervention into the Missouri Crisis debate was an aberration but not an accident. He retired from public life in 1801, having served out a second term as governor of New York during which this largest slave state north of Maryland finally enacted a law to gradually abolish slav-ery. Jay served in the 1780s as the inaugural president of the state's pioneering antislavery organization, the New-York Manumission Society, and, at times, during his service in national government had expressed views that chal-lenged the interests and presumptions of slaveholders. He did not, however, take an active role in the complex legislative machinations that finally led to a gradual emancipation law in 1799.[8] After he completed his governorship, he kept a low political profile.[9]

As scions of the wealthy New York family intermarried with the colony's even more elite clans, slaveholding was an engrained fact of Jay life until the first decades of the nineteenth century. Dating to the Revolutionary War, John Jay's ideological skepticism about slavery mingled with paternalistic impulses to reward loyalty, emotional detachment, and a desire for obedient service.[10] During the first two decades of the new century, slaves and former slaves in his own household and in the extended Jay clan repeatedly asserted themselves. Although not an entirely new phenomenon in the family, independent-mindedness by Black servants posed additional challenges in an era when some members of the family, including John himself, sought to apply the principles behind gradual emancipation law to their own households. The enslaved did not and could not simply wait quietly for the Jays to do what he eventually did—manumit the last of his slaves.

Transitions, master to employer and enslaved to free, on the part of the Jays exhibited self-serving caution and produced trauma for enslaved people. During the early years of his retirement, John Jay's slaveholdings had dwindled to two—Clarinda and her daughter, Zilpah. Clarinda had been a member of the household of John's father, Peter, during the Revolutionary War. Her daughter, Zilpah, born in the 1790s, was raised in John's household.[11] The two women would not go unscathed in their journey out of bondage. In 1809, after Zilpah became pregnant in her teen years, John banished her from the household by selling her to his sister-in-law Judith Livingston Watkins for a projected period of several years.

After Zilpah's young child died, Clarinda implored John to allow Zilpah to return from Manhattan to Bedford. At first John rebuffed her. After a female servant named Roseanna departed from the household in the spring of 1811, John relented. John described in a tone at once vivid and willfully reserved Clarinda's effort to engineer the return of her daughter: "On the going away of Roasanna, she renewed her solicitations that we should take Zilpha to supply her place. she was <u>alone</u>—Zilpha was the <u>only</u> child she had left. she had been deprived of the others & &." Clarinda took considerable psychological, emotional, even material risks in confronting her master. She was a slave and, as far as she knew in 1811, would always be a slave. In the event, John granted that Clarinda's "considerations have weight." With his son Peter assisting in making the arrangements, he rented Zilpah's services on a monthly basis.[12]

Several years later, although Zilpah's pre-1799 birth did not legally entitle her to freedom under the state's original gradual emancipation statute, Jay applied the law's formula to Zilpah anyway. He drew up plans for her imminent manumission, based on an estimate that she now approached the age of twenty-five. This decision in March 1817 occurred in the same month that New York's state legislature prepared a final emancipation law, declaring all slaves in the state free ten years hence on July 4, 1827. How and when her mother, Clarinda, received her freedom is mysterious. The 1810 U.S. Census recorded Clarinda as a slave, the 1820 as free.[13] Slavery's legacy lingered. Clarinda served the family for the rest of her life, and Zilpah probably did as well. Slavery, if not the personal circumstances of inequality, had a finite end that could be tied symbolically to the nation's birth, a lesson that could reverberate far beyond New York's boundaries.[14]

The Rye, New York, estate of John's elderly brother Peter Jay provided John and Peter Augustus Jay with another glimpse into the changing social landscape, as slaves Caesar and Peet chafed against their situation. In April 1811, Peter Augustus reported to his father, without going into detail, that "Uncle Peter has a great deal of trouble with his Servants. They become more & more ungovernable." Four months later, Peter Augustus observed candidly to his sister Maria, "Uncle cannot perceive that it is necessary to treat Slaves at the present day in a Manner different from that they were accustomed to fifty Years ago."[15]

Peter Augustus did not specify what sort of treatment Uncle Peter fruit-lessly attempted, but a vast gulf separated the world into which the elder Peter was born and raised and the world of his final years. When Uncle Peter was seven in 1741, authorities had burned slaves at the stake for an alleged plot to seize New York City. Now his nephew Peter Augustus was a counselor for a manumission society that pursued masters for cruelty to their slaves and lobbied for revisions to the law to further protect slaves from abusive masters. By 1811, the legal process of gradual emancipation had been under way for more than a decade and other restrictions on masters even longer.[16] The slaves in Rye may have consciously thought about such changes, or they may have just taken advantage of the weakening grip of a blind man well into his eighth decade. Managing the master-slave relationship in 1811 required a certain deftness and flexibility that took into account, if not for moral rea-sons than for practical ones, the narrowing parameters of slave ownership, as well as the personalities of the individual slaves.

Though a man from a different era himself, when John Jay visited his old-er brother's estate and assessed matters firsthand, he advised restraint and accommodation. John cautioned against dispatching Peet, a servant who had so many useful skills, while advising his brother to encourage another of the family's longtime slaves, Caesar, toward continued cooperativeness by offering him wages.[17] The retired gradual abolitionist who responded to Clarinda's pleas and would in time free his own slaves prodded his brother to adjust to reality for practical reasons. The ad hoc, conditional nature of free-dom negotiations became even clearer after Peter's death. In 1813, his widow,

Mary D. Jay, granted Peet his freedom, but Caesar would not receive his freedom until Mary died in 1824.[18] Different Jays from different generations drew different distinctions about their personal and moral obligations to the enslaved members of their households who registered their own needs and displeasures. The elder Peter Jay, despite his dependence on his slaves, lived in a bygone era. His widow availed herself of the flexibility still permitted to masters to decide if and when to manumit. John operated with a schedule in his head that mimicked the legal formula. His son Peter Augustus, meanwhile, navigated this family terrain—made more unstable because of the actions of Clarinda, Zilpah, Caesar, and Peet—informed by an active commitment to shaping emancipation's future. His explicit commitment to protecting and expanding the rights of free people of color would have a direct impact on his and his family's response to the Missouri controversy.

♠

Peter Augustus Jay participated in organized abolitionist activities during this period. Sponsored by his first cousin Peter Jay Munro, who was already an active member, Peter Augustus joined the New-York Manumission Society in 1798, when his father was still governor and gradual emancipation legislation still in process. Munro, who was something of a surrogate son to John Jay, was particularly active in the society's legal work, and also became president of the society in 1810. Peter Augustus was regularly listed as a counselor for the organization. Manumission Society lawyers helped broker the freedom of a variety of African American New Yorkers held in violation of New York's laws, which barred the importation of slaves into and the exportation of slaves out of the state. The society could not have done so without African Americans themselves bringing cases to their attention and providing evidence. Emancipation work was racially collaborative work.[19]

In the 1810s, Peter Augustus Jay attempted to patrol the political front with regard to slavery. He served as president of the Manumission Society in 1816. That same year, as a state legislator, Peter Augustus Jay fought unsuccessfully for a number of reforms, attempting to defend free Black voting rights and to improve legal protections for the children bound to serve their mother's masters under the terms of the 1799 gradual emancipation law.[20] In 1818, Peter warned New York senator Rufus King, soon to be a key figure in the Missouri controversy, of a troubling House bill that, in the name of enforcing the nation's withdrawal from the international slave trade, would have committed the federal government to trading in slaves by authorizing the sale of illegally imported slaves impounded by authorities. Peter Augustus decried specious racial distinctions, wondering why "if such conduct towards natives of Europe in a similar Situation would be an offence against the laws of nature & nations, it is less so toward natives of Africa."[21] The treatment, movement, equality, and citizenship of Black people—issues implicated in the sectional crisis just over the horizon—shaped Peter Augustus's public views on slavery. Indeed, in his public political work, unlike his dealings with his relatives, he was not constrained by the need to show deference to elderly family members.

As a delegate to the early republic's umbrella antislavery organization the American Convention for the Promotion of the Abolition of Slavery and Improving the Condition of the African Race, Peter Augustus helped beat back attempts to endorse newly emerging calls to colonize free Black people outside the boundaries of the United States. In 1818, a five-man subcommittee on colonization, on which Jay served, having sampled procolonizationist ideas, opined that colonization would thwart the "certain progress of those principles, which, if uninterrupted, will produce their universal emancipation." Free Black people in the slave states would become the special victims of colonization, marginalized and bullied to leave the country.[22]

John Jay's sons revered their founding father and his legacy. John and Peter Augustus shared an interest in politics and, in early 1819, strategized closely over Peter's attempts to gain an appointment to public office from Governor DeWitt Clinton.[23] It is unlikely that Peter took positions that contradicted his father's wishes. In the emerging national debate over slavery, however, Peter led. As the Missouri Crisis wore on in 1819, the timing of the Jays' responses suggests that the more famous father acted in concert with his more publicly engaged antislavery son. Together, they made a clear statement that the nation's founding documents and its moral obligation lined up squarely against the admission of Missouri as a slave state.

The Jays sought to stiffen the backs of northern congressmen after the initial 1819 congressional stalemate precipitated by their fellow New Yorker James Tallmadge Jr.'s attempt to impose a New York–style emancipation regime in states carved out of the Louisiana Purchase. Starting in late summer, abolitionists and other opponents of slavery's expansion from Maryland to Maine sought to demonstrate the public support for restricting slavery in Missouri.[24] On November 16, 1819, Peter addressed a packed meeting in New York City. Congress, Peter told the gathering of two thousand, had the necessary authority to block the extension of slavery and to make support of this goal a condition for admitting new states. He also discussed "in a feeling manner, the cruelties of slavery," as well as "the evils which would ultimately result to this country if not prohibited."

The New Yorkers went well beyond the immediate political question of Missouri's status to envision a nation without slavery at all, speaking in explicitly abolitionist terms.[25] Jay successfully motioned for the meeting to approve a set of resolutions emphatically opposing the admission of Missouri as a slave state and taking a strong position against the institution of slavery more generally. The preamble labeled "the existence of slavery in the United States . . . a great political, as well as moral evil." Thus, the federal government ought "to prohibit the admission of slavery into any state or territory hereafter to be formed or admitted into the Union" and thanked New York's senators and congressmen for taking the appropriate stand. In addition, the meeting issued an "Address to the American People," which concluded with the hope that the representatives of the states that had already abolished slavery would help other states to follow suit.[26] The meeting expressed no sympathy for the sorts of diffusion arguments made by Jefferson and antirestrictionists in Congress, who imagined that slavery would be rendered less fearful if allowed to spread.[27]

At virtually the same moment that Peter A. Jay helped to mobilize opposition to slavery in Missouri, his father inserted himself into the debate to further inculcate abolitionist goals into the northern side of the Missouri debate. On November 17, John Jay penned a letter to Elias Boudinot in response to an antislavery circular produced in New Jersey earlier in the month. Slavery "ought not to be introduced nor permitted in any of the new states, and . . . ought to be gradually diminished and finally abolished in all of them," declared the retired founder. He surely anticipated that Boudinot, a former Federalist congressman and cofounder of the American Bible Society, would make the letter public.[28] A retired founding father normally inclined to avoid political debate provided powerful symbolic support for his son's advocacy of a national emancipation process.

Significantly, the former chief justice of the U.S. Supreme Court also weighed in on the constitutionality of Congress imposing antislavery conditions on Missouri's admission. He read the slave-trade clause of the U.S. Constitution as denying Congress the power to interfere with the "migration and Importation" of slaves into "existing States" prior to 1808. Nonetheless, according to Jay, Congress retained the power to prevent the importation of slaves into new states at any time. After 1808, congressional regulation of the spread of slavery applied to all states "whether new or old." The retired nationalist asserted the primacy of the federal government to blunt the spread of slavery and implied congressional authority to ban the interstate slave trade as well.

John Jay's critique of slavery also emphasized the egalitarianism implications of American independence. He explained why Article 1, Section 9, of the Constitution used the phrase "such Persons" instead of "Slaves" when describing the importation of people: slavery was "Tolerat[ed]" at the time despite "its Discordancy with the Principles of the Revolution." Nonetheless, the institution was known to be "repugnant" to the values annunciated in the Declaration of Independence. Jay then copied directly into his letter Jefferson's famous phrases from the Declaration's preamble about self-evident egalitarian truths and unalienable rights. The spirit of the Revolution and opposition to Missouri's admission as a slave state were then one and the same.[29] In the context of this crisis, Jay was more Jeffersonian than Jefferson in his expression of these principles.

The seventy-four-year-old Jay's brief published remarks on Missouri lent support to northern congressmen, senators, and state legislators already digging their heels in against their southern opponents.[30] The publishers of a thirty-five-page pamphlet of anti-Missouri speeches rushed to append the Jay-Boudinot correspondence to the back of their publication under the heading *"The following letter contains the opinion of that great Civilian John Jay on the Constitutional authority of Congress."* The *New-England Galaxy & Masonic Magazine* opted for the more understated heading "Letter from the Venerable John Jay." Newspapers in New York, New Jersey, Vermont, and Rhode Island published all or parts of the letter.[31]

The New Yorker regarded gradual emancipation as a safe, effective, and replicable means of achieving the broader goal of ending American slavery. In a December 21, 1819, letter to Daniel Raymond, he expressed his approval of the pamphleteer's *The Missouri Question*. In that publication, Raymond denied that either colonization or westward extension of slavery would weaken the institution and emphatically identified gradual emancipation as the only viable means of ending the institution.[32] Whatever John Jay's and gradualism's shortcomings—self-serving for whites, dangerous, damaging, and degrading for Black people—the aging founder preached what he practiced in his comments on the Missouri Question.[33] Freedom, not slavery, should be passed on to the next generation of Black people and whites. John thus charted the same course for slavery's elimination from the American landscape that his son Peter supported in both political and abolitionist circles. Together, the Jays reclaimed the founding for the cause of emancipation.

Younger son William Jay's response to the Missouri Crisis, more religious and moralistic, portended the next phase in the family's abolitionism.

Missouri helped kindle the antislavery fire of thirty-year-old William Jay, who, with his wife and children, lived under the same roof with John Jay, Clarinda, Zilpah, and other servants. In 1819, William conveyed his own opposition to "the extension of slavery" in a letter to Boudinot. William used less restrained and more religious language than his father: "If our country is ever to be redeemed from the curse of slavery the present Congress must stand between the living and the dead and stay the plague." It was not the laws of the country but those of God that "the extension of slavery" violated. The peril was practical and moral. Once planted in the West, slavery would be difficult to eradicate, "poisoning the feelings of humanity" and undermining "civil society." Father and son surely discussed the crisis in their shared home. In his letter to Raymond, John expressed his own fears about the future, stating that there was no way to expand slavery "without doing violence" to the nation's "principles" and "depressing" its "power and prosperity." To father and sons, the Missouri confrontation constituted a grave national danger.[34]

Events in Washington, Missouri, and the North itself caused the Jay sons to focus in on principles of equality more than nation building. After the 36°30' compromise brokered Missouri's admission as a slave state, William recognized free Black civil rights as the next battleground.[35] He noted in his private diary's 1820 installment on that year's political events, "As if to insult the advocates of the rights of man & to burlesque all profession of liberty & equality so liberally made by the southern slave holders," Missouri's "constitution renders it penal for a free negro, to enter the State," a violation of the U.S. Constitution's privileges and immunities clause.[36] Despite overwhelming opposition in William's home state of New York, in 1821 another compromise eked through Congress, fig-leaf language requiring Missouri to agree to abide by the U.S. Constitution proving enough to garner the necessary votes for statehood.[37]

♠

In the short term, it fell to Peter Augustus Jay to carry the family's political torch into increasingly intense political headwinds blowing through the North in the Missouri Crisis's aftermath. New York's 1821 constitutional convention shattered any illusion that the state's broader political community wished for even gradual progress toward racial equality that free African Americans and Manumission Society members like Peter envisioned. As a delegate at the Albany gathering, Peter presented a petition from free Black Manhattanites to eliminate roadblocks to African American voting rights enacted by the legislature.[38] He soon found himself, however, trying to dissuade the convention from using a new constitution to entirely deprive all Black men of the right to vote. Jay reminded his colleagues that less than a year before the convention, the state legislature overwhelmingly encouraged its congressional delegation to reject the admission of Missouri because the proposed state's constitution flouted Black citizenship. He imagined "a hiss of scorn" rising up from the South over this hypocrisy. Jay felt stunned the convention would defy the principle of "natural equality of all men"—the Jeffersonian point that John Jay had affirmed in his Missouri letter.

Peter, however, recognized that his stance was as much a critique as it was a defense of the founders. Later in the convention, responding pointedly to the current "degraded" condition of African Americans, Peter asked, "Was it not by our fault, and the fault of our fathers?"[39] Having read in the newspaper Peter's speech, John Jay commented in a letter to his son, "in my opinion [it] does you Credit."[40] These brief words offered a paternal blessing to Peter's critique and his cause, tacitly accepting the premise that his own founding generation—indeed, he himself—had not done enough to improve the lives of African Americans. Citizenship was an afflicted people's due; white afflicters had a responsibility to take a stand.[41]

Stubborn hope for progress contended with anti-Black-citizenship alternatives. Only sixteen days after the close of the convention, Peter joined the company of his fellow abolitionists at a New York City session of the American Convention for Promoting the Abolition of Slavery, where he once again found himself beating back calls to consider African colonization.[42] The convention continued to imagine that a gradual emancipation program in the southern slave states was the nation's surest path forward to full emancipation. While acknowledging the "immense debt" that the nation owed African Americans, the convention fleshed out a vision of serfdom lasting southern Black people long enough to prepare themselves for "rational liberty."[43] Despite the evidence, the delegates clung to a vision of gradual social transformation whose limitations in the North were already becoming alarmingly apparent through disfranchisement, discrimination, harassment, poverty, and contempt.[44]

In the long term, the fiercer but less conventionally political William Jay, in collaboration with his own son John Jay II, would shed the family's gradualist mantle. Prior to his father's death in 1829, William had begun engaging the antislavery cause in earnest through calls for the gradual abolition of slavery in Washington, DC. During the years that he drafted a biography of his deceased father, William drew new conclusions, as the political, ideological, and reform landscapes shifted rapidly in the age of William Lloyd

Garrison's *Liberator*, Nat Turner's rebellion, and South Carolina's nullification gambit. He concluded that an immediate freedom was a far-safer means to achieve moral ends than continued mass southern enslavement, that colonizationism would not solve the problem, and that the evangelical Tappan brothers could sand down the roughest edges of the Garrisonians. The legal harassment by Connecticut authorities of white Connecticut schoolteacher Prudence Crandall for daring to teach Black girls and antiabolitionist riots in New York City deepened William's determination. His son John II, attending Columbia in Manhattan, was an eager abolitionist partner and was, if anything, more comfortable than his father with the emergent strain of antislavery fervor.[45] In fully and publicly embracing the immediate abolitionist cause, the younger Jays neither repudiated the founding father nor shed the lessons of Missouri. Indeed, William, from time to time, revisited the crisis and the first John Jay's stand in order to defend a more forthright radicalism.

The significance of John Jay's 1819 opposition to Missouri's admission as a slave state shifted for William over time. William included the entire John Jay–Elias Boudinot letter late in his lengthy, laudatory biography, but with only modest commentary. William published his *Life of John Jay* in 1833, when he was still determining his own place in a rapidly changing abolitionist landscape.[46] William's emphatic public embrace of immediatism, the 1835 book *An Inquiry into the Character and Tendency of the American Colonization, and American Anti-Slavery Societies* briefly revisited the Missouri Crisis. He took to task those who supported relocating American Black people to Africa for lining up behind Missouri's admission as a slave state, part of what Jay saw as the general pattern of colonizationist support for southern slavery.[47]

The deleterious effects of the Missouri Compromise were unmistakable to this fierce advocate for immediate abolition. In his 1839 treatise *A View of the Action of the Federal Government, in Behalf of Slavery*, Jay referred to the drawing of the Missouri Compromise line across the Louisiana Territory as "one of the most profligate and decided acts of the Federal Government in behalf of slavery." Jay asserted that the U.S. government "deliberately surrendered to all the cruelties and abominations of the system." He found it galling that the federal government could acknowledge its authority to ban the institution in the territories and then strike "a bargain between humanity and cruelty, religion and wickedness." The U.S. government, Jay argued in his book and elsewhere, did not have the power to intervene against slavery in the states, making the failure to act against slavery when it did have the power all the more damaging and disturbing.[48] Once a state, Missouri took its ignominious place among the slave states, which perpetuated the institution's perverse racism, pumped up demand for the internal slave trade, and contributed via the three-fifths clause of the U.S. Constitution to the South's overrepresentation in Congress.[49]

Across the years, William's demand for the immediate abolition of slavery drew scorn from the ranks of the colonizationist and clergy whose acceptance of southern slavery he skewered. To Dr. David Reese and Rev. Moses Stuart, William's radicalism betrayed his father's temperate preference for gradualist solutions. In an 1835 book specifically written to rebut William's denunciation of the American Colonization Society and support for the American Anti-slavery Society, Reese wrote that "zealots" had "perverted" Jay's "mind, so that, on this particular subject, he has become disqualified for sober thinking."[50] In 1850, Stuart conjured an image of the founder "look[ing] down with a mixture of sorrow and frowning, on a descendant who could exhort his countrymen to disregard and trample under foot the Constitution which his father had so signally helped to establish."[51] William privately seethed with anger over Reese's attack, while lashing back at Stuart by emphasizing the unequivocal denunciations of slavery John Jay had made as founding president of the New-York Manumission Society in 1780s.[52]

William Jay's counterpunching was not merely defensive. He policed his father's reputation, censuring John Jay biographers for not appreciating the full significance of the revered founder's opposition to slavery. Henry B. Renwick's 1841 biography of John Jay for Harper's Family Library praised John Jay's antislavery for avoiding the fanaticism of present-day abolitionists and not attempting to impose his opinions on other states.[53] William Jay publicly accused Harper's of currying favor with southern audiences by publishing a biography distorting John's record. He took Renwick to task for, among other things, downplaying the opinion expressed in John Jay's Missouri letter that Congress should block the admission of new slave states and had the authority to block the internal slave trade. More broadly, William decried "the sordid sacrifice of one of the brightest features of my father's character on the altar of slavery."[54]

In 1855, as the nation hurtled deeper into sectional crisis, William Jay quoted from his father's Missouri Crisis letter to once again combat aspersions cast on contemporary abolitionists by a John Jay biographer. This time William's target was Henry Flanders, author of a series on the lives of the chief justices, who lauded the founder for avoiding "folly and fanaticism" and "discountenanced all violent and impracticable schemes to promote" abolition.[55] William, in a letter originally published in the *New-York Evening*

Post and reprinted in William Lloyd Garrison's *Liberator*, took Flanders to task for ignoring John's position on denying the admission of new slave states and asserting federal power to ban the interstate slave trade. This evidence set the stage for William's broader claim that in 1855, someone who expressed the views and took the actions that his father had long ago would surely be counted as a fellow fanatic. William, whose own son John Jay II was a leading pro bono lawyer for fugitive slaves, felt quite certain that people of his father's generation would never have imagined "that, by a formal act of Congress, the office of a human blood-hound would be identified with that of a 'good citizen.'"[56] William's critique of Flanders exaggerated the consistency and fairness of John Jay's record on slavery. But the political stakes were far too high to let others bend the arc of his father's antislavery thinking toward morally bankrupt compromise with a southern interest that had consolidated power in the decades since 1819.

In William Jay's private view, his father stood on one side of history and Thomas Jefferson on the other, morally indefensible, side of history. In an 1853 letter to his longtime abolitionist comrade Gerrit Smith, William derided Jefferson as a "hypocrite in many things & <u>without conscience</u> on all things," who, during the Missouri Crisis, set himself absolutely against stopping slavery's spread. Quipped Jay, "I take him to have been almost as much an anti Slavery man as Daniel Webster," who had been the subject of Jay's disgust well before the Massachusetts senator's feckless coup de grace of supporting the Fugitive Slave Act as part of the Compromise of 1850.[57]

Ironically, during the controversy over the Kansas bill and popular sovereignty, William Jay's abolitionist son John Jay II vociferously defended the Missouri Compromise. The younger John Jay and his nascent proto-Republican allies held up the compromise as a bulwark against slavery's spread. In that formulation, it was Stephen A. Douglass's attack on the compromise line that betrayed the revolution. In an 1854 broadside coauthored with John P. Hale and Hiram Barney, John Jay II even enlisted Jefferson as an avatar for free-soil principles.[58] In this instance, his grandfather's 1819 letter opposing the admission of Missouri's admission as a slave state would have detracted from the compromise and, thus, went unremarked.

As the proslavery tide within the national government crested with the 1857 *Dred Scott* decision, John Jay and his 1819 letter gained renewed relevance. Under variations of the heading "John Jay versus Roger B. Taney," the *National Anti-Slavery Standard*, the *Liberator*, and the *National Era* all republished a piece from the *Philadelphia Times* that featured the first chief justice's letter to prove that the current chief justice perverted the founder's legacy. The introduction to the letter emphasized not only Jay's character and intelligence, but also his personal connection to George Washington, the greatest founder of them all. In presenting Jay's Missouri letter, the introduction noted that while it "was written during the controversy which terminated in the Missouri Compromise . . . it happens to hit the very point misdecided by the Judges of the present court"—specifically the right of Congress to regulate territorial slavery and the founding father's recognition of African American rights. Among the words italicized in the reprint of Jay's text was Jay's observation of slavery's "*discordancy with the principles of the Revolution.*" The article revived John Jay's stance in the Missouri Crisis to prove that Taney had defamed the founders.[59]

For William Jay, the *Dred Scott* decision intensified anticipation of divine retribution for America's sins and called into question whether the Union his father had helped forge had any moral justification left.[60] Even so, the former judge drew on his father's legacy to dismantle Taney's arguments. Columbia professor and legal theorist Francis Lieber requested information from the venerable abolitionist on the late-eighteenth-century roots of Black citizenship. Accusing Justice Taney of "audacious mendacity," Jay's nine pages of notes documented that at the time of the founding, free Black people not only were citizens but also exercised those rights with the express approval of the nation's founders. William paid close attention to chronology. Jefferson recorded his misgivings in *Notes on the State of Virginia* before the composition of the U.S. Constitution. The Articles of Confederation referred to "free citizens" and "free inhabitants," not to white ones in one place and "white & other free citizens" in another place. Free Black people had the right to vote under the 1777 New York Constitution, whose key author was John Jay. New York and Pennsylvania hosted antislavery organizations "presided over by Franklin & Jay" prior to the 1787 constitutional convention. All these facts belied the notion that the founders never imagined African American citizens.

The historical evidence William assembled in 1858 for Lieber also quoted John Jay's 1819 Missouri letter. In reproducing his father's quotation from the preamble of the Declaration of Independence, William double underlined and put in all caps the words "All Men" from the phrase "All men are created equal."[61] At stake was not the obliteration of a compromise line of dubious moral distinction, but rather the annihilation of the fundamental principle of humanity upon which the nation was founded. Filtered through John Jay in one time of crisis and repeated by William at the time of another crisis, Jefferson could be selectively deployed and effectively amplified. There was no such hope for Taney. As William Jay's life reached its final stages, the *Dred Scott* case did not come down to "John Jay *versus* Roger B. Taney," as the newspaper had put matters. It was John Jay *or* Roger B. Taney. Chief Justice Taney's logic negated that of former chief justice John Jay. Only one of the two men's vision of law and justice could prevail.

Frederick Douglass, in his 1859 eulogy for William Jay, quoted directly from the future abolitionist firebrand's 1819 letter to Elias Boudinot declaring that "Congress must stand between the living and the dead, and stay the plague."[62] The Jays did not succeed in convincing the nation's leaders to halt slavery's westward spread or to recognize the emancipationist view of the founding. The plague of slavery claimed its victims for decades. Meanwhile, the living and the dead, white and Black, remained connected. Those who lived in Jay households forged legacies of slavery and antislavery with—and in tension with—one another. The enslaved registered their autonomy, displeasure, and claims for recognition. The activism of Peter Augustus bolstered John's unequivocal expression of antislavery principles. That same expression fortified his younger son William's belief that radical abolitionism expressed essential features of his father's and the American Revolution's legacy. William Jay, upon his death, left in trust $1,000 to John Jay II to support his work on behalf of fugitive slaves and instructions that Zilpah Montgomery, whom his father manumitted in 1817, be buried upon her own death in the family's churchyard plot.[63] Two hundred years on from the Missouri Crisis, there is still no separating the living and the dead.

Notes

The author thanks Jason Duncan for providing the impetus to write this chapter and John Craig Hammond and Jeffrey Pasley for their editorial advice.

1. Thomas Jefferson to John Holmes, April 22, 1820, in *The Works of Thomas Jefferson*, ed. Paul Leicester Ford (New York: G. P. Putnam's Sons, 1905), 12:158–60; Annette Gordon-Reed and Peter S. Onuf, *"Most Blessed of the Patriarchs": Thomas Jefferson and the Empire of Imagination* (New York: Liveright, 2016), 7–8, 89, 288, 294; Joseph J. Ellis, *American Sphinx: The Character of Thomas Jefferson* (New York: Alfred A. Knopf, 1997), 264–73.

2. Modern full-length biographies of Jay have been surprisingly scarce, the most recent being Walter Stahr, *John Jay: Founding Father* (New York: Hambledon and London, 2005). For collective portraits of the founders that foreground Jay, see Richard B. Morris, *Seven Who Shaped Our Destiny: The Founding Fathers as Revolutionaries* (New York: Harper Torchbooks, 1973); Jack Rakove, *Revolutionaries: A New History of the Invention of America* (Boston: Houghton Mifflin Harcourt, 2010); and

Joseph J. Ellis, *The Quartet: Orchestrating the Second American Revolution, 1783–1789* (New York: Alfred A. Knopf, 2015).

3. "Bedford, West Chester County, N.Y.," *National Recorder* (Philadelphia), December 18, 1819; "Meeting to Oppose Slavery," *New-York Evening Post*, November 17, 1819; diary of William Jay, December 31, 1820, John Jay Homestead (hereafter referred to as JJH), Katonah, New York; Bayard Tuckerman, *William Jay and the Constitutional Movement for the Abolition of Slavery* (New York: Dodd, Mead, 1894), 28–29.

4. Manisha Sinha, *The Slave's Cause: A History of Abolition* (New Haven, CT: Yale University Press, 2016); Patrick Rael, *Eighty-Eight Years: The Long Death of Slavery in the United States, 1777–1865* (Athens: University of Georgia Press, 2015); and Ira Berlin, *The Long Emancipation: The Demise of Slavery in the United States* (Cambridge, MA: Harvard University Press, 2015), are three recent examples of this trend. For another innovative approach to intergenerational legacies, see Sarah Levine-Gronningsater, "Delivering Freedom: Gradual Emancipation, Black Legal Culture, and the Origins of Sectional Crisis in New York, 1758–1870" (PhD diss., University of Chicago, 2014).

5. Levine-Gronningsater, "Delivering Freedom."

6. See Paul J. Polgar, *Standard-Bearers of Equality: America's First Abolition Movement* (Chapel Hill: University of North Carolina Press, 2019), for an extraordinarily nuanced study of the first emancipation and its legacy; pages 242–47 specifically discuss the Missouri Crisis. William Pencak, "From 'Salt of the Earth' to 'Poison and Curse'? The Jay and Adams Families and the Construction of American Historical Memory," *Early American Studies* 2, no. 1 (2004): 228–65, comes closest among Jay scholars to conveying the interlocked nature of the family's story. Daniel C. Littlefield, "John Jay, the Revolutionary Generation, and Slavery," *New York History* 81, no. 1 (2000): 132; Richard B. Morris, *John Jay, the Nation, and the Court* (Boston: Boston University Press, 1967), 14; and Carol Brier, *Mr. Jay of Bedford: John Jay, The Retirement Years, 1801–1829* (Berwyn Heights, MD: Heritage Books, 2016), 292–95, take a less nuanced view of the transmission of antislavery legacies.

7. Gordon-Reed and Onuf, *"Most Blessed,"* is one of the most recent books to focus on Jefferson and slavery. See also Henry Wiencek, *Master of the Mountain: Thomas Jefferson and His Slaves* (New York: Farrar, Straus and Giroux, 2012). For an especially succinct statement of Jefferson's centrality to the subject of slavery and race in U.S. history, see David K. Shipler, "Jefferson Is America—and America Is Jefferson," *New York Times*, April 12, 1993.

8. See David N. Gellman, *Emancipating New York: The Politics of Slavery and Freedom, 1777–1827* (Baton Rouge: Louisiana State University Press, 2006) and *Liberty's Chain: The Jay Family, Slavery, and Emancipation, 1685–1912* (Ithaca, NY: Cornell University Press, forthcoming), for the details of gradual emancipation and Jay's activities.

9. In 1809 and 1810, Jay more or less deflected when British parliamentary antislavery activist William Wilberforce sought to enlist him in Anglo-American efforts to suppress the slave trade; William Wilberforce to JJ, August 1, 1809, Papers of John

Jay—Online Edition (hereafter PJJ), doc. 09282; John Jay (hereafter JJ) to Wilber-force, November 8, 1809, PJJ, doc. 09281; Wilberforce to JJ, July 18, 1810, PJJ, doc. 09277; JJ to Wilberforce, October 25, 1810, PJJ, doc. 09278. See Brier, *Mr. Jay of Bed-ford*; and Stahr, *John Jay*, chap. 15, on Jay during his long retirement.

10. For a succinct narrative of John Jay's approach to slaveholding during the Rev-olutionary War and the tragedy that in one instance ensued, see David N. Gellman, "Abbe's Ghost: Negotiating Slavery in Paris, 1783–1784," in *Experiencing Empire: Power, People, and Revolution in Early America*, ed. Patrick Griffin, 189–211 (Char-lottesville: University of Virginia Press, 2017).

11. Clarinda's and Zilpah's stories are told with particular sensitivity in Jan Hor-ton, "Listening for Clarinda," unpublished ms. report for John Jay Homestead His-toric Site (2000).

12. Peter Augustus Jay (hereafter PAJ) to Maria Jay Banyer (hereafter MJB), Oc-tober 21, 1809, PJJ, doc. 10046; Sarah Louisa Jay to John Jay (hereafter JJ), January 15, 1810, PJJ, doc. 09245; JJ to PAJ, April 16, May 8, 1811, March 9, 1813, PJJ, docs. 11518, 11519, 11555; PAJ to JJ, March 12, 1813, PJJ, doc. 06180.

13. JJ to PAJ, March 12, 1817, PJJ, doc. 90065; Horton, "Listening for Clarinda," 109–10; 1810 U.S. Census; 1820 U.S. Census, searched through Ancestry.com; the 1820 entry for "John Jay" requires entering "John Fay" in the search engine. Hor-ton, "Listening for Clarinda," is surprisingly silent on the entire subject of Clarinda's manumission, though eloquent on the conditions of the later years of Clarinda's life.

14. Polgar, *Standard-Bearers of Equality*, 6, 110, 242. For works that emphasize continuing inequality as a structural legacy of gradual emancipation, see Joanne Pope Melish, *Disowning Slavery: Gradual Emancipation and "Race" in New England, 1780–1860* (Ithaca, NY: Cornell University Press, 1998); and Leslie Marie Harris, *In the Shadow of Slavery: African Americans in New York City, 1626–1863* (Chicago: University of Chicago Press, 2003).

15. PAJ to JJ, April 5, 1811, PJJ, doc. 06155; PAJ to MJB, August 1,1811, PJJ, doc. 90199.

16. New-York Manumission Society Records, 1785–1849, https://cdm16694.con-tentdm.oclc.org/digital/collection/p15052coll5/id/31512; see specifically, November 17, 1807, January 15, 1811, 9:175–76, 268, 271. Among the many accounts of the events of 1741, two of the most accessible are Jill Lepore, *New York Burning: Liber-ty, Slavery, and Conspiracy in Eighteenth-Century Manhattan* (New York: Vintage, 2005); and Peter Charles Hoffer, *The Great New York Conspiracy of 1741: Slavery, Crime, and Colonial Law* (Lawrence: University Press of Kansas, 2003). For a general survey of slavery in New York City, see Graham Russell Hodges, *Root and Branch: African Americans in New York and East Jersey, 1613–1863* (Chapel Hill: University of North Carolina Press, 1999).

17. JJ to PAJ, October 24, 1811, PJJ, doc. 11525.

18. Transcription of Overseers of the Poor records, Rye, New York, January 14, 1814, Jay Heritage Society, Rye, NY; Will of Mary Jay, typed transcription; Will of (Blind) Peter Jay, typed transcription; Will of John Jay scan of handwritten copy, all in JJH files.

19. On Munro, see Louise V. North, "The 'Amiable' Children of John and Sarah Livingston Jay," 7–8, paper delivered at "Columbia's Legacy: Friends and Enemies in the New Nation," December 10, 2004, http://www.columbia.edu/cu/lweb/conferences/2004/john_jay/pdf/North.pdf; and Gellman, "Abbe's Ghost." New-York Manumission Society Records, 1785–1849, vols. 7 and 9. For evidence related to Munro's legal activities, see October 9, 1792, July 30, September 10, 1793, October 16, 1794, November 22, 1796, December 28, 1797, March 7[?], 1799, March 27, May 18, July 3, October 3, November 20, December 10, 1800, June 2, June 18, 1801, June 19, 1802, December 9, 1803, February 3, 1804, 7:14, 20, 34, 79, 105, 115–16, 154–55, 157, 167, 172, 174, 176, 191, 192, 194, 229, 249, 254. For indications of Peter Augustus Jay's involvement in the Manumission Society, see May 15, 1798, January 20, 1801, January 18, 1802, January 16, 1810, January 15, 1811, January 28, 1812, January 18, 1813, 9:10, 53, 73, 236, 271, 302, 327; see also 7:206–8. In addition, see Polgar, *Standard-Bearers of Equality*, 89, 103–20; and Gellman, *Emancipating New York*, 162–64, 203–5. On the limits of the kind of legal activism and cross-racial alliances pursued by the Manumission Society, see Martha S. Jones, "Time, Space, and Jurisdiction in Atlantic World Slavery: The Volunbrun Household in Gradual Emancipation New York," *Law and History Review* 29, no. 4 (2011): 1031–60.

20. *Journal of the Assembly of the State of New-York* (Albany: J. Buel, 1816), 3, 163, 211, 222, 264, 272, 357, 370–71, 382, 587, 604, 616; *Journal of the Senate of the State of New-York* (Albany: J. Buel, 1816), 229; Levine-Gronningsater, "Delivering Freedom," 123–24, 253–54; "Observation on draft of law concerning Slaves and Servants," in Elizabeth Clarkson Jay Papers, Manuscripts and Special Collections, New York State Library, contains a marked-up copy of the proposed bill. I am grateful to Sarah Gronningsater for sharing her digital photos of this document. "Extract of a letter from Albany, dated April 6," *New-York Evening Post*, April 9, 1816. For comments critical of legal obstructions to African American voting, see "Oppression" and "The Letter Continued," *New-York Courier*, March 25, April 10, 1816. In the midst of the frustrating 1816 session, Jay did win one small victory, successfully advancing a bill to cover the full costs of subsidizing the dwindling number of former slaves who had received their freedom after being confiscated from loyalist during the Revolutionary War. See *Journal of the Assembly* (1816), 50, 60–61, 419; *Journal of the Senate* (1816), 113–15, 126, 145; and "An Act Concerning the Maintenance of Certain Persons, Formerly Slaves," March 22, 1816, in *Laws of the State of New-York* (Albany: J. Buel, 1816), 37.

21. Peter A. Jay, February 13, 1818 (draft), in Correspondence, 1772–1841, box 1, John Jay Ide Collection, New-York Historical Society.

22. *The American Convention for Promoting the Abolition of Slavery and Improving the Condition of the African Race: Minutes, Constitution, Addresses, Memorials, Resolutions, Reports, Committees and Anti-Slavery Tracts* (New York: Bergman, 1969), 2:640, 649–56, 655 (quote); Polgar, *Standard-Bearers of Equality*, 287–88.

23. PAJ to JJ, January 28, March 18, April 15, 1819, PJJ, docs. 06224, 06226, 06231; JJ to PAJ, February 2, March 16 and 21, April 13 and 20, May 25, 1819, PJJ docs. 13425, 13424, 13515, 06230, 11591, 13426.

24. Sinha, *Slave's Cause*, 186–87; Sean Wilentz, *The Rise of American Democracy: Jefferson to Lincoln* (New York: W. W. Norton, 2005), 231. See also John Craig Hammond, "President, Planter, Politician: James Monroe, the Missouri Crisis, and the Politics of Slavery," *Journal of American History* 105, no. 4 (2019): 848–49. Hammond remarks on public meetings that emphasized the theme of limiting slavery's extension in territories and future states.

25. My reading thus supports the emphasis by Sinha, *Slave's Cause*, 187–90; and Polgar, *Standard-Bearers of Equality*, 243–45, on the abolitionist terms of the debate not fully appreciated by other historians.

26. Accounts of the meeting include "Meeting to Oppose Slavery," *New-York Evening Post*, November 17, 1819; *National Advocate* (New York), November 18, 1819; "Interesting Meeting," *Salem (MA) Gazette*, November 23, 1819; and "Slavery," *Boston Patriot and Daily Chronicle*. News of the meeting spread all the way to Edwardsville, Illinois, near St. Louis, Missouri ("Meeting to Oppose Slavery," *Edwardsville (IL) Spectator*, December 25, 1819. See also John Jay [1875–1928], *Memorials of Peter A. Jay: Compiled for His Descendants* (printed for private circulation, 1929), 94.

27. Matthew Mason, *Slavery & Politics in the Early Republic* (Chapel Hill: University of North Carolina Press, 2006), 180, 204–5; Ellis, *American Sphinx*, 269.

28. For a profile of Boudinot, see Jonathan J. Den Hartog, *Patriotism & Piety: Federalist Politics and Religious Struggle in the New American Nation* (Charlottesville: University of Virginia Press, 2015), 93–115.

29. JJ to Elias Boudinot, November 17, 1819 (draft), PJJ, doc. 08767; *National Recorder*, December 18, 1819; William Jay, *Life of John Jay: With Selections from His Correspondence and Miscellaneous Papers* (New York: J. and J. Harper, 1833), 1:452–53; Stahr, *John Jay*, 372–73.

30. Joseph L. Arbena, "Politics or Principle? Rufus King and the Opposition to Slavery, 1785–1825," *Essex Institute Historical Collections* 101 (January 1965): 56–77; Leonard L. Richards, *The Slave Power: The Free North and Southern Domination, 1780–1860* (Baton Rouge: Louisiana State University Press, 2000), 49–51.

31. *Papers Relative to the Restriction of Slavery. Speeches of Mr. King, in the Senate, and Messrs. Taylor & Talmadge, in the House of Representatives, of the United States, On the Bill for Authorising the People of the Territory of Missouri to Form a Constitution and State Government, and for the Admission of the Same into the Union in the Session of 1818-19* (Philadelphia: Hall and Atkinson, 1819); *New-England Galaxy & Masonic Magazine* 2, no. 14 (1819): 2; Stahr, *John Jay*, 373; "To the Editor of the Trenton Federalist," *New York Daily Advertiser*, December 15, 1819; "Slavery in Missouri," *Rhode Island American*, December 17, 1819; "To the Editor of the Trenton Federalist," *American* (New York), December 18, 1819; "From the Philadelphia Aurora: Extension of Slavery," *Vermont Journal* (Windsor), December 20, 1819; "To the Editor of the Trenton Federalist," *Centinel of Freedom* (Newark, NJ), January 4, 1820.

32. In JJ to Daniel Raymond, December 21, 1819, in *Life of John Jay*, by William Jay, 2:405–6, Jay expressed approval of Daniel Raymond, *The Missouri Question* (Baltimore: Schaeffer & Maund, 1819); on gradual emancipation see p. 35 of the pamphlet.

33. For historical evaluations of gradual emancipation in the North, see Gellman, *Emancipating New York*; Melish, *Disowning Slavery*; Harris, *In the Shadow of Slavery*; and Polgar, *Standard-Bearers of Equality*.

34. WJ to Boudinot, quoted in Tuckerman, *William Jay*, 28–29; Stephen P. Budney, *William Jay: Abolitionist & Anticolonialist* (Westport, CT: Praeger, 2005), 20–21. Den Hartog, *Patriotism & Piety*, 191 and 186–200 generally, emphasizes William's more avowedly religious approach to politics than his older brother's and also notes that the Missouri letter was "his first known objection to slavery."

35. Wilentz, *Rise of American Democracy*, 232–35.

36. WJ, diary, December 31, 1820.

37. Wilentz, *Rise of American Democracy*, 235–36; David N. Gellman and David Quigley, eds., *Jim Crow New York: A Documentary History of Race and Citizenship, 1777–1877* (New York: New York University Press, 2003), 84–86; Gellman, *Emancipating New York*, 209; Glover Moore, *The Missouri Controversy, 1819–1821* (Lexington: University Press of Kentucky, 1966), 138–39, 142–59.

38. Nathaniel H. Carter and William L. Stone, eds., *Report of the Proceedings and Debates of the Convention of 1821, Assembled for the Purpose of Amending the Constitution of the State of New-York* (Albany, NY: E. and E. Hosford, 1821), 134–35.

39. For Jay's speeches to the convention quoted here, see *Jim Crow New York*, 111–14, 138–42, 179.

40. JJ to PAJ, October 16, 1821, PJJ, doc. 11609; see also PAJ to JJ, October 10, November 15 and 22, 1821, PJJ, docs. 06251, 06253, 06254.

41. Here, I perhaps diverge somewhat from Polgar, *Standard-Bearer of Equality*, in the tight connection he describes between gradual emancipation and egalitarian visions of citizenship. Though I agree with the thrust of the argument, Peter Augustus Jay poignantly acknowledged in these remarks the cracks built into the foundation of this legacy.

42. *American Convention*, 780, 783–85. See Polgar, *Standard-Bearer of Equality*, 290–98, on tension over colonization with the American Convention.

43. *American Convention*, 748, 790–98, 792 (quotes); Mason, *Slavery & Politics*, 206.

44. For ample evidence, see *Jim Crow New York*; Hodges, *Root and Branch*; Harris, *In the Shadow of Slavery*; Melish, *Disowning Slavery*; and Polgar, *Standard-Bearers of Equality*, 236–42.

45. I base this account of emerging immediatism on my forthcoming biographical study, *Liberty's Chain*. Scholarly studies of William Jay are few, far between, and inadequate; they include Tuckerman, *William Jay*; Robert A. Trendel, *William Jay: Churchman, Public Servant, Reformer* (New York: Arno Press, 1982); and Budney, *William Jay*. There are no full-length studies of John Jay II, though a good introduction can be found in Jared Odessky, "'Possessed of but One Idea Himself': John Jay II's Challenges to Columbia on Slavery and Race," Columbia University & Slavery, https://columbiaandslavery.columbia.edu/content/possessed -one-idea-himself-john-jay-iis-challenges-columbia-slavery-and-race.

46. Jay, *Life of John Jay*, 1:452–53.

47. William Jay, *An Inquiry into the Character and Tendency of the American Colonization, and American Anti-Slavery Societies*, 4th ed. (New York: R. G. Williams, 1837), 49–50, 82, 106, 108.

48. William Jay, *A View of the Action of the Federal Government, in Behalf of Slavery* (New York: J. S. Taylor, 1839), 27–28, 183–84.

49. Jay, *View of the Action of the Federal Government*, 15, 64, 72, 135, mentions Missouri.

50. David M. Reese, *Letters to the Hon. William Jay, Being a Reply to His "Inquiry into the American Colonization and American Anti-slavery Societies"* (New York: Leavitt, Lord, 1835), vi–vii.

51. Moses Stuart, *Conscience and the Constitution with Remarks on the Recent Speech of the Hon. Daniel Webster in the Senate of the United State on the Subject of Slavery* (1850; reprint, New York: Negro University Press, 1969), 63.

52. WJ to John Jay II, June 3, 1835, WJ to PAJ, June 11, 1835, John Jay Papers, Butler Library, Rare Books and Manuscripts, Columbia University, New York; William Jay, *Reply to Remarks of Rev. Moses Stuart, Lately a Professor in the Theological Seminary at Andover, of Hon. John Jay and an Examination of His Scriptural Exegesis, Contained in his Recent Pamphlet . . .* (New York: John A. Gray, 1850).

53. Henry B. Renwick, *Lives of Jay and Hamilton* (New York: Harper & Brothers, 1841), 140–42.

54. "From the New-York American. Renwick's Life of John Jay," *Liberator*, February 19, 1841; William Jay Scrapbook, JJH.

55. Henry Flanders, *The Lives and Times of the Chief Justices of the Supreme Court of the United States*, 1st ser., *John Jay—John Rutledge* (Philadelphia: Lippincot, Grambo, 1855), 216, 218.

56. "Chief Justice Jay's Views of Slavery," *Liberator*, May 25, 1855.

57. WJ to Gerrit Smith, July 15, 1853, Smith Papers, Special Collections Research Center, Syracuse University Libraries (quoted with permission), Syracuse, NY. For William Jay's public criticism of Daniel Webster's approach to slavery and sectional politics, see William Jay, *The Creole Case, and Mr. Webster's Despatch; with the Comments of the N.Y. American* (New York: Office of "New-York American," 1842); "Letter from Hon. Wm. Jay to the Hon W. M. Nelson, Member of Congress," *National Anti-Slavery Standard*, March 28, 1850; "FUGITIVE SLAVES. Address of Hon. William Jay before the Anniversary of the American and Foreign Anti-Slavery Society," William Jay Scrapbook, JJH.

58. John P. Hale, Hiram Barney, and John Jay II, "Free Democratic Address to the People of the State of New York," October 1854, Broadside, American Antiquarian Society, Worcester, MA.

59. "John Jay versus Roger B. Taney," *National Anti-Slavery Standard*, May 9, 1857; "John Jay, First Chief Justice of the United States, versus Roger B. Taney, the Present Chief Justice," *National Era* (Washington, DC), April 30, 1857; "John Jay vs. Robert B. Taney: The First Chief Justice of the United States vs. the Present Chief Justice," *Liberator*, May 15, 1857. See also "The Contrasts: Rynders and Clarkson, Taney and Jay, Buchanan and Washington," *National Anti-Slavery Standard*, September 5, 1857.

60. WJ to Gerrit Smith, August 12, 1857, Smith Papers.

61. William Jay to Francis Lieber, March 9, 1858, Papers of Francis Lieber, Huntington Library, San Marino, CA.

62. Frederick Douglass, *Eulogy of the Late Hon. Wm. Jay, By Frederick Douglass, Delivered on the Invitation of the Colored Citizens of New York City, in Shiloh Presbyterian Church, New York, May 12, 1859* (Rochester: Press of A. Strong, 1859), 24.

63. William Jay, Last Will and Testament, signed April 14, 1858; William Jay, Codicil to Last Will and Testament, written May 15, 1858, and signed July 1, 1858; scans of handwritten documents shared by JJH with author.

10. John Quincy Adams, the Missouri Crisis, and the Long Politics of Slavery

David Waldstreicher

Wᴛʜ ʀᴇsᴘᴇᴄᴛ ᴛᴏ the crisis of 1819–21, John Quincy Adams is something of a cipher. Serving as secretary of state at the time, present at key cabinet meetings, his diary provides many of the most quotable quotes for students of the Missouri Compromise and its aftermath. Yet he's usually not seen as a significant actor in the controversy. Rather, he seems at most an informant, commentator, maybe an after-the-fact thought leader. He called the episode a "title page to a great and tragic volume" and later predicted civil war as an outcome, but he didn't man any barricades. Celebrating his prescience about the inevitability of civil war over slavery works if we care only what he was thinking, not what he was doing.[1] What was his role in the politics of slavery over the long haul, and where does Missouri fit in his later, now much-admired conversion to antislavery politics?

In his fine recent biography titled *The Lost Founding Father*, William J. Cooper has posed the particular place of Adams in U.S. history as a kind of bridge between the Revolution and the Civil War: "In a fundamental sense," Cooper writes, "the last major figure of the founding generation had become [by the mid-1830s] the first of the destroying generation." Last, lost, or both, Cooper is right: But was it just a coincidence or irony that Adams turned out to be this figure? The Missouri Crisis stands in the chronological middle of Adams's political career. It might seem to be a moment of transition—but from what to what? Because he has posited Adams as a founder, it becomes difficult for Cooper to acknowledge current preferences for the late, dissenting John Quincy Adams, the scourge of Congress. He helps us see the problem, however, precisely because of his neo-revisionist skepticism about antislavery politics. Even so, Cooper leaves intact the dilemma that has informed all writing on the sixth president's long career. Leading historians and biographers have not solved the puzzle. They have usually stressed an antislavery awakening, a transformation, but have struggled to account for it. Samuel Flagg Bemis posited two brilliant careers and celebrated Adams as the founder of American foreign policy for what he did at the time of the Missouri controversy and as president, and he even identified "the hidden issue . . . of slavery" as central in the election of 1828, but by dividing the story of domestic politics between the end of his first volume and the beginning of his second, he underestimated the presidency and how Adams got there. This set the stage for more disturbing, if realistic, accounts of Adams's valley of despair. In his prizewinning monograph *The Making of the Monroe Doctrine* (1975), Ernest R. May picked at Bemis's sutures, ratifying the credit Adams deserved for the doctrine but using his diary to show how Adams and the rest of the cabinet spent these years jockeying to succeed Monroe. Sordid court dynamics and personal interest explained as much as ideology. Leonard L. Richards, Paul C. Nagel, and other biographers of the 1980s and 1990s psychologized, stressing the personal demons, tragedies, and revenge motive for how the cautious nationalist became an antislavery tribune. Meanwhile, scholarship still more critical of American diplomacy, especially by William Earl Weeks, revised Bemis's triumph and the valley between the two careers into a tragedy: a compromise not only on slavery but also on imperialism.[2]

The seemingly irreconcilable tendencies to celebrate Adams's consistency or blame him for his midcareer failings reach an epitome in the work of Sean Wilentz. In a telling moment in his recent study *No Property in Man: Slavery and Antislavery at the Nation's Founding*, Wilentz depicts John Quincy Adams as "openly antagonistic to slavery" in 1804 because he remarked in a Senate debate about the status of slavery and the slave trade in Louisiana that "the Constitution does not recognize slavery—it contains no such word." This "great circumlocution" had deliberately excluded slavery from the nation's charter.[3] Wilentz admits no contradiction between his mocking treatment of Adams as a backward-looking neo-Federalist in his Jackson-defending epic *The Rise of American Democracy* (2006) and his recent celebration of Adams as part of a grand antislavery tradition that begins with the Constitution— again, as in Cooper, the founders' saving (or is it "destroying"?) grace. It is almost as if we have returned to the nineteenth-century abolitionist celebration of "Old Man Eloquent"—if we can forget that in other recent writings Wilentz continues to damn Adams and his father for engaging in "high-minded idealism" instead of pragmatic partisanship.[4]

Wilentz admits that Adams was "not yet an antislavery stalwart" in 1804, but the prolepsis is a rhetorical move that downplays the more relevant fact that Adams was only slightly pushing back against proslavery constitution-alism on the Senate floor in 1804. Adams had argued that restricting slavery and the slave trade in the recently purchased Louisiana Territory was not at all something the Senate should be doing when considering a treaty and annexation. He insisted that barring the slave trade wasn't constitutional, having objected to other enabling legislation on that basis while supporting—against every member of his own party—Louisiana's admission to the Union. He was declaring the Constitution neutral, at best, with proslavery effects, on the suddenly politicized matter of its future in an expanding Southwest. He wasn't trying to end slavery; he was seeking, desperately, to depoliticize slav-ery. That's why he was spending his evenings reading Raynal on the natural history of the West Indies. Slavery was wrong in the abstract, he had mused, but "as connected with commerce, it has important uses."[5] The young sen-ator stuck to his sense of what the national bargain entailed, over his party, his region, and his own beliefs about slavery. Expansion, and the nation, was what mattered.

As a test case, John Quincy Adams actually disproves the notion of a "no property in man" antislavery time bomb placed by the founders in the Constitution, though his fealty to a broader and deeper version of the idea of an antislavery and nationalist American Revolution of 1776 did later prove useful to antislavery activists as well as to Abraham Lincoln. A bet-ter understanding of the slow development of Adams's antislavery politics suggests that Adams had to probe, question, and even reject in a spirit of disillusionment slavery's actual place in the Constitution in order to forge an effective antislavery politics. He had to raise the spirit of the Declaration of Independence over conventional readings of the letter of the Constitution. And he had to stick with his preference for the nation and the long view over partisan politics and the short-term strategies that led directly to legislative gridlock, incompetent presidents, and yet another safety-valve imperial war that helped win elections.[6]

Adams was more than a failed president remade by the politics of slavery. He helped make the politics of slavery at both ends, pre- and post-Missouri. Insofar as the keys to national politics lay in silencing the politics of slavery, then spinning it, then explaining what silence and spin had done, he proved, in the long run, skilled, if not flawlessly, at all three. Among other things, it's a great example why "democracy" is not sufficient to explain American political history without an equally rigorous reckoning with the versions of nationalism and slavery politics that figures like Adams mediated with more and less success. Adams moved from a nationalism that compromised and silenced slavery to an antislavery nationalism. The move was not simply gradual, however: events during 1819–21 thrust him toward antislavery politics ideologically but backward practically. He came to embody the studied silence of a Constitution he came to view with increasing skepticism, and that silence allowed him to remain a National Republican standard-bearer and to become president. The Missouri Crisis proved a fulcrum in his career, setting the stage for the "failure" that came of his statesmanlike success. He helped make the compromise, understood what he had done, and elaborated on it in those most quotable of quotations in his diary. This key punctuation in his career can help us understand slavery as politics and governance. It also points to the peculiarly American tradition of practicing that politics while also denying its existence and blaming it on others.

♠

First things first. The beginnings of Adams's career matter—and so does his father's career. Even before 1776 the senior John Adams had prided himself on his ability to get along with southerners like Thomas Jefferson. He was among the first to realize that silence on slavery would be the price of intercolonial unity and, later, independence. In the Continental Congress he repeatedly noted southern colleagues' restlessness as matters of representation, taxation, and military service led to policy debates that could affect the future of slavery. In response, he sought to tamp down the issue, expressing resignation or a wish that the question at hand would be compromised. Adams's specific political roles during the war and the 1780s reinforced his sense of the delicate geopolitics of slavery and his preference for balance in the service of national unity. He promoted sectional balance in the officer corps of the Continental army. He insisted on distance from foreign powers and argued in a learned treatise that America's new republican governments were radical enough when considered in light of world history.[7] While John Quincy Adams served as his father's secretary in Paris, he had little to no reason to believe that the duty of a statesman or diplomat in a republican confederation required him to condemn slavery. If anything, it might require abjuring such excesses.

The younger Adams made his name by developing his father's revolutionary nationalism publicly and eloquently. In his July 1787 commencement address at Harvard, he ascribed the "critical period, when the whole nation is groaning," to the failure of "national credit," the foundation of "national grandeur." Economic distress in Massachusetts could ultimately be understood as the "erosion of the bands of union which connected us to our sister states, [which] have been shamefully relaxed by a selfish and contracted principle," an unwillingness to pay taxes to retire the Revolutionary War debt. Localism was the problem, thinking bigger the solution. When Massachusetts folk abided by their agreements, the "radiant sun of our union" would not only reappear but begin, again, to protect "the wretched object of tyranny and persecution in every corner of the globe." This was a call to republican virtue, to be sure, but one that deliberately emphasized national union over the rather specific events in Massachusetts that summer of Shays's Rebellion.[8]

The years John Quincy Adams had spent abroad confirmed his nascent American exceptionalism as well as his sense that what Americans had in common trumped any relationship that might be forged with particular European nations. At a time when his father, now vice president, was being attacked as a closet monarchist, Anglophile, and old-fashioned champion of "balanced," insufficiently democratic constitutions, John Quincy insisted in his first published newspaper essays that the U.S. Constitution (which he had actually at first opposed in 1787) had the virtues of both the British and the new French constitutions "without the evils of both." He gained the attention of the rest of the Washington administration with thorough defenses of the neutrality policy as the only sure guide against partisanship and "foreign usurpation." Earlier than most, and more consistently, he defined both British and French influence in America as "the shameful fetters of a foreign bondage."[9]

Successes in the arena of nonpartisan statesmanship affected the younger man's sense of who he was and could be. When Washington offered John Quincy a position abroad, he worried about leaving the center of the action, but his father argued, apparently from experience, that a diplomatic post would develop his connections to "able Men in the southern and middle States as well as in the northern ones." In 1795, during the increasingly strained period in Anglo-American relations, he responded anxiously to the sectional cast of politics, construing British undersecretary Hammond's attempt to sound him out as a kind of seduction: "What sort of soul does this man think I have? He talked about the Virginians, the Southern People, the democrats; but I let him know that I consider them all in no other light than as Americans." Six months later, he wrote his brother of his worry that a war with Great Britain would split the country: "All my hopes of national felicity and glory have invariably been founded upon the continuance of the union. . . . Much as I must disapprove of the general tenor of southern politics," he wrote, "I would rather even yield to their unreasonable pretensions and suffer much for their wrongs, than break the chain that binds us together." Without union, the United States would be swamped by the European powers anyway. During these years Adams contemplated quitting the diplomatic corps and settling in the South, perhaps in Georgia. The next year he shocked his parents by marrying Louisa Catherine Johnson, the daughter of a prominent Maryland merchant, whom he met in London.[10]

Watching U.S. politics from his post in Berlin during his father's presidency, Adams remained aloof from the Anglophile and Francophile extremes. He shared his father's pride in avoiding war with France: "You were not the man of any party, but of the whole nation," he wrote, in a turn of phrase that would become a mantra. News of Gabriel's Rebellion spurred him to write to his brother that "those absurd principles of unlimited democracy which the people of the southern states . . . encouraged, are producing their natural fruits, and if the planters have not discovered the inconsistency of holding in one hand the rights of man and in the other a scourge for the back of slaves, their negroes have proven themselves better logicians than their masters." Nevertheless, he hoped the "dreaded catastrophe" of Haiti would not recur: the eastern states should help put down any slave rebellion. While he imagined a Black Haiti itself in a possible alliance with the United States, as indeed a kind of proof of the new dispensation—a postcolonial new world beyond "metropolis and colony, or in other words master and servant"—he saw Caribbean revolt in terms of its implications for American independence, not the future of African slavery. Slave revolt was most interesting insofar as it became another way to convince southerners the error of their political ways, though he feared that nothing short of actual insurrection would force "democratisers of the Old Dominion" to "feel their need of assistance from their sister states, [and] the importance of the Union to them."[11]

When he returned to the United States and won a seat in the Massachusetts state senate, Adams participated with his brother in the *Port Folio* circle and shared in its culturally specific Federalist nostalgia. He saw the need to "look coolly" at the possibility that the federal Union might not last, though he did not think that Jefferson (with whom he had discussed slavery in Paris fifteen years earlier) had disunion in mind.[12] He scolded his brother Thomas, for example, for a piece that sneered at Washington DC's southern sensibilities. He did, however, follow closely the revelations by James Thomson Callendar about Sally Hemings and published anonymously a parody of Jefferson's alleged paternity of her children.

Dear Thomas, deem it no disgrace
With slaves to mend thy breed,

Nor let the wench's smutty face
Deter thee from thy deed.

Prefaced by a quote from Jefferson's *Notes on the State of Virginia* about a young country and its *"generative force of nature,"* this very free translation of a Horatian ode about a master in love with his slave mocked Jefferson as a would-be emperor whose inflated sense of self-worth, like Nero, allowed him to break his own rules, abetted by hack journalists.[13]

Elevated in 1803 to the U.S. Senate, John Quincy Adams had found a political home in New England Federalism, partly by necessity. Yet consider how careful and scrupulous he was being. He was the lone Federalist senator to vote both to admit the territory and against limiting slavery in Louisiana. This may have confused a lot of people; to judge from some recent scholarship, it still does.[14] Adams's fellow Federalists were not at all impressed with the junior senator's semantic accuracy or his muted distaste for slavery when he wasn't supporting his party, his region, or the actual antislavery legislation that was on the table. What they could not have missed was that Adamsian attitudes toward American diplomacy and empire dovetailed with Jeffersonian expansionism. He also found himself newly in tune with an administration that seemed committed to neutrality in order to best protect American interests and borders. Besides, he believed that a U.S. senator should seek to represent the interests of the entire nation. While other New Englanders canvassed against Jefferson in the election of 1804, John Quincy Adams conferred at the White House about foreign affairs, explaining in letters to his father why his seeming apostasy made sense.[15]

In the meantime, he tried to fashion a constructive critique of planter ascendancy that would preserve balance and the Union. He wrote a speech defending the Ely amendment: a proposal, originating in the Massachusetts assembly, to eliminate the three-fifths clause. But he did not actually deliver it on the Senate floor: instead, he published a revised and extended version anonymously in a Boston newspaper. As an electioneering piece that raked New England Jeffersonians for kowtowing to Virginians, the "Publius Valerius" series is notable both for its structural analysis of slaveholders' political power and for its well-developed argument for constitutional adjustment in a permanent union.[16]

Adams did not try to argue his way out of the implications of the Louisiana Purchase, which he was known to have supported. New England's present and future decline in power was "founded in nature." The real question was whether southern power would be "enjoyed with moderation." Things had not worked out as anticipated in 1787: slaveholders reaped their representation but without the federal taxation that had been part of the deal, since no direct tax had been passed except during the war scare of 1798, during the Adams administration.[17] As a result, representation in the United States had turned "unequal and oppressive" to states holding few or no slaves: "At present the people of the United States consist of two classes. A privileged order of slave-holding Lords, and a race of men degraded to a lower station, merely because they are not slave-holders." Northerners had representation by numbers but planters by numbers plus property, so "we are doubly taxed, and they are doubly represented." It was a vicious cycle: less representation meant less power to determine economic policy and taxes. How else could one explain the election of a president who identified cities, not slaves, as sores on the body politic?

Besides, the reopening of the slave trade by South Carolina meant that the Constitution, as it currently operated, "makes the highest privilege of freedom the purchase of accumulated slavery." Jeffersonians who argued that the Ely amendment insulted the slave states and endangered the Union made a "slavish" argument, "the language of a negro driver." A good constitutional amendment restoring balance to representation and taxation would actually save the Union. The speech he had drafted for the Senate debate made the argument for constitutional change even more pointedly. The compromise of 1787 was no longer fair. The South was more than safe: it was in the saddle. All sections had "a deep a permanent and a paramount interest in *Union*." Planter interest in the Union should allow for an adjustment. For his own part, he avoided politicizing slavery with respect to other issues that came before the Senate, including trade with Haiti and slave-trade abolition. Impressed by a young Henry Clay's speech against the slave trade, he wrote in his diary that "I took, and intend to take, no part in the debates on this subject."[18]

Looking back, Adams identified the Chesapeake affair and the embargo crisis in 1807 as a decisive moment in his political career. He decided to attend a Republican-sponsored town meeting in Boston, making his affiliation with the administration quite visible. Yet particularly because he had never publicly (or under his own name) engaged in Federalist denunciations of the Virginian "negro president," as the other Massachusetts senator did, he could plausibly insist on his own consistency. He supported the administration, he told a friend, because the nature of the Federalists' opposition, in time of war, could lead to civil war and the subservence of the Atlantic states to Britain. At a time when he was hearing rumors of a secession plot, he wrote to Harrison Gray Otis, an alleged plotter, of the need to consider the whole Union objectively. For Adams, New England disunionism was not only misguided but also "British usurpation," a deliberate effort to divide the sections and undermine the nation. The recurrent "Essex Junto" controversy, which has since seemed mythical or even comical, was deadly serious, even foundational, to Adams. Twenty years later, he spent some of the waning weeks of his presidency writing a book-length corrective to Otis's attempt to deny the existence of a New England conspiracy, arguing that if anything he himself deserved credit for the end of the embargo because of his timely conception of the extent of the crisis. He had gone directly to President Jefferson with news of the plot, arguing that the embargo be repealed to combat the secret Federalist-British negotiations. His efforts were particularly appreciated by Secretary of State James Madison, who compared Massachusetts's rapid unseating of Adams as senator to the backbiting he and Jefferson received from the likes of John Randolph, who repeatedly called them soft on federal threats to the South and slavery. Before it became clear that he would be consoled with a diplomatic post, Adams wrote in his diary that he had "sacrificed" himself to "the Constitution."[19]

In short, Adams early on had, in substance, the analysis of the slave power—but he held back. Why? The answer lies in his unionism, by which light he saw not only political parties but also sectionally specific appeals. For the next decade, Adams bewailed partisan Federalist dissent as "British" usurpation. What we begin to see in 1806–7 is John Quincy Adams, the son of a former president and leading revolutionary, functioning as a pedigreed proof of the nationalism of National Republicans at a time of rising sectionalism. In this important sense, the roots of his role in the Missouri Crisis go back decades. His genuine expertise on both Massachusetts and Britain reinforced the party's increasingly common sense that antislavery noises were really British threats. New England Federalism's willingness to justify or wink at British impressment proved its hypocrisy. The slave trade was admittedly terrible, but abolitionists in England and the United States were factional and impressment just as bad as slavery. This theme runs through his letters as well as his diary.

Adams consistently bewailed the British threat and the partisan nature of Federalist dissent, so much so that he came to function as an exception that proved the rule for the Jeffersonians. His expertise on both Massachusetts and Britain reinforced the party's sense of the threat to the Union. Reading from St. Petersburg of his senatorial successor's attempt to derail Louisiana statehood in 1811, he wrote home that though he loved his native region, he could as easily settle on the banks of the Red River. The continent was destined to be one nation. "The relative proportion of power between the different members of the Union is as insignificant, as the same question between the North End and the South End" of Boston. In the same series of letters, he reflected on the relationship between his own political philosophy and that of his father. John Adams had been more consistently concerned about how social questions could corrupt a republic, but "*Union* is to me what the *balance* is to you, and without this there can be no good government among mankind in any state, so without that there can be no good government among the people of North America in the state in which God has been pleased to place them."[20]

For years he had been especially appalled at the impressment of sailors and some New England leaders' willingness to justify it as the cost of doing business, or even a British right. When the time came, he did not hesitate to call it a just cause for war. British sailors were their Helots; they were kidnapped "like African negroes," and by 1812 he called it "manstealing" to Madame de Stael and any other European who would listen. Everything he read while in St. Petersburg confirmed his predictions. The impressment issue informed his unwillingness to give any ground at Ghent regarding American demands for compensation for liberated slaves. They were private property. To concede British rights to tamper with American bodies would mean caving in to British imperial pretensions. He swallowed and broadcast the American line that British officers had "taken" slaves during the War of 1812 only to sell them in the West Indies. If slaves could be enticed, he asked Lord Liverpool, where were the limits to war?

Postwar efforts to cooperate against the slave trade also foundered, for Adams, upon questions of sovereignty. One could not trust the British to board American ships or try American citizens. The idea that ships of all nations could be boarded by each other was an example of British "impudence," he explained to a "disappointed" William Wilberforce. Later he went so far as to worry that the disposition of Africans liberated from illegal slavers would interfere with states' rights to determine their free or bound status. Only in 1823 did he find a way to get around the impressment comparison—by defining slave traders as pirates at war with the world.[21]

First provided a face-saving ambassadorship to Russia after the Massachusetts Senate canned him, Adams's consistency, his sectional identity, and his loyalty to the regime earned him the coveted State Department post in Monroe's administration. The prior two secretaries of state—Virginians—had proceeded directly to the presidency. There was considerable irony in the structural position Adams had come to play among National Republicans. He was the New England man in the cabinet, there for sectional balance as well as his manifest skills, and thus suspect, but he was also a one-man argument for the flourishing of nationalism, and the end of partisanship and sectionalism, in the Era of Good Feelings.

The self-evident breakdown of the Virginia chain of succession, however, helped turn the Monroe presidency into an eight-year presidential campaign, affecting dynamics inside a cabinet stuffed with would-be successors, as well as in the Congress, where Henry Clay nursed his wounds and looked for allies. Relying especially on Adams's diary, Ernest F. May brilliantly analyzed how the secretary of state's careful distancing from Britain in the seemingly bold Monroe Doctrine reflected his need to seem unlike a Yankee Anglophile (much less an antislavery one) in the lead-up to the election of 1824. The secretary's stalwart refusal to enter a concord regarding the slave trade reflected the same dynamics.[22]

In this way, Adams came to play a key role in National Republicanism's bid to bind the nation together and secure a partisan antipartisan future.[23] The politicization of slavery that had already occurred during the war threatened that vision, whether in the southern Old Republican proslavery states' rights version or in a northern antislavery qua anti-Virginia key. Most striking in this phase of Adams's career was his political success in working with Madison and Monroe—even at the expense of southerners Henry Clay, John C. Calhoun, and William H. Crawford.

When General Andrew Jackson crossed the border and almost provoked a war with England and Spain, that trio proved ready, with good reason, to disavow Jackson and his insistence that border security and slave property justified aggressive action against the Seminoles and their freelance English allies.[24] But Adams sized up the geopolitics and the domestic politics and defended Jackson's actions. In his widely circulated public letter to consul William Erving, he depicted the British men Jackson tried and executed as at the head of a "negro-Indian banditti," "parti-colored forces" in the service of a possible British invasion. Everyone knew that Great Britain used "savages" to fight Americans: they had caused every Indian war since 1776. Arbuthnot and Armbrister were "political filters to fugitive slaves and Indian outlaws," and the laws of war entitled Jackson to hang them without the court-martial he provided. To his father Adams wrote that it had been justifiable self-defense on Jackson's part. Besides, partisan attacks on Jackson were really directed at *him*.[25]

Together, Jackson and Adams pried Florida and more from Spain. As diplomatic historians like William Earl Weeks and James E. Lewis Jr. have shown us, the Transcontinental Treaty was a key context for the Missouri Crisis and *the* key one for Adams. The Missouri controversy arose at the moment—an extended moment, just like that of Missouri—of Adams's real diplomatic triumph, but one that remained vulnerable. Because of various complications, the ratification of the Adams-Onís Treaty by the Senate and by Spain was almost as drawn out as that of the Missouri statehood legislation.

But in light of Deborah Rosen's recent book and other work on Jackson and expansion, we need to push this interpretation a bit further. Just as much as Jackson, Adams had taken advantage of the fugitive-slave issue in Florida and combined it with emergency "war" powers to provoke an easily won conflict with Spain to expand the nation. No wonder Adams saw Jackson as an ally and attacks on the general, as he put it in the letter to his father, as really about him. Adams's immediate success at growing the nation in a southwesterly direction is part of what made the question of slavery in a new state so momentous in 1819, part of why more northerners were unwilling to go along with more slave states.[26] In this real sense, Adams helped cause the Missouri Crisis. Southern-dominated National Republicanism succeeded all too well in 1819 because it had Adams and Adams had it.

In discussions within the cabinet, Adams took the position that slavery restriction for Missouri was unconstitutional and inconsistent with the Louisiana Purchase Treaty. He continued to worry that Missouri would derail the Spanish treaty. The pressures mounted. On January 3, 1820, he wrote in his diary that Missouri was "yet in a state of chaos in my mind." He asked his wife, Louisa Catherine, to insert a request in one of her regular letters to his father begging him not to be quoted on Missouri, even in the decidedly unlikely event that the eighty-four-year-old John Adams would break his entire life's practice and write something antislavery for public consumption. "Mr. A," wrote Louisa to her father-in-law, "has never given any opinion on this business and is not at all pleased to be drawn into it as long as he can possibly avoid it." Louisa herself had already become a factor just by sitting in the Senate gallery, where, listening to an attack on restriction, "even my Countenance was watched" for clues as to her husband's sympathies. On February 4, 1820, John Quincy wondered if Rufus King was thinking disunion, for any politician so willing to condemn slavery in public should realize "it must end in that." Yet a week later he wrote that he would have to be prepared for an active role in the crisis.[27]

The orator and statesman felt himself drawn in. The problem with the restrictionists' arguments was that they were not bold enough. All the passion lay with the proslavery side, he mused. He foresaw a new arrangement of parties—never a good thing to an Adams. Still, "this is a question between the rights of human nature and the Constitution of the United States. Probably both will suffer by the issue of this controversy." During a gripping evening with John C. Calhoun, he came face-to-face with the emerging positive good argument on behalf of slavery expansion. "He said he did not think it would produce a dissolution of the Union, but if it should the South would be from necessity compelled to form and Alliance Offensive and Defensive with Britain." The founding fiction that slavery would die of its own accord or wither from the end of the international slave trade had clearly faded if the cabinet colleague he most admired for his intelligence and devotion to the republic found a neocolonial dependence on Great Britain preferable to a union in which slavery existed on sufferance, banned from the western future. That evening he composed the first of the now much-quoted predictions of civil war and emancipation: "Slavery is the great and foul stain upon the North-American Union; and it is a contemplation worthy of the most exalted soul, whether its total abolition is or is not practicable. . . . This object is vast in its compass—awful in its prospects, sublime and beautiful in its issue. A Life devoted to it would be nobly spent or sacrificed." Nine days later, on March 4, Adams joined a cabinet majority advising the president that slavery restriction in territories was, in fact, constitutional.[28]

His own position had flipped, but clarified. Slavery questions were restricted to the states where slavery existed; where it did not yet exist was a different matter. Missouri was ambiguous, so a deal was inevitable. "The fault is in the Constitution of the United States, which has sanctioned a dishonorable compromise with slavery." The dishonor lay in the conflict with the Declaration of Independence, which had grounded the American Revolution in the consent of the governed. Yet now it was clearer than ever that "slave representation has governed the Union." Maybe he should not have signed on to the compromise by failing to object to it in the cabinet meetings. Maybe he could propose a constitutional convention that would address the problem.[29]

In public, however, he stayed out of the line of fire. Revealingly, in his diary he expressed increased admiration for Rufus King's stance while (in a striking instance of projection) noting that it scotched any hopes the sixty-nine-year-old New York Federalist might still have of becoming president.

Meanwhile, the debates in Congress continued to slow consideration of the Spanish treaty. Missouri was "a flaming sword that waves round on all sides and cuts in every direction," including across his desk as questions suddenly arose about slavery in Florida or, someday, Texas. What did he think? If we read the diary literally, or look for consistency or ideology, he appears ambivalent but leaning more and more antislavery. But what he thought mattered less than what he said—and didn't say—in public. He stayed out of the line of fire. He was a cabinet officer, not a congressman; he maintained secrecy, but documented everything. He spoke differently to different colleagues on the matter, or literally divided himself: as a "servant of the whole union" he had to represent the interests of all, but as an "eastern man" he certainly expected resolutions against slavery in the next wave of territories.[30]

It was only the second Missouri Crisis, over the new constitution that banned free Black people, that made Adams sure what side he was on, though he was hardly more forthcoming or public about it. The new Missouri constitution that deprived free Black people of rights was unconstitutional and had to be resisted, he said to congressmen privately. His most explicit predictions of disunion, "servile war," and the end of slavery date from this period: "If the dissolution of the Union must come, let it come from no other cause than this," he wrote in his diary on November 29, 1820.[31] But it did not come, and three months later he could write that while constitutional conflict would return, this was not the proper time. Not at all coincidentally, he was already beginning to talk about his presidential prospects with supporters, even while predicting that slavery in the territories would be the decisive issue in the 1824 contest.

The year 1821 instead saw the defining statement of his first career, a July 4 address in Washington, DC, that depicted "conquest and servitude" as "mingled up in every part of the social existence" of Britain—not the United States. The settlement of New England, by contrast, which stood in for the entire nation, involved the purchase of Indian lands and a social compact "in which conquest and servitude had no part." The Declaration of Independence delegitimized nation formation based "upon conquest. It swept away the rubbish of accumulated centuries of servitude." The United States stood for natural and equal rights. It was not an empire; "her glory is not dominion, but liberty." What have you done for the benefit of mankind? Adams asked rhetorically of Britain, and in an aside he actually said that we won't ask who invented the steamboat and the cotton gin—the same American inventions that were spreading African slavery faster than ever. Russian minister Pierre de Poletica, a friend of Adams from St. Petersburg days, was so appalled by the Anglophobia and wishful thinking in this "virulent diatribe" that he sent home a copy of the published oration with his own marginalia: "How about your two million black slaves who cultivate a great expanse of your territory for your particular and exclusive advantage? You forget the poor Indians whom you have not ceased to spoil. You forget your conduct toward Spain."[32]

Adams sent a copy of the address to his friend Edward Everett and gloated that certain "Eastern politicians" had not appreciated his drubbing of the English: those same characters had been against him ever since his 1787 address (a remark that reveals just how much he understood his career as a series of rhetorical occasions). Instead, he had served "my country" and two presidents from Virginia, though he had "never flattered her prejudices." While he gained fame for his foreign policy successes, he identified all the more with the National Republicans and tried to push for internal improvements, which he still thought possible under the current regime. The Louisiana Purchase had changed the Constitution, he surmised in his diary, and Virginians made it happen, so "Virginian constitutional scruples were accommodating things." Post–Missouri Compromise, what's striking is his continued optimism about union with slavery and insistence that he wasn't, couldn't possibly be, a sectionalist. The Constitution could be adjusted if necessary. In classic politician fashion, he thought that everything would be all right in the short-enough term. Diary eloquence notwithstanding, Missouri proved no fire bell in the night for John Quincy Adams. If his ears had rung, he got used to the sound.[33]

The Missouri Compromise, in this sense, was for Adams another transcontinental treaty, a bargain worthwhile even if not of his own making, even if it dirtied the Constitution and put off a likely reckoning. Yet in part because he had played both sides, Adams's own room for maneuver narrowed as the election of 1824 neared. Supporters in the South wanted to hear that he had opposed the Tallmadge Amendment, so he went back to his earliest diary entries for proof, ignoring what had come after. He told South Carolinian George McDuffie that his opinions had been greatly misrepresented: he had never favored restriction; he was just against the Missouri Constitution as a violation of both the U.S. Constitution and the Louisiana treaty. Adams confided in one supporter that he thought the opposition to the Anglo-American slave-trade convention had been scared up only "to raise a popular clamor against me." He told his wife that even the controversy over the Amelia Island expedition against slave traders had served instrumentally "to bar my access to the next Presidency." Unlike his cabinet rivals, he "should be President of not a section, nor of a faction, but of the whole Union."[34]

His coy "Macbeth policy" of allowing himself to be chosen rather than building a tight network reflected more than a disinclination to campaign or create a political party: it included a resolve to "indulge no sectional antipathies," a tendency he equated with partisanship. To Robert Walsh, who had declared him the favorite of the "universal Yankee nation," he wrote, "I have no more certainty of being the choice of the Yankee than of the Virginia Nation. I have been too much and too long the servant of the whole union to be the favorite of any one part of it. The whole course of my political life has been that of crossing partial interests whether sectional, political or geographical." As if this wasn't clear enough, he reminded Walsh how unpopular he was with Massachusetts Federalists and that he owed his appointments to Virginia presidents so it would be "ingratitude" as well as "illiberality" to have prejudices against Virginia. He avoided all comment on slavery-related matters in 1824: when friends northern or southern wrote to him for such a statement, noted biographer Samuel Flagg Bemis, "he would not even answer their letters." Adams, in other words, remained confident that "slave representation" and expansion could be managed—and that he was the one to manage them.[35]

The problem was that post-Missouri, as Robert P. Forbes and Richard R. John have observed, any ambitious federal policy called attention to slavery, at a moment of southern slavery's simultaneous rapid growth in the Southwest and seeming vulnerability in the Southeast. Presidents Madison and Monroe had hit this wall repeatedly even as they helped build it. President Adams tried to be neutral on slavery-related issues, and indeed not to raise them at all, but the fears of so many white southerners during his presidency, and the political hay they made by voicing them, were every bit as real as the apparent spread of antislavery sentiment that inspired them. Robert Hayne of South Carolina pounced on the Panama Congress, insisting quite specifically that the appointment of Pennsylvanian John Sergeant—a strident Missouri slavery restrictionist—as the envoy proved that diplomatic relations with emancipating republics raised "domestic questions." Georgia refused to reconsider the fraudulent Treaty of Indian Springs, in an episode that foreshadowed the nullification crisis but did not become a confrontation because Adams simply did not have the political capital to insist on his constitutional authority—especially when he was already suspected to be antislavery. Congressional allies came begging for assurances that his administration would not emancipate. JQA had lived, politically, by equivocating on slavery issues; now he was dying by it.[36]

He could not advocate for union and a vigorous, activist state while drawing regional distinctions. The problem may be seen in his response to the Negro Seamen's Act in 1825, which he found undoubtedly unconstitutional and not a little outrageous. Carolinians wanted assurances about slave property, but they had put it out of his hands by patently contradicting the rights of free Black people. Yet he should not force a confrontation. "To be silent, is not to interfere with state rights; and not to interfere, renounces no right of ourselves and others." His version of the federal consensus, which presumed neutrality and silence, had lost the initiative. Since Missouri, the politics of slavery had been renovated by his partisan opponents, in a proslavery key. They were making the links between slavery and politics—and in the process undoing his agenda. So slavery remained off-limits for as long as he remained in the White House, including in the campaign of 1828.[37]

It was only after the presidency that he began to think more on the structural factors that had made him, and perhaps his father too, a one-term nonpartisan president. Current events provided enough grist for him to work out his revision of American political history. By 1831–32 and the nullification crisis, the former president had developed a historical analysis positing the irreducible conflict between slavery and national sovereignty. The key move was to complete his evolution from loyalty to the Constitution as it was to emphasizing the Declaration of Independence as a preexisting *national* compact.[38]

The final essential rhetorical building blocks for Adams's antislavery nationalism came together in the wake of the Second Seminole War and the issue of Texas annexation. In 1836, national politics had entered back into his areas of special expertise: war and peace, treaties, borders, sovereignty. "There was an appropriation of 80,000 dollars for suppressing the hostilities of the Seminole Indians, the authority for which was nothing more than a Letter from the Secretary of War to the Chair of the Committee on Ways and Means," he noted in his diary on January 6, 1836, twelve days before James Henry Hammond silenced him with the gag rule. As he mulled the implications of an undebated, undeclared war, and proceeded to demand documents from the administration on Texas, he noted to a constituent that the ongoing petition debate had not allowed him "to speak a tenth part of my mind." It was not that he failed to rail like an abolitionist about the fallacy of property in man under the laws of God and nature. That wasn't his job, not under the Constitution. He had something else in mind, something potentially more dangerous to the proslavery consensus in Washington. "I did not start the question whether in the event of a servile insurrection and war Congress would not have complete and unlimited control over the whole subject of slavery, even to the emancipation of all the slaves in the State where such insurrection should break out, and for the suppression of which the freemen of Plymouth and Norfolk counties, Massachusetts, should be called by Acts of Congress to pour out their treasures and to shed their blood. Had I spoken my mind on those two points," Adams wrote, "the sturdiest of the abolitionists would have disavowed the sentiments of their champion."[39]

If Adams could not raise these constitutional questions in the context of a debate over slavery in Washington, DC, or the right of petition, he could still raise them in the different context of war and the war powers of Congress—avoiding, in the process, any reference to Massachusetts. The "Negro and Indian War, already raging within our borders," and the likelihood of a "Mexican War" over Texas, had possibilities that the slave trade in Washington, DC, or even the gag rule did not precisely because they illustrated slavery's tendency to ramify across realms of public policy, to recur during international crises, and above all to complicate expansion. A seemingly minor issue of funds for Second Seminole War refugees in Georgia and Alabama crystallized the argument for wartime emancipation. That issue allowed him to link the petitions debate with the larger problem of slavery as national governance.

He undid the great silence about slavery as governance and as an institution that was far from static but rather had changed and grown as a result of policy. Appropriations for refugees, Adams argued on the floor of the House on May 25, 1836, had only ever been approved by Congress twice: for the Florida Territory in the First Seminole War and for victims of the Caracas earthquake of 1812, both inapplicable precedents. The only conceivable justification for congressional action lay in the war powers under the Constitution. That power lay with Congress, and it was "tremendous." And it was the very reason he had wanted to explain his vote a few weeks earlier against the Pinckney Committee's first resolution on the matter of antislavery petitions. Congress could not declare that it had no power to interfere with slavery because to do so would disavow its own constitutional responsibilities in time of war. Anyone who was for national defense—anyone who was for union—had to admit that Congress had these powers. Anyone who remembered the War of 1812, Adams said, gesturing in the process to his own shining moment of loyalty, knew that the very arguments he had made on behalf of Congress in the Treaty of Ghent against the right of the British to carry away slaves presumed the ability to deal with slaves and to regulate the comings and goings of slaves and other persons, even if those powers had almost always been exercised to insist that the chains stay on. If Congress could not deal with slavery, it could not make treaties. If it could not make treaties, it could not make war or peace, much less protect slave property in time of war.[40]

To govern the Union was to govern slavery. The exercise of national state power could and would infringe on the claimed rights of slaveholders. The example of 1812 opened up the actual relationship between war and slavery, so apparent in every American war yet so muted in the whitened memory of them. A civil war, indeed, was under way in Mexico between nationals who had abolished slavery and settlers who wanted to reintroduce it. This was "a war of aggression, of conquest, of slave making."[41] The new, second, Seminole conflict obviously replayed the drama of slave raids that had spurred the First Seminole War eighteen years before. Drawing an apocalyptic vision of North American conflict and possible European interference, the former president drew on his encyclopedic knowledge of diplomatic history and his own record of service to insist that the present and predictable future wars, like past ones, would require the government to protect slave property—or, if necessary, sacrifice slave property.

Where does this leave us in our quest to understand this enigmatic "lost founding founder" and the Missouri Crisis?

In a real sense, John Quincy Adams was a representative as well as leading figure in the crisis. He might be said to have moved toward, first, antislavery principles as a result of Missouri, yet that change in thinking remained private. He helped the compromise happen by both what he did and what he did not do, in the cabinet and in public. The experience of 1819–21 confirmed his earlier sense of slavery as an issue not to be touched by statesmen with nationalist agendas. This sensibility—and the heightened suspicions others had of him—shaped his presidential campaign and his presidency, enabling both while nevertheless setting him up for failure. Reflecting on that failure, he reached for the alternative: a politics that highlighted, that theorized, that voiced instead of silencing, how slavery was connected to other aspects of American politics. It wasn't abolitionism; it was what abolitionism required to succeed.

For current scholarship, Adams shows the importance of treating slavery as normal politics—not just as institution, or ideology, or social movement, or version of capitalism—and as bound up organically and institutionally, not merely strategically, with partisan and nationalist agendas earlier, more consistently, and more deeply than our existing narratives of democratization allow. Perhaps the Missouri Crisis was not so much the pivot or the beginning of sectional politics as it was the epitome of the politics of slavery between the first and second American Revolutions, the first and second American civil wars, the first and second American emancipations, the first and second reconstructions.[42] Like the state of Missouri itself, the crisis stands in the middle, chronologically as well as geographically, both cause and consequence of a Union with continental ambitions built on slavery, on the denial of slavery's nature and of slavery's significance as politics, and on the antislavery denial of that denial.

Notes

1. John Quincy Adams Diary, January 10, 11, 1820, *The Diaries of John Quincy Adams: A Digital Collection* (Boston: Massachusetts Historical Society, 2004), http://www.masshist.org/jqadiaries (hereafter referred to as JQA Diary).

2. William J. Cooper, *The Lost Founding Father: John Quincy Adams and the Transformation of American Politics* (New York: Liveright, 2017), 305; Samuel Flagg Bemis, *John Quincy Adams and the Foundations of American Foreign Policy* (New York: Alfred A. Knopf, 1949) and *John Quincy Adams and the Union* (New York: Alfred A. Knopf, 1956); Ernest R. May, *The Making of the Monroe Doctrine* (Cambridge, MA: Belknap Press of Harvard University Press, 1975); Leonard L. Richards, *The Life and Times of Congressman John Quincy Adams* (New York: Oxford University Press, 1986); Paul C. Nagel, *John Quincy Adams: A Public Life, a Private Life* (New York: Alfred A. Knopf, 1997); William Earl Weeks, *John Quincy Adams and American Global Empire* (Lexington: University Press of Kentucky, 1992); Richard H. Immerman, *Empire of Liberty: A History of American Imperialism from Benjamin Franklin to Paul Wolfowitz* (Princeton, NJ: Princeton University Press, 2009), chap. 2; Stephen M. Chambers, *No God but Gain: The Untold Story of Cuban Slavery, the Monroe Doctrine, and the Making of the United States* (New York: Verso, 2015). For overviews and a review of the literature, see David Waldstreicher, "John Quincy Adams: The Life, the Diary and the Biographers," in *A Companion to John Adams and John Quincy Adams*, ed. Waldstreicher, 241–62 (Malden, MA: Wiley-Blackwell, 2013); and David Waldstreicher and Matthew Mason, eds., *John Quincy Adams and the Politics of Slavery: Selections from the Diary* (New York: Oxford University Press, 2017), ix–xxi.

3. Sean Wilentz, *No Property in Man: Slavery and Antislavery at the Nation's Founding* (Cambridge, MA: Harvard University Press, 2018), 177, 180.

4. In his self-serving review in the *Atlantic* of Nancy Isenberg and Andrew Burstein's excellent joint biography, *The Problem of Democracy: The Presidents Adams Confront the Cult of Personality* (New York: Viking, 2019), John Quincy does nothing right until he supposedly embraces a political party as well as abolition in the late 1830s. Wilentz, "The Problem with High-Minded Politics," *Atlantic*, May 2019, https://www.theatlantic.com/magazine/archive/2019/05/john-adams-john-quincy-adams-political-parties/586018/. Strangely, Wilentz took a more gradualist approach,

leaning on Leonard L. Richards's 1986 study of the congressional years, in his review of Nagel's biography in 1997, at least as revised and republished in his 2018 essay collection. In the introduction to that collection, however, Adams remains the epitome of disastrous antipartisanship. Wilentz, *The Politicians and the Egalitarians: The Hidden History of American Politics* (New York: W. W. Norton, 2018), 28, 125–47.

5. Everett S. Brown, ed., *William Plumer's Memorandum of Proceedings in the United States Senate, 1803–1807* (New York: Macmillan, 1923), 119; Bemis, *Adams and the Foundations*, 118–23; John Craig Hammond, *Slavery, Freedom and Expansion in the Early American West* (Charlottesville: University of Virginia Press, 2007), 36; Waldstreicher and Mason, *Adams and the Politics of Slavery*, 14–18. In *Profiles in Courage* (New York: Harper & Brothers, 1956), 27–44, Senator John F. Kennedy, himself angling for southern support, declared Adams's stance against his party and section during the Louisiana debates to be admirable and principled. But he didn't call it antislavery.

6. That Wilentz never gave any Federalists any such credit for getting slavery right when writing about *The Rise of American Democracy: Jefferson to Lincoln* (New York: W. W. Norton, 2005), instead lambasting their opposition to the extension of slavery and to what they were beginning to call the "slave power" as merely partisan and sectional pique, suggests there is more at stake here than a leading historian's ability to contradict himself on the virtues of partisan loyalty. Wilentz's preference for winning strategies in short-term party politics—and denunciations of "idealist" alternatives—has more than a little to do with his miscomprehension of Adams and his place in the politics of slavery. So does his apparent insistence that we must have our useful and ideologically consistent founders wherever we can find or make them. Interpretively speaking, Wilentz indulges in a particular kind of originalism when he states that the Constitution is clear on something because of something that is not in the text (antislavery intentions). One admiring reviewer, Walter Russell Mead, picked up on this gleefully: "Wilentz is not an originalist himself, but the historical methods he employs here to uncover the intended meaning of the Constitution are exactly those that originalists use. Lawyers and jurists looking to develop arguments that will impress conservative judges would be well advised to study the tools Wilentz deploys to such great effect." https://www.foreignaffairs.com/reviews/capsule-review/2018-10-16/no-property-man-slavery-and-antislavery-nations-founding. To pick out one precedent, the counterfactually significant lack of a clause guaranteeing property in man, and to declare that decisive, is an interpretive mode of rather dubious pedigree. It's the mirror image of Roger Taney's infamous *Dred Scott* decision, which stated that because the founders did not say Black people were citizens, they never could be citizens. Similarly, Allen C. Guelzo has taken to the *National Review* to claim antislavery to be the true collective original intention of the framers, highlighting the same John Quincy Adams quote of 1804. (Those who argue otherwise are "postmodern" and "anti-constitutionalist sensationalists," self-evidently on the wrong side of the culture war. Guelzo, "The Constitution Was Never Proslavery," https://www.nationalreview.com/magazine/2019/05/06/the-constitution-was-never-pro-slavery/.) Wilentz has doubled down on this interpretive mode in a *New York Times* op-ed on the Electoral College. Because no proslavery intentions can be detected

in the convention's late discussions about the Electoral College (the key issues of representation in the House and Senate had already been decided, with compromises over slavery), the Electoral College is somehow free of that taint that slavery left on democracy in the United States. Wilentz, "The Electoral College Was Not a Proslavery Ploy," *New York Times*, April 4, 2019. It's especially ironic that originalists would turn to John Quincy Adams and the abolitionists, since they themselves spent the early nineteenth century experimenting with both sides of the debate about just how proslavery or antislavery the Revolution or the Constitution had been. Their thinking evolved as they looked for opportunities to push back against the southern-stacked deck of national politics under the Constitution, which allowed two senators for every state regardless of population and for three-fifths of slaves to be represented in Congress, affecting everything the legislature could do and every presidential election under the electoral college. Antislavery activists came out on both sides of the debate about whether the Constitution's silence implied slavery's absence from American law, or whether the Constitution deliberately strengthened the "slave power." Given the ambiguity of the silence, it shouldn't be surprising that some, like John Quincy Adams and Frederick Douglass, even changed their mind. Aaron R. Hall and Simon Gilhooley argue that what we think of as originalism itself emerged from this debate. Hall, "'Plant Yourselves on Its Primal Granite': Slavery, History and the Antebellum Roots of Originalism," *Law and History Review* 37, no. 3 (2019): 743–61; Gilhooley, *The Antebellum Origins of the Modern Constitution: Slavery and the Spirit of the American Founding* (New York: Cambridge University Press, 2020).

7. John Adams to Joseph Hawley, November 25, 1775, in *John Adams: Revolutionary Writings, 1775–1783*, ed. Gordon S. Wood (New York: Library of America, 2011), 36; David Waldstreicher, *Slavery's Constitution: From Revolution to Ratification* (New York: Hill and Wang, 2009), 51–52; Wendy H. Wong, "John Adams, Diplomat," and Karen N. Barzilay, "John Adams in the Continental Congress," in *Companion to John Adams and John Quincy Adams*, ed. Waldstreicher, 78–101, 125–41; Gordon S. Wood, "The Relevance and Irrelevance of John Adams," in *Revolutionary Characters* (New York: Penguin Press, 2006), 173–202. See also Arthur Scherr, *John Adams, Slavery, and Race: Ideas, Politics, and Diplomacy in an Age of Crisis* (Santa Barbara, CA: Praeger, 2018).

8. John Quincy Adams, "An Oration, Delivered at the Public Commencement in the University of Cambridge, in New England," *Columbian Magazine* 1 (September 1787): 625–28.

9. JQA, "Publicola," "Marcellus," and "Columbus," in *Writings of John Quincy Adams*, ed. Worthington Chauncey Ford (New York: Macmillan, 1913) (hereafter referred to as *WJQA*), 1:91, 159; Robert A. East, *John Quincy Adams: The Critical Years, 1785–1794* (New York: Bookman Associates, 1962), 31, 142.

10. JQA Diary, December 1, 1795, also in Waldstreicher and Mason, *Adams and the Politics of Slavery*, 10–12; Charles N. Edel, *Nation Builder: John Quincy Adams and the Grand Strategy for the Republic* (Cambridge, MA: Harvard University Press, 2014), 59; JQA to Charles Adams, June 9, 1796, in *WJQA*, 1:493–94; Bemis, *Adams and the Foundations*, 87; Nagel, *John Quincy Adams*, 97.

11. JQA to JA, November 25, 1800, JQA to William Vans Murray, March 20 and July 14, 1798, to Thomas Boylston Adams, July 11, November 25, December 3, 1800, to William Vans Murray, December 16, 1800, in *WJQA*, 2:271, 386, 398, 485–86n; JQA Diary, January 28, 1802. Compare Ronald Angelo Johnson, *Diplomacy in Black and White: John Adams, Toussaint Louverture, and Their Atlantic World Alliance* (Athens: University of Georgia Press, 2014), who interprets John Adams's Haiti policy as more intentionally pro-Black and antislavery than seems warranted by the evidence. If Thomas Jefferson's policy proved a departure, John Quincy Adams provided no record of seeing it that way.

12. Adams to William Vans Murray, April 7, 1801, in *WJQA*, 2:525–26; *Diary of John Quincy Adams*, ed. David Grayson Allen et al. (Cambridge, MA: Belknap Press of Harvard University Press, 1981), 1:262.

13. JQA to Rufus King, October 8, 1802, in *WJQA*, 3:7; "Original Poetry. For the Port Folio. Horace, Book II, Ode 4," *Port-Folio* 2:43 (October 30, 1802); Horace, *The Complete Odes and Epodes*, trans. David West (New York: Oxford University Press, 1997), 59; Linda K. Kerber, *Federalists in Dissent: Imagery and Ideology in Jeffersonian America* (Ithaca, NY: Cornell University Press, 1971), 25–26n, 51; Catherine O'Donnell Kaplan, *Men of Letters in the Early Republic: Cultivating Forums of Citizenship* (Chapel Hill: University of North Carolina Press, 2008), 145–46.

14. For example, despite citing an earlier version of this paper, Jan Ellen Lewis reports this as "Adams's emergence as an opponent of slavery" and the three-fifths clause before summarizing as "a bit incoherent" his arguments of 1804. Lewis, "What Happened to the Three Fifths Clause: The Relationship Between Women and Slaves in Constitutional Thought, 1787–1866," *Journal of the Early Republic* 37, no. 1 (2017): 10–12. See also Wilentz, *No Property in Man*, 180.

15. Robert R. Thompson, "John Quincy Adams, Apostate: From 'Outrageous Federalist' to 'Republican Exile,' 1801–1809," *Journal of the Early Republic* 11, no. 2 (1991): 161–83; JQA to JA, November 3, [November 1804], in *WJQA*, 3:78, 79.

16. Leonard L. Richards considers Adams's arguments in the debate on the Ely amendment an important moment in the evolution of the "numbers argument" against slave representation. Richards, *The Slave Power: The Free North and Southern Domination, 1780–1860* (Baton Rouge: Louisiana State University Press, 2000), 44–45. The speech did not appear in the Senate's printed debates. Most Adams scholars believe he did not deliver it and then rewrote the substance and published under "Publius Valerius" in the Boston *Repertory*. For the Ely amendment, see Kevin Vrevich, "Mr. Ely's Amendment: Massachusetts Federalists and the Politicization of Slave Representation," *American Nineteenth-Century History* 19, no. 2 (2018): 159–78.

17. For an analysis that would support Adams's reasoning, see Robin L. Einhorn, *American Taxation, American Slavery* (Chicago: University of Chicago Press, 2006).

18. "Publius Valerius," in *WJQA*, 3:49–50, 59, 70–71, 73; "Proposed Amendment to the Constitution on Representation [December 1804]," in *WJQA*, 3:88; JQA Diary, December 17, 1804, January 21, 1805, February 20 and December 24, 1806, January 15, 1807.

19. JQA to Harrison Gray Otis, March 31, 1808, to Orchard Cook, November 25, 1808, to Nahum Parker, December 8 and 15, 1808, to William Plumer, October 16, 1809, in *WJQA*, 4:193, 255–56, 258–59, 340–41; Henry Adams, ed., *Documents Relating to New England Federalism* (1877; reprint, Boston: Little, Brown, 1905), 11–13, 107–330; JQA Diary, January 20, April 23, 1808, May 31, 1820.

20. JQA to William Plumer, August 16, 1809, to Abigail Adams, June 30, 1811, to John Adams, August 31 and October 31, 1811, in *WJQA*, 3:341, 4:127–28, 208–9, 267.

21. Adams to Albert Gallatin and Richard Rush, November 2, 1818, in *WJQA*, 6:470–71; JQA Diary, November 10, 1812, September 1, 1814, June 6, 1817, October 30, 1818, March 12 and 16, 1819, December 4, 1821, June 19, 1823; Bemis, *Adams and the Foundation*, 428. Gallatin had first proposed the piracy definition at Ghent nine years earlier: Charles Francis Adams, ed., *Memoirs of John Quincy Adams* (Philadelphia: J. B. Lippincott, 1874–77), 3:97.

22. May, *Making of the Monroe Doctrine*, 180–84. Stephen Chambers argues that Adams finessed American desires to keep trade open with Cuba: Adams "wed the resurrection of his political career to the products of the slave trade," and the Monroe Doctrine was "crafted to protect the illegal slave trade," but in Chambers's account Adams then suddenly breaks with this and pushes the slave-trade accord to appease the British. Chambers, *No God but Gain*, 50, 119, 125.

23. For the dynamics of partisan antipartisanship in the early republic, see David Waldstreicher, *In the Midst of Perpetual Fetes: The Making of American Nationalism, 1776–1820* (Chapel Hill: University of North Carolina Press, 1997), 201–7. For an application to a later period suggesting its continued importance, see Adam I. P. Smith, "Partisan Politics and the Public Sphere: The Civil War North," *American Nineteenth Century History* 2, no. 2 (2001): 182–203.

24. JA to Monroe, July 8, 1818, to Onís, July 23, 1818, in *WJQA*, 6:384, 387. Recently, historians have come to recognize the centrality of the fugitive slave issue in the borderlands to the ensuing First Seminole War and to Jackson's designs in the region. David S. Heidler and Jeanne T. Heidler, *Old Hickory's War: Andrew Jackson and the Quest for Empire* (Mechanicsburg, PA: Stackpole Books, 1996), 64–76; Adam Rothman, *Slave Country: American Expansion and the Origins of the Deep South* (Cambridge, MA: Harvard University Press, 2005), 166, 220; Deborah A. Rosen, *Border Law: The First Seminole War and American Nationhood* (Cambridge, MA: Harvard University Press, 2015).

25. *Mr. Adams's Defense of General Jackson's Conduct in the Seminole War* (n.p., 1818), 5, 9, 13–14; Erving letter in *WJQA*, 6:477, 482, 488, 499–500; JQA to John Adams, December 14, 1819, in *WJQA*, 6:528–32. Experts remain divided over whether Adams's actions and words were propaganda or a consistent extension of his ideology. For Adams's defense of Jackson as a crisis of conscience and a betrayal of his own principles, see Weeks, *Adams and American Global Empire*, 124–25. For Adams's consistent policy goals, see James E. Lewis Jr., *The American Union and the Problem of Neighborhood: The United States and the Collapse of the Spanish Empire, 1783–1829* (Chapel Hill: University of North Carolina Press, 1998) and *John*

Quincy Adams: Policymaker for the Union (Wilmington, DE: SR Books, 2001); and the more celebratory account in Bemis, *Adams and the Foundations*. Lynn Hudson Parsons splits the difference by describing Adams as brilliant but clueless: Parsons, *John Quincy Adams* (Madison, WI: Madison House, 1998), 142–43.

26. Lewis, *John Quincy Adams*, 62–63.

27. JQA Diary, January 2 and 3, February 4, 11, 27, 1820; Matthew Mason, "John Quincy Adams and the Tangled Politics of Slavery," in *Companion to John Adams and John Quincy Adams*, ed. Waldstreicher, 406–7; Judith S. Graham et al., eds., *Diary and Autobiographical Writings of Louisa Catherine Adams*, 2:462, 464, 472 (Cambridge, MA: Belknap Press of Harvard University Press, 2013).

28. Adams to James Monroe, 1820, in *WJQA*, 7:1–2; Diary, January 8, February 24, March 3 and 4, 1820; Chandra Miller, "'Title Page to a Great and Tragic Volume': The Impact of the Missouri Crisis on Slavery, Race and Republicanism in the Thought of John C. Calhoun and John Quincy Adams," *Missouri Historical Review* 94, no. 4 (2000): 365–88.

29. JQA Diary, March 3, 1820; the complete entry also appears in David Waldstreicher, ed., *The Diaries of John Quincy Adams, 1779–1848* (New York: Library of America, 2017), 1:537–46.

30. JQA Diary, February 23, March 3, 5, 31, April 9, 1820; Adams to Jonathan Jennings, July 17, 1820, to John D. Heath, January 7, 1822, in *WJQA*, 7:53, 191–93.

31. JQA Diary, November 29, 1820; Miller, "'Title Page to a Great and Tragic Volume,'" 380–85; Mason, "John Quincy Adams and the Tangled Politics of Slavery," 406–7.

32. JQA Diary, February 28, 1821; Adams, *An Address Delivered at the Request of the Committee of Citizens if Washington; On the Occasion of Reciting the Declaration of Independence, on the Fourth of July, 1821* (Washington, DC, 1821), 9–10, 21, 28, 31. Bemis, *Adams and the Foundations*, 357–58. For an analysis that compares the logic of the July 4 address with the Monroe Doctrine, noting that both simultaneously separated Indians from foreign policy and made slavery a foreign problem, see Gretchen Murphy, *Hemispheric Imaginings: The Monroe Doctrine and Narratives of U.S. Empire* (Durham, NC: Duke University Press, 2005), 33–60.

33. Adams to Everett, January 31, 1822, in *WJQA*, 7:200–201, 205; JQA, "The Macbeth Policy," in *WJQA*, 7:356–62; JQA Diary, October 20 and November 17, 1821, January 31, 1822. Alexander Smyth of Virginia raised Adams's votes on Louisiana and the slave trade in 1803–4, prompting Adams to reply with an address and a pamphlet: "To the Freeholders of Washington, Wythe, Grayson, Russell, Tazewell, Lee and Scott Counties, Virginia," in *WJQA*, 7:335–54.

34. Diary, October 1, 1822, May 1, 20, 24, 29, 1824; Adams to John D. Heath, January 7, 1822, to Charles Jared Ingersoll, June 3, Robert Walsh, July 15, 1822, to Louisa Catherine Adams, October 7, 1822, in *WJQA*, 7:191–95, 261–65, 281–82, 318.

35. Adams, "The Macbeth Policy," in *WJQA*, 7:359–60; Adams to Robert Walsh, November 27, 1822, in *WJQA*, 7:332; Mason, "John Quincy Adams and the Politics of Slavery," 408; David Callahan, "The Elections of 1824 and 1828" and Catherine Allgor and Margery Heffron, "A Monarch in the Republic: Louisa Catherine Johnson

Adams and Court Culture in Early Washington City," in *Companion to John Adams and John Quincy Adams*, ed. Waldstreicher, 325, 463–66; Bemis, *Adams and the Union*, 26–27, 70–71. I am especially indebted to Callahan for his argument that "the superb political arts that Adams had used in 1824 sowed the seeds of his defeat in the election of 1828."

36. Robert Pierce Forbes, *The Missouri Compromise and its Aftermath: Slavery and the Meaning of America* (Chapel Hill: University of North Carolina Press, 2007), 9, 190–92, 195–96; Richard R. John, "Affairs of Office: The Executive Departments, the Election of 1828, and the Making of the Democratic Party," in *The Democratic Experiment: New Directions in American Political History*, ed. Meg Jacobs, William J. Novak, and Julian E. Zelizer, 50–84 (Princeton, NJ: Princeton University Press, 2003); Padraig Riley, "The Presidency of John Quincy Adams," in *Companion to John Adams and John Quincy Adams*, ed. Waldstreicher, 335–36; William W. Freehling, *Prelude to Civil War: The Nullification Controversy in South Carolina* (New York: Harper & Row, 1966), 141; JQA Diary, September 11, 1826. For the structural constraints Adams faced in trying to consolidate Monrovian policies, see especially Stephen Skowronek, *The Politics Presidents Make: Leadership from John Adams to George Bush* (Cambridge, MA: Belknap Press of Harvard University Press, 1993), 110–27.

37. JQA Diary, November 21, 1825, January 11 and September 11, 1826. Bemis suggested that "the most significant issue in the Presidential campaign of 1828 was the hidden issue . . . the issue of slavery" (*Adams and the Union*, 147), but recent accounts seem to ignore that contention, with the important exception of Daniel Walker Howe, *What God Hath Wrought: The Transformation of the United States, 1815–1848* (New York: Oxford University Press, 2007). Lynn Hudson Parsons admits the force of the three-fifths clause in 1828 but declares that the "new era" of democracy and modern politics was cause and effect of Jackson's victory. But Donald Ratcliffe has argued persuasively that Adams's coalition in 1824 was popular and perhaps even a majority. Parsons, *The Birth of Modern Politics: Andrew Jackson, John Quincy Adams, and the Election of 1828* (New York: Oxford University Press, 2009), 128; Ratcliffe, "Popular Preferences in the Presidential Election of 1824," *Journal of the Early Republic* 34, no. 1 (2014): 45–78.

38. For more on this phase of Adams's evolution and the writing projects in which he worked out this version of history, see David Waldstreicher, "Slavery, Voice and Loyalty: John Quincy Adams as the First Revisionist," in *Historian in Chief: How Presidents Interpret the Past to Shape the Future*, ed. Seth Cotlar and Richard J. Ellis, 65–73 (Charlottesville: University of Virginia Press, 2019).

39. Diary, January 6 and 18, 1836; Adams to Solomon Lincoln, April 4, 1836, in *The Selected Writings of John and John Quincy Adams*, ed. Adrienne Koch and William Peden (New York: Alfred A. Knopf, 1946), 383; Charles Francis Adams Jr., "John Quincy Adams and Martial Law," *Proceedings of the Massachusetts Historical Society*, 2nd ser., 15 (1901–2): 439.

40. For the treaty power as the link between Adams's earlier denial of (British) wartime emancipation and his later embrace of it, see James Oakes, *The Scorpion's*

Sting: Antislavery and the Coming of the Civil War (New York: W. W. Norton, 2014), 136–39, 150–54.

41. Adams, *Speech of John Quincy Adams, on the Joint Resolution for Distributing Rations to the Distressed Fugitives from Indian Hostilities in the States of Alabama and Georgia, Delivered in the House of Representatives, Wednesday, May 15, 1836* (Washington, DC, 1836), 3–4, 7–8. A year and a half later, Adams referred to this speech as "by far the most noted speech that I ever made." Diary, November 20, 1837.

42. For further reflections on this theme, see David Waldstreicher and Van Gosse, "Introduction: Black Politics and U.S. Politics in the Age of Revolutions, Emancipations, and Reconstructions," in *Revolutions and Reconstructions: Black Politics in the Long Nineteenth Century*, ed. Gosse and Waldstreicher, 1–23 (Philadelphia: University of Pennsylvania Press, 2020).

11. Daniel Raymond, Mathew Carey, the Missouri Crisis, and the Global 1820s

Andrew Shankman

IN HIS FAMOUS reaction to the Missouri Crisis, Thomas Jefferson likened the searing national conflict over whether Missouri should enter the Union as a slave state to "a fire-bell in the night," which "awakened and filled me with terror." It was a terror so great that even if by spring 1820 the alarm had "hushed . . . for the moment," the former president feared that it was "a reprieve only" and even likely "the knell of the union."[1] This chapter argues that during the 1820s, there was no reprieve, that the conflict the Missouri Crisis began did not end, that the fire bell never stopped ringing. Missouri was followed by related but much more extensive conflicts in the United States, the Caribbean, and Latin America. During the 1820s these domestic and global conflicts destroyed the political party poised in 1820 to dominate the nation's politics, a group known as the National Republicans.

The National Republicans came to prominence as they led the nation into war in 1812, and victory in that war established them as national political leaders. After the war, the National Republicans planned to heal all sectional conflicts and usher in an unprecedented epoch of national harmony. Yet over the course of the 1820s, the fire bell that sounded in Missouri signaled conditions that made the National Republicans' plans for the nation impossible to realize. By the end of the 1820s, sectional conflicts over the place and future of slavery in the United States, and southern fears about the impact of the Latin American revolutions on the survival of slavery everywhere, led many southern politicians and slaveholders to loath and distrust the National Republicans' policies and aspirations. Profound sectional conflict obliterated the National Republicans' expectation that they could produce a harmonious, national public good that would meet the needs of all citizens in all social classes, states, regions, and sections.

In order to understand the impact of the Missouri Crisis, and the way the crisis intersected with subsequent national, hemispheric, and global events to produce such disastrous effects for the National Republicans, this chapter's first section briefly explains what the National Republicans expected to accomplish, particularly with their political economy, which they called the American System. After this brief discussion, the chapter's second section explores the ideas of two of the movement's key thinkers, Daniel Raymond of Baltimore and Mathew Carey of Philadelphia. Raymond was fairly well known and reasonably well respected in 1819. Carey was extremely well known and universally respected, the most prominent and prolific economic thinker associated with the National Republicans at the time of the Missouri Crisis. Seeing the crisis through their eyes, through the frameworks of thought they produced, helps us to understand why the National Republicans' project perished in the decade of events that began in Missouri.

Prior to the Missouri Crisis, nothing they had written suggested that Raymond and Carey would differ on any important public issue. However, with pamphlets in 1819 and 1820, respectively, Raymond and Carey disagreed about the Missouri Crisis, the most pressing issue of the day. Raymond opposed allowing Missouri to enter the Union as a slave state, while Carey supported it.[2] Raymond's and Carey's responses to the crisis, and Carey's efforts to preserve the core goal of national harmony in the decade that followed, provide a microcosmic look at a larger process. Raymond's response to Missouri placed him on the margins of the National Republican movement, while Carey's showed him to be at its very center. Yet as Carey championed National Republican policies after 1821, he came to conclude that slaveholders had no interest in National Republican policies or the harmonious sectional relationships National Republicans believed they could forge. Carey's experience of this unceasing southern opposition radicalized him, and he lost all confidence in the assumptions of the National Republican Party. When a National Republican as mainstream as Carey moved so much closer to an outlier like Raymond, it meant that the National Republican movement was in grave danger.

The chapter's third section explores the angry and violent national and hemispheric confrontations between and within slave-owning and non-slave-owning regions that occurred in the wake of the Missouri Compromise. After the Missouri Compromise, slavery remained at the center of politics in the United States, and because it did the slave South did not behave in the 1820s as Carey expected. It did not, in large part, due to the tremendous impact hemispheric events had on those determined to preserve slavery. As a result, the United States participated in a global conflict over the place and future of slavery in the Americas. The most committed U.S. advocates for slavery experienced the aftermath of the Missouri Crisis globally, and their reaction to the impact of this global 1820s caused Carey to become as hostile to slavery and slave owners at the end of the decade as Raymond was at the beginning.

The chapter's brief final section considers how Raymond and Carey can help us to understand not just why the National Republican movement failed, but also why the northern antislavery politics that began to develop in the 1820s and 1830s so often advanced a racist hatred of African Americans. As people such as Raymond and Carey turned against slavery over the course of the 1820s, they refused to accept the necessary condition for national harmony—approval, or at least acceptance, of the enslavement of men and women. Yet by refusing a central requirement for the success of the National Republican Party, Raymond and Carey also had to confront the issue of race and the prospect of a biracial republic of freedom. Like so many others turning against slavery during the 1820s, Raymond's and Carey's attitudes regarding race revealed an unwillingness to imagine biracial freedom and citizenship.

▲

The National Republican movement included many of the most famous political figures among Jefferson's followers, men such as Henry Clay, John C. Calhoun, John Quincy Adams, James Monroe, and others nearly as well known at the time like Charles Fenton Mercer, Richard Rush, Mathew Carey, and Hezekiah Niles. National Republicans served as congressmen, senators, cabinet secretaries, and vice presidents, and two were elected president. Like Jefferson, National Republicans believed that republican institutions could survive only if republican citizens remained independent. Independence required more than the right to vote, equality before the law, and constitutional protection of individual rights. Citizens also needed material independence: control of enough productive property to be free from coercion and manipulation by fellow citizens and governments. Jefferson's classic assumption was that a republic should remain almost exclusively agrarian. A nation of farmer, patriarchal heads of household was the ideal republican citizenry, and President Jefferson intended his domestic and foreign policy, from the Louisiana Purchase to his commercial trade wars with Britain and France, to protect and preserve a nation of farmers.[3]

National Republicans worried that Jefferson's agrarian vision would produce the very dependence it was meant to prevent. They feared that with the end of the Napoleonic Wars, international demand for U.S. agriculture would plummet as European nations began to restore their agricultural output. Glutted global markets would cause a cascade of rural failure and poverty. The solution was to create a much more diverse and dynamic domestic market that encouraged agriculture, commerce, and manufacturing. Henry Clay called this plan the American System. He expected the American System to foster national harmony by bringing the domestic production of all regions of the nation into mutually beneficial and reciprocal commercial relationships. With this dynamic domestic market, republican citizens would be less dependent on foreign markets. After 1815, the National Republicans confidently expected to wield cutting-edge political economy and pioneering use of statistics to create the conditions that would preserve a republic of independent citizens.[4]

The "American System" was a shorthand term for the series of interlocking policies the National Republicans enacted under their two presidents, James Monroe and John Quincy Adams, assisted by Henry Clay, who served as Speaker of the House and then, under Quincy Adams, as secretary of state. In 1816 Congress passed the nation's first protective tariff to stimulate domestic manufacturing. A rising population of manufacturers, National Republicans believed, would increase the domestic demand for domestic agriculture. The National Republicans also championed internal improvements (infrastructure) at both the national and the state levels. The National Road was a quintessential example of this policy, as was New York's commitment, beginning in 1817, to building the Erie Canal. To encourage widespread access to credit and banking, the National Republicans rechartered the Bank of the United States in 1816 and encouraged states to also charter banks. They expected the national bank and its branches to work harmoniously with the state banks to steadily, but never recklessly, increase the paper-money supply and extend credit to all the industrious producers who would take advantage of the new opportunities the American System provided. The result would be a society and economy far more diverse and dynamic than Jefferson's agrarian republic. Craftsmen, merchants, and bankers would be independent citizens while helping to preserve that status for the nation's farmers. With growing confidence between 1816 and 1819, National Republicans believed that all economic actors in all regions would find markets inside the nation, and wealth, prosperity, and national harmony would result. Jefferson's fire bell, then, held nothing but terror for the National Republican project. How could a politics and a political economy of national harmony survive what Jefferson described as a "geographical line coinciding with a marked principle, moral and political [that] once conceived and held up to the angry passions of men, will never be obliterated; and every new iteration will mark it deeper and deeper?"[5]

♦

A fine way to explore how the Missouri Crisis initiated a series of events that destroyed the National Republican fantasy of harmony is to look closely at two of those economic thinkers and statistical compilers the National Republican movement attracted, political economists, authors, and National Republican activists Daniel Raymond and Mathew Carey. In his 1819 pamphlet *The Missouri Question*, Daniel Raymond denounced human bondage using the starkest terms, writing that "slavery is the greatest curse our country is afflicted with . . . a cancer which is corroding the morals and political vitals of our country."[6] At the same time that he was writing his brief pamphlet, he was also working on his 470-page tome *Thoughts on Political Economy*, which he published the next year. Raymond's position on Missouri emerged from his systematic, yet decidedly idiosyncratic, conception of political economy, a conception that, though it marked him as an outlier in the National Republican movement, he believed provided the best possible version of the American System.

At the heart of Raymond's thought was the distinction he drew between "plunder" and "political economy." Not only were they distinct systems of economic action, but they also existed, or were meant to exist, at different periods in history. Plunder was the economic policy of the ancients, which for Raymond meant those living before about the mid-sixteenth century. Thus, Persia, Greece, and Rome were cultures of plunder producing "a history of pillage and rapine . . . for the purpose of wrestling from their weaker neighbors their substance and of reducing them to slavery." War to acquire riches through violent dominion was the quintessence of the culture of plunder and the only method, Raymond insisted, for increasing wealth known to the ancients. Right from the start, Raymond connected plunder with slavery. Conditions only worsened during "the middle or dark ages," which were reducible entirely to "a history of plunder, carnage, and desolation . . . of violence and rapine."[7]

The alternative to plunder was political economy, which became possible in the recent past after "the continent of Europe became parceled out among distinct nations of nearly equal power." Prior to this development, political economy had been unknown. With these new conditions, the residents of these new largely equal nations had to make their own lands more productive since they could no longer violently seize the property, labor, and freedom of others.[8] The modern science of political economy allowed enlightened people to leave behind plunder and the violent and exploitative actions that brought slavery into the world.

Yet one modern development threatened this humane age: the discovery and conquest of the Americas. That conquest provided Europeans a vast new space to practice plunder, and so "unfortunately for humanity the system of violence and rapine . . . was revived and transferred to the new world, with tenfold horror." The foundations of the present in the United States were laid, Raymond wrote, as entire peoples "were plundered, laid waste, and depopulated. . . . [T]he wretched inhabitants were seized by violence, apportioned among the captors, and reduced to slavery. . . . [U]nfortunately for [our] country, and long and deeply shall we deplore it, [it is] not free from the deadly sin of having participated in the violence and outrage committed upon the African race. Our fathers and ourselves have tasted the forbidden fruit, and the curse resteth upon us."[9]

For Raymond, political economy was not merely a series of preferred policies. It was the science of making land and labor more productive without coercion, while creating conditions where all enjoyed the fruits of their labor. Political economy, therefore, was fundamentally Christian, while plunder was anti-Christian, for political economy obligated all to labor and thereby accept the postlapsarian judgement that "in the sweat of thy face shalt though eat bread" (Gen. 3:19), a phrase that Raymond repeated throughout his treatise. The policies of a nation practicing political economy and rejecting plunder stigmatized those exploiting others, for "the science of political economy points out a road to national wealth in direct opposition to that of plunder and conquest, the two can never exist together in harmony."[10]

Essential to Raymond's idea of political economy was the distinction he drew between "national wealth" and "individual wealth." Raymond defined individual wealth as "the possession of property of the use of which the owner can obtain a quantity of the necessaries and comforts of life." Political economy existed to provide individual wealth for every citizen. Raymond provided national wealth a particular and idiosyncratic definition, and his definition allowed him to judge as insupportable all sorts of economic practices, policies, and institutions that were considered essential by virtually all slave owners. Raymond argued that national wealth rose only as every citizen acquired individual wealth, for "a capacity for acquiring by labor the necessities and comforts of life for all its citizens, is as high a degree of national wealth, as any nation ever did, or ever can hope to obtain." If some citizens enjoyed far more of the comforts than they could consume and a great many possessed too few, individual wealth might be great, but national wealth was diminished by each citizen who did not enjoy sufficient individual wealth. In those cases, "individual wealth is often national poverty," and plunder had supplanted political economy.[11]

To pursue political economy, statesmen needed to use the nation-state's power. They had to enact policies even when they did not produce individual wealth for certain powerful sections of the population as rapidly as others might. One policy prized by the powerful southern section was free trade, the opposition to a protective tariff. With free trade, according to Raymond, those exporting raw materials maximized individual wealth, but at the expense of the consumption power of the nation's craftsmen and the nation's manufacturing capacity. Rising individual wealth, therefore, reduced national wealth while also making the nation's smaller farmers dependent on foreign markets. A protective tariff, the cornerstone of the American System, would promote manufacturing, the more reliable domestic market, and the consumption power of craftsmen and small farmers. Free trade augmented "the power of one class of citizens over the destinies of another, [and so] produce[d] to a certain extent, the condition, if not physically at least morally, of lord and vassal, master and slave."[12]

Yet ending free trade, a policy that slave states by 1820 considered a vital interest, was only the start of the power Raymond believed the nation-state had. Raymond insisted that property rights were not absolute. It was axiomatic that "the public interests are paramount to individual interests," and "when a political economist has shown that public and private interests are opposed, he has made out a case, in which the interposition of the government is necessary; he cannot be required to prove that private interests ought to give way—this is to be taken for granted." Those who disagreed, said Raymond, "seem to suppose that the right of property is absolute in the individual, [but] individual right to property is never absolute, but always relative and conditional. . . . [T]he right to property is merely conventional . . . subject to such regulation as may be made respecting it, with a view to the general interests of the whole nation." Raymond went so far as to argue for "the right of the public to take any man's property from him, whenever it becomes necessary for the public good." In order to maximize national wealth, statesmen could "interfere with the private interests of the individual, or a class of individuals," to promote "in a greater degree, the interests of a larger class of individuals," for doing so was "beneficial to the nation, and will promote national wealth."[13]

The promotion of national wealth also justified extensive public expenditure on internal improvements or, as Raymond called them, "public works." Raymond also praised banks, which would circulate money, and so his thinking fitted well with the American System's commitment to rechartering the Bank of the United States while also encouraging the extensive growth of state-chartered banks. The powerful national government that built the National Republicans' American System would pursue political economy and promote national wealth. That was the obligation of modern governments, Raymond insisted. It was "the duty of the legislator to find employment for all the people, and if he cannot find them employment in agriculture and commerce, he must set them to manufacturing. . . . He is not to permit one half of the nation to remain idle and hungry, in order that the other half, may buy goods where they may be had cheapest."[14]

To allow half "to remain idle and hungry" when political economy could prevent it was to practice plunder. Yet Raymond concluded, in 1820 the United States practiced plunder rather than political economy. Private monopolies provided privileged citizens advantages and so were "conducive to individual, but prejudicial to national wealth." Another example of plunder was "the act of incorporation . . . for the purpose of giving the members an artificial power, which they would not possess in their individual capacities." Public authority had to remain paramount over all corporations, for "the very object . . . of the act of incorporation is to produce inequality either in rights or the division of property." Without public authority, private corporations became instruments of plunder, "an artificial combination, or amalgamation . . . artificial engines of power contrived by the rich for the purpose of increasing their already too great ascendency."[15]

Yet beyond any of these examples, slavery embodied every aspect of plunder. Slavery depended on artificial laws that benefited the few at the expense of a vast many. Slavery was the unchecked violent imposition of power that allowed a small group to enjoy wealth produced by the labor of others. And it was the forcible manipulation of public policy to promote individual wealth at the expense of national wealth. Slavery was such a shameful example of plunder that it was a fair question "among the learned whether more good or evil has resulted to mankind from the discovery of America."[16]

Slavery, Raymond claimed, had such a "pernicious influence" on national wealth that the harm it did to the nation and every citizen was "of greater magnitude than the mere suffering of the slaves themselves." Raymond insisted that slavery disastrously distorted population growth in the United States. He argued that the white population increased twice as fast in free states as in slave states, while the population of the enslaved increased faster than that of free Black people. Though the South had richer soil, that advantage did not produce growing populations of free, productive citizens, the source of national wealth as Raymond defined it. Slavery caused increasing concentration of wealth while preventing its redistribution in the form of wages and desirable employment. Without this circulation of wealth, slavery produced extensive individual wealth at the expense of national wealth. Raymond insisted that "had there never been a slave in the southern states [the] population at this day would have been much more numerous than it is. . . . [T]he country would have been in a much higher state of cultivation, and instead of being covered with the miserable huts of slaves would have been covered with the neat and comfortable dwellings of free, brave, and hardy yeomanry." It was manifest that the "evils of slavery always fall heavily on the lower classes of society, who are the most numerous."[17]

Since this system of plunder diminished national wealth and allowed the slave population to increase at a faster rate than the southern white population, the spread of slavery would magnify the problem. Public policy to promote the expansion of slavery was the quintessence of plunder—the promotion of individual wealth and the assault on national wealth. Should slavery expand, the outcome, Raymond insisted, would be apocalyptic. Poverty and inequality would increase as a beleaguered white population shrank and an angry and enslaved population grew to eclipse it, until ultimately "it must at no distant day, terminate in insurrections and servile wars, shocking even in imagination."[18]

As he excoriated slavery, Raymond returned to his insistence that property rights were conditional, subject to the needs of national wealth. Such claims in the midst of a sustained denunciation of slavery made explosive language orders of magnitude more so. Raymond scornfully rejected the presumption of "the advocates of slavery, [who] take it for granted, that they have an absolute, unconditional, indefeasible right to what they call their property in their slaves." "The property holders have not an absolute unconditional right to their property," Raymond informed slave owners, for "their right is subordinate to that of the nation." It was merely "the positive laws of the state" that allowed a slave owner to "have a right or interest in the bones and sinews of his fellow man." When such laws promoted individual wealth and diminished national wealth, they could be repealed, for "the interest and rights of the individual slave holder is subordinate to that of the public, and whenever the public interest require it, he is bound to set his slave free."[19] Every aspect of Raymond's argument in *Thoughts on Political Economy* made slavery the archetype of plunder, and so the negation of political economy and the public good. Of course, Daniel Raymond opposed slavery in Missouri. That was the most minimal aspect of a total opposition in which he championed the American System as exemplary political economy, a political economy that could succeed only in a world without slavery.

So why did Mathew Carey, as much a National Republican and an American System man as Daniel Raymond, take the opposite position on Missouri? Raymond was a systematic and idiosyncratic thinker, while Carey was neither. Instead, he wrote shorter pieces, though many more of them, for the press and in pamphlets. Raymond was a genuine outlier among those economic thinkers promoting the American System in the early years of the National Republican movement. Carey was firmly in that movement's mainstream; his ideas were similar to those of leading National Republicans such as Henry Clay, John C. Calhoun, Charles Fenton Mercer, and John Quincy Adams, many of whom were slave owners or who studiously avoided publicly criticizing slavery.[20] Carey's approach to political economy was not to conceive a system in a massive book, but instead to boost, to form and join organizations, and to seek to unite the different and differing economic actors inhabiting a nation that had been divided by region since its inception, divisions that were exacerbated by the War of 1812.

In the years immediately preceding the Missouri Crisis, Carey argued that a national political economy built on a protective tariff, internal improvements, and a rapid but regulated expansion of credit and banking could eliminate sectional tensions exposed by the war. This political economy could also address the political and economic weaknesses of the nation that had been apparent since at least the failure of the Embargo Act of 1807. Above all, Carey hoped to solve the nation's New England problem—that New England was an alienated and bitter region of potential secession, convinced that the South and West were hostile to commerce and using their grip on national power to pursue an unendurable course for the nation.[21]

In 1814–15, as the National Republican movement began to dominate national politics, nothing appeared more dangerous than the New England problem. To a significant extent, the political economy of mainstream

National Republicans was intended to resolve the New England problem, and addressing it shaped Carey's writing in the half decade before 1820. Carey's writings between 1814 and 1819 were intended to accomplish two things. First, he addressed New England directly, literally offering an olive branch. He argued that New England was mistaken in its fears about the attitudes toward commerce in the rest of the nation. Second, he sought to prove that claim by explaining the glories that would come from developing a diverse and vibrant domestic market and by championing, though in nothing like the sustained rigor of Raymond, the policies necessary to achieve it. Carey, then, was one of the earliest and most prominent supporters of the American System.[22]

Carey believed that Napoleon's defeat had ushered in "a new epoch." Since the 1790s the international demand for American grain had been artificially high. Now European economies would return to normal and demand would plummet. The United States had to turn inward, Carey insisted, and create domestic markets for its agriculture. The American System would foster that market and intersectional economic relationships, which would diminish New England's hostility. Protective tariffs would stimulate manufacturing and create a rising population of nonagricultural producers, who would consume the output of American farmers. Internal improvements, encouraged by both the national government and the states, would connect producers across the nation. And the spectacular growth in state banking would allow local figures who understood local needs to supply credit where it was most needed, facilitating economic production. The American System would preserve Jefferson's empire of liberty composed of independent citizen heads of household while creating a vibrant domestic market in which, collectively, those households became much more diverse sources of domestic production.

For Carey, slavery was crucial to the American System and the egalitarian social outcomes that he expected for the republic's white male citizen heads of household. He incorporated slavery into his vision of political economy to show that one could champion the economic interests of New England and the slave regions. But Carey did not support slavery just as a short-term tactic to solve bitter postwar sectional conflicts. He believed that slave staple production was essential for the development of the sizable domestic market he wanted the American System to create. A primary goal of the American System was to lessen the nation's dependence on foreign, especially British, markets. Creating a robust population of nonagricultural producers would also produce a domestic market for the agricultural output of both free and enslaved labor. As regimes of both free and slave labor grew, Carey was confident they would grow more interdependent, and that interdependence would be increasingly beneficial. One big boost, particularly in the early stages of American industrial development, would be the captured consumption by the enslaved, whose very concentration would create deep and immediate markets that could only much more slowly develop elsewhere as internal improvements painstakingly established commercial connections. The American System would draw upon and harmonize the economic interests and strengths of all regions and labor systems. At its core, the American System would facilitate "the transportation of raw materials from the southern states to the middle and eastern states, and of manufactured articles from the latter to the former."[23]

Carey's political economy, and indeed the National Republican movement more broadly, had as their primary purpose to solve the New England problem. Judged by this initial overriding purpose, the movement succeeded brilliantly. With the growth of its textile industry, by the mid-1820s New England was well on its way to fully integrating into a national political economy and to forging the intersectional connections between slave-grown southern staples and northern manufacturing that Carey and the National Republicans had hoped for. By the mid-1820s a much more nationalist New England had fully embraced protection and gloried in its status as a manufacturing center. None of that had seemed likely in 1814.[24]

What Carey had not expected in 1814 was that the South, particularly its slaveholders, who in 1814 he associated with nation building, warfare, and the political economy of the American System, would produce some of the severest critics of the political economy he championed. Yet the conflicts surrounding the Missouri Crisis showed that Carey's strongest opponents were not in New England. As the Missouri Crisis developed, the strongest criticisms of the American System came from southerners who denounced the protective tariff and demanded free trade. Some also insisted that the doctrine of implied powers that allowed the national government to incorporate a bank could lead to claims that it could circumvent, or even overrule, local magistracy essential for the protection and expansion of slavery. The national government chartering corporations that could act within states, but that might not be regulated by state laws, created special and unique fears for slave states. Their labor systems depended on state-level policies and laws and a constitutional understanding that slave states alone could oversee the policing of the people enslaved within their borders. Expansive constitutional interpretations, which could conjure up a national bank when it could be found in no clause of the Constitution, could lead to other even more frightening uses of national power, particularly since national representatives from northern states could likely be wielding that power. As even Henry Clay acknowledged, if the national government could create a banking corporation using implied powers, many could plausibly fear "that the chain of cause and effect is without end, that if we argue from a power expressly granted to all others, which might be convenient or necessary to its execution, there are no bounds to the power of this government." Those concerns led North Carolina congressman Nathanial Macon to exclaim one year before the Missouri Crisis, "Examine the Constitution of the U.S. . . . and then tell me if Congress can establish banks, make roads and canals, whether they cannot free all the slaves in the U.S. . . . If Congress can make canals, they can with more propriety emancipate."[25]

Carey was intensely frustrated by this southern mistrust of the American System, for he believed it was the best ally of those committed to slavery. That thinking shaped his stance on Missouri. Missouri provided an opportunity to prove to slave owners once and for all that they had nothing to fear from the American System. By opposing restriction in Missouri, Carey could show that his political economy meshed seamlessly with the needs and interests of slave owners. Indeed, Carey argued that he endorsed slavery in Missouri precisely because he was such a staunch advocate of the American System. Carey hoped that his support for Missouri's entrance as a slave state would solidify the coalition of National Republicans led by southern statesmen who championed the American System.

Thus, Carey had high hopes in 1821 as Missouri entered the Union as a slave state. Once slave owners saw that their interests aligned with the American System, then slavery would play a vital role in the nation's economic future. Yet slavery was valuable for Carey if and only if it could fully fit within the American System. If slave owners refused to see what seemed obvious to Carey, if their thorough commitment to slavery became their reason to oppose his political economy, then Carey might well have to make a painful choice. But with the Missouri Crisis resolved, with the nation poised to experience the benefits of his policies over the course of the next decade, Carey was sanguine that he would never have to decide between slavery without the American System or the American System without slavery.

♦

How wrong Carey was. Over the course of the 1820s, from his perspective slave owners continued to irrationally exaggerate the threat the American System posed to slavery. Carey always overestimated the degree of compatibility between the American System and the needs of slave owners. Some of their opposition and fear was inherent and structural. Slavery was a labor regime based in positive state laws that depended on state-level institutions maintaining absolute authority over the bodies of the enslaved. Expansive interpretations of national power that led to concrete institutions functioning as intrusions by the nation-state within states' borders contained the potential for disruption. Nathanial Macon was not entirely wrong, and imagine if he had read Daniel Raymond. He well might have. William Branch Giles, who served as Virginia's senator and governor, did, and he pronounced Raymond a "fanatic" in the *Richmond Enquirer* while equating his ideas with the goals of John Quincy Adams and Henry Clay.[26]

But these abstract, though certainly real, concerns depended on following abstruse discussions of political theory, federalism, the nature of corporations, and political economy. Such rarefied matters were bolstered by much less abstract and tangible circumstances and conditions in the aftermath of the Missouri Crisis. They contributed greatly to many slave owners concluding that the American System threatened slavery in ways that Carey could never really understand, let alone confront. These concerns eluded Carey because he did not experience the 1820s as so many southern slaveholders did: as a series of earth-shattering global catastrophes that made most white southerners feel far more vulnerable and isolated by 1832 than they had felt in the months just after the Missouri Compromise.

A fine way to understand the terrifying and reinforcing series of domestic and global events that shaped the 1820s for so many slave owners is to begin in 1817 on Amelia Island, a speck of land off the coast of Spanish Florida. By 1817 the Latin American revolts against Spain were almost a decade old. In 1817 none of the revolutionary movements had taken a formal stance against slavery. But the year before Simón Bolívar had fled in defeat to Haiti, where he promised to abolish slavery in Venezuela in exchange for aid.[27] For the United States, Haiti had been a terrifying outlier since the 1790s, but this agreement suggested a new willingness by Haitians directly to confront slavery and racial injustice in the Americas.[28] The Haitian government imagined an emancipatory possibility in Latin America, though Bolívar was a slave owner and revolutionary leaders in Venezuela were just as interested in slavery as the Spanish Empire was.[29]

In the same year that Haiti sought to influence the Latin American revolutions, it created a new constitution proclaiming Haiti free soil for any person of color who could get there. That year a significant slave revolt in Barbados led to, on average, a month of newspaper coverage in the United States.[30]

That was the context for the events on Amelia Island, a context that invited the sorts of fears about the future of slavery that Carey always considered exaggerated. In 1817 Latin American revolutionaries, including Venezuelans, now with Bolívar's promise, assisted in the seizure of Amelia Island to harass the Spanish and perhaps to strike at Cuba. Liberated Cuba was a terrifying prospect for U.S. slave owners, as Cuba, with the end of slavery in Haiti, had dramatically increased slavery and sugar production in the previous two decades. Liberated Cuba threatened to be everything Haiti was, but even closer to the North American mainland.[31]

The administration of President James Monroe was able to piece things together and worried about the seemingly new willingness of Haiti to confront racial injustice. The Monroe administration saw Amelia Island as a far too close example of the potential for the upheaval in the collapsing Spanish Empire to unsettle white dominion over matters of race. Writing from Charleston, South Carolina, on May 23, 1817, Joel Poinsett, already an acknowledged expert on the situation in Latin America and later U.S. minister to Mexico, explained to Acting Attorney General Richard Rush that revolutionary forces had again united under Bolívar. Therefore, Poinsett stressed, "it would be important to know the connection existing between this chief and the authorities of San Domingo [Haiti]; and the number of negroes in arms." Rush repeated these questions virtually word for word to Caesar Rodney and John Graham, special commissioners of the United States to South America.[32]

Rising fears about Haiti and the potential disruption of U.S. slavery turned Amelia Island into a specter (in addition to briefly becoming a haven for the slave trade) for both the Monroe administration and the public.[33] In justifying U.S. seizure of the island, Secretary of State John Quincy Adams explained to Rodney and Graham that "a body of blacks from St. Domingo" had assisted Mexico and Venezuela in overrunning Amelia Island, which had "become a receptacle for fugitive negroes." President Monroe proclaimed it "an asylum for fugitive slaves from the neighboring states," which, Adams added, made it a haven for "lawless plunderers of every nation and color." Within a few months of the Amelia Island episode, Adams was asking his special envoy to Venezuela to discover "the present effects and probable consequences of the emancipation of the slaves."[34]

Amelia Island was frightening enough to disrupt a general enthusiasm in the United States for revolution in Latin America, revolutions, it should be repeated, that had not yet done anything formally to free slaves. Newspapers, including the National Intelligencer of Washington, DC, the closest thing there was to an administration organ and national paper of record, and particularly southern papers, especially in Georgia, denounced the actions of the revolutionaries and emphasized their Haitian connection.[35] Fears about direct assaults on slavery sparked by Amelia Island became only more central due to the Missouri Crisis, which suggested that global threats were being reinforced by domestic ones. Thus, Carey's confidence about what he could accomplish in the 1820s depended on a prospect he could not have conceived: What would happen if during the 1820s much of the world began to look like Amelia Island, and what if Haiti went from being an outlier to a leading indicator?[36]

Over the course of the 1820s, slave owners could believe that was precisely what was happening. In the immediate aftermath of the Missouri Crisis, the revolutionary disruptions in Latin America began to weaken and even destroy slavery. Armed people of color, often slaves and former slaves, became a new normal, and several thousands of them were vital to the revolutions' successes as they made the prerevolutionary status quo untenable. Between 1821 and 1831 Chile and Mexico abolished slavery outright, while Uruguay, Colombia, Bolivia, Peru, and Venezuela enacted gradual emancipation laws. In Argentina and Paraguay slavery was seriously weakened.[37]

Those predisposed to be alarmed could imagine Haiti influencing global events as early as 1822, the year in which white South Carolinians had no doubt that Denmark Vesey, a man with Caribbean connections, led a slave uprising in Charleston. Amelia Island appeared to be everywhere. Carey expected the Missouri Compromise to calm southern fears about slavery's future and give him all the time he needed to show them the splendors of the American System. As he confidently proclaimed in his 1820 antirestriction pamphlet, "If Missouri is admitted with the right to decide the future of slavery in the state then we have nothing to fear."[38] Instead, within a year of that compromise, South Carolina was enacting its Negro Seamen's Acts. Terrified of any Black sailors arriving from the revolutionary South Atlantic, South Carolina's lawmakers used the language of contagion to imprison free Black seamen upon arrival.[39]

The fear of global contagion, and a plausible future in which virtually the only enslaving polities were the U.S. southern states, led to much greater attention to the dangers posed by opponents of slavery, both free and unfree. A year after Vesey, U.S. newspapers covered the slave uprising in Demerara (present-day Guyana) for about three times as long as they had the 1816 Barbados rising.[40] This growing anxiety about the course of events was part of the context for the presidential election of 1824 and charges of a corrupt bargain that brought the National Republicans John Quincy Adams and Henry Clay to power. For southerners fearful of the American System, the apparent national and international threats to slavery appeared to be connected. In 1825 the most prominent advocates of the American System took control of the executive branch. Yet just as terrifying, many southerners believed the National Republicans were endorsing the Latin American revolutions, revolutions that, after 1825, began to horrify many supporters of slavery.

Since 1817 Clay had been the most prominent U.S. advocate for independence in Latin America. His earliest use of the term "American System" came in a congressional speech envisaging an American zone of allied republics that could allow republican citizens in nations north and south to free themselves from the markets of monarchies.[41] Though the cooler-headed John Quincy Adams had never been as enthusiastic, almost immediately his presidency became closely associated with the most frightening features of the now clearly emancipatory Latin American revolutions.[42] Adams's first year in office—1825—was bracketed by two speeches, his inaugural address in March and his annual message to Congress in December. In his inaugural, Adams famously equated liberty with power and called for an extensive commitment to the American System spearheaded by a newly vigorous national government. The address was a proud distillation of National Republican ideas and ideals. It came as many slave owners were already fearful of the claims for federal power, the expansive constitutional interpretation that justified that power, and the prospect of national political figures acting in ways that could disrupt state institutions and the sole authority of state lawmakers and slave owners to govern enslaved bodies.[43]

In the December message to Congress, John Quincy Adams announced his intention to send U.S. representatives to the 1826 Panama Conference, the meeting of American republics convened by Bolívar to discuss relations among the newly independent neighboring nations and, many white southerners feared, plans to liberate Cuba. At the conference many delegates would be men of color, possibly even former slaves.[44] Adams's announcement provoked extensive outrage and helped to draw even more tightly connections that slave owners had steadily been making since Missouri. As Virginia congressman John Floyd, the future supporter of nullification and governor of the Old Dominion during Nat Turner's revolt, fulminated, "Who can tell what this Congress of Panama will lead to?" Floyd could certainly guess. "Shall we be told by this Congress," he asked the House of Representatives, "that *every* man on this continent is entitled to liberty? Shall we not be called on to consult what amount of men and money will be requisite to liberate Porto Rico and Cuba? And to settle what shall be the condition of Hayti? All these subjects will be debated, in full conclave, and will be settled *by vote*."[45]

Floyd also made clear that the Adams administration's participation in the conference was keeping alive slave owners' anger over Missouri. After all, Floyd explained, John Sergeant, the vociferous proponent of restriction in Missouri (and National Republican vice presidential candidate in 1832), was to be one of the two commissioners sent to Panama, and "we are acquainted with that Gentleman here. We know him as the great champion of the Missouri question. . . . That was a really important question. . . . I thought then, that if the question had been pressed farther than it was it would have put an end to this union; and I still believe that if these gentlemen had carried their point the union would have been gone." Floyd made sure to associate Sergeant with Rufus King, the New York senator that antirestrictionists accused of provoking the Missouri Crisis to win the presidency or, failing that, to revive the dreams of the Hartford Convention. It mattered a great deal, Floyd thundered, that back in 1819, Sergeant had been "supported by Mr. King," just as it mattered in 1826 that the administration sending Sergeant to Panama also employed King "at present [as] our minister to London."[46]

Reaction by slave owners to the destruction of slavery in Latin America and against participation in the Panama Conference was so powerful, both in Congress, which debated participation for months, and in southern newspapers that the John Quincy Adams administration sought to reassure. In instructions to the two conference delegates, Richard Anderson of Kentucky and Sergeant of Pennsylvania, Secretary of State Clay directed them to make it clear that the United States would oppose any effort to liberate Cuba or disrupt slavery there. Clay especially emphasized the danger posed by Black soldiers. When it came to maintaining the status quo in Cuba, the United States would align with the monarchies of Spain and the holy alliance against its fellow American republics, especially *"Colombia, on account of the character of a portion of the troops of that Republic."*[47]

Administration supporters in Congress defended U.S. participation by arguing that they could make a better case in person that abolition must not spread so close to the U.S. South. Yet these efforts to placate accomplished little. By the mid-1820s Carey was rapidly losing confidence that southerners would ever understand the virtues and splendors of the American System as they denounced protective tariffs and railed against federally sponsored internal improvements.[48] Carey tried to reassure them, writing essays about the value of slave labor to a national economy and a diverse domestic market.[49]

Yet he showed no evidence that he understood the 1820s as so many slave owners did: as a decade when National Republicans were pursuing a dangerous vision of political economy and the power of the national government, while recklessly encouraging a globally disruptive revolutionary contagion welcomed by Haiti. The end of the 1820s saw Carey abandon all hopes for the South as he began to view slavery much as Raymond always had. He became a vocal supporter of colonization and joined the Pennsylvania Colonization Society.[50] Thus, for Carey, the nullification crisis, South Carolina's attempt to gut the American System, was the final example of slave owners' refusal to do what was best for both the nation and the southern slave region.

Yet for many white southerners, these years only intensified the reinforcing connections of local, national, and global events. By 1829 the Latin American revolutions were unambiguously emancipatory. It was easy to conclude that American republics with so many recently emancipated citizens would excite David Walker to address them in his mighty *Appeal to the Colored Citizens of the World, but in Particular Those of the United States of America* in 1829, a year in which it was lost on nobody that many of the newly free were also soldiers and armed. Walker hoped to challenge southern whites by distributing his appeal using the turbulent, revolutionary waterways plied by antislavery seamen. His efforts led to responses similar to the Negro Seamen's Acts, with North Carolina and Georgia joining South Carolina in quarantining free Black sailors.[51] One year after Walker published his *Appeal*, the Whig Party in Britain regained power and announced laws and regulations mandating greater racial equality in the empire, producing the expectation of emancipation throughout the British West Indies, an expectation realized beginning in 1833. And, of course, one year after the British Whigs' triumph came publication of the first issue of William Lloyd Garrison's *Liberator* and Nat Turner's rebellion. Many southerners conveniently blamed Turner on Walker and Garrison, who could, in turn, be seen as stimulated by the global events, which allowed it all to be connected back to Haiti. Turner's was not the only uprising of 1831, as slaves also engaged in a massive revolt in Jamaica. By 1831 the appetite for terrifying news was all but insatiable, and the events in Jamaica received an average of five months of coverage in southern newspapers. By 1832–33, with slavery abolished in much of Latin America and disappearing in the British Caribbean, to many southern U.S. slave owners Haiti appeared to be setting the agenda far more than Governor Floyd's Virginia, which, in the debates after the Turner revolt, concluded that republican revolution did not, must not, mean slavery's abolition.[52]

In 1820 Carey had thought the Missouri Compromise would provide slave owners all the assurance they needed that their needs were best advanced by the American System. By 1831 Carey saw no possibility to pursue the American System with slavery. After South Carolina's nullification of the protective tariff, it was clear, Carey fulminated, that "the southern states have been from the commencement of the government a millstone around the neck of the other states."[53] He came to that conclusion by a very different way than Raymond had. But by the early 1830s, faced with having to choose between his cherished American System and slavery, Carey could now agree with Raymond that slavery was toxic. The mainstream booster had joined the idiosyncratic outlier.

In doing so, Carey provided perhaps the profoundest irony of the National Republican movement. By 1833, all of his efforts led Carey to see no other way except to abandon the far too powerful phalanx of slave owners. The only solution was a Northern Confederacy. In his 1833 pamphlet *Prospects beyond the Rubicon*, Carey called for the states north of Virginia to secede from the Union. By the nullification crisis, Carey had so abandoned the National Republican mainstream that all he could do was fantasize about re-creating the New England problem on a far-grander scale.[54]

What Carey could never do was experience the 1820s as so many white southern supporters of slavery did, as a global catastrophe in which Haiti appeared to be winning. By 1832 many slave owners easily understood the anxiety of the pre-emancipatory Bolívar, who, before he ever imagined having to go to Haiti, paused to consider the potential consequences of what he was undertaking. In 1810, as he embarked on his life's work, Bolívar presciently worried about outcomes, writing, "A great volcano lies at our feet. Who shall restrain the oppressed classes? Slavery will break its yoke, each shade of complexion will seek mastery."[55]

That volcano did erupt, certainly by 1826, the year of the Panama Conference. In the midst of debate about U.S. participation, Louisiana congressman William Brent explained why so many southerners could never trust people like Carey, who promoted dangerous economic ideas and frightening prospects of expansive national power, while also seeming to encourage the convulsions to the south. As Congress debated whether to attend the conference that was the result of those convulsions, and as John Floyd revived the specter of Missouri, National Republican Brent perceptively described the nightmares of the John Quincy Adams administration's critics. They feared, he explained, the liberation of Cuba. If Cuba was freed, and likely by an army that included former slaves, "is it not reasonable for us to suppose that part of its population, as in the other South American Republics, would all be declared free; and, if so, with the black population of Mexico on the frontier of Louisiana, and Haiti and Cuba for neighbors, what would be the condition of the Southern planters?"[56] By the end of the global 1820s, defenders of U.S. slavery saw the disruption created by the American System and the disruption of global abolition as connected. They were convinced that the policies and expansive claims of National Republicans like Carey fed a general destructive recklessness moving inexorably closer to the southern states.

♠

Between the Missouri Compromise and the nullification crisis, options narrowed considerably for the National Republicans. It became impossible to claim an easy compatibility between slavery and the American System. Settlement of the slavery question in Missouri did not usher in a period when slavery was peripheral to American politics. Instead, the aftermath of the Missouri Crisis saw a decade of titanic transformation. At its end, the U.S. southern states were some of the few polities left anywhere in the world where slavery was legal. Slave owners knew it; they obsessed over it. They could and certainly did connect advocacy for the American System with the eruption of Bolívar's volcano.

Daniel Raymond was an idiosyncratic outlier in 1820, and Mathew Carey was much more representative of the political-economy thinking of National Republicans. But the events of the 1820s confounded Carey's expectations of how slave owners would act and shattered his confidence that National Republican policies could harmoniously connect regions of free and enslaved labor. As a result, by 1831 Carey did what he did not do in 1820—identify slave owners and slave states as the primary source of the nation's problems. By the end of the 1820s, Carey denounced slavery as loudly as Raymond had at the beginning. The aftermath of the Missouri Crisis, the long global 1820s, meant that the National Republican project never had a chance. At the end of the decade, possibilities had shrunk and lines had hardened. Over the course of Andrew Jackson's presidency, his Democratic Party destroyed the American System, while more and more northerners came to loathe slavery.

Yet a consideration of Daniel Raymond, Mathew Carey, the Missouri Crisis, the National Republican project, the centrality of race and slavery, and the global 1820s cannot be left there. In 1819 Raymond excoriated slavery, and Carey joined him in doing so by 1831. But the way they embraced antislavery convictions helps us to comprehend why a vitriolic racism shaped much of the mainstream antislavery politics that arose in the antebellum North.

Those who grew outraged by the slave South from a perspective of political economy, from a sense of grievance over economic opportunities lost, rarely shared the values of antiracists such as David Walker or moral-imperative, immediate abolitionists like William Lloyd Garrison. Raymond and Carey help us to understand a northern politics that grew more significant, even dominant, over the next few decades, a politics that was antislavery while also being profoundly anti-Black and hostile to the possibility of a biracial society of republican freedom.

In *Thoughts on Political Economy*, Raymond argued (much as Andrew Johnson would sixty-seven years later) that the true victims of slavery were poor whites, while slavery in fact benefited the enslaved. Raymond believed that the enslaved population increased faster than the white population in slave states because the accumulation of vast individual wealth at the expense of national wealth gave slave owners the resources to provide for slaves. Yet, Raymond claimed, in free states the white population increased much faster than the Black. Raymond was confident that this disparity proved a general Black inferiority. It was clear that "the blacks do not stand upon equal footing with the whites in any respect whatever." Once slavery, in Raymond's view an artificial boost—an advantage—was removed, former slaves would have to fend for themselves. That would solve the terrifying prospect of Black slaves overwhelming free whites, for "by doing justice to the slaves in manumitting them their rapid increase will be greatly restrained." Because those of African descent "are more degraded," once left to their own devices, once granted a freedom they were incapable of managing, some would likely survive. But enslavement was the primary source of their fecundity. After slavery most freed people would prove "idle and worthless, they would dwindle away and become extinct."[57]

Ending slavery would end the problem of race. It would allow white citizens, who deserved and were capable of benefiting from their freedom, to enjoy national wealth in an egalitarian white man's republic. For Raymond, the path to a republic of free whites meant ending slavery, the artificial stimulant of the inferior Black population. For Carey, as he took the opposite view of Raymond over Missouri, slavery was justified there precisely because he agreed that Black people were naturally inferior. Threatening the integrity of the Union over slavery made no sense, Carey argued. It was appropriate to make use of 1.5 million slaves to aid the "prosperity and comfort [of] millions of a better race." Whites were superior to Black people, whether enslaved or free, which was why Missouri should be allowed to have slavery and exclude free Black people, who were "depraved in their morals, debased in intellect, and unqualified to perform the duties of citizens." For Raymond, Black inferiority made slavery a mortal threat since it artificially increased a dangerous population while undermining and degrading a superior one. For Carey, Black inferiority justified his harmonious melding of slavery and the American System—a national political economy that would use enslaved bodies to provide "peace and prosperity [for] eight million free-men and Christians."[58] On opposite sides over Missouri, there was never disagreement between Raymond and Carey that the U.S. republic was for whites only. That conviction was fundamental to both men's vision of a re-public of liberty, equality, and freedom. In coming together by the end of the global 1820s, Raymond and Carey helped to articulate an antislavery of virulent negrophobia that, despite the efforts of many abolitionists, Black and white, shaped a new mainstream in the states where Carey fantasized about a Northern Confederacy.[59]

Notes

1. Thomas Jefferson to John Holmes, April 22, 1820, in *The Portable Thomas Jefferson*, ed. Merrill D. Peterson (New York: Penguin Books, 1975), 568.

2. Daniel Raymond, *The Missouri Question* (Baltimore: Schaeffer and Maund, 1819); A Pennsylvanian, *Considerations on the Impropriety and Inexpediency of Renewing the Missouri Question* (Philadelphia: Mathew Carey, 1820).

3. Drew R. McCoy, *The Elusive Republic: Political Economy in Jeffersonian America* (Chapel Hill: University of North Carolina Press, 1980); Peter S. Onuf, "The Empire of Liberty: Land of the Free and Home of the Slave," in *The World of the Revolutionary American Republic: Land, Labor, and the Conflict for a Continent*, ed. Andrew Shankman (New York: Routledge, 2014), 195–217.

4. Drew McCoy, "An Unfinished Revolution: The Quest for Economic Independence in the Early Republic," in *The American Revolution: Its Character and Limits*, ed. Jack P. Greene (New York: New York University Press, 1987), 131–48; Andrew Shankman, "Neither Infinite Wretchedness nor Positive Good: Mathew Carey and Henry Clay on Political Economy and Slavery during the Long 1820s," in *Contesting Slavery: The Politics of Bondage and Freedom in the New American Nation*, ed. John Craig Hammond and Matthew Mason (Charlottesville: University of Virginia Press, 2011), 247–66; Andrew Shankman, "Capitalism, Slavery, and the New Epoch: Mathew Carey's 1819," in *Slavery's Capitalism: A New History of Economic Development*, ed. Sven Beckert and Seth Rockman (Philadelphia: University of Pennsylvania Press, 2016), 243–61; Martin Ohman, "The Statistical Turn in Early American Political Economy: Mathew Carey and the Authority of Numbers," *Early American Studies* 11, no. 3 (2013): 486–515; Douglas Egerton, *Charles Fenton Mercer and the Trial of National Conservatism* (Jackson: University Press of Mississippi, 1989); Andrew

Shankman, "John Quincy Adams and National Republicanism," in *A Companion to John Adams and John Quincy Adams*, ed. David Waldstreicher (Malden, MA: Wiley-Blackwell, 2013), 263–80; Charles Sellers, *The Market Revolution: Jacksonian America, 1815–1846* (New York: Oxford University Press, 1991), 70–102.

5. Peterson, *Portable Thomas Jefferson*, 568.

6. Raymond, *The Missouri Question*, 3.

7. Daniel Raymond, *Thoughts on Political Economy* (Baltimore: Fielding Lucas Jr., 1820), 10–11.

8. Raymond, *Thoughts on Political Economy*, 13.

9. Raymond, *Thoughts on Political Economy*, 14, 15, 17.

10. Raymond, *Thoughts on Political Economy*, 22–23.

11. Raymond, *Thoughts on Political Economy*, 28 (Raymond wrote this definition in all capital letters), 37, 28, 34–36.

12. Raymond, *Thoughts on Political Economy*, 127, 233, 241.

13. Raymond, *Thoughts on Political Economy*, 275, 347, 348–49, 373.

14. Raymond, *Thoughts on Political Economy*, 288–91, 346, 366–67, 377.

15. Raymond, *Thoughts on Political Economy*, 323, 325, 426–30.

16. Raymond, *Thoughts on Political Economy*, 434.

17. Raymond, *Thoughts on Political Economy*, 435, 438–41.

18. Raymond, *Thoughts on Political Economy*, 441–42.

19. Raymond, *Thoughts on Political Economy*, 451–54.

20. See chapter 10 by David Waldstreicher in this volume.

21. Kevin Gannon, "Escaping 'Mr. Jefferson's Plan of Destruction': New England Federalists and the Idea of a Northern Confederacy, 1803–1804," *Journal of the Early Republic* 21 no. 3 (2001): 414–43; Richard Buel, *America on the Brink: How the Political Struggle over the War of 1812 Almost Destroyed the Young Republic* (New York: Palgrave, 2005); Mark Peterson, *The City-State of Boston: The Rise and Fall of an Atlantic Power, 1630–1865* (Princeton, NJ: Princeton University Press, 2019), 420–22, 426–43.

22. Mathew Carey, *The Olive Branch; or, Faults on Both Sides, Federal and Democratic: A Serious Appeal on the Necessity of Mutual Forgiveness and Harmony* (Philadelphia: M. Carey, 1814). Carey compiled his essays on political economy written between 1814 and 1820 in *Essays on Political Economy; or, The Most Certain Means of Promoting the Wealth, Resources, and Happiness of Nations: Applied Particularly to the United States* (Philadelphia, 1822).

23. Carey, *Essays on Political Economy*, 67.

24. Lindsay Schakenbach, "From Discontented Bostonians to Patriotic Industrialists: The Boston Associates and the Transcontinental Treaty, 1790–1825," *American Quarterly* 84, no. 3 (2011): 377–401; Peterson, *City-State of Boston*, 444–46, 465–78. For regional variations on nationalism, see Benjamin Park, *American Nationalisms: Imagining the Union in the Age of Revolutions, 1783–1833* (New York: Cambridge University Press, 2018).

25. Shankman, "Capitalism, Slavery, and the New Epoch," 250–52.

26. "Political Disquisitions No. VII," *Richmond (VA) Enquirer*, August 26, 1825.

27. John Lynch, *Spanish American Revolutions, 1808–1826* (New York: W. W. Norton, 1973), 209.

28. Ashli White, *Encountering Revolution: Haiti and the Making of the Early Republic* (Baltimore: Johns Hopkins University Press, 2010); Mathew J. Clavin, *Toussaint Louverture and the American Civil War: The Promise and Peril of a Second Haitian Revolution* (Philadelphia: University of Pennsylvania Press, 2010).

29. Lynch, *Spanish American Revolutions*, 192, 196, 202–03.

30. Edward Bartlett Rugemer, *The Problem of Emancipation: The Caribbean Roots of the American Civil War* (Baton Rouge: Louisiana State University Press, 2008); Edward Bartlett Rugemer, "Caribbean Slave Revolts and the Origins of the Gag Rule: A Contest between Abolitionism and Democracy, 1797–1835," in *Contesting Slavery*, ed. Hammond and Mason, 94–113, 103.

31. Ada Ferrer, *Freedom's Mirror: Cuba and Haiti in the Age of Revolution* (Cambridge: Cambridge University Press, 2014).

32. Joel Poinsett to Richard Rush, May 23, 1817, in *Diplomatic Correspondence of the United States Concerning the Independence of the Latin-American Nations*, ed. William R. Manning, 2 vols. (New York: Oxford University Press, 1925), 1:39, 44.

33. Jennifer Heckard, "The Crossroads of Empire: The 1817 Liberation of Amelia Island, East Florida" (PhD diss., University of Connecticut, 2006), particularly chap. 5; Craig Hollander, "Against a Sea of Troubles: Slave Trade Suppressionism during the Early Republic (PhD diss., Johns Hopkins University, 2013), 31–32, 50–86. See also Jane G. Landers, *Atlantic Creoles in the Age of Revolutions* (Cambridge, MA: Harvard University Press, 2010), 131–37; Frank Lawrence Owsley Jr. and Gene Smith, *Filibusters and Expansionists: Jeffersonian Manifest Destiny, 1800–1821* (Tuscaloosa: University of Alabama Press, 1997), 14, 125–34; James G. Cusick, *The Other War of 1812: The Patriot War and the American Invasion of Spanish East Florida* (Gainesville: University Press of Florida, 2003), 171, 269–70; and Deborah Rosen, *Border Law: The First Seminole War and American Nationhood* (Cambridge, MA: Harvard University Press, 2015), 22–23, 163.

34. *Diplomatic Correspondence of the United States*, 1:48, 58.

35. Heckard, "Crossroads of Empire," 147–48; Caitlin Fitz, *Our Sister Republics: The United States in an Age of American Revolutions* (New York: Liveright, 2016), 111–12.

36. Valuable for thinking about global connections and the transcending of borders in this revolutionary period are Janet Polasky, *Revolutions without Borders: The Call to Liberty in the Atlantic World* (New Haven, CT: Yale University Press, 2015); and Landers, *Atlantic Creoles*.

37. Peter Blanchard, "The Slave Soldiers of Spanish South America: From Independence to Abolition," in *Arming Slaves: From Classical Times to the Modern Age*, ed. Christopher Leslie Brown and Philip D. Morgan (New Haven, CT: Yale University Press, 2006), 255–73; Lynch, *Spanish American Revolutions*, 85–86, 104, 116, 155, 224, 245, 289, 332.

38. A Pennsylvanian, *Considerations on the Impropriety and Inexpediency*, 4.

39. Michael A. Schoeppner, "Status across Borders: Roger Taney, Black British Subjects, and a Diplomatic Antecedent to the *Dred Scott* Decision," *Journal of American History* 100, no. 1 (2013): 46–67; Kay Wright Lewis, *A Curse upon the Nation: Race, Freedom, and Extermination in America and the Atlantic World* (Athens: University of Georgia Press, 2017), 74–82; Carl Lawrence Paulus, *The Slaveholding Crisis: Fear of Insurrection and the Coming of the Civil War* (Baton Rouge: Louisiana State University Press, 2017), 42; Clavin, *Toussaint Louverture*, 33–34; Douglas Egerton, *He Shall Go Out Free: The Lives of Denmark Vesey* (New York: Rowman and Littlefield, 2004).

40. Rugemer, "Caribbean Slave Revolts," 103.

41. James F. Hopkins, ed., *The Papers of Henry Clay*, 10 vols. (Lexington: University Press of Kentucky, 1959–91), 2:519–20.

42. James Lewis, *The American Union and the Problem of Neighborhood: The United States and the Collapse of the Spanish Empire, 1783–1829* (Chapel Hill: University of North Carolina Press, 1998).

43. Harry L. Watson, *Liberty and Power: The Politics of Jacksonian America* (New York: Hill and Wang, 1991), 83; Sean Wilentz, *The Rise of American Democracy: Jefferson to Lincoln* (New York: W. W. Norton, 2005), 258–59; Daniel Walker Howe, *What Hath God Wrought: The Transformation of America, 1815–1848* (New York: Oxford University Press, 2007), 251–55.

44. Fitz, *Our Sister Republics*, chap. 6; Piero Gleijeses, "The Limits of Sympathy: The United States and the Independence of Spanish America," *Journal of Latin American Studies* 24, no. 3 (1992): 481–505.

45. *The Register of Debates in Congress* (Gales and Seaton, 1827), 19th Cong., 1st sess., 1124–25 (emphasis in the original), https://memory.loc.gov/ammem/amlaw/lwrdlink.html#anchor19.

46. *Register of Debates*, 1293–95; John Craig Hammond, "President, Planter, Politician: James Monroe, the Missouri Crisis, and the Politics of Slavery," *Journal of American History* 105, no. 4 (2019): 843–67; Paul D. Naish, *Slavery and Silence: Latin America and the U.S. Slave Debate* (Philadelphia: University of Pennsylvania Press, 2017), 39–54.

47. Hopkins, *Papers of Henry Clay*, 5:331–34 (emphasis in the original).

48. John L. Larson, *Internal Improvement: National Public Works and the Promise of Popular Government in the Early United States* (Chapel Hill: University of North Carolina Press, 2001), esp. chap. five.

49. Shankman, "Neither Infinite Wretchedness," 258–59.

50. Beverly C. Tomek, *Colonization and Its Discontents: Emancipation, Emigration, and Antislavery in Antebellum Pennsylvania* (New York: New York University Press, 2011), 61, 63.

51. Peter Thompson, "David Walker's Nationalism—and Thomas Jefferson's," *Journal of the Early Republic* 37, no. 1 (2017): 47–80, 61.

52. Rugemer, "Caribbean Slave Revolts"; K. Lewis, *Curse upon the Nation*, 83–89; Paulus, *Slaveholding Crisis*, 45, 52–54, 60, 63, 69, 77, 80; Eva Sheppard Wolf, *Race and Liberty in the New Nation: Emancipation in Virginia from the Revolution to Nat*

Turner's Rebellion (Baton Rouge: Louisiana State University Press, 2006), esp. chaps. 5–6; Christopher Tomlins, "Revulsions of Capital: Slavery and Political Economy in the Epoch of the Turner Rebellion, Virginia, 1829–1832," in *American Capitalism: New Histories*, ed. Sven Beckert and Christine Desan (New York: Columbia University Press, 2018), 195–217; Tyson Reader, "Liberty with the Sword: Jamaican Maroons, Haitian Revolutionaries, and American Liberty," *Journal of the Early Republic* 37, no. 1 (2017): 81–115.

53. Mathew Carey, "Prospects beyond the Rubicon," (Philadelphia, 1833), 17–19, 21–23.

54. Carey, "Prospects beyond the Rubicon."

55. Bolivar quoted in Lynch, *Spanish American Revolutions*, 23.

56. Brent quoted in Gleijeses, "Limits of Sympathy," 499.

57. Raymond, *Thoughts on Political Economy*, 443, 448, 450, 460.

58. Carey, "Considerations on the Impropriety and Inexpediency," 5, 54–55.

59. John Frederick Bell, "Confronting Colorism: Interracial Abolition and the Consequences of Colorism," *Journal of the Early Republic* 39, no. 2 (2019): 239–65.

INDEX

Note: illustrations are indicated by *fig.* and tables by *t*